# SEVEN PLAYS BY SEAN O'CASEY

# Seven Plays
## by
# Sean O'Casey

*Selected, with an*
*Introduction and Notes by*

## RONALD AYLING

*Professor of English at the University of Alberta*

St. Martin's Press          New York

Play texts © Eileen O'Casey
Introduction and editorial matter © Ronald Ayling 1985

First edition of *The Shadow of a Gunman* and *Juno and the Paycock* 1925
First edition of *The Plough and the Stars* 1926
First edition of *The Silver Tassie* 1928
First edition of *Red Roses for Me* 1942
First edition of *Cock-a-Doodle Dandy* 1949
First edition of *The Bishop's Bonfire* 1955

All plays first published by The Macmillan Press Ltd

The editor and publishers wish to thank
Mrs Eileen O'Casey for permission to
reproduce the play texts.

ISBN 0–312–71323–1

Library of Congress Cataloging in Publication Data
O'Casey, Sean, 1880–1964.
   Seven plays.
   Bibliography: p.
   Includes index.
   Contents: The shadow of a gunman—Juno and the
paycock—The plough and the stars—[etc.]
   I. Ayling, Ronald, 1932–   . II. Title.
PR6029.C33A6  1985     822'.912      85–2167
ISBN 0–312–71323–1

*To Wole Soyinka*
*true heir to Sean O'Casey's legacy*

# Contents

# List of Plates

1. Michael Pennington as the tenement poet Donal Davoren in the 1981 Royal Shakespeare production of *The Shadow of a Gunman* at The Warehouse, London, directed by Michael Bogdanov. Photograph © Donald Cooper.
2. Sara Allgood as Juno with her indolent paycock played by Arthur Sinclair in *Juno and the Paycock* at the Royalty Theatre, 1926. Photograph © Mander and Mitchenson, Theatre Collection.
3. Gerard Murphy as Johnny Boyle and Judi Dench as Juno in the Royal Shakespeare Company production of *Juno and the Paycock* at the Aldwych Theatre, 1980, directed by Trevor Nunn. Photograph © Donald Cooper.
4. *The Plough and the Stars*, directed by Bill Bryden at the Olivier Theatre, 1977, with J. G. Devlin (Peter Flynn), Anna Manahan (Bessie Burgess), Harry Webster (Barman), Cyril Cusack (Fluther Good), Carmel McSharry (Mrs Gogan) and Bryan Murray (the Young Covey). Photograph © Donald Cooper.
5. *The Plough and the Stars*, directed by Bill Bryden at the Olivier Theatre, 1977, with Susan Fleetwood (Nora Clitheroe) and Nora Connolly (Mollser). Photograph © Donald Cooper.
6. The Fortune Theatre programme for the first performance of *The Plough and the Stars*, 1926. Photograph © Mander and Mitchenson, Theatre Collection.
7. The 1972 production of *The Silver Tassie* at the Abbey Theatre, directed by Hugh Hunt. Photograph © Fergus Bourke.
8. The Royal Shakespeare Company production of *The Silver Tassie* at the Aldwych Theatre, 1969, directed by David Jones. Bruce Myers (Barney Bagnal), Robert Oates (3rd Soldier), Ben Kingsley (The Croucher), John Kane (1st Soldier) and Richard Moore (Harry Heegan). Photograph © Donald Cooper.
9. *Red Roses for Me* at the Lyric Theatre, 1972, directed by Mary McCracken. Photograph © Lyric Theatre.

10. *Red Roses for Me* at the Abbey Theatre, 1980, directed by Hugh
    Hunt. Photograph © Fergus Bourke.
11. A scene from the English Stage Company's production of
    *Cock-a-Doodle Dandy* at the Royal Court Theatre, 1959, with
    Norman Rodway (The Messenger) and Berto Pasuka (The
    Cock). Photograph © Mander and Mitchenson, Theatre Collec-
    tion.
12. The design by Michael O'Herlithy for Act I of *The Bishop's
    Bonfire*. Photograph © Mander and Mitchenson, Theatre Collec-
    tion.

Every effort has been made to trace all the copyright-holders, but if
any have been inadvertently overlooked the publishers will be pleased
to make the necessary arrangements at the first opportunity.

# Acknowledgements

In the compilation of 'Notes on the Plays' I am especially appreciative of the invaluable assistance of Michael J. Durkan and of significant hints as well as helpful information from four of my colleagues in the English Department at the University of Alberta – Professors Christopher Gordon-Craig, Raymond J. S. Grant, Gerry McCaughey, and Hassan Qureshi – as well as from Mr Craig McLuckie. Professor W. A. Armstrong's Notes to *Cock-a-Doodle Dandy*, in *Classic Irish Drama* (London, 1964), the *Notes on Sean O'Casey's Juno and the Paycock* by Valerie L. Barnish (London, 1971) and the York Notes to *Juno and the Paycock* compiled by Dr Barbara Hayley (London, 1981) have also been most helpful. Last but not least, I am grateful for the much tried patience as well as the kindly encouragement of Sarah Mahaffy.

R.A.

# Introduction

## I

It is perhaps surprising that only one really comprehensive selection of plays by Sean O'Casey appeared in print during a long playwriting life that spanned the forty-seven years from 1917 to his death in 1964. That collection, entitled *Selected Plays of Sean O'Casey*, was chosen by the author himself – supposedly to celebrate his seventieth birthday, though it came out four years too late for that anniversary; published in New York in 1954, its circulation was limited and mostly within the United States. However restricted its readership, we shall subsequently return to the contents of this anthology in order to consider the aesthetic validity of the selection.

A number of other one-volume collections of O'Casey's dramas were printed during his lifetime: most notably, *Five Irish Plays* in 1935, *Three Plays* in 1957, *Five One-Act Plays* the following year and, in 1965, *Three More Plays*, which, though it appeared after O'Casey's death, had been approved and supervised through the press by him. A quick glance at the contents of each of these books, however, reveals that none of them was meant to be either representative or truly comprehensive, though each collection had an immediate rationale. O'Casey had produced for publication only five Irish plays up to 1935 and five one-act works up to 1958; the edition of *Three Plays* gathered together for the first time his trilogy of full-length Dublin dramas centred round the internecine Anglo-Irish conflict and the subsequent Civil War (covering, in the three writings, many of the major historical events in Ireland during the fateful years from 1915 to 1922); finally, *Three More Plays* was the playwright's first opportunity to publish *Purple Dust* and *Red Roses for Me* in revised versions that embodied a number of significant changes made since their publication in 1951 in the third volume of his *Collected Plays*. Though each of these gatherings had its own rationale, then, none of them could be said to make a sustained attempt to encompass either the various creative periods through which O'Casey's drama had progressed or to realise the rich variety of thematic and formal preoccupations that characterised it at different times. Only the *Selected Plays of Sean O'Casey*, indeed, can be said to have made an effective (though possibly, unconscious) shot at both objectives.

In a foreword to the volume O'Casey was vague about his own self-selection, saying somewhat ingenuously of the plays concerned,

> I don't know why I selected them any more than I know why I wrote them. To explain these things would be to explain life and that [neither] you, nor I, nor anyone else can do. For better or worse, they are part of the Will to life. The nine plays represent my varying mood in outlook on life and in the varying manners and techniques of the stage.

In theme and form alike, this variety is certainly well realised. The nine works (seven full-length and two one-act dramas) include five of the seven plays in the present anthology (the dates are of first publication): *The Shadow of a Gunman* (1925), *Juno and the Paycock* (1925), *The Plough and the Stars* (1926), *The Silver Tassie* (1928) and *Red Roses for Me* (1942). In addition, O'Casey chose to include *Within the Gates* (1933), *Purple Dust* (1940) and two late one-act dramas: *Bedtime Story* and *Time to Go* (both first published in 1951).

The two full-length plays chosen by O'Casey in 1954 but excluded from the present collection are *Within the Gates* and *Purple Dust*. Today we can see the former to be one of the more ponderous of the dramatist's experiments, a historically significant large-scale exercise in collective (and occasionally choric) drama and his most ambitious attempt to harness expressionist techniques to realise group experience. Though several remarkable poetic effects resulted from this experiment – particularly in some of the revue-like song-and-dance routines – the modified but none the less challenging expressionism of *The Silver Tassie* and *Red Roses for Me* seem, with hindsight, to be much more successful in practice. *Within the Gates*, for all its difficult and laborious genesis and its subsequent radical revisions, remains an honourable experiment that is now chiefly of value, aesthetically, because its radical features bore fruit in later allegorical writings by the dramatist. Before he could perfect his technique, however, he had to proceed by trial and error. The sprightly stylisation in later plays such as *Cock-a-Doodle Dandy* may well owe much of its lightness of touch to the protracted writing and rewriting of *Within the Gates* and the less anguished but none the less large-scale revisions to *Purple Dust*.

The exclusion of *Purple Dust* from the present collection may be more surprising, for it has received a good deal of critical commendation in recent years and a number of successful stage productions; indeed, its lengthy off-Broadway presentation at the Cherry Lane Theatre from 1956 to 1957 – where it ran for over four hundred performances – became the longest run for any of O'Casey's plays (*Juno and the Paycock*, whose 1925–6 run of 202 performances in London's West End remains the most successful O'Casey production in England to date, had previously held the record for the longest O'Casey run anywhere). The crucial importance of *Purple Dust* for the playwright's subsequent creative development cannot be overstressed, yet what it led to has, I believe, more intrinsic aesthetic value. Written from 1938 to 1940, it is basically a series of revue-like sketches employing songs, comic routines, and some hilarious pantomimic dialogue and action. It is very funny at times, but its major value lies not in its own worth but in the new direction to which it points: its admixture of satiric knockabout and stylised fantasy – in exaggerated actions as well as in stage setting – was an original vein of theatrical expression to which O'Casey would return in later more assured dramatic pieces like *Cock-a-Doodle Dandy* and *The Bishop's Bonfire*. The attendant return to an Irish locale and a largely Irish cast of characters was also of great value to O'Casey's artistry because, as he was to acknowledge in an essay on *Cock-a-Doodle Dandy* when it was first staged in New York in 1958, 'like Joyce, it is only through an Irish scene that my imagination can weave a way'.[1] Though *Purple Dust* has its advocates among the critics and has received significant stage productions from such prestigious theatre companies as the Berliner Ensemble and the Théâtre National Populaire as well as off-Broadway box office success, it is essentially a minor if often funny fantasy.

The two works in the present volume that are missing from the 1954 *Selected Plays of Sean O'Casey* are *Cock-a-Doodle Dandy* (1949), then O'Casey's most recent full-length play, and the then still-to-be-published *The Bishop's Bonfire* (1955). Otherwise, for all his disavowal, it can be seen that the author's choices were indeed intended to present a representative selection, not only of varying moods, manners and techniques, but of all stages of his playwriting career from 1923 until 1954. If the omission of *Cock-a-Doodle Dandy* – which he often referred to as his own especial favourite among his dramatic creations – be thought surprising, the reason may in part be explained by the reluctance of his American publisher but five years previously to print that title because he feared that its satire might give offence to some Roman Catholic readers in the USA; this supposition may perhaps be buttressed by the omission of another play earlier refused publication in New York – that is, *The Star Turns Red* (1940). However, the exclusion of the latter work, as of *Oak Leaves and Lavender* (1946), may more properly have been his own recognition of their limited success as overtly didactic dramatic experiments that are far too strongly tied to the particular social and political circumstances from which they sprang.

Still, the omission of *Cock-a-Doodle Dandy* remains a puzzle; without it, the *Selected Plays* edition lacks a significant dimension in so far as O'Casey's late period of avant-garde experimentation is concerned. It is true that the inclusion in the anthology of two late one-act pieces written since *Cock-a-Doodle Dandy* and – in the case of *Time to Go* – sharing that allegorical satire's thematic concerns and stylisation, may well have been O'Casey's attempt to realise in the selection something of the flavour and technique of the last phase of his playwriting. *Time to Go* does, indeed, realise on a small scale the symbolic conflict within this original form of modern morality play as well as something of the hilarious Aristophanic satire of *Cock-a-Doodle Dandy*. For the present selection, however, *Cock-a-Doodle Dandy* is included as the finest example of the last phase of O'Casey's dramaturgical exploration. It is perhaps best approached in conjunction with *The Bishop's Bonfire*, the major work that immediately followed it and with which it shares many of the same ideas and formal preoccupations; indeed, the two plays realise variations on related themes, depicting fluctuating attitudes of hope and despair in the face of Ireland's immediate post-Second World War obscurantism and its retreat from many of the realities of modern life. The quiet (and somewhat bittersweet) Chekhovian atmosphere of *The Bishop's Bonfire* is effectively juxtaposed to the boisterous verve and gusto of *Cock-a-Doodle Dandy*; together, the two comedies effectively represent the series of plays written in his last years that embody his lifelong love–hate relationship with his native land. *The Drums of Father Ned* (1960) may afford a more optimistic vision and a more expansive gallery of comic characters, *Behind the Green Curtains* (1961) a more savage indictment of moral and intellectual cowardice in an Ireland still living in isolation from the modern world, but neither they nor the other two plays of O'Casey's last period (*Figuro in the Night* and *The Moon Shines on Kylenamoe*, both first published in 1961) begin to approach either *Cock-a-Doodle Dandy* or *The Bishop's Bonfire* in comic ingenuity, depth of compassion or sheer variety of theatrical invention. To appreciate fully the artistic superiority of the seven plays assembled in the present volume, however, it may perhaps be best to approach them in the context of O'Casey's dramatic evolution.

## II

Four earlier apprentice plays by O'Casey[2] had been turned down by the Abbey Theatre, Dublin, before *The Shadow of a Gunman* was submitted to the same theatre in November 1922, accepted in February 1923, and staged in April. Subtitled 'A Tragedy in Two Acts', the play is set in the slums of Dublin in 1920, during the Anglo-Irish War that followed the Easter Rising of 1916, when brutal raids and counter-raids by the Irish Republican Army and the Black and Tans viciously tore apart Dublin's teeming tenement world – a community long battered by poverty, disease and the close-packed living conditions only too familiar to O'Casey, his neighbours and fellow workers. *Juno and the Paycock*, a three-act play whose background is the civil war of 1922, appeared on the Abbey stage early in March 1924 and was published with *The Shadow of a Gunman* in 1925. The two main characters in *Juno and the Paycock* are 'Captain' Jack and Mrs Juno Boyle, whose family's dissensions, struggles and eventual disintegration parallel the national situation. The play shows even more clearly than its predecessor the hardships suffered by Dublin's tenement dwellers; though the civil war, which followed hard upon the Anglo-Irish guerrilla war, seriously exacerbated the situation, it is apparent that the city's slums had long been the setting for a horrifying dehumanising process in which poverty, malnutrition and disease ravage the slum dwellers.

Soon after *Juno and the Paycock* was completed O'Casey began to write a play about the Easter Rising of 1916 to complete a trilogy centred on the war of independence. An ironic attitude to patriotic hero worship and a bitter juxtaposition of ideals and actuality were integral to the earlier works; the playwright's disillusionment with nationalist politics in the wake of the civil war was, however, epitomised in *The Plough and the Stars*, a four-act drama first staged at the Abbey Theatre in February 1926. Presenting political and social events in Dublin immediately before and during the Easter Week Rising of 1916, this chronicle play is a group drama which focuses upon the inhabitants of a large tenement house. As with the two previous works the play's life-enhancing values are embodied in various tenement women while the majority of the menfolk attempt to escape from harsh reality in alcoholic fantasies, gambling and nationalistic dreams. While both of the earlier dramas had ended with violent death and a grotesque atmosphere bordering on farce, the final curtain in *The Plough and the Stars* falls on a devastated tenement attic room, from which Dublin is seen burning in the distance while the British soldiers, who have occupied the tenement at the point of a bayonet, sit drinking tea onstage to the accompaniment of a chorus from the popular First World War song 'Keep the Home Fires Burning'. The horrifying impact of the fighting and of slum life is graphically realised in the action, but O'Casey's critical attitude towards the revolutionary soldiers (as well as the 'invading' government troops) and the aims and ideas they profess in the course of the action occasioned hostility in the Abbey during the play's first week's run in February 1926.

The first of O'Casey's full-length plays to embody to a perceptible degree non-naturalistic devices and stylisation of language and action, *The Plough and the Stars* survived the immediate protests and extensive attacks in the press to become the most often revived play in the Abbey Theatre's history; elsewhere, throughout the world, the play comes a close second to *Juno and the Paycock* in the frequency of stage revivals, despite its large cast of characters and ambitious scene changes. *The Shadow of a Gunman* became popular with Abbey audiences after an initial run of only four performances in April 1923; *Juno and the Paycock* eclipsed its popularity, however, becoming an immediate box-office success the following spring. For the first time in the history of the Abbey a play's run was extended for a second week. Like the first staged play, *Juno and the Paycock* was often revived in subsequent seasons. It has since become the second-most popular play in the Theatre's repertoire. The immediate and persisting popularity of O'Casey's Abbey Theatre trilogy has not been confined to Ireland alone: *Juno and the Paycock* and *The Plough and the Stars*, in particular, are very often performed in other English-speaking countries and, in more recent years, have had marked theatrical success in Europe, especially in West and East Germany.

Throughout its stage history outside Ireland, *The Shadow of a Gunman* has been overshadowed by its two immediate successors; and this phenomenon has even extended to its publishing record. The play was the last of the trilogy to be performed in London – it did not appear in the West End until late in May 1927, following well in the rear of *Juno* and *The Plough*, works that had been critically well received there in, respectively, November 1925 and May 1926 – and was immediately as well as unfavourably compared with the other two works, which reviewers, unaccountably, took to have preceded it in order of composition. I say 'unaccountably' for dramatic critics should, presumably, be expected to know something of the recent stage history of works they review, but it is only fair to admit that, were commentators to have consulted the first printed edition of *The Shadow of a Gunman* for such assistance, they would have received no help whatsoever. O'Casey's first book of plays – published in both London and New York on 10 February 1925 – was entitled *Two Plays*; both on the title-page and in the order of presentation within the volume itself, *Juno and the Paycock* preceded *The Shadow of a Gunman*. The dates of the first stage productions of both plays were omitted from the first edition of *Two Plays* though they were added to later reissues of the work. Subsequent reprintings of *The Shadow of a Gunman* in various collections of his dramatic writings invariably placed it out of chronological order. In *Five Irish Plays* (first published in 1935), in the first volume of O'Casey's *Collected Plays* (1949), as well as in the much reissued paperback collection *Three Plays* (1957) and, finally, the latest (and the first fully comprehensive), five-volume edition of *The Complete Plays of Sean O'Casey* (1984), O'Casey's first staged play appeared, in each case, second in the order of succession, after *Juno and the Paycock*, written eighteen-months later. It is therefore hardly surprising that many readers have assumed that its illustrious successor preceded it in order of composition.

Published in New York in 1954, the *Selected Plays of Sean O'Casey*, to which reference has already been made, is the only anthology published in the playwright's lifetime in which *The Shadow of a Gunman* appears first, in its correct chronological order. The present selection of *Seven Plays* is the first English edition to follow suit, allowing the play to be seen as O'Casey's brilliant if still somewhat uncertain earliest study of internecine strife and guerrilla warfare in Dublin's slum tenements. In its smaller-scaled structure (its two-act form was to be followed by the three acts of *Juno* and the four acts of *The Plough*, *The Silver Tassie* and *Red Roses for Me*) as well as in its basic theme and characters, it provides a lively as well as instructive introduction to its author's dramatic *oeuvre*. Each of these plays, deeply rooted as they are in Dublin working-class life, realises an idiosyncratic portrait-gallery of almost Dickensian proportions at times, saturated in an imaginative tenement idiom heightened by the inimitable bluster and blarney that became O'Casey's linguistic trademark.

In recent years *The Shadow of a Gunman* has begun to attain critical acclaim somewhat similar to that accorded the other two early Abbey Theatre plays, really coming into its own in 1980 when important and critically well-received stage revivals in England and Ireland became a significant part of celebrations commemorating the centenary of its author's birth.[3] Immature it may be, in places, and the pantomimic elements are overdone at times, but in no way is it theatrically naive; indeed, O'Casey's innate sense of stagecraft is immediately apparent in performance, and the still impressive interweaving of farcical elements with more serious, and at times potentially tragic, experience – particularly towards the end of the second act of *The Shadow of a Gunman* – realises in a minor key an original technique subsequently used even more masterfully in *Juno and the Paycock*, *The Plough and the Stars*, *The Silver Tassie* and *Red Roses for Me*.

What is perhaps the most remarkable feature about these dramas, viewed like this as a sequence in order of composition, is not so much the audacious enlargement of scope in itself in each new work as it is the author's courageous willingness to experiment in so varied and ambitious a manner with each of them. Having mastered a predominantly realistic mode in *Juno and the Paycock*, each subsequent play attempts, in varying ways, to open up the drama to realise wider and more disparate experience and encompass something of an epic dimension. The move is from restrictive tenement interiors and private domestic concerns to larger and more public settings and group experience – or, rather, in the plays after *Juno*, to set the one world against the other: to juxtapose the experience of a massed political rally outside a well-patronised tavern in Act II of *The Plough* with the domestic world of the Clitheroe family elsewhere in the play or, as in the second act of *The Silver Tassie* (the four-act drama that immediately followed *The Plough*), to throw into relief the mass horror of the trenches in Flanders during the First World War against a microcosm of squabbling small-time tenement life in the play's other three acts. In a final analysis, the enduring dramatic qualities of the first three plays rest primarily upon their highly original tragi-comic structure, range of grotesque characterisation, and vivid idiomatic speech. Each shows an increasing impatience with stage naturalism.

O'Casey's growing desire to broaden theme and form in his stage writings was given ambitious scope in *The Silver Tassie*, which must surely rank as the most crucial of his plays since it severed his connections with the Abbey Theatre and left him a playwright without a theatre. Started toward the end of 1926 and completed at the beginning of 1928, it was his first play to be written outside Ireland (he had settled in London in 1926); it also marked another departure in containing the first stage setting located outside his native land. A searing indictment of the First World War and its terrible effects on the minds and bodies of its many victims, three of its four acts are situated in Dublin settings and most of its characters are Irish men and women, mostly of slum origin. The second act, however, takes place just behind the British front line in Flanders; the characters there are a combination of Cockney and Dublin soldiers, the language is a mixture of realistic demotic speech and stylised plainsong chant, while the drama encompasses a *melange* of disparate styles and expressionistic techniques.

This mixture appears to have disconcerted the Abbey Theatre directors when the play was submitted to them in the summer of 1928; their refusal to produce it was followed by a heated controversy from which W. B. Yeats's original letter of rejection and O'Casey's impassioned counterattack have become famous.[4] Yeats's attack on propaganda in drama is an excellent piece of criticism, but it seems curiously wide of the mark in relation to *The Silver Tassie* – and his objections to the intrusion of the author's views into the drama could apply as much to O'Casey's earlier Abbey plays (which Yeats praises in his critique) as to the play on the First World War. Here, as in Yeats's subsequent onslaught on Wilfred Owen's war poetry, strong personal attitudes towards the European conflict seem to have coloured his outlook. In turn, his rejection not only prevented the Abbey's production of *The Tassie*, but, widely publicised in the press, the criticisms of a Nobel Prize winner (the poet had been so honoured but four years previously) did enormous damage to O'Casey's reputation and for many years impeded critical recognition of his later experimental dramas as well as financial backing for their stage presentation in Britain and the United States. In the case of *The Tassie*, however, there was only an initial wait of eighteen months before the work was produced on an ambitious and lavish scale by the celebrated impresario C. B. Cochran; the result was a critical success but a box-office failure, the production lasting only twenty-six performances. This presentation at the Apollo Theatre, London, in October 1929 was remarkable in many ways: directed by Raymond Massey and starring Charles Laughton, the striking set for Act II was designed by Augustus John while Martin Shaw supervised the choral interludes that were an impressive feature of the second act. George Bernard Shaw, who in correspondence with Lady Gregory had earlier defended the play against Yeats's criticisms, was greatly impressed by the London première, as was T. E. Lawrence (of Arabia) and also Lady Gregory, who wrote to Yeats from London: 'I am troubled because having seen the play I believe we [at the Abbey] ought to have accepted it.' On 12 August 1935, seven years after its original submission to the Abbey Theatre and three years after Lady Gregory's death, the play was performed there, and Yeats and O'Casey were reconciled.

The Abbey's rejection of *The Tassie* in 1928 severed his last personal as well as professional links with Ireland. Henceforth he was an experimental dramatist without a theatre workshop, and his subsequent plays for many years usually received either neglect or mediocre productions. The 1930s was a decade of experimentation for him. *Within the Gates*, published in 1933, was staged in London and New York the following year. Two plays followed in print in 1940: *The Star Turns Red* and *Purple Dust*. The first is an impassioned but strident piece of revolutionary rhetoric, the second an essentially lightweight romp. In these plays of O'Casey's 'middle period', as it might be called, the overriding ambition is to broaden the imaginative horizons for drama, which O'Casey believed had been narrowed by slice-of-life realism and the 'sober and exact imitation of life' naturalism that the playwright associated with the William Archer school of dramatic criticism. Believing that the 'beauty, fire and poetry of drama' had 'perished in a storm of fake realisms', O'Casey wanted a 'new form in drama' that would

> take qualities found in classical, romantic and expressionistic plays, . . . blend them together, breathe the breath of life into the

new form and create a new drama. It will give rise to a new form of acting, a new form of production, a new response in the audience. . . . Gay, farcical, comic or tragical, it must be, not the commonplace portrayal of the trivial events in the life of this man or that woman, but a commentary of life itself.

Above all, the dramatist wanted to reach beyond the individual and the personal to a more universal experience, believing as he did that there is 'a deeper life than the life we see with the open ear and the open eye, and this is the life important and the life everlasting. And this life can be caught from the group rather than from the individual.'[5]

As might be expected, the fortunes of O'Casey's later plays on stage have been varied and unpredictable. The varying admixture of disparate styles has undoubtedly troubled many stage directors; in addition, the extravagant demands made of set-designers, coupled with the need for good ensemble acting (often with a large cast) including, at times, choral incantation and other highly specialised requirements, have restricted both the number and success of performances of *The Silver Tassie*, *Red Roses for Me* and *Cock-a-Doodle Dandy*. Indeed, the increasingly high cost of mounting productions that will do adequate justice to the author's imaginative demands makes such theatrical ventures less viable today than when the plays were originally conceived.

A controversial drama throughout its history (in print as well as in performance), *The Silver Tassie* is probably O'Casey's most challenging and expansive play, in artistic and financial terms alike. If it has given rise to heated critical debate from the very beginning, it can also be argued that its few stage appearances have included several memorable productions that have in themselves provoked critical commentary of an unusually high order. Several of the more venturesome spirits in the theatrical world have been provoked to tackle the work by its very unusual qualities. The 1929 world première in London was a case in point, though it was to be another twenty-four years before a similarly ambitious stage presentation of the play was to be undertaken. In formal audacity and unusual admixture of styles, O'Casey's drama was for many years ahead of the theatrical practice of his time; more recently, however, practical as well as theoretical advances have been reflected in much praised innovative productions of several of these experimental works. Of

writings in this collection, *The Silver Tassie* has undoubtedly bene-
fited the most from these developments. Fritz Kortner's Berlin
presentation of this play in 1953 can now be seen as the imaginative
start for subsequent large-scale German exploration of O'Casey's
more radical work. Full-scale critical revaluation of *The Silver Tassie*
as a viable stage play, however, has proceeded from more recent
English-language productions, particularly those by the Royal
Shakespeare Company, in London in September 1969, and by the
Abbey Theatre Company in Dublin three years later; the reception
accorded the former presentation by the leading English dramatic
critics was especially interesting in that many hitherto hostile views
were modified and a new awareness shown for the richness of the
drama for an ensemble company familiar with 'epic' or Brechtian
staging.

It is quite a different matter in so far as the stage realisation of the
three later plays in the present anthology is concerned. The variety of
inventiveness is perhaps the most striking feature of these writings:
vaudeville routines mingle with lyricism, pantomime is juxtaposed
with expressionist or agitprop effects, and more conventional tragic
experience is to be found alongside unabashedly melodramatic
elements. While the present-day theatre shows itself to be increasingly competent in handling such disparate material, *Red Roses for
Me*, *Cock-a-Doodle Dandy* and *The Bishop's Bonfire* have yet to receive
imaginative stage presentations in the English-speaking world in any
way comparable to those later productions of *The Silver Tassie* that
have just been cited, or, indeed, worthy of comparison with European
productions of these later works. There are several honourable
exceptions – including the work of the Lyric Theatre in Belfast,
particularly in its two stagings of *Red Roses for Me*, and of the Abbey
Theatre in its productions of *The Star Turns Red* and *Purple Dust* – but
these are not enough.

After completing *The Star Turns Red* and *Purple Dust* in 1940,
O'Casey turned aside from both knockabout fantasy and polemical
allegory to look back with some nostalgia to scenes from his early
manhood. *Red Roses for Me*, published in 1942, is his most directly
autobiographical play. Its leading figure, Ayamonn Breydon, is an
idealised self-portrait whose relationships with his mother and the
local clergyman, together with his troubled love affair with a timid
Roman Catholic girl, are autobiographical ingredients drawn from

O'Casey's life within the Protestant community of Saint Barnabas in the somewhat isolated East Wall district of Dublin's dockland. The plot of *Red Roses for Me* is similar to that of *The Harvest Festival*, one of the early apprentice plays that preceded *The Shadow of a Gunman* on the Abbey stage. At a time of widespread hardship and industrial unrest the Protestant worker–hero is killed helping to lead a strike of railway workers. His friend, the local Protestant rector, wants to hold the funeral in his church, but in order to do so, he is forced to clash with bigoted parishioners who side with the employers in the violent struggle. In *The Harvest Festival* a similar conflict within the Select Vestry led to the defeat of the vicar and to the funeral held within the trade-union community; in *Red Roses* the minister overcomes strong opposition to keep the church open to all men of goodwill, whether or not their political and social views coincide with his or with those of the majority within the church.

*Red Roses for Me*, though perhaps too self-consciously literary in dialogue at times, has several moments of intense poetic beauty; its symbolism is often dramatically effective while the transformation scene in Act III (where song, dance and lighting are used to project a heightened visionary experience somewhat akin to a Joycean epiphany) is a successful fusion of expressionism and more traditional theatrical modes. In this episode, which takes place close by a bridge spanning the River Liffey, the setting sun literally and symbolically transforms the visual drabness of the scene as the accompanying dance sequence concretely embodies the change from despair to joy for the beggars on the bridge. Similarly, the revolutionary hero's words and actions subsequently transform, however briefly, the passive hopelessness of the slum dwellers into resolute resistance to the brutality of the strike-breaking police forces. Though there are several scenes of uproarious comedy (especially in Act II), a quieter elegiac atmosphere that is new to O'Casey's drama suffuses the later episodes, especially the final closing scene outside the darkened church that holds Breydon's coffin. The subtle mood created in such scenes was not to resurface in his work until he wrote *The Bishop's Bonfire* ('a sad play within the tune of a polka') twelve years later.

*Red Roses for Me* was O'Casey's first play for seventeen years to have its stage première in his native city (he had to wait another twelve years for the next); it was produced at the Olympia Theatre, Dublin, in March 1943. Its first professional presentation in London, in

February 1946, was not only a modest box-office success, but it also enabled O'Casey to see it onstage – the first time he had been able to see one of his new plays in performance since *Within the Gates* in 1934 – and, as a result, to make practical alterations that were incorporated in the revised edition of the play printed in the third volume of his *Collected Plays* in 1951.

After the Second World War came to an end in 1945 O'Casey went on writing his autobiography, completed a play on the Battle of Britain entitled *Oak Leaves and Lavender*, and revised his two most experimental 'middle period' dramas, *The Silver Tassie* and *Within the Gates*, in the hope that new stage versions of them would be published once the wartime paper restrictions were lifted. (These versions were printed in the second volume of his *Collected Plays*, issued in 1949.) While engaged in these activities, the playwright found his mind continually preoccupied with contemporary events in his native land, where he saw a heightened sense of puritanism inhibiting life and sexual relationships and creating a literary censorship stricter than anywhere else in western Europe. During the 1940s and 1950s O'Casey followed developments in Ireland with something approaching horror as well as disgust. He was bitterly disappointed that the country, after a quarter of a century of independence, had become what to his mind was a backward-looking and predominantly bourgeois theocratic state deliberately isolated from the more progressive social and political developments in the post-war world. Though understanding why the Republic had remained neutral during a war whose anti-Fascist nature made him a committed partisan, O'Casey became increasingly impatient with the renewed spirit of Jansenist puritanism there, together with a revival of what was in his view a dangerously superstitious religiosity and concomitant hostility to the socially ameliorative welfare programmes everywhere apparent in Britain and elsewhere after 1945. This impatience pervades all his late dramatic writings.

The new atmosphere of fear and clerical domination was reminiscent of certain experiences he had had as a young man in the Gaelic League, when Roman Catholic priests had interfered with League dances and similar social occasions, and when otherwise courageous citizens had capitulated without a struggle to clerical pressure. News reports from Ireland in 1947 also spoke of witch-hunts (actual witches being in question), a superstitious fear of the traditionally held magical power of women still being strong in many rural areas;

moreover, such superstitious beliefs were in some cases supported rather than opposed by the local clergy. O'Casey wrote to the American drama critic George Jean Nathan on 10 September 1947 that his new play would, 'if it be successful, hit at the present tendency of Eire to return to primitive beliefs, and Eire's preoccupation with Puritanism. I hope it will be gay, with a sombre thread of seriousness through it', adding later (in a letter of 31 October to Nathan): 'I've almost finished my play . . . it's a kind of Morality play, with Evil and Good contending with each other, but, I think, on different lines [from orthodox morality drama]. In fact, I'm thinking of giving it the subtitle of "An Immorality Play in Three Scenes".'

O'Casey sought to realise this atmosphere in a drama whose main thrust is primarily satirical. *Cock-a-Doodle Dandy*, first published in 1949, presents the rumbustious world of vaudeville knockabout comedy as well as Aristophanic fantasy. Temporarily abandoning any attempt to realise in action a positive social transformation such as was seen at the end of *The Star Turns Red* or in the Liffey bridge scene in *Red Roses for Me*, O'Casey concentrates on satiric exposure of the negative and life-denying forces in modern Irish life. In this respect the move is towards the mode of burlesque and comic exaggeration found originally in *Purple Dust*, though there is subtler handling of diverse theatrical modes in *Cock-a-Doodle Dandy*. There is, too, a finer structural control – the work is rigorously designed, in fact – a more supple poetic language is made use of, and the characterisation is varied and vigorous. In an article, entitled 'O'Casey's Credo', published in the *New York Times* on 9 November 1958 (and intended to introduce the play to New York theatregoers) he declared: 'The play is symbolical in more ways than one. The action manifests itself in Ireland, the mouths that speak are Irish mouths; but the spirit is to be found in action everywhere', adding, 'The Cock in the play, of course, is the joyful active spirit of life as it weaves a way through the Irish scene.' O'Casey emphasised in the same essay that 'in spite of the fanciful nature of the play, almost all the incidents are factual'. A letter of 27 December 1949 to Nathan substantiates this claim and concludes: 'I've records of them all. Poor oul' Eire!'

All O'Casey's late plays, from *The Bishop's Bonfire* in 1955 to his three last plays published in 1961, are, similarly, studies of the stultifying conditions of contemporary life in rural Ireland. Each one contains a good deal of satire directed at the narrow-minded materialism of the middle-class businessmen running the country with the support of the Church establishment. As in *The Star Turns Red*, there are courageous priests who stand out against the heavy repressive measures of the organised powers in Church and State (Father Boheroe in *The Bishop's Bonfire* and the spirit of Father Ned in *The Drums of Father Ned*, for instance), but these are merely isolated examples. O'Casey's outlook in these works varies from optimistic vision – as in *The Drums of Father Ned* and *Figuro in the Night*, where the younger generation gains a new freedom from political and sexual repression – to varying degrees of realistic recognition of the powerful entrenchment of the reactionary forces. In *Cock-a-Doodle Dandy* and *The Bishop's Bonfire* the more enlightened young people are forced to leave the country, after various unsuccessful attempts to liberalise the way of life in their rural communities. The bonfire to celebrate the return to Ballyoonagh of a local man who has become a bishop is, symbolically, to be fuelled by banned books.

One of the more forward-looking characters in *The Bishop's Bonfire* speaks of the Irish Republic as 'a fly-away country'. It is not surprising that, in a nation seeking to retrench the rights and privileges of long-established vested interests, and one invariably looking to a reactionary colonial past for its social ideals, emigration should exact a heavy toll among the more venturesome citizens. In such a country, the combination of small-time businessmen with organised powers of Church and State successfully stifles what visionary dreams and aspirations still exist among the few adventurous spirits that remain. In the same play, attempting to combat what seems like a universal apathy and a sense of hopeless compliance with the powers-that-be, one of the more liberal priests urges his countrymen to resist; having been successful thirty years earlier in liberating themselves from colonial domination, they now need to free themselves from a small-time huckster mentality that seems to coexist naturally with a complacent pietism (the speech recalls the lament of W. B. Yeats more than forty years earlier when, in the poem 'September 1913', he wrote that 'Romantic Ireland' was 'dead and gone' in an increasingly mercantile-mad world whose values were merely to 'fumble in a greasy till/And add the halfpence to the pence/And prayer to shivering prayer'). 'You've escaped from the dominion of the big house with the lion and the unicorn on its front', says O'Casey's Father Boheroe, 'don't let yourselves sink beneath the meaner dominion of the big shop with the cross and shamrock on its gable.'

Starting with *Cock-a-Doodle Dandy*, O'Casey's last nine plays may, loosely, be said to constitute the final period of O'Casey's playwriting career. Each of them offers variations on similar social themes. Artistically, they are a mixed bag: *The Drums of Father Ned* and *Figuro in the Night*, for all their infectious spirits and comic gusto, are lightweight works while *Behind the Green Curtains* is weighed down by its overly didactic message. In *Cock-a-Doodle Dandy* and *The Bishop's Bonfire*, on the other hand, there is a brilliant synthesis of varied dramatic styles, a renewed interest in celebrating the contradictory nature of the human spirit, and subtle variations of mood and atmosphere that deserve recognition alongside the earlier Dublin masterpieces.

Ireland has altered a great deal in the twenty years following the playwright's death and many of the changes would have pleased him. However different the moral and social climate nowadays, the better plays from this period retain their literary and dramatic relevance if for no more than the theatrical vivacity of their satire and of the various non-illusionist techniques devised to project the crazy kaleidoscope (as O'Casey envisaged it) of post-war Irish life, let alone the vitality of the dialogue and of characterisation. If the first five plays in the present collection are 'chronicle' plays embodying the recent past in what is now the Irish Republic (in the first three works, this troubled past also approaches something akin to the hideous present in Northern Ireland), the later writings are symbolic plays whose thematic and aesthetic concerns are timeless, invoking as they do the worlds of the medieval morality play and of Aristophanic comedy as well as elements from the music-hall and vaudeville traditions.

*The Bishop's Bonfire* was given its world première in Dublin in February 1955; directed by Tyrone Guthrie and with Cyril Cusack in the lead, it was given a favourable reception by visiting London critics and an extended stage run, despite clerical disapproval. In December the same year *Red Roses* opened in New York, the first O'Casey play on Broadway in twenty-two years. In November 1958, New York was to see *Cock-a-Doodle Dandy* on the stage of the Carnegie Hall Playhouse. It was, unfortunately, a poor production and it was not until a full decade after its initial appearance in print and on the amateur stage that the work received a presentation in any way worthy of its imaginative powers: this was the 1959 production by George Devine for the English Stage Company, then still riding a crest of fame for its championing of John Osborne's *Look Back in Anger* three years earlier. Designed as a special presentation for the Edinburgh Festival – where it achieved critical as well as popular success – *Cock-a-Doodle Dandy* was given a London run later in September 1959 at the Royal Court Theatre. Notable revivals of the play since then include the German-language version by the Berliner Ensemble in January 1971 and Irish productions by the Lyric Theatre, Belfast (November 1975), and, in August 1977, the Abbey Theatre. London theatregoers saw *The Bishop's Bonfire* in a weak production at the Mermaid Theatre in July of 1961. It is still very much an open question whether or not either of these late plays has yet received a presentation fully matching the imaginative challenge they extend to the contemporary theatre: certainly, in the English-speaking theatre one looks in vain – as yet – for the audacious flair of Peter Brook's famed staging of *A Midsummer Night's Dream* to be exhibited in an O'Casey production. Yet it is some such response that these late plays clearly demand.

In an editorial written specifically for the O'Casey Centenary Number of the *Irish University Review* (Spring 1980), Christopher Murray made the justifiable claim that the 'reputation of Sean O'Casey . . . remains at a consistently high level', instancing the frequency and range of stage productions, translations of his writings and the growth of critical and scholarly attention paid to his work. Four years later – and twenty years since the playwright's death – this claim, if anything, is strengthened by recent developments. A new unabridged edition of the autobiographies, published in 1980, has been followed by the appearance of the first *Complete Plays of Sean O'Casey* in five volumes (1984), while the present anthology is the first fully annotated edition of seven major plays that are in the forefront of O'Casey's achievement as a dramatist. On the continent the entire corpus of dramatic writings has been (and is) receiving theatrical revaluation;[6] in England, recent productions of the first three plays and of *The Silver Tassie* by the two London-based national companies – the National Theatre and the Royal Shakespeare Company – have occasioned considerable critical reassessment;[7] in Ireland, north as well as south, the Lyric and Abbey Theatres have set about redressing the persistent theatrical neglect there of all O'Casey's dramas since *The Plough and the Stars*. At long last things are moving, but there is still a long way to go in theatrical as well as critical exploration.

# NOTES

1. Sean O'Casey, 'O'Casey's Credo', *New York Times*, 9 November 1958; reprinted in *Blasts and Benedictions* (London and New York, 1967) pp. 142–5.
2. These plays of O'Casey's 'apprenticeship' are *The Frost in the Flower* (probably two-act; written *c*. 1918–19, rejected by the Abbey Theatre in 1919; rewritten the same year and again rejected in January 1920), *The Harvest Festival* (three-act; 1919, rejected in January 1920 and partially revised in 1920), *The Crimson in the Tricolour* (three-act; written 1920–1, rejected October 1922 and considered subsequently for possible rewriting as a comedy), and the one-act *The Seamless Coat of Kathleen* (1922, rejected April 1922).
3. Two productions of *The Shadow of a Gunman* were particularly important during the O'Casey centenary celebrations: The Royal Shakespeare Company's presentation that opened at The Other Place in Stratford-upon-Avon on 26 March 1980 and that by the Abbey Theatre, Dublin, that opened on 8 May 1980.
4. Both articles may be found in the first volume of *The Letters of Sean O'Casey*, vol. I: *1910–1941*, ed. David Krause (New York and London, 1975) pp. 267–8 and 271–3.
5. These quotations are taken from O'Casey's essay 'From Within the Gates', first published in the *New York Times*, 21 October 1934; reprinted in *Blasts and Benedictions*, pp. 113–14, 116.
6. There is as yet no adequate account of the full extent of this exploration but knowledge of the many German productions in recent years is salutary: see Manfred Pauli's *Sean O'Casey: Drama, Poesie, Wirklichkeit* (Berlin, 1977) pp. 250ff.; this book is also valuable for the many photographs of these productions.
7. Many instances of such critical revaluation could be given but it may be sufficient to quote the following examples: on the NT's *Juno and the Paycock*, see Sean Day-Lewis, *Daily Telegraph* (23 April 1966), Hugh Leonard, *Plays and Players* (June 1966) and *Times Educational Supplement* (10 June 1966); on the RSC's *The Silver Tassie* see Irving Wardle, *The Times* (11 September 1969), and another special article by him entitled 'A Neglected Masterpiece' in *The Times* (13 September), Peter Lewis, *Daily Mail* (11 September 1969), Caryl Brahms, *Guardian* (11 September 1969), J. W. Lambert, *Sunday Times* (14 September 1969) and Frank Marcus, *Sunday Telegraph* (14 September 1969); on the RSC's *Shadow of a Gunman* see Michael Billington, *Guardian* (2 April 1980) and T. P. Matheson, *Times Literary Supplement* (11 April 1980); on the RSC's *Juno and the Paycock* see Ned Chaillet, *The Times* (8 October 1980) and Derek Mahon, *Times Literary Supplement* (17 October 1980). Many more reviews could be instanced, as well as quite contrary critical opinions, of course.

# Textual Note

Something should be said about the textual provenance of these seven plays. In each case the text is the latest or 'final' edition approved for publication by the dramatist. Six of the seven texts are to be found in the versions that are printed in the *Complete Plays of Sean O'Casey* (1984); the seventh, that of *Red Roses for Me*, appears in the fourth and last version of the play authorised by the playwright shortly before his death.

For the first three plays – *The Shadow of a Gunman*, *Juno and the Paycock* and *The Plough and the Stars* – the text printed here is virtually identical with that printed in the first volume of O'Casey's *Collected Plays* (1949) and subsequently reprinted in 1957 in the paperbound edition entitled *Three Plays*. Only a few very minor alterations were made to the first editions of each of them. There seems little doubt that the reason for this was that, before each one of the first three full-length plays made its appearance in print, it was given a major stage production (with the playwright in close attendance) by a Dublin acting company then at its peak of achievement as an ensemble acting group; the dramatist was thereby enabled to incorporate changes, made in the light of practical theatre conditions, into the text of the first editions of each of them – in the *Two Plays* of 1925, for *The Shadow of a Gunman* and *Juno and the Paycock*, and in the 1926 edition of *The Plough and the Stars*.

The case was quite different for several of the later plays, however, where publication preceded stage performance: *The Silver Tassie* and *Red Roses for Me* – first printed in 1928 and 1942, respectively – were both subsequently revised after the playwright had seen professional productions of them in London. *The Silver Tassie* appears in the present collection in the 'stage version' (as it was described by the author) first printed in the second volume of his *Collected Plays* in 1949. In each of the four acts there are a number of changes from the text first printed in 1928; these alterations, though made between 1946 and 1947, were based primarily on observations of the 1929 London première and on the production ideas of Raymond Massey, its stage director, with whom the dramatist worked closely at the time. The 'stage version' differs in about thirty instances from the first edition; about half of these alterations are embodied in the stage directions, a strong indication of the influence of practical considerations on O'Casey's stagecraft. Two of the more significant revisions are, first, the addition of O'Casey's 'Notes' to facilitate stage production (which, in the present edition, as in the 1949 version, precede the actual text of the play itself) and, secondly, the fairly extensive rewriting of the conclusion to the final scene of the drama.[1]

*Red Roses for Me* has an even more complicated textual history. There are in print four different versions of the play, though only three of them warrant much attention, textually. These three versions are the first edition of 1942, the thoroughly revised text first published in 1951 in the third volume of O'Casey's *Collected Plays* (this is the text retained for the *Complete Plays* edition of 1984) and the slightly amended version of this text that was first printed in *Three More Plays* (1965); it is the last text, which, though it was published a year after the playwright's death, was in fact approved and supervised through the press by him, that is followed in the present collection.

All four acts of the first edition of *Red Roses for Me* were revised once the dramatist had an opportunity – which did not occur for four years after publication – to see the work on stage. The London première of 1946 enjoyed not only a distinct critical success but a modest box-office one as well, the production being twice transferred to theatres in the West End. O'Casey's revisions, meant to improve this production, were never in fact used in it but first saw the light of day in 1951 when the play was reprinted in his *Collected Plays* edition. Most of the changes were of a minor order, many being cuts and rewriting of dialogue to make the speech rhythms more attuned to oral delivery. A number of more significant alterations were made to Act IV, however, including the deletion of an extremely funny incident (which, despite its hilarity, was thought to impede the dramatic action) and the recasting of several other scenes. The changes tighten the action and dialogue considerably, making the version more theatrically effective, though the main outline of the work is unaffected.

Subsequently, following a New York production of *Red Roses for Me* in 1955, for which the playwright made further revisions, the Dramatists Play Service Inc. of New York brought out what might be called an acting edition in August 1956. This is a curious mixture of material from the 1951 text with some additional revisions and, in at least one scene in Act IV, a reversion to material in the 1942 text that had been changed for the 1951 edition. This New York version was not supervised through the press by the playwright, as were each of the other three versions. The last one of these, which may be called the final authorised version, is that first printed in *Three More Plays*: it is, basically, the 1951 text with the addition of a brief episode in Act III that was first introduced into the 1956 New York edition; otherwise, none of the other departures from the 1951 text that are to be found in the 1956 script were reprinted in this final version, followed in the present anthology.[2]

The original 1949 text of *Cock-a-Doodle Dandy* remained unchanged (save for the correction of occasional printing errors, which included the attribution of a speech to the wrong character) when it was reissued in the fourth volume of *Collected Plays* in 1951; it is the latter text which is here reprinted. *The Bishop's Bonfire* appeared in only one edition during its creator's lifetime; the present anthology follows this text, which made its appearance in print in June 1955, some four months after its stage première in Dublin. O'Casey was too ill to visit his native city for this production but some changes were incorporated into the printed text in the light of correspondence between the playwright and Tyrone Guthrie, the stage director, on the one hand, and O'Casey and Cyril Cusack, who took the part of Codger Sleehaun, on the other hand.

## NOTES

1. A copy of the first edition of *The Silver Tassie* incorporating O'Casey's manuscript corrections for the 1949 'stage version' is to be found in the Berg Collection of the New York Public Library. Examination of the differences between the two versions affords a valuable exercise in practical stagecraft: see Ronald Ayling and Michael J. Durkan, *Sean O'Casey: A Bibliography* (London, 1978; Seattle, 1979) pp. 87–8, and Heinz Kosok, 'The Revision of *The Silver Tassie*', *Sean O'Casey Review*, v (1978) 15–18.
2. For specific details of the various textual changes, see Ayling and Durkan, *Sean O'Casey: A Bibliography*, pp. 67, 90 and 134; and also Heinz Kosok, 'The Three Versions of *Red Roses for Me*', *O'Casey Annual No. 1* (London, 1982) pp. 141–7.

# Sean O'Casey: A Chronology

1880 (30 Mar) Born John Casey in Dublin, the youngest of a large family of whom five survived childhood.

c. 1891 Introduced to the theatre at the age of eleven by occasional visits with his brother Isaac, called 'Archie' in the playwright's autobiography, to the Queen's Theatre, Dublin (mostly vaudeville and Dion Boucicault).

c. 1894 Starts work at fourteen in the stockroom of a hardware shop. Had various clerical jobs until he became a manual labourer in his late teens, an occupation he kept until 1925, when he became a full-time writer. His longest job was a nine-year period as labourer on the Great Northern Railway of Ireland (GNRI), 1902–11.

c. 1895 Acts part of Father Dolan in an amateur production of Boucicault's *The Shaughran* at the Mechanics Theatre, Abbey Street; this theatre became the Abbey Theatre in 1904.

c. 1902 Begins work as a labourer on the GNRI.

1906 Joins Gaelic League and learns Irish; soon becomes branch secretary and Gaelicises name to Sean O Cathasaigh.

1907 (25 May) First published work an article on Irish educational system in *The Peasant and Irish Ireland*.

1909 (4 Jan) Irish Transport and General Workers' Union founded.

1911 Jim Larkin founds union newspaper, the *Irish Worker*, to which O'Casey subsequently contributes. Irish railways strike – the background to *Red Roses for Me*. Dismissed from his job at GNRI for refusing to resign from trade union.

1913 (15 Aug) Large-scale lock-out of union men by Dublin employers, with appalling consequences for working people during the seven months it lasts; profoundly influences the playwright's political and social thinking. Secretary of the Women and Children's Relief Fund during the lock-out.

1913    (Oct) Irish Citizen Army (ICA) formed by trade union to protect its members from police brutality.

(25 Nov) Irish Volunteers founded: a nationalist organisation with several prominent anti-labour men in its ranks.

1914    (Mar) ICA reorganised, with O'Casey as its secretary. He draws up its Constitution, endorsed in March. Although this document stressed the nationalist as well as socialist basis of the ICA, O'Casey opposed too-close ties with the Volunteers because of anti-union elements in the latter. He resigned from the ICA on 17 July 1914, when his motion to make the Countess Markievicz choose between the two bodies (she belonged to both) was defeated by the Executive Committee.

1916    (Jan) Publishes 'The Grand Oul' Dame Britannia', one of the most popular anti-war ballads in Ireland; despite its success as a broadside publication, many Irishmen join the British Army to fight in France – the background to *The Silver Tassie*. Many other satirical poems and love-songs published, off and on, from 1916 to 1918.

(24 Apr–29 Apr) The Volunteers and ICA rise in armed rebellion against the British authorities – the background to *The Plough and the Stars*.

1917–21  Guerrilla warfare in Ireland between the Irish Republican Army (the IRA, successor to the banned nationalist bodies) and the British forces; counter-terrorism by the Black and Tans – background to *The Shadow of a Gunman*.

1918    Death of O'Casey's sister Isabella in January and of his mother in November. About this time he writes his first play, for an amateur group, but its satire of the group's members prevents its production. This two-act play, *The Frost in the Flower*, was submitted to, and rejected by, the Abbey Theatre sometime during the period 1918–19.

1919    (Mar) O'Casey's first major publication, *The Story of the Irish Citizen Army* – much censored by the military authorities. Writes a second play, in three acts, *The Harvest Festival*, and revises *The Frost in the Flower* in accordance with recommendations by the Abbey Theatre.

1920    (26 Jan) The Abbey rejects both plays. O'Casey shares a one-room tenement flat with Michael O Maolain at 35, Mountjoy Square, the setting for *The Shadow of a Gunman*.

1921    Writes three-act play *The Crimson in the Tricolour*.

(6 Dec) Peace Treaty signed, partitioning the country into an independent Irish Free State and a Northern six counties within the United Kingdom.

1922–3   Civil War in the South over the terms of the Treaty – background to *Juno and the Paycock*.

1922    (28 Sept) The Abbey rejects *The Crimson in the Tricolour*.

(17 Nov) Completes *The Shadow of a Gunman* and submits typescript to the Abbey.

1923    (25 Feb) The Abbey accepts the play and gives it a run of four performances at the very end of its season (from 12 Apr).

1924    (3 Mar) *Juno and the Paycock* becomes the most popular play in the Abbey's twenty-year history.

(7 June) First visit to Lady Gregory's house at Coole Park, in Clare–Galway.

1925    (10 Feb) *Two Plays* (*Juno* and *Shadow of a Gunman*) published in London and New York.

(16 Nov) English première of *Juno* at the Royalty Theatre, London.

1926    (8 Feb) Riots during first week of Abbey production of *The Plough and the Stars*. O'Casey visits London to receive the Hawthornden Prize (for *Juno*); he lives in England for the rest of his life.

(15 Mar) American première of *Juno* at Mayfair Theatre in New York.

(Apr) Publication of *The Plough* in London and New York.

(12 May) English première of the same play at the Fortune Theatre, London.

1927    (27 May) The Court Theatre, London, presents the English première of *Shadow of a Gunman*.

(23 Sept) Marries Eileen Carey Reynolds.

(27 Nov) *The Plough* is given its American première at the Hudson Theatre, New York.

1928     Son Breon born. (20 Apr) The Abbey rejects *The Silver Tassie*; (12 June) play published.

1929     (11 Oct) C. B. Cochran presents *The Silver Tassie* at the Apollo Theatre, London.

(24 Oct) American première of *The Silver Tassie* at the Irish Theatre, New York.

1930     (22 Sept) Alfred Hitchcock's film of *Juno* (with Sara Allgood) released.

1932     Refuses invitation by Yeats and Shaw to be a founder member of the Irish Academy of Letters.

1934     (Autumn) Visits USA for New York production of *Within the Gates* (published 24 Nov 1933).

1935     (15 Jan) Second son Niall born.

(12 Aug) Abbey production of *The Silver Tassie* provokes vociferous clerical opposition.

(29 Oct) Publication of *Five Irish Plays*.

1937     (5 Mar) Publication of *The Flying Wasp*, a collection of contentious articles on the contemporary theatre.

(15 Mar) John Ford's film of *The Plough*, starring Barry Fitzgerald and Barbara Stanwyck, released.

1939     (3 Mar) Publication of *I Knock at the Door* (banned in Eire), the first of six volumes of autobiography.

(28 Sept) Daughter Shivaun born.

1940     (Jan) Barry Fitzgerald and Sara Allgood appear together for the last time in a revival of *Juno* at the Mansfield Theatre, New York.

1942     (17 Feb) *Red Roses for Me* published in London.

1943     (15 Mar) Olympia Theatre production of *Red Roses* is the first O'Casey première in Dublin for seventeen years.

1946     (26 Feb) London production of *Red Roses* has a modest success at the Embassy Theatre and is later twice transferred to other theatres in the West End.

1947     (26 May) Revival of *The Silver Tassie* at the Gaiety Theatre, Dublin.

1949     (8 Apr) *Cock-a-Doodle Dandy* published; (10 Dec) its world première at the People's Theatre, Newcastle-upon-Tyne.

(21 July) New York revival of *The Silver Tassie* at the

Carnegie Hall Playhouse (runs for eighty performances). (11 Nov) First two volumes of *Collected Plays* issued in London.

1950     (30 Jan) American première of *Cock-a-Doodle Dandy*, directed by Margo Jones, in Dallas, Texas.

1951     (25 Apr) *Red Roses* is given its US première at the Playhouse in Houston, Texas.

(17 July) Third and Fourth volumes of *Collected Plays* issued in London.

(24 Sept) Abbey Theatre revives *The Silver Tassie*.

1953     (20 June) Berlin production of the same play, directed by Fritz Kortner, provokes protests and controversy.

1954     (29 Oct) Publication of *Sunset and Evening Star* brings six-volume autobiographical sequence to a close.

1955     (28 Feb) *The Bishop's Bonfire* produced in Dublin by Tyrone Guthrie at the Gaiety Theatre; (24 June) play published in London.

(28 Dec) *Red Roses for Me* opens in New York at the Booth Theatre, the first O'Casey play on Broadway for twenty-two years.

1956     (Mar) *The Green Crow*, a collection of old and new essays, published in New York (English edition issued in Feb the following year).

(Oct) *Mirror in My House*, a two-volume edition (and the first collected one) of O'Casey's autobiography, published in New York.

1957     (1 Jan) Niall dies of leukaemia.

1958     (Feb) Playwright forced to withdraw his latest play, *The Drums of Father Ned*, from the Dublin International Theatre Festival when Archbishop of Dublin objects to works by James Joyce and O'Casey in the programme. The Festival has to be abandoned when Samuel Beckett withdraws his mime plays in protest.

(12 Nov) Carnegie Hall Playhouse presentation of *Cock-a-Doodle Dandy* is the play's New York première.

1959     (Sept) Presented by George Devine's English Stage Company, *Cock-a-Doodle Dandy* is the success of the year's Edinburgh Festival; (17 Sept) production opens at the Royal Court Theatre, London.

1960     Dramatist's eightieth birthday celebrated by publication of two major critical studies. Refuses several honours, including a CBE and at least three honorary degrees.

1961　(1 June) Last three plays published.

(26 July) *The Bishop's Bonfire* is given its English première at the Mermaid Theatre, London.

1962　(16 Aug) O'Casey Festival opens at the Mermaid with a production of *Purple Dust*, followed by *Red Roses* (5 Sept) and *The Plough* (26 Sept).

1964　The Abbey Theatre presents *Juno* (20 Apr) and *The Plough* (27 Apr) in London as the Irish contribution to the World Theatre Festival.

(18 Sept) Dies in Torquay of a heart attack.

1966　Increased theatrical interest over several years (particularly on the continent of Europe) culminates in 1966 with production of *Purple Dust* by the Berliner Ensemble and by the Théâtre National Populaire, Paris, and of *Juno* (directed by Laurence Olivier) by the National Theatre at the Old Vic, London. Dublin eventually sees *The Drums of Father Ned* at the Olympia Theatre in June.

1967　(12 Jan) *Blasts and Benedictions*, a posthumous collection of essays and stories, published in London and New York.

1969　(10 Sept) Royal Shakespeare Company production of *The Silver Tassie* at the Aldwych Theatre, London, has great critical success.

O'Casey's papers are acquired for the Berg Collection at the New York Public Library.

1971　(Jan) Berliner Ensemble follows up its earlier stage success with *Purple Dust* (a production in the company's repertoire for over twelve years) by presenting *Cock-a-Doodle Dandy*.

(23 Sept) Eileen O'Casey publishes memoir entitled *Sean*.

1975　(27 Mar) *The Letters of Sean O'Casey*, vol. I (1910–41) issued.

1977　(20 Sept) *The Plough* revived in London at the Olivier Theatre by the National Theatre Company.

1980　Centenary year sees publication of a new two-volume paperback edition of the *Autobiographies* (7 Mar) and of O'Casey's earliest extant play, *The Harvest Festival* (30 Mar); *The letters of Sean O'Casey*, vol. II (1942–54) issued late in the summer. Significant anniversary productions in England and Ireland include the Royal Shakespeare Company's *Juno* in London (with Judi Dench as Juno) and *Shadow of a Gunman* in Stratford-upon-Avon; and new and well-received productions of *Shadow of a Gunman* and *Red Roses for Me* by the Abbey Theatre.

1981   (26 Mar) New edition of the *Autobiographies* (the first with an index) issued in London.

1984   First edition of O'Casey's *Complete Plays* published, in five volumes.

---

## FIRST PRODUCTIONS

*The Shadow of a Gunman*, 12 April 1923, Abbey Theatre, Dublin
*Juno and the Paycock*, 3 March 1924, Abbey Theatre, Dublin
*The Plough and the Stars*, 8 February 1926, Abbey Theatre, Dublin
*The Silver Tassie*, 11 October 1929, Apollo Theatre, London
*Red Roses for Me*, 15 March 1943, Olympia Theatre, Dublin
*Cock-a-Doodle Dandy*, 10 December 1949, People's Theatre, Newcastle-upon-Tyne
*The Bishop's Bonfire*, 28 February 1955, Gaiety Theatre, Dublin

# The Shadow of a Gunman

## A Tragedy in Two Acts

1

## CHARACTERS

DONAL DAVOREN
SEUMAS SHIELDS, a pedlar
TOMMY OWENS         Residents in
ADOLPHUS GRIGSON    the tenement
MRS GRIGSON
MINNIE POWELL
MR MULLIGAN, the landlord
MR MAGUIRE, soldier of the IRA
MRS HENDERSON ⎱ residents of an
MR GALLOGHER ⎰ adjoining tenement
AN AUXILIARY

## PLACE AND TIME

A room in a tenement in Hilljoy Square, Dublin.

Some hours elapse between the two acts. The period of the play is May 1920.

## ACT I

*A return room\* in a tenement house in Hilljoy Square.\* At the back two
large windows looking out into the yard; they occupy practically the whole
of the back wall-space. Between the windows is a cupboard, on the top of
which is a pile of books. The doors are open, and on these are hanging a
number of collars and ties. Running parallel with the windows is a stretcher
bed; another runs at right angles along the wall at right. At the head of this
bed is a door leading to the rest of the house. The wall on the left runs
diagonally, so that the fireplace – which is in the centre – is plainly visible.
On the mantelshelf to the right is a statue of the Virgin, to the left a statue of
the Sacred Heart, and in the centre a crucifix. Around the fireplace are a
few common cooking utensils. In the centre of the room is a table, on which
are a typewriter, a candle and candlestick, a bunch of wild flowers in a
vase, writing materials and a number of books. There are two chairs, one
near the fireplace and one at the table. The aspect of the place is one of
absolute untidiness, engendered on the one hand by the congenital
slovenliness of* SEUMAS SHIELDS, *and on the other by the temperament of*
DONAL DAVOREN, *making it appear impossible to effect an improvement in
such a place.*

DAVOREN *is sitting at the table typing. He is about thirty. There is in his
face an expression that seems to indicate an eternal war between weakness
and strength; there is in the lines of the brow and chin an indication of a
desire for activity, while in his eyes there is visible an unquenchable
tendency towards rest. His struggle through life has been a hard one, and his
efforts have been handicapped by an inherited and self-developed devotion
to 'the might of design, the mystery of colour, and the belief in the
redemption of all things by beauty everlasting'.\* His life would drive him
mad were it not for the fact that he never knew any other. He bears upon his
body the marks of the struggle for existence and the efforts towards
self-expression.*

SEUMAS SHIELDS, *who is in the bed next the wall to the right, is a heavily
built man of thirty-five; he is dark-haired and sallow-complexioned. In
him is frequently manifested the superstition, the fear and the malignity of
primitive man.*

DAVOREN [*lilting an air as he composes*].

Or when sweet Summer's ardent arms outspread,
Entwined with flowers,
Enfold us, like two lovers newly wed,
Thro' ravish'd hours –
Then sorrow, woe and pain lose all their powers,
For each is dead, and life is only ours.*

*A woman's figure appears at the window and taps loudly on one of the panes; at the same moment there is loud knocking at the door.*

VOICE OF WOMAN AT WINDOW. Are you awake, Mr Shields – Mr Shields, are you awake? Are you goin' to get up today at all, at all?

VOICE AT THE DOOR. Mr Shields, is there any use of callin' you at all? This is a nice nine o'clock: do you know what time it is, Mr Shields?

SEUMAS [*loudly*]. Yus!

VOICE AT THE DOOR. Why don't you get up, then, an' not have the house turned into a bedlam* tryin' to waken you?

SEUMAS [*shouting*]. All right, all right, all right! The way these oul' ones bawl at a body!* Upon my soul! I'm beginnin' to believe that the Irish People are still in the stone age. If they could they'd throw a bomb at you.

DAVOREN. A land mine exploding under the bed is the only thing that would lift you out of it.

SEUMAS [*stretching himself*]. Oh-h-h. I was fast in the arms of Morpheus* – he was one of the infernal deities, son of Somnus,* wasn't he?

DAVOREN. I think so.

SEUMAS. The poppy was his emblem, wasn't it?

DAVOREN. Ah, I don't know.

SEUMAS. It's a bit cold this morning, I think, isn't it?

DAVOREN. It's quite plain I'm not going to get much quietness in this house.

SEUMAS [*after a pause*]. I wonder what time it is?

DAVOREN. The Angelus* went some time ago.

SEUMAS [*sitting up in bed suddenly*]. The Angelus! It couldn't be that late, could it? I asked them to call me at nine so that I could get Mass before I went on my rounds. Why didn't you give us a rap?

DAVOREN. Give you a rap! Why, man, they've been thundering at the door and hammering at the window for the past two hours, till the house shook to its very foundations, but you took less notice of the infernal din that I would take of the strumming of a grasshopper.

SEUMAS. There's no fear of you thinking of any one else when you're at your poetry. The land of Saints and Scholars 'ill shortly be a land of bloody poets. [*Anxiously*] I suppose Maguire has come and gone?

DAVOREN. Maguire? No, he hasn't been here – why, did you expect him?

SEUMAS [*in a burst of indignation*]. He said he'd be here at nine. 'Before the last chime has struck,' says he, 'I'll be coming in on the door,' and it must be – what time is it now?

DAVOREN. Oh, it must be half-past twelve.

SEUMAS. Did anybody ever see the like of the Irish People? Is there any use tryin' to do anything in this country? Have everything packed and ready, have everything packed and ready, have . . .

DAVOREN. And have you everything packed and ready?

SEUMAS. What's the use of having anything packed and ready when he didn't come? [*He rises and dresses himself.*] No wonder this unfortunate country is as it is, for you can't depend upon the word of a single individual in it. I suppose he was too damn lazy to get up; he wanted the streets to be well aired first. – Oh, Kathleen ni Houlihan, you way's a thorny way.*

DAVOREN. Ah me! alas, pain, pain ever, for ever!*

SEUMAS. That's from Shelley's *Prometheus Unbound*. I could never agree with Shelley, not that there's anything to be said against him as a poet – as a poet – but . . .

DAVOREN. He flung a few stones through stained-glass windows.

SEUMAS. He wasn't the first nor he won't be the last to do that, but the stained-glass windows – more than ever of them – are here still, and Shelley is doing a jazz dance down below. [*He gives a snarling laugh of pleasure.*]

DAVOREN [*shocked*]. And you actually rejoice and are exceedingly glad that, as you believe, Shelley, the sensitive, high-minded, noble-hearted Shelley, is suffering the tortures of the damned.

SEUMAS. I rejoice in the vindication of the Church and Truth.

DAVOREN. Bah. You know as little about truth as anybody else, and you care as little about the Church as the least of those that profess her faith; your religion is simply the state of being afraid that God will torture your soul in the next world as you are afraid the Black and Tans* will torture your body in this.

SEUMAS. Go on, me boy; I'll have a right laugh at you when both of us are dead.

DAVOREN. You're welcome to laugh as much as you like at me when both of us are dead.

SEUMAS [*as he is about to put on his collar and tie*]. I don't think I need to wash meself this morning; do I look all right?

DAVOREN. Oh, you're all right; it's too late now to start washing yourself. Didn't you wash yourself yesterday morning?

SEUMAS. I gave meself a great rub yesterday. [*He proceeds to pack various articles into an attaché case – spoons, forks, laces, thread, etc.*] I think I'll bring out a few of the braces too; damn it, they're worth sixpence each; there's great stuff* in them – did you see them?

DAVOREN. Yes, you showed them to me before.

SEUMAS. They're great value; I only hope I'll be able to get enough o' them. I'm wearing a pair of them meself – they'd do Cuchullian,* they're so strong. [*Counting the spoons*] There's a dozen in each of these parcels – three, six, nine – damn it, there's only eleven in this one. I better try another Three, six, nine – my God, there's only eleven in this one too, and one of them bent! Now I suppose I'll have to go through the whole bloody lot of them, for I'd never be easy in me mind thinkin' there'd be more than a dozen in some o' them. And still we're looking for freedom – ye gods, it's a glorious country! [*He lets one fall, which he stoops to pick up.*] Oh, my God, there's the braces after breakin'.

DAVOREN. That doesn't look as if they were strong enough for Cuchullian.

SEUMAS. I put a heavy strain on them too sudden. There's that fellow Maguire never turned up, either; he's almost too lazy to wash himself. [*As he is struggling with the braces the door is hastily shoved in and* MAGUIRE *rushes in with a handbag.*] This is a nice nine o'clock. What's the use of you coming at this hour o' the day? Do you think we're going to work be moonlight? If you weren't goin' to come at nine couldn't you say you weren't . . .

MAGUIRE. Keep your hair on;* I just blew in to tell you that I couldn't go today at all. I have to go to Knocksedan.*

SEUMAS. Knocksedan! An' what, in the name o' God, is bringin' you to Knocksedan?

MAGUIRE. Business, business. I'm going out to catch butterflies.

SEUMAS. If you want to make a cod* of anybody, make a cod of somebody else, an' don't be tryin' to make a cod o' me. Here I've had everything packed an' ready for hours; you were to be here at nine, an' you wait till just one o'clock to come rushin' in like a mad

bull to say you've got to go to Knocksedan! Can't you leave
Knockesdan till tomorrow?

MAGUIRE. Can't be did, can't be did, Seumas; if I waited till tomorrow
all the butterflies might be dead. I'll leave this bag here till this
evening. [*He puts the bag in a corner of the room.*] Goodbye . . . ee.*
[*He is gone before* SEUMAS *is aware of it.*]

SEUMAS [*with a gesture of despair*]. Oh, this is a hopeless country!
There's a fellow that thinks that the four cardinal virtues are not to
be found outside an Irish Republic. I don't want to boast about
myself – I don't want to boast about myself, and I suppose I could
call meself as good a Gael as some of those that are knocking about
now* – but I remember the time when I taught Irish six nights
a week, when in the Irish Republican Brotherhood* I paid me rifle
levy* like a man, an' when the Church refused to have anything to
do with James Stephens,* I tarred a prayer for the repose of his soul
on the steps of the Pro-Cathedral.* Now, after all me work for Dark
Rosaleen,* the only answer you can get from a roarin' Republican
to a simple question is 'Goodbye . . . ee.' What, in the name o' God,
can be bringin' him to Knocksedan?

DAVOREN. Hadn't you better run out and ask him?

SEUMAS. That's right, that's right – make a joke about it! That's the
Irish People all over – they treat a joke as a serious thing and a
serious thing as a joke. Upon me soul, I'm beginning to believe that
the Irish People aren't, never were, an' never will be fit for
self-government. They made Balor of the Evil Eye* King of
Ireland, an' so signs on it there's neither conscience nor honesty
from one end of the country to the other. Well, I hope he'll have a
happy day in Knocksedan. [*A knock at the door.*] Who's that?
[*Another knock. Irritably*] Who's that; who's there?

DAVOREN [*more irritably*]. Halt and give the countersign – damn it,
man, can't you go and see?

SEUMAS *goes over and opens the door. A man of about sixty is revealed,
dressed in a faded blue serge suit; a half tall hat* is on his head. It is evident
that he has no love for* SEUMAS, *who denies him the deference he believes is
due from a tenant to a landlord. He carries some papers in his hand.*

THE LANDLORD [*ironically*]. Good day, Mr Shields; it's meself that
hopes you're feelin' well – you're lookin' well, anyhow – though you
can't always go be looks nowadays.

SEUMAS. It doesn't matter whether I'm lookin' well or feelin' well; I'm all right, thanks be to God.

THE LANDLORD. I'm very glad to hear it.

SEUMAS. It doesn't matter whether you're glad to hear it or not, Mr Mulligan.

THE LANDLORD. You're not inclined to be very civil, Mr Shields.

SEUMAS. Look here, Mr Mulligan, if you come here to raise an argument, I've something to do – let me tell you that.

THE LANDLORD. I don't come here to raise no argument; a person ud have small gains argufyin' with you – let me tell you that.

SEUMAS. I've no time to be standin' here gostherin'* with you – let me shut the door, Mr Mulligan.

THE LANDLORD. You'll not shut no door till you've heard what I've got to say.

SEUMAS. Well, say it then, an' go about your business.

THE LANDLORD. You're very high an' mighty, but take care you're not goin' to get a drop. What a baby you are not to know what brings me here! Maybe you thought I was goin' to ask you to come to tea.

DAVOREN. Ah me! alas, pain, pain ever, for ever!

SEUMAS. Are you goin' to let me shut the door, Mr Mulligan?

THE LANDLORD. I'm here for me rent; you don't like the idea of bein' asked to pay your just an' lawful debts.

SEUMAS. You'll get your rent when you learn to keep your rent-book in a proper way.

THE LANDLORD. I'm not goin' to take any lessons from you, anyhow.

SEUMAS. I want to have no more talk with you, Mr Mulligan.

THE LANDLORD. Talk or no talk, you owe me eleven weeks' rent, an' its marked down again' you in black an' white.

SEUMAS. I don't care a damn if it was marked down in green, white, an' yellow.*

THE LANDLORD. You're a terribly independent fellow, an' it ud be fitter for you to be less funny an' stop tryin' to be billickin'* honest an' respectable people.

SEUMAS. Just you be careful what you're sayin', Mr Mulligan. There's law in the land still.

THE LANDLORD. Be me sowl* there is, an' you're goin' to get a little of it now. [*He offers the papers to* SEUMAS.] Them's for you.

SEUMAS [*hesitating to take them*]. I want to have nothing to do with you, Mr Mulligan.

THE LANDLORD [*throwing the papers in the centre of the room*]. What am I better? It was the sorry day I ever let you come into this house. Maybe them notices to quit will stop your writin' letters to the papers about me an' me house.

DAVOREN. For goodness' sake, bring the man in, and don't be discussing the situation like a pair of primitive troglodytes.*

SEUMAS [*taking no notice*]. Writing letters to the papers is my business, an' I'll write as often as I like, when I like, an' how I like.

THE LANDLORD. You'll not write about this house at all events. You can blow* about the state of the yard, but you took care to say nothin' about payin' rent: oh no, that's not in your line. But since you're not satisfied with the house, you can pack up an' go to another.

SEUMAS. I'll go, Mr Mulligan, when I think fit, an' no sooner.

THE LANDLORD. Not content with keeping the rent, you're startin' to bring in lodgers – [*to* DAVOREN] not that I'm sayin' anythin' again' you, sir. Bringin' in lodgers without as much as be your leave – what's the world comin' to at all that a man's house isn't his own? But I'll soon put a stop to your gallop, for on the twenty-eight of the next month out you go, an' there'll be few sorry to see your back.

SEUMAS. I'll go when I like.

THE LANDLORD. I'll let you see whether you own the house or no.

SEUMAS. I'll go when I like!

THE LANDLORD. We'll see about that.

SEUMAS. We'll see.

THE LANDLORD. Ay, we'll see. [THE LANDLORD *goes out and* SEUMAS *shuts the door.*]

THE LANDLORD [*outside*]. Mind you, I'm in earnest; you'll not stop in this house a minute longer than the twenty-eight.

SEUMAS [*with a roar*]. Ah, go to hell!

DAVOREN [*pacing the room as far as the space will permit*]. What in the name of God persuaded me to come to such a house as this?

SEUMAS. It's nothing when you're used to it; you're too thin-skinned altogether. The oul' sod's got the wind up* about you, that's all.

DAVOREN. Got the wind up about me!

SEUMAS. He thinks you're on the run. He's afraid of a raid, and that his lovely property'll be destroyed.

DAVOREN. But why, in the name of all that's sensible, should he think that I'm on the run?

SEUMAS. Sure they all think you're on the run. Mrs Henderson thinks it, Tommy Owens thinks it, Mrs an' Mr Grigson thinks it, an'

Minnie Powell thinks it too. [*Picking up his attaché case*] I'd better be off if I'm goin' to do anything today.

DAVOREN. What are we going to do with these notices to quit?

SEUMAS. Oh, shove them up on the mantelpiece behind one of the statues.

DAVOREN. Oh, I mean what action shall we take?

SEUMAS. I haven't time to stop now. We'll talk about them when I come back. . . . I'll get me own back on that oul' Mulligan yet. I wish to God they would come an' smash his rookery* to pieces, for it's all he thinks of, and, mind you, oul' Mulligan would call himself a descendant of the true Gaels of Banba* – [*as he goes out*]

Oh, proud were the chieftains of famed Inisfail.
Is truagh gan oidher 'na Vfarradh.
The stars of our sky an' the salt of our soil –*

Oh, Kathleen ni Houlihan, your way's a thorny way! [*He goes out.*]

DAVOREN [*returning to the table and sitting down at the typewriter*]. Oh, Donal Og O'Davoren, your way's a thorny way. Your last state is worse than your first. Ah me, alas! Pain, pain ever, for ever. Like thee, Prometheus, no change, no pause, no hope. Ah, life, life, life! [*There is a gentle knock at the door.*] Another Fury* come to plague me now! [*Another knock, a little louder.*] You can knock till you're tired.

*The door opens and* MINNIE POWELL *enters with an easy confidence one would not expect her to possess from her gentle way of knocking. She is a girl of twenty-three, but the fact of being forced to earn her living, and to take care of herself, on account of her parents' early death, has given her a force and an assurance beyond her years. She has lost the sense of fear (she does not know this), and, consequently, she is at ease in all places and before all persons, even those of a superior education, so long as she meets them in the atmosphere that surrounds the members of her own class. Her hair is brown, neither light nor dark, but partaking of both tints according to the light or shade she may happen to be in. Her well-shaped figure – a rare thing in a city girl – is charmingly dressed in a brown tailor-made costume, her stockings and shoes are a darker brown tint than the costume, and all are crowned by a silk tam-o' shanter* of a rich blue tint.*

MINNIE. Are you in, Mr Shields?

DAVOREN [*rapidly*]. No, he's not, Minnie; he's just gone out – if you run out quickly you're sure to catch him.

MINNIE. Oh, it's all right, Mr Davoren, you'll do just as well; I just come in for a drop o' milk for a cup o' tea; I shouldn't be troublin' you this way, but I'm sure you don't mind.

DAVOREN [*dubiously*]. No trouble in the world; delighted, I'm sure. [*Giving her the milk*] There, will you have enough?

MINNIE. Plenty, lashins,* thanks. Do you be all alone all the day, Mr Davoren?

DAVOREN. No, indeed; I wish to God I was.

MINNIE. It's not good for you then. I don't know how you like to be by yourself – I couldn't stick it long.

DAVOREN [*wearily*]. No?

MINNIE. No, indeed; [*with rapture*] there's nothin' I'm more fond of than a Hooley.* I was at one last Sunday – I danced rings round me! Tommy Owens was there – you know Tommy Owens, don't you?

DAVOREN. I can't say I do.

MINNIE. D'ye not? The little fellow that lives with his mother in the two-pair back* – [*ecstatically*] he's a gorgeous melodeon* player!

DAVOREN. A gifted son of Orpheus, eh?

MINNIE [*who never heard of Orpheus*]. You've said it, Mr Davoren: the son of poor oul' Battie Owens, a weeshy,* dawny,* bit of a man that was never sober an' was always talkin' politics. Poor man, it killed him in the long run.

DAVOREN. A man should always be drunk, Minnie, when he talks politics – it's the only way in which to make them important.

MINNIE. Tommy takes after the oul' fellow, too; he's talk from morning till night when he has a few jars in him. [*Suddenly; for like all of her class,* MINNIE *is not able to converse very long on the one subject, and her thoughts spring from one thing to another.*] Poetry is a grand thing, Mr Davoren, I'd love to be able to write a poem – a lovely poem on Ireland an' the men o' '98.*

DAVOREN. Oh, we've had enough of poems, Minnie, about '98, and of Ireland, too.

MINNIE. Oh, there's a thing for a Republican to say! But I know what you mean: it's time to give up the writing an' take to the gun. [*Her roving eye catches sight of the flowers in the vase.*] What's Mr Shields doin' with the oul' weeds?

DAVOREN. Those aren't Shields', they're mine. Wild flowers is a kindlier name for them, Minnie, than weeds. These are wild violets, this is an *Arum maculatum*, or wake robin, and these are celandines, a very beautiful flower related to the buttercups. [*He quotes*]

> One day, when Morn's half-open'd eyes
> Were bright with Spring sunshine –
> My hand was clasp'd in yours, dear love,
> And yours was clasp'd in mine –
> We bow'd as worshippers before
> The Golden Celandine.*

MINNIE. Oh, aren't they lovely, an' isn't the poem lovely, too! I wonder, now, who she was.

DAVOREN [*puzzled*]. She, who?

MINNIE. Why, the . . . [*Roguishly*] Oh, be the way you don't know.

DAVOREN. Know? I'm sure I don't know.

MINNIE. It doesn't matter, anyhow – that's your own business; I suppose I don't know her.

DAVOREN. Know her – know whom?

MINNIE [*shyly*]. Her whose hand was clasped in yours, an' yours was clasped in hers.

DAVOREN. Oh, that – that was simply a poem I quoted about the celandine, that might apply to any girl – to you, for instance.

MINNIE [*greatly relieved, coming over and sitting beside* DAVOREN]. But you have a sweetheart, all the same, Mr Davoren, haven't you?

DAVOREN. I? No, not one, Minnie.

MINNIE. Oh, now, you can tell that to some one else; aren't you a poet an' aren't all the girls fond o' poets?

DAVOREN. That may be, but all the poets aren't fond of girls.

MINNIE. They are in the story-books, ay, and fond of more than one, too. [*With a questioning look*] Are you fond of them, Mr Davoren?

DAVOREN. Of course I like girls, Minnie, especially girls who can add to their charms by the way in which they dress, like you, for instance.

MINNIE. Oh, now, you're on for coddin' me, Mr Davoren.

DAVOREN. No, really, Minnie, I'm not; you are a very charming little girl indeed.

MINNIE. Then if I'm a charmin' little girl, you ought to be able to write a poem about me.

DAVOREN [*who has become susceptible to the attractiveness of* MINNIE, *catching her hand*]. And so I will, so I will, Minnie; I have written them about girls not half so pretty as yourself.

MINNIE. Ah, I knew you had one, I knew you had one now.

DAVOREN. Nonsense. Every girl a poet writes about isn't his sweetheart; Annie Laurie* wasn't the sweetheart of Bobbie Burns.

MINNIE. You needn't tell me she wasn't; 'An' for bonnie Annie Laurie I'd lay me down an' die.' No man ud lay down an' die for any but a sweetheart, not even for a wife.

DAVOREN. No man, Minnie, willingly dies for anything.

MINNIE. Except for his country, like Robert Emmet.*

DAVOREN. Even he would have lived on if he could; he died not to deliver Ireland. The British Government killed him to save the British nation.

MINNIE. You're only jokin' now; you'd die for your country.

DAVOREN. I don't know so much about that.

MINNIE. You would, you would, you would – I know what you are.

DAVOREN. What am I?

MINNIE [*in a whisper*]. A gunman on the run!

DAVOREN [*too pleased to deny it*]. Maybe I am, and maybe I'm not.

MINNIE. Oh, I know, I know, I know. Do you never be afraid?

DAVOREN. Afraid! Afraid of what?

MINNIE. Why, the ambushes of course; *I'm* all of a tremble when I hear a shot go off, an' what must it be in the middle of the firin'?

DAVOREN [*delighted at* MINNIE'S *obvious admiration; leaning back in his chair, and lighting a cigarette with placid affectation*]. I'll admit one does be a little nervous at first, but a fellow gets used to it after a bit, till, at last, a gunman throws a bomb as carelessly as a schoolboy throws a snowball.

MINNIE [*fervently*]. I wish it was all over, all the same. [*Suddenly, with a tremor in her voice*] You'll take care of yourself, won't you, won't you, Donal – I mean, Mr Davoren?

DAVOREN [*earnestly*]. Call me Donal, Minnie; we're friends, great friends now – [*putting his arm around her*] go on, Minnie, call me Donal, let me hear you say Donal.

MINNIE. The place badly needs a tidyin' up . . . Donal – there now, are you satisfied? [*Rapidly, half afraid of* DAVOREN'S *excited emotions*] But it really does, it's in an awful state. Tomorrow's a half-day, an' I'll run in an' straighten it up a bit.

DAVOREN [*frightened at the suggestion*]. No, no, Minnie, you're too pretty for that sort of work; besides, the people of the house would be sure to start talking about you.

MINNIE. An' do you think Minnie Powell cares whether they'll talk or no? She's had to push her way through life up to this without help from any one, an' she's not goin' to ask their leave, now, to do what she wants to do.

DAVOREN [*forgetting his timidity in the honest joy of appreciating the independent courage of* MINNIE]. My soul within art thou, Minnie! A pioneer in action as I am a pioneer in thought. The two powers that shall 'grasp this sorry scheme of things entire, and mould life nearer to the heart's desire'.* Lovely little Minnie, and brave as well; brave little Minnie, and lovely as well!

*His disengaged hand lifts up her bent head, and he looks earnestly at her; he is stooping to kiss her, when* TOMMY OWENS *appears at the door, which* MINNIE *has left partially open.* TOMMY *is about twenty-five years of age. He is small and thin; his words are uttered in a nasal drawl; his voice is husky, due to frequent drinks and perpetual cigarette-smoking. He tries to get rid of the huskiness by an occasional cough.* TOMMY *is a hero-worshipper, and, like many others, he is anxious to be on familiar terms with those who he thinks are braver than he is himself, and whose approbation he tries to win by an assumption equal to their own. He talks in a staccato manner. He has a few drinks taken – it is too early to be drunk – that make him talkative. He is dressed in a suit of dungarees,* and gives a gentle cough to draw attention to his presence.*

TOMMY. I seen nothin' – honest – thought you was learnin' to typewrite – Mr Davoren teachin' you. I seen nothin' else – s'help me God!

MINNIE. We'd be hard put to it if we minded* what you seen, Tommy Owens.

TOMMY. Right, Minnie, Tommy Owens has a heart – Evenin', Mr Davoren – don't mind me comin' in – I'm Tommy Owens – live up in the two-pair back, workin' in Ross an' Walpole's – Mr Shields knows me well; you needn't be afraid o' me, Mr Davoren.

DAVOREN. Why should I be afraid of you, Mr Owens, or of anybody else?

TOMMY. Why should you, indeed? We're all friends here – Mr Shields knows me well – all you've got to say is, 'Do you know Tommy

Owens?' an' he'll tell you the sort of a man Tommy Owens is.
There's no flies on Tommy* – got me?

MINNIE. For goodness' sake, Tommy, leave Mr Davoren alone – he's
got enough burgeons* on him already.

TOMMY. Not a word, Minnie, not a word – Mr Davoren understands
me well, as man to man. It's 'Up the Republic' all the time – eh, Mr
Davoren?

DAVOREN. I know nothing about the Republic; I have no connection
with the politics of the day, and I don't want to have any
connection.

TOMMY. You needn't say no more – a nod's as good as a wink to a blind
horse* – you've no meddlin' or makin' with it, good, bad, or
indifferent, pro nor con; I know it an' Minnie knows it – give me
your hand. [*He catches* DAVOREN'S *hand.*] Two firm hands clasped
together will all the power outbrave of the heartless English tyrant,
the Saxon coward an' knave. That's Tommy Owens' hand, Mr
Davoren, the hand of a man, a man – Mr Shields knows me well.
[*He breaks into song.*]

> High upon the gallows tree stood the noble-hearted three,
> By the vengeful tyrant stricken in their bloom;
> But they met him face to face with the spirit of their race,
> And they went with souls undaunted to their doom!

MINNIE [*in an effort to quell his fervour*]. Tommy Owens, for goodness'
sake . . .

TOMMY [*overwhelming her with a shout*].

> God save Ireland ses the hayros, God save Ireland ses we all,
> Whether on the scaffold high or the battle-field we die.
> Oh, what matter when for Ayryinn dear we fall!*

[*Tearfully*] Mr Davoren, I'd die for Ireland!

DAVOREN. I know you would, I know you would, Tommy.

TOMMY. I never got a chance – they never gave me a chance – but all
the same I'd be there if I was called on – Mr Shields knows that – ask
Mr Shields, Mr Davoren.

DAVOREN. There's no necessity, Tommy; I know you're the right stuff
if you got the chance, but remember that he also serves who only
stands and waits.*

TOMMY [*fiercely*]. I'm bloody well tired o' waitin' – we're all tired o' waiting'. Why isn't every man in Ireland out with the IRA? Up with the barricades, up with the barricades; it's now or never, now an' for ever, as Sarsfield said at the battle o' Vinegar Hill.\* Up with the barricades – that's Tommy Owens – an' a penny buys a whistle. Let them as thinks different say different – what do you say, Mr Davoren?

DAVOREN. I say, Tommy, you ought to go up and get your dinner, for if you wait much longer it won't be worth eating.

TOMMY. Oh, damn the dinner; who'd think o' dinner an' Ireland fightin' to be free – not Tommy Owens, anyhow. It's only the Englishman who's always thinkin' of his belly.

MINNIE. Tommy Owens!

TOMMY. Excuse me, Miss Powell, in the ardure ov me anger I disremembered\* there was a lady present.

*Voices are heard outside, and presently* MRS HENDERSON *comes into the room, followed by* MR GALLOGHER, *who, however, lingers at the door, too timid to come any further.* MRS HENDERSON *is a massive woman in every way; massive head, arms, and body; massive voice, and a massive amount of self-confidence. She is a mountain of good nature, and during the interview she behaves towards* DAVOREN *with deferential self-assurance. She dominates the room, and seems to occupy the whole of it. She is dressed poorly but tidily, wearing a white apron and a large shawl.* MR GALLOGHER, *on the other hand, is a spare little man with a spare little grey beard and a thin, nervous voice. He is dressed as well as a faded suit of blue will allow him to be. He is obviously ill at ease during his interview with* DAVOREN. *He carries a hard hat, much the worse for wear, under his left arm, and a letter in his right hand.*

MRS HENDERSON [*entering the room*]. Come along in, Mr Gallicker, Mr Davoren won't mind; it's him as can put you in the way o' havin' your wrongs righted; come on in, man, an' don't be so shy – Mr Davoren is wan ov\* ourselves that stands for govermint ov the people with the people by the people. You'll find you'll be as welcome as the flowers in May. Good evenin', Mr Davoren, an' God an' His holy angels be between you an' all harm.

TOMMY [*effusively*]. Come on, Mr Gallicker, an' don't be a stranger – we're all friends here – anything special to be done or particular advice asked, here's your man here.

DAVOREN [*subconsciously pleased, but a little timid of the belief that he is connected with the gunmen*]. I'm very busy just now, Mrs Henderson, and really . . .

MRS HENDERSON [*mistaking the reason of his embarrassment*]. Don't be put out, Mr Davoren, we won't keep you more nor* a few minutes. It's not in me or in Mr Gallicker to spoil sport. Him an' me was young once, an' knows what it is to be strolling at night in the pale moonlight, with arms round one another. An' I wouldn't take much an' say there's game in Mr Gallicker still, for I seen, sometimes, a dangerous cock* in his eye. But we won't keep you an' Minnie long asunder; he's the letter an' all written. You must know, Mr Davoren – excuse me for not introducin' him sooner – this is Mr Gallicker, that lives in the front drawin'-room ov number fifty-five, as decent an' honest an' quiet a man as you'd meet in a day's walk. An' so signs on it, it's them as 'ill be imposed upon – read the letter, Mr Gallicker.

TOMMY. Read away, Mr Gallicker, it will be attended to, never fear; we know our own know,* eh, Mr Davoren?

MINNIE. Hurry up, Mr Gallicker, an' don't be keeping Mr Davoren.

MRS HENDERSON. Give him time, Minnie Powell. Give him time. You must know in all fairity,* Mr Davoren, that the family livin' in the next room to Mr Gallicker – the back drawin'-room, to be particular – am I right or am I wrong, Mr Gallicker?

MR GALLOGHER. You're right, Mrs Henderson, perfectly right, indeed – that's the very identical room.

MRS HENDERSON. Well, Mr Davoren, the people in the back drawin'-room, or, to be more particular, the residents – that's the word that's writ in the letter – am I right or am I wrong, Mr Gallicker?

MR GALLOGHER. You're right, Mrs Henderson, perfectly accurate – that's the very identical word.

MRS HENDERSON. Well, Mr Davoren, the residents in the back drawin'-room, as I aforesaid, is nothin' but a gang o' tramps that oughtn't to be allowed to associate with honest, decent, quiet, respectable people. Mr Gallicker has tried to reason with them, and make them behave themselves – which in my opinion they never will – however, that's only an opinion, an' not legal – ever since they have made Mr Gallicker's life a HELL! Mr Gallicker, am I right or am I wrong?

MR GALLOGHER. I'm sorry to say you're right, Mrs Henderson, perfectly right – not a word of exaggeration.

MRS HENDERSON. Well, now, Mr Gallicker, seein' as I have given Mr Davoren a fair account ov how you're situated, an' ov these tramps' cleverality, I'll ask you to read the letter, which I'll say, not because you're there, or that you're a friend o' mine, is as good a letter as was decomposed by a scholar. Now, Mr Gallicker, an' don't forget the top sayin'.*

MR GALLOGHER *prepares to read;* MINNIE *leans forward to listen;* TOMMY *takes out a well-worn notebook and a pencil stump, and assumes a very important attitude.*

TOMMY. One second. Mr Gallicker, is this the twenty-first or twenty-second?

MR GALLOGHER. The twenty-first, sir.

TOMMY. Thanks; proceed, Mr Gallicker.

MR GALLOGHER [*with a few preliminary tremors, reads the letter. Reading*].

### To All To Whom These Presents Come, Greeting

Gentlemen of the Irish Republican Army . . .

MRS HENDERSON. There's a beginnin' for you, Mr Davoren.

MINNIE. That's some swank.*

TOMMY. There's a lot in that sayin', mind you; it's a hard wallop at the British Empire.

MRS HENDERSON [*proudly*]. Go on, Mr Gallicker.

MR GALLOGHER [*reading*].

I wish to call your attention to the persecution me and my family has to put up with in respect of and appertaining to the residents of the back drawing-room of the house known as fifty-five, Saint Teresa Street, situate in the Parish of St Thomas, in the Borough and City of Dublin. This persecution started eighteen months ago – or to be precise – on the tenth day of the sixth month, in the year nineteen hundred and twenty.

MRS HENDERSON. That's the word I was trying to think ov – precise – it cuts the ground from under their feet – so to speak.
MR GALLOGHER [*reading*].

We, the complainants, resident on the ground floor, deeming it disrespectable . . .

MRS HENDERSON [*with an emphatic nod*]. Which it was.
MR GALLOGHER [*reading*].

Deeming it disrespectable to have an open hall door, and to have the hall turned into a playground, made a solemn protest, and, in consequence, we the complainants aforesaid has had no peace ever since. Owing to the persecution, as aforesaid specified, we had to take out a summons again them some time ago as there was no Republican Courts* then; but we did not proceed again them as me and my wife – to wit, James and Winifred Gallogher – has a strong objection to foreign Courts* as such. We had peace for some time after that, but now things have gone from bad to worse. The name calling and the language is something abominable . . .

MRS HENDERSON [*holding out her hand as a constable would extend his to stop a car that another may pass*]. Excuse me, Mr Gallicker, but I think the word 'shockin'' should be put in there after abominable; for the language used be these tramps has two ways o' bein' looked at – for it's abominable to the childer* an' shockin' to your wife – am I right or am I wrong, Mr Davoren?
TOMMY [*judicially*]. Shockin' is a right good word, with a great deal o' meanin', an' . . .
MRS HENDERSON [*with a deprecating gesture that extinguishes TOMMY*]. Tommy, let Mr Davoren speak; whatever Mr Davoren ses, Julia Henderson'll abide be.
DAVOREN [*afraid to say anthing else*]. I think the word might certainly be introduced with advantage.
MRS HENDERSON. Go over there, Mr Gallicker, an' put in the word shockin', as aforesaid. [GALLOGHER *goes over to the table, and with a great deal of difficulty enters the word.*]
TOMMY [*to MR GALLOGHER as he writes*]. Ey, there's two k's in shockin'!
MR GALLOGHER [*reading*].

The language is something abominable and shocking. My wife has often to lock the door of the room to keep them from assaulting her. If you would be so kind as to send some of your army or police down to see for themselves we would give them full particulars. I have to be always from home all day, as I work with Mr Hennessy, the harness maker of the Coombe, who will furnish all particulars as to my unvarnished respectability, also my neighbours. The name of the resident-tenant who is giving all this trouble and who, pursuant to the facts of the case aforesaid mentioned, will be the defendant, is Dwyer. The husband of the aforesaid Mrs Dwyer, or the aforesaid defendant, as the case may be, is a seaman, who is coming home shortly, and we beg The Irish Republican Army to note that the said Mrs Dwyer says he will settle us when he comes home. While leaving it entirely in the hands of the gentlemen of The Republican Army, the defendant, that is to say, James Gallogher of fifty-five St Teresa Street, ventures to say that he thinks he has made out a Primmy Fashy Case* against Mrs Dwyer and all her heirs, male and female as aforesaid mentioned in the above written schedule.

*NB*. If you send up any of your men, please tell them to bring their guns. I beg to remain the humble servant and devoted admirer of the Gentlemen of the Irish Republican Army.

Witness my hand this tenth day of the fifth month of the year nineteen hundred and twenty.

                                                    JAMES GALLOGHER

MR GALLOGHER [*with a modest cough*]. Ahem.
MRS HENDERSON. There's a letter for you, Mr Davoren!
TOMMY. It's the most powerfullest letter I ever heard read.
MINNIE. It wasn't you, really, that writ it, Mr Gallicker?
MRS HENDERSON. Sinn Fein Amhain:* him an' him only, Minnie, I seen him with me own two eyes when me an' Winnie – Mrs Gallicker, Mr Davoren, aforesaid as appears in the letter – was havin' a chat be the fire.
MINNIE. You'd never think it was in him to do it.
MRS HENDERSON. An' to think that the likes ov such a man is to have the sowl-case* worried out ov him by a gang o' tramps; but it's in good hands now, an' instead ov them settlin' yous, Mr Gallicker, it's yous 'ill settle them. Give the letter to Mr Davoren, an' we'll be goin'. [GALLOGHER *gives the letter to* DAVOREN.]

MRS HENDERSON [*moving towards the door*]. I hope you an' Mr Shields is gettin' on all right together, Mr Davoren.

DAVOREN. Fairly well, thanks, Mrs Henderson. We don't see much of each other. He's out during the day, and I'm usually out during the evening.

MRS HENDERSON. I'm afraid he'll never make a fortune out ov what he's sellin'. He'll talk above an hour over a pennorth o' pins. Every time he comes to our place I buy a package o' hairpins from him to give him a little encouragement. I 'clare* to God I have as many pins now as ud make a wire mattress for a double bed. All the young divils about the place are beginnin' to make a jeer ov him, too; I gave one ov them a mallavogin'* the other day for callin' him oul' hairpins!

MR GALLOGHER [*venturing an opinion*]. Mr Shields is a man of exceptional mental capacity, and is worthy of a more dignified position.

MRS HENDERSON. Them words is true, Mr Gallicker, and they aren't. For to be wise is to be a fool, an' to be a fool is to be wise.

MR GALLOGHER [*with deprecating tolerance*]. Oh, Mrs Henderson, that's a parrotox.

MRS HENDERSON. It may be what a parrot talks, or a blackbird, or, for the matter of that, a lark – but it's what Julia Henderson thinks, any . . . whisht, is that a *Stop Press*? [*Outside is heard the shriek of a newsboy calling 'Stop Press'.*]

MRS HENDERSON. Run out, Tommy, an' get it till we see what it is.

TOMMY. I haven't got a make.*

MRS HENDERSON. I never seen you any other way, an' you'll always be the same if you keep follyin' your Spearmints, an' your Bumble Bees an' your Night Patrols. [*Shouting to someone outside*] Is that a *Stop Press*, Mrs Grigson?

VOICE OUTSIDE. Yis; an ambush out near Knocksedan.

MRS HENDERSON. That's the stuff to give them. [*Loudly*] Was there anybody hurted?

VOICE OUTSIDE. One poor man killed – some chap named Maguire, the paper says.

DAVOREN [*agitated*]. What name did she say?

MINNIE. Maguire; did you know him, Mr Davoren?

DAVOREN. Yes – no, no; I didn't know him, no, I didn't know him, Minnie.

MINNIE. I wonder is it the Maguire that does be with Mr Shields?

DAVOREN. Oh no, not at all, it couldn't be.

MRS HENDERSON. Knocksedan? That's in the County Sligo, now, or I'm greatly mistaken – am I right, Mr Gallicker, or am I wrong?

MR GALLOGHER [*who knows perfectly well that it is in the County Dublin, but dare not correct* MRS HENDERSON]. That's where it is – Knocksedan, that's the very identical county.

MRS HENDERSON. Well, I think we better be makin' a move, Mr Gallicker; we've kep' Mr Davoren long enough, an' you'll find the letter'll be in good hans.

MR GALLOGHER *and* MRS HENDERSON *move towards the door, which when he reaches it* MR GALLOGHER *grips, hesitates, buttons his coat, and turns to* DAVOREN.

MR GALLOGHER. Mr Davoren, sir, on behalf ov meself, James Gallicker, an' Winifred, Mrs Gallicker, wife ov the said James, I beg to offer, extend an' furnish our humble an' hearty thanks for your benevolent goodness in interferin' in the matter specified, particularated* an' expanded upon in the letter, mandamus* or schedule, as the case may be. An' let me interpretate* to you on behalf ov meself an' Winifred Gallicker, that whenever you visit us you will be supernally positive ov a hundred thousand welcomes – ahem.

MRS HENDERSON [*beaming with pride for the genius of her friend*]. There's a man for you, Mr Davoren! You forgot to mention Biddy and Shaun, Mr Gallicker – [*to* DAVOREN] his two children – it's himself has them trained well. It ud make your heart thrill like an alarm clock to hear them singin' 'Faith ov Our Fathers' an' 'Wrap the Green Flag Roun Me'.

MR GALLOGHER [*half aplogetically and half proudly*]. Faith an' Fatherland, Mrs Henderson, Faith and Fatherland.

MRS HENDERSON. Well, good-day, Mr Davoren, an' God keep you an' strengthen all the men that are fightin' for Ireland's freedom. [*She and* GALLOGHER *go out.*]

TOMMY. I must be off too; so long, Mr Davoren, an' remember that Tommy Owens only waits the call. [*He goes out too.*]

DAVOREN. Well, Minnie, we're by ourselves once more.

MINNIE. Wouldn't that Tommy Owens give you the sick – only waitin' to hear the call! Ah, then it'll take all the brass bands in the country to blow the call before Tommy Owens ud hear it. [*She looks at her wristlet watch.*] Sacred Heart, I've only ten minutes to get back to work! I'll have to fly! Quick, Mr Davoren, write me name in typewritin' before I go – just 'Minnie'. [DAVOREN *types the name.*]

MINNIE[*shyly but determinedly*]. Now yours underneath – just 'Donal'. [DAVOREN *does so.*] Minnie, Donal; Donal, Minnie; goodbye now.

DAVOREN. Here, what about your milk?

MINNIE. I haven't time to take it now. [*Slyly*] I'll come for it this evening. [*They both go towards the door.*]

DAVOREN. Minnie, the kiss I didn't get.

MINNIE. What kiss?

DAVOREN. When we were interrupted; you know, you little rogue, come, just one.

MINNIE. Quick, then.

DAVOREN *kisses her and she runs out.* DAVOREN *returns thoughtfully to the table.*

DAVOREN. Minnie, Donal; Donal, Minnie. Very pretty, but very ignorant. A gunman on the run! Be careful, be careful, Donal Davoren. But Minnie is attracted to the idea, and I am attracted to Minnie. And what danger can there be in being the shadow of a gunman?

CURTAIN

## ACT II

*The same as in Act I. But it is now night.* SEUMAS *is in the bed that runs along the wall at back.* DAVOREN *is seated near the fire, to which he has drawn the table. He has a fountain pen in his hand, and is attracted towards the moon, which is shining in through the windows. An open writing-pad is on the table of* DAVOREN's *elbow. The bag left by* MAGUIRE *is still in the same place.*

DAVOREN.

> The cold chaste moon, the Queen of Heaven's bright isles,
> Who makes all beautiful on which she smiles;
> That wandering shrine of soft yet icy flame,
> Which ever is transformed yet still the same.*

Ah, Shelley, Shelley, you yourself were a lovely human orb shining through clouds of whirling human dust. 'She makes all beautiful on which she smiles.' Ah, Shelley, she couldn't make this thrice accursed room beautiful. Her beams of beauty only make its horrors more full of horrors still. There is an ugliness that can be made beautiful, and there is an ugliness that can only be destroyed, and this is part of that ugliness. Donal, Donal, I fear your last state is worse than your first. [*He lilts a verse, which he writes on the pad before him.*]

> When night advances through the sky with slow
>     And solemn tread
> The queenly moon looks down on life below,
>     As if she read
> Man's soul, and in her scornful silence said:
>     All beautiful and happiest things are dead.*

SEUMAS [*sleepily*]. Donal, Donal, are you awake? [*A pause.*] Donal, Donal, are you asleep?
DAVOREN. I'm neither awake nor asleep: I'm thinking.
SEUMAS. I was just thinkin', too – I was just thinkin' too, that Maguire is sorry now that he didn't come with me instead of going to Knocksedan. He caught something besides butterflies – two of them he got, one through each lung.

DAVOREN. The Irish people are very fond of turning a serious thing into a joke; that was a serious affair – for poor Maguire.

SEUMAS [*defensively*]. Why didn't he do what he arranged to do? Did he think of me when he was goin' to Knocksedan? How can he expect me to have any sympathy with him now?

DAVOREN. He can hardly expect that now that he's dead.

SEUMAS. The Republicans'll do a lot for him, now. How am I goin' to get back the things he has belongin' to me, either? There's some of them in that bag over there, but that's not quarter of what he had; an' I don't know where he was stoppin', for he left his old digs* a week or so ago – suppose there's nothing to be said about my loss; I'm to sing dumb.

DAVOREN. I hope there's nothing else in the bag, besides thread and hairpins.

SEUMAS. What else ud be in it? . . . I can't sleep properly ever since they put on this damned curfew.* A minute ago I thought I heard some of the oul' ones standin' at the door; they won't be satisfied till they bring a raid on the house; an' they never begin to stand at the door till after curfew. . . . Are you gone to bed, Donal?

DAVOREN. No; I'm trying to finish this poem.

SEUMAS [*sitting up in bed*]. If I was you I'd give that game up; it doesn't pay a working man to write poetry. I don't profess to know much about poetry – I don't profess to know much about poetry – about poetry – I don't know much about the pearly glint of the morning dew, or the damask sweetness of the rare wild rose, or the subtle greenness of the serpent's eye – but I think a poet's claim to greatness depends upon his power to put passion in the common people.

DAVOREN. Ay, passion to howl for his destruction. The People! Damn the people! They live in the abyss, the poet lives on the mountain-top; to the people there is no mystery of colour: it is simply the scarlet coat of the soldier; the purple vestments of a priest; the green banner of a party; the brown or blue overalls of industry. To them the might of design is a three-roomed house or a capacious bed. To them beauty is for sale in a butcher's shop. To the people the end of life is the life created for them; to the poet the end of life is the life that he creates for himself; life has a stifling grip upon the people's throat – it is the poet's musician. The poet ever strives to save the people; the people ever strive to destroy the poet. The people view life through creeds, through customs, and through necessities; the poet views creeds, customs, and necessities through life. The people . . .

SEUMAS [*suddenly, and with a note of anxiety in his voice*]. Whisht!*
What's that? Is that the tappin' again?

DAVOREN. Tappin'. What tappin'?

SEUMAS [*in an awed whisper*]. This is the second night I heard that tappin! I believe it bodes no good to me. There, do you hear it again – a quiet, steady, mysterious tappin' on the wall.

DAVOREN. I hear no tappin'.

SEUMAS. It ud be better for me if you did. It's a sure sign of death when nobody hears it but meself.

DAVOREN. Death! What the devil are you talking about, man?

SEUMAS. I don't like it at all; there's always something like that heard when one of our family dies.

DAVOREN. I don't know about that; but I know there's a hell of a lot of things heard when one of your family lives.

SEUMAS. God between us an' all harm! Thank God I'm where I ought to be – in bed. . . . It's always best to be in your proper place when such things happen – Sacred Heart! There it is again; do you not hear it now?

DAVOREN. Ah, for God's sake go asleep.

SEUMAS. Do you believe in nothing?

DAVOREN. I don't believe in tappin'.

SEUMAS. Whisht, it's stopped again; I'll try to go asleep for fear it ud begin again.

DAVOREN. Ay, do; and if it starts again I'll be sure to waken you up. [*A pause.*]

SEUMAS. It's very cold tonight. Do you feel cold?

DAVOREN. I thought you were goin' asleep?

SEUMAS. The bloody cold won't let me. . . . You'd want a pair of pyjamas on you. [*A pause.*] Did you ever wear pyjamas, Donal?

DAVOREN. No, no, no.

SEUMAS. What kind of stuff is in them?

DAVOREN [*angrily*]. Oh, it depends on the climate; in India, silk; in Italy, satin; and the Eskimo wears them made from the skin of the Polar bear.

SEUMAS [*emphatically*]. If you take my advice you'll get into bed – that poem is beginnin' to get on your nerves.

DAVOREN [*extinguishing the candle with a vicious blow*]. Right; I'm going to bed now, so you can shut up.

*Visibility is still maintained from the light of the moon.*

SEUMAS. I was goin' to say something when you put out the light – what's this it was? – um, um, oh, ay: when I was comin' in this evenin' I saw Minnie Powell goin' out. If I was you I wouldn't have that one comin' in here.

DAVOREN. She comes in; I don't bring her in, do I?

SEUMAS. The oul' ones'll be talkin', an' once they start you don't know how it'll end. Surely a man that has read Shelley couldn't be interested in an ignorant little bitch that thinks of nothin' but jazz dances, foxtrots, picture-theatres an' dress.

DAVOREN. Right glad I am that she thinks of dress, for she thinks of it in the right way, and makes herself a pleasant picture to the eye. Education has been wasted on many persons, teaching them to talk only, but leaving them with all their primitive instincts. Had poor Minnie received an education she would have been an artist. She is certainly a pretty girl. I'm sure she is a good girl, and I believe she is a brave girl.

SEUMAS. A Helen of Troy come to live in a tenement! You think a lot about her simply because she thinks a lot about you, an' she thinks a lot about you because she looks upon you as a hero – a kind o' Paris . . . she'd give the world an' all to be gaddin' about with a gunman. An' what ecstasy it ud give her if after a bit you were shot or hanged; she'd be able to go about then – like a good many more – singin', 'I do not mourn me darlin' lost, for he fell in his Jacket Green.'* An' then, for a year an' a day, all round her hat she'd wear the Tricoloured Ribbon O, till she'd pick up an' marry someone else – possibly a British Tommy with a Mons Star.* An' as for bein' brave, it's easy to be that when you've no cause for cowardice; I wouldn't care to have me life dependin' on brave little Minnie Powell – she wouldn't sacrifice a jazz dance to save it.

DAVOREN [*sitting on the bed and taking off his coat and vest, preparatory to going to bed*]. There; that's enough about Minnie Powell. I'm afraid I'll soon have to be on the run out of this house, too; it is becoming painfully obvious that there is no peace to be found here.

SEUMAS. Oh, this house is all right; barrin' the children, it does be quiet enough. Wasn't there children in the last place you were in too?

DAVOREN. Ay, ten; [*viciously*] and they were all over forty. [*A pause as* DAVOREN *is removing his collar and tie.*]

SEUMAS. Everything is very quiet now; I wonder what time is it?

DAVOREN. The village cock hath thrice done salutation to the morn.*

SEUMAS. Shakespeare, *Richard III*, Act v, Scene iii. It was Ratcliff said that to Richard just before the battle of Bosworth. . . . How peaceful the heavens look now with the moon in the middle; you'd never think there were men prowlin' about tryin' to shoot each other. I don't know how a man who has shot anyone can sleep in peace at night.

DAVOREN. There's plenty of men can't sleep in peace at night now unless they know that they have shot somebody.

SEUMAS. I wish to God it was all over. The country is gone mad. Instead of counting their beads now they're countin' bullets; their Hail Marys and Paternosters* are burstin' bombs – burstin' bombs, an' the rattle of machine-guns; petrol is their holy water; their Mass is a burnin' buildin'; their De Profundis* is 'The Soldiers' Song',* an' their creed is, I believe in the gun almighty, maker of heaven an' earth – an' it's all for 'the glory o' God an' the honour o' Ireland'.

DAVOREN. I remember the time when you yourself believed in nothing but the gun.

SEUMAS. Ay, when there wasn't a gun in the country; I've a different opinion now when there's nothin' but guns in the country. . . . An' you daren't open your mouth, for Kathleen ni Houlihan is very different now to the woman who used to play the harp an' sing 'Weep on, weep on, your hour is past', for she's a ragin' divil now, an' if you only look crooked at her you're sure of a punch in th' eye. But this is the way I look at it – I look at it this way: You're not goin' – you're not goin' to beat the British Empire – the British Empire, by shootin' an occasional Tommy at the corner of an occasional street. Besides, when the Tommies have the wind up – when the Tommies have the wind up they let bang at everything they see – they don't give a God's curse who they plug.*

DAVOREN. Maybe they ought to get down off the lorry and run to the Records Office to find out a man's pedigree before they plug him.

SEUMAS. It's the civilians that suffer; when there's an ambush they don't know where to run. Shot in the back to save the British Empire, an' shot in the breast to save the soul of Ireland. I'm a Nationalist meself, right enough – a Nationalist right enough, but all the same – I'm a Nationalist right enough; I believe in the freedom of Ireland, an' that England has no right to be here, but I draw the line when I hear the gunmen blowin' about* dyin' for the people, when it's the people that are dyin' for the gunmen! With all due respect to the gunmen, I don't want them to die for me.

DAVOREN. Not likely; you object to any one of them deliberately dying for you for fear that one of these days you might accidentally die for one of them.

SEUMAS. You're one of the brave fellows that doesn't fear death.

DAVOREN. Why should I be afraid of it? It's all the same to me how it comes, where it comes, or when it comes. I leave fear of death to the people that are always praying for eternal life; 'Death is here and death is there, death is busy everywhere.'

SEUMAS. Ay, in Ireland. Thanks be to God I'm a daily communicant. There's a great comfort in religion; it makes a man strong in time of trouble an' brave in time of danger. No man need be afraid with a crowd of angels round him; thanks to God for His Holy religion!

DAVOREN. You're welcome to your angels; philosophy is mine; philosophy that makes the coward brave; the sufferer defiant; the weak strong; the . . .

*A volley of shots is heard in a lane that runs parallel with the wall of the back-yard. Religion and philosophy are forgotten in the violent fear of a nervous equality.*

SEUMAS. Jesus, Mary, an' Joseph, what's that?

DAVOREN. My God, that's very close.

SEUMAS. Is there no Christianity at all left in the country?

DAVOREN. Are we ever again going to know what peace and security are?

SEUMAS. If this continues much longer I'lll be nothing but a galvanic battery o' shocks.

DAVOREN. It's dangerous to be in and it's equally dangerous to be out.

SEUMAS. This is a dangerous spot to be in with them windows; you couldn't tell the minute a bullet ud come in through one of them – through one of them, an' hit the – hit the – an' hit the . . .

DAVOREN [*irritably*]. Hit the what, man?

SEUMAS. The wall.

DAVOREN. Couldn't you say that at first without making a song about it?

SEUMAS [*suddenly*]. I don't believe there's horses in the stable at all.

DAVOREN. Stable! What stable are you talking about?

SEUMAS. There's a stable at the back of the house with an entrance

from the yard; it's used as a carpenter's shop. Didn't you often hear
the peculiar noises at night? They give out that it's the horses
shakin' their chains.

DAVOREN. And what is it?

SEUMAS. Oh, there I'll leave you!*

DAVOREN. Surely you don't mean . . .

SEUMAS. But I do mean it.

DAVOREN. You do mean what?

SEUMAS. I wouldn't – I wouldn't be surprised – wouldn't be surprised
– surprised . . .

DAVOREN. Yes, yes, surprised – go on.

SEUMAS. I wouldn't be surprised if they were manufacturin' bombs
there.

DAVOREN. My God, that's a pleasant comtemplation! The sooner I'm
on the run out of this house the better. How is it you never said
anything about this before?

SEUMAS. Well – well, I didn't want – I didn't want to – to . . .

DAVOREN. You didn't want to what?

SEUMAS. I didn't want to frighten you.

DAVOREN [*sarcastically*]. You're bloody kind!

*A knock at the door; the voice of* MRS GRIGSON *heard.*

MRS GRIGSON. Are you asleep, Mr Shields?

SEUMAS. What the devil can she want at this hour of the night? [*To* MRS
GRIGSON] No, Mrs Grigson, what is it?

MRS GRIGSON. [*opening the door and standing at the threshold. She is a
woman about forty, but looks much older. She is one of the cave-dwellers
of Dublin, living as she does in a tenement kitchen, to which only an
occasional sickly beam of sunlight filters through a grating in the yard;
the consequent general dimness of her abode has given her the habit of
peering through half-closed eyes. She is slovenly dressed in an old skirt
and bodice; her face is grimy, not because her habits are dirty — for,
although she is untidy, she is a clean woman — but because of the smoky
atmosphere of her room. Her hair is constantly falling over her face,
which she is frequently removing by rapid movements of her right hand*].
He hasn't turned up yet, an' I'm stiff with the cold waitin' for him.

SEUMAS. Mr Grigson, is it?

MRS GRIGSON. Adolphus, Mr Shields, after takin' his tea at six o'clock

– no, I'm tellin' a lie – it was before six, for I remember the Angelus was ringin' out an' we sittin' at the table – after takin' his tea he went out for a breath o' fresh air, an' I haven't seen sign or light* of him since. 'Clare to God me heart is up in me mouth, thinkin' he might be shot be the Black an' Tans.

SEUMAS. Aw, he'll be all right, Mrs Grigson. You ought to go to bed an' rest yourself; it's always the worst that comes into a body's mind; go to bed, Mrs Grigson, or you'll catch your death of cold.

MRS GRIGSON. I'm afraid to go to bed, Mr Shields, for I'm always in dread that some night or another, when he has a sup taken,* he'll fall down the kitchen stairs an' break his neck. Not that I'd be any the worse if anything did happen to him, for you know the sort he is, Mr Shields; sure he has me heart broke.

SEUMAS. Don't be downhearted, Mrs Grigson; he may take a thought one of these days an' turn over a new leaf.

MRS GRIGSON. Sorra leaf Adolphus 'll ever turn over, he's too far gone in the horns* for that now. Sure no one ud mind him takin' a pint or two, if he'd stop at that, but he won't; nothin' could fill him with beer, an' no matter how much he may have taken, when he's taken more he'll always say, 'Here's the first today.'

DAVOREN [*to* SEUMAS]. Christ! Is she going to stop talking there all the night?

SEUMAS. 'Sh, she'll hear you; right enough, the man has the poor woman's heart broke.

DAVOREN. And because he has her heart broken, she's to have the privilege of breaking everybody else's.

MRS GRIGSON. Mr Shields.

SEUMAS. Yes?

MRS GRIGSON. Do the insurance companies pay if a man is shot after curfew?

SEUMAS. Well, now, that's a thing I couldn't say, Mrs Grigson.

MRS GRIGSON [*plaintively*]. Isn't he a terrible man to be takin' such risks, an' not knowin' what'll happen to him? He knows them Societies* only want an excuse to do people out of their money – is it after one, now, Mr Shields?

SEUMAS. Aw, it must be after one, Mrs Grigson.

MRS GRIGSON [*emphatically*]. Ah, then, if I was a young girl again I'd think twice before gettin' married. Whisht! There's somebody now – it's him, I know be the way he's fumblin'. [*She goes out a little way. Stumbling steps are heard in the hall. Outside.*] Is that you, Dolphie, dear? [*After a few moments* ADOLPHUS GRIGSON *with* MRS GRIGSON *holding his arm, stumbles into the room.*] Dolphie, dear, mind yourself.

GRIGSON [*he is a man of forty-five, but looks, relatively, much younger than* MRS GRIGSON. *His occupation is that of a solicitor's clerk. He has all the appearance of being well fed; and, in fact, he gets most of the nourishment,* MRS GRIGSON *getting just enough to give her strength to do the necessary work of the household. On account of living most of his life out of the kitchen, his complexion is fresh, and his movements, even when sober, are livelier than those of his wife. He is comfortably dressed; heavy topcoat, soft trilby hat, a fancy coloured scarf about his neck, and he carries an umbrella*]. I'm all right; do you see anything wrong with me?

MRS GRIGSON. Of course you're all right, dear; there's no one mindin' you.*

GRIGSON. Mindin' me, is it, mindin' me? He'd want to be a good thing that ud mind me. There's a man here – a man, mind you, afraid av nothin' – not in this bloody house anyway.

MRS GRIGSON [*imploringly*]. Come on downstairs, Dolphie, dear; sure there's not one in the house ud say a word to you.

GRIGSON. Say a word to me, is it? He'd want to be a good thing that ud say anything to Dolphus Grigson. [*Loudly*] Is there anyone wants to say anything to Dolphus Grigson? If there is, he's here – a man, too – there's no blottin' it out – a man.

MRS GRIGSON. You'll wake everybody in the house; can't you speak quiet?

GRIGSON [*more loudly still*]. What do I care for anybody in the house? Are they keepin' me: are they givin' me anything? When they're keepin' Grigson it'll be time enough for them to talk. [*With a shout*] I can tell them Adolphus Grigson wasn't born in a bottle!

MRS GRIGSON [*tearfully*]. Why do you talk like that, dear? We all know you weren't born in a bottle.

GRIGSON. There's some of them in this house think Grigson was born in a bottle.

DAVOREN [*to* SEUMAS]. A most appropriate place for him to be born in.

MRS GRIGSON. Come on down to bed, now, an' you can talk about them in the mornin'.

GRIGSON. I'll talk about them, now; do you think I'm afraid of them? Dolphus Grigson's afraid av nothin', creepin' or walkin' – if there's any one in the house thinks he's fit to take a fall out av* Adolphus

Grigson, he's here – a man; they'll find that Grigson's no soft thing.

DAVOREN. Ah me, alas! Pain, pain ever, for ever.

MRS GRIGSON. Dolphie, dear, poor Mr Davoren wants to go to bed.

DAVOREN. Oh, she's terribly anxious about poor Mr Davoren, all of a sudden.

GRIGSON [*stumbling towards* DAVOREN, *and holding out his hand*]. Davoren! He's a man. Leave it there, mate. You needn't be afraid av Dolphus Grigson; there never was a drop av informer's blood in the whole family av Grigson. I don't know what you are or what you think, but you're a man, an' not like some of the goughers* in this house, that ud hang you. Not referrin' to you, Mr Shields.

MRS GRIGSON. Oh, you're not deludin' to Mr Shields.

SEUMAS. I know that, Mr Grigson; go on down, now, with Mrs Grigson, an' have a sleep.

GRIGSON. I tie myself to no woman's apron-strings, Mr Shields; I know how to keep Mrs Grigson in her place; I have the authority of the Bible for that. I know the Bible from cover to cover, Mr Davoren, an' that's more than some in this house could say. And what does the Holy Scripture say about woman? It says, 'The woman shall be subject to her husband', an' I'll see that Mrs Grigson keeps the teachin' av the Holy Book in the letter an' in the spirit. If you're ever in trouble, Mr Davoren, an' Grigson can help – I'm your man – have you me?

DAVOREN. I have you, Mr Grigson, I have you.

GRIGSON. Right; I'm an Orangeman, an' I'm not ashamed av it, an' I'm not afraid av it, but I can feel for a true man, all the same – have *you* got me, Mr Shields?

SEUMAS. Oh, we know you well, Mr Grigson; many a true Irishman was a Protestant – Tone, Emmet an' Parnell.*

GRIGSON. Mind you, I'm not sayin' as I agree with them you've mentioned, Mr Shields, for the Bible forbids it, an' Adolphus Grigson 'll always abide be the Bible. Fear God an' honour the King – that's written in Holy Scripture, an' there's no blottin' it out. [*Pulling a bottle out of his pocket*] But here, Mr Davoren, have a drink, just to show there's no coolness.

DAVOREN. No, no, Mr Grigson, it's late now to take anything. Go on down with Mrs Grigson, and we can have a chat in the morning.

GRIGSON. Sure you won't have a drink?

DAVOREN. Quite sure – thanks all the same.

GRIGSON [*drinking*]. Here's the first today! To all true men, even if

they were born in a bottle. Here's to King William, to the battle av
the Boyne;* to the Hobah Black Chapter – that's my Lodge, Mr
Davoren; an' to the Orange Lily O. [*Singing in a loud shout*]

> An' dud ya go to see the show, each rose an'
>     pinkadilly O,
> To feast your eyes an' view the prize won be the
>     Orange Lily O.
> The Vic'roy there, so debonair, just like a daffadilly O,
> With Lady Clarke, blithe as a lark, approached the
>     Orange Lily O.
>         Heigh Ho the Lily O,
>         The Royal, Loyal Lily O,
> Beneath the sky what flower can vie with Erin's
>     Orange Lily O!

DAVOREN. Holy God, isn't this terrible!
GRIGSON [*singing*].

> The elated Muse, to hear the news, jumped like a
>     Connaught filly O,
> As gossip Fame did loud proclaim the triumph av
>     the Lily O.
> The Lowland field may roses yield, gay heaths the
>     Highlands hilly O;
> But high or low no flower can show like Erin's
>     Orange Lily O.
>         Heigh Ho the Lily O,
>         The Royal, Loyal Lily O,
> Beneath the sky what flower can vie with Erin's Or . . .*

*While* GRIGSON *has been singing, the sound of a rapidly moving motor is
heard, faintly at first, but growing rapidly louder, till it apparently stops
suddenly somewhere very near the house, bringing* GRIGSON's *song to an
abrupt conclusion. They are all startled, and listen attentively to the
throbbing of the engines, which can be plainly heard.* GRIGSON *is
considerably sobered, and anxiously keeps his eyes on the door.* SEUMAS *sits
up in bed and listens anxiously.* DAVOREN, *with a shaking hand, lights the
candle, and begins to search hurriedly among the books and papers on the
table.*

GRIGSON [*with a tremor in his voice*]. There's no need to be afraid, they couldn't be comin' here.

MRS GRIGSON. God forbid! It ud be terrible if they came at this hour ov the night.

SEUMAS. You never know, Mrs Grigson; they'd rush in on you when you'd be least expectin' them. What, in the name o' God, is goin' to come out of it all? Nobody now cares a traneen* about the orders of the Ten Commandments; the only order that anybody minds now is, 'Put your hands up.' Oh, it's a hopeless country.

GRIGSON. Whisht; do you hear them talking outside at the door? You're sure of your life nowhere now; it's just as safe to go everywhere as it is to anywhere. An' they don't give a damn whether you're a loyal man or not. If you're a Republican they make you sing 'God Save the King', an' if you're loyal they'll make you sing 'The Soldiers' Song'. The singin' ud be all right if they didn't make you dance afterwards.

MRS GRIGSON. They'd hardly come here unless they heard something about Mr Davoren.

DAVOREN. About me! What could they hear about me?

GRIGSON. You'll never get some people to keep their mouths shut. I was in the Blue Lion this evening, an' who do you think was there, blowin' out av him, but that little blower,* Tommy Owens; there he was tellin' everybody that *he* knew where there was bombs; that *he* had a friend that was a General in the IRA; that *he* could tell them what the Staff* was thinkin' av doin'; that *he* could lay his hand on tons av revolvers; that they wasn't a mile from where he was livin', but that *he* knew his own know, an' would keep it to himself.

SEUMAS. Well, God blast the little blower, anyway; it's the like ov him that deserves to be plugged! [*To* DAVOREN] What are you lookin' for among the books, Donal?

DAVOREN. A letter that I got today from Mr Gallogher and Mrs Henderson; I'm blessed if I know where I put it.

SEUMAS [*peevishly*]. Can't you look for it in the mornin'?

DAVOREN. It's addressed to the Irish Republican Army, and, considering the possibility of a raid, it would be safer to get rid of it.

*Shots again heard out in the lane, followed by shouts of 'Halt, halt, halt!'*

GRIGSON. I think we had better be gettin' to bed, Debby; it's not right to be keepin' Mr Davoren an' Mr Shields awake.

SEUMAS. An' what made them give you such a letter as that; don't they
know the state the country is in? An' you were worse to take it.
Have you got it?

DAVOREN. I can't find it anywhere; isn't this terrible!

GRIGSON. Goodnight, Mr Davoren; goodnight, Mr Shields.

MRS GRIGSON. Goodnight, Mr Shields; goodnight, Mr Davoren.


*They go out.* SEUMAS *and* DAVOREN *are too much concerned about the letter
to respond to their goodnights.*


SEUMAS. What were you thinkin' of when you took such a letter as
that? Ye gods, has nobody any brains at all, at all? Oh, this is a
hopeless country. Did you try in your pockets?

DAVOREN [*searching in his pockets*]. Oh, thanks be to God, here it is.

SEUMAS. Burn it now, an', for God's sake, don't take any letters like
that again. . . . There's the motor goin' away; we can sleep in peace
now for the rest of the night. Just to make sure of everything now,
have a look in that bag o' Maguire's: not that there can be anything
in it.

DAVOREN. If there's nothing in it, what's the good of looking?

SEUMAS. It won't kill you to look, will it?


DAVOREN *goes over to the bag, puts it on the table, opens it, and jumps
back, his face pale and limbs trembling.*


DAVOREN. My God, it's full of bombs, Mills bombs!*

SEUMAS. Holy Mother of God, you're jokin'!

DAVOREN. If the Tans come you'll find whether I'm jokin' or no.

SEUMAS. Isn't this a nice pickle to be in? St Anthony, look down on us!

DAVOREN. There's no use of blaming St Anthony; why did you let
Maguire leave the bag here?

SEUMAS. Why did I let him leave the bag here; why did I let him leave
the bag here! How did I know what was in it? Didn't I think there
was nothin' in it but spoons an' hairpins? What'll we do now;
what'll we do now? Mother o' God, grant there'll be no raid tonight.
I knew things ud go wrong when I missed Mass this mornin'.

DAVOREN. Give over your praying and let us try to think of what is best
to be done. There's one thing certain: as soon as morning comes I'm
on the run out of this house.

SEUMAS. Thinkin' of yourself, like the rest of them. Leavin' me to bear
the brunt of it.

DAVOREN. And why shouldn't you bear the brunt of it? Maguire was
no friend of mine; besides, it's your fault; you knew the sort of man
he was, and you should have been on your guard.

SEUMAS. Did I know he was a gunman; did I know he was a gunman,
did I know he was a gunman? Did . . .

DAVOREN. Do you mean to tell me that . . .

SEUMAS. Just a moment . . .

DAVOREN. You didn't know . . .

SEUMAS. Just a moment . . .

DAVOREN. That Maguire was connected with . . .

SEUMAS [*loudly*]. Just a moment; can't . . .

DAVOREN. The Republican Movement? What's the use of trying to tell
damn lies!

MINNIE POWELL *rushes into the room. She is only partly dressed, and has
thrown a shawl over her shoulders. She is in a state of intense excitement.*

MINNIE. Mr Davoren, Donal, they're all round the house; they must
be goin' to raid the place; I was lookin' out of the window an' I seen
them; I do be on the watch every night; have you anything? If you
have . . .

*There is heard at street door a violent and continuous knocking, followed by
the crash of glass and the beating of the door with rifle butts.*

MINNIE. There they are, there they are, there they are!

DAVOREN *reclines almost fainting on the bed;* SEUMAS *sits up in an attitude of
agonised prayerfulness;* MINNIE *alone retains her presence of mind. When
she sees their panic she becomes calm, though her words are rapidly spoken,
and her actions are performed with decisive celerity.*

MINNIE. What is it; what have you got; where are they?

DAVOREN. Bombs, bombs, bombs; my God! in the bag on the table
there; we're done, we're done!

SEUMAS. Hail, Mary, full of grace – pray for us miserable sinners –
Holy St Anthony, do you hear them batterin' at the door – now an'

at the hour of our death – say an act of contrition, Donal – there's
the glass gone!

MINNIE. I'l take them to my room; maybe they won't search it; if they
do aself,* they won't harm a girl. Goodbye . . . Donal. [*She glances
lovingly at* DAVOREN – *who is only semi-conscious – as she rushes out
with the bag.*]

SEUMAS. If we come through this I'll never miss a Mass again! If it's the
Tommies* it won't be so bad, but if it's the Tans, we're goin' to
have a terrible time.

*The street door is broken open and heavy steps are heard in the hall,
punctuated with shouts of "Old the light 'ere', 'Put 'em up', etc. An*
AUXILIARY *opens the door of the room and enters, revolver in one hand and
electric torch in the other. His uniform is black, and he wears a black beret.*

AUXILIARY. 'Oo's 'ere?

SEUMAS [*as if he didn't know*]. Who – who's that?

AUXILIARY [*peremptorily*]. 'Oo's 'ere?

SEUMAS. Only two men, mister; me an' me mate in t'other bed.

AUXILIARY. Why didn't you open the door?

SEUMAS. We didn't hear you knockin', sir.

AUXILIARY. You must be a little awd* of 'earing, ay?

SEUMAS. I had rheumatic fever a few years ago, an' ever since I do be a
– I do be a little deaf sometimes.

AUXILIARY [*to* DAVOREN]. 'Ow is it you're not in bed?

DAVOREN. I was in bed; when I heard the knockin' I got up to open the
door.

AUXILIARY. *You're* a koind blowke* you are. Deloighted, like, to have
a visit from us, ay? Ay? [*Threatening to strike him*] Why down't you
answer?

DAVOREN. Yes, sir.

AUXILIARY. What's your name?

DAVOREN. Davoren, Dan Davoren, sir.

AUXILIARY. You're not an Irishman, are you?

DAVOREN. I-I-I was born in Ireland.

AUXILIARY. Ow, you were, were you; Irish han' proud of it, ay? [*To*
SEUMAS] What's *your* name?

SEUMAS. Seuma . . . Oh no; Jimmie Shields, sir.

AUXILIARY. Ow, you're a Selt [*he means a Celt*], one of the Seltic race that speaks a lingo of its ahn,* and that's going to overthrow the British Empire – I don't think! 'Ere, where's your gun?

SEUMAS. I never had a gun in me hand in me life.

AUXILIARY. Now; you wouldn't know what a gun is if you sawr one, I suppowse. [*Displaying his revolver in a careless way*] 'Ere, what's that?

SEUMAS. Oh, be careful, please, be careful.

AUXILIARY. Why, what 'ave I got to be careful abaht?

SEUMAS. The gun; it-it-it might go off.

AUXILIARY. An' what prawse* if it did; it can easily be relowded. Any ammunition 'ere? What's in that press? [*He searches and scatters contents of press.*]

SEUMAS. Only a little bit o' grub; you'll get nothin' here, sir; no one in the house has any connection with politics.

AUXILIARY. Now? I've never met a man yet that didn't say that, but we're a little bit too ikey* now to be kidded with that sort of talk.

SEUMAS. May I go an' get a drink o' water?

AUXILIARY. You'll want a barrel of watah before you're done with us. [*The* AUXILIARY *goes about the room examining places*] 'Ello, what's 'ere? A statue o' Christ! An' a Crucifix! You'd think you was in a bloomin' monastery.

MRS GRIGSON *enters, dressed disorderly and her hair awry.*

MRS GRIGSON. They're turning the place upside-down. Upstairs an' downstairs they're makin' a litter of everything! I declare to God, it's awful what law-abidin' people have to put up with. An' they found a pint bottle of whisky under Dolphie's pillow, an' they're drinkin' every drop ot it – an' Dolphie'll be like a devil in the mornin' when he finds he has no curer.*

AUXILIARY [*all attention when he hears the word 'whiskey'*]. A bottle of whisky, ay? 'Ere, where do you live – quick, where do you live?

MRS GRIGSON. Down in the kitchen – an' when you go down will you ask them not to drink – oh, he's gone without listenin' to me. [*While* MRS GRIGSON *is speaking the* AUXILIARY *rushes out.*]

SEUMAS [*anxiously to* MRS GRIGSON]. Are they searchin' the whole house, Mrs Grigson?

MRS GRIGSON. They didn't leave a thing in the kitchen that they didn't flitter* about the floor; the things in the cupboard, all the little odds an' ends that I keep in the big box, an . . .

SEUMAS. Oh, they're a terrible gang of blaguards* – did they go upstairs? – they'd hardly search Minnie Powell's room – do you think, would they, Mrs Grigson?

MRS GRIGSON. Just to show them the sort of a man he was, before they come in, Dolphie put the big Bible on the table, open at the First Gospel of St Peter, second chapter, an' marked the thirteenth to the seventeenth verse in red ink – you know the passages, Mr Shields – [*quoting*]

'Submit yourselves to every ordinance of man for the Lord's sake: whether it be to the king, as supreme; or unto governors, as unto them that are sent by him for the punishment of evildoers, an' for the praise of them that do well. . . . Love the brotherhood. Fear God. Honour the King.'

An' what do you think they did, Mr Shields? They caught a hold of the Bible an' flung it on the floor – imagine that, Mr Shields – flingin' the Bible on the floor! Then one of them says to another – 'Jack,' says he, 'have you seen the light; is your soul saved?' An' then they grabbed hold of poor Dolphie, callin' him Mr Moody an' Mr Sankey* an' wanted him to offer up a prayer for the Irish Republic! An' when they were puttin' me out, there they had the poor man sittin' up in bed, his hands crossed on his breast, his eyes lookin' up at the ceilin', an' he singin' a hymn – 'We shall meet in the Sweet Bye an' Bye – an' all the time, Mr Shields, there they were drinkin' his whisky; there's torture for you, an' they all laughin' at poor Dolphie's terrible sufferin's.

DAVOREN. In the name of all that's sensible, what did he want to bring whisky home with him for? They're bad enough sober, what'll they be like when they're drunk?

MRS GRIGSON [*plaintively*]. He always brings a drop home with him – he calls it his medicine.

SEUMAS [*still anxious*]. They'll hardly search all the house; do you think they will, Mrs Grigson?

MRS GRIGSON. An' we have a picture over the mantlepiece of King William crossing the Boyne, an' do you know what they wanted to make out, Mr Shields, that it was Robert Emmet, an' the picture of a sacret society!

SEUMAS. She's not listenin' to a word I'm sayin'! Oh, the country is hopeless an' the people is hopeless.

DAVOREN. For God's sake tell her to go to hell out of this – she's worse than the Auxsie.*

SEUMAS [*thoughtfully*]. Let her stay where she is; it's safer to have a woman in the room. If they come across the bombs I hope to God Minnie'll say nothin'.

DAVOREN. We're a pair of pitiable cowards to let poor Minnie suffer when we know that we and not she are to blame.

SEUMAS. What else can we do, man? Do you want us to be done in? If you're anxious to be riddled, I'm not. Besides, they won't harm her, she's only a girl, an' so long as she keeps her mouth shut it'll be all right.

DAVOREN. I wish I could be sure of that.

SEUMAS. D'ye think are they goin', Mrs Grigson? What are they doin' now?

MRS GRIGSON [*who is standing at the door, looking out into the hall*]. There's not a bit of me that's not shakin' like a jelly!

SEUMAS. Are they gone upstairs, Mrs Grigson? Do you think, Mrs Grigson, will they soon be goin'?

MRS GRIGSON. When they were makin' poor Dolphie sit up in the bed, I 'clare to God I thought every minute I'd hear their guns goin' off, an' see poor Dolphie stretched out dead in the bed – whisht, God bless us, I think I hear him moanin'!

SEUMAS. You might as well be talking to a stone! They're all hopeless, hopeless, hopeless! She thinks she hears him moanin'! It's bloody near time somebody made him moan!

DAVOREN [*with a sickly attempt at humour*]. He's moaning for the loss of his whisky.

*During the foregoing dialogue the various sounds of a raid — orders, the tramping of heavy feet, the pulling about of furniture, etc. — are heard. Now a more definite and sustained commotion is apparent. Loud and angry commands of 'Go on', 'Get out and get into the lorry', are heard, mingled with a girl's voice — it is* MINNIE's *— shouting bravely, but a little hysterically, 'Up the Republic.'*

MRS GRIGSON [*from the door*]. God save us, they're takin' Minnie, they're takin' Minnie Powell! [*Running out*] What in the name of God can have happened?

SEUMAS. Holy Saint Anthony grant that she'll keep her mouth shut.

DAVOREN [*sitting down on the bed and covering his face with his hands*].

We'll never again be able to lift up our heads if anything happens to Minnie.

SEUMAS. For God's sake keep quiet or somebody'll hear you; nothin'll happen to her, nothin' at all – it'll be all right if she only keeps her mouth shut.

MRS GRIGSON [*running in*]. They're after gettin'* a whole lot of stuff in Minnie's room! Enough to blow up the whole street, a Tan says! God tonight, who'd have ever thought that of Minnie Powell!

SEUMAS. Did she say anything, is she sayin' anything, what's she sayin', Mrs Grigson?

MRS GRIGSON. She's shoutin' 'Up the Republic' at the top of her voice. An' big Mrs Henderson is fightin' with the soldiers – she's after nearly knockin' one of them down, an' they're puttin' her into the lorry too.

SEUMAS. God blast her! Can she not mind her own business? What does she want here – didn't she know there was a raid on? Is the whole damn country goin' mad? They'll open fire in a minute an' innocent people'll be shot!

DAVOREN. What way are they using Minnie, Mrs Grigson; are they rough with her?

MRS GRIGSON. They couldn't be half rough enough; the little hussy, to be so deceitful; she might as well have had the house blew up! God tonight, who'd think it was in Minnie Powell!

SEUMAS. Oh, grant she won't say anything!

MRS GRIGSON. There they're goin' away now; ah, then I hope they'll give that Minnie Powell a coolin'.

SEUMAS. God grant she won't say anything! Are they gone, Mrs Grigson?

MRS GRIGSON. With her fancy stockin's, an' her pom-poms, an' her crêpe-de-chine blouses! I knew she'd come to no good!

SEUMAS. God grant she'll keep her mouth shut! Are they gone, Mrs Grigson?

MRS GRIGSON. They're gone, Mr Shields, an' here's poor Dolphie an' not a feather astray on him. Oh, Dolphie, dear, you're all right, thanks to God; I thought you'd never see the mornin'.

GRIGSON [*entering without coat or vest*]. Of course I'm all right; what ud put a bother on Dolphie Grigson? – not the Tans anyway!

MRS GRIGSON. When I seen you stretched out on the bed, an' you . . . singin' a hymn . . .

GRIGSON [*fearful of possible humiliation*]. Who was singin' a hymn?

D'ye hear me talkin' to you – where did you hear me singing' a hymn?

MRS GRIGSON. I was only jokin', Dolphie, dear; I . . .

GRIGSON. Your place is below, an' not gosterin' here to men; down with you quick! [MRS GRIGSON *hurriedly leaves the room. Nonchalantly taking out his pipe, filling it, lighting it, and beginning to smoke*]. Excitin' few moments, Mr Davoren; Mrs G lost her head completely – panic-stricken. But that's only natural, all women is very nervous. The only thing to do is to show them that they can't put the wind up you; show the least sign of fright an' they'd walk on you, simply walk on you. Two of them come down – 'Put them up', revolvers under your nose – you know, the usual way. 'What's all the bother about?' says I, quite calm. 'No bother at all,' says one of them, 'only this gun might go off an' hit somebody – have you me?' says he. 'What if it does,' says I; 'a man can only die once, an' you'll find Grigson won't squeal.' 'God, you're a cool one,' says the other, 'there's no blottin' it out.'

SEUMAS. That's the best way to take them; it only makes thing worse to show that you've got the wind up. 'Any ammunition here?' says the fellow that come in here. 'I don't think so,' says I, 'but you better have a look,' 'No back talk,' says he, 'or you might get plugged.' 'I don't know of any clause', says I, 'in the British Constitution that makes it a crime for a man to speak in his own room', – with that, he just had a look round, an' off he went.

GRIGSON. If a man keeps a stiff upper front – Merciful God, there's an ambush!

*Explosions of two bursting bombs are heard on the street outside the house, followed by fierce and rapid revolver fire. People are heard rushing into the hall, and there is general clamour and confusion.* SEUMAS *and* DAVOREN *cower down in the room;* GRIGSON, *after a few moments' hesitation, frankly rushes out of the room to what he conceives to be the safer asylum of the kitchen. A lull follows, punctured by an odd rifle-shot; then comes a peculiar and ominous stillness, broken in a few moments by the sounds of voices and movement. Questions are heard being asked:* 'Who was it was killed?' 'Where was she shot?' *which are answered by:* 'Minnie Powell'; 'She went to jump off the lorry an' she was shot'; 'She's not dead, is she?'; 'They say she's dead – shot through the buzzom!'

DAVOREN [*in a tone of horror-stricken doubt*]. D'ye hear what they're sayin', Shields, d'ye hear they're sayin' – Minnie Powell is shot.

SEUMAS. For God's sake speak easy, an' don't bring them in here on top of us again.

DAVOREN. Is that all you're thinking of? Do you realise that she has been shot to save us?

SEUMAS. Is it my fault; am I to blame?

DAVOREN. It is your fault and mine, both; oh, we're a pair of dastardly cowards to have let her do what she did.

SEUMAS. She did it off her own bat* – we didn't ask her to do it.

MRS GRIGSON *enters. She is excited and semi-hysterical, and sincerely affected by the tragic occurence.*

MRS GRIGSON [*falling down in a sitting posture on one of the beds*]. What's goin' to happen next! Oh, Mr Davoren, isn't it terrible, isn't it terrible! Minnie Powell, poor little Minnie Powell's been shot dead! They were raidin' a house a few doors down, an' had just got up in their lorries to go away, when they was ambushed. You never heard such shootin'! An' in the thick of it, poor Minnie went to jump off the lorry she was on, an' she was shot through the buzzom. Oh, it was horrible to see the blood pourin' out, an' Minnie moanin'. They found some paper in her breast, with 'Minnie' written on it, an' some other name they couldn't make out with the blood; the officer kep' it. The ambulance is bringin' her to the hospital, but what good's that when she's dead! Poor little Minnie, poor little Minnie Powell, to think of you full of a life a few minutes ago, an' now she's dead!

DAVOREN. Ah me, alas! Pain, pain, pain ever, for ever! It's terrible to think that little Minnie is dead, but it's still more terrible to think that Davoren and Shields are alive! Oh, Donal Davoren, shame is your portion now till the silver cord is loosened and the golden bowl be broken.* Oh, Davoren, Donal Davoren, poet and poltroon,* poltroon and poet!

SEUMAS [*solemnly*]. I knew something ud come of the tappin' on the wall!

CURTAIN

# Juno and the Paycock

## A Tragedy in Three Acts

# CHARACTERS

'CAPTAIN' JACK BOYLE

JUNO BOYLE, his wife

JOHNNY BOYLE ⎱ their children
MARY BOYLE   ⎰

'JOXER' DALY                         residents in
                                     the tenement
MRS MAISIE MADIGAN

'NEEDLE' NUGENT, a tailor

MRS TANCRED

JERRY DEVINE

CHARLES BENTHAM, a schoolteacher

AN IRREGULAR MOBILISER

TWO IRREGULARS

A COAL-BLOCK VENDOR

A SEWING-MACHINE MAN

TWO FURNITURE-REMOVAL MEN

TWO NEIGHBOURS

# PLACE AND TIME

*Act I*. The living apartment of a two-roomed tenancy of the Boyle
   family, in a tenement house in Dublin.

*Act II*. The same.

*Act III*. The same.

A few days elapse between Acts I and II, and two months between Acts
   II and III.

During Act III the curtain is lowered for a few minutes to denote the
   lapse of one hour. Period of the play, 1922.

# ACT I

The living-room of a two-room tenancy occupied by the Boyle family in a tenement house in Dublin. Left, a door leading to another part of the house; left of door a window looking into the street; at back a dresser; farther to right at back, a window looking into the back of the house. Between the window and the dresser is a picture of the Virgin; below the picture, on a bracket, is a crimson bowl in which a floating votive light is burning. Farther to the right is a small bed partly concealed by cretonne hangings strung on a twine. To the right is the fireplace; near the fireplace is a door leading to the other room. Beside the fireplace is a box containing coal. On the mantelshelf is an alarm clock lying on its face. In a corner near the window looking into the back is a galvanised bath. A table and some chairs. On the table are breakfast things for one. A teapot is on the hob and a frying-pan stands inside the fender. There are a few books on the dresser and one on the table. Leaning against the dresser is a long-handled shovel – the kind invariably used by labourers when turning concrete or mixing mortar. JOHNNY BOYLE is sitting crouched beside the fire. MARY with her jumper off – it is lying on the back of a chair – is arranging her hair before a tiny mirror perched on the table. Beside the mirror is stretched out the morning paper, which she looks at when she isn't gazing into the mirror. She is a well-made and good-looking girl of twenty-two. Two forces are working in her mind – one, through the circumstances of her life, pulling her back; the other, through the influence of books she has read, pushing her forward. The opposing forces are apparent in her speech and her manners, both of which are degraded by her environment, and improved by her acquaintance – slight though it be – with literature. The time is early forenoon.

MARY [*looking at the paper*]. On a little by-road, out beyant* Finglas,* he was found.

MRS BOYLE *enters by door on right; she has been shopping and carries a small parcel in her hand. She is forty-five years of age, and twenty years ago she must have been a pretty woman; but her face has now assumed that look which ultimately settles down upon the faces of the women of the working-class; a look of listless monotony and harassed anxiety, blending with an expression of mechanical resistance. Were circumstances favourable, she would probably be a handsome, active and clever woman.*

MRS BOYLE. Isn't he come in yet?

MARY. No, mother.

MRS BOYLE. Oh, he'll come in when he likes; struttin' about the town like a paycock* with Joxer, I suppose. I hear all about Mrs Tancred's son is in this mornin's paper.

MARY. The full details are in it this mornin'; seven wounds he had – one entherin' the neck, with an exit wound beneath the left shoulder-blade; another in the left breast penethratin' the heart, an'. . . .

JOHNNY [*springing up from the fire*]. Oh, quit readin' for God's sake! Are yous losin' all your feelin's? It'll soon be that none of you'll read anythin' that's not about butcherin'! [*He goes quickly into the room on the left.*]

MARY. He's gettin' very sensitive, all of a sudden!

MRS BOYLE. I'll read it myself, Mary, by an' by, when I come home. Everybody's sayin' that he was a Diehard* – thanks be to God that Johnny had nothin' to do with him this long time. . . . [*Opening the parcel and taking out some sausages, which she places on a plate*] Ah, then, if that father o' yours doesn't come in soon for his breakfast, he may go without any; I'll not wait much longer for him.

MARY. Can't you let him get it himself when he comes in?

MRS BOYLE. Yes, an' let him bring in Joxer Daly along with him? Ay, that's what he'd like an' that's what he's waitin' for – till he thinks I'm gone to work, an' then sail in with the boul'* Joxer, to burn all the coal an' dhrink all the tea in the place, to show them what a good Samaritan he is! But I'll stop here till he comes in, if I have to wait till tomorrow mornin'.

VOICE OF JOHNNY INSIDE. Mother!

MRS BOYLE. Yis?

VOICE OF JOHNNY. Bring us in a dhrink o' wather.

MRS BOYLE. Bring in that fella a dhrink o' wather, for God's sake, Mary.

MARY. Isn't he big an' able enough to come out an' get it himself?

MRS BOYLE. If you weren't well yourself you'd like somebody to bring you in a dhrink o' wather. [*She brings in drink and returns.*] Isn't it terrible to have to be waitin' this way! You'd think he was bringin' twenty poun's a week into the house the way he's going on. He wore out the Health Insurance long ago, he's afther wearin' out the unemployment dole, an', now he's thryin' to wear out me! An' constantly singin', no less, when he ought always to be on his knees offerin' up a Novena* for a job!

MARY [*tying a ribbon fillet-wise around her head*]. I don't like this ribbon, Ma; I think I'll wear the green – it looks betther than the blue.

MRS BOYLE. Ah, wear whatever ribbon you like, girl, only don't be botherin' me. I don't know what a girl on strike wants to be wearin' a ribbon round her head for, or silk stockin's on her legs either; it's wearin' them things that make the employers think they're givin' yous too much money.

MARY. The hour is past now when we'll ask the employers' permission to wear what we like.

MRS BOYLE. I don't know why you wanted to walk out* for Jennie Claffey; up to this you never had a good word for her.

MARY. What's the use of belongin' to a Trades Union if you won't stand up for your principles? Why did they sack her? It was a clear case of victimisation. We couldn't let her walk the streets, could we?

MRS BOYLE. No, of course yous couldn't – yous wanted to keep her company. Wan victim wasn't enough. When the employers sacrifice wan victim, the Trades Unions go wan betther be sacrificin' a hundred.

MARY. It doesn't matther what you say, Ma – a principle's a principle.

MRS BOYLE. Yis; an' when I go into oul' Murphy's tomorrow, an' he gets to know that, instead o' payin' all, I'm goin' to borry* more, what'll he say when I tell him a principle's a principle? What'll we do if he refuses to give us any more on tick*?

MARY. He daren't refuse – if he does, can't you tell him he's paid?

MRS BOYLE. It's lookin' as if he was paid, whether he refuses or no.

JOHNNY *appears at the door on left. He can be plainly seen now; he is a thin, delicate fellow, something younger than* MARY. *He has evidently gone through a rough time. His face is pale and drawn; there is a tremulous look of indefinite fear in his eyes. The left sleeve of his coat is empty, and he walks with a slight halt.*

JOHNNY. I was lyin' down; I thought yous were gone. Oul' Simon Mackay is thrampin' about like a horse over me head, an' I can't sleep with him – they're like thunder-claps in me brain! The curse o' – God forgive me for goin' to curse!

MRS BOYLE. There, now; go back an' lie down again an' I'll bring you in a nice cup o' tay.

JOHNNY. Tay, tay, tay! You're always thinkin' o' tay. If a man was dyin', you'd thry to make him swally a cup o' tay! [*He goes back.*]

MRS BOYLE. I don't know what's goin' to be done with him. The bullet he got in the hip in Easter Week* was bad enough; but the bomb that shatthered his arm in the fight in O'Connell Street* put the finishin' touch on him. I knew he was makin' a fool of himself. God knows I went down on me bended knees to him not to go agen the Free State.*

MARY. He stuck to his principles, an', no matter how you may argue, ma, a principle's a principle.

VOICE OF JOHNNY. Is Mary goin' to stay here?

MARY. No, I'm not goin' to stay here; you can't expect me to be always at your beck an' call, can you?

VOICE OF JOHNNY. I won't stop here be meself!

MRS BOYLE. Amn't I nicely handicapped with the whole o' yous! I don't know what any o' yous ud do without your ma. [*To* JOHNNY] Your father'll be here in a minute, an' if you want anythin,' he'll get it for you.

JOHNNY. I hate assin' him for anythin' . . . He hates to be assed to stir. . . . Is the light lightin' before the picture o' the Virgin?

MRS BOYLE. Yis, yis! The wan inside to St Anthony isn't enough, but he must have another wan to the Virgin here!

JERRY DEVINE *enters hastily. He is about twenty-five, well set, active and earnest. He is a type, becoming very common now in the Labour Movement, of a mind knowing enough to make the mass of his associates, who know less, a power, and too little to broaden that power for the benefit of all.* MARY *seizes her jumper and runs hastily into room left.*

JERRY [*breathless*]. Where's the Captain, Mrs Boyle, where's the Captain?

MRS BOYLE. You may well ass a body that: he's wherever Joxer Daly is – dhrinkin' in some snug* or another.

JERRY. Father Farrell is just afther stoppin' to tell me to run up an' get him to go to the new job that's goin' on in Rathmines; his cousin is foreman o' the job, an' Father Farrell was speakin' to him about poor Johnny an' his father bein' so idle so long, an' the foreman told

Father Farrell to send the Captain up an' he'd give him a start – I
wondher where I'd find him?

MRS BOYLE. You'll find he's ayther in Ryan's or Foley's.

JERRY. I'll run round to Ryan's – I know it's a great house o' Joxer's.
[*He rushes out.*]

MRS BOYLE [*piteously*]. There now, he'll miss that job, or I know for
what! If he gets win' o' the word, he'll not come back till evenin', so
that it'll be too late. There'll never be any good got out o' him so
long as he goes with that shouldher-shruggin' Joxer. I killin' meself
workin', an' he sthruttin' about from mornin' till night like a
paycock!

*The steps of two persons are heard coming up a flight of stairs. They are the
footsteps of* CAPTAIN BOYLE *and* JOXER. CAPTAIN BOYLE *is singing in a
deep, sonorous, self-honouring voice.*

THE CAPTAIN. Sweet Spirit, hear me prayer! Hear . . . oh . . . hear . . .
me prayer . . . hear, oh, hear . . . Oh, he . . . ar . . . oh, he . . . ar
. . . me . . . pray . . . er!*

JOXER [*outside*]. Ah, that's a darlin' song, a daaarlin' song!

MRS BOYLE [*viciously*]. Sweet spirit hear his prayer! Ah, then, I'll take
me solemn affeydavey,* it's not for a job he's prayin'! [*She sits down
on the bed so that the cretonne hangings hide her from the view of those
entering.*]

*The* CAPTAIN *comes in. He is a man of about sixty; stout, grey-haired and
stocky. His neck is short, and his head looks like a stone ball that one
sometimes sees on top of a gate-post. His cheeks, reddish-purple, are puffed
out, as if he were always repressing an almost irrepressible ejaculation. On
his upper lip is a crisp, tightly cropped moustache; he carries himself with
the upper part of his body slightly thrown back, and his stomach slightly
thrust forward. His walk is a slow, consequential strut. His clothes are
dingy, and he wears a faded seaman's-cap with a glazed peak.*

BOYLE [*to* JOXER, *who is still outside*]. Come on, come on in, Joxer; she's
gone out long ago, man. If there's nothing else to be got, we'll
furrage out a cup o' tay, anyway. It's the only bit I get in comfort
when she's away. 'Tisn't Juno should be her pet name at all, but
Deirdre of the Sorras,* for she's always grousin'.*

JOXER *steps cautiously into the room. He may be younger than the*
CAPTAIN *but he looks a lot older. His face is like a bundle of crinkled paper;*
*his eyes have a cunning twinkle; he is spare and loosely built; he has a habit*
*of constantly shrugging his shoulders with a peculiar twitching movement,*
*meant to be ingratiating. His face is invariably ornamented with a grin.*

JOXER. It's a terrible thing to be tied to a woman that's always
grousin'. I don't know how you stick it – it ud put years on me. It's a
good job she has to be so ofen away, for [*with a shrug*] when the cat's
away, the mice can play!

BOYLE [*with a commanding and complacent gesture*]. Pull over to the fire,
Joxer, an' we'll have a cup o' tay in a minute.

JOXER. Ah, a cup o' tay's a darlin' thing, a daaarlin' thing – the cup
that cheers but doesn't* . . . [JOXER'*s rhapsody is cut short by the sight*
*of* MRS BOYLE *coming forward and confronting the two cronies. Both are*
*stupefied.*]

MRS BOYLE [*with sweet irony – poking the fire, and turning her head to*
*glare at* JOXER]. Pull over to the fire, Joxer Daly, an' we'll have a cup
o' tay in a minute! Are you sure, now, you wouldn't like an egg?

JOXER. I can't stop, Mrs Boyle; I'm in a desperate hurry, a desperate
hurry.

MRS BOYLE. Pull over to the fire, Joxer Daly; people is always far more
comfortabler here than they are in their own place. [JOXER *makes*
*hastily for the door.*]

BOYLE [*stirs to follow him; thinks of something to relieve the situation –*
*stops, and says suddenly*] Joxer!

JOXER [*at door ready to bolt*]. Yis?

BOYLE. You know the foreman o' that job that's goin' on down in
Killesther, don't you, Joxer?

JOXER [*puzzled*]. Foreman – Killesther?

BOYLE [*with a meaning look*]. He's a butty* o' yours, isn't he?

JOXER [*the truth dawning on him*]. The foreman at Killesther – oh yis,
yis. He's an oul' butty o' mine – oh, he's a darlin' man, a daarlin'
man.

BOYLE. Oh, then, it's a sure thing. It's a pity we didn't go down at
breakfast first thing this mornin' – we might ha' been working now;
but you didn't know it then.

JOXER [*with a shrug*]. It's betther late than never.

BOYLE. It's nearly time we got a start, anyhow; I'm fed up knockin'
round, doin' nothin'. He promised you – gave you the straight tip?

JOXER. Yis. 'Come down on the blow o' dinner',* says he, 'an' I'll start
you, an' any friend you like to brin' with you.' 'Ah,' says I, 'you're a
darlin' man, a daaarlin' man.'

BOYLE. Well, it couldn't come at a betther time – we're a long time
waitin' for it.

JOXER. Indeed we were; but it's a long lane that has no turnin'.

BOYLE. The blow-up for dinner is at one – wait till I see what time it
'tis. [*He goes over to the mantelpiece, and gingerly lifts the clock.*]

MRS BOYLE. Min' now, how you go on fiddlin' with that clock – you
know the least little thing sets it asthray.

BOYLE. The job couldn't come at a betther time; I'm feelin' in great
fettle, Joxer. I'd hardly believe I ever had a pain in me legs, an' last
week I was nearly crippled with them.

JOXER. That's betther an' betther; ah, God never shut wan door but
He opened another!

BOYLE. It's only eleven o'clock; we've lashins o' time.* I'll slip on me
oul' moleskins afther breakfast, an' we can saunther down at our
ayse. [*Putting his hand on the shovel*] I think, Joxer, we'd betther
bring our shovels?

JOXER. Yis, Captain, yis; it's betther to go fully prepared an' ready for
all eventualities. You bring your long-tailed shovel, an' I'll bring
me navvy. We mighten' want them, an', then agen, we might: for
want of a nail the shoe was lost, for want of a shoe the horse was lost,
an' for want of a horse the man was lost* – aw, that's a darlin'
proverb, a daaarlin' . . . [*As Joxer is finishing his sentence,* MRS BOYLE
*approaches the door and* JOXER *retreats hurriedly. She shuts the door
with a bang.*]

BOYLE [*suggestively*]. We won't be long pullin' ourselves together agen
when I'm working for a few weeks. [MRS BOYLE *takes no notice.*] The
foreman on the job is an oul' butty o' Joxer's; I have an idea that I
know him meself. [*Silence*] . . . There's a button off the back o' me
moleskin trousers. . . . If you leave out a needle an' thread I'll sew
it on meself. . . . Thanks be to God, the pains in me legs is gone,
anyhow!

MRS BOYLE [*with a burst*]. Look here, Mr Jackie Boyle, them yarns
won't go down with Juno. I know you an' Joxer Daly of an oul' date,
an' if you think you're able to come it over me with them fairy tales,
you're in the wrong shop.

BOYLE [*coughing subduedly to relieve the tenseness of the situation*].
U-u-u-ugh!

MRS BOYLE. Butty o' Joxer's! Oh, you'll do a lot o' good as long as you continue to be a butty o' Joxer's!

BOYLE. U-u-u-ugh!

MRS BOYLE. Shovel! Ah, then, me boyo, you'd do far more work with a knife an' fork than ever you'll do with a shovel! If there was e'er a genuine job goin' you'd be dh'other way about – not able to lift your arms with the pains in your legs! Your poor wife slavin' to keep the bit in your mouth, an' you gallivantin'* about all the day like a paycock!

BOYLE. It ud be betther for a man to be dead, betther for a man to be dead.

MRS BOYLE [*ignoring the interruption*]. Everybody callin' you 'Captain', an' you only wanst on the wather, in an oul' collier from here to Liverpool, when anybody, to listen or look at you, ud take you for a second Christo For Columbus!

BOYLE. Are you never goin' to give us a rest?

MRS BOYLE. Oh, you're never tired o' lookin' for a rest.

BOYLE. D'ye want to dhrive me out o' the house?

MRS BOYLE. It ud be easier to dhrive you out o' the house than to dhrive you into a job. Here, sit down an' take your breakfast – it may be the last you'll get, for I don't know where the next is goin' to come from.

BOYLE. If I get this job we'll be all right.

MRS BOYLE. Did ye see Jerry Devine?

BOYLE [*testily*]. No, I didn't see him.

MRS BOYLE. No, but you seen Joxer. Well, he was here lookin' for you.

BOYLE. Well, let him look!

MRS BOYLE. Oh, indeed, he may well look, for it ud be hard for him to see you, an' you stuck in Ryan's snug.

BOYLE. I wasn't in Ryan's snug – I don't go into Ryan's.

MRS BOYLE. Oh, is there a mad dog there? Well, if you weren't in Ryan's you were in Foley's.

BOYLE. I'm telling you for the last three weeks I haven't tasted a dhrop of intoxicatin' liquor. I wasn't in ayther wan snug or dh'other – I could swear that on a prayer-book – I'm as innocent as the child unborn!

MRS BOYLE. Well, if you'd been in for your breakfast you'd ha' seen him.

BOYLE [*suspiciously*]. What does he want me for?

MRS BOYLE. He'll be back any minute an' then you'll soon know.

BOYLE. I'll dhrop out an' see if I can meet him.

MRS BOYLE. You'll sit down an' take your breakfast, an' let me go to me work, for I'm an hour late already waitin' for you.

BOYLE. You needn't ha' waited, for I'll take no breakfast – I've a little spirit left in me still!

MRS BOYLE. Are you goin' to have your breakfast – yes or no?

BOYLE [*too proud to yield*]. I'll have no breakfast – yous can keep your breakfast. [*Plaintively*] I'll knock out* a bit somewhere, never fear.

MRS BOYLE. Nobody's goin' to coax you – don't think that. [*She vigorously replaces the pan and the sausages in the press.*]

BOYLE. I've a little spirit left in me still.


JERRY DEVINE *enters hastily.*


JERRY. Oh, here you are at last! I've been searchin' for you everywhere. The foreman in Foley's told me you hadn't left the snug with Joxer ten minutes before I went in.

MRS BOYLE. An' he swearin' on the holy prayer-book that he wasn't in no snug!

BOYLE [*to* JERRY]. What business is it o' yours whether I was in a snug or no? What do you want to be gallopin' about afther me for? Is a man not allowed to leave his house for a minute without havin' a pack o' spies, pimps an' informers cantherin' at his heels?

JERRY. Oh, you're takin' a wrong view of it, Mr Boyle; I simply was anxious to do you a good turn. I have a message for you from Father Farrell: he says that if you go to the job that's on in Rathmines, an' ask for Foreman Mangan, you'll get a start.

BOYLE. That's all right, but I don't want the motions of me body to be watched the way an ashtronomer ud watch a star. If you're folleyin' Mary aself, you've no pereeogative* to be folleyin' me. [*Suddenly catching his thigh*] U-ugh, I'm afther gettin' a terrible twinge in me right leg!

MRS BOYLE. Oh, it won't be very long now till it travels into your left wan. It's miraculous that whenever he scents a job in front of him, his legs begin to fail him! Then, me bucko, if you lose this chance, you may go an' furrage for yourself!

JERRY. This job'll last for some time too, Captain, an' as soon as the foundations are in, it'll be cushy* enough.

BOYLE. Won't it be a climbin' job? How d'ye expect me to be able to go up a ladder with these legs? An', if I get up aself, how am I goin' to get down agen?

MRS BOYLE [*viciously*]. Get wan o' the labourers to carry you down in a hod! You can't climb a laddher, but you can skip like a goat into a snug!

JERRY. I wouldn't let myself be let down that easy, Mr Boyle; a little exercise, now, might do you all the good in the world.

BOYLE. It's a docthor you should have been, Devine – maybe you know more about the pains in me legs than meself that has them?

JERRY [*irritated*]. Oh, I know nothin' about the pains in your legs; I've brought the message that Father Farrell gave me, an' that's all I can do.

MRS BOYLE. Here, sit down an' take your breakfast, an' go an' get ready; an' don't be actin' as if you couldn't pull a wing out of a dead bee.

BOYLE. I want no breakfast, I tell you; it ud choke me afther all that's been said. I've a little spirit left in me still.

MRS BOYLE. Well, let's see your spirit, then, an' go in at wanst an' put on your moleskin trousers!

BOYLE [*moving towards the door on left*]. It ud be betther for a man to be dead! U-ugh! There's another twinge in me other leg! Nobody but meself knows the sufferin' I'm goin' through with the pains in these legs o' mine! [*He goes into the room on left as* MARY *comes out with her hat in her hand.*]

MRS BOYLE. I'll have to push off now, for I'm terrible late already, but I was determined to stay an' hunt that Joxer this time. [*She goes off.*]

JERRY. Are you going out, Mary?

MARY. It looks like it when I'm putting on my hat, doesn't it?

JERRY. The bitther word agen, Mary.

MARY. You won't allow me to be friendly with you; if I thry, you deliberately misundherstand it.

JERRY. I didn't always misundherstand it; you were often delighted to have the arms of Jerry around you.

MARY. If you go on talkin' like this, Jerry Devine, you'll make me hate you!

JERRY. Well, let it be either a weddin' or a wake!* Listen, Mary, I'm standin' for the Secretaryship of our Union. There's only one opposin' me; I'm popular with all the men, an' a good speaker – all are sayin' that I'll get elected.

MARY. Well?

JERRY. The job's worth three hundred an' fifty pounds a year, Mary.
You an' I could live nice an' cosily on that; it would lift you out o'
this place an' . . .

MARY. I haven't time to listen to you now – I have to go. [*She is going
out, when* JERRY *bars the way.*]

JERRY [*appealingly*]. Mary, what's come over you with me for the last
few weeks? You hardly speak to me, an' then only a word with a face
o' bitherness on it. Have you forgotten, Mary, all the happy
evenins that were as sweet as the scented hawthorn that sheltered
the sides o' the road as we saunthered through the country?

MARY. That's all over now. When you get your new job, Jerry, you
won't be long findin' a girl far betther than I am for your
sweetheart.

JERRY. Never, never, Mary! No matther what happens, you'll always
be the same to me.

MARY. I must be off; please let me go, Jerry.

JERRY. I'll go a bit o' the way with you.

MARY. You needn't, thanks; I want to be by meself.

JERRY [*catching her arm*]. You're goin' to meet another fella; you've
clicked with* someone else, me lady!

MARY. That's no concern o' yours, Jerry Devine; let me go!

JERRY. I saw yous comin' out o' the Cornflower Dance class, an' you
hangin' on his arm – a thin, lanky strip of a Micky Dazzler,* with a
walkin' stick an' gloves!

VOICE OF JOHNNY [*loudly*]. What are you doin' there – pullin' about
everything!

VOICE OF BOYLE [*loudly and viciously*]. I'm puttin' on me moleskin
trousers!

MARY. You're hurtin' me arm! Let me go, or I'll scream, an' then
you'll have the oul' fella out on top of us!

JERRY. Don't be so hard on a fella, Mary, don't be so hard.

BOYLE [*appearing at the door*]. What's the meanin' of all this
hillabaloo?*

MARY. Let me go, let me go!

BOYLE. D'ye hear me – what's all this hillabaloo about?

JERRY [*plaintively*]. Will you not give us one kind word, one kind
word, Mary?

BOYLE. D'ye hear me talkin' to yous? What's all this hillabaloo for?

JERRY. Let me kiss your hand, your little, tiny, white hand!

BOYLE. Your little, tiny, white hand – are you takin' leave o' your

senses, man? [MARY *breaks away and rushes out.*] This is a nice goin's
on in front of her father!

JERRY. Ah, dhry up, for God's sake! [*He follows* MARY.]

BOYLE. Chiselurs* don't care a damn now about their parents, they're
bringin' their father's grey hairs down with sorra to the grave,* an'
laughin' at it. Ah, I suppose it's just the same everywhere – the
whole worl's in a state o' chassis!* [*He sits by the fire.*] Breakfast!
Well, they can keep their breakfast for me. Not if they went down
on their bended knees would I take it – I'll show them I've a little
spirit in me still! [*He goes over to the press, takes out a plate and looks at
it.*] Sassige! Well, let her keep her sassige. [*He returns to the fire,
takes up the teapot and gives it a gentle shake.*] The tea's wet right
enough. [*A pause; he rises, goes to the press, takes out the sausage, puts
it on the pan, and puts both on the fire. He attends the sausage with a
fork. Singing*]

> When the robins nest agen,
> And the flowers are in bloom,
> When the Springtime's sunny smile seems to banish all
> > sorrow an' gloom;
> Then me bonny blue-ey'd lad, if me heart be true till then –
> He's promised he'll come back to me,
> When the robins nest agen!*

[*He lifts his head at the high note, and then drops his eyes to the pan.
Singing*]

> When the . . .

*Steps are heard approaching; he whips the pan off the fire and puts it under
the bed, then sits down at the fire. The door opens and a bearded man
looking in says*

You don't happen to want a sewin' machine?

BOYLE [*furiously*]. No, I don't want e'er a sewin' machine! [*He returns
the pan to the fire, and commences to sing again. Singing*]

> When the robins nest agen,
> And the flowers they are in bloom,
> He's . . .

[*A thundering knock is heard at the street door.*] There's a terrible tatheraraa\* – that's a stranger – that's nobody belongin' to the house. [*Another loud knock.*]

JOXER [*sticking his head in at the door*]. Did ye hear them tatherarahs?

BOYLE. Well, Joxer, I'm not deaf.

JOHNNY [*appearing in his shirt and trousers at the door on left; his face is anxious and his voice is tremulous*]. Who's that at the door; who's that at the door? Who gave that knock – d'ye yous hear me – are yous deaf or dhrunk or what?

BOYLE [*to* JOHNNY]. How the hell do I know who 'tis? Joxer, stick your head out o' the window an' see.

JOXER. An' mebbe get a bullet in the kisser?\* Ah, none o' them thricks for Joxer! It's betther to be a coward than a corpse!

BOYLE [*looking cautiously out of the window*]. It's a fella in a thrench coat.

JOHNNY. Holy Mary, Mother o' God, I . . .

BOYLE. He's goin' away – he must ha' got tired knockin'. [*Johnny returns to the room on left.*]

BOYLE. Sit down an' have a cup o' tay, Joxer.

JOXER. I'm afraid the missus ud pop in on us agen before we'd know where we are. Somethin's tellin' me to go at wanst.

BOYLE. Don't be superstitious, man; we're Dublin men, an' not boyos that's only afther comin' up from the bog o' Allen\* – though if she did come in, right enough, we'd be caught like rats in a thrap.

JOXER. An' you know the sort she is – she wouldn't listen to reason – an' wanse bitten twice shy.

BOYLE [*going over to the window at back*]. If the worst came to the worst, you could dart out here, Joxer; it's only a dhrop of a few feet to the roof of the return room,\* an' the first minute she goes into dh'other room I'll give you the bend, an' you can slip in an' away.

JOXER [*yielding to the temptation*]. Ah, I won't stop very long anyhow. [*Picking up a book from the table*] Whose is the buk?

BOYLE. Aw, one o' Mary's; she's always readin' lately – nothin' but thrash, too. There's one I was lookin' at dh'other day: three stories, *The Doll's House, Ghosts*, an' *The Wild Duck*\* – buks only fit for chiselurs!

JOXER. Didja ever rade *Elizabeth*, or *Th' Exile o' Sibayria?*\* . . . Ah, it's a darlin' story, a daarlin' story!

BOYLE. You eat your sassige, an' never min' *The' Exile o' Sibayria*.

*Both sit down;* BOYLE *fills out tea, pours gravy on* JOXER's *plate, and keeps the sausage for himself.*

JOXER. What are you wearin' your moleskin trousers for?

BOYLE. I have to go to a job, Joxer. Just afther you'd gone, Devine kem runnin' in to tell us that Father Farrell said if I went down to the job that's goin' on in Rathmines I'd get a start.

JOXER. Be the holy, that's good news!

BOYLE. How is it good news? I wondher if you were in my condition, would you call it good news?

JOXER. I thought . . .

BOYLE. You thought! You think too sudden sometimes, Joxer. D'ye know, I'm hardly able to crawl with the pains in me legs!

JOXER. Yis, yis; I forgot the pains in your legs. I know you can do nothin' while they're at you.

BOYLE. You forget; I don't think any of yous realise the state I'm in with the pains in my legs. What ud happen if I had to carry a bag o' cement?

JOXER. Ah, any man havin' the like of them pains id be down an' out, down an' out.

BOYLE. I wouldn't mind if he had said it to meself; but, no, oh no, he rushes in an' shouts it out in front o' Juno, an' you know what Juno is, Joxer. We all know Devine knows a little more than the rest of us, but he doesn't act as if he did; he's a good boy, sober, able to talk an' all that, but still . . .

JOXER. Oh ay; able to argufy, but still . . .

BOYLE. If he's runnin' afther Mary, aself, he's not goin' to be runnin' afther me. Captain Boyle's able to take care of himself. Afther all, I'm not gettin' brought up on Virol.\* I never heard him usin' a curse; I don't believe he was ever dhrunk in his life – sure he's not like a Christian at all!

JOXER. You're afther takin' the word out o' me mouth – afther all, a Christian's natural, but he's unnatural.

BOYLE. His oul' fella was just the same – a Wicklow man.\*

JOXER. A Wicklow man! That explains the whole thing. I've met many a Wicklow man in me time, but I never met wan that was any good.

BOYLE. 'Father Farrell', says he, 'sent me down to tell you.' Father Farrell! . . . D'ye know, Joxer, I never like to be beholden to any o' the clergy.

JOXER. It's dangerous, right enough.

BOYLE. If they do anything for you, they'd want you to be livin' in the Chapel* . . . I'm goin' to tell you somethin', Joxer, that I wouldn't tell to anybody else – the clergy always had too much power over the people in this unfortunate country.

JOXER. You could sing that if you had an air to it!

BOYLE [*becoming enthusiastic*] Didn't they prevent the people in '47* from seizin' the corn, an' they starvin'; didn't they down Parnell;* didn't they say that hell wasn't hot enough nor eternity long enough to punish the Fenians?* We don't forget, we don't forget them things, Joxer. If they've taken everything else from us, Joxer, they've left us our memory.

JOXER [*emotionally*]. For mem'ry's the only friend that grief can call its own, that grief . . . can . . . call . . . its own!

BOYLE. Father Farrell's beginnin' to take a great intherest in Captain Boyle; because of what Johnny did for his country, says he to me wan day. It's a curious way to reward Johnny be makin' his poor oul' father work. But that's what the clergy want, Joxer – work, work, work for me an' you; havin' us mulin'* from mornin' till night, so that they may be in betther fettle when they come hoppin' round for their dues! Job! Well, let him give his job to wan of his hymn-singin', prayer-spoutin', craw-thumpin'* Confraternity* men!

*The voice of a* COAL-BLOCK VENDOR *is heard chanting in the street.*

VOICE OF THE COAL VENDOR. Blocks . . . coal-blocks! Blocks . . . coal-blocks!

JOXER. God be with the young days when you were steppin' the deck of a manly ship, with the win' blowin' a hurricane through the masts, an' the only sound you'd hear was 'Port your helm!' an' the only answer, 'Port it is, sir!'

BOYLE. Them was days, Joxer, them was days. Nothin' was too hot or too heavy for me then. Sailin' from the Gulf o' Mexico to the Antanartic Ocean. I seen things, I seen things, Joxer, that no mortal man should speak about that knows his Catechism. Ofen, an' ofen, when I was fixed to the wheel with a marlin-spike,* an' the win's blowin' fierce an' the waves lashin' an' lashin', till you'd think every minute was goin' to be your last, an' it blowed – blew is the right word, Joxer, but blowed is what the sailors use. . . .

JOXER. Aw, it's a darlin' word, a daarlin' word.

BOYLE. An', as it blowed, I ofen looked up at the sky an' assed meself the question – what is the stars, what is the stars?

VOICE OF THE COAL VENDOR. Any blocks, coal-blocks; blocks, coal-blocks!

JOXER. Ah, that's the question, that's the question – what is the stars?

BOYLE. An' then, I'd have another look, an' I'd ass meself – what is the moon?

JOXER. Ah, that's the question – what is the moon, what is the moon?

*Rapid steps are heard coming towards the door.* BOYLE *makes desperate efforts to hide everything;* JOXER *rushes to the window in a frantic effort to get out;* BOYLE *begins to innocently lilt 'Oh, me darlin' Jennie, I will be thrue to thee', when the door is opened, and the black face of the* COAL VENDOR *appears.*

THE COAL VENDOR. D'yez want any blocks?

BOYLE [*with a roar*]. No, we don't want any blocks!

JOXER [*coming back with a sigh of relief*]. That's afther puttin' the heart across me – I could ha' sworn it was Juno. I'd betther be goin', Captain; you couldn't tell the minute Juno'd hop in on us.

BOYLE. Let her hop in; we may as well have it out first as at last. I've made up me mind – I'm not goin' to do only what she damn well likes.

JOXER. Them sentiments does you credit, Captain; I don't like to say anything as between man an' wife, but I say as a butty, as a butty, Captain, that you've stuck it too long, an' that it's about time you showed a little spunk.

> How can a man die betther than facin' fearful odds,
> For th' ashes of his fathers an' the temples of his gods?*

BOYLE. She has her rights – there's no denyin' it, but haven't I me rights too?

JOXER. Of course you have – the sacred rights o' man!

BOYLE. Today, Joxer, there's goin' to be issued a proclamation be me, establishin' an independent Republic, an' Juno'll have to take an oath of allegiance.

JOXER. Be firm, be firm, Captain; the first few minutes'll be the worst: if you gently touch a nettle it'll sting you for your pains; grasp it like a lad of mettle, an' as soft as silk remains!*

VOICE OF MRS BOYLE OUTSIDE. Can't stop, Mrs Madigan – I haven't a minute!

JOXER [*flying out of the window*]. Holy God, here she is!

BOYLE [*packing the things away with a rush in the press*]. I knew that fella ud stop till she was in on top of us! [*He sits down by the fire.*]

MRS BOYLE [*enters hastily; she is flurried and excited*]. Oh, you're in – you must have been only afther comin' in?

BOYLE. No, I never went out.

MRS BOYLE. It's curious, then, you never heard the knockin'. [*She puts her coat and hat on bed.*]

BOYLE. Knockin'? Of course I heard the knockin'.

MRS BOYLE. An' why didn't you open the door, then? I suppose you were so busy with Joxer that you hadn't time.

BOYLE. I haven't seen Joxer since I seen him before. Joxer! What ud bring Joxer here?

MRS BOYLE. D'ye mean to tell me that the pair of yous wasn't collogin' together* here when me back was turned?

BOYLE. What ud we be collogin' together about? I have somethin' else to think of besides collogin' with Joxer. I can swear on all the holy prayer-books . . .

MRS BOYLE. That you weren't in no snug! Go on in at wanst now, an' take off that moleskin trousers o' yours, an' put on a collar an' tie to smarten yourself up a bit. There's a visitor comin' with Mary in a minute, an' he has great news for you.

BOYLE. A job, I suppose; let us get wan first before we start lookin' for another.

MRS BOYLE. That's the thing that's able to put the win' up you. Well, it's no job, but news that'll give you the chance o' your life.

BOYLE. What's all the mysthery about?

MRS BOYLE. G'win an' take off the moleskin trousers when you're told! [BOYLE *goes into room on left.* MRS BOYLE *tidies up the room, puts the shovel under the bed, and goes to the press.*] Oh, God bless us, looka the way everything's thrun* about! Oh, Joxer was here, Joxer was here!

MARY *enters with* CHARLIE BENTHAM; *he is a young man of twenty-five, tall, good-looking, with a very high opinion of himself generally. He is dressed in a brown coat, brown knee-breeches, grey stockings, a brown sweater, with a deep blue tie; he carries gloves and a walking-stick.*

MRS BOYLE [*fussing round*]. Come in, Mr Bentham; sit down, Mr Bentham, in this chair; it's more comfortabler than that, Mr Bentham. Himself'll be here in a minute; he's just takin' off his trousers.

MARY. Mother!

BENTHAM. Please don't put yourself to any trouble, Mrs Boyle – I'm quite all right here, thank you.

MRS BOYLE. An' to think of you knowin' Mary, an' she knowin' the news you had for us, an' wouldn't let on; but it's all the more welcomer now, for we were on our last lap!

VOICE OF JOHNNY INSIDE. What are you kickin' up all the racket for?

BOYLE [*roughly*]. I'm takin' off me moleskin trousers!

JOHNNY. Can't you do it, then, without lettin' th' whole house know you're takin' off your trousers? What d'ye want puttin' them on an' takin' them off again?

BOYLE. Will you let me alone, will you let me alone? Am I never goin' to be done thryin' to please th' whole o' yous?

MRS BOYLE [*to* BENTHAM]. You must excuse th' state o' the' place, Mr Bentham; th' minute I turn me back that man o' mine always makes a litther o' th' place, a litther o' th' place.

BENTHAM. Don't worry, Mrs Boyle; it's all right, I assure . . .

BOYLE [*inside*]. Where's me braces; where in th' name o' God did I leave me braces? . . . Ay, did you see where I put me braces?

JOHNNY [*inside, calling out*]. Ma, will you come in here an' take da away ou' o' this or he'll dhrive me mad.

MRS BOYLE [*going towards the door*]. Dear, dear, dear, that man'll be lookin' for somethin' on th' day o' Judgement. [*Looking into room and calling to* BOYLE] Look at your braces, man, hangin' round your neck!

BOYLE [*inside*]. Aw, Holy God!

MRS BOYLE [*calling*]. Johnny, Johnny, come out here for a minute.

JOHNNY. Ah, leave Johnny alone, an' don't be annoyin' him!

MRS BOYLE. Come on, Johnny, till I inthroduce you to Mr Bentham. [*To* BENTHAM] My son, Mr Bentham; he's after goin' through the mill. He was only a chiselur of a Boy Scout* in Easter Week, when he got hit in the hip; and his arm was blew off in the fight in O'Connell Street. [JOHNNY *comes in.*] Here he is, Mr Bentham; Mr Bentham, Johnny. None can deny he done his bit for Irelan', if that's goin' to do him any good.

JOHNNY [*boastfully*]. I'd do it agen, ma, I'd do it agen; for a principle's a principle.

MRS BOYLE. Ah, you lost your best principle, me boy, when you lost your arm; them's the only sort o' principles that's any good to a workin' man.

JOHNNY. Ireland only half free'll never be at peace while she has a son left to pull a trigger.

MRS BOYLE. To be sure, to be sure – no bread's a lot betther than half a loaf. [*Calling loudly in to* BOYLE] Will you hurry up there?

BOYLE *enters in his best trousers, which aren't too good, and looks very uncomfortable in his collar and tie.*

MRS BOYLE. This is my husband; Mr Boyle, Mr Bentham.

BENTHAM. Ah, very glad to know you, Mr Boyle. How are you?

MRS BOYLE. Ah, I'm not too well at all; I suffer terrible with pains in me legs. Juno can tell you there what . . .

MRS BOYLE. You won't have many pains in your legs when you hear what Mr Bentham has to tell you.

BENTHAM. Juno! What an interesting name! It reminds one of Homer's glorious story of ancient gods and heroes.

BOYLE. Yis, doesn't it? You see, Juno was born an' christened in June; I met her in June; we were married in June, an' Johnny was born in June, so wan day I says to her, 'You should ha' been called Juno', an' the name stuck to her ever since.

MRS BOYLE. Here, we can talk o' them things agen; let Mr Bentham say what he has to say now.

BENTHAM. Well, Mr Boyle, I suppose you'll remember a Mr Ellison of Santry – he's a relative of yours, I think.

BOYLE [*viciously*]. Is it that prognosticator an' procrastinator! Of course I remember him.

BENTHAM. Well, he's dead, Mr Boyle . . .

BOYLE. Sorra many'll* go into mournin' for him.

MRS BOYLE. Wait till you hear what Mr Bentham has to say, an' then, maybe, you'll change your opinion.

BENTHAM. A week before he died he sent for me to write his will for him. He told me that there were two only that he wished to leave his property to: his second cousin, Michael Finnegan of Santry, and John Boyle, his first cousin, of Dublin.

BOYLE [*excitedly*]. Me, is it me, me?

BENTHAM. You, Mr Boyle; I'll read a copy of the will that I have here with me, which has been duly filed in the Court of Probate. [*He takes a paper from his pocket and reads*]

6th February 1922

This is the last Will and Testament of William Ellison, of Santry, in the County of Dublin. I hereby order and wish my property to be sold and divided as follows:

£20 to the St Vincent de Paul Society.*

£60 for Masses for the repose of my soul (5*s.* for each Mass).

The rest of my property to be divided between my first and second cousins.

I hereby appoint Timothy Buckly, of Santry, and Hugh Brierly, of Coolock, to be my Executors.

(*Signed*) WILLIAM ELLISON
HUGH BRIERLY
TIMOTHY BUCKLY
CHARLES BENTHAM, NT*

BOYLE [*eagerly*]. An' how much'll be comin' out of it, Mr Bentham?

BENTHAM. The Executors told me that half of the property would be anything between £1500 and £2000.

MARY. A fortune, father, a fortune!

JOHNNY. We'll be able to get out o' this place now, an' go somewhere we're not known.

MRS BOYLE. You won't have to trouble about a job for awhile, Jack.

BOYLE [*fervently*]. I'll never doubt the goodness o' God agen.

BENTHAM. I congratulate you, Mr Boyle [*They shake hands.*]

BOYLE. An' now, Mr Bentham, you'll have to have a wet.

BENTHAM. A wet?

BOYLE. A wet – a jar – a boul!*

MRS BOYLE. Jack, you're speakin' to Mr Bentham, an' not to Joxer.

BOYLE [*solemnly*]. Juno . . . Mary . . . Johnny . . . we'll have to go into mournin' at wanst. . . . I never expected that poor Bill ud die so sudden. . . . Well, we all have to die some day . . . you, Juno, today . . . an' me, maybe, tomorrow. . . . It's sad, but it can't be helped. . . . *Requiescat in pace* . . . or, usin' our oul' tongue like St Patrick or St Bridget, *Guh sayeree jeea ayera*!*

MARY. Oh, father, that's not Rest in Peace; that's God save Ireland.

BOYLE. U-u-ugh, it's all the same – isn't it a prayer? . . . Juno, I'm done with Joxer; he's nothin' but a prognosticator an' a . . .

JOXER [*climbing angrily through the window and bounding into the room*]. You're done with Joxer, are you? Maybe you thought I'd stop on the roof all the night for you! Joxer out on the roof with the win' blowin' through him was nothin' to you an' your friend with the collar an' tie!

MRS BOYLE. What in the name o' God brought you out on the roof; what were you doin' there?

JOXER [*ironically*]. I was dhreamin' I was standin' on the bridge of a ship, an' she sailin' the Antartic Ocean, an' it blowed, an' blowed, an' I lookin' up at the sky an' sayin', what is the stars, what is the stars?

MRS BOYLE [*opening the door and standing at it*]. Here, get ou' o' this, Joxer Daly; I was always thinkin' you had a slate off.*

JOXER [*moving to the door*]. I have to laugh every time I look at the deep-sea sailor; an' a row on a river ud make him sea-sick!

BOYLE. Get ou' o' this before I take the law into me own hands!

JOXER [*going out*]. Say aw rewaeawr,* but not goodbye. Lookin' for work, an' prayin' to God he won't get it! [*He goes.*]

MRS BOYLE. I'm tired tellin' you what Joxer was; maybe now you see yourself the kind he is.

BOYLE. He'll never blow the froth off a pint o' mine agen, that's a sure thing. Johnny . . . Mary . . . you're to keep yourselves to yourselves for the future. Juno, I'm done with Joxer. . . . I'm a new man from this out. . . . [*Clasping* MRS BOYLE's *hand, and singing emotionally*]

O, me darlin' Juno, I will be thrue to thee;
Me own, me darlin' Juno, you're all the world to me.*

CURTAIN

## ACT II

*The same, but the furniture is more plentiful, and of a vulgar nature. A glaringly upholstered armchair and lounge; cheap pictures and photos everywhere. Every available spot is ornamented with huge vases filled with artificial flowers. Crossed festoons of coloured paper chains stretch from end to end of ceiling. On the table is an old attaché case. It is about six in the evening, and two days after the First Act.* BOYLE, *in his shirt-sleeves, is voluptuously stretched on the sofa; he is smoking a clay pipe. He is half asleep. A lamp is lighting on the table. After a few moments' pause the voice of* JOXER *is heard singing softly outside at the door – 'Me pipe I'll smoke, as I dhrive me moke\* —.are you there, Mor . . . ee . . . ar . . . i . . . teee!'*

BOYLE [*leaping up, takes a pen in his hand and busies himself with papers*].
    Come along, Joxer, me son, come along.
JOXER [*putting his head in*]. Are you be yourself?
BOYLE. Come on, come on; that doesn't matther; I'm masther now,
    an' I'm goin' to remain masther. [JOXER *comes in.*]
JOXER. How d'ye feel now, as a man o' money?
BOYLE [*solemnly*]. It's a responsibility, Joxer, a great responsibility.
JOXER. I suppose 'tis now, though you wouldn't think it.
BOYLE. Joxer, han' me over that attackey\* case on the table there.
    [JOXER *hands the case.*] Ever since the Will was passed I've run
    hundreds o' dockyments through me han's – I tell you, you have to
    keep your wits about you. [*He busies himself with papers.*]
JOXER. Well, I won't disturb you; I'll dhrop in when . . .
BOYLE [*hastily*]. It's all right, Joxer, this is the last one to be signed
    today. [*He signs a paper, puts it into the case, which he shuts with a
    snap, and sits back pompously in the chair.*] Now, Joxer, you want to
    see me; I'm at your service – what can I do for you, me man?
JOXER. I've just dhropped in with the three pouns five shillings that
    Mrs Madigan riz on the blankets an' table\* for you, an' she says
    you're to be in no hurry payin' it back.
BOYLE. She won't be long without it; I expect the first cheque for a
    couple o' hundhred any day. There's the five bob\* for yourself – go
    on, take it, man; it'll not be the last you'll get from the Captain.
    Now an' agen we have our differ, but we're there together all the
    time.

JOXER. Me for you, an' you for me, like the two Musketeers.*

BOYLE. Father Farrell stopped me today an' tole me how glad he was I fell in for the money.

JOXER. He'll be stoppin' you ofen enough now; I suppose it was 'Mr' Boyle with him?

BOYLE. He shuk me be the han' . . .

JOXER [*ironically*]. I met with Napper Tandy, an' he shuk me be the han'!*

BOYLE. You're seldom asthray, Joxer, but you're wrong shipped this time. What you're sayin' of Father Farrell is very near to blasfeemey. I don't like anyone to talk disrespectful of Father Farrell.

JOXER. You're takin' me up wrong, Captain; I wouldn't let a word be said agen Father Farrell – the heart o' the rowl,* that's what he is; I always said he was a darlin' man, a daarlin' man.

BOYLE. Comin' up the stairs who did I meet but that bummer,* Nugent. 'I seen you talkin' to Father Farrell', says he, with a grin on him. 'He'll be folleyin' you,' says he, 'like a Guardian Angel from this out' – all the time the oul' grin on him, Joxer.

JOXER. I never seen him yet but he had the oul' grin on him!

BOYLE. 'Mr Nugent,' says I, 'Father Farrell is a man o' the people, an', as far as I know the History o' me country, the priests was always in the van of the fight for Irelan's freedom.'

JOXER [*fervently*].

> Who was it led the van, Soggart Aroon?*
> Since the fight first began, Soggart Aroon?

BOYLE. 'Who are you tellin'?' says he. 'Didn't they let down the Fenians, an' didn't they do in Parnell? An' now . . .' 'You ought to be ashamed o' yourself,' says I, interruptin' him, 'not to know the History o' your country.' An' I left him gawkin'* where he was.

JOXER. Where ignorance 's bliss 'tis folly to be wise*; I wondher did he ever read *The Story o' Ireland*.*

BOYLE. Be J. L. Sullivan? Don't you know he didn't.

JOXER. Ah, it's a darlin' buk, a daarlin' buk!

BOYLE. You'd betther be goin', now, Joxer; his Majesty, Bentham'll be here any minute, now.

JOXER. Be the way things is lookin', it'll be a match between him an'

Mary. She's thrun over Jerry altogether. Well, I hope it will, for he's a darlin' man.

BOYLE. I'm glad you think so – I don't. [*Irritably*] What's darlin' about him?

JOXER [*nonplussed*]. I only seen him twiced; if you want to know me, come an' live with me.

BOYLE. He's too dignified for me – to hear him talk you'd think he knew as much as a Boney's Oraculum.* He's given up his job as teacher, an' is goin' to become a solicitor in Dublin – he's been studyin' law. I suppose he thinks I'll set him up, but he's wrong shipped. An' th' other fella – Jerry's as bad. The two o' them ud give you a pain in your face, listenin' to them; Jerry believin' in nothin', an' Bentham believin' in everythin'. One that says all is God an' no man; an' th' other that says all is man an' no God!

JOXER. Well, I'll be off now.

BOYLE. Don't forget to dhrop down afther awhile; we'll have a quiet jar, an' a song or two.

JOXER. Never fear.

BOYLE. An' tell Mrs Madigan that I hope we'll have the pleasure of her organisation at out little enthertainment.

JOXER. Righto; we'll come down together. [*He goes out.*]

JOHNNY *comes from room on left, and sits down moodily at the fire.* BOYLE *looks at him for a few moments, and shakes his head. He fills his pipe.*

VOICE OF MRS BOYLE AT THE DOOR. Open the door, Jack; this thing has me nearly kilt with the weight.

BOYLE *opens the door.* MRS BOYLE *enters carrying the box of a gramophone, followed by* MARY *carrying the horn and some parcels.* MRS BOYLE *leaves the box on the table and flops into a chair.*

MRS BOYLE. Carryin' that from Henry Street was no joke.

BOYLE. U-u-ugh, that's a grand-lookin' insthrument – how much was it?

MRS BOYLE. Pound down, an' five to be paid at two shillin's a week.

BOYLE. That's reasonable enough.

MRS BOYLE. I'm afraid we're runnin' into too much debt; first the furniture, an' now this.

BOYLE. The whole lot won't be much out of £2000.

MARY. I don't know what you wanted a gramophone for – I know Charlie hates them; he says they're destructive of real music.

BOYLE. Desthructive of music – that fella ud give you a pain in your face. All a gramophone wants is to be properly played; its thrue wondher is only felt when everythin's quiet – what a gramophone wants is dead silence!

MARY. But, father, Jerry says the same; afther all, you can only appreciate music when your ear is properly trained.

BOYLE. That's another fella ud give you a pain in your face. Properly thrained! I suppose you couldn't appreciate football unless your fut was properly thrained.

MRS BOYLE [*to* MARY]. Go on in ower that an' dress or Charlie'll be in on you, an' tea nor nothin'll be ready. [MARY *goes into room left.*]

MRS BOYLE [*arranging table for tea*]. You didn't look at your new gramophone, Johnny?

JOHNNY. 'Tisn't gramophones I'm thinking of.

MRS BOYLE. An' what is it you're thinkin' of, allanna?*

JOHNNY. Nothin', nothin', nothin'.

MRS BOYLE. Sure, you must be thinkin' of somethin'; it's yourself that has yourself the way y'are; sleepin' wan night in me sisther's, an' the nex' in your father's brother's – you'll get no rest goin' on that way.

JOHNNY. I can rest nowhere, nowhere, nowhere.

MRS BOYLE. Sure, you're not thryin' to rest anywhere.

JOHNNY. Let me alone, let me alone, let me alone, for God's sake. [*A knock at street door.*]

MRS BOYLE [*in a flutter*]. Here he is; here's Mr Bentham!

BOYLE. Well, there's room for him; it's a pity there's not a brass band to play him in.

MRS BOYLE. We'll han' the tea round, an' not be clusthered round the table, as if we never seen nothin'. [*Steps are heard approaching, and* MRS BOYLE, *opening the door, allows* BENTHAM *to enter.*] Give your hat an' stick to Jack, there . . . sit down, Mr Bentham . . . no, not there . . . in th' easy chair be the fire . . . there, that's bether. Mary'll be out to you in a minute.

BOYLE [*solemnly*]. I seen be the paper this mornin' that Consols* was down half per cent. That's serious, min' you, an' shows the whole counthry's in a state o' chassis.

MRS BOYLE. What's Consols, Jack?

BOYLE. Consols? Oh, Consols is – oh, there's no use tellin' women what Consols is – th' wouldn't undherstand.

BENTHAM. It's just as you were saying, Mrs Boyle. [MARY *enters, charmingly dressed*.] Oh, good evening, Mary; how pretty you're looking!

MARY [*archly*]. Am I?

BOYLE. We were just talkin' when you kem in, Mary; I was tellin' Mr Bentham that the whole counthry's in a state o' chassis.

MARY [*to* BENTHAM]. Would you prefer the green or the blue ribbon round me hair, Charlie?

MRS BOYLE. Mary, your father's speakin'.

BOYLE [*rapidly*]. I was jus' tellin' Mr Bentham that the whole country's in a state o' chassis.

MARY. I'm sure you're frettin', da, whether it is or no.

MRS BOYLE. With all our churches an' religions, the worl's not a bit the betther.

BOYLE [*with a commanding gesture*]. Tay! [MARY *and* MRS BOYLE *dispense the tea.*]

MRS BOYLE. An' Irelan's takin' a leaf out o' the worl's buk; when we got the makin' of our own laws* I thought we'd never stop to look behind us, but instead of that we never stopped to look before us! If the people ud folley up their religion betther there'd be a betther chance for us – what do you think Mr Bentham?

BENTHAM. I'm afraid I can't venture to express an opinion on that point, Mrs Boyle; dogma has no attraction for me.

MRS BOYLE. I forgot you didn't hold with us: what's this you said you were?

BENTHAM. A Theosophist,* Mrs Boyle.

MRS BOYLE. An' what in the name o' God's a Theosophist?

BOYLE. A Theosophist, Juno, 's a – tell her, Mr Bentham, tell her.

BENTHAM. It's hard to explain in a few words: Theosophy's founded on the Vedas,* the religious books of the East. Its central theme is the existence of an all-pervading Spirit – the Life-Breath. Nothing really exists but this one Universal Life-Breath. And whatever even seems to exist separately from this Life-Breath, doesn't really exist at all. It is all vital force in man, in all animals, and in all vegetation. This Life-Breath is called the Prawna.*

MRS BOYLE. The Prawna! What a comical name!

BOYLE. Prawna; yis, the Prawna. [*Blowing gently through his lips*] That's the Prawna!

MRS BOYLE. Whist, whist, Jack.

BENTHAM. The happiness of man depends upon his sympathy with this Spirit. Men who have reached a high state of excellence are called Yogi.* Some men become Yogi in a short time, it may take others millions of years.

BOYLE. Yogi! I seen hundhreds of them in the streets o' San Francisco.

BENTHAM. It is said by these Yogi that if we practise certain mental exercises we would have powers denied to others – for instance, the faculty of seeing things that happen miles and miles away.

MRS BOYLE. I wouldn't care to meddle with that sort o' belief; it's a very curious religion, altogether.

BOYLE. What's curious about it? Isn't all religions curious? – if they weren't, you wouldn't get any one to believe them. But religions is passin' away – they've had their day like everything else. Take the real Dublin people, f'rinstance: they know more about Charlie Chaplin* an' Tommy Mix* than they do about SS. Peter an' Paul!

MRS BOYLE. You don't believe in ghosts, Mr Bentham?

MARY. Don't you know he doesn't, mother?

BENTHAM. I don't know that, Mary. Scientists are beginning to think that what we call ghosts are sometimes seen by persons of a certain nature. They say that sensational actions, such as the killing of a person, demand great energy, and that energy lingers in the place where the action occurred. People may live in the place and see nothing, when someone may come along whose personality has some peculiar connection with the energy of the place, and, in a flash, the person sees the whole affair.

JOHNNY [*rising swiftly, pale and affected*]. What sort o' talk is this to be goin' on with? Is there nothin' betther to be talkin' about but the killin' o' people? My God, isn't it bad enough for these things to happen without talkin' about them! [*He hurriedly goes into the room on left.*]

BENTHAM. Oh, I'm very sorry, Mrs Boyle; I never thought . . .

MRS BOYLE [*apologetically*]. Never mind, Mr Bentham, he's very touchy. [*A frightened scream is heard from* JOHNNY *inside.*] Mother of God, what's that? [*He rushes out again, his face pale, his lips twitching, his limbs trembling.*]

JOHNNY. Shut the door, shut the door, quick, for God's sake! Great God, have mercy on me! Blessed Mother o' God, shelter me, shelther your son!

MRS BOYLE [*catching him in her arms*]. What's wrong with you? What ails you? Sit down, sit down, here, on the bed . . . there now . . . there now.

MARY. Johnny, Johnny, what ails you?

JOHNNY. I seen him, I seen him . . . kneelin' in front o' the statue . . . merciful Jesus, have pity on me!

MRS BOYLE [*to* BOYLE]. Get him a glass o' whisky . . . quick, man, an' don't stand gawkin'. [BOYLE *gets the whisky.*]

JOHNNY. Sit here, sit here, mother . . . between me an' the door.

MRS BOYLE. I'll sit beside you as long as you like, only tell me what was it came across you at all?

JOHNNY [*after taking some drink*]. I seen him. . . . I seen Robbie Tancred kneelin' down before the statue . . . an' the red light shinin' on him . . . an' when I went in . . . he turned an' looked at me . . . an' I seen the woun's bleedin' in his breast. . . . Oh, why did he look at me like that? . . . it wasn't my fault that he was done in. . . . Mother o' God, keep him away from me!

MRS BOYLE. There, there, child, you've imagined it all. There was nothin' there at all – it was the red light you seen, an' the talk we had put all the rest into your head. Here, dhrink more o' this – it'll do you good. . . . An', now, stretch yourself down on the bed for a little. [*To* BOYLE] Go in, Jack, an' show him it was only in his own head it was.

BOYLE. [*making no move*]. E-e-e-e-eh; it's all nonsense; it was only a shadda he saw.

MARY. Mother o' God, he made me heart lep!

BENTHAM. It was simply due to an overwrought imagination – we all get that way at times.

MRS BOYLE. There, dear, lie down in the bed, an' I'll put the quilt across you . . . e-e-e-eh, that's it . . . you'll be as right as the mail in a few minutes.

JOHNNY. Mother, go into the room an' see if the light's lightin' before the statue.

MRS BOYLE [*to* BOYLE]. Jack, run in an' see if the light's lightin' before the statue.

BOYLE [*to* MARY]. Mary, slip in an' see if the light's lightin' before the statue. [MARY *hesitates to go in.*]

BENTHAM. It's all right; Mary, I'll go. [*He goes into the room; remains for a few moments, and returns.*] Everything's just as it was – the light burning bravely before the statue.

BOYLE. Of course; I knew it was all nonsense. [*A knock at the door. Going to open the door*] E-e-e-e-eh.

*He opens it, and* JOXER, *followed by* MRS MADIGAN, *enters.* MRS MADIGAN
*is a strong, dapper little woman of about forty-five; her face is almost
always a widespread smile of complacency. She is a woman who, in
manner at least, can mourn with them that mourn, and rejoice with them
that do rejoice. When she is feeling comfortable, she is inclined to be
reminiscent; when others say anything, or following a statement made by
herself, she has a habit of putting her head a little to one side, and nodding it
rapidly several times in succession, like a bird pecking at a hard berry.
Indeed, she has a good deal of the bird in her, but the bird instinct is by no
means a melodious one. She is ignorant, vulgar and forward, but her heart
is generous withal. For instance, she would help a neighbour's sick child;
she would probably kill the child, but her intention would be to cure it; she
would be more at home helping a drayman to lift a fallen horse. She is
dressed in a rather soiled grey dress and a vivid purple blouse; in her hair is
a huge comb, ornamented with huge coloured beads. She enters with a
gliding step, beaming smile and nodding head.* BOYLE *receives them
effusively.*

BOYLE. Come on in, Mrs Madigan; come on in; I was afraid you
weren't comin'. . . . [*Slyly*] There's some people able to dhress, ay,
Joxer?

JOXER. Fair as the blossoms that bloom in the May, an' sweet as the
scent of the new-mown hay. . . . Ah, well she may wear them.

MRS MADIGAN [*looking at* MARY.]. I know some as are as sweet as the
blossoms that bloom in the May – oh, no names, no pack dhrill.

BOYLE. An' now I'll inthroduce the pair o' yous to Mary's intended:
Mr Bentham, this is Mrs Madigan, an oul' back-parlour neighbour,
that, if she could help it at all, ud never see a body shuk!

BENTHAM [*rising, and tentatively shaking the hand of* MRS MADIGAN].
I'm sure, it's a great pleasure to know you, Mrs Madigan.

MRS MADIGAN. An, I'm goin' to tell you, Mr Bentham, you're goin' to
get as nice a bit o' skirt* in Mary, there, as ever you seen in your
puff.* Not like some of the dhressed-up dolls that's knockin' about
lookin' for men when it's a skelpin* they want. I remember, as well
as I remember yestherday, the day she was born – of a Tuesday, the
25th o' June, in the year 1901, at thirty-three minutes past wan in
the day by Foley's clock, the pub at the corner o' the street. A cowld
day it was too, for the season o' the year, an' I remember sayin' to
Joxer, there, who I met comin' up th' stairs, that the new arrival in
Boyle's ud grow up a hardy chiselur if it lived, an' that she'd be

somethin' one o' these days that nobody suspected, an' so signs on it,* here she is today, goin' to be married to a young man lookin' as if he'd be fit to commensurate in any position in life it ud please God to call him!

BOYLE [*effusively*]. Sit down, Mrs Madigan, sit down, me oul' sport. [*To* BENTHAM] This is Joxer Daly, Past Chief Ranger of the Dear Little Shamrock Branch of the Irish National Foresters, an oul' front-top neighbour, that never despaired, even in the darkest days of Ireland's sorra.

JOXER. *Nil desperandum*,* Captain, *nil desperandum*.

BOYLE. Sit down, Joxer, sit down. The two of us was ofen in a tight corner.

MRS BOYLE. Ay, in Foley's snug!

JOXER. An' we kem out of it flyin', we kem out of it flyin', Captain.

BOYLE. An' now for a dhrink – I know yous won't refuse an oul' friend.

MRS MADIGAN [*to* MRS BOYLE]. Is Johnny not well, Mrs . . . .

MRS BOYLE [*warningly*]. S-s-s-sh.

MRS MADIGAN. Oh, the poor darlin'.

BOYLE. Well, Mrs Madigan, is it tea or what?

MRS MADIGAN. Well, speakin' for meself, I jus' had me tea a minute ago, an' I'm afraid to dhrink any more – I'm never the same when I dhrink too much tay. Thanks, all the same, Mr Boyle.

BOYLE. Well, what about a bottle o' stout or a dhrop o' whiskey?

MRS MADIGAN. A bottle o' stout ud be a little too heavy for me stummock afther me tay. . . . A-a-ah, I'll thry the ball o' malt.* [BOYLE *prepares the whisky*.] There's nothin' like a ball o' malt occasional like – too much of it isn't good. [*To* BOYLE, *who is adding water*] Ah, God, Johnny, don't put too much wather on it! [*She drinks*.] I suppose yous'll be lavin' this place.

BOYLE. I'm looking for a place near the sea; I'd like the place that you might say was me cradle, to be me grave as well. The sea is always callin' me.

JOXER. She is callin', callin', callin', in the win' an' on the sea.

BOYLE. Another dhrop o' whisky, Mrs Madigan?

MRS MADIGAN. Well, now, it ud be hard to refuse seein' the suspicious times that's in it.

BOYLE [*with a commanding gesture*]. Song! . . . Juno . . . Mary . . . 'Home to our Mountains'!*

MRS MADIGAN [*enthusiastically*]. Hear, hear!

JOXER. Oh, tha's a darlin' song, a daarlin' song!

MARY [*bashfully*]. Ah no, da; I'm not in a singin' humour.

MRS MADIGAN. Gawn* with you, child, an' you only goin' to be marrid;
I remember as well as I remember yestherday – it was on a lovely
August evenin', exactly, accordin' to date, fifteen years ago, come
the Tuesday folleyin' the nex' that's comin' on, when me own man –
*the Lord be good to him* – an' me was sittin' shy together in a doty
little nook* on a counthry road, adjacent to The Stiles. 'That'll
scratch your lovely, little white neck', says he, ketchin' hould of a
danglin' bramble branch, holdin' clusters of the loveliest flowers
you ever seen, an' breakin' it off, so that his arm fell, accidental like,
roun' me waist, an' as I felt it tightenin', an tightenin', an'
tightenin', I thought me buzzom was every minute goin' to burst
out into a roystherin' song about

> The little green leaves that were shakin' on the threes,
> The gallivantin' buttherflies, an' buzzin' o' the bees!

BOYLE. Ordher for the song!

MRS BOYLE. Come on, Mary – we'll do our best.

MRS BOYLE *and* MARY *stand up, and choosing a suitable position, sing
simply* 'Home to our Mountains'.* *They bow to the company, and return
to their places.*

BOYLE [*emotionally, at the end of the song*]. 'Lull . . . me . . . to . . .
rest!'

JOXER [*clapping his hands*]. Bravo, bravo! Darlin' girulls, darlin'
girulls!

MRS MADIGAN. Juno, I never seen you in betther form.

BENTHAM. Very nicely rendered indeed.

MRS MADIGAN. A noble call, a noble call!

MRS BOYLE. What about yourself, Mrs Madigan?

*After some coaxing,* MRS MADIGAN *rises, and in a quavering voice sings the
following verse:*

> If I were a blackbird I'd whistle and sing;
> I'd follow the ship that my thrue love was in;
> An' on the top riggin', I'd there build me nest,
> An' at night I would sleep on me Willie's white breast!

*Becoming husky, amid applause, she sits down.*

MRS MADIGAN. Ah, me voice is too husky now, Juno; though I
remember the time when Maisie Madigan could sing like a
nightingale at matin' time. I remember as well as I remember
yestherday, at a party given to celebrate the comin' of the first
chiselur to Annie an' Benny Jimeson – who was the barber, yous
may remember, in Henrietta Street, that, afther Easter Week, hung
out a green, white an' orange pole, an' then, when the Tans started
their jazz dancin', whipped it in agen, an' stuck out a red, white an'
blue wan instead, givin' as an excuse that a barber's pole was strictly
non-political – singin' 'An' You'll Remember Me'* with the top
notes quiverin' in a dead hush of pethrified attention, folleyed be a
clappin' o' han's that shuk the tumblers on the table, an' capped by
Jimeson, the barber, sayin' that it was the best rendherin' of 'You'll
Remember Me' he ever heard in his natural!
BOYLE [*peremptorily*]. Ordher for Joxer's song!
JOXER. Ah no, I couldn't; don't ass me, Captain.
BOYLE. Joxer's song, Joxer's song – give us wan of your shut-eyed
wans.
JOXER [*settles himself in his chair; takes a drink; clears his throat; solemnly
closes his eyes, and begins to sing in a very querulous voice*].

> She is far from the lan' where her young hero sleeps,
> An' lovers around her are sighing [*He hesitates.*]
> An' lovers around her are sighin' . . . sighin' . . .
>      sighin' . . . [*A pause.*]

BOYLE [*imitating* JOXER].

> And lovers around her are sighing!*

What's the use of you thryin' to sing the song if you don't know it?
MARY. Thry another one, Mr Daly – maybe you'd be more fortunate.
MRS MADIGAN. Gawn, Joxer; thry another wan.
JOXER [*starting again*].

> I have heard the mavis singin' his love song to the morn;
> I have seen the dew-dhrop clingin' to the rose jus' newly born;
>      but . . . but . . . [*frantically*] To the rose jus' newly born . . .
>      newly born . . . born.*

JOHNNY. Mother, put on the gramophone, for God's sake, an' stop Joxer's bawlin'.

BOYLE [*commandingly*]. Gramophone! . . . I hate to see fellas thryin' to do what they're not able to do. [BOYLE *arranges the gramophone, and is about to start it, when voices are heard of persons descending the stairs.*]

MRS BOYLE [*warningly*]. Whisht,* Jack, don't put it on, don't put it on yet; this must be poor Mrs Tancred comin' down to go to the hospital – I forgot all about them bringin' the body to the church tonight. Open the door, Mary, an' give them a bit o' light.


MARY *opens the door, and* MRS TANCRED — *a very old woman, obviously shaken by the death of her son* — *appears, accompanied by several* NEIGHBOURS. *The first few phrases are spoken before they appear.*


FIRST NEIGHBOUR. It's a sad journey we're goin' on, but God's good, an' the Republicans* won't be always down.

MRS TANCRED. Ah, what good is that to me now? Whether they're up or down – it won't bring me darlin' boy from the grave.

MRS BOYLE. Come in an' have a hot cup o' tay, Mrs Tancred, before you go.

MRS TANCRED. Ah, I can take nothin' now, Mrs Boyle – I won't be long afther him.

FIRST NEIGHBOUR. Still an' all, he died a noble death, an' we'll bury him like a king.

MRS TANCRED. An' I'll go on livin' like a pauper. Ah, what's the pains I suffered bringin' him into the world to carry him to his cradle, to the pains I'm sufferin' now, carryin' him out o' the world to bring him to his grave!

MARY. It would be better for you not to go at all, Mrs Tancred, but to stay at home beside the fire with some o' the neighbours.

MRS TANCRED. I seen the first of him, an' I'll see the last of him.

MRS BOYLE. You'd want a shawl, Mrs Tancred; it's a cowld night, an' the win's blowin' sharp.

MRS MADIGAN [*rushing out*]. I've a shawl above.

MRS TANCRED. Me home is gone now; he was me only child, an' to think that he was lyin' for a whole night stretched out on the side of a lonely counthry lane, with his head, his darlin' head, that I ofen kissed an' fondled, half hidden in the wather of a runnin' brook.

An' I'm told he was the leadher of the ambush where me nex' door neighbour, Mrs Mannin', lost her Free State soldier son.* An' now here's the two of us oul' women, standin' one on each side of a scales o' sorra, balanced be the bodies of our two dead darlin' sons. [MRS MADIGAN *returns, and wraps a shawl around her.*] God bless you, Mrs Madigan. . . . [*She moves slowly towards the door.*] Mother o' God, Mother o' God, have pity on the pair of us! . . . O Blessed Virgin, where were you when me darlin' son was riddled with bullets, when me darlin' son was riddled with bullets! . . . Sacred Heart of the Crucified Jesus, take away our hearts o' stone . . . an' give us hearts o' flesh!* . . . Take away this murdherin' hate . . . an' give us Thine own eternal love! [*They pass out of the room.*]

MRS BOYLE [*explanatorily to* BENTHAM]. That was Mrs Tancred of the two-pair back; her son was found, e'er yesterday, lyin' out beyant Finglas riddled with bullets. A Diehard he was, be all accounts. He was a nice quiet boy, but lattherly he went to hell, with his Republic first, an' Republic last an' Republic over all. He often took tea with us here, in the oul' days, an' Johnny, there, an' him used to be always together.

JOHNNY. Am I always to be havin' to tell you that he was no friend o' mine? I never cared for him, an' he could never stick me. It's not because he was Commandant of the Battalion that I was Quarther-Masther of, that we were friends.

MRS BOYLE. He's gone now – the Lord be good to him! God help his poor oul' creature of a mother, for no matther whose friend or enemy he was, he was her poor son.

BENTHAM. The whole thing is terrible, Mrs Boyle; but the only way to deal with a mad dog is to destroy him.

MRS BOYLE. An' to think of me forgettin' about him bein' brought to the church tonight, an' we singing' an' all, but it was well we hadn't the gramophone goin', anyhow.

BOYLE. Even if we had aself. We've nothin' to do with these things, one way or t'other. That's the Government's business, an' let them do what we're payin' them for doin'.

MRS BOYLE. I'd like to know how a body's not to mind these things; look at the way they're afther leavin' the people in this very house. Hasn't the whole house, nearly, been massacreed? There's young Dougherty's husband with his leg off; Mrs Travers that had her son blew up be a mine in Inchegeela, in County Cork; Mrs Mannin' that lost wan of her sons in an ambush a few weeks ago, an' now, poor Mrs Tancred's only child gone west with his body made a

collandher* of. Sure, if it's not our business, I don't know whose
business it is.

BOYLE. Here, there, that's enough about them things; they don't
affect us, an' we needn't give a damn. If they want a wake, well, let
them have a wake.* When I was a sailor, I was always resigned to
meet with a wathery grave; an' if they want to be soldiers, well,
there's no use o' them squealin' when they meet a soldier's fate.

JOXER. Let me like a soldier fall – me breast expandin' to th' ball!*

MRS BOYLE. In wan way, she deserves all she got; for lately, she let th'
Diehards make an open house of th' place; an' for th' last couple of
months, either when th' sun was risin' or when th' sun was settin',
you had CID* men burstin' into your room, assin' you where were
you born, where were you christened, where were you married, an'
where would you be buried!

JOHNNY. For God's sake, let us have no more o' this talk.

MRS MADIGAN. What about Mr Boyle's song before we start th'
gramophone?

MARY [*getting her hat, and putting it on*]. Mother, Charlie and I are goin'
out for a little sthroll.

MRS BOYLE. All right, darlin'.

BENTHAM [*going out with* MARY]. We won't be long away, Mrs Boyle.

MRS MADIGAN. Gwan, Captain, gwan.

BOYLE. E-e-e-e-eh, I'd want to have a few more jars in me, before I'd
be in fettle for singin'.

JOXER. Give us that poem you writ t'other day. [*To the rest*] Aw, it's a
darlin' poem, a daarlin' poem.

MRS BOYLE. God bless us, is he startin' to write poetry!

BOYLE [*rising to his feet*]. E-e-e-e-eh. [*He recites in an emotional,
consequential manner the following verses*]

> Shawn an' I were friends, sir, to me he was all in all.
> His work was very heavy and his wages were very small.
> None betther on th' beach as Docker, I'll go bail,
> 'Tis now I'm feelin' lonely, for today he lies in jail.
> He was not what some call pious – seldom at church
>     or prayer;
> For the greatest scoundrels I know, sir, goes every
>     Sunday there.
> Fond of his pint – well, rather, but hated the Boss
>     by creed
> But never refused a copper* to comfort a pal in need.

E-e-e-e-eh. [*He sits down.*]

MRS MADIGAN. Grand, grand; you should folly* that up, you should folly that up.

JOXER. It's a daarlin' poem!

BOYLE [*delightedly*]. E-e-e-e-eh.

JOHNNY. Are yous goin' to put on th' gramophone tonight, or are yous not?

MRS BOYLE. Gwan, Jack, put on a record.

MRS MADIGAN. Gwan, Captain, gwan.

BOYLE. Well, yous'll want to keep a dead silence.

*He sets a record, starts the machine, and it begins to play 'If You're Irish Come into the Parlour'.* As the tune is in full blare, the door is suddenly opened by a brisk, little bald-headed man, dressed circumspectly in a black suit; he glares fiercely at all in the room; he is 'NEEDLE' NUGENT, a tailor. He carries his hat in his hand.*

NUGENT [*loudly, above the noise of the gramophone*]. Are yous goin' to have that thing bawlin' an' the funeral of Mrs Tancred's son passin' the house? Have none of yous any respect for the Irish people's National regard for the dead? [BOYLE *stops the gramophone.*]

MRS BOYLE. Maybe, Needle Nugent, it's nearly time we had a little less respect for the dead, an' a little more regard for the livin'.

MRS MADIGAN. We don't want you, Mr Nugent, to teach us what we learned at our mother's knee. You don't look yourself as if you were dyin' of grief; if y'ass Maisie Madigan anything, I'd call you a real thrue Diehard an' live-soft Republican, attendin' Republican funerals in the day, an' stoppin' up half the night makin' suits for the Civic Guards*!

*Persons are heard running down the street, some saying 'Here it is, here it is.' NUGENT withdraws, and the rest, except JOHNNY, go to the window looking into the street, and look out. Sounds of a crowd coming nearer are heard; portion are singing*

> To Jesus' Heart all burning
> With fervent love for men,
> My heart with fondest yearning
> Shall raise its joyful strain.
> While ages course along,

Blest be with loudest song
The Sacred Heart of Jesus
By every heart and tongue.

MRS BOYLE. Here's the hearse, here's the hearse!

BOYLE. There's t'oul' mother walkin' behin' the coffin.

MRS MADIGAN. You can hardly see the coffin with the wreaths.

JOXER. Oh, it's a darlin' funeral, a daarlin' funeral!

MRS MADIGAN. We'd have a betther view from the street.

BOYLE. Yes – this place ud give you a crick in your neck.

*They leave the room, and go down.* JOHNNY *sits moodily by the fire. A* YOUNG MAN *enters; he looks at* JOHNNY *for a moment.*

YOUNG MAN. Quarther-Masther Boyle.

JOHNNY [*with a start*]. The Mobiliser!

YOUNG MAN. You're not at the funeral?

JOHNNY. I'm not well.

YOUNG MAN. I'm glad I've found you; you were stoppin' at your aunt's; I called there but you'd gone. I've to give you an ordher to attend a Battalion Staff meetin' the night afther tomorrow.

JOHNNY. Where?

YOUNG MAN. I don't know; you're to meet me at the Pillar* at eight o'clock; then we're to go to a place I'll be told of tonight; there we'll meet a mothor that'll bring us to the meeting. They think you might be able to know somethin' about them that gave the bend* where Commandant Tancred was shelterin'.

JOHNNY. I'm not goin', then. I know nothing about Tancred.

YOUNG MAN [*at the door*]. You'd better come for you own sake – remember your oath.

JOHNNY [*passionately*]. I won't go! Haven't I done enough for Ireland! I've lost me arm, an' me hip's desthroyed so that I'll never be able to walk right agen! Good God, haven't I done enough for Ireland?

YOUNG MAN. Boyle, no man can do enough for Ireland! [*He goes.*]

*Faintly in the distance the crowd is heard saying*

Hail, Mary, full of grace, the Lord is with Thee;
Blessed art Thou amongst women, and blessed [*etc.*]

CURTAIN

## ACT III

*The same as Act II. It is about half-past six on a November evening; a bright fire burns in the grate; MARY, dressed to go out, is sitting on a chair by the fire, leaning forward, her hands under her chin, her elbows on her knees. A look of dejection, mingled with uncertain anxiety, is on her face. A lamp, turned low, is lighting on the table. The votive light under the picture of the Virgin gleams more redly than ever. MRS BOYLE is putting on her hat and coat. It is two months later.*

MRS BOYLE. An' has Bentham never even written to you since – not one line for the past month?

MARY [*tonelessly*]. Not even a line, mother.

MRS BOYLE. That's very curious. . . . What came between the two of yous at all? To leave you so sudden, an' yous so great together. . . . To go away t' England, an' not to even leave you his address. . . . The way he was always bringin' you to dances, I thought he was mad afther you. Are you sure you said nothin' to him?

MARY. No, mother – at least nothing that could possibly explain his givin' me up.

MRS BOYLE. You know you're a bit hasty at times, Mary, an' say things you shouldn't say.

MARY. I never said to him what I shouldn't say, I'm sure of that.

MRS BOYLE. How are you sure of it?

MARY. Because I love him with all my heart and soul, mother. Why, I don't know; I often thought to myself that he wasn't the man poor Jerry was, but I couldn't help loving him, all the same.

MRS BOYLE. But you shouldn't be frettin' the way you are; when a woman loses a man, she never knows what she's afther losin', to be sure, but, then, she never knows what she's afther gainin', either. You're not the one girl of a month ago – you look like one pinin' away. It's long ago I had a right to bring you to the doctor, instead of waitin' till tonight.

MARY. There's no necessity, really, mother, to go to the doctor; nothing serious is wrong with me – I'm run down and disappointed, that's all.

MRS BOYLE. I'll not wait another minute; I don't like the look of you at all. . . . I'm afraid we made a mistake in throwin' over poor Jerry. . . . He'd have been betther for you than that Bentham.

MARY. Mother, the best man for a woman is the one for whom she has the most love, and Charlie had it all.

MRS BOYLE. Well, there's one thing to be said for him – he couldn't have been thinkin' of the money, or he wouldn't ha' left you . . . it must ha' been somethin' else.

MARY [*wearily*]. I don't know, mother . . . only I think . . .

MRS BOYLE. What d'ye think?

MARY. I imagine . . . he thought . . . we weren't . . . good enough for him.

MRS BOYLE. An' what was he himself, only a school teacher? Though I don't blame him for fightin' shy of people like that Joxer fella an' that oul' Madigan wan* – nice sort o' people for your father to inthroduce to a man like Mr Bentham. You might have told me all about this before now, Mary; I don't know why you like to hide everything from your mother; you knew Bentham, an' I'd ha' known nothin' about it if it hadn't bin for the Will; an' it was only today, afther long coaxin', that you let out that he's left you.

MARY. It would have been useless to tell you – you wouldn't understand.

MRS BOYLE [*hurt*]. Maybe not. . . . Maybe I wouldn't understand. . . . Well, we'll be off now. [*She goes over to door left, and speaks to* BOYLE *inside.*] We're goin' now to the doctor's. Are you goin' to get up this evenin'?

BOYLE [*from inside*]. The pains in me legs is terrible! It's me should be poppin' off to the doctor instead o' Mary, the way I feel.

MRS BOYLE. Sorra mend you!* A nice way you were in last night – carried in in a frog's march, dead to the world. If that's the way you'll go on when you get the money it'll be the grave for you, an asylum for me and the Poorhouse for Johnny.

BOYLE. I thought you were goin'?

MRS BOYLE. That's what has you as you are – you can't bear to be spoken to. Knowin' the way we are, up to our ears in debt, it's a wondher you wouldn't ha' got up to go to th' solicitor's an' see if we could ha' gotten a little o' the money even.

BOYLE [*shouting*]. I can't be goin' up there night, noon an' mornin', can I? He can't give the money till he gets it, can he? I can't get blood out of a turnip,* can I?

MRS BOYLE. It's nearly two months since we heard of the Will, an' the money seems as far off as ever. . . . I suppose you know we owe twenty pouns to oul' Murphy?

BOYLE. I've a faint recollection of you tellin' me that before.

MRS BOYLE. Well, you'll go over to the shop yourself for the things in future – I'll face him no more.

BOYLE. I thought you said you were goin'?

MRS BOYLE. I'm goin' now; come on, Mary.

BOYLE. Ey, Juno, ey!

MRS BOYLE. Well, what d'ye want now?

BOYLE. Is there e're a bottle o' stout left?

MRS BOYLE. There's two o' them here still.

BOYLE. Show us in one o' them an' leave t'other there till I get up. An' throw us in the paper that's on the table, an' the bottle o' Sloan's Liniment* that's in th' drawer.

MRS BOYLE [*getting the liniment and the stout*]. What paper is it you want – the *Messenger*?

BOYLE. *Messenger*! The *News o' the World*!* [MRS BOYLE *brings in the things asked for, and comes out again.*]

MRS BOYLE [*at door*]. Mind the candle, now, an' don't burn the house over our heads. I left t'other bottle o' stout on the table. [*She puts bottle of stout on table. She goes out with* MARY. *A cork is heard popping inside.*]

*A pause; then outside the door is heard the voice of* JOXER *lilting softly: 'Me pipe I'll smoke, as I dhrive me moke . . . are you . . . there . . . Mor . . . ee . . . ar . . . i . . . teee!' A gentle knock is heard, and after a pause the door opens, and* JOXER, *followed by* NUGENT, *enters.*

JOXER. Be God, they must be all out; I was thinkin' there was somethin' up when he didn't answer the signal. We seen Juno an' Mary goin', but I didn't see him, an' it's very seldom he escapes me.

NUGENT. He's not goin' to escape me – he's not goin' to be let go to the fair altogether.

JOXER. Sure, the house couldn't hould them lately; an' he goin' about like a mastherpiece of the Free State counthry; forgettin' their friends; forgettin' God – wouldn't even lift his hat passin' a chapel!* Sure they were bound to get a dhrop! An' you really think there's no money comin' to him afther all?

NUGENT. Not as much as a red rex,* man; I've been a bit anxious this long time over me money, an' I went up to the solicitor's to find out all I could – ah, man, they were goin' to throw me down the stairs. They toul' me that the oul' cock himself had the stairs worn away comin' up afther it, an' they black in the face tellin' him he'd get nothin'. Some way or another that the Will is writ he won't be entitled to get as much as a make!*

JOXER. Ah, I thought there was somethin' curious about the whole thing; I've bin havin' sthrange dhreams for the last couple o' weeks. An' I notice that that Bentham fella doesn't be comin' here now – there must be somethin' on the mat there too. Anyhow, who, in the name o' God, ud leave anythin' to that oul' bummer? Sure it ud be unnatural. An' the way Juno an' him's been throwin' their weight about for the last few months! Ah, him that goes a borrowin' goes a sorrowin'!*

NUGENT. Well, he's not goin' to throw his weight about in the suit I made for him much longer. I'm tellin' you seven pouns aren't to be found growin' on the bushes these days.

JOXER. An' there isn't hardly a neighbour in the whole street that hasn't lent him money on the strength of what he was goin' to get, but they're after backing the wrong horse. Wasn't it a mercy o' God that I'd nothin' to give him! The softy I am, you know, I'd ha' lent him me last juice!* I must have had somebody's good prayers. Ah, afther all, an honest man's the noblest work o' God!* [BOYLE *coughs inside.*] Whisht, damn it, he must be inside in bed.

NUGENT. Inside o' bed or outside of it, he's goin' to pay me for that suit, or give it back – he'll not climb up my back* as easily as he thinks.

JOXER. Gwan in at wanst, man, an' get it off him, an' don't be a fool.

NUGENT [*going to door left, opening it and looking in*]. Ah, don't disturb yourself, Mr Boyle; I hope you're not sick?

BOYLE. Th' oul' legs, Mr Nugent, the oul' legs.

NUGENT. I just called over to see if you could let me have anything off the suit?

BOYLE. E-e-e-eh, how much is this it is?

NUGENT. It's the same as it was at the start – seven pouns.

BOYLE. I'm glad you kem, Mr Nugent; I want a good heavy topcoat – Irish frieze, if you have it. How much would a topcoat like that be, now?

NUGENT. About six pouns.

BOYLE. Six pouns – six an' seven, six an' seven is thirteen – that'll be thirteen pounds I'll owe you.

JOXER *slips the bottle of stout that is on the table into his pocket.* NUGENT *rushes into the room, and returns with suit on his arm; he pauses by the door.*

NUGENT. You'll owe me no thirteen pouns. Maybe you think you're betther able to owe it than pay it!

BOYLE [*frantically*]. Here, come back to hell ower that – where're you goin' with them clothes o' mine?

NUGENT. Where am I goin' with them clothes o' yours? Well, I like your damn cheek!

BOYLE. Here, what am I goin' to dhress meself in when I'm goin' out?

NUGENT. What do I care what you dhress yourself in! You can put yourself in a bolsther cover, if you like. [*He goes towards the other door, followed by* JOXER.]

JOXER. What'll he dhress himself in! Gentleman Jack an' his frieze coat! [*They go out.*]

BOYLE [*inside*]. Ey, Nugent; ey, Mr Nugent, Mr Nugent! [*After a pause* BOYLE *enters hastily, buttoning the braces of his moleskin trousers; his coat and vest are on his arm; he throws these on a chair and hurries to the door on right.*] Ey, Mr Nugent, Mr Nugent!

JOXER [*meeting him at the door*]. What's up, what's wrong, Captain?

BOYLE. Nugent's been here an' took away me suit – the only things I had to go out in!

JOXER. Tuk your suit – for God's sake! An' what were you doin' while he was takin' them?

BOYLE. I was in bed when he stole in like a thief in the night, an' before I knew even what he was thinkin' of, he whipped them from the chair an' was off like a redshank!*

JOXER. An' what, in the name o' God, did he do that for?

BOYLE. What did he do it for? How the hell do I know what he done it for? – jealousy an' spite, I suppose.

JOXER. Did he not say what he done it for?

BOYLE. Amn't I afther tellin' you that he had them whipped up an' was gone before I could open me mouth?

JOXER. That was a very sudden thing to do; there mus' be somethin' behin' it. Did he hear anythin', I wondher?

BOYLE. Did he hear anythin'? – you talk very queer, Joxer – what could he hear?

JOXER. About you not gettin' the money, in some way or t'other?

BOYLE. An' what ud prevent me from gettin' th' money?

JOXER. That's jus' what I was thinkin' – what ud prevent you from gettin' the money – nothin', as far as I can see.

BOYLE [*looking round for bottle of stout, with an exclamation*]. Aw, holy God!

JOXER. What's up, Jack?

BOYLE. He must have afther lifted the bottle o' stout that Juno left on the table!

JOXER [*horrified*]. Ah no, ah no; he wouldn't be afther doin' that now.

BOYLE. An' who done it then? Juno left a bottle o' stout here, an' it's gone – it didn't walk, did it?

JOXER. Oh, that's shockin'; ah, man's inhumanity to man makes countless thousands mourn!*

MRS MADIGAN [*appearing at the door*]. I hope I'm not disturbin' you in any discussion on your forthcomin' legacy – if I may use the word – an' that you'll let me have a barny* for a minute or two with you, Mr Boyle.

BOYLE [*uneasily*]. To be sure, Mrs Madigan – an oul' friend's always welcome.

JOXER. Come in the evenin', come in th' mornin'; come when your assed, or come without warnin'*, Mrs Madigan.

BOYLE. Sit down, Mrs Madigan.

MRS MADIGAN [*ominously*]. Th' few words I have to say can be said standin'. Puttin' aside all formularies,* I suppose you remember me lendin' you some time ago three pouns that I raised on blankets an' furniture in me uncle's?*

BOYLE. I remember it well. I have it recorded in me book – three pouns five shillings from Maisie Madigan, raised on articles pawned; an' item: fourpence, given to make up the price of a pint, on th' principle that no bird ever flew on wan wing; all to be repaid at par, when the ship comes home.

MRS MADIGAN. Well, ever since I shoved in the blankets I've been perishing with th' cowld, an' I've decided, if I'll be too hot in th' next' world aself, I'm not goin' to be too cowld in this wan; an' consequently, I want me three pouns if you please.

BOYLE. This is a very sudden demand, Mrs Madigan, an' can't be met; but I'm willin' to give you a receipt in full, in full.

MRS MADIGAN. Come on, out with th' money, an' don't be jack-actin'.

BOYLE. You can't get blood out of a turnip, can you?

MRS MADIGAN [*rushing over and shaking him*]. Gimme me money, y'oul' reprobate, or I'll shake the worth of it out of you!

BOYLE. Ey, houl' on, there; houl' on, there! You'll wait for your money now, me lassie!

MRS MADIGAN [*looking around the room and seeing the gramophone*]. I'll
wait for it, will I? Well, I'll not wait long; if I can't get th' cash, I'll
get th' worth of it. [*She snatches up the gramophone.*]

BOYLE. Ey, ey, there, wher'r you goin' with that?

MRS MADIGAN. I'm goin' to th' pawn to get me three quid five shillins;
I'll brin' you th' ticket, an' then you can do what you like, me
bucko.

BOYLE. You can't touch that, you can't touch that! It's not my
property, an' it's not ped for yet!

MRS MADIGAN. So much th' better. It'll be an ayse to me conscience,
for I'm takin' what doesn't belong to you. You're not goin' to be
swankin' it like a paycock with Maisie Madigan's money – I'll pull
some o' th' gorgeous feathers out o' your tail! [*She goes off with the
gramophone.*]

BOYLE. What's th' world comin' to at all? I ass you, Joxer Daly, is
there any morality left anywhere?

JOXER. I wouldn't ha' believed it, only I seen it with me own two eyes.
I didn't think Maisie Madigan was that sort of woman; she has
either a sup taken,* or she's heard somethin'.

BOYLE. Heard somethin' – about what, if it's not any harm to ass you?

JOXER. She must ha' heard some rumour or other that you weren't
goin' to get th' money.

BOYLE. Who says I'm not goin' to get th' money?

JOXER. Sure, I don't know – I was only sayin'.

BOYLE. Only sayin' what?

JOXER. Nothin'.

BOYLE. You were goin' to say somethin' – don't be a twisther.*

JOXER [*angrily*]. Who's a twisther?

BOYLE. Why don't you speak your mind, then?

JOXER. You never twisted yourself – no, you wouldn't know how!

BOYLE. Did you ever know me to twist; did you ever know me to twist?

JOXER [*fiercely*]. Did you ever do anythin' else! Sure, you can't believe
a word that comes out o' your mouth.

BOYLE. Here, get out, ower o' this; I always knew you were a
prognosticator an' a procrastinator!

JOXER [*going out as* JOHNNY *comes in*]. The anchor's weighed,
farewell, ree. . .mem. . .ber . . . me.* Jacky Boyle, Esquire,
infernal rogue an' damned liar.

JOHNNY. Joxer an' you at it agen? – when are you goin' to have a little
respect for yourself, an' not be always makin' a show of us all?

BOYLE. Are you goin' to lecture me now?

JOHNNY. Is mother back from the doctor yet, with Mary?

[MRS BOYLE *enters; it is apparent from the serious look on her face that something has happened. She takes off her hat and coat without a word and puts them by. She then sits down near the fire, and there is a few moments' pause.*

BOYLE. Well, what did the doctor say about Mary?

MRS BOYLE [*in an earnest manner and with suppressed agitation*]. Sit down here, Jack; I've something to say to you . . . about Mary.

BOYLE [*awed by her manner*]. About . . . Mary?

MRS BOYLE. Close that door there and sit down here.

BOYLE [*closing the door*]. More throuble in our native land, is it? [*He sits down.*] Well, what is it?

MRS BOYLE. It's about Mary.

BOYLE. Well, what about Mary – there's nothin' wrong with her, is there?

MRS BOYLE. I'm sorry to say there's a gradle* wrong with her.

BOYLE. A gradle wrong with her! [*Peevishly*] First Johnny an' now Mary; is the whole house goin' to become an hospital! It's not consumption, is it?

MRS BOYLE. No . . . it's not consumption . . . it's worse.

JOHNNY. Worse! Well, we'll have to get her into some place ower this, there's no one here to mind her.

MRS BOYLE. We'll all have to mind her now. You might as well know now, Johnny, as another time. [*To* BOYLE] D'ye know what the doctor said to me about her, Jack?

BOYLE. How ud I know – I wasn't there, was I?

MRS BOYLE. He told me to get her married at wanst.

BOYLE. Married at wanst! An' why did he say the like o' that?

MRS BOYLE. Because Mary's goin' to have a baby in a short time.

BOYLE. Goin' to have a baby! – my God, what'll Bentham say when he hears that?

MRS BOYLE. Are you blind, man, that you can't see that it was Bentham that has done this wrong to her?

BOYLE [*passionately*]. Then he'll marry her, he'll have to marry her!

MRS BOYLE. You know he's gone to England, an' God knows where he is now.

BOYLE. I'll folly him, I'll folly him, an' bring him back, an' make him do her justice. The scoundrel, I might ha' known what he was, with his Yogees an' his Prawna!

MRS BOYLE. We'll have to keep it quiet till we see what we can do.

BOYLE. Oh, isn't this a nice thing to come on top o' me, an' the state I'm in! A pretty show I'll be to Joxer an' to that oul' wan, Madigan! Amn't I afther goin' through enough without havin' to go through this!

MRS BOYLE. What you an' I'll have to go through'll be nothin' to what poor Mary'll have to go through; for you an' me is middlin' old, an' most of our years is spent; but Mary'll have maybe forty years to face an' handle, an' every wan of them'll be tainted with a bitther memory.

BOYLE. Where is she? Where is she till I tell her off? I'm tellin' you when I'm done with her she'll be a sorry girl!

MRS BOYLE. I left her in me sister's till I came to speak to you. You'll say nothin' to her, Jack; ever since she left school she's earned her livin', an' your fatherly care never throubled the poor girl.

BOYLE. Gwan, take her part agen her father! But I'll let you see whether I'll say nothin' to her or no! Her an' her readin'! That's more o' th' blasted nonsense that has the house fallin' on top of us! What did th' likes of her, born in a tenement house, want with readin'? Her readin's afther bringin' her to a nice pass – oh, it's madnin', madnin', madnin'!

MRS BOYLE. When she comes back say nothin' to her, Jack, or she'll leave this place.

BOYLE. Leave this place! Ay, she'll leave this place, an' quick too!

MRS BOYLE. If Mary goes, I'll go with her.

BOYLE. Well, go with her! Well, go, th' pair o' yous! I lived before I seen yous, an' I can live when yous are gone. Isn't this a nice thing to come rollin' in on top o' me afther all your prayin' to St Anthony an' the Little Flower!* An' she's a Child o' Mary,* too – I wonder what'll the nuns think of her now? An' it'll be bellows'd all over th' disthrict before you could say Jack Robinson; an' whenever I'm seen they'll whisper, 'That's th' father of Mary Boyle that had th' kid be th' swank* she used to go with; d'ye know, d'ye know?' To be sure they'll know – more about it than I will meself!

JOHNNY. She should be dhriven out o' th' house she's brought disgrace on!

MRS BOYLE. Hush, you, Johnny. We needn't let it be bellows'd all over the place; all we've got to do is to leave this place quietly an' go somewhere where we're not known an' nobody'll be th' wiser.

BOYLE. You're talkin' like a two-year-oul', woman. Where'll we get a place ou' o' this – places aren't that easily got.

MRS BOYLE. But, Jack, when we get the money . . .

BOYLE. Money – what money?

MRS BOYLE. Why, oul' Ellison's money, of course.

BOYLE. There's no money comin' from oul' Ellison, or any one else. Since you've heard of wan throuble, you might as well hear of another. There's no money comin' to us at all – the Will's a wash-out!

MRS BOYLE. What are you sayin', man – no money?

JOHNNY. How could it be a wash-out?

BOYLE. The boyo that's afther doin' it to Mary done it to me as well. The thick* made out the Will wrong; he said in th' Will, only first cousin an' second cousin, instead of mentionin' our names, an' now any one that thinks he's a first cousin or second cousin t'oul Ellison can claim the money as well as me, an' they're springin' up in hundreds, an' comin' from America an' Australia, thinkin' to get their whack* out of it, while all the time the lawyers is gobblin' it up, till there's not as much as ud buy a stockin' for your lovely daughter's baby!

MRS BOYLE. I don't believe it, I don't believe it, I don't believe it!

JOHNNY. Why did you say nothin' about this before?

MRS BOYLE. You're not serious, Jack; you're not serious!

BOYLE. I'm tellin' you the scholar, Bentham, made a banjax* o' th' Will; instead o' sayin', 'th' rest o' me property to be divided between me first cousin, Jack Boyle, an' me second cousin Mick Finnegan, o' Santhry', he writ down only, 'me first an' second cousins', an' the world an' his wife are afther th' property now.

MRS BOYLE. Now I know why Bentham left poor Mary in th' lurch; I can see it all now – oh, is there not even a middlin' honest man left in th' world?

JOHNNY [to BOYLE]. An' you let us run into debt, an' you borreyed money from everybody to fill yourself with beer! An' now you tell us the whole thing's a washout! Oh, if it's thrue, I'm done with you, for you're worse than me sisther Mary!

BOYLE. You hole your tongue, d'ye hear? I'll not take any lip from you. Go an' get Bentham if you want satisfaction for all that's afther happenin' us.

JOHNNY. I won't hole me tongue, I won't hole me tongue! I'll tell you what I think of you, father an' all as you are . . . you . . .

MRS BOYLE. Johnny, Johnny, Johnny, for God's sake, be quiet!

JOHNNY. I'll not be quiet, I'll not be quiet; he's a nice father, isn't he? is it any wondher Mary went asthray, when . . .

MRS BOYLE. Johnny, Johnny, for my sake be quiet – for your mother's sake!

BOYLE. I'm goin' out now to have a few dhrinks with th' last few makes I have, an' tell that lassie o' yours not to be here when I come back; for if I lay me eyes on her, I'll lay me hans on her, an' if I lay me hans on her, I won't be accountable for me actions!

JOHNNY. Take care somebody doesn't lay his hans on you – y'oul' . . .

MRS BOYLE. Johnny, Johnny!

BOYLE [*at door, about to go out*]. Oh, a nice son, an' a nicer daughter, I have. [*Calling loudly upstairs*] Joxer, Joxer, are you there?

JOXER [*from a distance*]. I'm here, More. . .ee. . .aar. . .i. . .tee!

BOYLE. I'm goin' down to Foley's – are you comin'?

JOXER. Come with you? With that sweet call me heart is stirred; I'm only waiting for the word, an' I'll be with you, like a bird! [BOYLE *and* JOXER *pass the door going out.*]

JOHNNY [*throwing himself on the bed*]. I've a nice sisther, an' a nice father, there's no bettin' on it. I wish to God a bullet or a bomb had whipped me ou' o' this long ago! Not one o' yous, have any thought for me!

MRS BOYLE [*with passionate remonstrance*]. If you don't whisht, Johnny, you'll drive me mad. Who has kep' th' home together for the past few years – only me? An' who'll have to bear th' biggest part o' this throuble but me? – but whinin' an' whingin' isn't goin' to do any good.

JOHNNY. You're to blame yourself for a gradle of it – givin' him his own way in everything, an' never assin' to check him, no matther what he done. Why didn't you look afther th' money? why . . .

*There is a knock at the door;* MRS BOYLE *opens it;* JOHNNY *rises on his elbow to look and listen; two men enter.*

FIRST MAN. We've been sent up be th' Manager of the Hibernian Furnishing Company, Mrs Boyle, to take back the furniture that was got a while ago.

MRS BOYLE. Yous'll touch nothin' here – how do I know who yous are?

FIRST MAN [*showing a paper*]. There's the ordher, ma'am. [*Reading*] A
chest o' drawers, a table, wan easy an' two ordinary chairs; wan
mirror; wan chesterfield divan, an' a wardrobe an' two vases. [*To
his comrade*] Come on, Bill, it's afther knockin'-off time already.

JOHNNY. For God's sake, mother, run down to Foley's an' bring father
back, or we'll be left without a stick. [*The men carry out the table.*]

MRS BOYLE. What good would it be? – you heard what he said before
he went out.

JOHNNY. Can't you thry? He ought to be here, an' the like of this goin'
on.

MRS BOYLE *puts a shawl around her, as* MARY *enters.*

MARY. What's up, mother? I met a man carryin' away the table, an'
everybody's talking about us not gettin' the money after all.

MRS BOYLE. Everythin's gone wrong, Mary, everythin'. We're not
gettin' a penny out o' the Will, not a penny – I'll tell you all when I
come back; I'm goin' for your father. [*She runs out.*]

JOHNNY [*to* MARY, *who has sat down by the fire*]. It's a wondher you're
not ashamed to show your face here, afther what has happened.

JERRY *enters slowly; there is a look of earnest hope on his face. He looks at*
MARY *for a few moments.*

JERRY [*softly*]. Mary! [MARY *does not answer.*] Mary, I want to speak to
you for a few moments, may I? [MARY *remains silent;* JOHNNY *goes
slowly into room on left.*] Your mother has told me everything, Mary,
and I have come to you. . . . I have come to tell you, Mary, that my
love for you is greater and deeper than ever. . . .

MARY [*with a sob*]. Oh, Jerry, Jerry, say no more; all that is over now;
anything like that is impossible now!

JERRY. Impossible? Why do you talk like that, Mary?

MARY. After all that has happened.

JERRY. What does it matter what has happened? We are young enough
to be able to forget all those things. [*He catches her hand*] Mary,
Mary, I am pleading for your love. With Labour, Mary, humanity
is above everything; we are the Leaders in the fight for a new life. I
want to forget Bentham, I want to forget that you left me – even for
a while.

MARY. Oh, Jerry, Jerry, you haven't the bitter word of scorn for me after all.

JERRY [*passionately*]. Scorn! I love you, love you, Mary!

MARY [*rising, and looking him in the eyes*]. Even though . . .

JERRY. Even though you threw me over for another man; even though you gave me many a bitter word!

MARY. Yes, yes, I know; but you love me, even though . . . even though . . . I'm . . . goin' . . . goin' . . . [*He looks at her questioningly, and fear gathers in his eyes.*] Ah, I was thinkin' so. . . . You don't know everything!

JERRY [*poignantly*]. Surely to God, Mary, you don't mean that . . . that . . . that . . .

MARY. Now you know all, Jerry; now you know all!

JERRY. My God, Mary, have you fallen as low as that?

MARY. Yes, Jerry, as you say, I have fallen as low as that.

JERRY. I didn't mean it that way, Mary . . . it came on me so sudden, that I didn't mind what I was sayin'. . . . I never expected this – your mother never told me. . . . I'm sorry . . . God knows, I'm sorry for you, Mary.

MARY. Let us say no more, Jerry; I don't blame you for thinkin' it's terrible. . . . I suppose it is. . . . Everybody'll think the same . . . it's only as I expected – your humanity is just as narrow as the humanity of the others.

JERRY. I'm sorry, all the same . . . I shouldn't have troubled you. . . . I wouldn't if I'd known. . . . If I can do anything for you . . . Mary . . . I will. [*He turns to go, and halts at the door.*]

MARY. Do you remember, Jerry, the verses you read when you gave the lecture in the Socialist Rooms some time ago, on Humanity's Strife with Nature?

JERRY. The verses – no; I don't remember them.

MARY. I do. They're runnin' in me head now –

> An' we felt the power that fashion'd
> All the lovely things we saw,
> That created all the murmur
> Of an everlasting law,
> Was a hand of force an' beauty,
> With an eagle's tearin' claw.

Then we saw our globe of beauty
Was an ugly thing as well,
A hymn divine whose chorus
Was an agonisin' yell;
Like the story of a demon,
That an angel had to tell;

Like a glowin' picture by a
Hand unsteady, brought to ruin;
Like her craters, if their deadness
Could give life unto the moon;
Like the agonising horror
Of a violin out of tune.*

[*There is a pause, and* JERRY *goes slowly out.*]

JOHNNY [*returning*]. Is he gone?

MARY. Yes. [*The two men re-enter.*]

FIRST MAN. We can't wait any longer for t'oul' fella – sorry, Miss, but we have to live as well as th' nex' man. [*They carry out some things.*]

JOHNNY. Oh, isn't this terrible! . . . I suppose you told him everything . . . couldn't you have waited for a few days? . . . he'd have stopped th' takin' of the things, if you'd kep' your mouth shut. Are you burnin' to tell every one of the shame you've brought on us?

MARY [*snatching up her hat and coat*]. Oh, this is unbearable! [*She rushes out.*]

FIRST MAN [*re-entering*]. We'll take the chest o' drawers next – it's the heaviest.

*The votive light flickers for a moment, and goes out.*

JOHNNY [*in a cry of fear*]. Mother o' God, the light's afther goin' out!

FIRST MAN. You put the win' up me the way you bawled that time. The oil's all gone, that's all.

JOHNNY [*with an agonising cry*]. Mother o' God, there's a shot I'm afther gettin'!

FIRST MAN. What's wrong with you, man? Is it a fit you're takin'?

JOHNNY. I'm afther feelin' a pain in me breast, like the tearin' by of a bullet!

FIRST MAN. He's goin' mad – it's a wondher they'd leave a chap like that here by himself.

*Two* IRREGULARS* *enter swiftly; they carry revolvers; one goes over to* JOHNNY; *the other covers the two furniture men.*

FIRST IRREGULAR [*to the men, quietly and incisively*]. Who are you? – what are yous doin' here? – quick!

FIRST MAN. Removin' furniture that's not paid for.

IRREGULAR. Get over to the other end of the room an' turn your faces to the wall – quick! [*The two men turn their faces to the wall, with their hands up.*]

SECOND IRREGULAR [*to* JOHNNY]. Come on, Sean Boyle, you're wanted; some of us have a word to say to you.

JOHNNY. I'm sick, I can't – what do you want with me?

SECOND IRREGULAR. Come on, come on; we've a distance to go, an' haven't much time – come on.

JOHNNY. I'm an oul' comrade – yous wouldn't shoot an oul' comrade.

SECOND IRREGULAR. Poor Tancred was an oul' comrade o' yours, but you didn't think o' that when you gave him away to the gang that sent him to his grave. But we've no time to waste; come on – here, Dermot, ketch his arm. [*To* JOHNNY] Have you your beads?*

JOHNNY. Me beads! Why do you ass me that, why do you ass me that?

SECOND IRREGULAR. Go on, go on, march!

JOHNNY. Are yous goin' to do in a comrade? – look at me arm, I lost it for Ireland.

SECOND IRREGULAR. Commandant Tancred lost his life for Ireland.

JOHNNY. Sacred Heart of Jesus, have mercy on me! Mother o' God, pray for me – be with me now in the agonies o' death! . . . Hail, Mary, full o' grace . . . the Lord is . . . with Thee.

*They drag out* JOHNNY BOYLE, *and the curtain falls. When it rises again the most of the furniture is gone.* MARY *and* MRS BOYLE, *one on each side, are sitting in a darkened room, by the fire; it is an hour later.*

MRS BOYLE. I'll not wait much longer . . . what did they bring him away in the mothor for? Nugent says he thinks they had guns . . . is me throubles never goin' to be over? . . . If anything ud happen to poor Johnny, I think I'd lose me mind. . . . I'll go to the Police Station, surely they ought to be able to do somethin'. [*Below is heard the sound of voices.*] Whisht, is that something? Maybe, it's your father, though when I left him in Foley's he was hardly able to lift his head. Whisht!

*A knock at the door, and the voice of* MRS MADIGAN, *speaking very softly:*

Mrs Boyle, Mrs Boyle. [MRS BOYLE *opens the door.*] Oh, Mrs Boyle,
God an' His Blessed Mother be with you this night!

MRS BOYLE [*calmly*]. What is it, Mrs Madigan? It's Johnny –
something about Johnny.

MRS MADIGAN. God send it's not, God send it's not Johnny!

MRS BOYLE. Don't keep me waitin', Mrs Madigan; I've gone through
so much lately that I feel able for anything.

MRS MADIGAN. Two polismen* below wantin' you.

MRS BOYLE. Wantin' me; an' why do they want me?

MRS MADIGAN. Some poor fella's been found, an' they think it's,
it's . . .

MRS BOYLE. Johnny, Johnny!

MARY [*with her arms round her mother*]. Oh, mother, mother, me poor,
darlin' mother.

MRS BOYLE. Hush, hush, darlin'; you'll shortly have your own
throuble to bear. [*To* MRS MADIGAN] An' why do the polis think it's
Johnny, Mrs Madigan?

MRS MADIGAN. Because one o' the doctors knew him when he was
attendin' with his poor arm.

MRS BOYLE. Oh, it's thrue, then; it's Johnny, it's me son, me own son!

MARY. Oh, it's thrue, it's thrue what Jerry Devine says – there isn't a
God, there isn't a God; if there was He wouldn't let these things
happen!

MRS BOYLE. Mary, you mustn't say them things. We'll want all the
help we can get from God an' His Blessed Mother now! These things
have nothin' to do with the Will o' God. Ah, what can God do agen
the stupidity o' men!

MRS MADIGAN. The polis want you to go with them to the hospital to
see the poor body – they're waitin' below.

MRS BOYLE. We'll go. Come, Mary, an' we'll never come back here
agen. Let your father furrage for himself now; I've done all I could
an' it was all no use – he'll be hopeless till the end of his days. I've
got a little room in me sisther's where we'll stop till your throuble is
over, an' then we'll work together for the sake of the baby.

MARY. My poor little child that'll have no father!

MRS BOYLE. It'll have what's far betther – it'll have two mothers.

A ROUGH VOICE SHOUTING FROM BELOW. Are yous goin' to keep us
waitin' for yous all night?

MRS MADIGAN [*going to the door, and shouting down*]. Take your hour, there, take your hour! If yous are in such a hurry, skip off, then, for nobody wants you here – if they did yous wouldn't be found. For you're the same as yous were undher the British Government – never where yous are wanted! As far as I can see, the Polis as Polis, in this city, is Null an' Void!

MRS BOYLE. We'll go, Mary, we'll go; you to see your poor dead brother, an' me to see me poor dead son!

MARY. I dhread it, mother, I dhread it!

MRS BOYLE. I forgot, Mary, I forgot; your poor oul' selfish mother was only thinkin' of herself. No, no, you mustn't come – it wouldn't be good for you. You go on to me sisther's an' I'll face th' ordeal meself. Maybe I didn't feel sorry enough for Mrs Tancred when her poor son was found as Johnny's been found now – because he was a Diehard! Ah, why didn't I remember that then he wasn't a Diehard or a Stater, but only a poor dead son! It's well I remember all that she said – an' it's my turn to say it now: What was the pain I suffered, Johnny, bringin' you into the world to carry you to your cradle, to the pains I'll suffer carryin' you out o' the world to bring you to your grave! Mother o' God, Mother o' God, have pity on us all! Blessed Virgin, where were you when me darlin' son was riddled with bullets, when me darlin' son was riddled with bullets? Sacred Heart o' Jesus, take away our hearts o' stone, and give us hearts o' flesh!* Take away this murdherin' hate, an' give us Thine own eternal love! [*They all go slowly out.*]

*There is a pause; then a sound of shuffling steps on the stairs outside. The door opens and* BOYLE *and* JOXER, *both of them very drunk, enter.*

BOYLE. I'm able to go no farther. . . . Two polis, ey . . . what were they doin' here, I wondher? . . . Up to no good, anyhow . . . an' Juno an' that lovely daughter o' mine with them. [*Taking a sixpence from his pocket and looking at it*] Wan single, solitary tanner left out of all I borreyed . . . [*He lets it fall.*] The last o' the Mohecans.* . . . The blinds is down, Joxer, the blinds is down!

JOXER [*walking unsteadily across the room, and anchoring at the bed*]. Put all . . . your throubles . . . in your oul' kit-bag . . . an' smile . . . smile . . . smile!*

BOYLE. The counthry'll have to steady itself . . . it's goin' . . . to hell. . . . Where'r all . . . the chairs . . . gone to . . . steady itself,

Joxer. . . . Chairs'll . . . have to . . . steady themselves. . . . No
matther . . . what any one may . . . say. . . . Irelan' sober . . . is
Irelan' . . . free.*

JOXER [*stretching himself on the bed*]. Chains . . . an' . . . slaveree* . . .
that's a darlin' motto . . . a daaarlin' . . . motto!

BOYLE. If th' worst comes . . . to th' worse . . . I can join a . . . flyin'
. . . column.* . . . I done . . . me bit . . . in Easther Week . . . had
no business . . . to . . . be . . . there . . . but Captain Boyle's
Captain Boyle!

JOXER. Breathes there a man with soul . . . so . . . de . . . ad . . . this
. . . me . . . o. . . .wn, me nat. . .ive l. . .an'!*

BOYLE [*subsiding into a sitting posture on the floor*]. Commandant Kelly
died . . . in them . . . arms . . . Joxer. . . . Tell me Volunteer
butties . . . says he . . . that . . . I died for . . . Irelan'!

JOXER. D'jever rade 'Willie . . . Reilly . . . an' His Own . . . Colleen
. . . Bawn?* It's a darlin' story, a daarlin' story!

BOYLE. I'm telling you . . . Joxer . . . th' whole worl's . . . in a
terr. . .ible state o' . . . chassis!


CURTAIN

# The Plough and the Stars

## A Tragedy in Four Acts

*To the gay laugh of my mother at the gate of the grave*

## CHARACTERS

JACK CLITHEROE (a bricklayer), Commandant
  in the Irish Citizen Army
NORA CLITHEROE, his wife
PETER FLYNN, a labourer; Nora's uncle     Residents in
THE YOUNG COVEY, a fitter; Clitheroe's cousin   the tenement
BESSIE BURGESS, a street fruit-vendor
MRS GOGAN, a charwoman
MOLLSER, her consumptive child
FLUTHER GOOD, a carpenter

LIEUTENANT LANGON (a civil servant), of the Irish Volunteers
CAPTAIN BRENNAN (a chicken-butcher), of the Irish Citizen Army
CORPORAL STODDART, of the Wiltshires
SERGEANT TINLEY, of the Wiltshires
ROSIE REDMOND, a daughter of 'the Digs'
A BAR-TENDER
A WOMAN
THE FIGURE IN THE WINDOW

## PLACE AND TIME

*Act I*. The living-room of the Clitheroe flat in a Dublin tenement.
*Act II*. A public-house, outside of which a meeting is being held.
*Act III*. The street outside the Clitheroe tenement.
*Act IV*. The room of Bessie Burgess.

*Time*. Acts I and II, November 1915; Acts III and IV, Easter Week,
  1916. A few days elapse between Acts III and IV.

## ACT I

*The home of the* CLITHEROES. *It consists of the front and back drawing-rooms in a fine old Georgian house, struggling for life against the assaults of time, and the more savage assaults of the tenants. The room shown is the back drawing-room, wide, spacious, and lofty. At back is the entrance to the front drawing-room. The space, originally occupied by folding doors, is now draped with casement cloth of a dark purple, decorated with a design in reddish-purple and cream. One of the curtains is pulled aside, giving a glimpse of front drawing-room, at the end of which can be seen the wide, lofty windows looking out into the street. The room directly in front of the audience is furnished in a way that suggests an attempt towards a finer expression of domestic life. The large fireplace on right is of wood, painted to look like marble (the original has been taken away by the landlord). On the mantelshelf are two candlesticks of dark carved wood. Between them is a small clock. Over the clock is hanging a calendar which displays a picture of 'The Sleeping Venus'.\* In the centre of the breast of the chimney hangs a picture of Robert Emmet.\* On the right of the entrance to the front drawing-room is a copy of 'The Gleaners', on the opposite side a copy of 'The Angelus'.\* Underneath 'The Gleaners' is a chest of drawers on which stands a green bowl filled with scarlet dahlias and white chrysanthemums. Near to the fireplace is a settee which at night forms a double bed for* CLITHEROE *and* NORA. *Underneath 'The Angelus' are a number of shelves containing saucepans and a frying-pan. Under these is a table on which are various articles of delf ware. Near the end of the room, opposite to the fireplace, is a gate-legged table, covered with a cloth. On top of the table a huge cavalry sword is lying. To the right is a door which leads to a lobby from which the staircase leads to the hall. The floor is covered with a dark green linoleum. The room is dim except where it is illuminated from the glow of the fire. Through the window of the room at back can be seen the flaring of the flame of a gasolene lamp giving light to workmen repairing the street. Occasionally can be heard the clang of crowbars striking the sets.* FLUTHER GOOD *is repairing the lock of door, right. A claw hammer\* is on a chair beside him, and he has a screwdriver in his hand. He is a man of forty years of age, rarely surrendering to thoughts of anxiety, fond of his 'oil'\* but determined to conquer the habit before he dies. He is square-jawed and harshly featured; under the left eye is a scar, and his nose is bent from a smashing blow received in a fistic battle long ago. He is bald, save for a few peeping tufts of reddish hair around his ears; and his upper lip is hidden by* *a scrubby red moustache, embroidered here and there with a grey hair. He is dressed in a seedy\* black suit, cotton shirt with a soft collar, and wears a very respectable little black bow. On his head is a faded jerry hat,\* which, when he is excited, he has a habit of knocking farther back on his head, in a series of taps. In an argument he usually fills with sound and fury generally signifying a row. He is in his shirt-sleeves at present, and wears a soiled white apron, from a pocket in which sticks a carpenter's two-foot rule. He has just finished the job of putting on a new lock, and, filled with satisfaction, he is opening and shutting the door, enjoying the completion of a work well done. Sitting at the fire, airing a white shirt, is* PETER FLYNN. *He is a little, thin bit of a man, with a face shaped like a lozenge; on his cheeks and under his chin is a straggling wiry beard of a dirty-white and lemon hue. His face invariably wears a look of animated anguish, mixed with irritated defiance, as if everybody was at war with him, and he at war with everybody. He is cocking his head in a way that suggests resentment at the presence of* FLUTHER, *who pays no attention to him, apparently, but is really furtively watching him.* PETER *is clad in a singlet, white whipcord knee breeches, and is in his stocking feet.*

*A voice is heard speaking outside of door, left (it is that of* MRS GOGAN).

MRS GOGAN [*outside*]. Who are you lookin' for, sir? Who? Mrs Clitheroe? . . . Oh, excuse me. Oh ay, up this way. She's out, I think: I seen her goin'. Oh, you've somethin' for her; oh, excuse me. You're from Arnott's.\* . . . I see. . . . You've a parcel for her. . . . Righto. . . . I'll take it. . . . I'll give it to her the minute she comes in. . . . It'll be quite safe. . . . Oh, sign that. . . . Excuse me. . . . Where? . . . Here? . . . No, there; righto. Am I to put Maggie or Mrs? What is it? You dunno? Oh, excuse me.

MRS GOGAN *opens the door and comes in. She is a doleful-looking little woman of forty, insinuating manner and sallow complexion. She is fidgety and nervous, terribly talkative, has a habit of taking up things that may be near her and fiddling with them while she is speaking. Her heart is aflame with curiosity, and a fly could not come into nor go out of the house without her knowing. She has a draper's parcel in her hand, the knot of the twine tying it is untied.* PETER, *more resentful of this intrusion than of* FLUTHER'S *presence, gets up from the chair, and without looking around, his head carried at an angry cock, marches into the room at back.*

MRS GOGAN [*removing the paper and opening the cardboard box it contains*]. I wondher what's this now? A hat! [*She takes out a hat, black, with decorations in red and gold.*] God, she's goin' to th' divil lately for style! That hat, now, cost more than a penny. Such notions of upperosity she's gettin'. [*Putting the hat on her head*] Oh, swank, what! [*She replaces it in parcel.*]

FLUTHER. She's a pretty little judy,* all the same.

MRS GOGAN. Ah, she is, an' she isn't. There's prettiness an' prettiness in it. I'm always sayin' that her skirts are a little too short for a married woman. An' to see her, sometimes of an evenin', in her glad-neck* gown would make a body's blood run cold. I do be ashamed of me life before her husband. An' th' way she thries to be polite, with her 'Good mornin', Mrs Gogan', when she's goin' down, an' her 'Good evenin', Mrs Gogan', when she's comin' up. But there's politeness an' politeness in it.

FLUTHER. They seem to get on well together, all th' same.

MRS GOGAN. Ah, they do, an' they don't. The pair o' them used to be like two turtle doves always billin' an' cooin'. You couldn't come into th' room but you'd feel, instinctive like, that they'd just been afther* kissin' an' cuddlin' each other. . . . It often made me shiver, for, afther all, there's kissin' an' cuddlin' in it. But I'm thinkin' he's beginnin' to take things more quietly; the mysthery of havin' a woman's a mysthery no longer. . . . She dhresses herself to keep him with her, but it's no use – afther a month or two, th' wondher of a woman wears off.

FLUTHER. I dunno, I dunno. Not wishin' to say anything derogatory, I think it's all a question of location: when a man finds th' wondher of a woman beginnin' to die, it's usually beginnin' to live in another.

MRS GOGAN. She's always grumblin' about havin' to live in a tenement house. 'I wouldn't like to spend me last hour in one, let alone live me life in a tenement', says she. 'Vaults', says she, 'that are hidin' th' dead, instead of homes that are sheltherin' th' livin'.' 'Many a good one', says I, 'was reared in a tenement house.' Oh, you know, she's a well-up little lassie, too; able to make a shillin' go where another would have to spend a pound. She's wipin' th' eyes of th' Covey an' poor oul' Pether – everybody knows that – screwin' every penny she can out o' them, in ordher to turn th' place into a babby-house.* An' she has th' life frightened out o' them; washin' their face, combin' their hair, wipin' their feet, brushin' their clothes, thrimmin' their nails, cleanin' their teeth – God Almighty, you'd think th' poor men were undhergoin' penal servitude.

FLUTHER [*with an exclamation of disgust*]. A-a-ah, that's goin' beyond th' beyonds in a tenement house. That's a little bit too derogatory.

PETER *enters from room, back, head elevated and resentful fire in his eyes; he is still in his singlet and trousers, but is now wearing a pair of unlaced boots – possibly to be decent in the presence of* MRS GOGAN. *He places the white shirt, which he has carried in on his arm, on the back of a chair near the fire, and, going over to the chest of drawers, he opens drawer after drawer, looking for something; as he fails to find it he closes each drawer with a snap; he pulls out pieces of linen neatly folded, and bundles them back again any way.*

PETER [*in accents of anguish*]. Well, God Almighty, give me patience!
[*He returns to room, back, giving the shirt a vicious turn as he passes.*]

MRS GOGAN. I wondher what he is foostherin'* for now?

FLUTHER. He's adornin' himself for th' meeting tonight. [*Pulling a handbill from his pocket and reading*] 'Great Demonstration an' torchlight procession around places in th' city sacred to th' memory of Irish Patriots, to be concluded be a meetin', at which will be taken an oath of fealty to th' Irish Republic. Formation in Parnell Square at eight o'clock.'* Well, they can hold it for Fluther. I'm up th' pole;* no more dhrink for Fluther. It's three days now since I touched a dhrop, an' I feel a new man already.

MRS GOGAN. Isn't oul' Peter a funny-lookin' little man? . . . Like somethin' you'd pick off a Christmas Tree. . . . When he's dhressed up in his canonicals, you'd wondher where he'd been got. God forgive me, when I see him in them, I always think he must ha' had a Mormon* for a father! He an' th' Covey can't abide each other; the' pair o' them is always at it, thryin' to best* each other. There'll be blood dhrawn one o' these days.

FLUTHER. How is it that Clitheroe himself, now, doesn't have anythin' to do with th' Citizen Army? A couple o' months ago, an' you'd hardly ever see him without his gun, an' th' Red Hand o' Liberty Hall* in his hat.

MRS GOGAN. Just because he wasn't made a Captain of. He wasn't goin' to be in anything where he couldn't be conspishuous. He was so cocksure o' being made one that he bought a Sam Browne* belt, an' was always puttin' it on an' standin' at th' door showing it off, till th' man came an' put out th' street lamps on him. God, I think he used to bring it to bed with him! But I'm tellin' you herself was delighted that that cock didn't crow, for she's like a cluckin' hen if he leaves her sight for a minute. [*While she is talking, she takes up book after book from the table, looks into each of them in a near-sighted way, and then leaves them back. She now lifts up the sword, and proceeds to examine it.*] Be th' look of it, this must ha' been a general's sword. . . . All th' gold lace an' th' fine figaries* on it. . . . Sure it's twiced too big for him.

FLUTHER. A-ah; it's a baby's rattle he ought to have, an' he as he is with thoughts tossin' in his head of what may happen to him on th' day o' judgement.

PETER *has entered, and seeing* MRS GOGAN *with the sword, goes over to her, pulls it resentfully out of her hands, and marches into the room, back, without speaking.*

MRS GOGAN [*as* PETER *whips the sword*]. Oh, excuse me! . . . [*To* FLUTHER] Isn't he th' surly oul' rascal!

FLUTHER. Take no notice of him. . . . You'd think he was dumb, but when you get his goat,* or he has a few jars up, he's vice versa. [*He coughs.*]

MRS GOGAN [*she has now sidled over as far as the shirt hanging on the chair*]. Oh, you've got a cold on you, Fluther.

FLUTHER [*carelessly.*] Ah, it's only a little one.

MRS GOGAN. You'd want to be careful, all th' same. I knew a woman, a big lump of a woman, red-faced an' round-bodied, a little awkward on her feet; you'd think, to look at her, she could put out her two arms an' lift a two-storied house on th' top of her head; got a ticklin' in her throat, an' a little cough, an' th' next mornin' she had a little catchin' in her chest, an' they had just time to wet her lips with a little rum, an' off she went. [*She begins to look at and handle the shirt.*]

FLUTHER [*a little nervously*]. It's only a little cold I have; there's nothing derogatory wrong with me.

MRS GOGAN. I dunno; there's many a man this minute lowerin' a pint, thinkin' of a woman, or pickin' out a winner, or doin' work as you're doin', while th' hearse dhrawn be th' horses with the black plumes is dhrivin' up to his own hall door, an' a voice that he doesn't hear is muttherin' in his ear, 'Earth to earth, an' ashes t' ashes, an' dust to dust.'

FLUTHER [*faintly*]. A man in th' pink o' health should have a holy horror of allowin' thoughts o' death to be festerin' in his mind, for [*with a frightened cough*] be God, I think I'm afther gettin' a little catch in me chest that time – it's a creepy thing to be thinkin' about.

MRS GOGAN. It is, an' it isn't; it's both bad an' good. . . . It always gives meself a kind o' threspassin'* joy to feel meself movin' along in a mournin' coach, an' me thinkin' that, maybe, th' next funeral 'll be me own, an' glad, in a quiet way, that this is somebody else's.

FLUTHER. An' a curious kind of a gaspin' for breath – I hope there's nothin' derogatory wrong with me.

MRS GOGAN [*examining the shirt*]. Frills on it, like a woman's petticoat.

FLUTHER. Suddenly gettin' hot, an' then, just as suddenly, gettin' cold.

MRS GOGAN [*holding out the shirt towards* FLUTHER]. How would you like to be wearin' this Lord Mayor's nightdhress, Fluther?

FLUTHER [*vehemently*]. Blast you an' your nightshirt! Is a man fermentin'* with fear to stick th' showin' off to him of a thing that looks like a shinin' shroud?

MRS GOGAN. Oh, excuse me!

PETER *has again entered, and he pulls the shirt from the hands of* MRS GOGAN, *replacing it on the chair. He returns to room.*

PETER [*as he goes out*]. Well, God Almighty, give me patience!

MRS GOGAN [*to* PETER]. Oh, excuse me!

*There is heard a cheer from the men working outside on the street, followed by the clang of tools being thrown down, then silence. The glare of the gasolene light diminishes and finally goes out.*

MRS GOGAN [*running into the back room to look out of the window*]. What's the men repairin' th' streets cheerin' for?

FLUTHER [*sitting down weakly on a chair*]. You can't sneeze but that oul' one wants to know th' why an' th' wherefore. . . . I feel as dizzy as bedamned! I hope I didn't give up th' beer too suddenly.

THE COVEY* *comes in by the door, right. He is about twenty-five, tall, thin, with lines on his face that form a perpetual protest against life as he conceives it to be. Heavy seams fall from each side of nose, down around his lips, as if they were suspenders keeping his mouth from falling. He speaks in*

*a slow, wailing drawl; more rapidly when he is excited. He is dressed in*
*dungarees, and is wearing a vividly red tie. He flings his cap with a gesture*
*of disgust on the table, and begins to take off his overalls.*

MRS GOGAN [*to* THE COVEY, *as she runs back into the room*]. What's after
happenin', Covey?

THE COVEY [*with contempt*]. Th' job's stopped. They've been mobilised
to march in th' demonstration tonight undher th' Plough an' th'
Stars.* Didn't you hear them cheerin', th' mugs! They have to
renew their political baptismal vows to be faithful *in seculo
seculorum.* *

FLUTHER [*forgetting his fear in his indignation*]. There's no reason to
bring religion into it. I think we ought to have as great a regard for
religion as we can, so as to keep it out of as many things as possible.

THE COVEY [*pausing in the taking off of his dungarees*]. Oh, you're one o'
the boys that climb into religion as high as a short Mass on Sunday
mornin's? I suppose you'll be singin' songs o' Sion an' songs o'
Tara* at th' meetin', too.

FLUTHER. We're all Irishmen, anyhow; aren't we?

THE COVEY [*with hand outstretched, and in a professional tone*]. Look
here, comrade, there's no such thing as an Irishman, or an
Englishman, or a German or a Turk; we're all only human bein's.
Scientifically speakin', it's all a question of the accidental gatherin'
together of mollycewels an' atoms.

PETER *comes in with a collar in his hand. He goes over to mirror, left, and*
*proceeds to try to put it on.*

FLUTHER. Mollycewels an' atoms! D'ye think I'm goin' to listen to you
thryin' to juggle Fluther's mind with complicated cunundhrums of
mollycewels an' atoms?

THE COVEY [*rather loudly*]. There's nothin' complicated in it. There's
no fear o' the Church tellin' you that mollycewels is a stickin'
together of millions of atoms o' sodium, carbon, potassium o'
idodide, etcetera, that, accordin' to th' way they're mixed, make a
flower, a fish, a star that you see shinin' in th' sky, or a man with a
big brain like me, or a man with a little brain like you!

FLUTHER [*more loudly still*]. There's no necessity to be raisin' your
voice; shoutin's no manifestin' forth* of a growin' mind.

PETER [*struggling with his collar*]. God, give me patience with this thing. . . . She makes these collars as stiff with starch as a shinin' band o' solid steel! She does it purposely to thry an' twart* me. If I can't get it on th' singlet, how, in th' Name o' God, am I goin' to get it on th' shirt?

THE COVEY [*loudly*]. There's no use o' arguin' with you; it's education you want, comrade.

FLUTHER. The Covey an' God made th' world, I suppose, wha'?

THE COVEY. When I hear some men talkin' I'm inclined to disbelieve that th' world's eight-hundhred million years old, for it's not long since th' fathers o' some o' them crawled out o' th' shelterin' slime o' the sea.

MRS GOGAN [*from room at back*]. There, they're afther formin' fours, an' now they're goin' to march away.

FLUTHER [*scornfully*]. Mollycewels! [*He begins to untie his apron.*] What about Adam an' Eve?

THE COVEY. Well, what about them?

FLUTHER [*fiercely*]. What about them, you?

THE COVEY. Adam an' Eve! Is that as far as you've got? Are you still thinkin' there was nobody in th' world before Adam and Eve? [*Loudly*] Did you ever hear, man, of th' skeleton of th' man o' Java?*

PETER [*casting the collar from him*]. Blast it, blast it, blast it!

FLUTHER [*viciously folding his apron*]. Ah, you're not goin' to be let tap your rubbidge o' thoughts into th' mind o' Fluther.

THE COVEY. You're afraid to listen to th' thruth!

FLUTHER. Who's afraid?

THE COVEY. You are!

FLUTHER. G'way, you wurum!

THE COVEY. Who's a worum?

FLUTHER. You are, or you wouldn't talk th' way you're talkin'.

THE COVEY. Th' oul', ignorant savage leppin' up in you, when science shows you that th' head of your god is an empty one. Well, I hope you're enjoyin' th' blessin' o' havin' to live be th' sweat of your brow.

FLUTHER. You'll be kickin' an' yellin' for th' priest yet, me boyo. I'm not goin' to stand silent an' simple listenin' to a thick like you makin' a maddenin' mockery o' God Almighty. It 'ud be a nice derogatory thing on me conscience, an' me dyin', to look back in rememberin' shame of talkin' to a word-weavin' little ignorant yahoo of a red flag Socialist!

MRS GOGAN [*she has returned to the front room, and has wandered around looking at things in general, and is now in front of the fireplace looking at the picture hanging over it*]. For God's sake, Fluther, dhrop it; there's always th' makin's of a row in th' mention of religion. . . . [*Looking at picture*] God bless us, it's a naked woman!

FLUTHER [*coming over to look at it*]. What's undher it? [*Reading*] 'Georgina: The Sleepin' Vennis'. Oh, that's a terrible picture; oh, that's a shockin' picture! Oh, th' one that got that taken, she must have been a prime lassie!

PETER [*who also has come over to look, laughing, with his body bent at the waist, and his head slightly tilted back*]. Hee, hee, hee, hee, hee!

FLUTHER [*indignantly, to* PETER]. What are you hee, hee-in' for? That's a nice thing to be hee, hee-in' at. Where's your morality, man?

MRS GOGAN. God forgive us, it's not right to be lookin' at it.

FLUTHER. It's nearly a derogatory thing to be in th' room where it is.

MRS GOGAN [*giggling hysterically*]. I couldn't stop any longer in th' same room with three men, afther lookin' at it! [*She goes out.*]

THE COVEY, *who has divested himself of his dungarees, throws them with a contemptuous motion on top of* PETER'S *white shirt.*

PETER [*plaintively*]. Where are you throwin' them? Are you thryin' to twart an' torment me again?

THE COVEY. Who's thryin' to twart you?

PETER [*flinging the dungarees violently on the floor*]. You're not goin' to make me lose me temper, me young Covey.

THE COVEY [*flinging the white shirt on the floor*]. If you're Nora's pet, aself,* you're not goin' to get your way in everything.

PETER [*plaintively, with his eyes looking up at the ceiling*]. I'll say nothin'. . . . I'll leave you to th' day when th' all-pitiful, all-merciful, all-lovin' God 'll be handin' you to th' angels to be rievin' an' roastin' you, tearin' an' tormentin' you, burnin' an' blastin' you!

THE COVEY. Aren't you th' little malignant oul' bastard, you lemon-whiskered oul' swine!

PETER *runs to the sword, draws it, and makes for* THE COVEY, *who dodges him around the table;* PETER *has no intention of striking, but* THE COVEY *wants to take no chance.*

THE COVEY [*dodging*]. Fluther, hold him, there. It's a nice thing to have a lunatic like this lashin' around with a lethal weapon! [THE COVEY *darts out of the room, right, slamming the door in the face of* PETER.]

PETER [*battering and pulling at the door*]. Lemme out, lemme out; isn't it a poor thing for a man who wouldn't say a word against his greatest enemy to have to listen to that Covey's twartin' animosities,* shovin' poor, patient people into a lashin' out of curses that darken his soul with th' shadow of th' wrath of th' last day!

FLUTHER. Why d'ye take notice of him? If he seen you didn't, he'd say nothin' derogatory.

PETER. I'll make him stop his laughin' an' leerin', jibin' an' jeerin' an' scarifyin' people with his corner-boy insinuations! . . . He's always thryin' to rouse me: if it's not a song, it's a whistle; if it isn't a whistle, it's a cough. But you can taunt an' taunt – I'm laughin' at you; he, hee, hee, hee, hee, heee!

THE COVEY [*singing through the keyhole*].

Dear harp o' me counthry, in darkness I found thee,
The dark chain of silence had hung o'er thee long –

PETER [*frantically*]. Jasus, d'ye hear that? D'ye hear him soundin' forth his divil-souled song o' provocation?

THE COVEY [*singing as before*].

When proudly, me own island harp, I unbound thee,
An' gave all thy chords to light, freedom an' song!*

PETER [*battering at door*]. When I get out I'll do for you, I'll do for you, I'll do for you!

THE COVEY [*through the keyhole*]. Cuckoo-oo!

NORA *enters by door, right. She is a young woman of twenty-two, alert, swift, full of nervous energy, and a little anxious to get on in the world. The firm lines of her face are considerably opposed by a soft, amorous mouth and gentle eyes. When her firmness fails her, she persuades with her feminine charm. She is dressed in a tailor-made costume, and wears around her neck a silver fox fur.*

NORA [*running in and pushing* PETER *away from the door*]. Oh, can I not
turn me back but th' two o' yous are at it like a pair o' fightin' cocks!
Uncle Peter . . . Uncle Peter . . . UNCLE PETER!

PETER [*vociferously*]. Oh, Uncle Peter, Uncle Peter be damned! D'ye
think I'm goin' to give a free pass* to th' young Covey to turn me
whole life into a Holy Manual o' penances an' martyrdoms?

THE COVEY [*angrily rushing into the room*]. If you won't exercise some
sort o' conthrol over that Uncle Peter o' yours, there'll be a funeral,
an' it won't be me that'll be in th' hearse!

NORA [*between* PETER *and* THE COVEY, *to* THE COVEY]. Are yous always
goin' to be tearin' down th' little bit of respectability that a body's
thryin' to build up? Am I always goin' to be havin' to nurse yous
into th' hardy habit o' thryin' to keep up a little bit of appearance?

THE COVEY. Why weren't you here to see th' way he run at me with th'
sword?

PETER. What did you call me a lemon-whiskered oul' swine for?

NORA. If th' two o' yous don't thry to make a generous altheration in
your goin's on, an' keep on thryin' t' inaugurate th' customs o' th'
rest o' th' house into this place, yous can flit* into other lodgin's
where your bowsey* battlin' 'ill* meet, maybe, with an encore.*

PETER [*to* NORA]. Would you like to be called a lemon-whiskered oul'
swine?

NORA. If you attempt to wag that sword of yours at anybody again, it'll
have to be taken off you an' put in a safe place away from babies that
don't know th' danger o' them things.

PETER [*at entrance to room, back*]. Well, I'm not goin' to let anybody
call me a lemon-whiskered oul' swine. [*He goes in.*]

FLUTHER [*trying the door*]. Openin' an' shuttin' now with a well-
mannered motion, like a door of a select bar in a high-class
pub.

NORA [*to* THE COVEY, *as she lays table for tea*]. An', once for all, Willie,
you'll have to thry to deliver yourself from th' desire of provokin'
oul' Pether into a wild forgetfulness of what's proper an' allowable
in a respectable home.

THE COVEY. Well, let him mind his own business, then. Yestherday I
caught him hee-hee-in' out of him an' he readin' bits out of
Jenersky's *Thesis on th' Origin, Development, an' Consolidation of th'
Evolutionary Idea of th' Proletariat.*

NORA. Now, let it end at that, for God's sake; Jack'll be in any minute,
an' I'm not goin' to have th' quiet of his evenin' tossed about in an

everlastin' uproar between you an' Uncle Pether. [*To* FLUTHER]
Well, did you manage to settle th' lock, yet, Mr Good?

FLUTHER [*opening and shutting door*]. It's betther than a new one, now,
Mrs Clitheroe; it's almost ready to open and shut of its own accord.

NORA [*giving him a coin*]. You're a whole man.* How many pints will
that get you?

FLUTHER [*seriously*]. Ne'er a one at all, Mrs Clitheroe, for Fluther's on
th' wather waggon now. You could stan' where you're stannin'
chantin', 'Have a glass o' malt, Fluther; Fluther, have a glass o'
malt', till th' bells would be ringin' th' ould year out an' th' New
Year in, an' you'd have as much chance o' movin' Fluther as a tune
on a tin whistle would move a deaf man an' he dead.

*As* NORA *is opening and shutting door,* MRS BESSIE BURGESS *appears at it.
She is a woman of forty, vigorously built. Her face is a dogged one,
hardened by toil, and a little coarsened by drink. She looks scornfully and
viciously at* NORA *for a few moments before she speaks.*

BESSIE. Puttin' a new lock on her door . . . afraid her poor neighbours
ud break through an' steal. . . . [*In a loud tone*] Maybe, now,
they're a damn sight more honest than your ladyship . . . checkin'
th' children playin' on th' stairs . . . gettin' on th' nerves of your
ladyship. . . . Complainin' about Bessie Burgess singin' her hymns
at night, when she has a few up. . . . [*She comes in half-way on the
threshold, and screams*] Bessie Burgess 'll sing whenever she damn
well likes! [NORA *tries to shut the door, but* BESSIE *violently shoves it in,
and, gripping* NORA *by the shoulders, shakes her.*] You little over-
dressed throllop,* you, for one pin I'd paste th' white face o' you!

NORA [*frightened*]. Fluther, Fluther!

FLUTHER [*running over and breaking the hold of* BESSIE *from* NORA].
Now, now, Bessie, Bessie, leave poor Mrs Clitheroe alone; she'd do
no one any harm, an' minds no one's business but her own.

BESSIE. Why is she always thryin' to speak proud things, an' lookin'
like a mighty one in th' congregation o' th' people!

NORA *sinks frightened on to the couch as* JACK CLITHEROE *enters. He is a
tall, well-made fellow of twenty-five. His face has none of the strength of
*NORA'S. It is a face in which is the desire for authority, without the power to
attain it.*

CLITHEROE [*excitedly*]. What's up? what's afther happenin'?

FLUTHER. Nothin', Jack. Nothin'. It's all over now. Come on, Bessie, come on.

CLITHEROE [*to* NORA]. What's wrong, Nora? Did she say anything to you?

NORA. She was bargin'* out of her, an' I only told her to g'up ower o' that to her own place; an' before I knew where I was, she flew at me like a tiger, an' thried to guzzle* me!

CLITHEROE [*going to door and speaking to* BESSIE]. Get up to your own place, Mrs Burgess, and don't you be interferin' with my wife, or it'll be th' worse for you. . . . Go on, go on!

BESSIE [*as* CLITHEROE *is pushing her out*]. Mind who you're pushin', now. . . . I attend me place o' worship, anyhow . . . not like some o' them that go to neither church, chapel nor meetin'-house. . . . If me son was home from th' threnches he'd see me righted.*

BESSIE *and* FLUTHER *depart, and* CLITHEROE *closes the door.*

CLITHEROE [*going over to* NORA, *and putting his arm round her*]. There, don't mind that old bitch, Nora, darling; I'll soon put a stop to her interferin'.

NORA. Some day or another, when I'm here be meself, she'll come in an' do somethin' desperate.

CLITHEROE [*kissing her*]. Oh, sorra fear* of her doin' anythin' desperate. I'll talk to her tomorrow when she's sober. A taste o' me mind that'll shock her into the sensibility of behavin' herself!

NORA *gets up and settles the table. She sees the dungarees on the floor and stands looking at them, then she turns to* THE COVEY, *who is reading* Jenersky's Thesis *at the fire.*

NORA. Willie, is that th' place for your dungarees?

THE COVEY [*getting up and lifting them from the floor*]. Ah, they won't do th' floor any harm, will they? [*He carries them into room, back.*]

NORA [*calling*]. Uncle Peter, now, Uncle Peter; tea's ready.

PETER *and* THE COVEY *come in from room, back; they all sit down to tea.* PETER *is in full dress of the* Foresters;* *green coat, gold braided; white breeches, top boots, frilled shirt. He carries the slouch hat, with the white ostrich plume, and the sword in his hands. They eat for a few moments in* *silence*, THE COVEY *furtively looking at* PETER *with scorn in his eyes*. PETER *knows it and is fidgety.*

THE COVEY [*provokingly*]. Another cut o' bread, Uncle Peter? [PETER *maintains a dignified silence.*]

CLITHEROE. It's sure to be a great meetin' tonight. We ought to go, Nora.

NORA [*decisively*]. I won't go, Jack; you can go if you wish.

THE COVEY. D'ye want th' sugar, Uncle Peter? [*A pause.*]

PETER [*explosively*]. Now, are you goin' to start your thryin' an' your twartin' again?

NORA. Now, Uncle Peter, you mustn't be so touchy; Willie has only assed* you if you wanted th' sugar.

PETER. He doesn't care a damn whether I want th' sugar or no. He's only thryin' to twart me!

NORA [*angrily, to* THE COVEY]. Can't you let him alone, Willie? If he wants the sugar, let him stretch his hand out an' get it himself!

THE COVEY [*to* PETER]. Now, if you want the sugar, you can stretch out your hand and get it yourself!

CLITHEROE. Tonight is th' first chance that Brennan has got of showing himself off since they made a Captain of him – why, God only knows. It'll be a treat to see him swankin' it at th' head of the Citizen Army carryin' th' flag of the Plough an' th' Stars. . . . [*Looking roguishly at* NORA] He was sweet on you, once, Nora?

NORA. He may have been. . . . I never liked him. I always thought he was a bit of a thick.

THE COVEY. They're bringin' nice disgrace on that banner now.

CLITHEROE [*remonstratively*]. How are they bringin' disgrace on it?

THE COVEY [*snappily*]. Because it's a Labour flag, an' was never meant for politics. . . . What does th' design of th' field plough, bearin' on it th' stars of th' heavenly plough, mean, if it's not Communism? It's a flag that should only be used when we're buildin' th' barricades to fight for a Workers' Republic!

PETER [*with a puff of derision*]. P-phuh.

THE COVEY [*angrily*]. What are you phuhin' out o' you for? Your mind is th' mind of a mummy. [*Rising*] I bdether go an' get a good place to have a look at Ireland's warriors passin' by. [*He goes into room, left, and returns with his cap.*]

NORA [*to* THE COVEY]. Oh, Willie, brush your clothes before you go.

THE COVEY. Oh, they'll do well enough.

NORA. Go an' brush them; th' brush is in th' drawer there.

THE COVEY *goes to the drawer, muttering, gets the brush, and starts to brush his clothes.*

THE COVEY [*singing at* PETER, *as he does so*].

> Oh, where's th' slave so lowly,
> Condemn'd to chains unholy,
> Who, could he burst his bonds at first,
> Would pine beneath them slowly?
>
> We tread th' land that . . . bore us,
> Th' green flag glitters . . . o'er us,
> Th' friends we've tried are by our side,
> An' th' foe we hate . . . before us!*

PETER [*leaping to his feet in a whirl of race*]. Now, I'm tellin' you, me young Covey, once for all, that I'll not stick any longer these tittherin' taunts of yours, rovin' around to sing your slights an' slandhers, reddenin' th' mind of man to th' thinkin' an' sayin' of things that sicken his soul with sin! [*Hysterical; lifting up a cup to fling at* THE COVEY] Be God, I'll –

CLITHEROE [*catching his arm*]. Now then, none o' that, none o' that!

NORA. Uncle Pether, Uncle Pether, UNCLE PETHER!

THE COVEY [*at the door, about to go out*]. Isn't that th' malignant oul' varmint!* Lookin' like th' illegitimate son of an illegitimate child of a corporal in th' Mexican army! [*He goes out.*]

PETER [*plaintively*]. He's afther leavin' me now in such a state of agitation that I won't be able to do meself justice when I'm marchin' to th' meetin'.

NORA [*jumping up*]. Oh, for God's sake, here, buckle your sword on, and go to your meetin', so that we'll have at least one hour of peace! [*She proceeds to belt on the sword.*]

CLITHEROE [*irritably*]. For God's sake hurry him up ou' o' this, Nora.

PETER. Are yous all goin' to thry to start to twart me now?

NORA [*putting on his plumed hat*]. S-s-sh. Now, your hat's on, your house is thatched,* off you pop! [*She gently pushes him from her.*]

PETER [*going, and turning as he reaches the door*]. Now, if that young Covey –

NORA. Go on, go on. [*He goes.*]

CLITHEROE *sits down in the lounge, lights a cigarette, and looks thoughtfully into the fire.* NORA *takes the things from the table, placing them on the chest of drawers. There is a pause, then she swiftly comes over to him and sits beside him.*

NORA [*softly*]. A penny for them, Jack!

CLITHEROE. Me? Oh, I was thinkin' of nothing.

NORA. You were thinkin' of th' . . . meetin' . . . Jack. When we were courtin' an' I wanted you to go, you'd say, 'Oh, to hell with meetin's,' an' that you felt lonely in cheerin' crowds when I was absent. An' we weren't a month married when you began that you couldn't keep away from them.

CLITHEROE. Oh, that's enough about th' meetin'. It looks as if you wanted me to go th' way you're talkin'. You were always at me to give up th' Citizen Army, an' I gave it up; surely that ought to satisfy you.

NORA. Ay, you gave it up – because you got th' sulks when they didn't make a Captain of you. It wasn't for my sake, Jack.

CLITHEROE. For your sake or no, you're benefitin' by it, aren't you? I didn't forget this was your birthday, did I? [*He puts his arms around her.*] And you liked your new hat; didn't you, didn't you? [*He kisses her rapidly several times.*]

NORA [*panting*]. Jack, Jack; please, Jack! I thought you were tired of that sort of thing long ago.

CLITHEROE. Well, you're finding out now that I amn't tired of it yet, anyhow, Mrs Clitheroe doesn't want to be kissed, sure she doesn't? [*He kisses her again.*] Little, little red-lipped Nora!

NORA [*coquettishly removing his arm from around her*]. Oh, yes, your little, little red-lipped Nora's a sweet little girl when th' fit seizes you; but your little, little red-lipped Nora has to clean your boots every mornin', all the same.

CLITHEROE [*with a movement of irritation*]. Oh, well, if we're goin' to be snotty!* [*A pause.*]

NORA. It's lookin' like as if it was you that was goin' to be . . . snotty! Bridlin' up with bittherness, th' minute a body attempts t' open her mouth.

CLITHEROE. Is it any wondher, turnin' a tendher sayin' into a meanin' o' malice an' spite!

NORA. It's hard for a body to be always keepin' her mind bent on makin' thoughts that'll be no longer than th' length of your own satisfaction. [*A pause. Standing up*] If we're goin' to dhribble th' time away sittin' here like a pair o' cranky mummies, I'd be as well sewin' or doin' something about th' place. [*She looks appealingly at him for a few moments; he doesn't speak. She swiftly sits down beside him, and puts her arm around his neck. Imploringly*] Ah, Jack, don't be so cross!

CLITHEROE [*doggedly*]. Cross? I'm not cross; I'm not a bit cross. It was yourself started it.

NORA [*coaxingly*]. I didn't mean to say anything out o' the way. You take a body up too quickly, Jack. [*In an ordinary tone as if nothing of an angry nature had been said*] You didn't offer me me evenin' allowance yet.

CLITHEROE *silently takes out a cigarette for her and himself and lights both.*

NORA [*trying to make conversation*]. How quiet th' house is now; they must be all out.

CLITHEROE [*rather shortly*]. I suppose so.

NORA [*rising from the seat*]. I'm longin' to show you me new hat, to see what you think of it. Would you like to see it?

CLITHEROE. Ah, I don't mind.

NORA *suppresses a sharp reply, hesitates for a moment, then gets the hat, puts it on, and stands before* CLITHEROE.

NORA. Well, how does Mr Clitheroe like me new hat?

CLITHEROE. It suits you, Nora, it does right enough. [*He stands up, puts his hand beneath her chin, and tilts her head up. She looks at him roguishly. He bends down and kisses her.*]

NORA. Here, sit down, an' don't let me hear another cross word out of you for th' rest o' the night. [*They sit down.*]

CLITHEROE [*with his arms around her*]. Little, little, red-lipped Nora!

NORA [*with a coaxing movement of her body towards him*]. Jack!

CLITHEROE [*tightening his arms around her*]. Well?

NORA. You haven't sung me a song since our honeymoon. Sing me one now, do . . . please, Jack!

CLITHEROE. What song? 'Since Maggie Went Away'?

NORA. Ah, no, Jack, not that; it's too sad. 'When You Said You Loved Me.'

*Clearing his throat,* CLITHEROE *thinks for a moment and then begins to sing.* NORA, *putting an arm around him, nestles her head on his breast and listens delightedly.*

CLITHEROE [*singing verses following to the air of 'When You and I Were Young, Maggie'*]:

> Th' violets were scenting th' woods, Nora,
>     Displaying their charm to th' bee,
> When I first said I lov'd only you, Nora,
>     An' you said you lov'd only me!

> Th' chestnut blooms gleam'd through th' glade, Nora,
>     A robin sang loud from a tree,
> When I first said I lov'd only you, Nora,
>     An' you said you lov'd only me!

> Th' golden-rob'd daffodils shone, Nora,
>     An' danc'd in th' breeze on th' lea,
> When I first said I lov'd only you, Nora,
>     An' you said you lov'd only me!

> Th' trees, birds, an' bees sang a song, Nora,
>     Of happier transports to be,
> When I first said I lov'd only you, Nora,
>     An' you said you lov'd only me!

NORA *kisses him. A knock is heard at the door, right; a pause as they listen.* NORA *clings closely to* CLITHEROE. *Another knock, more imperative than the first.*

CLITHEROE. I wonder who can that be, now?
NORA [*a little nervous*]. Take no notice of it, Jack; they'll go away in a minute. [*Another knock, followed by a voice.*]
VOICE. Commandant Clitheroe, Commandant Clitheroe, are you there? A message from General Jim Connolly.*
CLITHEROE. Damn it, it's Captain Brennan.

NORA [*anxiously*]. Don't mind him, don't mind, Jack. Don't break our happiness. . . . Pretend we're not in. Let us forget everything tonight but our two selves!

CLITHEROE [*reassuringly*]. Don't be alarmed, darling; I'll just see what he wants, an' send him about his business.

NORA [*tremulously*]. No, no. Please, Jack; don't open it. Please, for your own little Nora's sake!

CLITHEROE [*rising to open the door*]. Now don't be silly, Nora.

CLITHEROE *opens the door, and admits a young man in the full uniform of the Irish Citizen Army – green suit; slouch green hat caught up at one side by a small Red Hand badge; Sam Browne belt, with a revolver in the holster. He carries a letter in his hand. When he comes in he smartly salutes* CLITHEROE. *The young man is* CAPTAIN BRENNAN.

CAPT. BRENNAN [*giving the letter to* CLITHEROE]. A dispatch from General Connolly.

CLITHEROE [*reading. While he is doing so,* BRENNAN'S *eyes are fixed on* NORA, *who droops as she sits on the lounge*].

Commandant Clitheroe is to take command of the eighth battalion of the ICA which will assemble to proceed to the meeting at nine o'clock. He is to see that all units are provided with full equipment; two days' rations and fifty rounds of ammunition. At two o'clock a.m. the army will leave Liberty Hall for a reconnaissance attack on Dublin Castle.

COM.-GEN. CONNOLLY*

CLITHEROE. I don't understand this. Why does General Connolly call me Commandant?

CAPT. BRENNAN. Th' Staff appointed you Commandant, and th' General agreed with their selection.

CLITHEROE. When did this happen?

CAPT. BRENNAN. A fortnight ago.

CLITHEROE. How is it word was never sent to me?

CAPT. BRENNAN. Word was sent to you. . . . I meself brought it.

CLITHEROE. Who did you give it to, then?

CAPT. BRENNAN [*after a pause*]. I think I gave it to Mrs Clitheroe, there.

CLITHEROE. Nora, d'ye hear that?

NORA *makes no answer.*

CLITHEROE [*there is a note of hardness in his voice*]. Nora . . . Captain
  Brennan says he brought a letter to me from General Connolly, and
  that he gave it to you. . . . Where is it? What did you do with it?
NORA [*running over to him, and pleadingly putting her arms around him*].
  Jack, please, Jack, don't go out tonight an' I'll tell you; I'll explain
  everything. . . . Send him away, an' stay with your own little
  red-lipp'd Nora.
CLITHEROE [*removing her arms from around him*]. None o' this
  nonsense, now; I want to know what you did with th' letter?

NORA *goes slowly to the lounge and sits down.*

CLITHEROE [*angrily*]. Why didn't you give me th' letter? What did you
  do with it? . . . [*He shakes her by the shoulder.*] What did you do with
  th' letter?
NORA [*flaming up*]. I burned it, I burned it! That's what I did with it! Is
  General Connolly an' th' Citizen Army goin' to be your only care? Is
  your home goin' to be only a place to rest in? Am I goin' to be only
  somethin' to provide merry-makin' at night for you? Your vanity'll
  be th' ruin of you an' me yet. . . . That's what's movin' you:
  because they've made an officer of you, you'll make a glorious cause
  of what you're doin', while your little red-lipp'd Nora can go on
  sittin' here, makin' a companion of th' loneliness of th' night!
CLITHEROE [*fiercely*]. You burned it, did you? [*He grips her arm.*] Well,
  me good lady –
NORA. Let go – you're hurtin' me!
CLITHEROE. You deserve to be hurt. . . . Any letter that comes to me
  for th' future, take care that I get it. . . . D'ye hear – take care that I
  get it!

*He goes to the chest of drawers and takes out a Sam Browne belt, which he
puts on, and then puts a revolver in the holster. He puts on his hat, and
looks towards* NORA. *While this dialogue is proceeding, and while*
CLITHEROE *prepares himself,* BRENNAN *softly whistles 'The Soldiers'
Song'.* *

CLITHEROE [*at door, about to go out*]. You needn't wait up for me; if I'm
  in at all, it won't be before six in th' morning.

NORA [*bitterly*]. I don't care if you never come back!
CLITHEROE [*to* CAPTAIN BRENNAN]. Come along, Ned.

*The go out; there is a pause.* NORA *pulls her new hat from her head and with
a bitter movement flings it to the other end of the room. There is a gentle
knock at door, right, which opens, and* MOLLSER *comes into the room. She
is about fifteen, but looks to be about ten, for the ravages of consumption
have shrivelled her up. She is pitifully worn, walks feebly, and frequently
coughs. She goes over to* NORA.

MOLLSER [*to* NORA]. Mother's gone to th' meetin', an' I was feelin'
   terrible lonely, so I come down to see if you'd let me sit with you,
   thinkin' you mightn't be goin' yourself. . . . I do be terrible afraid
   I'll die sometime when I'm be meself. . . . I often envy you, Mrs
   Clitheroe, seein' th' health you have, an' th' lovely place you have
   here, an' wondherin' if I'll ever be sthrong enough to be keepin' a
   home together for a man. Oh, this must be some more o' the Dublin
   Fusiliers flyin' off to the front.

*Just before* MOLLSER *ceases to speak, there is heard in the distance the music
of a brass band playing a regiment to the boat on the way to the front. The
tune that is being played is 'It's a Long Way to Tipperary';* as the band
comes to the chorus, the regiment is swinging into the street by* NORA'S *house,
and the voices of the soldiers can be heard lustily singing the chorus of the
song.*

   It's a long way to Tipperary, it's a long way to go;
   It's a long way to Tipperary, to th' sweetest girl I know!
   Goodbye, Piccadilly; farewell, Leicester Square.
   It's a long, long way to Tipperary, but my heart's right there!

NORA *and* MOLLSER *remain silently listening. As the chorus ends and the
music is faint in the distance again,* BESSIE BURGESS *appears at door, right,
which* MOLLSER *has left open.*

BESSIE [*speaking in towards the room*]. There's th' men marchin' out
   into th' dhread dimness o' danger, while th' lice is crawlin' about
   feedin' on th' fatness o' the land! But you'll not escape from th'
   arrow that flieth be night, or th' sickness that wasteth be day.* . . .
   An' ladyship an' all, as some o' them may be, they'll be scattered
   abroad, like th' dust in th' darkness!

BESSIE *goes away;* NORA *steals over and quietly shuts the door. She comes back to the lounge and wearily throws herself on it beside* MOLLSER.

MOLLSER [*after a pause and a cough*]. Is there anybody goin', Mrs Clitheroe, with a titther* o' sense?

CURTAIN

## ACT II

*A commodious public house at the corner of the street in which the meeting is
being addressed from Platform no. 1. It is the south corner of the public
house that is visible to the audience. The counter, beginning at back about
one-fourth of the width of the space shown, comes across two-thirds of the
length of the stage, and, taking a circular sweep, passes out of sight to left.
On the counter are beer-pulls, glasses, and a carafe. The other three-fourths
of the back is occupied by a tall, wide, two-paned window. Beside this
window at the right is a small, box-like, panelled snug. Next to the snug is
a double swing door, the entrance to that particular end of the house. Farther
on is a shelf on which customers may rest their drinks. Underneath the
windows is a cushioned seat. Behind the counter at back can be seen the
shelves running the whole length of the counter. On these shelves can be seen
the end (or the beginning) of rows of bottles. The* BARMAN *is seen wiping the
part of the counter which is in view.* ROSIE *is standing at the counter toying
with what remains of a half of whisky\* in a wine-glass. She is a sturdy,
well-shaped girl of twenty; pretty, and pert in manner. She is wearing a
cream blouse, with an obviously suggestive glad-neck;\* a grey tweed dress,
brown stockings and shoes. The blouse and most of the dress are hidden by a
black shawl. She has no hat, and in her hair is jauntily set a cheap,
glittering, jewelled ornament. It is an hour later.*

BARMAN [*wiping counter*]. Nothin' much doin' in your line tonight,
Rosie?

ROSIE. Curse o' God on th' haporth,\* hardly, Tom. There isn't much
notice taken of a pretty petticoat of a night like this. . . . They're all
in a holy mood. Th' solemn-lookin' dials\* on th' whole o' them an'
they marchin' to th' meetin'. You'd think they were th' glorious
company of th' saints, an' th' noble army of martyrs thrampin'
through th' sthreets of paradise. They're all thinkin' of higher
things than a girl's garthers. . . . It's a tremendous meetin'; four
platforms they have – there's one o' them just outside opposite th'
window.

BARMAN. Oh, ay; sure when th' speaker comes [*motioning with his
hand*] to th' near end, here, you can see him plain, an' hear nearly
everythin' he's spoutin' out of him.\*

ROSIE. It's no joke thryin' to make up fifty-five shillin's a week for
your keep an' laundhry, an' then taxin' you a quid for your own

room if you bring home a friend for th' night. . . . If I could only
put by a couple of quid for a swankier outfit, everythin' in th'
garden ud look lovely –
BARMAN. Whisht, till we hear what he's sayin'.

*Through the window is silhouetted the figure of a tall man who is speaking
to the crowd. The* BARMAN *and* ROSIE *look out of the window and listen.*

THE VOICE OF THE MAN. It is a glorious thing to see arms in the hands of
Irishmen. We must accustom ourselves to the thought of arms, we
must accustom ourselves to the sight of arms, we must accustom
ourselves to the use of arms. . . . Bloodshed is a cleansing and
sanctifying thing, and the nation that regards it as the final horror
has lost its manhood. . . . There are many things more horrible
than bloodshed, and slavery is one of them!*

*The figure moves away towards the right, and is lost to sight and hearing.*

ROSIE. It's th' sacred thruth, mind you, what that man's afther sayin'.
BARMAN. If I was only a little younger, I'd be plungin' mad into th'
middle of it!
ROSIE [*who is still looking out of the window*]. Oh, here's the two gems
runnin' over again for their oil!

PETER *and* FLUTHER *enter tumultuously. They are hot, and full and hasty
with the things they have seen and heard. Emotion is bubbling up in them,
so that when they drink, and when they speak, they drink and speak with
the fullness of emotional passion.* PETER *leads the way to the counter.*

PETER [*splutteringly to* BARMAN]. Two halves . . . [*To* FLUTHER] A
meetin' like this always makes me feel as if I could dhrink Loch
Erinn dhry!
FLUTHER. You couldn't feel any way else at a time like this when th'
spirit of a man is pulsin' to be out fightin' for th' thruth with his feet
thremblin' on th' way, maybe to th' gallows, an' his ears tinglin'
with th' faint, far-away sound of burstin' rifle-shots that'll maybe
whip th' last little shock o' life out of him that's left lingerin' in his
body!
PETER. I felt a burnin' lump in me throat when I heard th' band playin'
'The Soldiers' Song'* rememberin' last hearin' it marchin' in

military formation with th' people starin' on both sides at us, carryin' with us th' pride an' resolution o' Dublin to th' grave of Wolfe Tone.*

FLUTHER. Get th' Dublin men goin' an' they'll go on full force for anything that's thryin' to bar them away from what they're wantin', where th' slim thinkin' counthry boyo ud limp away from th' first faintest touch of compromisation!

PETER [*hurriedly to the* BARMAN]. Two more, Tom! . . . [*To* FLUTHER] Th' memory of all th' things that was done, an' all th' things that was suffered be th' people, was boomin' in me brain. . . . Every nerve in me body was quiverin' to do somethin' desperate!

FLUTHER. Jammed as I was in th' crowd, I listened to th' speeches patherin' on th' people's head, like rain fallin' on th' corn; every derogatory thought went out o' me mind, an' I said to meself, 'You can die now, Fluther, for you've seen th' shadow-dhreams of th' past leppin' to life in th' bodies of livin' men that show, if we were without a tither o' courage for centuries, we're vice versa now!' Looka here. [*He stretches out his arm under* PETER'S *face and rolls up his sleeve.*] The blood was BOILIN' in me veins!

*The silhouette of the tall figure again moves into the frame of the window speaking to the people.*

PETER [*unaware, in his enthusiasm, of the speaker's appearance, to* FLUTHER]. I was burnin' to dhraw me sword, an' wave an' wave it over me –

FLUTHER [*overwhelming* PETER]. Will you stop your blatherin' for a minute, man, an' let us hear what he's sayin'!

VOICE OF THE MAN. Comrade soldiers of the Irish Volunteers and of the Citizen Army, we rejoice in this terrible war. The old heart of the earth needed to be warmed with the red wine of the battle-fields. . . . Such august homage was never offered to God as this: the homage of millions of lives given gladly for love of country. And we must be ready to pour out the same red wine in the same glorious sacrifice, for without shedding of blood there is no redemption!*

*The figure moves out of sight and hearing.*

FLUTHER [*gulping down the drink that remains in his glass, and rushing out*]. Come on, man; this is too good to be missed!

PETER *finishes his drink less rapidly, and as he is going out wiping his mouth with the back of his hand he runs into* THE COVEY *coming in. He immediately erects his body like a young cock, and with his chin thrust forward, and a look of venomous dignity on his face, he marches out.*

THE COVEY [*at counter*]. Give us a glass o' malt,\* for God's sake, till I stimulate meself from the shock o' seein' th' sight that's afther goin' out!

ROSIE [*all business, coming over to the counter, and standing near* THE COVEY]. Another one for me, Tommy; [*to the* BARMAN] th' young gentleman's ordherin' it in th' corner of his eye.

*The* BARMAN *brings the drink for* THE COVEY, *and leaves it on the counter.* ROSIE *whips it up.*

BARMAN. Ay, houl' on there, houl' on there, Rosie!

ROSIE [*to the* BARMAN]. What are you houldin' on out o' you for? Didn't you hear th' young gentleman say that he couldn't refuse anything to a nice little bird? [*To* THE COVEY] Isn't that right, Jiggs?\* [THE COVEY *says nothing.*] Didn't I know, Tommy, it would be all right? It takes Rosie to size a young man up, an' tell th' thoughts that are thremblin' in his mind. Isn't that right, Jiggs?

THE COVEY *stirs uneasily, moves a little farther away, and pulls his cap over his eyes.*

ROSIE [*moving after him*]. Great meetin' that's gettin' held outside. Well, it's up to us all, anyway, to fight for our freedom.

THE COVEY [*to* BARMAN]. Two more, please. [*To* ROSIE] Freedom! What's th' use o' freedom, if it's not economic freedom?

ROSIE [*emphasising with extended arm and moving finger*]. I used them very words just before you come in. 'A lot o' thricksters,' says I, 'that wouldn't know what freedom was if they got it from their mother.' . . . [*To* BARMAN] Didn't I, Tommy?

BARMAN. I disremember.

ROSIE. No, you don't disremember. Remember you said, yourself, it was all 'only a flash in th' pan'. Well, 'flash in th' pan, or no flash in th' pan,' says I, 'they're not goin' to get Rosie Redmond,' says I, 'to fight for freedom that wouldn't be worth winnin' in a raffle!'

THE COVEY. There's only one freedom for th' workin' man: conthrol o'

th' means o' production, rates of exchange, an' th' means of
disthribution. [*Tapping* ROSIE *on the shoulder*] Look here, comrade,
I'll leave here tomorrow night for you a copy of Jenersky's *Thesis on
the Origin, Development, an' Consolidation of the Evolutionary Idea of
the Proletariat.*

ROSIE [*throwing off her shawl on to the counter, and showing an
exemplified glad neck, which reveals a good deal of a white bosom*]. If
y'ass Rosie, it's heartbreakin' to see a young fella thinkin' of
anything, or admirin' anything, but silk thransparent stockin's
showin' off the shape of a little lassie's legs!

THE COVEY, *frightened, moves a little away.*

ROSIE [*following on*]. Out in th' park in th' shade of a warm summery
evenin', with your little darlin' bridie to be, kissin' an' cuddlin' [*she
tries to put her arm around his neck*], kissin' an' cuddlin', ay?

THE COVEY [*frightened*]. Ay, what are you doin'? None o' that, now;
none o' that. I've something else to do besides shinannickin' afther*
Judies! [*He turns away, but* ROSIE *follows, keeping face to face with
him.*]

ROSIE. Oh, little duckey, oh, shy little duckey! Never held a mot's
hand,* an' wouldn't know how to tittle* a little Judy! [*She clips him
under the chin.*] Tittle him undher th' chin, tittle him undher th'
chin!

THE COVEY [*breaking away and running out*]. Ay, go on, now; I don't
want to have any meddlin' with a lassie like you!

ROSIE [*enraged*]. Jasus, it's in a monasthery some of us ought to be,
spendin' our holidays kneelin' on our adorers,* tellin' our beads,
an' knockin' hell out of our buzzums!

THE COVEY [*outside*]. Cuckoo-oo!

PETER *and* FLUTHER *come in again, followed by* MRS GOGAN, *carrying a
baby in her arms. They go over to the counter.*

PETER [*with plaintive anger*]. It's terrible that young Covey can't let me
pass without proddin' at me! Did you hear him murmurin' 'cuckoo'
when we were passin'?

FLUTHER [*irritably*]. I wouldn't be everlastin' cockin' me ear to hear
every little whisper that was floatin' around about me! It's my rule
never to lose me temper till it would be dethrimental to keep it.
There's nothin' derogatory in th' use o' th' word 'cuckoo', is there?

PETER [*tearfully*]. It's not th' word; it's th' way he says it: he never says it straight out, but murmurs it with curious quiverin' ripples, like variations on a flute!

FLUTHER. Ah, what odds if he gave it with variations on a thrombone! [*To* MRS GOGAN] What's yours goin' to be, ma'am?

MRS GOGAN. Ah, a half o' malt, Fluther.

FLUTHER [*to* BARMAN]. Three halves, Tommy. [*The* BARMAN *brings the drinks.*]

MRS GOGAN [*drinking*]. The Foresthers' is a gorgeous dhress! I don't think I've seen nicer, mind you, in a pantomime. . . . Th' loveliest part of th' dhress, I think, is th' osthrichess plume. . . . When yous are goin' along, an' I see them wavin' an' noddin' an' waggin', I seem to be lookin' at each of yous hangin' at th' end of a rope, your eyes bulgin' an' your legs twistin' an' jerkin', gaspin' an' gaspin' for breath while yous are thryin' to die for Ireland!

FLUTHER. If any o' them is hangin' at the end of a rope, it won't be for Ireland!

PETER. Are you goin' to start th' young Covey's game o' proddin' an' twartin' a man? There's not many that's talkin' can say that for twenty-five years he never missed a piligrimage to Bodenstown!*

FLUTHER. You're always blowin' about goin' to Bodenstown. D'ye think no one but yourself ever went to Bodenstown?

PETER [*plaintively*]. I'm not blowin' about it; but there's not a year that I go there but I pluck a leaf off Tone's grave, an' this very day me prayer-book is nearly full of them.

FLUTHER [*scornfully*]. Then Fluther has a vice versa opinion of them that put ivy leaves into their prayer-books, scabbin' it on* th' clergy, an' thryin' to out-do th' haloes o' th' saints be lookin' as if he was wearin' around his head a glittherin' aroree boree allis!* [*Fiercely*] Sure, I don't care a damn if you slep' in Bodenstown! You can take your breakfast, dinner, an' tea on th' grave in Bodenstown, if you like, for Fluther!

MRS GOGAN. Oh, don't start a fight, boys, for God's sake; I was only sayin' what a nice costume it is – nicer than th' kilts, for, God forgive me, I always think th' kilts is hardly decent.

FLUTHER. Ah, sure, when you'd look at him, you'd wondher whether th' man was makin' fun o' th' costume, or th' costume was makin' fun o' th' man!

BARMAN. Now, then, thry to speak asy,* will yous? We don't want no shoutin' here.

THE COVEY *followed by* BESSIE BURGESS *comes in. They go over to the opposite end of the counter, and direct their gaze on the other group.*

THE COVEY [*to* BARMAN]. Two glasses o' malt.

PETER. There he is, now; I knew he wouldn't be long till he folleyed me in.

BESSIE [*speaking to* THE COVEY, *but really at the other party*]. I can't for th' life o' me undherstand how they can call themselves Catholics, when they won't lift a finger to help poor little Catholic Belgium.*

MRS GOGAN [*raising her voice*]. What about poor little Catholic Ireland?

BESSIE [*over to* MRS GOGAN]. You mind your own business, ma'am, an' stupefy your foolishness be gettin' dhrunk.

PETER [*anxiously*]. Take no notice of her; pay no attention to her. She's just tormentin' herself towards havin' a row with somebody.

BESSIE. There's a storm of anger tossin' in me heart, thinkin' of all th' poor Tommies, an' with them me own son, dhrenched in water an' soaked in blood, gropin' their way to a shattherin' death, in a shower o' shells! Young men with th' sunny lust o' life beamin' in them, layin' down their white bodies, shredded into torn an' bloody pieces, on th' althar that God Himself has built for th' sacrifice of heroes!

MRS GOGAN. Isn't it a nice thing to have to be listenin' to a lassie an' hangin' our heads in a dead silence, knowin' that some persons think more of a ball of malt than they do of th' blessed saints.

FLUTHER. Whisht; she's always dangerous an' derogatory when she's well oiled. Th' safest way to hindher her from havin' any enjoyment out of her spite, is to dip our thoughts into the fact of her bein' a female person that has moved out of th' sight of ordinary sensible people.

BESSIE. To look at some o' th' women that's knockin' about, now, is a thing to make a body sigh. . . . A woman on her own, dhrinkin' with a bevy* o' men, is hardly an example to her sex. . . . A woman dhrinkin' with a woman is one thing, an' a woman dhrinkin' with herself is still a woman – flappers* may be put in another category altogether – but a middle-aged married woman makin' herself th' centre of a circle of men is as a woman that is loud an' stubborn, whose feet abideth not in her own house.*

THE COVEY [*to* BESSIE]. When I think of all th' problems in front o' th' workers, it makes me sick to be lookin' at oul' codgers goin' about dhressed up like green-accoutred figures gone asthray out of a toyshop!

PETER. Gracious God, give me patience to be listenin' to that blasted young Covey proddin' at me from over at th' other end of th' shop!

MRS GOGAN [*dipping her finger in the whisky, and moistening with it the lips of her baby*]. Cissie Gogan's a woman livin' for nigh on twenty-five years in her own room, an' beyond biddin' th' time o' day to her neighbours, never yet as much as nodded her head in th' direction of other people's business, while she knows some as are never content unless they're standin' senthry over other people's doin's!

BESSIE *is about to reply, when the tall, dark figure is again silhouetted against the window, and the voice of the speaker is heard speaking passionately.*

VOICE OF SPEAKER. The last sixteen months have been the most glorious in the history of Europe. Heroism has come back to the earth. War is a terrible thing, but war is not an evil thing. People in Ireland dread war because they do not know it. Ireland has not known the exhilaration of war for over a hundred years. When war comes to Ireland she must welcome it as she would welcome the Angel of God!*

*The figure passes out of sight and hearing.*

THE COVEY [*towards all present*]. Dope, dope. There's only one war worth havin': th' war for th' economic emancipation of th' proletariat.

BESSIE. They may crow away out o' them; but it ud be fitther for some o' them to mend their ways, an' cease from havin' scouts out watchin' for th' comin' of th' St Vincent de Paul man,* for fear they'd be nailed lowerin' a pint of beer, mockin' th' man with an angel face, shinin' with th' glamour of deceit an' lies!

MRS GOGAN. An' a certain lassie standin' stiff behind her own door with her ears cocked listenin' to what's being said, stuffed till she's sthrained with envy of a neighbour thryin' for a few little things that may be got be hard sthrivin' to keep up to th' letther an' th' law, an' th' practices of th' Church!

PETER [*to* MRS GOGAN]. If I was you, Mrs Gogan, I'd parry her jabbin' remarks be a powerful silence that'll keep her tantalisin' words from penethratin' into your feelin's. It's always betther to leave these people to th' vengeance o' God!

BESSIE. Bessie Burgess doesn't put up to know much, never havin' a swaggerin' mind, thanks be to God, but goin' on packin' up knowledge accordin' to her conscience: precept upon precept, line upon line; here a little, an there a little.* But [*with a passionate swing of her shawl*], thanks be to Christ, she knows when she was got, where she was got, an' how she was got; while there's some she knows, decoratin' their finger with a well-polished weddin' ring, would be hard put to it if they were assed to show their weddin' lines!*

MRS GOGAN [*plunging out into the centre of the floor in a wild tempest of hysterical rage*]. Y' oul' rip of a blasted liar, me weddin' ring's been well earned be twenty years be th' side o' me husband, now takin' his rest in heaven, married to me be Father Dempsey, in th' Chapel o' Saint Jude's, in th' Christmas Week of eighteen hundhred an' ninety-five; an' any kid, livin' or dead, that Jinnie Gogan's had since, was got between th' bordhers of th' Ten Commandments! . . . An' that's more than some o' you can say that are kep' from th' dhread o' desthruction be a few drowsy virtues, that th' first whisper of temptation lulls into a sleep, that'll know one sin from another only on th' day of their last anointin', an' that use th' innocent light o' th' shinin' stars to dip into th' sins of a night's diversion!

BESSIE [*jumping out to face* MRS GOGAN, *and bringing the palms of her hands together in sharp claps to emphasise her remarks*]. Liar to you, too, ma'am, y' oul' hardened threspasser on other people's good nature, wizenin' up your soul in th' arts o' dodgeries, till every dhrop of respectability in a female is dhried up in her, lookin' at your ready-made manoeuverin' with th' menkind!

BARMAN. Here, there; here, there; speak asy there. No rowin' here, no rowin' here, now.

FLUTHER [*trying to calm* MRS GOGAN]. Now Jinnie, Jinnie, it's a derogatory thing to be smirchin' a night like this with a row; it's rompin' with th' feelin's of hope we ought to be, instead o' bein' vice versa!

PETER [*trying to quiet* BESSIE]. I'm terrible dawny,* Mrs Burgess, an' a fight leaves me weak for a long time afterwards. . . . Please, Mrs

Burgess, before there's damage done, try to have a little·respect for yourself.

BESSIE [*with a push of her hand that sends* PETER *tottering to the end of the shop*]. G'way, you little sermonising, little yella-faced, little consequential, little pudgy, little bum, you!

MRS GOGAN [*screaming*]. Fluther, leggo! I'm not goin' to keep an unresistin' silence, an' her scattherin' her festherin' words in me face, stirrin' up every dhrop of decency in a respectable female, with her restless rally o' lies that would make a saint say his prayer backwards!

BESSIE [*shouting*]. Ah, everybody knows well that th' best charity that can be shown to you is to hide th' thruth as much as our thrue worship of God Almighty will allow us!

MRS GOGAN [*frantically*]. Here, houl' th' kid, one o' yous; houl' th' kid for a minute! There's nothin' for it but show this lassie a lesson or two. . . . [*To* PETER] Here, houl' th' kid, you. [*Before* PETER *is aware of it, she places the infant in his arms.*]

MRS GOGAN [*to* BESSIE, *standing before her in a fighting attitude*]. Come on, now, me loyal lassie, dyin' with grief for little Catholic Belgium! When Jinnie Gogan's done with you, you'll have a little leisure lyin' down to think an' pray for your king an' counthry!

BARMAN [*coming from behind the counter, getting between the women, and proceeding to push them towards the door*]. Here, now, since yous can't have a little friendly argument quietly, you'll get out o' this·place in quick time. Go on, an' settle your differences somewhere else – I don't want to have another endorsement on me licence.

PETER [*anxiously, over to* MRS GOGAN]. Here, take your kid back, ower this. How nicely I was picked, now, for it to be plumped into me arms!

THE COVEY. She knew who she was givin' it to, maybe.

PETER [*hotly to* THE COVEY]. Now, I'm givin' you fair warnin', me young Covey, to quit firin' your jibes an' jeers at me. . . . For one o' these days, I'll run out in front o' God Almighty an' take your sacred life!

BARMAN [*pushing* BESSIE *out after* MRS GOGAN]. Go on, now; out you go.

BESSIE [*as she goes out*]. If you think, me lassie, that Bessie Burgess has an untidy conscience, she'll soon show you to th' differ!

PETER [*leaving the baby down on the floor*]. Ay, be Jasus, wait there, till I give her back her youngster! [*He runs to the door.*] Ay, there, ay!

[*He comes back.*] There, she's afther goin' without her kid. What are we goin' to do with it, now?

THE COVEY. What are we goin' to do with it? Bring it outside an' show everybody what you're afther findin'!

PETER [*in a panic to* FLUTHER]. Pick it up, you, Fluther, an' run afther her with it, will you?

FLUTHER. What d'ye take Fluther for? You must think Fluther's a right gom.* D'ye think Fluther's like yourself, destitute of a titther of undherstandin'?

BARMAN [*imperatively to* PETER]. Take it up, man, an' run out afther her with it, before she's gone too far. You're not goin' to leave th' bloody thing here, are you?

PETER [*plaintively, as he lifts up the baby*]. Well, God Almighty, give me patience with all th' scorners, tormentors, an' twarters that are always an' ever thryin' to goad me into prayin' for their blindin' an' blastin' an' burnin' in th' world to come! [*He goes out.*]

FLUTHER. God, it's a relief to get rid o' that crowd. Women is terrible when they start to fight. There's no holdin' them back. [*To* THE COVEY] Are you goin' to have anything?

THE COVEY. Ah, I don't mind if I have another half.

FLUTHER [*to* BARMAN]. Two more, Tommy, me son. [*The* BARMAN *gets the drinks.*]

FLUTHER. You know, there's no conthrollin' a woman when she loses her head.

ROSIE *enters and goes over to the counter on the side nearest to* FLUTHER.

ROSIE [*to* BARMAN]. Divil a use o' havin' a thrim* little leg on a night like this; things was never worse. . . . Give us a half till tomorrow, Tom, duckey.

BARMAN [*coldly*]. No more tonight, Rosie; you owe me for three already.

ROSIE [*combatively*]. You'll be paid, won't you?

BARMAN. I hope so.

ROSIE. You hope so! Is that th' way with you, now?

FLUTHER [*to* BARMAN]. Give her one; it'll be all right.

ROSIE [*clapping* FLUTHER *on the back*]. Oul' sport!

FLUTHER. Th' meetin' should be soon over, now.

THE COVEY. Th' sooner th' better. It's all a lot o' blasted nonsense, comrade.

FLUTHER. Oh, I wouldn't say it was all nonsense. Afther all, Fluther can remember th' time, an' him only a dawny chiselur, bein' taught at his mother's knee to be faithful to th' Shan Van Vok!*

THE COVEY. That's all dope, comrade; th' sort o' thing that workers are fed on be th' Boorzwawzee.*

FLUTHER [*a little sharply*]. What's all dope? Though I'm sayin' it that shouldn't: [*catching his cheek with his hand, and pulling down the flesh from the eye*] d'ye see that mark there, undher me eye? . . . A sabre slice from a dragoon in O'Connell Street! [*Thrusting his head forward towards* ROSIE] Feel that dint in th' middle o' me nut!

ROSIE [*rubbing* FLUTHER's *head, and winking at* THE COVEY]. My God, there's a holla!*

FLUTHER [*putting on his hat with quiet pride*]. A skelp* from a bobby's* baton at a Labour meetin' in th' Phoenix Park!

THE COVEY. He must ha' hitten you in mistake. I don't know what you ever done for th' Labour movement.

FLUTHER [*loudly*]. D'ye not? Maybe, then, I done as much, an' know as much about th' Labour Movement as th' chancers* that are blowin' about it!

BARMAN. Speak easy, Fluther, thry to speak easy.

THE COVEY. There's no necessity to get excited about it, comrade.

FLUTHER [*more loudly*]. Excited? Who's gettin' excited? There's no one gettin' excited! It would take something more than a thing like you to flutther a feather o' Fluther. Blatherin', an', when all is said, you know as much as th' rest in th' wind up!

THE COVEY. Well, let us put it to th' test, then, an' see what you know about th' Labour Movement: what's the mechanism of exchange?

FLUTHER [*roaring, because he feels he is beaten*]. How th' hell do I know what it is? There's nothin' about that in th' rules of our Thrades Union!

BARMAN. For God's sake, thry to speak easy, Fluther.

THE COVEY. What does Karl Marx* say about th' Relation of Value to th' Cost o' Production?

FLUTHER [*angrily*]. What th' hell do I care what he says? I'm Irishman enough not to lose me head be follyin' foreigners!

BARMAN. Speak easy, Fluther.

THE COVEY. It's only waste o' time talkin' to you, comrade.

FLUTHER. Don't be comradin' me, mate. I'd be on me last legs if I wanted you for a comrade.

ROSIE [*to* THE COVEY]. It seems a highly rediculous thing to hear a thing that's only an inch or two away from a kid, swingin' heavy words about he doesn't know th' meanin' of, an' uppishly thryin' to down a man like Misther Fluther here, that's well flavoured in th' knowledge of th' world he's livin' in.

THE COVEY [*savagly to* ROSIE]. Nobody's askin' you to be buttin' in with your prate.* . . . I have you well taped,* me lassie. . . . Just you keep your opinions for your own place. . . . It'll be a long time before th' Covey takes any insthructions or reprimandin' from a prostitute!

ROSIE [*wild with humiliation*]. You louse, you louse, you! . . . You're no man. . . . You're no man. . . . I'm a woman, anyhow, an' if I'm a prostitute aself, I have me feelin's. . . . Thryin' to put his arm around me a minute ago, an' givin' me th' glad eye, th' little wrigglin' lump o' desolation turns on me now, because he saw there was nothin' doin'. . . . You louse, you! If I was a man, or you were a woman, I'd bate th' puss* o' you!

BARMAN. Ay, Rosie, ay! You'll have to shut your mouth altogether, if you can't learn to speak easy!

FLUTHER [*to* ROSIE]. Houl' on there, Rosie; houl' on there. There's no necessity to flutther yourself when you're with Fluther. . . . Any lady that's in th' company of Fluther is goin' to get a fair hunt. . . . This is outside your province. . . . I'm not goin' to let you demean yourself be talkin' to a tittherin' chancer. . . . Leave this to Fluther – this is a man's job. [*to* THE COVEY] Now, if you've anything to say, say it to Fluther, an', let me tell you, you're not goin' to be pass-remarkable* to any lady in my company.

THE COVEY. Sure I don't care if you were runnin' all night afther your Mary o' th' Curlin' Hair, but, when you start tellin' luscious lies about what you done for th' Labour Movement, it's nearly time to show y'up!

FLUTHER [*fiercely*]. Is it you show Fluther up? G'way, man, I'd beat two o' you before me breakfast!

THE COVEY [*contemptuously*]. Tell us where you bury your dead, will you?

FLUTHER [*with his face stuck into the face of* THE COVEY]. Sing a little less on th' high note, or, when I'm done with you, you'll put a Christianable consthruction on things, I'm tellin' you!

THE COVEY. You're a big fella, you are.

FLUTHER [*tapping* THE COVEY *threateningly on the shoulder*]. Now, you're temptin' Providence when you're temptin' Fluther!

THE COVEY [*losing his temper, and bawling*]. Easy with them hands, there, easy with them hands! You're startin' to take a little risk when you commence to paw the Covey!

FLUTHER *suddenly springs into the middle of the shop, flings his hat into the corner, whips off his coat, and begins to paw the air.*

FLUTHER [*roaring at the top of his voice*]. Come on, come on, you lowser;* put your mits up now, if there's a man's blood in you! Be God, in a few minutes you'll see some snots* flyin' around, I'm tellin' you. . . . When Fluther's done with you, you'll have a vice versa opinion of him! Come on, now, come on!

BARMAN [*running from behind the counter and catching hold of* THE COVEY]. Here, out you go, me little bowsey.* Because you got a couple o' halves you think you can act as you like. [*He pushes* THE COVEY *to the door.*] Fluther's a friend o' mine, an' I'll not have him insulted.

THE COVEY [*struggling with the* BARMAN]. Ay, leggo, leggo there; fair hunt, give a man a fair hunt!* One minute with him is all I ask; one minute alone with him, while you're runnin' for th' priest an' th' doctor.

FLUTHER [*to the* BARMAN]. Let him go, let him go, Tom! let him open th' door to sudden death if he wants to!

BARMAN [*to* THE COVEY]. Go on, out you go an' do th' bowsey somewhere else. [*He pushes* THE COVEY *out and comes back.*]

ROSIE [*getting* FLUTHER'*s hat as he is putting on his coat*]. Be God, you put th' fear o' God in his heart that time! I thought you'd have to be dug out of him. . . . Th' way you lepped out without any of your fancy side-steppin'! 'Men like Fluther', say I to meself, 'is gettin' scarce nowadays.'

FLUTHER [*with proud complacency*]. I wasn't goin' to let meself be malignified* by a chancer. . . . He got a little bit too derogatory for Fluther. . . . Be God, to think of a cur like that comin' to talk to a man like me!

ROSIE [*fixing on his hat*]. Did j'ever!

FLUTHER. He's lucky he got off safe. I hit a man last week, Rosie, an' he's fallin' yet!

ROSIE. Sure, you'd ha' broken him in two if you'd ha' hitten him one clatther!*

FLUTHER [*amorously, putting his arm around* ROSIE]. Come on into th' snug, me little darlin', an' we'll have a few dhrinks before I see you home.

ROSIE. Oh, Fluther, I'm afraid you're a terrible man for th' women.

*They go into the snug as* CLITHEROE, CAPTAIN BRENNAN, *and* LIEUTEN-
ANT LANGON *of the Irish Volunteers enter hurriedly.* CAPTAIN BRENNAN
*carries the banner of the Plough and the Stars, and* LIEUTENANT LANGON
*a green, white, and orange Tricolour. They are in a state of emotional
excitement. Their faces are flushed and their eyes sparkle; they speak
rapidly, as if unaware of the meaning of what they said. They have been
mesmerised by the fervency of the speeches.*

CLITHEROE [*almost pantingly*]. Three glasses o' port! [*The* BARMAN
  *brings the drinks.*]
CAPT. BRENNAN. We won't have long to wait now.
LIEUT. LANGON. Th' time is rotten ripe for revolution.
CLITHEROE. You have a mother, Langon.
LIEUT. LANGON. Ireland is greater than a mother.
CAPT. BRENNAN. You have a wife, Clitheroe.
CLITHEROE. Ireland is greater than a wife.
LIEUT. LANGON. Th' time for Ireland's battle is now – th' place for
  Ireland's battle is here.

*The tall, dark figure again is silhouetted against the window. The three
men pause and listen.*

VOICE OF THE MAN. Our foes are strong, but strong as they are, they
  cannot undo the miracles of God, who ripens in the heart of young
  men the seeds sown by the young men of a former generation. They
  think they have pacified Ireland; think they have foreseen everything; think they have provided against everything; but the fools,
  the fools, the fools! – they have left us our Fenian dead, and, while
  Ireland holds these graves, Ireland, unfree, shall never be at
  peace!*
CAPT. BRENNAN [*catching up the Plough and the Stars*]. Imprisonment
  for th' Independence of Ireland!
LIEUT. LANGON [*cathing up the Tricolour*]. Wounds for th' Independence of Ireland!
CLITHEROE. Death for th' Independence of Ireland!
THE THREE [*together*]. So help us God!

*They drink. A bugle blows the Assembly.\* They hurry out. A pause.*
FLUTHER *and* ROSIE *come out of the snug;* ROSIE *is linking* FLUTHER, *who is a little drunk. Both are in a merry mood.*

ROSIE. Come on home, ower o' that, man. Are you afraid or what? Are you goin' to come home, or are you not?
FLUTHER. Of course I'm goin' home. What ud ail me that I wouldn't go?
ROSIE [*lovingly*]. Come on, then, oul' sport.
OFFICER'S VOICE [*giving command outside*]. Irish Volunteers, by th' right, quick march!
ROSIE [*putting her arm round* FLUTHER *and singing*]

> I once had a lover, a tailor, but he could do nothin' for me,
> An' then I fell in with a sailor as strong an' as wild as th' sea.
> We cuddled an' kissed with devotion, till th' night from th'
>     mornin' had fled;
> An' there, to our joy, a bright bouncin' boy
> Was dancin' a jig in th' bed!
>
> Dancin' a jig in th' bed, an' bawlin' for
>     butther an' bread.
> An' there, to our joy, a bright bouncin' boy
> Was dancin' a jig in th' bed!

[*They go out with their arms round each other.*]
CLITHEROE'S VOICE [*in command outside*]. Dublin Battalion of the Irish Citizen Army, by th' right, quick march!

CURTAIN

# ACT III

*The corner house in a street of tenements: it is the home of the* CLITHEROES. *The house is a long, gaunt, five-storey tenement; its brick front is chipped and scarred with age and neglect. The wide and heavy hall door, flanked by two pillars, has a look of having been charred by a fire in the distant past. The door lurches a little to one side, disjointed by the continual and reckless banging when it is being closed by most of the residents. The diamond-paned fanlight is destitute of a single pane, the framework alone remaining. The windows, except the two looking into the front parlour (*CLITHEROE's *room), are grimy, and are draped with fluttering and soiled fragments of lace curtains. The front parlour windows are hung with rich, comparatively, casement cloth. Five stone steps lead from the door to the path on the street. Branching on each side are railings to prevent people from falling into the area.\* At the left corner of the house runs a narrow lane, bisecting the street, and connecting it with another of the same kind. At the corner of the lane is a street lamp.*

*As the house is revealed,* MRS GOGAN *is seen helping* MOLLSER *to a chair, which stands on the path beside the railings, at the left side of the steps. She then wraps a shawl around* MOLLSER's *shoulders. It is some months later.*

MRS GOGAN [*arranging shawl around* MOLLSER]. Th' sun'll do you all th' good in th' world. A few more weeks o' this weather, an' there's no knowin' how well you'll be. . . . Are you comfy, now?

MOLLSER [*weakly and wearily*]. Yis, ma; I'm all right.

MRS GOGAN. How are you feelin'?

MOLLSER. Betther, ma, betther. If th' horrible sinkin' feelin' ud go, I'd be all right.

MRS GOGAN. Ah, I wouldn't put much pass\* on that. Your stomach maybe's out of ordher. . . . Is th' poor breathin' any betther, d'ye think?

MOLLSER. Yis, yis, ma; a lot betther.

MRS GOGAN. Well, that's somethin' anyhow. . . . With th' help o' God, you'll be on th' mend from this out. . . . D'your legs feel any sthronger undher you, d'ye think!

MOLLSER [*irritably*]. I can't tell, ma. I think so. . . . A little.

MRS GOGAN. Well, a little aself is somethin'. . . . I thought I heard you coughin' a little more than usual last night. . . . D'ye think you were?

MOLLSER. I wasn't, ma, I wasn't.

MRS GOGAN. I thought I heard you, for I was kep' awake all night with th' shootin'. An' thinkin' o' that madman, Fluther, runnin' about through th' night lookin' for Nora Clitheroe to bring her back when he heard she'd gone to folly* her husband, an' in dhread any minute he might come staggerin' in covered with bandages, splashed all over with th' red of his own blood, an' givin' us barely time to bring th' priest to hear th' last whisper of his final confession, as his soul was passin' through th' dark doorway o' death into th' way o' th' wondherin' dead. . . . You don't feel cold, do you?

MOLLSER. No, ma; I'm all right.

MRS GOGAN. Keep your chest well covered, for that's th' delicate spot in you . . . if there's any danger, I'll whip you in again. . . . [*Looking up the street*] Oh, here's th' Covey an' oul' Pether hurryin' along. God Almighty, sthrange things is happenin' when them two is pullin' together.

THE COVEY *and* PETER *come in, breathless and excited.*

MRS GOGAN [*to the two men*]. Were yous far up th' town? Did yous see any sign o' Fluther or Nora? How is things lookin'? I hear they're blazin' away out o' th' GPO. That th' Tommies is sthretched in heaps around Nelson's Pillar an' th' Parnell Statue,* an' that th' pavin' sets in O'Connell Street is nearly covered be pools o' blood.

PETER. We seen no sign o' Nora or Fluther anywhere.

MRS GOGAN. We should ha' held her back be main force from goin' to look for her husband. . . . God knows what's happened to her – I'm always seein' her sthretched on her back in some hospital, moanin' with th' pain of a bullet in her vitals, an' nuns thryin' to get her to take a last look at th' crucifix!

THE COVEY. We can do nothin'. You can't stick your nose into O'Connell Street, an' Tyler's is on fire.

PETER. An' we seen th' Lancers –

THE COVEY [*interrupting*]. Throttin' along, heads in th' air; spurs an' sabres jinglin', an' lances quiverin', an' lookin' as if they were assin'* themselves, 'Where's these blighters, till we get a prod at them?' when there was a volley from th' Post Office that stretched half o' them, an' sent th' rest gallopin' away wondherin' how far they'd have to go before they'd feel safe.

PETER [*rubbing his hands*]. 'Damn it,' says I to meself, 'this looks like business!'

THE COVEY. An' then out comes General Pearse* an' his staff, an', standin' in th' middle o' th' street, he reads th' Proclamation.

MRS GOGAN. What proclamation?

PETER. Declarin' an Irish Republic.

MRS GOGAN. Go to God!

PETER. The gunboat *Helga*'s shellin' Liberty Hall, an' I hear the people livin' on th' quays had to crawl on their bellies to Mass with th' bullets that were flyin' around from Boland's Mills.

MRS GOGAN. God bless us, what's goin' to be th' end of it all!

BESSIE [*looking out of the top window*]. Maybe yous are satisfied now; maybe yous are satisfied now. Go on an' get guns if yous are men – Johnny get your gun, get your gun, get your gun! Yous are all nicely shanghaied* now; th' boyo hasn't a sword on his thigh now!* Oh, yous are all nicely shanghaied now!

MRS GOGAN [*warningly to* PETER *and* THE COVEY]. S-s-sh, don't answer her. She's th' right oul' Orange bitch! She's been chantin' 'Rule, Britannia' all th' mornin'.

PETER. I hope Fluther hasn't met with any accident, he's such a wild card.

MRS GOGAN. God grant it; but last night I dreamt I seen gettin' carried into th' house a sthretcher with a figure lyin' on it, stiff an' still, dhressed in th' habit of St Francis. An' then, I heard th' murmurs of a crowd no one could see sayin' th' litany for th' dead; an' then it got so dark that nothin' was seen but th' white face of th' corpse, gleamin' like a white wather-lily floatin' on th' top of a dark lake. Then a tiny whisper thrickled into me ear, sayin', 'Isn't the face very like th' face o' Fluther?' an' then, with a thremblin' flutther, th' dead lips opened, an' although I couldn't hear, I knew they were sayin', 'Poor oul' Fluther, afther havin' handed in his gun at last, his shakin' soul moored in th' place where th' wicked are at rest* an' th' weary cease from throublin'.'

PETER [*who has put on a pair of spectacles, and has been looking down the street*]. Here they are, be God, here they are; just afther turnin' th' corner – Nora an' Fluther!

THE COVEY. She must be wounded or something – he seems to be carryin' her.

FLUTHER *and* NORA *enter.* FLUTHER *has his arm around her and is half* *leading, half carrying her in. Her eyes are dim and hollow, her face pale and strained-looking; her hair is tossed,\* and her clothes are dusty.*

MRS GOGAN [*running over to them*]. God bless us, is it wounded y'are, Mrs Clitheroe, or what?

FLUTHER. Ah, she's all right, Mrs Gogan; only worn out from thravellin' an' want o' sleep. A night's rest, now, an' she'll be as fit as a fiddle. Bring her in, an' make her lie down.

MRS GOGAN [*to* NORA]. Did you hear e'er a whisper o' Mr Clitheroe?

NORA [*wearily*]. I could find him nowhere, Mrs Gogan. None o' them would tell me where he was. They told me I shamed my husband an' th' women of Ireland be carryin' on as I was. . . . They said th' women must learn to be brave an' cease to be cowardly. . . . Me who risked more for love than they would risk for hate. . . . [*Raising her voice in hysterical protest*] My Jack will be killed, my Jack will be killed! . . . He is to be butchered\* as a sacrifice to th' dead!

BESSIE [*from upper window*]. Yous are all nicely shanghaied now! Sorra mend th' lasses that have been kissin' an' cuddlin' their boys into th' sheddin' of blood! . . . Fillin' their minds with fairy tales that had no beginnin', but, please God, 'll have a bloody quick endin'! . . . Turnin' bitther into sweet, an' sweet into bitther. . . . Stabbin' in th' back\* th' men that are dyin' in th' threnches for them! It's a bad thing for any one that thries to jilt\* th' Ten Commandments, for judgements are prepared\* for scorners an' sthripes for th' back o' fools! [*Going away from window as she sings*]

> Rule, Britannia, Britannia rules th' waves,
> Britons never, never, never shall be slaves!

FLUTHER [*with a roar up at the window*]. Y'ignorant oul' throllop, you!

MRS GOGAN [*to* NORA]. He'll come home safe enough to you, you'll find, Mrs Clitheroe; afther all, there's a power o'\* women that's handed over sons an' husbands to take a runnin' risk in th' fight they're wagin'.

NORA. I can't help thinkin' every shot fired 'll be fired at Jack, an' every shot fired at Jack 'll be fired at me. What do I care for th' others? I can think only of me own self. . . . An' there's no woman gives a son or a husband to be killed – if they say it, they're lyin', lyin', against God, Nature, an' against themselves! . . . One blasted hussy at a barricade told me to go home an' not be thryin' to dishearten th' men. . . . That I wasn't worthy to bear a son to a man that was out fightin' for freedom. . . . I clawed at her, an' smashed her in th' face till we were separated. . . . I was pushed down th' street, an' I cursed them – cursed the rebel ruffians an' Volunteers that had dhragged me ravin' mad into th' sthreets to seek me husband!

PETER. You'll have to have patience, Nora. We all have to put up with twarthers an' tormentors in this world.

THE COVEY. If they were fightin' for anything worth while, I wouldn't mind.

FLUTHER [*to* NORA]. Nothin' derogatory 'll happen to Mr Clitheroe. You'll find, now, in th' finish up it'll be vice versa.

NORA. Oh, I know that wherever he is, he's thinkin' of wantin' to be with me. I know he's longin' to be passin' his hand through me hair, to be caressin' me neck, to fondle me hand an' to feel me kisses clingin' to his mouth. . . . An' he stands wherever he is because he's brave? [*Vehemently*] No, but because he's a coward, a coward, a coward!

MRS GOGAN. Oh, they're not cowards anyway.

NORA [*with denunciatory anger*]. I tell you they're afraid to say they're afraid! . . . Oh, I saw it, I saw it, Mrs Gogan. . . . At th' barricade in North King Street I saw fear glowin' in all their eyes. . . . An' in th' middle o' th' sthreet was somethin' huddled up in a horrible tangled heap. . . . His face was jammed again th' stones, an' his arm was twisted round his back. . . . An' every twist of his body was a cry against th' terrible thing that had happened to him. . . . An' I saw they were afraid to look at it. . . . An' some o' them laughed at me, but th' laugh was a frightened one. . . . An' some o' them shouted at me, but th' shout had in it th' shiver o' fear. . . . I tell you they were afraid, afraid, afraid!

MRS GOGAN [*leading her towards the house*]. Come on in, dear. If you'd been a little longer together, th' wrench asundher wouldn't have been so sharp.

NORA. Th' agony I'm in since he left me has thrust away every rough thing he done, an' every unkind word he spoke; only th' blossoms that grew out of our lives are before me now; shakin' their colours before me face, an' breathin' their sweet scent on every thought springin' up in me mind, till, sometimes, Mrs Gogan, sometimes I think I'm goin' mad!

MRS GOGAN. You'll be a lot better when you have a little lie down.

NORA [*turning towards* FLUTHER *as she is going in*]. I don't know what I'd have done, only for Fluther.* I'd have been lyin' in th' streets, only for him. . . . [*As she goes in*] They have dhriven away th' little happiness life had to spare for me. He has gone from me for ever, for ever. . . . Oh, Jack, Jack, Jack!

*She is led in by* MRS GOGAN, *as* BESSIE *comes out with a shawl around her shoulders. She passes by them with her head in the air. When they have gone in, she gives a mug of milk to* MOLLSER *silently.*

FLUTHER. Which of yous has th' tossers?*

THE COVEY. I have.

BESSIE [*as she is passing them to go down the street*]. You an' your Leadhers an' their sham-battle soldiers has landed a body in a nice way, havin' to go an' ferret out a bit o' bread God knows where. . . . Why aren't yous in th' GPO if yous are men? It's paler an' paler yous are gettin'. . . . A lot o' vipers, that's what th' Irish people is! [*She goes out.*]

FLUTHER. Never mind her. . . . [*To* THE COVEY] Make a start an' keep us from th' sin o' idleness. [*To* MOLLSER] Well, how are you today, Mollser, oul' son? What are you dhrinkin', milk?

MOLLSER. Grand, Fluther, grand, thanks. Yis, milk.

FLUTHER. You couldn't get a betther thing down you. . . . This turn-up has done one good thing, anyhow; you can't get dhrink anywhere, an' if it lasts a week, I'll be so used to it that I won't think of a pint.

THE COVEY [*who has taken from his pocket two worn coins and a thin strip of wood about four inches long*]. What's th' bettin'?

PETER. Heads, a juice.

FLUTHER. Harps, a tanner.*

THE COVEY *places the coins on the strip of wood, and flips them up into the air. As they jingle on the ground the distant boom of a big gun is heard. They stand for a moment listening.*

FLUTHER. What th' hell's that?

THE COVEY. It's like th' boom of a big gun!

FLUTHER. Surely to God they're not goin' to use artillery on us?

THE COVEY [*scornfully*]. Not goin'! [*Vehemently*] Wouldn't they use anything on us, man?

FLUTHER. Aw, holy Christ, that's not playin' th' game!

PETER [*plaintively*]. What would happen if a shell landed here now?

THE COVEY [*ironically*]. You'd be off to heaven in a fiery chariot.

PETER. In spite of all th' warnin's that's ringin' around us, are you goin' to start your pickin' at me again?

FLUTHER. Go on, toss them again, toss them again. . . . Harps, a tanner.

PETER. Heads, a juice. [THE COVEY *tosses the coins.*]

FLUTHER [*as the coins fall*]. Let them roll, let them roll. Heads, be God!

BESSIE *runs in excitedly. She has a new hat on her head, a fox-fur round her neck over her shawl, three umbrellas under her right arm, and a box of biscuits under her left. She speaks rapidly and breathlessly.*

BESSIE. They're breakin' into th' shops, they're breakin' into th' shops! Smashin' th' windows, battherin' in th' doors, an' whippin' away everything! An' th' Volunteers is firin' on them. I seen two men an' a lassie pushin' a piano down th' sthreet, an' th' sweat rollin' off them thryin' to get it up on th' pavement; an' an oul' wan that must ha' been seventy lookin' as if she'd dhrop every minute with th' dint o' heart beatin', thryin' to pull a big double bed out of a broken shop-window! I was goin' to wait till I dhressed meself from th' skin out.

MOLLSER [*to* BESSIE, *as she is going in*]. Help me in, Bessie; I'm feelin' curious.

BESSIE *leaves the looted things in the house, and, rapidly returning, helps* MOLLSER *in.*

THE COVEY. Th' selfishness of that one – she waited till she got all she could carry before she'd come to tell anyone!

FLUTHER [*running over to the door of the house and shouting in to* BESSIE]. Ay, Bessie, did you hear of e'er a pub gettin' a shake up?

BESSIE [*inside*]. I didn't hear o' none.

FLUTHER [*in a burst of enthusiasm*]. Well, you're goin' to hear of one soon!

THE COVEY. Come on, man, an' don't be wastin' time.

PETER [*to them as they are about to run off*]. Ay, ay, are you goin' to leave me here?

FLUTHER. Are you goin' to leave yourself here?

PETER [*anxiously*]. Didn't yous hear her sayin' they were firin' on them?

THE COVEY AND FLUTHER [*together*]. Well?

PETER. Supposin' I happened to be potted?

FLUTHER. We'd give you a Christian burial, anyhow.

THE COVEY [*ironically*]. Dhressed up in your regimentals.

PETER [*to* THE COVEY, *passionately*]. May th' all-lovin' God give you a hot knock one o' these days, me young Covey, tuthorin' Fluther up now to be tiltin' at me, an' crossin' me with his mockeries an' jibin'!

*A fashionably dressed, middle-aged, stout woman comes hurriedly in, and makes for the group. She is almost fainting with fear.*

WOMAN. For Gawd's sake, will one of you kind men show any safe way for me to get to Wrathmines?* . . . I was foolish enough to visit a friend, thinking the howl* thing was a joke, and now I cawn't get a car or a tram to take me home – isn't it awful?

FLUTHER. I'm afraid, ma'am, one way is as safe as another.

WOMAN. And what am I gowing to do? Oh, isn't this awful? . . . I'm so different from others. . . . The mowment I hear a shot, my legs give way under me – I cawn't stir, I'm paralysed – isn't it awful?

FLUTHER [*moving away*], It's a derogatory way to be, right enough, ma'am.

WOMAN [*catching* FLUTHER's *coat*]. Creeping along the street there, with my head down and my eyes half shut, a bullet whizzed past within an inch of my nowse. . . . I had to lean against the wall for a long time, gasping for breath – I nearly passed away – it was awful! . . . I wonder, would you kind men come some of the way and see me safe?

FLUTHER. I have to go away, ma'am, to thry an' save a few things from th' burnin' buildin's.

THE COVEY. Come on, then, or there won't be anything left to save. [THE COVEY *and* FLUTHER *hurry away*.]

WOMAN [*to* PETER]. Wasn't it an awful thing for me to leave my friend's house? Wasn't it an idiotic thing to do? . . . I haven't the slightest idea where I am. . . . You have a kind face, sir. Could you possibly come and pilot me in the direction of Wrathmines?

PETER [*indignantly*]. D'ye think I'm goin' to risk me life throttin' in front of you? An' maybe get a bullet that would gimme a game* leg or something that would leave me a jibe an' a jeer to Fluther an' th' young Covey for th' rest o' me days! [*With an indignant toss of his head he walks into the house.*]

WOMAN [*going out*]. I know I'll fall down in a dead faint if I hear another shot go off anyway near me – isn't it awful?

MRS GOGAN *comes out of the house pushing a pram before her. As she enters the street,* BESSIE *rushes out, follows* MRS GOGAN, *and catches hold of the pram, stopping* MRS GOGAN's *progress.*

BESSIE. Here, where are you goin' with that? How quick you were, me lady, to clap your eyes on th' pram. . . . Maybe you don't know that Mrs Sullivan, before she went to spend Easther with her people in Dunboyne,* gave me sthrict injunctions to give an accasional look to see if it was still standin' where it was left in th' corner of th' lobby.

MRS GOGAN. That remark of yours, Mrs Bessie Burgess, requires a little considheration, seein' that th' pram was left on our lobby, an' not on yours; a foot or two a little to th' left of th' jamb* of me own room door; nor is it needful to mention th' name of th' person that gave a squint to see if it was there th' first thing in th' mornin', an' th' last thing in th' stillness o' th' night; never failin' to realise that her eyes couldn't be goin' wrong, be sthretchin' out her arm an' runnin' her hand over th' pram, to make sure that th' sight was no deception! Moreover, somethin's tellin' me that th' runnin' hurry of an inthrest you're takin' in it now is a sudden ambition to use th' pram for a purpose that a loyal woman of law an' ordher would stagger away from! [*She gives the pram a sudden push that pulls* BESSIE *forward.*]

BESSIE [*still holding the pram*]. There's not as much as one body in th' house that doesn't know that it wasn't Bessie Burgess that was always shakin' her voice complainin' about people leavin' bassinettes in th' way of them that, week in an' week out, had to pay their rent, an' always had to find a regular accommodation for her own furniture in her own room. . . . An' as for law an' ordher, puttin' aside th' harp an' shamrock, Bessie Burgess 'll have as much respect as she wants for th' lion an' unicorn!

PETER [*appearing at the door*]. I think I'll go with th' pair of yous an' see th' fun. A fella might as well chance it, anyhow.

MRS GOGAN [*taking no notice of* PETER, *and pushing the pram on another step*]. Take your rovin' lumps o' hands from pattin' th' bassinette, if you please, ma'am; an', steppin' from th' threshold of good manners, let me tell you, Mrs Burgess, that it's a fat wondher to Jennie Gogan that a lady-like singer o' hymns like yourself would lower her thoughts from sky-thinkin' to stretch out her arm in a sly-seekin' way to pinch anything dhriven asthray in th' confusion of th' battle our boys is makin' for th' freedom of their counthry!

PETER [*laughing and rubbing his hands together*]. Hee, hee, hee, hee, hee! I'll go with th' pair o' yous an' give yous a hand.

MRS GOGAN [*with a rapid turn of her head as she shoves the pram forward*]. Get up in th' prambulator an' we'll wheel you down.

BESSIE [*to* MRS GOGAN]. Poverty an' hardship has sent Bessie Burgess to abide with sthrange company, but she always knew them she had to live with from backside to breakfast time;* an' she can tell them, always havin' had a Christian kinch* on her conscience, that a passion for thievin' an' pinchin' would find her soul a foreign place to live in, an' that her present intention is quite th' lofty-hearted one of pickin' up anything shaken up an' scatthered about in th' loose confusion of a general plundher!

*By this time they have disappeared from view.* PETER *is following, when the boom of a big gun in the distance brings him to a quick halt.*

PETER. God Almighty, that's th' big gun again! God forbid any harm would happen to them, but sorra mind I'd mind* if they met with a dhrop* in their mad endeyvours to plundher an' desthroy.

*He looks down the street for a moment, then runs to the hall door of the house, which is open, and shuts it with a vicious pull; he then goes to the chair in which* MOLLSER *had sat, sits down, takes out his pipe, lights it and begins to smoke with his head carried at a haughty angle.* THE COVEY *comes staggering in with a ten-stone sack of flour on his back. On the top of the sack is a ham. He goes over to the door, pushes it with his head, and finds he can't open it; he turns slightly in the direction of* PETER.

THE COVEY [*to* PETER]. Who shut th' door? . . . [*He kicks at it.*] Here, come on an' open it, will you? This isn't a mot's* hand bag I've got on me back.

PETER. Now, me young Covey, d'ye think I'm goin' to be your lackey?

THE COVEY [*angrily*]. Will you open th' door, y'oul' –

PETER [*shouting*]. Don't be assin' me to open any door, don't be assin' me to open any door for you. . . . Makin' a shame an' a sin o' th' cause that good men are fightin' for. . . . Oh, God forgive th' people that, instead o' burnishin' th' work th' boys is doin' today with quiet honesty an' patience, is revilin' their sacrifices with a riot of lootin' an' roguery!

THE COVEY. Isn't your own eyes leppin' out o' your head with envy that you haven't th' guts to ketch a few o' th' things that God is givin' to His chosen people? . . . Y'oul' hypocrite, if everyone was blind you'd steal a cross off an ass's back!

PETER [*very calmly*]. You're not going to make me lose me temper; you can go on with your proddin' as long as you like; goad an' goad an' goad away; hee, hee, heee! I'll not lose me temper. [*Somebody opens door and* THE COVEY *goes in.*]

THE COVEY [*inside, mockingly*]. Cuckoo-oo!

PETER [*running to the door and shouting in a blaze of passion as he follows* THE COVEY *in*]. You lean, long, lanky lath of a lowsey bastard. . . . [*Following him in*] Lowsey bastard, lowsey bastard!

BESSIE *and* MRS GOGAN *enter, the pride of a great joy illuminating their faces.* BESSIE *is pushing the pram, which is filled with clothes and boots; on the top of the boots and clothes is a fancy table, which* MRS GOGAN *is holding on with her left hand, while with her right hand she holds a chair on the top of her head. They are heard talking to each other before they enter.*

MRS GOGAN [*outside*]. I don't remember ever havin' seen such lovely pairs as them, [*they appear*] with th' pointed toes an' th' cuban heels.*

BESSIE. They'll go grand with th' dhresses we're afther liftin', when we've stitched a sthray bit o' silk to lift th' bodices up a little higher, so as to shake th' shame out o' them, an' make them fit for women that hasn't lost themselves in th' nakedness o' th' times. [*They fussily carry in the chair, the table, and some of the other goods. They return to bring in the rest.*]

PETER [*at door, sourly to* MRS GOGAN]. Ay, you. Mollser looks as if she was goin' to faint, an' your youngster is roarin' in convulsions in her lap.

MRS GOGAN [*snappily*]. She's never any other way but faintin'!

*She goes to go in with some things in her arms, when a shot from a rifle rings out. She and* BESSIE *make a bolt for the door, which* PETER, *in a panic, tries to shut before they have got inside.*

MRS GOGAN. Ay, ay, ay, you cowardly oul' fool, what are you thryin' to shut th' door on us for?

*They retreat tumultuously inside. A pause; then* CAPTAIN BRENNAN *comes in supporting* LIEUTENANT LANGON, *whose arm is around* BRENNAN's *neck.* LANGON's *face, which is ghastly white, is momentarily convulsed with spasms of agony. He is in a state of collapse, and* BRENNAN *is almost carrying him. After a few moments* CLITHEROE, *pale, and in a state of calm nervousness, follows, looking back in the direction from which he came, a rifle, held at the ready, in his hands.*

CAPT. BRENNAN [*savagely to* CLITHEROE]. Why did you fire over their heads? Why didn't you fire to kill?

CLITHEROE. No, no, Bill; bad as they are they're Irish men an' women.

CAPT. BRENNAN [*savagely*]. Irish be damned! Attackin' an' mobbin' th' men that are riskin' their lives for them. If these slum lice gather at our heels again, plug one o' them, or I'll soon shock them with a shot or two meself!

LIEUTENANT LANGON [*moaningly*]. My God, is there ne'er an ambulance knockin' around anywhere? . . . Th' stomach is ripped out o' me; I feel it – o-o-oh, Christ!

CAPT. BRENNAN. Keep th' heart up, Jim; we'll soon get help, now.

NORA *rushes wildly out of the house and flings her arms round the neck of* CLITHEROE *with a fierce and joyous insistence. Her hair is down, her face is haggard, but her eyes are agleam with the light of happy relief.*

NORA. Jack, Jack, Jack; God be thanked . . . be thanked. . . . He has been kind and merciful to His poor handmaiden. . . . My Jack, my own Jack, that I thought was lost is found, that I thought was dead is alive again!* . . . Oh, God be praised for ever, evermore! . . . My poor Jack. . . . Kiss me, kiss me, Jack, kiss your own Nora!

CLITHEROE [*kissing her, and speaking brokenly*]. My Nora; my little, beautiful Nora, I wish to God I'd never left you.

NORA. It doesn't matter – not now, not now, Jack. It will make us dearer than ever to each other. . . . Kiss me, kiss me again.

CLITHEROE. Now, for God's sake, Nora, don't make a scene.

NORA. I won't, I won't; I promise, I promise, Jack; honest to God. I'll be silent an' brave to bear th' joy of feelin' you safe in my arms again. . . . It's hard to force away th' tears of happiness at th' end of an awful agony.

BESSIE [*from the upper window*]. Th' Minsthrel Boys aren't feelin' very comfortable now. Th' big guns has knocked all th' harps out of their hands.* General Clitheroe'd rather be unlacin' his wife's bodice than standin' at a barricade. . . . An' th' professor of chicken-butcherin' there, finds he's up against somethin' a little tougher even than his own chickens, an' that's sayin' a lot!

CAPT. BRENNAN [*up to* BESSIE]. Shut up, y'oul' hag!

BESSIE [*down to* BRENNAN]. Choke th' chicken, choke th' chicken, choke th' chicken!

LIEUTENANT LANGON. For God's sake, Bill, bring me some place where me wound 'll be looked afther. . . . Am I to die before anything is done to save me?

CAPT. BRENNAN [*to* CLITHEROE]. Come on, Jack. We've got to get help for Jim, here – have you no thought for his pain an' danger?

BESSIE. Choke th' chicken, choke th' chicken, choke th' chicken!

CLITHEROE [*to* NORA]. Loosen me, darling, let me go.

NORA [*clinging to him*]. No, no, no, I'll not let you go! Come on, come up to our home, Jack, my sweetheart, my lover, my husband, an' we'll forget th' last few terrible days! . . . I look tired now, but a few hours of happy rest in your arms will bring back th' bloom of freshness again, an' you will be glad, you will be glad, glad . . . glad!

LIEUTENANT LANGON. Oh, if I'd kep' down only a little longer, I mightn't ha' been hit! Everyone else escapin', an' me gettin' me belly ripped assundher! . . . I couldn't scream, couldn't even scream. . . . D'ye think I'm really badly wounded, Bill? Me clothes seem to be all soakin' wet. . . . It's blood . . . My God, it must be me own blood!

CAPT. BRENNAN [*to* CLITHEROE]. Go on, Jack, bid her goodbye with another kiss, an' be done with it! D'ye want Langon to die in me arms while you're dallyin' with your Nora?

CLITHEROE [*to* NORA]. I must go, I must go, Nora. I'm sorry we met at all. . . . It couldn't be helped – all other ways were blocked be th' British. . . . Let me go, can't you, Nora? D'ye want me to be unthrue to me comrades?

NORA. No, I won't let you go. . . . I want you to be thrue to me, Jack. . . . I'm your dearest comrade; I'm your thruest comrade. . . . They only want th' comfort of havin' you in th' same danger as themselves. . . . Oh, Jack, I can't let you go!

CLITHEROE. You must, Nora, you must.

NORA. All last night at th' barricades I sought you, Jack. . . . I didn't think of th' danger – I could only think of you. . . . I asked for you everywhere. . . Some o' them laughed. . . . I was pushed away, but I shoved back. . . . Some o' them even sthruck me . . . an' I screamed an' screamed your name!

CLITHEROE [*in fear her action would give him future shame*]. What possessed you to make a show of yourself, like that? . . . What way d'ye think I'll feel when I'm told my wife was bawlin' for me at th' barricades? What are you more than any other woman?

NORA. No more, maybe; but you are more to me than any other man, Jack. . . . I didn't mean any harm, honestly, Jack. . . . I couldn't help it. . . . I shouldn't have told you. . . . My love for you made me mad with terror.

CLITHEROE [*angrily*]. They'll say now that I sent you out th' way I'd have an excuse to bring you home. . . . Are you goin' to turn all th' risks I'm takin' into a laugh?

LIEUTENANT LANGON. Let me lie down, let me lie down, Bill; th' pain would be easier, maybe, lyin' down. . . Oh, God, have mercy on me!

CAPT. BRENNAN [*to* LANGON]. A few steps more, Jim, a few steps more; thry to stick it for a few steps more.

LIEUTENANT LANGON. Oh, I can't, I can't, I can't!

CAPT. BRENNAN [*to* CLITHEROE]. Are you comin', man, or are you goin' to make an arrangement for another honeymoon? . . . If you want to act th' renegade, say so, an' we'll be off!

BESSIE [*from above*]. Runnin' from th' Tommies – choke th' chicken. Runnin' from th' Tommies – choke th' chicken!

CLITHEROE [*savagely to* BRENNAN]. Damn you, man, who wants to act th' renegade? [*To* NORA] Here, let go your hold; let go, I say!

NORA [*clinging to* CLITHEROE, *and indicating* BRENNAN]. Look, Jack, look at th' anger in his face; look at th' fear glintin' in his eyes. . . . He himself's afraid, afraid, afraid! . . . He wants you to go th' way he'll have th' chance of death sthrikin' you an' missin' him! . . . Turn round an' look at him, Jack, look at him, look at him! . . . His very soul is cold . . . shiverin' with th' thought of what may happen to him. . . . It is his fear that is thryin' to frighten you from recognisin' th' same fear that is in your own heart!

CLITHEROE [*struggling to release himself from* NORA]. Damn you, woman, will you let me go!

CAPT. BRENNAN [*fiercely, to* CLITHEROE]. Why are you beggin' her to let you go? Are you afraid of her, or what? Break her hold on you, man, or go up, an' sit on her lap! [CLITHEROE *trying roughly to break her hold.*]

NORA [*imploringly*]. Oh, Jack . . . Jack . . . Jack!

LIEUTENANT LANGON [*agonisingly*]. Brennan, a priest; I'm dyin', I think, I'm dyin'!

CLITHEROE [*to* NORA]. If you won't do it quietly, I'll have to make you! [*To* BRENNAN] Here, hold this gun, you, for a minute. [*He hands the gun to* BRENNAN.]

NORA [*pitifully*]. Please, Jack. . . . You're hurting me, Jack. . . . Honestly. . . . Oh, you're hurting . . . me! . . . I won't, I won't, I won't! . . . Oh, Jack, I gave you everything you asked of me. . . . Don't fling me from you, now!

*He roughly loosens her grip, and pushes her away from him.* NORA *sinks to the ground and lies there.*

NORA [*weakly*]. Ah, Jack . . . Jack . . . Jack!

CLITHEROE [*taking the gun back from* BRENNAN]. Come on, come on.

*They go out.* BESSIE *looks at* NORA *lying on the street, for a few moments, then, leaving the window, she comes out, runs over to* NORA, *lifts her up in her arms, and carries her swiftly into the house. A short pause, then down the street is heard a wild, drunken yell; it comes nearer, and* FLUTHER *enters, frenzied, wild-eyed, mad, roaring drunk. In his arms is an earthen half-gallon jar of whisky; streaming from one of the pockets of his coat is the arm of a new tunic shirt; on his head is a woman's vivid blue hat with gold lacing, all of which he has looted.*

FLUTHER [*singing in a frenzy*].

Fluther's a jolly good fella! . . . Fluther's a jolly good fella!
Up th' rebels! . . . That nobody can deny!

[*He beats on the door.*] Get us a mug or a jug, or somethin', some o'

yous, one o' yous, will yous, before I lay one o' yous out! . . .
[*Looking down the street*] Bang an' fire away for all Fluther
cares. . . . [*Banging at door*] Come down an' open th' door, some of
yous, one of yous, will yous, before I lay some o' yous out! . . . Th'
whole city can topple home to hell, for Fluther!

*Inside the house is heard a scream from* NORA, *followed by a moan.*

FLUTHER [*singing furiously*].

> That nobody can deny, that nobody can deny,
> For Fluther's a jolly good fella, Fluther's a jolly good fella,
> Fluther's a jolly good fella. . . . Up th' rebels! That nobody
> can deny!

[*His frantic movements cause him to spill some of the whisky out of the
jar.*] Blast you, Fluther, don't be spillin' th' precious liquor! [*He
kicks at the door.*] Ay, give us a mug or a jug, or somethin', one o'
yous, some o' yous, will yous, before I lay one o' yous out!

*The door suddenly opens, and* BESSIE, *coming out, grips him by the collar.*

BESSIE [*indignantly*]. You bowsey, come in ower o' that. . . . I'll
thrim* your thricks o' dhrunken dancin' for you, an' none of us
knowin' how soon we'll bump into a world we were never in before!
FLUTHER [*as she is pulling him in*]. Ay, th' jar, th' jar, th' jar!

*A short pause, then again is heard a scream of pain from* NORA. *The door
opens and* MRS GOGAN *and* BESSIE *are seen standing at it.*

BESSIE. Fluther would go, only he's too dhrunk. . . . Oh, God, isn't it
a pity he's so dhrunk! We'll have to thry to get a docthor
somewhere.
MRS GOGAN. I'd be afraid to go. . . . Besides, Mollser's terrible bad. I
don't think you'll get a docthor to come. It's hardly any use goin'.
BESSIE [*determinedly*]. I'll risk it. . . . Give her a little of Fluther's
whisky. . . . It's th' fright that's brought it on her so soon. . . . Go
on back to her, you.

MRS GOGAN *goes in, and* BESSIE *softly closes the door. She is moving forward, when the sound of some rifle shots, and the tok, tok, tok of a distant machine-gun brings her to a sudden halt. She hesitates for a moment, then she tightens her shawl round her, as if it were a shield, then she firmly and swiftly goes out.*

BESSIE [*as she goes out*]. Oh, God, be Thou my help in time o' throuble.
   An' shelter me safely in th' shadow of Thy wings!*

CURTAIN

## ACT IV

*The living-room of* BESSIE BURGESS. *It is one of two small attic rooms (the other, used as a bedroom, is to the left), the ceiling slopes up towards the back, giving to the apartment a look of compressed confinement. In the centre of the ceiling is a small skylight. There is an unmistakable air of poverty bordering on destitution. The paper on the walls is torn and soiled, particularly near the fire where the cooking is done, and near the washstand where the washing is done. The fireplace is to the left. A small armchair near fire. One small window at back. A pane of this window is starred by the entrance of a bullet. Under the window to the right is an oak coffin standing on two kitchen chairs. Near the coffin is a home-manufactured stool, on which are two lighted candles. Beside the window is a worn-out dresser on which is a small quantity of delf. Tattered remains of cheap lace curtains drape the window. Standing near the window on left is a brass standard lamp with a fancy shade; hanging on the wall near the same window is a vividly crimson silk dress, both of which have been looted. A door on left leading to the bedroom. Another opposite giving a way to the rest of the house. To the left of this door a common washstand. A tin kettle, very black, and an old saucepan inside the fender. There is no light in the room but that given from the two candles and the fire. The dusk has well fallen, and the glare of the burning buildings in the town can be seen through the window, in the distant sky.* THE COVEY *and* FLUTHER *have been playing cards, sitting on the floor by the light of the candles on the stool near the coffin. When the curtain rises* THE COVEY *is shuffling the cards,* PETER *is sitting in a stiff, dignified way beside him, and* FLUTHER *is kneeling beside the window, cautiously looking out. It is a few days later.*

FLUTHER [*furtively peeping out of the window*]. Give them a good shuffling. . . . Th' sky's gettin' reddher an' reddher. . . . You'd think it was afire. . . . Half o' th' city must be burnin'.

CLITHEROE. If I was you, Fluther, I'd keep away from that window. . . . It's dangerous, an', besides, if they see you, you'll only bring a nose on th' house.*

PETER. Yes; an' he knows we had to leave our own place th' way they were riddlin' it with machine-gun fire. . . . He'll keep on pimpin'* an' pimpin' there, till we have to fly out o' this place too.

FLUTHER [*ironically*]. If they make any attack here, we'll send you out in the green an' glory uniform, shakin' your sword over your head, an' they'll fly before you as th' Danes flew before Brian Boru!*

THE COVEY [*placing the cards on the floor, after shuffling them*]. Come on, an' cut. [FLUTHER *comes over, sits on floor, and cuts the cards.*]

THE COVEY [*having dealt the cards*]. Spuds* up again. [NORA *moans feebly in room on left.*]

FLUTHER. There, she's at it again. She's been quiet for a long time, all th' same.

THE COVEY. She was quiet before, sure, an' she broke out again worse than ever. . . . What was led that time?

PETER. Thray o' Hearts, Thray o' Hearts, Thray o' Hearts.

FLUTHER. It's damned hard lines to think of her dead-born kiddie lyin' there in th' arms o' poor little Mollser. Mollser snuffed it* sudden too, afther all.

THE COVEY. Sure she never got any care. How could she get it, an' th' mother out day an' night lookin' for work, an' her consumptive husband leavin' her with a baby to be born before he died!

VOICES IN A LILTING CHANT TO THE LEFT IN A DISTANT STREET. Red Cr. . .oss, Red Cr. . .oss! . . . Ambu. . .lance, Ambu. . .lance!

THE COVEY [*to* FLUTHER]. Your deal, Fluther.

FLUTHER [*shuffling and dealing the cards*]. It'll take a lot out o' Nora – if she'll ever be th' same.

THE COVEY. Th' docthor thinks she'll never be th' same; thinks she'll be a little touched here. [*He touches his forehead.*] She's ramblin' a lot; thinkin' she's out in th' counthry with Jack; or gettin' his dinner ready for him before he comes home; or yellin' for her kiddie. All that, though, might be th' chloroform she got. . . . I don't know what we'd have done only for oul' Bessie; up with her for th' past three nights, hand runnin'.*

FLUTHER. I always knew there was never anything really derogatory wrong with poor oul' Bessie. [*To* PETER, *who is taking a trick*] Ay, houl' on, there, don't be so damn quick – that's my thrick.

PETER. What' your thrick? It's my thrick, man.

FLUTHER [*loudly*]. How is it your thrick?

PETER [*answering as loudly*]. Didn't I lead th' deuce!

FLUTHER. You must be gettin' blind, man; don't you see th' ace?

BESSIE [*appearing at the door of room, left; in a tense whisper*]. D'ye want to waken her again on me, when she's just gone asleep? If she wakes will yous come an' mind her? If I hear a whisper out o' one o' yous again, I'll . . . gut yous!

THE COVEY [*in a whisper*]. S-s-s-h. She can hear anything above a whisper.

PETER [*looking up at the ceiling*]. Th' gentle an' merciful God'll give th' pair o' yous a scawldin' an' a scarifyin' one o' these days!

FLUTHER *takes a bottle of whiskey from his pocket, and takes a drink.*

THE COVEY [*to* FLUTHER]. Why don't you spread that out*, man, an' thry to keep a sup for tomorrow?

FLUTHER. Spread it out? Keep a sup for tomorrow? How th' hell does a fella know there'll be any tomorrow? If I'm goin' to be whipped away, let me be whipped away* when it's empty, an' not when it's half full! [*To* BESSIE, *who has seated herself in an armchair at the fire*] How is she, now, Bessie?

BESSIE. I left her sleeping quietly. When I'm listenin' to her babblin', I think she'll never be much betther than she is. Her eyes have a hauntin' way of lookin' in instead of lookin' out, as if her mind had been lost alive in madly minglin' memories of th' past. . . . [*Sleepily*] Crushin' her thoughts . . . together . . . in a fierce . . . an' fanciful . . . [*she nods her head and starts wakefully*] idea that dead things are livin', an' livin' things are dead. . . . [*With a start*] Was that a scream I heard her give? [*Reassured*] Blessed God, I think I hear her screamin' every minute! An' it's only there with me that I'm able to keep awake.

THE COVEY. She'll sleep, maybe, for a long time, now. Ten there.

FLUTHER. Ten here. If she gets a long sleep, she might be all right. Peter's th' lone five.

THE COVEY. Whisht! I think I hear somebody movin' below. Whoever it is, he's comin' up.

*A pause. Then the door opens and* CAPT. BRENNAN *comes into the room. He has changed his uniform for a suit of civvies.* *His eyes droop with the heaviness of exhaustion; his face is pallid and drawn. His clothes are dusty and stained here and there with mud. He leans heavily on the back of a chair as he stands.*

CAPT. BRENNAN. Mrs Clitheroe; where's Mrs Clitheroe? I was told I'd find her here.

BESSIE. What d'ye want with Mrs Clitheroe?

CAPT. BRENNAN. I've a message, a last message for her from her husband.

BESSIE. Killed! He's not killed, is he!

CAPT. BRENNAN [*sinking stiffly and painfully on to a chair*]. In th' Imperial Hotel;* we fought till th' place was in flames. He was shot through th' arm, an' then through th' lung. . . . I could do nothin' for him – only watch his breath comin' an' goin' in quick, jerky gasps, an' a tiny sthream o' blood thricklin' out of his mouth, down over his lower lip. . . . I said a prayer for th' dyin', an' twined his rosary beads around his fingers. . . . Then I had to leave him to save meself. . . . [*He shows some holes in his coat.*] Look at th' way a machine-gun tore at me coat, as I belted out o' the buildin' an' darted across th' sthreet for shelter. . . . An' then, I seen the Plough an' th' Stars fallin' like a shot as th' roof crashed in, an' where I'd left poor Jack was nothin' but a leppin' spout o' flame!

BESSIE [*with partly repressed vehemence*]. Ay, you left him! You twined his Rosary beads round his fingers, an' then you run like a hare to get out o' danger!

CAPT. BRENNAN. I took me chance as well as him. . . . He took it like a man. His last whisper was to 'Tell Nora to be brave; that I'm ready to meet my God, an' that I'm proud to die for Ireland.' An' when our General* heard it he said that 'Commandant Clitheroe's end was a gleam of glory.' Mrs Clitheroe's grief will be a joy when she realises that she has had a hero for a husband.

BESSIE. If you only seen her, you'd know to th' differ.

NORA *appears at door, left. She is clad only in her nightdress; her hair, uncared for some days, is hanging in disorder over her shoulders. Her pale face looks paler still because of a vivid red spot on the tip of each cheek. Her eyes are glimmering with the light of incipient insanity; her hands are nervously fiddling with her nightgown. She halts at the door for a moment, looks vacantly around the room, and then comes slowly in. The rest do not notice her till she speaks.*

NORA [*in a quiet and monotonous tone*]. No . . . Not there, Jack. . . . I can feel comfortable only in our own familiar place beneath th' bramble tree. . . . We must be walking for a long time; I feel very, very tired. . . . Have we to go farther, or have we passed it by? [*Passing her hand across her eyes*] Curious mist on my eyes. . . . Why don't you hold my hand, Jack. . . . [*Excitedly*] No, no, Jack, it's not. Can't you see it's a goldfinch. Look at th' black-satiny wings with th' gold bars, an' th' splash of crimson on its head. . . . [*Wearily*] Something ails me, something ails me. . . . Don't kiss me like that; you take my breath away, Jack. . . . Why do you frown at me? . . . You're going away, and [*frightened*] I can't follow you. Something's keeping me from moving. . . . [*crying out*] Jack, Jack, Jack!

BESSIE [*who has gone over and caught* NORA'*s arm*]. Now, Mrs Clitheroe, you're a terrible woman to get up out of bed. . . . You'll get cold if you stay here in them clothes.

NORA. Cold? I'm feelin' very cold; it's chilly out here in th' counthry. . . . [*Looking around frightened*] What place is this? Where am I?

BESSIE [*coaxingly*]. You're all right, Nora; you're with friends, an' in a safe place. Don't you know your uncle an' your cousin, an' poor oul' Fluther?

PETER [*about to go over to* NORA]. Nora, darlin', now –

FLUTHER [*pulling him back*]. Now, leave her to Bessie, man. A crowd 'll only make her worse.

NORA [*thoughtfully*]. There is something I want to remember, an' I can't. [*With agony*] I can't, I can't, I can't! My head, my head! [*Suddenly breaking from* BESSIE, *and running over to the men, and gripping* FLUTHER *by the shoulders*] Where is it? Where's my baby? Tell me where you've put it, where've you hidden it? My baby, my baby; I want my baby! My head, my poor head. . . . Oh, I can't tell what is wrong with me. [*Screaming*] Give him to me, give me my husband!

BESSIE. Blessin' o' God on us, isn't this pitiful!

NORA [*struggling with* BESSIE]. I won't go away for you; I won't. Not till you give me back my husband. [*Screaming*] Murderers, that's what yous are; murderers, murderers!

BESSIE. S-s-sh. We'll bring Mr Clitheroe back to you, if you'll only lie down an' stop quiet. . . . [*Trying to lead her in*] Come on, now, Nora, an' I'll sing something to you.

NORA. I feel as if my life was thryin' to force its way out of my body. . . . I can hardly breathe . . . I'm frightened, I'm frightened, I'm frightened! For God's sake, don't leave me, Bessie. Hold my hand, put your arms around me!

FLUTHER [*to* BRENNAN]. Now you can see th' way she is, man.

PETER. An' what way would she be if she heard Jack had gone west?

THE COVEY [*to* PETER]. Shut up, you, man!

BESSIE [*to* NORA]. We'll have to be brave, an' let patience clip away th' heaviness of th' slow-movin' hours, rememberin' that sorrow may

endure for th' night, but joy cometh in th' mornin'.* . . . Come on
in, an' I'll sing to you, an' you'll rest quietly.

NORA [*stopping suddenly on her way to the room*]. Jack an' me are goin'
out somewhere this evenin'. Where I can't tell. Isn't it curious I
can't remember. . . . Maura, Maura, Jack, if th' baby's a girl; any
name you like, if th' baby's a boy! . . . He's there. [*Screaming*] He's
there, an' they won't give him back to me!

BESSIE. S-ss-s-h, darlin', s-ssh. I won't sing to you, if you're not quiet.

NORA [*nervously holding* BESSIE]. Hold my hand, hold my hand, an'
sing to me, sing to me!

BESSIE. Come in an' lie down, an' I'll sing to you.

NORA [*vehemently*]. Sing to me, sing to me; sing, sing!

BESSIE [*singing as she leads* NORA *into room*].

> Lead, kindly light, amid th' encircling gloom,
>     Lead Thou me on;
> Th' night is dark an' I am far from home,
>     Lead Thou me on.
> Keep Thou my feet; I do not ask to see
> Th' distant scene – one step enough for me.
>
> So long that Thou hast blessed me, sure Thou still
>     Wilt lead me on;

[*They go in. Singing in room*]

> O'er moor an' fen, o'er crag an' torrent, till
>     Th' night is gone.
> An' in th' morn those angel faces smile
> That I have lov'd long since, an' lost awhile!*

THE COVEY [*to* BRENNAN]. Now that you've seen how bad she is, an'
that we daren't tell her what has happened till she's betther, you'd
best be slippin' back to where you come from.

CAPT. BRENNAN. There's no chance o' slippin' back now, for th'
military are everywhere: a fly couldn't get through. I'd never have
got here, only I managed to change me uniform for what I'm
wearin'. . . . I'll have to take me chance, an' thry to lie low here for
a while.

THE COVEY [*frightened*]. There's no place here to lie low. Th' Tommies
'll be hoppin' in here, any minute!

PETER [*aghast*]. An' then we'd all be shanghaied!

THE COVEY. Be God, there's enough afther happenin' to us!

FLUTHER [*warningly, as he listens*]. Whisht, whisht, th' whole
o' yous. I think I heard th' clang of a rifle butt on th' floor of th'
hall below. [*All alertness.*] Here, come on with th' cards again.
I'll deal. [*He shuffles and deals the cards to all.*] Clubs up. [*To*
BRENNAN] Thry to keep your hands from shakin', man. You lead,
Peter. [*As* PETER *throws out a card*] Four o' Hearts led.

*The door opens and* CORPORAL STODDART *of the Wiltshires enters in full
war kit; steel helmet, rifle and bayonet, and trench-tool.** He looks round
the room. A pause and a palpable silence.*

FLUTHER [*breaking the silence*]. Two tens an' a five.

CORPORAL STODDART. 'Ello. [*Indicating the coffin*] This the stiff?

THE COVEY. Yis.

CORPORAL STODDART. Who's gowing with it? Ownly one allowed to
gow with it, you know.

THE COVEY. I dunno.

CORPORAL STODDART. You dunnow?

THE COVEY. I dunno.

BESSIE [*coming into the room*]. She's afther slippin' off to sleep again,
thanks be to God. I'm hardly able to keep me own eyes open. [*To the
soldier*] Oh, are yous goin' to take away poor little Mollser?

CORPORAL STODDART. Ay; 'oo's agowing with 'er?

BESSIE. Oh, th' poor mother, o' course. God help her, it's a terrible
blow to her!

FLUTHER. A terrible blow? Sure, she's in her element now, woman,
mixin' earth to earth, an' ashes t'ashes an' dust to dust, an' revellin'
in plumes an' hearses, last days an' judgements!

BESSIE [*falling into chair by the fire*]. God bless us! I'm jaded!

CORPORAL STODDART. Was she plugged?

THE COVEY. Ah, no; died o' consumption.

CORPORAL STODDART. Ow, is that all? Thought she moight 'ave been
plugged.

THE COVEY. Is that all? Isn't it enough? D'ye know, comrade, that
more die o' consumption than are killed in th' wars? An' it's all
because of th' system we're livin' undher?

CORPORAL STODDART. Ow, I know. I'm a Sowcialist moiself, but I 'as to do my dooty.

THE COVEY [*ironically*]. Dooty! Th' only dooty of a Socialist is th' emancipation of th' workers.

CORPORAL STODDART. Ow, a man's a man, an 'e 'as to foight for 'is country, 'asn't 'e?

FLUTHER [*aggressively*]. You're not fightin' for your counthry here, are you?

PETER [*anxiously, to* FLUTHER]. Ay, ay, Fluther, none o' that, none o' that!

THE COVEY. Fight for your counthry! Did y'ever read, comrade, Jenersky's *Thesis on the Origin, Development, an' Consolidation of th' Evolutionary Idea of the Proletariat*?

CORPORAL STODDART. Ow, cheese it,* Paddy, cheese it!

BESSIE [*sleepily*]. How is things in th' town, Tommy?

CORPORAL STODDART. Ow, I fink it's nearly hover. We've got 'em surrounded, and we're clowsing in on the bloighters. Ow, it was only a little bit of a dawg-foight.

*The sharp ping of the sniper's rifle is heard, followed by a squeal of pain.*

VOICES TO THE LEFT IN A CHANT. Red Cr. . .oss, Red Cr. . .oss! Ambu. . .lance, Ambu. . .lance!

CORPORAL STODDART [*excitedly*]. Christ, that's another of our men 'it by that blawsted sniper! 'E's knocking abaht 'ere, somewheres. Gawd, when we get th' bloighter, we'll give 'im the cold steel, we will. We'll jab the belly aht of 'im, we will!

MRS GOGAN *comes in tearfully, and a little proud of the importance of being directly connected with death.*

MRS GOGAN [*to* FLUTHER]. I'll never forget what you done for me, Fluther, goin' around at th' risk of your life settlin' everything with th' undhertaker an' th' cemetery people. When all me own were afraid to put their noses out, you plunged like a good one through hummin' bullets, an' they knockin' fire out o' th' road, tinklin' through th' frightened windows, an' splashin' themselves to pieces on th' walls! An' you'll find, that Mollser, in th' happy place she's gone to, won't forget to whisper, now an' again, th' name o' Fluther.

CORPORAL STODDART. Git it aht, mother, git it aht.

BESSIE [*from the chair*]. It's excusin' me you'll be, Mrs Gogan, for not stannin' up, seein' I'm shaky on me feet for want of a little sleep, an' not desirin' to show any disrespect to poor little Mollser.

FLUTHER. Sure, we all know, Bessie, that it's vice versa with you.

MRS GOGAN [*to* BESSIE]. Indeed, it's meself that has well chronicled, Mrs Burgess, all your gentle hurryin's to me little Mollser, when she was alive, bringin' her somethin' to dhrink, or somethin' t'eat, an' never passin' her without liftin' up her heart with a delicate word o' kindness.

CORPORAL STODDART [*impatiently, but kindly*]. Git it aht, git it aht, mother.

THE COVEY, FLUTHER, BRENNAN, *and* PETER *carry out the coffin, followed by* MRS GOGAN.

CORPORAL STODDART [*to* BESSIE, *who is almost asleep*]. 'Ow many men is in this 'ere 'ouse? [*No answer. Loudly*] 'Ow many men is in this 'ere 'ouse?

BESSIE [*waking with a start*]. God, I was nearly asleep! . . . How many men? Didn't you see them?

CORPORAL STODDART. Are they all that are in the 'ouse?

BESSIE. Oh, there's none higher up, but there may be more lower down. Why?

CORPORAL STODDART. All men in the district 'as to be rounded up. Somebody's giving 'elp to the snipers, an' we 'as to take precautions. If I 'ad my woy, I'd make 'em all join hup,* and do their bit! But I suppowse they and you are all Shinners.*

BESSIE [*who has been sinking into sleep, waking up to a sleepy vehemence*]. Bessie Burgess is no Shinner, an' never had no thruck with anything spotted be th' fingers o' th' Fenians; but always made it her business to harness herself for Church whenever she knew that 'God Save the King' was goin' to be sung at t'end of th' service; whose only son went to th' front in th' first contingent of the Dublin Fusiliers, an' that's on his way home carryin' a shatthered arm that he got fightin' for his king an' counthry!

*Her head sinks slowly forward again.* PETER *comes into the room; his body is stiffened and his face is wearing a comically indignant look. He walks to and fro at the back of the room, evidently repressing a violent desire to speak angrily. He is followed in by* FLUTHER, THE COVEY, *and* BRENNAN, *who slinks into an obscure corner of the room, nervous of notice.*

FLUTHER [*after an embarrassing pause*]. Th' air in th' sthreet outside's shakin' with the firin' o' rifles an' machine-guns. It must be a hot shop* in th' middle o' th' scrap.

CORPORAL STODDART. We're pumping lead in on 'em from every side, now; they'll soon be shoving up th' white flag.

PETER [*with a shout*]. I'm tellin' you either o' yous two lowsers 'ud make a betther hearse-man than Peter; proddin' an' pokin' at me an' I helpin' to carry out a corpse!

FLUTHER. It wasn't a very derogatory thing for th' Covey to say that you'd make a fancy hearse-man,* was it?

PETER [*furiously*]. A pair o' redjesthered* bowseys pondherin' from mornin' till night on how they'll get a chance to break a gap through th' quiet nature of a man that's always endeavourin' to chase out of him any sthray thought of venom against his fella-man!

THE COVEY. Oh, shut it, shut it, shut it!

PETER. As long as I'm a livin' man, responsible for me thoughts, words, an' deeds to th' Man above,* I'll feel meself instituted to fight again' th' sliddherin'* ways of a pair o' picaroons,* whisperin', concurrin', concoctin', an' conspirin' together to rendher me unconscious of th' life I'm thryin' to live!

CORPORAL STODDART [*dumbfounded*]. What's wrong, Daddy; wot 'ave they done to you?

PETER [*savagely to the* CORPORAL]. You mind your own business! What's it got to do with you, what's wrong with me?

BESSIE [*in a sleepy murmur*]. Will yous thry to conthrol yourselves into quietness? Yous'll waken her . . . up . . . on . . . me . . . again. [*She sleeps.*]

FLUTHER. Come on, boys, to th' cards again, an' never mind him.

CORPORAL STODDART. No use of you gowing to start cawds; you'll be gowing out of 'ere, soon as Sergeant comes.

FLUTHER. Goin' out o' here? An' why're we goin' out o' here?

CORPORAL STODDART. All men in district to be rounded up, and 'eld in till the scrap is hover.

FLUTHER. An' where're we goin' to be held in?

CORPORAL STODDART. They're puttin' 'em in a church.

THE COVEY. A church?

FLUTHER. What sort of a church? Is it a Protestan' Church?

CORPORAL STODDART. I dunnow; I suppowse so.

FLUTHER [*dismayed*]. Be God, it'll be a nice thing to be stuck all night in a Protestan' Church!

CORPORAL STODDART. Bring the cawds; you moight get a chance of a goime.

FLUTHER. Ah, no, that wouldn't do. . . . I wondher? [*After a moment's thought*] Ah, I don't think we'd be doin' anything derogatory be playin' cards in a Protestan' Church.

CORPORAL STODDART. If I was you I'd bring a little snack with me; you moight be glad of it before the mawning. [*Sings*]

> I do loike a snoice mince poy,
> I do loike a snoice mince poy!

*The snap of the sniper's rifle rings out again, followed simultaneously by a scream of pain.* CORPORAL STODDART *goes pale, and brings his rifle to the ready, listening.*

VOICES CHANTING TO THE RIGHT. Red Cro. . .ss, Red Cro. . .ss! Ambu. . .lance, Ambu. . .lance!

SERGEANT TINLEY *comes rapidly in, pale, agitated, and fiercely angry.*

CORPORAL STODDART [*to* SERGEANT]. One of hour men 'it, Sergeant?

SERGEANT TINLEY. Private Taylor; got 'it roight through the chest, 'e did; an 'ole in front of 'im as 'ow you could put your fist through, and 'arf 'is back blown awoy! Dum-dum bullets they're using. Gang of Hassassins potting at us from behind roofs. That's not playing the goime: why down't they come into the owpen and foight fair!

FLUTHER [*unable to stand the slight*]. Fight fair! A few hundhred scrawls o' chaps* with a couple o' guns an' rosary beads, again' a hundhred thousand thrained men with horse, fut, an' artillery . . . an' he wants us to fight fair! [*To* SERGEANT] D'ye want us to come out in our skins an' throw stones?

SERGEANT TINLEY [*to* CORPORAL]. Are these four all that are 'ere?

CORPORAL STODDART. Four; that's all, Sergeant.

SERGEANT TINLEY [*vindictively*]. Come on, then; get the blighters aht. [*To the men*]. 'Ere, 'op it aht! Aht into the streets with you, and if a

snoiper sends another of our men west, you gow with 'im! [*He
catches* FLUTHER *by the shoulder*] Gow on, git aht!

FLUTHER. Eh, who are you chuckin', eh?

SERGEANT TINLEY [*roughly*]. Gow on, git aht, you blighter.

FLUTHER. Who are you callin' a blighter to, eh? I'm a Dublin man,
born an' bred in th' city, see?

SERGEANT TINLEY. I down't care if you were Broin Buroo; git aht, git
aht.

FLUTHER [*halting as he is going out*]. Jasus, you an' your guns! Leave
them down, an' I'd beat th' two o' yous without sweatin'!

PETER, BRENNAN, THE COVEY, *and* FLUTHER, *followed by the soldiers, go
out.* BESSIE *is sleeping heavily on the chair by the fire. After a pause,* NORA
*appears at door, left, in her nightdress. Remaining at door for a few
moments she looks vaguely around the room. She then comes in quietly, goes
over to the fire, pokes it, and puts the kettle on. She thinks for a few
moments, pressing her hand to her forehead. She looks questioningly at the
fire, and then at the press at back. She goes to the press, opens it, takes out a
soiled cloth and spreads it on the table. She then places things for tea on the
table.*

NORA. I imagine th' room looks very odd somehow. . . . I was nearly
forgetting Jack's tea. . . . Ah, I think I'll have everything done
before he gets in. . . . [*She lilts gently, as she arranges the table*]

> Th' violets were scenting th' woods, Nora,
>    Displaying their charms to th' bee,
> When I first said I lov'd only you, Nora,
>    An' you said you lov'd only me.

> Th' chestnut blooms gleam'd through th' glade, Nora,
>    A robin sang loud from a tree,
> When I first said I lov'd only you, Nora,
>    An' you said you lov'd only me.

[*She pauses suddenly, and glances round the room.*]

NORA [*doubtfully*]. I can't help feelin' this room very strange. . . .
What is it? . . . What is it? . . . I must think . . . I must thry to
remember. . . .

VOICES CHANTING IN A DISTANT STREET. Ambu. . .lance, Ambu. . .lance! Red Cro. . .ss, Red Cro. . .ss!

NORA [*startled and listening for a moment, then resuming the arrangement of the table*].

> Trees, birds, an' bees sang a song, Nora,
> Of happier transports to be,
> When I first said I lov'd only you, Nora,
> An' you said you lov'd only me.

*A burst of rifle fire is heard in a street near by, followed by the rapid rok, tok, tok of a machine-gun.*

NORA [*staring in front of her and screaming*]. Jack, Jack, Jack! My baby, my baby, my baby!

BESSIE [*waking with a start*]. You divil, are you afther gettin' out o' bed again! [*She rises and runs towards* NORA, *who rushes to the window, which she frantically opens.*]

NORA [*at window, screaming*]. Jack, Jack, for God's sake, come to me!

SOLDIERS [*outside, shouting*]. Git away, git away from that window, there!

BESSIE [*seizing hold of* NORA]. Come away, come away, woman, from that window!

NORA [*struggling with* BESSIE]. Where is it; where have you hidden it? Oh, Jack, Jack, where are you?

BESSIE [*imploringly*]. Mrs Clitheroe, for God's sake, come away!

NORA [*fiercely*]. I won't; he's below. Let . . . me . . . go! You're thryin' to keep me from me husband. I'll follow him. Jack, Jack, come to your Nora!

BESSIE. Hus-s-sh, Nora, Nora! He'll be here in a minute. I'll bring him to you, if you'll only be quiet – honest to God, I will.

*With a great effort* BESSIE *pushes* NORA *away from the window, the force used causing her to stagger against it herself. Two rifle shots ring out in quick succession.* BESSIE *jerks her body convulsively; stands stiffly for a moment, a look of agonised astonishment on her face, then she staggers forward, leaning heavily on the table with her hands.*

BESSIE [*with an arrested scream of fear and pain*]. Merciful God, I'm shot, I'm shot, I'm shot! . . . Th' life's pourin' out o' me! [*To* NORA]

I've got this through . . . through you . . . through you, you bitch,
you! . . . O God, have mercy on me! . . . [*To* NORA] You wouldn't
stop quiet, no, you wouldn't, you wouldn't, blast you! Look at
what I'm afther gettin', look at what I'm afther gettin' . . . I'm
bleedin' to death, an' no one's here to stop th' flowin' blood!
[*Calling*] Mrs Gogan, Mrs Gogan! Fluther, Fluther, for God's sake,
somebody, a doctor, a doctor!

*She staggers frightened towards the door, to seek for aid, but, weakening
half-way across the room, she sinks to her knees, and bending forward,
supports herself with her hands resting on the floor.* NORA *is standing rigidly
with her back to the wall opposite, her trembling hands held out a little from
the sides of her body, her lips quivering, her breast heaving, staring wildly
at the figure of* BESSIE.

NORA [*in a breathless whisper*]. Jack, I'm frightened. . . . I'm frightened, Jack. . . . Oh, Jack, where are you?
BESSIE [*moaning*]. This is what's afther comin' on me for nursin' you
day an' night. . . . I was a fool, a fool, a fool! Get me a dhrink o'
wather, you jade, will you? There's a fire burnin' in me blood!
[*Pleadingly*] Nora, Nora, dear, for God's sake, run out an' get Mrs
Gogan, or Fluther, or somebody to bring a doctor, quick, quick,
quick! [*As* NORA *does not stir*] Blast you, stir yourself, before I'm
gone!
NORA. Oh, Jack, Jack, where are you?
BESSIE [*in a whispered moan*]. Jesus Christ, me sight's goin'! It's all
dark, dark! Nora, hold me hand! [BESSIE's *body lists over and she
sinks into a prostrate position on the floor.*] I'm dyin', I'm dyin' . . . I
feel it. . . . Oh God, oh God! [*She feebly sings*]

> I do believe, I will believe
>     That Jesus died for me;
> That on th' cross He shed His blood,
>     From sin to set me free. . . .
>
> I do believe . . . I will believe
>     . . . Jesus died . . . me;
> . . . th' cross He shed . . . blood,
>     From sin . . . free.

*She ceases singing, and lies stretched out, still and very rigid. A pause. Then* MRS GOGAN *runs hastily in.*

MRS GOGAN [*quivering with fright*]. Blessed be God, what's afther happenin'? [*To* NORA] What's wrong, child, what's wrong? [*She sees* BESSIE, *runs to her and bends over the body.*] Bessie, Bessie! [*She shakes the body*] Mrs Burgess, Mrs Burgess! [*She feels* BESSIE's *forehead.*] My God, she's as cold as death. They're afther murdherin' th' poor inoffensive woman!

SERGEANT TINLEY *and* CORPORAL STODDART *enter agitatedly, their rifles at the ready.*

SERGEANT TINLEY [*excitedly*]. This is the 'ouse. That's the window!
NORA [*pressing back against the wall*]. Hide it, hide it; cover it up, cover it up!
SERGEANT TINLEY [*going over to the body*]. 'Ere, what's this? Who's this? [*Looking at* BESSIE] Oh Gawd, we've plugged one of the women of the 'ouse.
CORPORAL STODDART. Whoy the 'ell did she gow to the window? Is she dead?
SERGEANT TINLEY. Oh, dead as bedamned. Well, we couldn't afford to toike any chawnces.
NORA [*screaming*]. Hide it, hide it; don't let me see it! Take me away, take me away, Mrs Gogan!

MRS GOGAN *runs into room, left, and runs out again with a sheet which she spreads over the body of* BESSIE.

MRS GOGAN [*as she spreads the sheet*]. Oh, God help her, th' pooor woman, she's stiffenin' out as hard as she can! Her face has written on it th' shock o' sudden agony, an' her hands is whitenin' into th' smooth shininess of wax.
NORA [*whimperingly*]. Take me away, take me away; don't leave me here to be lookin' an' lookin' at it!
MRS GOGAN [*going over to* NORA *and putting her arm around her*]. Come on with me, dear, an' you can doss in poor Mollser's bed, till we gather some neighbours to come an' give th' last friendly touches to Bessie in th' lonely layin' of her out. [MRS GOGAN *and* NORA *go slowly out.*]

CORPORAL STODDART [*who has been looking around, to* SERGEANT TINLEY]. Tea here, Sergeant. Wot abaht a cup of scald?*

SERGEANT TINLEY. Pour it aht, Stoddart, pour it aht. I could scoff* anything just now.

CORPORAL STODDART *pours out two cups of tea, and the two soldiers begin to drink. In the distance is heard a bitter burst of rifle and machine-gun fire, interspersed with the boom, boom of artillery. The glare in the sky seen through the window flares into a fuller and a deeper red.*

SERGEANT TINLEY. There gows the general attack on the Powst Office.

VOICES IN A DISTANT STREET. Ambu. . .lance, Ambu. . .lance! Red Cro. . .ss, Red Cro. . .ss!

*The voices of soldiers at a barricade outside the house are heard singing*

> They were summoned from the 'illside,
> They were called in from the glen,
> And the country found 'em ready
> At the stirring call for men.
> Let not tears add to their 'ardship,
> As the soldiers pass along,
> And although our 'eart is breaking,
> Make it sing this cheery song.

SERGEANT TINLEY AND CORPORAL STODDART [*joining in the chorus, as they sip the tea*]

> Keep the 'owme fires burning,
> While your 'earts are yearning;
> Though your lads are far away
> They dream of 'owme;
> There's a silver loining
> Through the dark cloud shoining,
> Turn the dark cloud inside out,
> Till the boys come 'owme!*

CURTAIN

# The Silver Tassie

## A Tragi-Comedy in Four Acts

## (Stage Version)

*To Eileen*
*with the yellow daffodils*
*in the green vase*

# CHARACTERS
(in order of appearance)

SYLVESTER HEEGAN
MRS HEEGAN, his wife
SIMON NORTON
SUSIE MONICAN
MRS FORAN
TEDDY FORAN, her husband
HARRY HEEGAN, DCM, Heegan's son
JESSIE TAITE
BARNEY BAGNAL
THE CROUCHER
1ST SOLDIER
2ND SOLDIER
3RD SOLDIER
4TH SOLDIER
THE CORPORAL
THE VISITOR
THE STAFF-WALLAH
1ST STRETCHER-BEARER
2ND STRETCHER-BEARER
3RD STRETCHER-BEARER
1ST CASUALTY
2ND CASUALTY
SURGEON FORBY MAXWELL
THE SISTER OF THE WARD

# PLACE AND TIME

*Act I*. Room in Heegan's home.
*Act II*. Somewhere in France (later on).
*Act III*. Ward in a Hospital (a little later on).
*Act IV*. Room in Premises of Avondale Football Club (later on still).

NOTES*

The Croucher's make-up should come as close as possible to a death's head, a skull; and his hands should show like those of a skeleton's. He should sit somewhere *above* the group of soldiers; preferably to one side, on the left, from viewpoint of audience, so as to overlook the soldiers. He should look languid, as if very tired of life.

The group of soldiers – Act II – should enter in a close mass, as if each was keeping the other from falling, utterly weary and tired out. They should appear as if they were almost locked together.

The soldiers' last response to the Staff-Wallah's declaration, namely, 'To the Guns!' should have in these three words the last high notes of 'The Last Post'.

The song sung at the end of the play should be given to the best two (or one) singers in the cast. If, on the other hand, there be no passable singer among the players, the song should be omitted.

Perhaps a more suitable spiritual than 'Sweet Chariot' would be chosen for Harry to sing. For instance, 'Keep Inchin' Along', or 'Keep Me from Sinkin' Down'.

The chants in the play are simple Plain Song. The first chant is given in full as an example of the way in which they are sung. In the others, the dots . . . indicate that the note preceding them should be sustained till the music indicates a change. There are three parts in each chant: the Intonation; the Meditation; and the Ending. After a little practice, they will be found to be easy to sing. The soldiers having the better voices should be selected to intone the chants, irrespective of the numbers allotted to them as characters in the book of the play.

## ACT I

*The eating, sitting, and part sleeping room of the* HEEGAN *family. A large window at back looks on to a quay, from which can be seen the centre mast of a steamer, at the top of which gleams a white light. Another window at right looks down on a side street. Under the window at back, plumb in the centre, is a stand, the legs gilded silver and the top gilded gold; on the stand is a purple velvet shield on which are pinned a number of silver medals surrounding a few gold ones. On each side of the shield is a small vase holding a bunch of artificial flowers. The shield is draped with red and yellow ribbons. To the left of the stand is a bed covered with a bedspread of black striped with vivid green. To the right of the stand is a dresser and chest of drawers combined. The fireplace is to the left. Beside the fireplace is a door leading to a bedroom, another door which gives access to the rest of the house and the street, on the right. At the corner left is a red-coloured stand resembling an easel, having on it a silver-gilt framed picture photograph of* HARRY HEEGAN *in football dress, crimson jersey with yellow collar and cuffs and a broad yellow belt, black stockings, and yellow football boots. A table on which are a half-pint bottle of whisky, a large parcel of bread and meat sandwiches, and some copies of English illustrated magazines.*

SYLVESTER HEEGAN *and* SIMON NORTON *are sitting by the fire.* SYLVESTER HEEGAN *is a stockily built man of sixty-five; he has been a docker all his life since first the muscles of his arms could safely grip a truck, and even at sixty-five the steel in them is only beginning to stiffen.*

SIMON NORTON *is a tall man, originally a docker too, but by a little additional steadiness, a minor effort towards self-education, a natural, but very slight superior nimbleness of mind, has risen in the Company's estimation and has been given the position of checker, a job entailing as many hours of work as a docker, almost as much danger, twice as much responsibility, and a corresponding reduction in his earning powers. He is not so warmly, but a little more circumspectly dressed than* SYLVESTER, *and in his manner of conduct and speech there is a hesitant suggestion of greater refinement than in those of* SYLVESTER, *and a still more vague indication that he is aware of it. This timid semi-conscious sense of superiority, which* SIMON *sometimes forgets, is shown frequently by a complacent stroking of a dark beard which years are beginning to humiliate. The night is cold, and* SIMON *and* SYLVESTER *occasionally stretch longingly towards the fire. They are fully dressed and each has his topcoat and hat beside him, as if ready to go out at a moment's notice.* SUSIE MONICAN *is standing at the table polishing a Lee-Enfield rifle with a chamois cloth; the butt of the rifle is* resting on the table. *She is a girl of twenty-two, well-shaped limbs, challenging breasts, all of which are defiantly hidden by a rather long dark blue skirt and bodice buttoning up to the throat, relieved by a crimson scarf around her neck, knotted in front and falling down her bosom like a man's tie. She is undeniably pretty, but her charms are almost completely hidden by her sombre, ill-fitting dress, and the rigid manner in which she has made her hair up declares her unflinching and uncompromising modesty. Just now she is standing motionless, listening intently, looking towards the door on right.*

MRS HEEGAN *is standing at the window at right, listening too, one hand pulling back the curtain, but her attention, taken from the window, is attracted to the door. She is older than* SYLVESTER, *stiffened with age and rheumatism; the end of her life is unknowingly lumbering towards a rest: the impetus necessity has given to continual toil and striving is beginning to slow down, and everything she has to do is done with a quiet mechanical persistence. Her inner ear cannot hear even a faint echo of a younger day. Neither* SYLVESTER *nor* SIMON *has noticed the attentive attitude of* MRS HEEGAN *or* SUSIE, *for* SYLVESTER, *with one arm outstretched crooked at the elbow, is talking with subdued intensity to* SIMON.

SYLVESTER. I seen him do it, mind you. I seen him do it.
SIMON. I quite believe you, Sylvester.
SYLVESTER. Break a chain across his bisseps! [*With a pantomime action*] Fixes it over his arm . . . bends it up . . . a little strain . . . snaps in two . . . right across his bisseps!
SUSIE. Shush you, there!

MRS HEEGAN *goes out with troubled steps by door. The rest remain still for a few moments.*

SYLVESTER. A false alarm.
SIMON. No cause for undue anxiety; there's plenty of time yet.
SUSIE [*chanting as she resumes the polishing of rifle*].

> Man walketh in a vain shadow, and disquieteth himself
>    in vain:
> He heapeth up riches, and cannot tell who shall gather
>    them.*

[*She sends the chant in the direction of* SYLVESTER *and* SIMON, SUSIE *coming close to the two men and sticking an angry face in between them.*]
When the two of yous standin quiverin' together on the dhread day of the Last Judgement, how will the two of yous feel if yous have nothin' to say but 'he broke a chain across his bisseps'? Then the two of you'll know that the wicked go down into hell, an' all the people who forget God!* [*She listens a moment, and leaving down the rifle, goes out by door left.*]

SYLVESTER. It's persecutin', that tambourine theology of Susie's. I always get a curious, sickenin' feelin', Simon, when I hear the Name of the Supreme Bein' tossed into the quietness of a sensible conversation.

SIMON. The day he won the Cross Country Championship of County Dublin, Syl, was a day to be chronicled.

SYLVESTER. In a minor way, yes, Simon. But the day that caps the chronicle was the one when he punched the fear of God into the heart of Police Constable 63 C under the stars of a frosty night on the way home from Terenure.

SIMON. Without any exaggeration, without any exaggeration, mind you, Sylvester, that could be called a memorable experience.

SYLVESTER. I can see him yet [*he gets up, slides from side to side, dodging and parrying imaginary blows*] glidin' round the dazzled Bobby, cross-ey'd tryin' to watch him.

SIMON [*tapping his pipe resolutely on the hob*]. Unperturbed, mind you, all the time.

SYLVESTER. An' the hedges by the road-side standin' stiff in the silent cold of the air, the frost beads on the branches glistenin' like toss'd-down diamonds from the breasts of the stars, the quietness of the night stimulated to a fuller stillness by the mockin' breathin' of Harry, an' the heavy, ragin' pantin' of the Bobby, an' the quickenin' beats of our own hearts afraid, of hopin' too little or hopin' too much. [*During the last speech by* SYLVESTER, SUSIE *has come in with a bayonet, and has commenced to polish it.*

SUSIE. We don't go down on our knees often enough; that's why we're not able to stand up to the Evil One: we don't go down on our knees enough. . . . I can hear some persons fallin' with a splash of sparks into the lake of everlastin' fire. . . . An account of every idle word shall be given at the last day.* [*She goes out again with rifle. Bending towards* SIMON *and* SYLVESTER *as she goes*]. God is listenin' to yous; God is listenin' to yous!

SYLVESTER. Dtch, dtch, dtch. People ought to be forcibly restrained from constantly cannonadin' you with the name of the Deity.

SIMON. Dubiety never brush'd a thought into my mind, Syl, while I was waitin' for the moment when Harry would stretch the Bobby hors dee combaa on the ground.

SYLVESTER [*resuming his pantomime actions*]. There he was staggerin', beatin' out blindly, every spark of energy panted out of him, while Harry feinted, dodg'd, side-stepp'd, then suddenly sail'd in an' put him asleep with . . .

SIMON. A right-handed hook to the jaw! ⎫
SYLVESTER. A left-handed hook to the jaw! ⎬ [*Together.*]

SYLVESTER [*after a pause*]. A left-handed hook to the jaw, Simon.

SIMON. No, no, Syl, a right-handed hook to the jaw.

MRS FORAN *runs quickly in by the door with a frying-pan in her hand, on which is a steak. She comes to the fire, pushing, so as to disturb the two men. She is one of the many gay, careworn women of the working-class.*

MRS FORAN [*rapidly*]. A pot of clothes is boilin' on the fire above, an' I knew yous wouldn't mind me slappin' a bit of a steak on here for a second to show him, when he comes in before he goes away, that we're mindful of his needs, an' I'm hopeful of a dream tonight that the sea's between us, not lookin' very haggard in the mornin' to find the dream a true one. [*With satisfied anticipation*]

> For I'll be single again, yes, I'll be single again;
> An' I eats what I likes, . . . an' I drinks what I likes,
> An' I likes what I likes, when I'm –

[*Stopping suddenly*] What's the silence for?

SYLVESTER [*slowly and decidedly*]. I was at the fight, Simon, an' I seen him givin' a left-handed hook to the jaw.

MRS FORAN. What fight?

SIMON [*slowly and decidedly*]. I was there too, an' I saw him down the Bobby with a right-handed hook to the jaw.

MRS FORAN. What Bobby?

SYLVESTER. It was a close up, an' I don't know who'd know better if it wasn't the boy's own father.

MRS FORAN. What boy . . . what father?

SYLVESTER. Oh, shut up, woman, an' don't be smotherin' us with a shower of questions.

SUSIE [*who has entered on the last speech, and has started to polish a soldier's steel helmet*]. Oh, the miserableness of them that don't know the things that belong unto their peace. They try one thing after another, they try everything, but they never think of trying God. [*Coming nearer to them.*] Oh, the happiness of knowing that God's hand has pick'd you out for heaven. [*To* MRS FORAN] What's the honey-pot kiss of a lover to the kiss of righteousness and peace?

MRS FORAN, *embarrassed, goes over to window.*

SUSIE [*turning to* SIMON]. Simon, will you not close the dandy door of the public house and let the angels open the pearly gates of heaven for you?

SYLVESTER. We feel very comfortable where we are, Susie.

SUSIE. Don't mock, Sylvester, don't mock. You'd run before a great wind, tremble in an earthquake, and flee from a fire; so don't treat lightly the still, small voice calling you to repentance and faith.*

SYLVESTER [*with appeal and irritation*]. Oh, do give over worryin' a man, Susie.

SUSIE. God shows His love by worrying, and worrying, and worrying the sinner. The day will come when you will call on the mountains to cover you,* and then you'll weep and gnash your teeth that you did not hearken to Susie's warning. [*Putting her hands appealingly on his shoulders*] Sylvester, if you pray long enough and hard enough, and deep enough, you'll get the power to fight and conquer Beelzebub.

MRS FORAN. I'll be in a doxological mood tonight, not because the kingdom of heaven'll be near me, but because my husband'll be far away, and tomorrow [*singing*]

> I'll be single again, yes, single again;
> An' I goes where I likes, an' I does what I likes,
> An' I likes what I likes now I'm single again!

SIMON. Go on getting Harry's things ready, Susie, and defer the dosing of your friends with canticles till the time is ripe with rest for them to listen quietly.

SIMON *and* SYLVESTER *are very self-conscious during* SUSIE's *talk to them.* SIMON *empties his pipe by tapping the head on the hob of the grate. He then blows through it. As he is blowing through it,* SYLVESTER *is emptying his by tapping it on the hob; as he is blowing it* SIMON *taps his again; as* SIMON *taps* SYLVESTER *taps with him, and then they look into the heads of the pipes and blow together.*

SUSIE. It must be mercy or it must be judgement: if not mercy today it may be judgement tomorrow. He is never tired of waiting and waiting and waiting; and watching and watching and watching; and knocking and knocking and knocking for the sinner – you, Sylvester, and you, Simon – to turn from his wickedness and live.* Oh, if the two of you only knew what it was to live! Not to live leg-staggering an' belly-creeping among the pain-spotted and sin-splashed desires of the flesh; but to live, oh, to live swift-flying from a holy peace to a holy strength, and from holy strength to a holy joy, like the flashing flights of a swallow in the deep beauty of a summer sky.

SIMON *and* SYLVESTER *shift about, self-conscious and uneasy.*

SUSIE [*placing her hand first on* SIMON's *shoulder and then on* SYLVESTER's]. The two of you God's elegant swallows; a saved pair, a loving pair strong-wing'd, freed from the gin of the snarer, tip of wing to tip of wing, flying fast or darting swift together to the kingdom of heaven.

SIMON [*expressing a protecting thought to* SYLVESTER]. One of the two of us should go out and hunt back the old woman from the perishing cold of watching for the return of Harry.

SYLVESTER. She'll be as cold as a naked corpse, an' unstinted watchin' won't bring Harry back a minute sooner. I'll go an' drive her back. [*He rises to go.*] I'll be back in a minute, Susie.

SIMON [*hurriedly*]. Don't bother, Syl, I'll go; she won't be farther than the corner of the street; you go on toasting yourself where you are. [*He rises.*] I'll be back in a minute, Susie.

MRS FORAN [*running to the door*]. Rest easy the two of you, an' I'll go, so as to give Susie full time to take the sin out of your bones an' put you both in first-class form for the kingdom of heaven. [*She goes out.*]

SUSIE. Sinners that jeer often add to the glory of God: going out, she gives you, Sylvester, and you, Simon, another few moments, precious moments – oh, how precious, for once gone, they are gone for ever – to listen to the warning from heaven.

SIMON [*suddenly*]. Whisht, here's somebody coming, I think?

SYLVESTER. I'll back this is Harry comin' at last. [*A pause as the three listen.*] No, it's nobody.

SIMON. Whoever it was 's gone by.

SUSIE. Oh, Syl, oh, Simon, don't try to veil the face of God with an evasion. You can't, you can't cod God. This may be your last chance before the pains of hell encompass the two of you. Hope is passing by; salvation is passing by, and glory arm-in-arm with her. In the quietness left to you go down on your knees and pray that they come into your hearts and abide with you for ever. . . . [*With fervour, placing her left hand on* SIMON'*s shoulder and her right hand on* SYLVESTER'*s, and shaking them*] Get down on your knees, get down on your knees, get down on your knees and pray for conviction of sin, lest your portion in David become as the portion of the Canaanites, the Amorites, the Perizzites, and the Jebusites!

SYLVESTER. Eh, eh, Susie; cautious now – you seem to be forgettin' yourself.

SIMON. Desist, Susie, desist. Violence won't gather people to God. It only ingenders hostility to what you're trying to do.

SYLVESTER. You can't batter religion into a man like that.

SIMON. Religion is love, but that sort of thing is simply a nullification of religion.

SUSIE. Bitterness and wrath in exhortation is the only hope of rousing the pair of yous into a sense of coming and everlasting penalties.

SYLVESTER. Well, give it a miss, give it a miss to me now. Don't try to claw me into the kingdom of heaven. An' you only succeed in distempering piety when you try to mangle it into a man's emotions.

SIMON. Heaven is all the better, Susie, for being a long way off.

SYLVESTER. If I want to pray I do it voluntarily, but I'm not going to be goaded an' goaded into it.

SUSIE. I go away in a few days to help to nurse the wounded, an' God's merciful warnings may depart along with me, then sin'll usher the two of you into Gehenna for all eternity. Oh, if the two of you could only grasp the meaning of the word eternity! [*Bending down and looking up into their faces*] Time that had no beginning and never can have an end – an' there you'll be – two cockatrices creeping together, a desolation, an astonishment, a curse and a hissing from everlasting to everlasting. [*She goes into room.*]

SYLVESTER. Cheerful, what! Cockatrices – be-God, that's a good one, Simon!

SIMON. Always a trying thing to have to listen to one that's trying to push the kingdom of God into a reservation of a few yards.

SYLVESTER. A cockatrice! Now where did she manage to pick up that term of approbation, I wonder?

SIMON. From the Bible. An animal somewhere mentioned in the Bible, I think, that a serpent hatched out of a cock's egg.*

SYLVESTER. A cock's egg! It couldn't have been the egg of an ordinary cock. Not the male of what we call a hen?

SIMON. I think so.

SYLVESTER. Well, be-God, that's a good one! You know Susie'll have to be told to disintensify her soul-huntin', for religion even isn't an excuse for saying that a man'll become a cockatrice.

SIMON. In a church, somehow or other, it seems natural enough, and even in the street it's all right, for one thing is as good as another in the wide-open ear of the air, but in the delicate quietness of your own home it, it –

SYLVESTER. Jars on you!

SIMON. Exactly!

SYLVESTER. If she'd only confine her glory-to-God business to the festivals, Christmas, now, or even Easter, Simon, it would be recommendable; for a few days before Christmas, like the quiet raisin' of a curtain, an' a few days after, like the gentle lowerin' of one, there's nothing more . . . more –

SIMON. Appropriate . . .

SYLVESTER. Exhilaratin' than the singin' of the 'Adestay Fidellis'.*

SIMON. She's damned pretty, an' if she dressed herself justly, she'd lift some man's heart up, an' toss down many another. It's a mystery now, what affliction causes the disablement, for most women of that kind are plain, an' when a woman's born plain she's born good. I wonder what caused the peculiar bend in Susie's nature? Narrow your imagination to the limit and you couldn't call it an avocation.

SYLVESTER [*giving the head of his pipe a sharp, quick blow on the palm of his hand to clear it*]. Adoration.

SIMON. What?

SYLVESTER. Adoration, Simon, accordin' to the flesh . . . She fancied Harry and Harry fancied Jessie, so she hides her rage an' loss in the love of a scorchin' Gospel.

SIMON. Strange, strange.

SYLVESTER. Oh, very curious, Simon.

SIMON. It's a problem, I suppose.

SYLVESTER. An inconsolable problem, Simon.

MRS FORAN *enters by door, helping in* MRS HEEGAN, *who is pale and shivering with cold.*

MRS HEEGAN [*shivering and shuddering*]. U-u-uh, I feel the stream of blood that's still trickling through me old veins icifyin' fast; u-uh.

MRS FORAN. Madwoman, dear, to be waitin' out there on the quay an' a wind risin' as cold as a stepmother's breath, piercin' through your old bones, mockin' any effort a body would make to keep warm, an' [*suddenly rushing over to the fireplace in an agony of dismay, scattering* SIMON *and* SYLVESTER, *and whipping the frying-pan off the fire*] – The steak, the steak; I forgot the blasted steak an' onions fryin' on the fire! God Almighty, there's not as much as a bead of juice left in either of them. The scent of the burnin' would penetrate to the street, an' not one of you'd stir a hand to lift them out of danger. Oh, look at the condition they're in. Even the gospel-gunner couldn't do a little target practice by helpin' the necessity of a neighbour. [*As she goes out*] I can hear the love for your neighbours almost fizzlin' in your hearts.

MRS HEEGAN [*pushing in to the fire, to* SIMON *and* SYLVESTER]. Push to the right and push to the left till I get to the fosterin' fire. Time eatin' his heart out, an' no sign of him yet. The two of them, the two of my legs is numb . . . an' the wind's risin' that'll make the sea heave an' sink under the boat tonight, under shaded lights an' the submarines about. [SUSIE *comes in, goes over to window, and looks out.*] Hours ago the football match must have been over, an' no word of him yet, an' all drinkin' if they won, an' all drinkin' if they lost; with Jessie hitchin' on him, an' no one thinkin' of me an' the maintenance money.

SYLVESTER. He'll come back in time; he'll have to come back; he must come back.

SIMON. He got the goals, Mrs Heegan, that won the last two finals, and it's only fair he'd want to win this, which'll mean that the Cup won before two –

SYLVESTER [*butting in*]. Times hand runnin'.

SIMON. Two times consecutively before, makin' the Cup the property of the Club.

SYLVESTER. Exactly!

MRS HEEGAN. The chill's residin' in my bones, an' feelin's left me just the strength to shiver. He's overstayed his leave a lot, an' if he misses now the tide that's waitin', he skulks behind desertion from the colours.

SUSIE. On Active Service that means death at dawn.

MRS HEEGAN. An' my governmental money grant would stop at once.

SUSIE. That would gratify Miss Jessie Taite, because you put her weddin' off with Harry till after the duration of the war, an' cut her out of the allowance.

SYLVESTER [*with a sickened look at* SIMON]. Dtch, Dtch, dtch, the way the women nag the worst things out of happenings! [*To the women*] My God Almighty, he'll be back in time an' fill yous all with disappointment.

MRS HEEGAN. She's coinin' money workin' at munitions, an' doesn't need to eye the little that we get from Harry; for one evening hurryin' with him to the pictures she left her bag behind, an goin' through it what would you think I found?

SUSIE. A saucy book, now, or a naughty picture?

MRS HEEGAN. Lion and Unicorn standin' on their Jew ay mon draw.* With all the rings an' dates, an' rules an' regulations.

SIMON. What was it, Mrs Heegan?

MRS HEEGAN. Spaced an' lined; signed an' signatured; nestlin' in a blue envelope to keep it warm.

SYLVESTER [*testily*]. Oh, sing it out, woman, an' don't be takin' the value out of what you're goin' to tell us.

MRS HEEGAN. A Post Office Savings Bank Book.

SYLVESTER. Oh, hairy enough, eh?

SIMON. How much, Mrs Heegan?

MRS HEEGAN. Pounds an' shillings with the pence missin'; backed by secrecy, an' security guaranteed by Act of Parliament.

SYLVESTER [*impatiently*]. Dtch, dtch. Yes, yes, woman, but how much was it?

MRS HEEGAN. Two hundred an' nineteen pounds, sixteen shillings an' no pence.

SYLVESTER. Be-God, a nice little nest-egg, right enough!

SUSIE. I hope in my heart that she came by it honestly, and that she remembers that it's as true now as when it was first spoken that it's harder for a camel to go through the eye of a needle than for a rich person to enter the kingdom of heaven.*

SIMON. And she hidin' it all under a veil of silence, when there wasn't the slightest fear of any of us bein' jealous of her.

*A tumult is heard on the floor over their heads, followed by a crash of breaking delf. They are startled, and listen attentively.*

MRS HEEGAN [*breaking the silence*]. Oh, there he's at it again. An' she sayin' that he was a pattern husband since he came home on leave, merry-making with her an' singin' dolorously the first thing every mornin'. I was thinkin' there'd be a rough house sometime over her lookin' so well after his long absence . . . you'd imagine now, the trenches would have given him some idea of the sacredness of life!

*Another crash of breaking delfware.*

MRS HEEGAN. An' the last week of his leave she was too fond of breakin' into song in front of him.

SYLVESTER. Well, she's gettin' it now for goin' round heavin' her happiness in the poor man's face.

*A crash, followed by screams from MRS FORAN.*

SUSIE. I hope he won't be running down here as he often does.

SIMON [*a little agitated*]. I couldn't stay here an' listen to that; I'll go up and stop him: he might be killing the poor woman.

MRS HEEGAN. Don't do anything of the kind, Simon; he might down you with a hatchet or something.

SIMON. Phuh, I'll keep him off with the left and hook him with the right. [*Putting on his hat and coat as he goes to the door.*] Looking prim and careless'll astonish him. Monstrous to stay here, while he may be killing the woman.

MRS HEEGAN [*to SIMON as he goes out*]. For God's sake mind yourself, Simon.

SYLVESTER [*standing beside closed door on right with his ear close to one of the panels, listening intently*]. Simon's a tidy little man with his fists, an' would make Teddy Foran feel giddy if he got home with his left hook. [*Crash.*] I wonder is that Simon knockin' down Foran, or Foran knockin' down Simon?

MRS HEEGAN. If he came down an' we had the light low, an' kept quiet, he might think we were all out.

SYLVESTER. Shush. I can hear nothin' now. Simon must have awed him. Quiet little man, but when Simon gets goin'. Shush? No, nothin' . . . . Something unusual has happened. O, oh, be-God!

_The door against which_ SYLVESTER _is leaning bursts suddenly in._ SYLVESTER _is flung headlong to the floor, and_ MRS FORAN, _her hair falling wildly over her shoulders, a cut over her eye, frantic with fear, rushes in and scrambles in a frenzy of haste under the bed._ MRS HEEGAN, _quickened by fear, runs like a good one, followed by_ SUSIE, _into the room, the door of which they bang after them._ SYLVESTER _hurriedly fights his way under the bed with_ MRS FORAN.

MRS FORAN [_speaking excitedly and jerkily as she climbs under the bed_]. Flung his dinner in to the fire – and then started to smash the little things in the room. Tryin' to save the dresser, I got a box in the eye. I locked the door on him as I rushed out, an' before I was half-way down, he had one of the panels flyin' out with – a hatchet!

SYLVESTER [_under the bed – out of breath_]. Whythehell didn'tyou sing out beforeyousent thedoor flyin' inontop o' me!

MRS FORAN. How could I an' I flyin' before danger to me – life?

SYLVESTER. Yes, an'you've got meinto a nice extremity now!

MRS FORAN. An' I yelled to Simon Norton when he had me – down, but the boyo only ran the faster out of the – house!

SYLVESTER. Oh, an' the regal-like way he went out to fight! Oh, I'm findin' out that everyone who wears a cocked hat isn't a Napoleon!

TEDDY FORAN, MRS FORAN'_s husband, enters by door, with a large fancy, vividly yellow-coloured bowl, ornamented with crimson roses, in one hand and a hatchet in the other. He is big and powerful, rough and hardy. A man who would be dominant in a public house, and whose opinions would be listened to with great respect. He is dressed in the khaki uniform of a soldier home on leave._

TEDDY. Under the bed, eh? Right place for a guilty conscience. I should have thrown you out of the window with the dinner you put before me. Out with you from under there, an' come up with your husband.

SUSIE [*opening suddenly door right, putting in her head, pulling it back and shutting door again*]. God is looking at you, God is looking at you!

MRS FORAN. I'll not budge an inch from where I am.

TEDDY [*looking under the bed and seeing* SYLVESTER]. What are you doin' there encouragin' her against her husband?

SYLVESTER. You've no right to be rippin' open the poor woman's life of peace with violence.

TEDDY [*with indignation*]. She's my wife, isn't she?

MRS FORAN. Nice thing if I lose the sight of my eye with the cut you gave me!

TEDDY. She's my wife, isn't she? An' you've no legal right to be harbourin' her here, keepin' her from her household duties. Stunned I was when I seen her lookin' so well after me long absence. Blowin' her sighin' in me face all day, an' she sufferin' the tortures of hell for fear I'd miss the boat!

SYLVESTER. Go on up to your own home; you've no right to be violatin' this place.

TEDDY. You'd like to make her your cheery amee,* would you? It's napoo, there, napoo,* you little pip-squeak. I seen you an' her goin' down the street arm-in-arm.

SYLVESTER. Did you expect to see me goin' down the street leg-in-leg with her?

TEDDY. Thinkin' of her Ring-papers* instead of her husband. [*To* MRS FORAN] I'll teach you to be rippling with joy an' your husband goin' away! [*He shows the bowl.*] Your weddin' bowl, look at it; pretty, isn't it? Take your last eyeful of it now, for it's goin' west quick!

SUSIE [*popping her head in again*]. God is watching you, God is watching you!

MRS FORAN [*appealingly*]. Teddy, Teddy, don't smash the poor weddin' bowl.

TEDDY [*smashing the bowl with a blow of the hatchet*]. It would be a pity, wouldn't it? Damn it, an' damn you. I'm off now to smash anything I missed, so that you'll have a gay time fittin' up the little home again by the time your loving husband comes back. You can come an' have a look, an' bring your mon amee if you like.

*He goes out, and there is a pause as* MRS FORAN *and* SYLVESTER *peep anxiously towards the door.*

SYLVESTER. Cautious, now cautious; he might be lurking outside that

door there, ready to spring on you the minute you show'd your
nose!

MRS FORAN. Me lovely little weddin' bowl, me lovely little weddin'
bowl!

TEDDY *is heard breaking things in the room above.*

SYLVESTER [*creeping out from under the bed*]. Oh, he is gone up. He was
a little cow'd, I think, when he saw me.

MRS FORAN. Me little weddin' bowl, wrapp'd in tissue paper, an' only
taken out for a few hours every Christmas – me poor little weddin'
bowl.

SUSIE [*popping her head in*]. God is watching – oh, he's gone!

SYLVESTER [*jubilant*]. Vanished! He was a little cow'd I think, when he
saw me.

MRS HEEGAN *and* SUSIE *come into the room.*

MRS FORAN. He's makin' a hash of every little thing we have in the
house, Mrs Heegan.

MRS HEEGAN. Go inside to the room, Mrs Foran, an' if he comes down
again, we'll say you ran out to the street.

MRS FORAN [*going into room*]. My poor little weddin' bowl that I might
have had for generations!

SUSIE [*who has been looking out of the window, excitedly*]. They're
comin', they're comin': a crowd with a concertina; some of them
carrying Harry on their shoulders, an' others are carrying that
Jessie Taite too, holding a silver cup in her hands. Oh, look at the
shameful way she's showing her legs to all who like to have a look at
them!

MRS HEEGAN. Never mind Jessie's legs – what we have to do is to hurry
him out to catch the boat.

*The sound of a concertina playing in the street outside has been heard, and
the noise of a marching crowd. The crowd stop at the house. Shouts are
heard — 'Up the Avondales!'; 'Up Harry Heegan and the Avondales!'
Then steps are heard coming up the stairs, and first SIMON NORTON enters,
holding the door ceremoniously wide open to allow HARRY to enter, with his
arm around JESSIE, who is carrying a silver cup joyously, rather than
reverentially, elevated, as a priest would elevate a chalice. HARRY is*

*wearing khaki trousers, a military cap stained with trench mud, a vivid
orange-coloured jersey with black collar and cuffs. He is twenty-three years
of age, tall, with the sinewy muscles of a manual worker made flexible by
athletic sport. He is a typical young worker, enthusiastic, very often
boisterous, sensible by instinct rather than by reason. He has gone to the
trenches as unthinkingly as he would go to the polling-booth. He isn't
naturally stupid; it is the stupidity of persons in high places that has
stupefied him. He has given all to his masters, strong heart, sound lungs,
healthy stomach, lusty limbs, and the little mind that education has
permitted to develop sufficiently to make all the rest a little more useful. He
is excited now with the sweet and innocent insanity of a fine achievement,
and the rapid lowering of a few drinks.*

JESSIE *is twenty-two or so, responsive to all the animal impulses of life.
Ever dancing around, in and between the world, the flesh, and the devil.
She would be happy climbing with a boy among the heather on Howth
Hill, and could play ball with young men on the swards of the Phoenix
Park. She gives her favour to the prominent and popular.* HARRY *is her
favourite: his strength and speed have won the Final for his club, he wears
the ribbon of the DCM.\*It is a time of spiritual and animal exaltation
for her.*

BARNEY BAGNAL, *a soldier mate of* HARRY's, *stands a little shyly near the
door, with a pleasant, good-humoured grin on his rather broad face. He is
the same age as* HARRY, *just as strong, but not so quick, less finely formed,
and not so sensitive; able to take most things quietly, but savage and wild
when he becomes enraged. He is fully dressed, with topcoat buttoned on
him, and he carries* HARRY's *on his arm.*

HARRY [*joyous and excited*].\* Won, won, won, be-God; by the odd
   goal in five. Lift it up, lift it up, Jessie, sign of youth, sign of
   strength, sign of victory!
MRS HEEGAN [*to* SYLVESTER]. I knew, now, Harry would come back in
   time to catch the boat.
HARRY [*to* JESSIE]. Leave it here, leave it down here, Jessie, under the
   picture, the picture of the boy that won the final.
MRS HEEGAN. A parcel of sandwiches, a bottle of whisky, an' some
   magazines to take away with you an' Barney, Harry.
HARRY. Napoo sandwiches, an' napoo magazines: look at the cup, eh?
   The cup that Harry won, won by the odd goal in five! [*To* BARNEY]
   The song that the little Jock used to sing, Barney, what was it? The
   little Jock we left shrivellin' on the wire after the last push.

BARNEY. 'Will ye no come back again?'

HARRY. No, no, the one we all used to sing with him, 'The Silver
Tassie'. [*Pointing to Cup*] There it is, the Silver Tassie, won by the
odd goal in five, kicked by Harry Heegan.

MRS HEEGAN. Watch your time, Harry, watch your time.

JESSIE. He's watching it, he's watching it – for God's sake don't get
fussy, Mrs Heegan.

HARRY. They couldn't take their beatin' like men. . . . Play the game,
play the game, why the hell couldn't they play the game? [*To*
BARNEY] See the President of the Club, Dr Forby Maxwell, shaking
hands with me, when he was giving me the cup, 'Well done,
Heegan!' The way they yell'd and jump'd when they put in the
equalising goal in the first half!

BARNEY. Ay, a fluke, that's what it was; a lowsey fluke.

MRS HEEGAN [*holding* HARRY's *coat up for him to put it on*]. Here, your
coat, Harry, slip it on while you're talkin'.

HARRY [*putting it on*]. All right, keep smiling, don't fuss. [*To the rest*]
Grousing the whole time they were chasin' the ball; an' when they
lost it, 'Referee, referee, offside, referee . . . foul there; ey, open
your eyes, referee!'

JESSIE. And we scream'd and shouted them down with 'Play the game,
Primrose Rovers, play the game!'

BARNEY. You ran them off their feet till they nearly stood still.

MRS FORAN [*has been peeping in timidly from the room and now comes in to
the rest*]. Somebody run up an' bring Teddy down for fear he'd be
left behind.

SYLVESTER [*to* HARRY]. Your haversack an' trench tools, Harry;
haversack first, isn't it?

HARRY [*fixing his haversack*]. Haversack, haversack, don't rush me.
[*To the rest*] But when I got the ball, Barney, once I got the ball, the
rain began to fall on the others. An' the last goal, the goal that put us
one ahead, the winning goal, that was a-a-eh-a stunner!

BARNEY. A beauty, me boy, a hot beauty.

HARRY. Slipping by the back rushing at me like a mad bull, steadying a
moment for a drive, seeing in a flash the goalie's hands sent with a
shock to his chest by the force of the shot, his half-stunned motion
to clear, a charge, and then carrying him, the ball and all with a rush
into the centre of the net!

BARNEY [*enthusiastically*]. Be-God, I did get a thrill when I seen you
puttin' him sittin' on his arse in the middle of the net!

MRS FORAN [*from the door*]. One of yous go up an' see if Teddy's ready to go.

MRS HEEGAN [*to* HARRY]. Your father'll carry your kit-bag, an' Jessie'll carry your rifle as far as the boat.

HARRY [*irritably*]. Oh, damn it, woman, give your wailin' over for a minute!

MRS HEEGAN. You've got only a few bare minutes to spare, Harry.

HARRY. We'll make the most of them, then. [*To* BARNEY] Out with one of them wine-virgins we got in 'The Mill in the Field', Barney, and we'll rape her in a last hot moment before we set out to kiss the guns!

SIMON *has gone into room and returned with a gun and a kit-bag. He crosses to where* BARNEY *is standing.*

BARNEY [*taking a bottle of wine from his pocket*]. Empty her of her virtues, eh?

HARRY. Spill it out, Barney, spill it out. . . . [*Seizing Silver Cup, and holding it towards* BARNEY] Here, into the cup, be-God. A drink out of the cup, out of the Silver Tassie!

BARNEY [*who has removed the cap and taken out the cork*]. Here she is now. . . . Ready for anything, stripp'd to the skin!

JESSIE. No double-meaning talk, Barney.

SUSIE [*haughtily, to* JESSIE]. The men that are defending us have leave to bow themselves down in the House of Rimmon,* for the men that go with the guns are going with God.

BARNEY *pours wine into the Cup for* HARRY *and into a glass for himself.*

HARRY [*to* JESSIE]. Jessie, a sup for you. [*She drinks from the Cup.*] An' a drink for me. [*He drinks.*] Now a kiss while our lips are wet. [*He kisses her.*] Christ, Barney, how would you like to be retreating from the fairest face and [*lifting* JESSIE's *skirt a little*] – and the trimmest, slimmest little leg in the parish? Napoo, Barney, to everyone but me!

MRS FORAN. One of you go up, an' try to get my Teddy down.

BARNEY [*lifting* SUSIE's *skirt a little*]. Napoo, Harry, to everyone but –

SUSIE [*angrily, pushing* BARNEY *away from her*]. You khaki-cover'd ape, you, what are you trying to do? Manhandle the lassies of France, if you like, but put on your gloves when you touch a woman that seeketh not the things of the flesh.

HARRY [*putting an arm round* SUSIE *to mollify her*]. Now, Susie, Susie, lengthen your temper for a passing moment, so that we may bring away with us the breath of a kiss to the shell-bullied air of the trenches. . . . Besides, there's nothing to be ashamed of – it's not a bad little leggie at all.

SUSIE [*slipping her arm round* HARRY's *neck, and looking defiantly at* BARNEY]. I don't mind what Harry does; I know he means no harm, not like other people. Harry's different.

JESSIE. You'll not forget to send me the German helmet home from France, Harry?

SUSIE [*trying to rest her head on* HARRY's *breast*]. I know Harry, he's different. It's his way. I wouldn't let anyone else touch me, but in some way or another I can tell Harry's different.

JESSIE [*putting her arm round* HARRY *under* SUSIE's *in an effort to dislodge it*]. Susie, Harry wants to be free to keep his arm round me during his last few moments here, so don't be pulling him about!

SUSIE [*shrinking back a little*]. I was only saying that Harry was different.

MRS FORAN. For God's sake, will someone go up for Teddy, or he won't go back at all!

TEDDY [*appearing at door*]. Damn anxious for Teddy to go back! Well, Teddy's goin' back, an' he's left everything tidy upstairs so that you'll not have much trouble sortin' things out. [*To* HARRY] The Club an' a crowd's waitin' outside to bring us to the boat before they go to the spread in honour of the final. [*Bitterly*] A party for them while we muck off to the trenches!

HARRY [*after a slight pause, to* BARNEY]. Are you game, Barney?

BARNEY. What for?

HARRY. To go to the spread* and hang the latch for another night?

BARNEY [*taking his rifle from* SIMON *and slinging it over his shoulder*]. No, no, napoo desertin' on Active Service. Deprivation of pay an' the rest of your time in the front trenches. No, no. We must go back.

MRS HEEGAN. No, no, Harry. You must go back.

SIMON, SYLVESTER AND SUSIE [*together*]. You must go back.

VOICES OF CROWD OUTSIDE. They must go back!

*The ship's siren is heard blowing.*

SIMON. The warning signal.

SYLVESTER. By the time they get there, they'll be unslinging the gangways!

SUSIE [*handing* HARRY *his steel helmet*]. Here's your helmet, Harry. [*He puts it on.*]

MRS HEEGAN. You'll all nearly have to run for it now!

SYLVESTER. I've got your kit-bag, Harry.

SUSIE. I've got your rifle.

SIMON. I'll march in front with the cup, after Conroy with the concertina.

TEDDY. Come on: ong avong to the trenches!

HARRY [*recklessly*]. Jesus, a last drink, then! [*He raises the Silver Cup, singing*]

> Gae bring to me a pint of wine,
> And fill it in a silver tassie;

BARNEY [*joining in vigorously*].

> . . . a silver tassie.

HARRY.

> That I may drink before I go,
> A service to my bonnie lassie.

BARNEY.

> . . . bonnie lassie.

HARRY.

> The boat rocks at the pier o' Leith,
> Full loud the wind blows from the ferry;
> The ship rides at the Berwick Law,
> An' I must leave my bonnie Mary!

BARNEY.

> . . . leave my bonnie Mary!

HARRY.

> The trumpets sound, the banners fly,
> The glittering spears are ranked ready;

BARNEY.

> . . . glittering spears are ranked ready;

HARRY.

> The shouts of war are heard afar,
> The battle closes thick and bloody.

BARNEY.

> . . . closes thick and bloody.

HARRY.         It's not the roar of sea or shore,
                  That makes me longer wish to tarry,
                  Nor shouts of war that's heard afar –
                  It's leaving thee, my bonnie lassie!

BARNEY.        . . . leaving thee, my bonnie lassie!*

TEDDY. Come on, come on. [SIMON, SYLVESTER, *and* SUSIE *go out.*]
VOICES OUTSIDE.

        Come on from your home to the boat;
        Carry on from the boat to the camp.

TEDDY *and* BARNEY *go out.* HARRY *and* JESSIE *follow; as* HARRY *reaches the door, he takes his arm from round* JESSIE *and comes back to* MRS HEEGAN.

VOICES OUTSIDE.

        From the camp up the line to the trenches.

HARRY. [*shyly and hurriedly kissing* MRS HEEGAN]. Well, goodbye, old
    woman.
MRS HEEGAN. Goodbye, my son.

HARRY *goes out. The chorus of 'The Silver Tassie', accompanied by a concertina, can be heard growing fainter till it ceases.* MRS FORAN *goes out timidly.* MRS HEEGAN *pokes the fire, arranges the things in the room, and then goes to the window and looks out. After a pause, the loud and long blast of the ship's siren is heard. The light on the masthead, seen through the window, moves slowly away, and* MRS HEEGAN *with a sigh, 'Ah dear', goes over to the fire and sits down. A slight pause, then* MRS FORAN *returns to the room.*

MRS FORAN. Every little bit of china I had in the house is lyin' above in
    a mad an' muddled heap like the flotsum an' jetsum of the seashore!
MRS HEEGAN [*with a deep sigh of satisfaction*]. Thanks be to Christ that
    we're after managin' to get the three of them away safely.

CURTAIN

## ACT II

*In the war zone: a scene of jagged and lacerated ruin of what was once a monastery. At back a lost wall and window are indicated by an arched piece of broken coping pointing from the left to the right, and a similar piece of masonry pointing from the right to the left. Between these two lacerated fingers of stone can be seen the country stretching to the horizon where the front trenches are. Here and there heaps of rubbish mark where houses once stood. From some of these, lean, dead hands are protruding. Further on, spiky stumps of trees which were once a small wood. The ground is dotted with rayed and shattered shell-holes. Across the horizon in the red glare can be seen the criss-cross pattern of the barbed wire bordering the trenches. In the sky sometimes a green star, sometimes a white star, burns. Within the broken archway to the left is an arched entrance to another part of the monastery, used now as a Red Cross station. In the wall, right, near the front is a stained-glass window, background green, figure of the Virgin, white-faced, wearing a black robe, lights inside making the figure vividly apparent. Farther up from this window is a life-size crucifix. A shell has released an arm from the cross, which has caused the upper part of the figure to lean forward with the released arm outstretched towards the figure of the Virgin. Underneath the crucifix on a pedestal, in red letters, are the words: 'Princeps Pacis'. Almost opposite the crucifix is a gunwheel to which* BARNEY *is tied. At the back, in the centre, where the span of the arch should be, is the shape of a big howitzer gun, squat, heavy underpart, with a long, sinister barrel now pointing towards the front at an angle of forty-five degrees. At the base of the gun a piece of wood is placed on which is chalked, 'Hyde Park Corner'. On another piece of wood near the entrance of the Red Cross station is chalked, 'No hawkers or street cries permitted here'. In the near centre is a brazier in which a fire is burning. Crouching above, on a ramp, is a soldier whose clothes are covered with mud and splashed with blood. Every feature of the scene seems a little distorted from its original appearance. Rain is falling steadily; its fall worried now and again by fitful gusts of a cold wind. A small organ is heard playing slow and stately notes as the curtain rises.*

*After a pause, the* CROUCHER, *without moving, intones dreamily:*

CROUCHER. And the hand of the Lord was upon me, and carried me out in the spirit of the Lord, and set me down in the midst of a valley.

And I looked and saw a great multitude that stood upon their feet, an exceeding great army.

And he said unto me, Son of man, can this exceeding great army
become a valley of dry bones?*

*The music ceases, and a voice, in the part of the monastery left standing,
intones, 'Kyr. . .ie . . . eleison. Kyr. . .ie . . . e. . .eleison', followed by
the answer: 'Christe . . . eleison'.* *

CROUCHER [*resuming*]. And I answered, O Lord God, thou knowest.
   And he said, prophesy, and say unto the wind, come from the four
   winds a breath and breathe upon these living that they may die.

*As he pauses the voice in the monastery is heard again: 'Gloria in excelsis
Deo et in terra pax hominibus bonae voluntatis.'* *

CROUCHER [*resuming*]. And I prophesied, and the breath came out of
   them, and the sinews came away from them, and behold a shaking,
   and their bones fell asunder, bone from his bone, and they died,
   and the exceeding great army became a valley of dry bones.

*The voice from the monastery is heard, clearly for the first half of the
sentence, then dying away towards the end: 'Accendat in nobis Dominus
ignem sui amoris, et flammam aeternae caritatis.'* *
   *A group of* SOLDIERS *come in from fatigue bunched together as if for
comfort and warmth. They are wet and cold, and they are sullen-faced.
They form a circle around the brazier and stretch their hands towards the
blaze.*

1ST SOLDIER. Cold and wet and tir'd.
2ND SOLDIER. Wet and tir'd and cold.
3RD SOLDIER. Tir'd and cold and wet.
4TH SOLDIER [*very like* TEDDY]. Twelve blasted hours of ammunition
   transport fatigue!
1ST SOLDIER. Twelve weary hours.
2ND SOLDIER. And wasting hours.
3RD SOLDIER. And hot and heavy hours.
1ST SOLDIER. Toiling and thinking to build the wall of force that blocks
   the way from here to home.
2ND SOLDIER. Lifting shells.
3RD SOLDIER. Carrying shells.
4TH SOLDIER. Piling shells.
1ST SOLDIER. In the falling, pissing rine and whistling wind.

2ND SOLDIER. The whistling wind and falling, drenching rain.

3RD SOLDIER. The God-dam rain and blasted whistling wind.

1ST SOLDIER. And the shirkers sife at home coil'd up at ease.

2ND SOLDIER. Shells for us and pianos for them.

3RD SOLDIER. Fur coats for them and winding-sheets for us.

4TH SOLDIER. Warm.

2ND SOLDIER. And dry.

1ST SOLDIER. An' 'appy. [*A slight pause.*]

BARNEY. An' they call it re-cu-per-at-ing!

1ST SOLDIER [*reclining near the fire*]. Gawd, I'm sleepy.

2ND SOLDIER [*reclining*]. Tir'd and lousy.

3RD SOLDIER [*reclining*]. Damp and shaking.

4TH SOLDIER [*murmuring, the rest joining him*]. Tir'd and lousy, an' wet an' sleepy, but mother call me early in the morning.

1ST SOLDIER [*dreamily*]. Wen I thinks of 'ome, I thinks of a field of dysies.

THE REST [*dreamily*]. Wen 'e thinks of 'ome, 'e thinks of a field of dysies.

1ST SOLDIER [*chanting dreamily*].

> I sees the missus paryding along Walham Green,
> Through the jewels an' silks on the costers' carts,
> Emmie a-pulling her skirts an' muttering,
> 'A balloon, a balloon, I wants a balloon',
> The missus a-tugging 'er on, an' sying,
> 'A balloon, for shime, an' your father fighting:
> You'll wait till 'e's 'ome, an' the bands a-plying!'

[*He pauses. Suddenly*]

> But wy'r we 'ere, wy'r we're – that's wot we wants
> to know!

2ND SOLDIER. God only knows – or else, perhaps, a red-cap.*

1ST SOLDIER [*chanting*].

> Tabs'll murmur, 'em an' 'aw, an' sy: 'You're 'ere
> because you're
> Point nine double o, the sixth platoon an' forty-eight
> battalion,

The Yellow Plumes that pull'd a bow at Crécy,*
And gave to fame a leg up on the path to glory;
Now with the howitzers of the Twenty-first Division,
Tiking life easy with the Army of the Marne,
An' all the time the battered Conchie* squeals,
"It's one or two men looking after business."'

3RD SOLDIER. An' saves his blasted skin!
1ST SOLDIER [*chanting*].

The padre gives a fag an' softly whispers:
'Your king, your country an' your muvver 'as you 'ere.'
An' last time 'ome on leave, I awsks the missus:
'The good God up in heaven, Bill, 'e knows,
An' I gets the seperytion moneys* reg'lar.'

[*He sits up suddenly.*]

But wy're we 'ere, wy're we 'ere – that's wot I wants to know!

THE REST [*chanting sleepily*].

Why 's 'e 'ere, why 's 'e 'ere – that's wot 'e
wants to know!

BARNEY [*singing to the air of second bar in chorus of 'Auld Lang Syne'*].

We're here because we're here, because we're here,
because we're here!


*Each slides into an attitude of sleep — even* BARNEY's *head droops a little.
The* CORPORAL, *followed by the* VISITOR, *appears at back. The*
VISITOR *is a portly man with a rubicund face; he is smiling to demonstrate
his ease of mind, but the lines are a little distorted with an ever-present sense
of anxiety. He is dressed in a semi-civilian, semi-military manner — dark
worsted suit, shrapnel helmet, a haversack slung round his shoulder, a
brown belt round his middle, black top boots and spurs, and he carries a
cane. His head is bent between his shoulders, and his shoulders are
crouched a little.*

VISITOR. Yes, tomorrow, I go a little farther. Penetrate a little deeper into danger. Foolish, yes, but then it's an experience; by God, it's an experience. The military authorities are damned strict – won't let a . . . man . . . plunge!

CORPORAL. In a manner of speakin', sir, only let you see the arses of the guns.

VISITOR [*not liking the remark*]. Yes, no; no, oh yes. Damned strict, won't let a . . . man . . . plunge! [*Suddenly, with alarm*] What's that, what was that?

CORPORAL. Wha' was what?

VISITOR. A buzz, I thought I heard a buzz.

CORPORAL. A buzz?

VISITOR. Of an aeroplane.

CORPORAL. Didn't hear. Might have been a bee.

VISITOR. No, no; don't think it was a bee. [*Arranging helmet with his hands*] Damn shrapnel helmet; skin tight; like a vice; hurts the head. Rather be without it; but, regulations, you know. Military authorities damn particular – won't let a . . . man . . . plunge!

VISITOR [*seeing* BARNEY]. Aha, what have we got here, what have we got here?

CORPORAL [*to* BARNEY]. 'Tshun!* [*To the* VISITOR] Regimental misdemeanour, sir.

VISITOR [*to* BARNEY]. Nothing much, boy, nothing much?

BARNEY [*chanting softly*].

> A Brass-hat pullin' the bedroom curtains
> Between himself, the world an' the Estaminay's*
>     daughter,
> In a pyjama'd hurry ran down an' phon'd
> A Tommy was chokin' an Estaminay cock,
> An' I was pinch'd as I was puttin' the bird
> Into a pot with a pint of peas.

CORPORAL [*chanting hoarsely*].

> And the hens all droop, for the loss has made
> The place a place of desolation!

VISITOR [*reprovingly, to the* CORPORAL]. Seriously, Corporal, seriously, please. Sacred, sacred: property of the citizen of a friendly State,

sacred. On Active Service, serious to steal a fowl, a cock. [*To*
BARNEY] The uniform, the cause, boy, the corps. *Infra dignitatem*,
boy, *infra dignitatem.* *

BARNEY. Wee, wee.

VISITOR [*pointing to reclining soldiers*]. Taking it easy, eh?

CORPORAL. Done in; transport fatigue, twelve hours.

VISITOR. Um, not too much rest, corporal. Dangerous. Keep 'em
moving much as possible. Too much rest – bad. Sap, sap, sap.

CORPORAL [*pointing to the left*]. Bit of monastery left intact. Hold
services there; troops off to front line. Little organ plays.

VISITOR. Splendid. Bucks 'em up. Gives 'em peace.

*A* STAFF OFFICER *enters suddenly, passing by the* VISITOR *with a springing
hop, so that he stands in the centre with the* VISITOR *on his right and the*
CORPORAL *on his left. He is prim, pert, and polished, superfine khaki
uniform, gold braid, crimson tabs, and gleaming top-boots. He speaks his
sentences with a gasping importance.*

CORPORAL [*stiffening*]. 'Shun! Staff!

SOLDIERS [*springing to their feet — the* CROUCHER *remains as he is, with a
sleepy alertness*]. Staff! 'Shun!

CORPORAL [*bellowing at the* CROUCHER]. Eh, you there: 'shun! Staff!

CROUCHER [*calmly*]. Not able. Sick. Privilege. Excused duty.

STAFF-WALLAH [*reading document*].


### BATTERY BRIGADE ORDERS, F.A., 31 D 2.

Units presently recuperating, parade eight o'clock p.m.

Attend Lecture organised by Society for amusement and mental
development, soldiers at front.

Subject: Habits of those living between Frigid Zone and Arctic
Circle.

Lecturer: Mr Melville Sprucer.

Supplementary Order: Units to wear gas-masks.

As you were.

*The* STAFF-WALLAH *departs as he came in with a springing hop. the*
VISITOR *and the* CORPORAL *relax, and stroll down towards the RC*

*Station.* * The soldiers relax too, seeking various positions of ease around the fire.*

VISITOR [*indicating the RC Station*]. Ah, in here. We'll just pop in here for a minute. And then pop out again. [*He and the* CORPORAL *go into the RC Station. A pause.*]

1ST SOLDIER [*chanting and indicating that he means the* VISITOR *by looking in the direction of the RC Station*].

> The perky bastard's cautious nibbling
> In a safe, safe shelter at danger queers me.
> Furiously feeling he's up to the neck in
> The whirl and the sweep of the front-line fighting.

2ND SOLDIER [*chanting*].

> In his full-blown, chin-strapp'd, shrapnel helmet,
> He'll pat a mug on the back and murmur,
> 'Here's a stand-fast Tauntonshire before me',
> And the mug,* on his feet, 'll whisper 'yessir'.

3RD SOLDIER [*chanting*].

> Like a bride, full-flush'd, 'e'll sit down and listen
> To every word of the goddam sermon,
> From the cushy-soul'd, word-spreading, yellow-
>       streaked dud.

BARNEY [*chanting*].

> Who wouldn't make a patch on a Tommy's backside.

[*A pause.*]

1ST SOLDIER. 'Ow long have we been resting 'ere?

2ND SOLDIER. A month.

3RD SOLDIER. Twenty-nine days, twenty-three hours, and [*looking at watch*] twenty-three minutes.

4TH SOLDIER. Thirty-seven minutes more'll make it thirty days.

CROUCHER.

Thirty days hath September, April, June, and
    November –
November – that's the month when I was born –
    November.
Not the beginning, not the end, but the middle of
    November.
Near the valley of the Thames, in the middle of
    November.
Shall I die at the start, near the end, in the middle of
    November?

1ST SOLDIER [*nodding towards the* CROUCHER]. One more scrap,* an'
    'e'll be Ay one in the kingdom of the Bawmy.*
2ND SOLDIER. Perhaps they have forgotten.
3RD SOLDIER. Forgotten.
4TH SOLDIER. Forgotten us.
1ST SOLDIER. If the blighters at the front would tame their grousing.
THE REST. Tame their grousing.*
2ND SOLDIER. And the wounded cease to stare their silent scorning.
THE REST. Passing by us, carried cushy* on the stretchers.
3RD SOLDIER. We have beaten out the time upon the duckboard.*
4TH SOLDIER. Stiff standing watch'd the sunrise from the firestep.
2ND SOLDIER. Stiff standing from the firestep watch'd the sunset.
3RD SOLDIER. Have bless'd the dark wiring of the top with curses.
2ND SOLDIER. And never a ray of leave.
3RD SOLDIER. To have a quiet drunk.
1ST SOLDIER. Or a mad mowment to rustle a judy.*

3RD SOLDIER *takes out a package of cigarettes; taking one himself he hands
the package round. Each takes one, and the man nearest to* BARNEY,
*kneeling up, puts one in his mouth and lights it for him. They all smoke
silently for a few moments, sitting up round the fire.*

2ND SOLDIER [*chanting very earnestly and quietly*].

Would God I smok'd an' walk'd an' watch'd th'
Dance of a golden Brimstone butterfly,
To the saucy pipe of a greenfinch resting
In a drowsy, brambled lane in Cumberland.

1ST SOLDIER.

> Would God I smok'd and lifted cargoes
> From the laden shoulders of London's river-way;
> Then holiday'd, roaring out courage and movement
> To the muscled machines of Tottenham Hotspur.*

3RD SOLDIER.

> To hang here even a little longer,
> Lounging through fear-swell'd, anxious moments;
> The hinderparts of the god of battles
> Shading our war-tir'd eyes from his flaming face.

BARNEY.

> If you creep to rest in a clos'd-up coffin,
> A tail of comrades seeing you safe home;
> Or be a kernel lost in a shell exploding –
> It's all, sure, only in a lifetime.

ALL TOGETHER.

> Each sparrow, hopping, irresponsible,
> Is indentur'd in God's mighty memory;
> And we, more than they all, shall not be lost
> In the forgetfulness of the Lord of Hosts.

*The* VISITOR *and the* CORPORAL *come from the Red Cross Station.*

VISITOR [*taking out a cigarette-case*]. Nurses too gloomy. Surgeons too serious. Doesn't do.

CORPORAL. All lying-down cases, sir. Pretty bad.

VISITOR [*who is now standing near the crucifix*]. All the more reason make things merry and bright. Lift them out of themselves. [*To the* SOLDIERS] See you all tomorrow at lecture?

1ST SOLDIER [*rising and standing a little sheepishly before the* VISITOR]. Yessir, yessir.

THE REST. Yessir, yessir.

VISITOR. Good. Make it interesting. [*Searching in pocket*] Damn it, have I none? Ah, saved.

*He takes a match from his pocket and is about to strike it carelessly on the arm of the crucifix, when the* 1ST SOLDIER, *with a rapid frightened movement, knocks it out of his hand.*

1ST SOLDIER [*roughly*]. Blarst you, man, keep your peace-white paws from that!

2ND SOLDIER. The image of the Son of God.

3RD SOLDIER. Jesus of Nazareth, the King of the Jews.

1ST SOLDIER [*reclining by the fire again*]. There's a Gawd knocking abaht somewhere.

4TH SOLDIER. Wants Him to be sending us over a chit in the shape of a bursting shell.

VISITOR. Sorry put it across you. [*To* CORPORAL] Too much time to think. Nervy. Time to brood, brood; bad. Sap. Sap. Sap. [*Walking towards where he came in*] Must return quarters; rough and ready. Must stick it. There's a war on. Cheerio. Straight down road instead of round hill: shorter?

CORPORAL. Less than half as long.

VISITOR. Safe?

CORPORAL. Yes. Only drop shells off and on, cross-roads. Ration party wip'd out week ago.

VISITOR. Go round hill. No hurry. General Officer's orders, no unnecessary risks. Must obey. Military Authorities damned particular – won't let a . . . man . . . plunge!

*He and the* CORPORAL *go off. The soldiers in various attitudes are asleep around the fire. After a few moments' pause, two* STRETCHER-BEARERS *come in slowly from left, carrying a casualty. They pass through the sleeping soldiers, going towards the Red Cross Station. As they go they chant a verse, and as the verse is ending, they are followed by another pair carrying a second casualty.*

1ST BEARERS [*chanting*].

> Oh, bear it gently, carry it soft –
> A bullet or a shell said stop, stop, stop.
> It's had its day, and it's left the play,
> Since it gamboll'd over the top, top, top.
> It's had its day, and it's left the play,
> Since it gamboll'd over the top.

2ND BEARERS [*chanting*].

> Oh, carry it softly, bear it gently –
> The beggar has seen it through, through, through.
> If it 'adn't been 'im, if it 'adn't been 'im,
> It might 'ave been me or you, you, you.
> If it 'adn't been 'im, if it 'adn't been 'im,
> It might 'ave been me or you.

VOICE [*inside RC Station*]. Easy, easy there; don't crowd.

1ST STRETCHER-BEARER [*to man behind*]. Woa, woa there, Bill, 'ouse full.

STRETCHER-BEARER [*behind, to those following*]. Woa, woa; traffic blocked. [*They leave the stretchers on the ground.*]

THE WOUNDED ON THE STRETCHERS [*chanting*].

> Carry on, carry on to the place of pain,
> Where the surgeon spreads his aid, aid, aid.
> And we show man's wonderful work, well done,
> To the image God hath mad, made, made,
> And we show man's wonderful work, well done,
> To the image God hath made!
>
> When the future hours have all been spent,
> And the hand of death is near, near, near,
> Then a few, few moments and we shall find
> There'll be nothing left to fear, fear, fear,
> Then a few, few moments and we shall find
> There'll be nothing left to fear.
>
> The power, the joy, the pull of life,
> The laugh, the blow, and the dear kiss,
> The pride and hope, the gain and loss,
> Have been temper'd down to this, this, this,
> The pride and hope, the gain and loss,
> Have been temper'd down to this.

1ST STRETCHER-BEARER [*to* BARNEY]. Oh, Barney, have they liced you up because you've kiss'd the Colonel's judy?

BARNEY. They lit on me stealin' Estaminay poulthry.

1ST STRETCHER-BEARER. A hen?
2ND STRETCHER-BEARER. A duck, again, Barney?
3RD STRETCHER-BEARER. A swan this time.
BARNEY [*chanting softly*].

> A Brass-hat pullin' the bedroom curtains
> Between himself, the world an' the Estaminay's daughter,
> In a pyjama'd hurry ran down and phon'd
> A Tommy was chokin' an Estaminay cock;
> An' I was pinch'd as I was puttin' the bird
> Into a pot with a pint of peas.

1ST STRETCHER-BEARER. The red-tabb'd squit!*
2ND STRETCHER-BEARER. The lousy map-scanner!
3RD STRETCHER-BEARER. We must keep up, we must keep up the
    morale of the awmy.
2ND STRETCHER-BEARER [*loudly*]. Does 'e eat well?
THE REST [*in chorus*]. Yes, 'e eats well?
2ND STRETCHER-BEARER. Does 'e sleep well?
THE REST [*in chorus*]. Yes, 'e sleeps well!
2ND STRETCHER-BEARER. Does 'e whore well?
THE REST [*in chorus*]. Yes, 'e whores well!
2ND STRETCHER-BEARER. Does 'e fight well?
THE REST [*in chorus*]. Napoo; 'e 'as to do the thinking for the Tommies!
VOICE [*from the RC Station*]. Stretcher Party – carry on!

*The* BEARERS *stoop with precision, attach their supports to the stretchers,
lift them up and march slowly into the RC Station, chanting.*

STRETCHER-BEARERS [*chanting*].

> Carry on – we've one bugled reason why –
> We've 'eard and answer'd the call, call, call.
> There's no more to be said, for when we are dead,
> We may understand it all, all, all.
> There's no more to be said, for when we are dead,
> We may understand it all.

*They go out, leaving the scene occupied by the* CROUCHER *and the soldiers
sleeping around the fire. The* CORPORAL *re-enters. He is carrying two*

*parcels. He pauses, looking at the sleeping soldiers for a few moments, then shouts.*

CORPORAL [*shouting*]. Hallo, there, you sleepy blighters! Number 2! a parcel; and for you, Number 3. Get a move on – parcels. [*The* SOLDIERS *wake up and spring to their feet.*] For you, Number 2. [*He throws a parcel to* 2ND SOLDIER.] Number 3. [*He throws the other parcel to* 3RD SOLDIER.]

3RD SOLDIER [*taking paper from around his parcel*]. Looks like a bundle of cigarettes.

1ST SOLDIER. Or a pack of cawds.

4TH SOLDIER. Or a prayer-book.

3RD SOLDIER [*astounded*]. Holy Christ, it is!

THE REST. What?

3RD SOLDIER. A prayer-book!

4TH SOLDIER. In a green plush cover with a golden cross.

CROUCHER. Open it at the Psalms and sing that we may be saved from the life and death of the beasts that perish.

BARNEY. *Per omnia saecula saeculorum.* *

2ND SOLDIER [*who has opened his parcel*]. A ball, be God!

4TH SOLDIER. A red and yellow coloured rubber ball.

1ST SOLDIER. And a note.

2ND SOLDIER [*reading*]. To play your way to the enemies' trenches when you all go over the top. Mollie.

1ST SOLDIER. See if it 'ops.

*The* 2ND SOLDIER *hops the ball, and then kicks it from him. The* CORPORAL *intercepts it, and begins to dribble it across the stage. The* 3RD SOLDIER *tries to take it from him. The* CORPORAL *shouts 'Offside, there!' They play for a few minutes with the ball, when suddenly the* STAFF-WALLAH *springs in and stands rigidly in centre.*

CORPORAL [*stiff to attention as he sees the* STAFF-WALLAH]. 'Shun. Staff!

*All the* SOLDIERS *stiffen. The* CROUCHER *remains motionless.*

CORPORAL [*shouting to the* CROUCHER]. You: 'shun. Staff!

CROUCHER. Not able. Sick. Excused duty.

STAFF-WALLAH [*reading document*].

> Brigade Orders, C/X 143. B/Y 341. Regarding gas-masks. Gas-masks to be worn round neck so as to lie in front $2\frac{1}{2}$ degrees from socket of left shoulder-blade, and $2\frac{3}{4}$ degrees from socket of right shoulder-blade, leaving bottom margin to reach $\frac{1}{4}$ of an inch from second button of lower end of tunic. Order to take effect from 6 a.m. following morning of date received.

> Dismiss! [*He hops out again, followed by* CORPORAL.]

1ST SOLDIER [*derisively*]. Comprenneemoy.

3RD SOLDIER. Tray bong.*

2ND SOLDIER [*who is standing in archway, back, looking scornfully after the* STAFF-WALLAH, *chanting*].

> Jazzing back to his hotel he now goes gaily,
> Shelter'd and safe where the clock ticks tamely.
> His backside warming a cushion, down-fill'd,
> Green clad, well splash'd with gold birds red-beak'd.

1ST SOLDIER.

> His last dim view of the front-line sinking
> Into the white-flesh'd breasts of a judy;
> Cuddling with proud, bright, amorous glances
> The thing salved safe from the mud of the trenches.

2ND SOLDIER.

> His tunic reared in the lap of comfort
> Peeps at the blood-stain'd jackets passing,
> Through colour-gay bars of ribbon jaunty,
> Fresh from a posh shop snug in Bond Street.*

CROUCHER.

> Shame and scorn play with and beat them,
> Till we anchor in their company;
> Then the decorations of security
> Become the symbols of self-sacrifice.

*A pause.*

2ND SOLDIER.

> A warning this that we'll soon be exiles
> From the freedom chance of life can give,
> To the front where you wait to be hurried breathless,
> Murmuring how, how do you do, to God.

3RD SOLDIER.

> Where hot with the sweat of mad endeavour,
> Crouching to scrape a toy-deep shelter,
> Quick-tim'd by hell's fast, frenzied drumfire
> Exploding in flaming death around us.

2ND SOLDIER.

> God, unchanging, heart-sicken'd, shuddering,
> Gathereth the darkness of the night sky
> To mask His paling countenance from
> The blood dance of His self-slaying children.

3RD SOLDIER.

> Stumbling, swiftly, cursing, plodding,
> Lumbering, loitering, stumbling, grousing,
> Through mud and rain, and filth and danger,
> Flesh and blood seek slow the front line.

2ND SOLDIER.

> Squeals of hidden laughter run through
> The screaming medley of the wounded –
> Christ, who bore the cross, still weary,
> Now trails a rope tied to a field gun.

*As the last notes of the chanting are heard the* CORPORAL *comes rapidly in; he is excited but steady; pale-faced and grim.*

CORPORAL. They attack. Along a wide front the enemy attacks. If they break through it may reach us even here.

SOLDIERS [*in chorus as they all put on gas-masks*]. They attack. The
  enemy attacks.
CORPORAL. Let us honour that in which we do put our trust.
SOLDIERS [*in chorus*].

> That it may not fail us in our time of need.

*The* CORPORAL *goes over to the gun and faces towards it, standing on the
bottom step. The* SOLDIERS *group around, each falling upon one knee, their
forms crouched in a huddled act of obeisance. They are all facing the gun
with their backs to the audience. The* CROUCHER *rises and joins them.*

CORPORAL [*singing*].

> Hail, cool-hardened tower of steel emboss'd
> With the fever'd, figment thoughts of man;
> Guardian of our love and hate and fear,
> Speak for us to the inner ear of God!

SOLDIERS.

> We believe in God and we believe in thee.

CORPORAL.

> Dreams of line, of colour, and of form;
> Dreams of music dead for ever now;
> Dreams in bronze and dreams in stone have gone
> To make thee delicate and strong to kill.

SOLDIERS.

> We believe in God and we believe in thee.

CORPORAL.

> Jail'd in thy steel are hours of merriment
> Cadg'd from the pageant-dream of children's play;
> Too soon of the motley stripp'd that they may sweat
> With them that toil for the glory of thy kingdom.

SOLDIERS.

We believe in God and we believe in thee.

CORPORAL.

Remember our women, sad-hearted, proud-fac'd.
Who've given the substance of their womb for shadows;
Their shrivel'd, empty breasts war tinselléd
For patient gifts of graves to thee.

SOLDIERS.

We believe in God and we believe in thee.

CORPORAL.

Dapple those who are shelter'd with disease,
And women labouring with child,
And children that play about the streets,
With blood of youth expiring in its prime.

SOLDIERS.

We believe in God and we believe in thee.

CORPORAL.

Tear a gap through the soul of our mass'd enemies;
Grant them all the peace of death;*
Blow them swiftly into Abram's bosom,
And mingle them with the joys of paradise!

SOLDIERS.

For we believe in God and we believe in thee.

*The sky has become vexd with a crimson glare, mixed with yellow streaks, and striped with pillars of rising brown and black smoke. The STAFF-WALLAH rushes in, turbulent and wild, with his uniform disordered.*

STAFF-WALLAH.

> The enemy has broken through, broken through,
>     broken through!
> Every man born of woman to the guns, to the guns.

SOLDIERS.

> To the guns, to the guns, to the guns!

STAFF-WALLAH.

> Those at prayer, all in bed; and the swillers drinking
>     deeply in the pubs.

SOLDIERS.

> To the guns, to the guns.

STAFF-WALLAH.

> All the batmen, every cook, every bitch's son that hides
> A whiff of courage in his veins,
> Shelter'd vigour in his body,
> That can run, or can walk, even crawl –
> Dig him out, dig him out, shove him on –

SOLDIERS.

> To the guns!

*The* SOLDIERS *hurry to their places led by the* STAFF-WALLAH *to the gun. The gun swings around and points to the horizon; a shell is swung into the breech and a flash indicates the firing of the gun, searchlights move over the red glare of the sky; the scene darkens, stabbed with distant flashes and by the more vivid flash of the gun which the* SOLDIERS *load and fire with rhythmical movements while the scene is closing. Only flashes are seen; no noise is heard.* *

CURTAIN

## ACT III

*The upper end of an hospital ward. At right angles from back wall are two beds, one covered with a red quilt and the other with a white one. From the centre of the head of each bed is an upright having at the top a piece like a swan's neck, curving out over the bed, from which hangs a chain with a wooden cross-piece to enable weak patients to pull themselves into a sitting posture. To the left of these beds is a large glass double-door which opens on to the ground: one of the doors is open and a lovely September sun, which is setting, gives a glow to the garden.*

*Through the door two poplar trees can be seen silhouetted against the sky. To the right of this door is another bed covered with a black quilt. Little white discs are fixed to the head of each bed: on the first is the number 26, on the second 27, and on the third 28. Medical charts hang over each on the wall. To the right is the fireplace, facing down the ward. Farther on, to the right of the fire, is a pedestal on which stands a statue of the Blessed Virgin; under the statue is written, 'Mater Misericordiae, ora pro nobis'.\* An easy-chair, on which are rugs, is near the fire. In the centre is a white, glass-topped table on which are medicines, drugs, and surgical instruments. On one corner is a vase of flowers. A locker is beside the head, and a small chair by the foot of each bed. Two electric lights, green-shaded, hang from the ceiling, and a bracket light with a red shade projects from the wall over the fireplace. It is dusk, and the two lights suspended from the ceiling are lighted. The walls are a brilliant white.*

SYLVESTER *is in the bed numbered '26'; he is leaning upon his elbow looking towards the glass door.*

SIMON, *sitting down on the chair beside bed numbered '27', is looking into the grounds.*

SYLVESTER [*after a pause*]. Be God, isn't it a good one!

SIMON. Almost, almost, mind you, Sylvester, incomprehensible.

SYLVESTER. To come here and find Susie Monican fashion'd like a Queen of Sheba. God moves in a mysterious way, Simon.

SIMON. There's Surgeon Maxwell prancing after her now.

SYLVESTER [*stretching to see*]. Heads together, eh? Be God, he's kissing her behind the trees! Oh, Susannah, Susannah, how are the mighty fallen, and the weapons of war perished!\*

HARRY HEEGAN *enters crouched in a self-propelled invalid chair; he wheels himself up to the fire.* SYLVESTER *slides down into the bed, and* SIMON *becomes interested in a book that he takes off the top of his locker.* HARRY *remains for a few moments beside the fire, and then wheels himself round and goes out as he came in;* SYLVESTER *raises himself in the bed, and* SIMON *leaves down the book to watch* HARRY.

SYLVESTER. Down and up, up and down.

SIMON. Up and down, down and up.

SYLVESTER. Never quiet for a minute.

SIMON. Never able to hang on to an easy second.

SYLVESTER. Trying to hold on to the little finger of life.

SIMON. Half-way up to heaven.

SYLVESTER. And him always thinking of Jessie.

SIMON. And Jessie never thinking of him.

SUSIE MONICAN, *in the uniform of a VAD\* nurse, enters the ward by the glass door. She is changed, for it is clear that she has made every detail of the costume as attractive as possible. She has the same assertive manner, but dignity and a sense of importance have been added. Her legs, encased in silk stockings, are seen (and shown) to advantage by her short and smartly cut skirt. Altogether she is now a very handsome woman. Coming in she glances at the bed numbered 28, then pauses beside* SYLVESTER *and* SIMON.

SUSIE. How is Twenty-eight?

SIMON AND SYLVESTER [*together*]. Travelling again.

SYLVESTER. Dumb, Susie, dumb.

SIMON. Brooding, Susie; brooding, brooding.

SYLVESTER. Cogitatin', Susie; cogitatin', cogitatin'.

SUSIE [*sharply, to* SYLVESTER]. It's ridiculous, Twenty-six, for you to be in bed. The Sister's altogether too indulgent to you. Why didn't you pair of lazy devils entice him down to sit and cogitate under the warm wing of the sun in the garden?

SYLVESTER. Considerin' the low state of his general health.

SIMON. Aided by a touch of frost in the air.

SYLVESTER. Thinkin' it over we thought it might lead –

SIMON. To him getting an attack of double pneumonia.

SYLVESTER AND SIMON [*together*]. An' then he'd go off like – [*they blow through their lips*] poof – the snuff of a candle!

SUSIE. For the future, during the period you are patients here, I am to be addressed as 'Nurse Monican', and not as 'Susie'. Remember that, the pair of you, please.

HARRY *wheels himself in again, crossing by her, and, going over to the fire, looks out into grounds.*

SUSIE [*irritatedly, to* SYLVESTER]. Number Twenty-six, look at the state of your quilt. You must make an effort to keep it tidy. Dtch, dtch, dtch, what would the Matron say if she saw it!

SIMON [*with a nervous giggle*]. He's an uneasy divil, Nurse Monican.

SUSIE [*hotly, to* SIMON]. Yours is as bad as his, Twenty-seven. You mustn't lounge on your bed; it must be kept perfectly tidy [*she smoothes the quilts*]. Please don't make it necessary to mention this again. [*To* HARRY] Would you like to go down for a little while into the garden, Twenty-eight?

HARRY *crouches silent and moody.*

SUSIE [*continuing*]. After the sober rain of yesterday it is good to feel the new grace of the yellowing trees, and to get the fresh smell of the grass.

HARRY *wheels himself round and goes out by the left.*

SUSIE [*to* SYLVESTER *as she goes out*]. Remember, Twenty-six, if you're going to remain in a comatose condition, you'll have to keep your bed presentable. [*A pause.*]

SYLVESTER [*mimicking* SUSIE]. Twenty-six, if you're going to remeen in a comatowse condition, you'll have to keep your bed in a tidy an' awdahly mannah.

SIMON. Dtch, dtch, dtch, Twenty-seven, it's disgriceful. And as long as you're heah, in the capacity of a patient, please remember I'm not to be addressed as 'Susie', but as 'Nurse Monican'.

SYLVESTER. Twenty-seven, did you tike the pills the doctah awdahed?

VOICE OF SUSIE [*left*]. Twenty-six!

SYLVESTER. Yes, Nurse?

VOICE OF SUSIE. Sister says you're to have a bawth at once; and you, Twenty-seven, see about getting it ready for him. [*A fairly long pause.*]

SYLVESTER [*angrily*]. A bawth: well, be God, that's a good one! I'm not in a fit condition for a bath! [*Another pause. Earnestly, to* SIMON]. You haven't had a dip now for nearly a week, while I had one only the day before yesterday in the late evening: it must have been you she meant, Simon.

SIMON. Oh, there was no dubiety about her bellowing out Twenty-six, Syl.

SYLVESTER [*excitedly*]. How the hell d'ye know, man, she didn't mix the numbers up?

SIMON. Mix the numbers up! How could the woman mix the numbers up?

SYLVESTER. How could the woman mix the numbers up! What could be easier than to say Twenty-six instead of Twenty-seven? How could the woman mix the numbers up! Of course the woman could mix the numbers up!

SIMON. What d'ye expect me to do – hurl myself into a bath that was meant for you?

SYLVESTER. I don't want you to hurl yourself into anything; but you don't expect me to plunge into a bath that maybe wasn't meant for me?

SIMON. Nurse Monican said Twenty-six, and when you can alter that, ring me up and let me know. [*A pause; then* SIMON *gets up and goes toward the bathroom door.*]

SYLVESTER [*snappily*]. Where are you leppin' to now?

SIMON. I want to get the bath ready.

SYLVESTER. You want to get the bawth ready! Turn the hot cock on, and turn the cold cock on for Number Twenty-six, mixin' them the way a chemist would mix his medicines – sit still, man, till we hear the final verdict.

SIMON *sits down again.* SUSIE *comes in left, and, passing to the door leading to grounds, pauses beside* SIMON *and* SYLVESTER.

SUSIE [*sharply*]. What are the two of you doing? Didn't I tell you, Twenty-six, that you were to take a bawth; and you, Twenty-seven, that you were to get it ready for him?

SYLVESTER [*sitting brightly up in bed*]. Oh, just goin' to spring up, Nurse Monican, when you popped in.

SUSIE. Well, up with you, then, and take it. [*To* SIMON] You go and get it ready for him. [SIMON *goes into the bathroom.*]

SYLVESTER [*venturing a last hope as* SUSIE *goes towards the entrance to grounds*]. I had a dip, Nurse, only the day before yesterday in the late evening.

SUSIE [*as she goes out*]. Have another one now, please.

*The water can be heard flowing in the bathroom, and a light cloud of steam*
*comes out by the door which* SIMON *has left open.*

SYLVESTER [*mimicking* SUSIE]. Have another one, now, please! One to
be taken before and after meals. The delicate audacity of the lip of
that one since she draped her shoulders with a crimson cape!

SIMON *appears and stands leaning against the side of the bathroom door.*

SIMON [*gloating*]. She's steaming away now, Sylvester, full cock.
SYLVESTER [*scornfully, to* SIMON]. Music to you, the gurgling of the
thing, music to you. Gaugin' the temperature for me. Dtch, dtch,
dtch [*sitting up*], an hospital's the last place that God made. Be damn
it, I wouldn't let a stuffed bird stay in one!
SIMON. Come on, man, before the hot strength bubbles out of it.
SYLVESTER [*getting out of bed*]. Have you the towels hot an' everything
ready for me to spring into?
SIMON [*with a bow*]. Everything's ready for your enjoyment, Sir.
SYLVESTER [*as he goes towards the bathroom*]. Can't they be content with
an honest to God cleanliness, an' not be tryin' to gild a man with
soap and water.
SIMON [*with a grin, as* SYLVESTER *passes*]. Can I do anything more for
you, Sir?
SYLVESTER [*almost inarticulate with indignation, as he goes in*]. Now I'm
tellin' you, Simon Norton, our cordiality's gettin' a little strained!

HARRY *wheels himself in, goes again to the fireplace, and looks into*
*grounds.* SIMON *watches him for a moment, takes a package of cigarettes*
*from his pocket and lights one.*

SIMON [*awkwardly, to* HARRY]. Have a fag,* Harry, oul' son?
HARRY. Don't want one; tons of my own in the locker.
SIMON. Like me to get you one?
HARRY. I can get them myself if I want one. D'ye think my arms are
lifeless as well as my legs?
SIMON. Far from that. Everybody's remarking what a great improve-
ment has taken place in you during the last few days.
HARRY. Everybody but myself.
SIMON. What with the rubbing every morning and the rubbing every
night, and now the operation tomorrow as a grand finally, you'll

maybe be in the centre of the football field before many months are out.

HARRY [*irritably*]. Oh, shut up, man! It's a miracle I want – not an operation. The last operation was to give life to my limbs, but no life came, and again I felt the horrible sickness of life only from the waist up. [*Raising his voice*] Don't stand there gaping at me, man. Did you never clap your eyes on a body dead from the belly down? Blast you, man, why don't you shout at me, 'While there's life there's hope'!

SIMON *edges away to his corner.* SUSIE *comes in by the glass door and goes over to the table.*

HARRY [*to* SUSIE]. A package of fags. Out of the locker. Will you, Susie?

SUSIE *goes to* HARRY's *locker, gets the cigarettes and gives them to him. As he lights the cigarette, his right arm gives a sudden jerk.*

SUSIE. Steady. What's this?

HARRY [*with a nervous laugh*]. Barred from my legs it's flowing back into my arms. I can feel it slyly creeping into my fingers.

VOICE OF PATIENT, OUT LEFT [*plaintively*]. Nurse!

SUSIE [*turning her head in direction of the voice*]. Shush, you Twenty-three; go asleep, go asleep.

HARRY. A soft, velvety sense of distance between my fingers and the things I touch.

SUSIE. Stop thinking of it. Brooding checks the chance of your recovery. A good deal may be imagination.

HARRY [*peevishly*]. Oh, I know the different touches of iron [*he touches the bed-rail*]; of wood [*he touches the chair*]; of flesh [*he touches his cheek*]; and to my fingers they're giving the same answers – a feeling of numb distance between me and the touches of them all.

VOICE OF PATIENT, OUT LEFT. Nurse!

SUSIE. Dtch, dtch. Go asleep, Twenty-three.

VOICE, OUT LEFT. The stab in the head is worse than ever, Nurse.

SUSIE. You've got your dose of morphia, and you'll get no more. You'll just have to stick it.

RESIDENT SURGEON FORBY MAXWELL *enters from the grounds. He is about* *thirty years of age, and good-looking. His white overalls are unbuttoned, showing war ribbons on his waistcoat, flanked by the ribbon of the DSO.\* He has a careless, jaunty air, and evidently takes a decided interest in* SUSIE. *He comes in singing softly:*

> Stretched on the couch, Jessie fondled her dress,
> That hid all her beauties just over the knee;
> And I wondered and said, as I sigh'd, 'What a shame,
> That there's no room at all on the couch there for me.'

SUSIE [*to* SURGEON MAXWELL]. Twenty-three's at it again.

MAXWELL. Uh, hopeless case. Half his head in Flanders. May go on like that for another month.

SUSIE. He keeps the patients awake at night.

SIMON. With his 'God have mercys on me', running after every third or fourth tick of the clock.

HARRY. 'Tisn't fair to me, 'tisn't fair to me; I must get my bellyful of sleep if I'm ever going to get well.

MAXWELL. Oh, the poor devil won't trouble any of you much longer.
[*Singing*]

> Said Jess, with a light in the side of her eyes,
> 'A shrewd, mathematical fellow like you,
> With an effort of thought should be able to make
> The couch wide enough for the measure of two.'

SUSIE. Dtch, dtch, Surgeon Maxwell.

MAXWELL [*singing*].

> I fixed on a plan, and I carried it through,
> And the eyes of Jess gleam'd as she whisper'd to me:
> 'The couch, made for one, that was made to hold two,
> Has, maybe, been made big enough to hold three!'

SURGEON MAXWELL *catches* SUSIE's *hand in his.* SYLVESTER *bursts in from the bathroom, and rushes to his bed, colliding with the* SURGEON *as he passes him.*

MAXWELL. Hallo, hallo there, what's this?

SYLVESTER [*flinging himself into bed, covering himself rapidly with the*

*clothes, blowing himself warm*]. Pooh, pooh, I feel as if I was sittin' on
the doorstep of pneumonia! Pooh, oh!

MAXWELL [*to* SYLVESTER]. We'll have a look at you in a moment,
Twenty-six, and see what's wrong with you.

SYLVESTER *subsides down into the bed, and* SIMON *edges towards the
entrance to the grounds, and stands looking into the grounds, or watching*
SURGEON MAXWELL *examining* SYLVESTER.

MAXWELL [*to* HARRY, *who is looking intently out into the grounds*]. Well,
how are we today, Heegan?

HARRY. I imagine I don't feel quite so dead in myself as I've felt these
last few days back.

MAXWELL. Oh, well, that's something.

HARRY. Sometimes I think I feel a faint, fluttering kind of a buzz in the
tops of my thighs.

MAXWELL [*touching* HARRY's *thigh*]. Where, here?

HARRY. No; higher up, doctor; just where the line is that leaves the
one part living and the other part dead.

MAXWELL. A buzz?

HARRY. A timid, faint, fluttering kind of a buzz.

MAXWELL. That's good. There might be a lot in that faint, fluttering
kind of a buzz.

HARRY [*after a pause*]. I'm looking forward to the operation tomorrow.

MAXWELL. That's the way to take it. While there's life there's hope
[*with a grin and a wink at* SUSIE]. And now we'll have a look at
Twenty-six.

HARRY, *when he hears 'While there's life there's hope', wheels himself
madly out left; half-way out he turns his head and stretches to look out into
the grounds, then he goes on.*

SUSIE. Will the operation tomorrow be successful?

MAXWELL. Oh, of course; very successful.

SUSIE. Do him any good, d'ye think?

MAXWELL. Oh, blast the good it'll do him.

SUSIE *goes over to* SYLVESTER *in the bed.*

SUSIE [*to* SYLVESTER]. Sit up. Twenty-six, Surgeon Maxwell wants to
examine you.

SYLVESTER [*sitting up with a brave effort but a woeful smile*]. Righto. In the pink!

SURGEON MAXWELL *comes over, twirling his stethoscope.* SIMON *peeps round the corner of the glass door.*

SUSIE [*to* SURGEON MAXWELL]. What was the cause of the row between the Matron and Nurse Jennings? [*To* SYLVESTER] Open your shirt, Twenty-six.

MAXWELL [*who has fixed the stethoscope in his ears, removing it to speak to* SUSIE]. Caught doing the tango in the Resident's arms in the Resident's room. Naughty girl, naughty girl. [*To* SYLVESTER] Say 'ninety-nine'.

SYLVESTER. Ninety-nine.

SUSIE. Oh, I knew something like this would happen. Daughter of a Dean, too.

MAXWELL [*to* SYLVESTER]. Say 'ninety-nine'.

SYLVESTER. Ninety-nine. U-u-uh, it's gettin' very cold here, sitting up!

MAXWELL [*to* SYLVESTER]. Again. Don't be frightened; breathe quietly.

SYLVESTER. Ninety-nine. Cool as a cucumber, Doctor. Ninety-nine.

MAXWELL [*to* SUSIE]. Damn pretty little piece. Not so pretty as you, though.

SYLVESTER [*to* SURGEON MAXWELL]. Yesterday Doctor Joyce, givin' me a run over, said to a couple of medical men that were with him lookin' for tips,* that the thing was apparently yieldin' to treatment, and that an operation wouldn't be necessary.

MAXWELL. Go on; ninety-nine, ninety-nine.

SYLVESTER. Ninety-nine, ninety-nine.

MAXWELL [*to* SUSIE]. Kicks higher than her head, and you should see her doing the splits.

SYLVESTER. [*to* SURGEON MAXWELL]. Any way of gettin' rid of it'll do for me, for I'm not one of them that'll spend a night before an operation in a crowd of prayers.

SUSIE. Not very useful things to be doing and poor patients awaiting attention.

MAXWELL [*putting stethoscope into pocket*]. He'll do all right; quite fit. Great old skin. [*To* SYLVESTER] You can cover yourself up, now. [*To* SUSIE] And don't tell me, Nurse Susie, that you've never felt a thrill

or left a bedside for a kiss in a corner. [*He tickles her under the arm.*]
Kiss in a corner, Nurse!

SUSIE [*pleased, but coy*]. Please don't, Doctor Maxwell, please.

MAXWELL [*tickling her again as they go out*]. Kiss in a corner;
ta-ra-ra-ra, kiss in a corner! [*A pause.*]

SYLVESTER [*to* SIMON]. Simon, were you listenin' to that conversation?

SIMON. Indeed I was.

SYLVESTER. We have our hands full, Simon, to keep alive. Think of
sinkin' your body to the level of a hand that, ta-ra-ra-ra, would
plunge a knife into your middle, haphazard, hurryin' up to run
away after a thrill from a kiss in a corner. Did you see me dizzied an'
wastin' me time pumpin' ninety-nines out of me, unrecognised,
quiverin' with cold an' equivocation!

SIMON. Everybody says he's a very clever fellow with the knife.

SYLVESTER. He'd gouge out your eye, saw off your arm, lift a load of
vitals out of your middle, rub his hands, keep down a terrible desire
to cheer lookin' at the ruin, an' say, 'Twenty-six, when you're a
little better, you'll feel a new man!'

MRS HEEGAN, MRS FORAN, *and* TEDDY *enter from the grounds.* MRS FORAN
*is leading* TEDDY, *who has a heavy bandage over his eyes, and is dressed in
the blue clothes of military hospitals.*

MRS FORAN [*to* TEDDY]. Just a little step here, Ted; upsh! That's it; now
we're on the earth again, beside Simon and Sylvester. You'd better
sit here. [*She puts him sitting on a chair.*]

SYLVESTER [*to* MRS HEEGAN *as she kisses him*]. Well, how's the old
woman, eh?

MRS HEEGAN. A little anxious about poor Harry.

SIMON. He'll be all right. Tomorrow'll tell a tale.

SUSIE [*coming in, annoyed*]. Who let you up here at this hour?
Twenty-eight's to have an operation tomorrow, and shouldn't be
disturbed.

MRS HEEGAN. Sister Peter Alcantara said we might come up, Nurse.

MRS FORAN [*loftily*]. Sister Peter Alcantara's authority ought to be
good enough, I think.

MRS HEEGAN. Sister Peter Alcantara said a visit might buck him up a
bit.

MRS FORAN. Sister Peter Alcantara knows the responsibility she'd incur by keeping a wife from her husband and a mother from her son.

SUSIE. Sister Peter Alcantara hasn't got to nurse him. And remember, nothing is to be said that would make his habit of introspection worse than it is.

MRS FORAN [*with dignity*]. Thanks for the warnin', Nurse, but them kind of mistakes is unusual with us.

SUSIE *goes out left, as* HARRY *wheels himself rapidly in. Seeing the group, he stops suddenly, and a look of disappointment comes on to his face.*

MRS HEEGAN [*kissing* HARRY]. How are you, son?

MRS FORAN. I brought Teddy, your brother in arms, up to see you, Harry.

HARRY [*impatiently*]. Where's Jessie? I thought you were to bring her with you?

MRS HEEGAN. She's comin' after us in a moment.

HARRY. Why isn't she here now?

MRS FORAN. She stopped to have a word in the grounds with someone she knew.

HARRY. It was Barney Bagnal, was it? Was it Barney Bagnal?

TEDDY. Maybe she wanted to talk to him about gettin' the VC.*

HARRY. What VC? Who's gettin' the VC?

TEDDY. Barney. Did he not tell you? [MRS FORAN *prods his knee.*] What's up?

HARRY [*intensely, to* TEDDY]. What's he gettin' it for? What's he gettin' the VC for?

TEDDY. For carryin' you wounded out of the line of fire. [MRS FORAN *prods his knee.*] What's up?

HARRY [*in anguish*]. Christ Almighty, for carryin' me wounded out of the line of fire!

MRS HEEGAN [*rapidly*]. Harry, I wouldn't be thinkin' of anything till we see what the operation'll do tomorrow.

SIMON [*rapidly*]. God, if it gave him back the use even of one of his legs.

MRS FORAN [*rapidly*]. Look at all the places he could toddle to, an' all the things he could do then with the prop of a crutch.

MRS HEEGAN. Even at the worst, he'll never be dependin' on anyone, for he's bound to get the maximum allowance.

SIMON. Two quid a week, isn't it?

SYLVESTER. Yes, a hundred per cent total incapacitation.

HARRY. She won't come up if one of you don't go down and bring her up.

MRS HEEGAN. She's bound to come up, for she's got your ukulele.

HARRY. Call her up, Simon, call her up – I must see Jessie.

SIMON *goes over to the door leading to the grounds, and looks out.*

MRS FORAN [*bending over till her face is close to* HARRY's]. The drawn look on his face isn't half as bad as when I seen him last.

MRS HEEGAN [*bending and looking into* HARRY's *face*]. Look, the hollows under his eyes is fillin' up, too.

TEDDY. I'm afraid he'll have to put Jessie out of his head, for when a man's hit in the spine . . . [MRS FORAN *prods his knee.*] What's up, woman?

HARRY [*impatiently, to* SIMON]. Is she coming? Can you see her anywhere?

SIMON. I can see someone like her in the distance, under the trees.

HARRY. Call her; can't you give her a shout, man?

SIMON [*calling*]. Jessie. Is that you, Jessie? Jessie-e!

MRS HEEGAN [*to* HARRY]. What time are you goin' under the operation?

HARRY [*to* SIMON]. Call her again, call her again, can't you!

SIMON [*calling*]. Jessie, Jessie-e!

TEDDY. Not much of a chance for an injury to the spine, for . . .

MRS FORAN [*putting her face close to* TEDDY's]. Oh, shut up, you!

HARRY. Why did you leave her in the grounds? Why didn't you wait till she came up with you?

MRS FORAN [*going over to* SIMON *and calling*]. Jessie, Jessie-e!

JESSIE'S VOICE [*in distance*]. Yehess!

MRS FORAN [*calling*]. Come up here at once; we're all waitin' for you!

JESSIE'S VOICE. I'm not going up!

MRS FORAN [*calling*]. Bring up that ukulele here at once, miss!

JESSIE'S VOICE. Barney'll bring it up!

HARRY, *who has been listening intently, wheels himself rapidly to where* SIMON *and* MRS FORAN *are, pushing through them hurriedly.*

HARRY [*calling loudly*]. Jessie! Jessie! Jessie-e!

MRS FORAN. Look at that, now; she's runnin' away, the young rip!

HARRY [*appealingly*]. Jessie, Jessie-e!

SUSIE *enters quickly from left. She goes over to* HARRY *and pulls him back from the door.*

SUSIE [*indignantly*]. Disgraceful! Rousing the whole ward with this commotion! Dear, dear, dear, look at the state of Twenty-eight. Come along, come along, please; you must all go at once.

HARRY. Jessie's coming up for a minute, Nurse.

SUSIE. No more to come up. We've had enough for one night, and you for a serious operation tomorrow. Come on, all out, please. [SUSIE *conducts* MRS HEEGAN, MRS FORAN, *and* TEDDY *out left.*]

MRS FORAN [*going out*]. We're goin', we're goin', thank you. A nice way to treat the flotsum and jetsum of the battlefields!

SUSIE [*to* HARRY]. To bed now, Twenty-eight, please. [*To* SIMON] Help me get him to bed, Twenty-seven.

SUSIE *pushes* HARRY *to his bed, right;* SIMON *brings portion of a bed-screen which he places around* HARRY, *hiding him from view.*

SUSIE [*turning to speak to* SYLVESTER, *who is sitting up in bed, as she arranges screen*]. You're going to have your little operation in the morning, so you'd better go to sleep too.

SYLVESTER *goes pale and a look of dismay and fear crawls over his face.*

SUSIE. Don't funk it now. They're not going to turn you inside out. It'll be over in ten minutes.

SYLVESTER [*with a groan*]. When they once get you down your only hope is in the infinite mercy of God!

SIMON. If I was you, Sylvester, I wouldn't take this operation too seriously. You know th' oul' song – Let Me Like a Soldier Fall!* If I was you, I'd put it completely out of me mind.

SYLVESTER [*subsiding on to the pillow – with an agonised look on his face*]. Let me like a soldier fall! Did anyone ever hear th' equal o' that! Put it out of me mind completely! [*He sits up, and glares at* SIMON]. Eh, you, look! If you can't think sensibly, then thry to think without talkin'! [*He sinks back on the pillow again.*] Let me like a soldier fall. Oh, it's not a fair trial for a sensible man to be stuck down in a world like this!

SYLVESTER *slides down till he lies prone and motionless on the bed.* HARRY *is in bed now.* SIMON *removes the screen, and* SUSIE *arranges* HARRY'S *quilt for the night.*

SUSIE [*to* SIMON]. Now run and help get the things together for supper. [SIMON *goes out left.*] [*Encouragingly to* HARRY] After the operation, a stay in the air of the Convalescent may work wonders.

HARRY. If I could mingle my breath with the breeze that blows from every sea, and over every land, they wouldn't widen me into anything more than the shrivell'd thing I am.

SUSIE [*switching off the two hanging lights, so that the red light over the fireplace alone remains*]. Don't be foolish, Twenty-eight. Wheeling yourself about among the beeches and the pines, when the daffodils are hanging out their blossoms, you'll deepen your chance in the courage and renewal of the country.

*The bell of a convent in grounds begins to ring for Compline.*

HARRY [*with intense bitterness*]. I'll say to the pine, 'Give me the grace and beauty of the beech'; I'll say to the beech, 'Give me the strength and stature of the pine.' In a net I'll catch butterflies in bunches; twist and mangle them between my fingers and fix them wriggling on to mercy's banner. I'll make my chair a Juggernaut, and wheel it over the neck and spine of every daffodil that looks at me, and strew them dead to manifest the mercy of God and the justice of man!

SUSIE [*shocked*]. Shush, Harry, Harry!

HARRY. To hell with you, your country, trees, and things, you jibbering jay!

SUSIE [*as she is going out*]. Twenty-eight!

HARRY [*vehemently*]. To hell with you, your country, trees, and things, you jibbering jay!

SUSIE *looks at him, pauses for a few moments, as if to speak, and then goes out.*

   *A pause; then* BARNEY *comes in by door from grounds. An overcoat covers his military hospital uniform of blue. His left arm is in a sling. Under his right arm he carries a ukulele, and in his hand he has a bunch of flowers. Embarrassed, he goes slowly to* HARRY'S *bed, drops the flowers at the foot, then he drops the ukulele there.*

BARNEY [*awkwardly*]. Your ukulele. An' a bunch of flowers from

Jessie. [HARRY *remains motionless on the bed.*] A bunch of flowers from Jessie, and . . . your . . . ukulele.

*The* SISTER OF THE WARD *enters, left, going to the chapel for Compline. She wears a cream habit with a white coif; a large set of rosary beads hangs from her girdle. She pauses on her way, and a brass crucifix flashes on her bosom.*

SISTER [*to* HARRY]. Keeping brave and hopeful, Twenty-eight?

HARRY [*softly*]. Yes, Sister.

SISTER. Splendid. And we've got a ukulele too. Can you play it, my child?

HARRY. Yes, Sister.

SISTER. Splendid. You must play me something when you're well over the operation. [*To* BARNEY] Standing guard over your comrade, Twenty-two, eh?

BARNEY [*softly and shyly*]. Yes, Sister.

SISTER. Grand. Forasmuch as ye do it unto the least of these my brethren, ye do it unto me.* Well, God be with you both, my children. [*To* HARRY] And Twenty-eight, pray to God for wonderful He is in His doing toward the children of men.* [*Calm and dignified she goes out into the grounds.*]

BARNEY [*pausing as he goes out left*]. They're on the bed; the ukulele, and the bunch of flowers from . . . Jessie.

*The* SISTERS *are heard singing in the Convent the hymn of Salve Regina:*

Salve Regina, mater misericordiae;
Vitae dulcedo et spes nostra, salve!
Ad te clamamus, exules filii Hevae;
Ad te suspiramus, gementes et flentes in hac lacrymarum valle.
Eia ergo Advocata nostra,
Illos tuos misericordes oculos ad nos converte,
Et Jesum, benedictum fructum ventris tui –*

HARRY. God of the miracles, give a poor devil a chance, give a poor devil a chance!

SISTERS.

Nobis post hoc exsilium ostende,
O clemens, o pia, o dulcis Virgo Maria!*

CURTAIN

## ACT IV

*A room off the dance-hall of the Avondale Football Club. At back, left,
cutting corners of the back and side walls, is the arched entrance, divided by
a slim pillar, to the dance-hall. This entrance is hung with crimson and
black striped curtains; whenever these are parted the dancers can be seen
swinging or gliding past the entrance if a dance be taking place at the time.
Over the entrance is a scroll on which is printed: 'Up the Avondales!' The
wall back has a wide, tall window which opens to the garden, in which the
shrubs and some sycamore trees can be seen. It is hung with apple-green
casement curtains, which are pulled to the side to allow the window to be
open as it is at present. Between the entrance to hall and the window is a
Roll of Honour containing the names of five menbers of the Club killed in
the war. Underneath the Roll of Honour a wreath of laurel tied with red
and black ribbon. To the front left is the fireplace. Between the fireplace
and the hall-entrance is a door on which is an oval white enamel disc with
'Caretaker' painted on it. To the right a long table, covered with a green
cloth, on which are numerous bottles of wine and a dozen glasses. On the
table, too, is a telephone. A brown carpet covers the floor. Two easy and
one ordinary chairs are in the room. Hanging from the ceiling are three
lanterns; the centre one is four times the length of its width, the ones at the side
are less than half as long as the centre lantern and hang horizontally; the
lanterns are black, with a broad red stripe running down the centre of the
largest and across those hanging at each side, so that, when they are lighted,
they suggest an illuminated black cross with an inner one of gleaming red.
The hall is vividly decorated with many coloured lanterns, looped with
coloured streamers.*

*When the scene is revealed the curtains are drawn, and the band can be
heard playing a foxtrot. Outside in the garden, near the window,* SIMON
*and* SYLVESTER *can be seen smoking, and* TEDDY *is walking slowly up and
down the path. The band is heard playing for a few moments, then the
curtains are pulled aside, and* JESSIE *with* BARNEY *holding her hand,
comes in and walks rapidly to the table where the wine is standing. They are
quickly followed by* HARRY. SIMON *and* SYLVESTER, *outside, watch those
in the room through the window.* BARNEY *wears a neat navy-blue suit, with
a rather high, stiff collar and black tie. Pinned on the breast of his
waistcoat are his war medals, flanked by the Victoria Cross.* HARRY *is also
wearing his medals.* JESSIE *has on a very pretty, rather tight-fitting dance
frock, with the sleeves falling widely to the elbow, and cut fairly low on her*

*breast. All the dancers, and* HARRY *too, wear coloured, fantastically shaped paper hats.*

JESSIE [*hot, excited, and uneasy, as with a rapid glance back she sees the curtains parted by* HARRY]. Here he comes prowling after us again! His watching of us is pulling all the enjoyment out of the night. It makes me shiver to feel him wheeling after us.

BARNEY. We'll watch for a chance to shake him off, an' if he starts again we'll make him take his tangled body somewhere else. [*As* HARRY *moves forward from the curtained entrance*] Shush, he's comin' near us. [*In a louder tone to* JESSIE] Red wine, Jessie, for you, or white wine?

. HARRY. Red wine first, Jessie, to the passion and the power and the pain of life, an' then a drink of white wine to the melody that is in them all!

JESSIE. I'm so hot.

HARRY. I'm so cold; white wine for the woman warm to make her cold; red wine for the man that's cold to make him warm!

JESSIE. White wine for me.

HARRY. For me the red wine till I drink to men puffed up with pride of strength, for even creeping things can praise the Lord!*

BARNEY [*gently to* HARRY, *as he gives a glass of wine to* JESSIE]. No more for you now, Harry.

HARRY [*mockingly*]. Oh, please, your lusty lordship, just another, an' if I seek a second, smack me well. [*Wheeling his chair viciously against* BARNEY] Get out, you trimm'd-up clod. There's medals on my breast as well as yours! [*He fills a glass*].

JESSIE. Let us go back to the dancing, Barney. [BARNEY *hesitates.*] Please, Barney, let us go back to the dancing!

HARRY. To the dancing, for the day cometh when no man can play.* And legs were made to dance, to run, to jump, to carry you from one place to another; but mine can neither walk, nor run, nor jump, nor feel the merry motion of a dance. But stretch me on the floor fair on my belly, and I will turn over on my back, then wriggle back again on to my belly; and that's more than a dead, dead man can do!

BARNEY. Jessie wants to dance, an' so we'll go, and leave you here a little.

HARRY. Cram pain with pain, and pleasure cram with pleasure. I'm going too. You'd cage me in from seeing you dance, and dance, and

dance, with Jessie close to you, and you so close to Jessie. Though you wouldn't think it, yes, I have – I've hammer'd out many a merry measure upon a polish'd floor with a sweet, sweet heifer. [*As* BARNEY *and* JESSIE *are moving away he catches hold of* JESSIE's *dress*] Her name? Oh, any name will do – we'll call her Jessie!

JESSIE. Oh, let me go. [*To* BARNEY] Barney, make him let me go, please.

BARNEY, *without a word, removes* HARRY's *hand from* JESSIE's *dress.* JESSIE *and* BARNEY *then go out to the dance-hall through the curtained entrance into the hall. After a moment's pause* HARRY *follows them into the hall.* SIMON *and* SYLVESTER *come in from the garden, leaving* TEDDY *still outside smoking and walking to and fro in the cautious manner of the blind.* SIMON *and* SYLVESTER *sit down near the fire and puff in silence for a few moments.*

SYLVESTER [*earnestly*]. I knew it. I knew it, Simon – strainin' an' strainin' his nerves; driftin' towards an hallucination!

SIMON. Jessie might try to let him down a little more gently, but it would have been better, I think, if Harry hadn't come here tonight.

SYLVESTER. I concur in that, Simon. What's a decoration to an hospital is an anxiety here.

SIMON. To carry life and colour to where there's nothing but the sick and helpless is right; but to carry the sick and helpless to where there's nothing but life and colour is wrong.

*The telephone bell rings.*

SYLVESTER. There's the telephone bell ringing.

SIMON. Oh, someone'll come in and answer it in a second.

SYLVESTER. To join a little strength to a lot of weakness is what I call sensible; but to join a little weakness to a lot of strength is what I call a . . .

SIMON. A cod.*

SYLVESTER. Exactly. [*The telephone continues to ring.*] That's the telephone ringin' still.

SIMON. Oh, someone'll come in and answer it in a second.

TEDDY *has groped his way to French window.*

TEDDY. The telephone's tinklin', boys.

SYLVESTER. Thanks, Teddy. We hear it, thanks. [*To* SIMON] When he got the invitation from the Committay to come, wearin' his decorations, me an' the old woman tried to persuade him that, seein' his condition, it was better to stop at home, an' let me represent him, but [*with a gesture*] no use!

TEDDY *resumes his walk to and fro.*

SIMON. It was natural he'd want to come, since he was the means of winning the Cup twice before for them, leading up to their keeping the trophy for ever by the win of a year ago.

SYLVESTER. To bring a boy so helpless as him, whose memory of agility an' strength time hasn't flattened down, to a place wavin' with joy an' dancin', is simply, simply –

SIMON. Devastating, I'd say.

SYLVESTER. Of course it is! Is that god-damn telephone goin' to keep ringin' all night?

MRS FORAN *enters from hall quickly.*

MRS FORAN. Miss Monican says that one of you is to answer the telephone, an' call her if it's anything important.

SYLVESTER [*nervously*]. I never handled a telephone in my life.

SIMON. I chanced it once and got so hot and quivery that I couldn't hear a word, and didn't know what I was saying myself.

MRS FORAN. Have a shot at it and see.

*The three of them drift over to the telephone.*

SYLVESTER. Chance it again, Simon, an' try to keep steady. [*As* SIMON *stretches his hand to the receiver*] Don't rush, don't rush, man, an' make a mess of it. Take it in your stride.

SIMON [*pointing to receiver*]. When you lift this down, you're connected, I think.

SYLVESTER. No use of thinkin' on this job. Don't you turn the handle first?

SIMON [*irritably*]. No, you don't turn no handle, man!

MRS FORAN. Let Simon do it now; Simon knows.

SIMON *tremblingly lifts down the receiver, almost letting it fall.*

SYLVESTER. Woa, woa, Simon; careful, careful!

SIMON [*speaking in receiver*]. Eh, hallo! Eh, listen there. Eh, hallo! listen.

SYLVESTER. You listen man, an' give the fellow at the other end a chance to speak.

SIMON. If you want me to manipulate the thing, let me manipulate it in tranquillity.

MRS FORAN [*to* SYLVESTER]. Oh, don't be puttin' him out, Sylvester.

SIMON [*waving them back*]. Don't be crushing in on me; give me room to manipulate the thing. [*Dead silence for some moments.*]

MRS FORAN. Are you hearin' anything from the other end?

SIMON. A kind of buzzing and a roaring noise. [SYLVESTER *suddenly gives the cord a jerk and pulls the receiver out of* SIMON's *hand. Angrily*] What the hell are you trying to do, man? You're after pulling it right out of my mit.

SYLVESTER [*heatedly*]. There was a knot or a twist an' a tangle in it that was keepin' the sound from travellin'.

SIMON. If you want me to work the thing properly, you'll have to keep yourself from interfering. [*Resuming surlily*] Eh, hallo, listen, yes? Ha! ha! ha! ha! Yes, yes, yes. No, no, no. Cheerio! Yes. Eh, hallo, listen, eh. Hallo.

SYLVESTER. What is it? What're they sayin'?

SIMON [*hopelessly, taking the receiver from his ear*]. I don't seem to be able to hear a damn sound.

SYLVESTER. An' Holy God, what are you yessin' and noin' and cheerioin' out of you for then?

SIMON. You couldn't stand here like a fool and say nothing, could you?

SYLVESTER. Show it to me, Simon, show it to me – you're not holdin' it at the proper angle.

MRS FORAN. Give it to Syl, Simon; it's a delicate contrivance that needs a knack in handlin'.

SYLVESTER [*as he is taking the receiver from* SIMON *and carefully placing it to his ear*]. You have always to preserve an eqwee-balance between the speakin' mouth and the hearin' ear. [*Speaking into receiver*] Hallo! Anybody there at the other end of this? Eh, wha's that? Yes, yes, I've got you. [*Taking the receiver from his ear and speaking to* SIMON *and* MRS FORAN] Something like wine, or dine, or shine, or something – an' a thing that's hummin'.

SIMON. I can see no magnificent meaning jumping out of that!

MRS FORAN. They couldn't be talkin' about bees, could they?

SYLVESTER [*scornfully*]. Bees! No, they couldn't be talkin' about bees! That kind of talk, Mrs Foran, only tends to confuse matters. Bees! Dtch, dtch, dtch – the stupidity of some persons is . . . terrifyin'!

SIMON. Ask them quietly what they want.

SYLVESTER [*indignantly*]. What the hell's the use of askin' them that, when I can hear something only like a thing that's hummin'?

MRS FORAN. It wouldn't be, now, comin', or even bummin'?

SYLVESTER. It might even possibly be drummin'. Personally, Mrs Foran, I think, since you can't help, you might try to keep from hinderin'.

SIMON. Put it back, Syl, where it was, an' if it rings again, we'll only have to slip quietly out of this.

MRS FORAN. Yes, put it back, an' say it never rang.

SYLVESTER. Where was it? Where do I put it back?

SIMON. On that thing stickin' out there. Nice and gently now.

SYLVESTER *cautiously puts receiver back. They look at the telephone for a few moments, then go back to the fire, one by one.* SYLVESTER *stands with his back to it;* SIMON *sits in a chair, over the back of which* MRS FORAN *leans.*

MRS FORAN. Curious those at the other end of the telephone couldn't make themselves understood.

SIMON. Likely they're not accustomed to it, and it's a bit difficult if you're not fully conscious of its manipulation.

SYLVESTER. Well, let them study an' study it then, or abide by the consequences, for we can't be wastin' time teachin' them.

*The curtains at entrance of dance-hall are pulled aside, and* TEDDY, *who has disappeared from the garden a little time before, comes in. As he leaves the curtains apart, the dancers can be seen gliding past the entrance in the movements of a tango.* TEDDY *comes down, looks steadily but vacantly towards the group around the fire, then goes over carefully to the table, where he moves his hand about till it touches a bottle, which he takes up in one hand, feeling it questioningly with the other.*

SIMON. How goes it, Teddy?

TEDDY [*with a vacant look towards them*]. Sylvester – Simon – Well.

What seest thou, Teddy? Thou seest not as man seeth. In the
garden the trees stand up; the green things showeth themselves and
fling out flowers of divers hues. In the sky the sun by day and the
moon and the stars by night – nothing. In the hall the sound of
dancing, the eyes of women, grey and blue and brown and black, do
sparkle and dim and sparkle again. Their white breasts rise and fall,
and rise again. Slender legs, from red and black, and white and
green, come out, go in again – nothing. Strain as you may, it
stretches from the throne of God to the end of the hearth of hell.

SIMON. What?

TEDDY. The darkness.

SIMON [*knowing not what to say*]. Yes, oh yes.

TEDDY [*holding up a bottle of wine*]. What colour, Syl? It's all the same,
but I like the red the best.

MRS FORAN [*going over to* TEDDY]. Just one glass, dear, and you'll sit
down quietly an' take it in sips.

MRS FORAN *fills a glass of wine for* TEDDY, *leads him to a chair, puts him
sitting down, and gives the glass of wine carefully to him. The band in the
hall has been playing, and through the parted curtains the dancers are seen
gliding past.* JESSIE *moves by now in the arms of* BARNEY, *and in a few
moments is followed along the side of the hall by* HARRY *wheeling himself in
his chair and watching them.* MRS FORAN *and the two men look on and
become attentive when among the dancers* SUSIE, *in the arms of* SURGEON
MAXWELL, JESSIE *partnered with* BARNEY, *and* HARRY *move past.*

SYLVESTER [*as* SUSIE *goes by*]. Susie Monican's lookin' game enough
tonight for anything.

SIMON. Hardly remindful of her one-time fear of God.

SYLVESTER [*as* JESSIE *goes by followed by* HARRY]. There he goes, still
followin' them.

SIMON. And Jessie's looking as if she was tired of her maidenhood,
too.

MRS FORAN. The thin threads holdin' her dress up sidlin' down over
her shoulders, an' her catchin' them up again at the tail end of the
second before it was too late.

SIMON [*grinning*]. And Barney's hand inching up, inching up to pull
them a little lower when they're sliding down.

MRS FORAN. Astonishin' the way girls are advertisin' their immodesty.
Whenever one of them sits down, in my heart I pity the poor men

havin' to view the disedifyin' sight of the full length of one leg couched over another.

TEDDY [*forgetful*]. A damn nice sight, all the same, I think.

MRS FORAN [*indignantly*]. One would imagine such a thought would jar a man's mind that had kissed goodbye to the sight of his eyes.

TEDDY. Oh, don't be tickin' off every word I say!

MRS FORAN [*after an astonished pause, whipping the glass out of* TEDDY'*s hand*]. Damn the drop more, now, you'll get for the rest of the evenin'.

*The band suddenly stops playing, and the couples seen just then through the doorway stop dancing and look attentively up the hall. After a slight pause,* HARRY *in his chair, pushed by* SUSIE, *comes in through the entrance: his face is pale and drawn, his breath comes in quick faint gasps, and his head is leaning sideways on the back of the chair.* MRS HEEGAN *is one side of* HARRY, *and* SURGEON MAXWELL, *who is in dinner-jacket style of evening dress, wearing his medals, including the DSO walks on the other.* HARRY *is wheeled over near the open window.* BARNEY *and* JESSIE, *standing in the entrance, look on and listen.*

MAXWELL. Here near the window. [*To* MRS HEEGAN] He'll be all right, Mrs Heegan, in a second; a little faint – too much excitement. When he recovers a little, I'd get him home.

HARRY [*faintly but doggedly*]. Napoo home, napoo. Not yet. I'm all right. I'll spend a little time longer in the belly of an hour bulgin' out with merriment. Carry on.

MAXWELL. Better for you to go home, Heegan.

HARRY. When they drink to the Club from the Cup – the Silver Tassie – that I won three times, three times for them – that first was filled to wet the lips of Jessie and of me – I'll go, but not yet. I'm all right; my name is yet only a shadow on the Roll of Honour.

MRS HEEGAN. Come home, Harry; you're gettin' your allowance only on the understandin' that you take care of yourself.

HARRY. Get the Cup. I'll mind it here till you're ready to send it round to drink to the Avondales – on the table here beside me. Bring the Cup; I'll mind it here on the table beside me.

MAXWELL. Get the Cup for him, someone.

SIMON *goes to the hall and returns with the Cup, which he gives to* HARRY.

HARRY [*holding the Cup out*]. A first drink again for me, for me alone this time, for the shell that hit me bursts for ever between Jessie and me. [*To* SIMON] Go on, man, fill out the wine!

MAXWELL [*to* SIMON]. A little – just a glass. Won't do him any harm. [*To* HARRY] Then you'll have to remain perfectly quiet, Heegan.

HARRY. The wine . . . fill out the wine!

SIMON [*to* HARRY]. Red wine or white?

HARRY. Red wine, red like the faint remembrance of the fires in France; red wine like the poppies that spill their petals on the breasts of the dead men. No, white wine, white like the stillness of the millions that have removed their clamours from the crowd of life. No, red wine; red like the blood that was shed for you and for many for the commission of sin!* [*He drinks the wine.*] Steady, Harry, and lift up thine eyes unto the hills.* [*Roughly to those around him*] What are you all gaping at?

MAXWELL. Now, now, Heegan – you must try to keep quiet.

SUSIE. And when you've rested and feel better, you will sing for us a Negro spiritual, and point the melody with the ukulele.

MRS HEEGAN. Just as he used to do.

SYLVESTER. Behind the trenches.

SIMON. In the rest-camps.

MRS FORAN. Out in France.

HARRY. Push your sympathy away from me, for I'll have none of it. [*He wheels his chair quickly towards the dance-hall.*] Go on with the dancing and keep the ball a-rolling. [*Calling loudly at the entrance*] Trumpets and drum begin! [*The band begins to play.*] Dance and dance and dance. [*He listens for a moment.*] Sink into merriment again, and sling your cares to God! [*He whirls round in the chair to the beat of the tune.* *Dancers are seen gliding past entrance.*] Dear God, I can't. [*He sinks sideways on his chair.*] I must, must rest. [*He quietly recites*]

> For a spell here I will stay,
> Then pack up my body and go –
> For mine is a life on the ebb,
> Yours a full life on the flow!

HARRY *goes over to far side of window and looks out into garden.* MRS HEEGAN *is on his right and* TEDDY *on his left;* SIMON *and* SYLVESTER *a little behind, looking on.* MRS FORAN *to the right of* MRS HEEGAN. SURGEON

MAXWELL *and* SUSIE, *who are a little to the front, watch for a moment, then the* SURGEON *puts his arm round* SUSIE *and the pair glide off into the dance-hall.*

*When* SURGEON MAXWELL *and* SUSIE *glide in to the motions of the dance through the entrance into the dance hall, the curtains are pulled together. A few moments' pause.* TEDDY *silently puts his hand on* HARRY's *shoulder, and they both stare into the garden.*

SIMON. The air'll do him good.

SYLVESTER. An' give him breath to sing his song an' play the ukulele.

MRS HEEGAN. Just as he used to do.

SYLVESTER. Behind the trenches.

SIMON. In the Rest Camps.

MRS FORAN. Out in France.

HARRY. I can see, but I cannot dance.

TEDDY. I can dance, but I cannot see.

HARRY. Would that I had the strength to do the things I see.

TEDDY. Would that I could see the things I've strength to do.

HARRY. The Lord hath given and the Lord hath taken away.

TEDDY. Blessed be the name of the Lord.*

MRS FORAN. I do love the ukulele, especially when it goes tinkle, tinkle, tinkle in the night-time.

SYLVESTER. Bringin' before you glistenin' bodies of blacks, coilin' themselves an' shufflin' an' prancin' in a great jungle dance; shakin' assegais an' spears to the rattle, rattle, rattle an' thud, thud, thud of the tom-toms.

MRS FORAN. There's only one possible musical trimmin' to the air of a Negro spiritual, an' that's the tinkle, tinkle, tinkle of a ukulele.

HARRY. The rising sap in trees I'll never feel.

TEDDY. The hues of branch or leaf I'll never see.

HARRY. There's something wrong with life when men can walk.

TEDDY. There's something wrong with life when men can see.

HARRY. I never felt the hand that made me helpless.

TEDDY. I never saw the hand that made me blind.

HARRY. Life came and took away the half of life.

TEDDY. Life took from me the half he left with you.

HARRY. The Lord hath given and the Lord hath taken away.

TEDDY. Blessed be the name of the Lord.

SUSIE *comes quickly in by entrance, goes over to the table and, looking at several bottles of wine, selects one. She is going hurriedly back, when, seeing* HARRY, *she goes over to him.*

SUSIE [*kindly*]. How are you now, Harry?

HARRY. All right, thank you.

SUSIE. That's good. [SUSIE *is about to hurry away, when* MRS FORAN *stops her with a remark.*]

MRS FORAN [*with a meaning gesture*]. He's takin' it cushy till you're ready to hear him singin' his Negro spiritual, Miss.

SUSIE. Oh, God, I'd nearly forgotten that. They'll be giving out the balloons at the next dance, and when that foxtrot's over he'll have to come in and sing us the spiritual.

MRS HEEGAN. Just as he used to do.

SIMON. Behind the trenches.

SYLVESTER. In the rest-camps.

MRS FORAN. Out in France.

SUSIE. As soon as the Balloon Dance is over, Harry, out through the garden and in by the front entrance with you, so that you'll be ready to start as they all sit down. And after the song, we'll drink to the Club from the Silver Tassie. [*She hurries back to the hall with the bottle of wine.*]

MRS FORAN. I'm longin' to hear Harry on the ukulele.

HARRY. I hope I'll be able to do justice to it.

MRS HEEGAN. Of course you will, Harry.

HARRY [*nervously*]. Before a crowd. Forget a word and it's all up with you.

SIMON. Try it over now, softly; the sound couldn't carry as far as the hall.

SYLVESTER. It'll give you confidence in yourself.

HARRY [*to* SIMON]. Show us the ukulele Simon.

SIMON *gets the ukulele and gives it to* HARRY.

TEDDY. If I knew the ukulele it might wean me a little way from the darkness.

HARRY *pulls a few notes, tuning the ukulele, then he softly sings:*

> Swing low, sweet chariot, comin' for to carry me home,
> Swing low, sweet chariot, comin' for to carry me home.

I looked over Jordan, what did I see, comin' for to carry
　　me home?
A band of angels comin' after me – comin' for to carry
　　me home.

*A voice in the hall is heard shouting through a megaphone.*

VOICE. Balloons will be given out now! Given out now – the balloons!
MRS FORAN [*excitedly*]. They're goin' to send up the balloons! They're
　going to let the balloons fly now!
HARRY [*singing*].

　　Swing low, sweet chariot, comin' for to carry me home.
　　Swing low, sweet chariot, comin' for to carry me home.

MRS FORAN [*as* HARRY *is singing*]. Miss Monican wants us all to see the
　flyin' balloons. [*She catches* TEDDY's *arm and runs with him into the
　hall.*]
SIMON. We must all see the flyin' balloons.
MRS HEEGAN [*running into hall*]. Red balloons and black balloons.
SIMON [*following* MRS HEEGAN]. Green balloons and blue balloons.
SYLVESTER [*following* SIMON]. Yellow balloons and puce balloons.

*All troop into the hall, leaving the curtains apart, and* HARRY *alone with
his ukulele. Through the entrance various coloured balloons that have been
tossed into the air can be seen, mid sounds of merriment and excitement.*

HARRY [*softly and slowly*].

　　Comin' for to carry me home.

*He throws the ukulele into an armchair, sits still for a moment then goes to
the table, takes up the Silver Cup, and wheels himself into the garden.
　After a pause* BARNEY *looks in, then enters pulling* JESSIE *by the hand,
letting the curtains fall together again. Then he goes quickly to window,
shuts and bolts it, drawing-to one half of the curtains, goes back to* JESSIE,
*catches her hand again, and tries to draw her towards the room on the left.
During the actions that follow the dance goes merrily on in the hall.*

JESSIE [*holding up a broken shoulder-strap and pulling back towards the hall* ]. Barney, no. God, I'd be afraid he might come in on us alone.

*Hands part the curtains and throw in coloured streamers that encircle* JESSIE *and* BARNEY.

BARNEY. Damn them! . . . He's gone, I tell you, to sing the song an' play the ukulele.

JESSIE [*excited and afraid*]. See, they're watching us. No, Barney. You mustn't. I'll not go! [BARNEY *seizes* JESSIE *in his arms and forces her towards the door on the left.*] You wouldn't be good. I'll not go into that room.

BARNEY. I will be good, I tell you! I just want to be alone with you for a minute. [BARNEY *loosens* JESSIE'*s other shoulder-strap, so that her dress leaves her shoulders and bosom bare.*]

JESSIE [*near the door left, as* BARNEY *opens it.*] You've loosened my dress – I knew you weren't going to be good. [*As she kisses him passionately*] Barney, Barney – you shouldn't be making me do what I don't want to do!

BARNEY [*holding her and trying to pull her into room*]. Come on, Jessie, you needn't be afraid of Barney – we'll just rest a few minutes from the dancing.

*At that part of the window uncurtained* HARRY *is seen peering in. He then wheels his chair back and comes on to the centre of the window-frame with a rush, bursting the catch and speeding into the room, coming to a halt, angry and savage, before* BARNEY *and* JESSIE.

HARRY. So you'd make merry over my helplessness in front of my face, in front of my face, you pair of cheats! You couldn't wait till I'd gone, so that my eyes wouldn't see the joy I wanted hurrying away from me over to another? Hurt her breast pulling your hand quick out of her bodice, did you? [*To* JESSIE] Saved you in the nick of time, my lady, did I? [*To* BARNEY] Going to enjoy yourself on the same little couch where she, before you formed an image in her eye, acted the part of an amateur wife, and I acted the part of an amateur husband – the black couch with the green and crimson butterflies, in the yellow bushes, where she and me often tired of the things you're dangling after now!

JESSIE. He's a liar, he's a liar, Barney! He often tried it on with coaxing first and temper afterwards, but it always ended in a halt that left him where he started.

HARRY. If I had my hands on your white neck I'd leave marks there that crowds of kisses from your Barney wouldn't moisten away.

BARNEY. You half-baked Lazarus, I've put up with you all the evening, so don't force me now to rough-handle the bit of life the Jerries left you as a souvenir!

HARRY. When I wanted to slip away from life, you brought me back with your whispered 'Think of the tears of Jess, think of the tears of Jess', but Jess has wiped away her tears in the ribbon of your Cross, and this poor crippled jest gives a flame of joy to the change; but when you get her, may you find in her the pressed-down emptiness of a whore!

BARNEY [*running over and seizing* HARRY]. I'll tilt the leaking life out of you, you jealous, peering pimp!*

JESSIE [*trying to hold* BARNEY *back*]. Barney, Barney, don't! don't!

HARRY [*appealingly*]. Barney, Barney! My heart – you're stopping it!

JESSIE [*running to entrance and shouting in*]. Help! Help! they're killing each other!

*In the hall the dance stops.* SURGEON MAXWELL *runs in, followed by* SUSIE, SIMON, SYLVESTER, MRS FORAN, MRS HEEGAN, *and lastly* TEDDY *finding his way over to the window. Dancers gather around entrance and look on.*

SURGEON MAXWELL, *running over, separates* BARNEY *from* HARRY.

MAXWELL. What's this? Come, come – we can't have this sort of thing going on.

MRS HEEGAN. He was throttlin' him, throttlin' a poor helpless creature, an' if anything happens, he and that painted slug Jessie Taite'll be held accountable!

MAXWELL. This can't be allowed to go on. You'll have to bring him home. Any more excitement would be dangerous.

MRS HEEGAN. This is what he gets from Jessie Taite for sittin' on the stairs through the yawnin' hours of the night, racin' her off to the play an' the pictures, an' plungin' every penny he could keep from me into presents for the consolidation of the courtship!

MAXWELL. Bring the boy home, woman, bring the boy home.

SYLVESTER [*fiercely to* JESSIE]. And money of mine in one of the gewgaws scintillatin' in her hair!

JESSIE. What gewgaw? What gewgaw?

*Coloured streamers are thrown in by those standing at entrance, which fall on and encircle some of the group around* HARRY.

SYLVESTER. The tiarara I gave you two Christmases ago with the yellow berries and the three flutterin' crimson swallows!

HARRY [*faintly and bitterly, with a hard little laugh*]. Napoo Barney Bagnal and napoo Jessie Taite. A merry heart throbs coldly in my bosom; a merry heart in a cold bosom – or is it a cold heart in a merry bosom? [*He gathers a number of the coloured streamers and winds them round himself and chair.*] Teddy! [HARRY *catches* TEDDY *by the sleeve and winds some more streamers round him.*] Sing a song, man, and show the stuff you're made of!

MAXWELL [*catching hold of* MRS HEEGAN'*s arm*]. Bring him home, woman. [MAXWELL *catches* SYLVESTER'*s arm.*] Get him home, man.

HARRY. Dear God, this crippled form is still your child. [*To* MRS HEEGAN] Dear mother, this helpless thing is still your son. Harry Heegan, me, who, on the football field, could crash a twelve-stone flyer off his feet. For this dear Club three times I won the Cup, and grieve in reason I was just too weak this year to play again. And now, before I go, I give you all the Cup, the Silver Tassie, to have and to hold for ever, evermore. [*From his chair he takes the Cup with the two sides hammered close together, and holds it out to them.*] Mangled and bruised as I am bruised and mangled. Hammered free from all its comely shape. Look, there is Jessie writ, and here is Harry, the one name safely separated from the other. [*He flings it on the floor.*] Treat it kindly. With care it may be opened out, for Barney there to drink to Jess, and Jessie there to drink to Barney.

TEDDY. Come, Harry, home to where the air is soft. No longer can you stand upon a hill-top; these empty eyes of mine can never see from one. Our best is all behind us – what's in front we'll face like men, dear comrade of the blood-fight and the battle-front!

HARRY. What's in front we'll face like men! [HARRY *goes out by the window,* SYLVESTER *pushing the chair,* TEDDY'*s hand on* HARRY'*s shoulder,* MRS HEEGAN *slowly following. Those left in the room watch them going out through the garden, turning to the right till they are all out of sight. As he goes out of window*] The Lord hath given and man hath taken away!

TEDDY [*heard from the garden*]. Blessed be the name of the Lord!

*The band in the hall begins to play again. Those in hall begin to dance.*

MAXWELL. Come on, all, we've wasted too much time already.

SUSIE [*to* JESSIE, *who is sitting quietly in a chair*]. Come on, Jessie – get your partner; [*roguishly*] you can have a quiet time with Barney later on.

JESSIE. Poor Harry!

SUSIE. Oh nonsense! If you'd passed as many through your hands as I, you'd hardly notice one. [*To* JESSIE] Jessie, Teddy Foran and Harry Heegan have gone to live their own way in another world. Neither I nor you can lift them out of it. No longer can they do the things we do. We can't give sight to the blind or make the lame walk. We would if we could. It is the misfortune of war. As long as wars are waged, we shall be vexed by woe; strong legs shall be made useless and bright eyes made dark. But we, who have come through the fire unharmed, must go on living.* [*Pulling* JESSIE *from the chair*] Come along, and take your part in life! [*To* BARNEY] Come along, Barney, and take your partner into the dance!

*Barney comes over, puts his arm round* JESSIE, *and they dance into the hall.* SUSIE *and* SURGEON MAXWELL *dance together. As they dance the waltz 'Over the Waves', some remain behind drinking. Two of these sing the song to the same tune as the dance.*

MAXWELL.

> Swing into the dance,
> Take joy when it comes, ere it go;
> For the full flavour of life
> Is either a kiss or a blow.
> He to whom joy is a foe,
> Let him wrap himself up in his woe;
> For he is a life on the ebb,
> We a full life on the flow.*

*All in the hall dance away with streamers and balloons flying.* SIMON *and* MRS FORAN *sit down and watch the fun through the entrance.* MRS FORAN *lights a cigarette and smokes. A pause as they look on.*

1. Michael Pennington as the tenement poet Donal Davoren in the 1981 Royal Shakespeare production of *The Shadow of a Gunman* at The Warehouse, London, directed by Michael Bogdanov.

2. Sara Allgood as Juno with her indolent paycock played by Arthur Sinclair in *Juno and the Paycock* at the Royalty Theatre, 1926.

3. Gerard Murphy as Johnny Boyle and Judi Dench as Juno in the Royal Shakespeare Company production of *Juno and the Paycock* at the Aldwych Theatre, 1980, directed by Trevor Nunn.

9. *Red Roses for Me* at the Lyric Theatre, 1972, directed by Mary McCracken.

10. *Red Roses for Me* at the Abbey Theatre, 1980, directed by Hugh Hunt.

7. The 1972 production of *The Silver Tassie* at the Abbey Theatre, directed by Hugh Hunt.

8. The Royal Shakespeare Company production of *The Silver Tassie* at the Aldwych Theatre, 1969, directed by David Jones. Left to right: Bruce Myers (Barney Bagnal), Robert Oates (3rd soldier), Ben Kingsley (The Croucher), John Kane (1st soldier) and Richard Moore (Harry Heegan).

5. *The Plough and the Stars*, directed by Bill Bryden at the Olivier Theatre, 1977, with Susan Fleetwood (Nora Clitheroe) and Nora Connolly (Mollser).

6. The Fortune Theatre programme for the first performance of *The Plough and the Stars*, 1926.

4. *The Plough and the Stars*, directed by Bill Bryden at the Olivier Theatre, 1977, with J. G. Devlin (Peter Flynn), Anna Manahan (Bessie Burgess), Harry Webster (Barman), Cyril Cusack (Fluther Good), Carmel McSharry (Mrs Gogan) and Bryan Murray (the Young Covey).

11. A scene from the English Stage Company's production of *Cock-a-Doodle Dandy* at the Royal Court Theatre, 1959, with Norman Rodway (The Messenger) and Berto Pasuka (The Cock).

12. Michael O'Herlithy's design for Act I of *The Bishop's Bonfire*, February, 1955.

MRS FORAN. It's a terrible pity Harry was too weak to stay an' sing his song, for there's nothing I love more than the ukulele's tinkle, tinkle in the night-time.

CURTAIN

## SONGS AND CHANTS IN *THE SILVER TASSIE*

### 1st CHANT

### 2nd CHANT

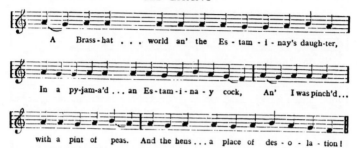

A Brass-hat . . . world an' the Es - tam - i - nay's daugh-ter,

In a py-jam-a'd . . . an Es-tam-i-na-y cock, An' I was pinch'd . . .

with a pint of peas. And the hens . . . a place of des - o - la - tion!

### 3rd CHANT

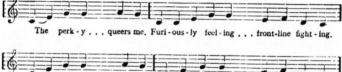

The perk - y . . . queers me. Furi - ous - ly feel - ing . . . front-line fight - ing.

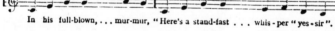

In his full-blown, . . . mur-mur, "Here's a stand-fast . . . whis - per "yes - sir".

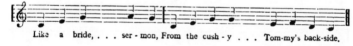

Like a bride, . . . ser - mon, From the cush - y . . . Tom-my's back-side.

### 4th CHANT

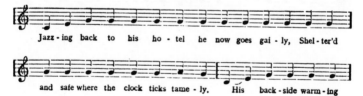

Jazz - ing back to his ho - tel he now goes gai - ly, Shel - ter'd

and safe where the clock ticks tame - ly. His back - side warm - ing

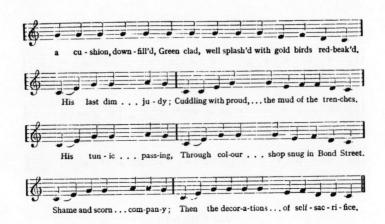

a cu-shion, down-fill'd, Green clad, well splash'd with gold birds red-beak'd.

His last dim . . . ju-dy; Cuddling with proud, . . . the mud of the tren-ches.

His tun-ic . . . pass-ing, Through col-our . . . shop snug in Bond Street.

Shame and scorn . . . com-pan-y; Then the decor-a-tions . . . of self-sac-ri-fice.

## 5th CHANT

A warn-ing . . . give, To the front . . . do, to God.

God, un-chang-ing, . . . night sky To mask . . . His self-slay-ing chil-dren.

Stumbling, swiftly . . . grous-ing, Through mud . . . seek slow the front line.

Squeals of hid-den . . . wounded—Christ who bore . . . tied to a field gun.

## WOULD GOD, I SMOK'D

Would God, I smok'd and walk'd and watch'd - - The dance of a
Would God, I smok'd and lift - ed car - goes From the lad - en
To hang here ev - en a lit - tle lon - ger, Loung - ing
If you creep to rest in a clos'd-up cof - fin, A tail of
Each spar - row, hop - ping, ir - re - sponsible, Is in - den - tur'd

gol - den Brim - stone but - ter - fly, - - To the
shoul - ders of Lon - don's riv - er - way; - - The
through fear - swell'd, anx - ious moments; The
com - rades see - ing you safe home; - Or a
in God's migh - ty mem - o - ry; - - And we,

sau - cy pipe of a green - finch rest - ing In a
holi - day'd, roar - ing out courage and move - ment To the
hin - der - parts of The god of bat - tles Shading our
ker - nel lost in a shell ex - plod - ing— It's all,
more than they all, shall not be lost In the for-

drowsy, brambled lane in Cumber - land. In Cumber - land.
mus - cled ma-chines of Tottenham Hotspur. Of Tottenham Hotspur,
war - tir'd eyes from his flam - ing face. From his flaming face.
sure, on - ly in a life - time. A life - time.
get - ful - ness of the Lord of Hosts. Of the Lord of Hosts.

## STRETCHER-BEARERS' SONG

Oh, bear it gent - ly, car - ry it soft - ly—A bull-et or a shell said stop, stop, stop. It's had its day, and it's left the play, Since it gam - boll'd ov - er the top, top, top. It's had its day and it's left the play, Since it gam - boll'd o - - ver the top.

## SONG TO THE GUN

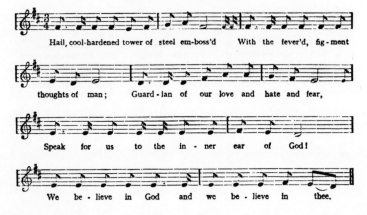

Hail, cool-hardened tower of steel em-boss'd With the fever'd, fig - ment thoughts of man; Guard - ian of our love and hate and fear, Speak for us to the in - ner ear of God! We be - lieve in God and we be - lieve in thee.

## THE ENEMY HAS BROKEN THROUGH

The en-em-y has brok-en through, brok-en through, brok-en through! Ev-ery man born of wo-man to the guns, to the guns. To the guns, to the guns, to the guns! Those at prayer, all in bed and the swillers drinking deeply in the pubs. To the guns, to the guns. All the bat-men, ev-ery cook, ev-ery bitch's son that hides A whiff of cour-age in his veins, Shelter'd vig-our in his bod-y, That can run, or can walk, ev-en crawl— · · · Dig him out, dig him out, shove him on— · · · To the guns!

### SURGEON'S SONG

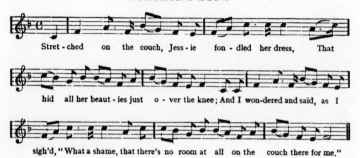

Stret - ched on the couch, Jess - ie fon - dled her dress, That
hid all her beaut - ies just o - ver the knee; And I won-dered and said, as I
sigh'd, "What a shame, that there's no room at all on the couch there for me."

# Red Roses for Me

## A Play in Four Acts

*To Dr J. D. Cummins*
*in memory of the grand chats*
*around his surgery fire.*

## CHARACTERS

MRS BREYDON

AYAMONN BREYDON, her son

EEADA

DYMPNA } Mrs Breydon's neighbours in the house

FINNOOLA

SHEILA MOORNEEN, Ayamonn's sweetheart

BRENNAN O' THE MOOR, owner of a few oul' houses

A SINGER, a young man with a good voice

ROORY O'BALACAUN, a zealous Irish Irelander

MULLCANNY, a mocker of sacred things

REV. E. CLINTON, Rector of St Burnupus

SAMUEL, verger to the church

INSPECTOR FINGLAS, of the Mounted Police, and the Rector's church-warden

DOWZARD

FOSTER } members of St Burnupus' Select Vestry

1ST MAN

2ND MAN } neighbours in the next house to Breydons'

3RD MAN

A LAMPLIGHTER

1ST RAILWAYMAN

2ND RAILWAYMAN

1ST WORKMAN

2ND WORKMAN

3RD WORKMAN

## PLACE AND TIME

*Act I*. Two-roomed home of the Breydons.

*Act II*. The same.

*Act III*. A Dublin street, beside a bridge over the river Liffey.

*Act IV*. Part of the grounds round the Protestant Church of St Burnupus.* In this Act the curtain is lowered for a few minutes to denote the passing of a few hours.

*Time*. A little while ago.

*My thanks to Bridgid Edwards for setting down the airs to the songs.*

# ACT I

*The front one of two rather dilapidated rooms in a poor working-class locality. The walls, whitewashed, are dwindling into a rusty yellowish tinge. The main door, leading to the hall, is at the back, a little towards the right. The fireplace is in the right-hand wall, and a brilliant fire is burning in the large, old-fashioned grate. In the centre of the room is an old ebony-hued table on which stands a one-wick oil-lamp, its chimney a litle smoky from the bad oil in the reservoir. Some books lie on the table, some paper, coloured chalks, a pen, and a small bottle of ink. In the left wall, up towards the back, is the door leading to the second room. Below this door is a horsehair sofa showing signs of old age. On it, to the head, is a neatly folded bundle of sheets and blankets, showing that it is used as a bed during the night. To the left of the main door at the back is a large basket used by actors when on tour. On the other side of this door is an ordinary kitchen dresser on which some of the crockery is on the ledge, for the upper shelf is filled with a row of books, by the look of them second-hand. Over the basket, on the wall, is tacked a childlike brightly-coloured pastel of what is meant to be a copy of one of Fra Angelico's angels blowing a curved and golden trumpet; and beside it is a small coloured reproduction of Constable's 'Cornfield'. In the same wall, towards the back, is a large, tall window, nearly reaching the ceiling, and, when one is in front of it, the top of a railway signal, with transverse arms, showing green and red lights, can be seen. Under this window, on a roughly made bench, stand three biscuit tins. In the first grows a geranium, in the second, musk, and in the third, a fuchsia. The discs of the geranium are extremely large and glowing; the tubular blooms of the golden musk, broad, gay, and rich; and the purple bells of the fuchsia, surrounded by their long white waxy sepals, seem to be as big as arum lilies. These crimson, gold, and purple flowers give regal tint to the poor room. Occasionally in the distance can be heard the whistle of an engine, followed by its strenuous puffing as it pulls at a heavy rake of goods wagons. A chair or two stand about the room.*

*It is towards the evening of a mid-spring day, and the hour would make it dusk, but it is darker than that, for the sky is cloudy and rain is falling heavily over the city.*

AYAMONN *and his mother are in the room when the scene shows itself. He is tall, well built, twenty-two or so, with deep brown eyes, fair hair, rather bushy, but tidily kept, and his face would remind an interested observer of a rather handsome, firm-minded, thoughtful, and good-humoured bulldog. His mother is coming up to fifty, her face brownish, dark eyes with a fine glint in them, and she bears on her cheeks and brow the marks of struggle and hard work. She is dressed in a black jacket, fitting close, marred by several patches, done very neatly, dark-blue skirt, a little faded, and rather heavily-soled boots. At the moment this is all covered with a rich blue velvet cloak, broidered with silver lace, and she is sitting on a kitchen chair covered with a dark-red, rather ragged cloth.*

AYAMONN *wears a bright-green silk doublet over which is a crimson velvet armless cloak bordered with white fur. The back part of the cloak is padded so as to form a big hump between his shoulders. Across his chest is a dark-green baldric from which hangs a scabbard. A cross-hilted sword is in his hand. On his head he has a black felt hat with narrow turned-up rims. A black band goes round the hat, and a crimson feather sticks up from it. His legs are in heavy, black, working corduroy trousers, and he wears heavy hobnailed boots. She and he are in an intensely listening attitude.*

MRS BREYDON [*whispering over to* AYAMONN]. She's gone; wanted to borra something else, I suppose. They're feverish with borrowing in this blessed house!

AYAMONN. Damn her for a troublesome fool! Where's this I was when the knock came?

MRS BREYDON. I was just goin' to say

>  Ay, an' for much more slaughter after this,
>  O God! forgive my sins, and pardon thee!

AYAMONN [*looking at the floor*]. Oh yes! [*He recites*]

>  What, will th' aspiring blood of Lancaster
>  Sink to the ground? I thought it would have mounted.
>  [*He holds the sword aloft, and stares at it.*] See how my sword
>      weeps for the poor king's death!
>  O, may such purple tears be always shed
>  For those that wish the downfall of our house!
>  If any spark of life be yet remaining, [*he stabs at the floor*]
>  Down, down to hell; and say I sent thee hither!*

*A knuckle-knock is heard at the door.* AYAMONN *and* MRS BREYDON *stiffen into a silent listening attitude. A fine baritone voice, husky with age, is heard speaking outside.*

VOICE. Is anyone in or out or what? [*Louder raps are given as* AYAMONN *steals over, and places his back to the door.*] Eh, in there – is there anyone movin', or is the oul' shack empty?

MRS BREYDON [*in a whisper*]. Oul' Brennan on the Moor.* He was here before, today. He's got his rent for his oul' houses, an' he wants to be told again that the Bank of Ireland's a safe place to put it.

AYAMONN [*warningly*]. Ssshush!

VOICE. No answer, eh? An' me afther seein' a light in th' window. Maybe they are out. For their own sakes, I hope they are; for it's hardly an honourable thing to gainsay a neighbour's knock.

*The sound of feet shuffling away is heard outside, and then there is silence for a few moments.*

MRS BREYDON. He's gone. He's always a bit lively the day he gets his rents. How a man, with his money, can go on livin' in two rooms in a house an' sthreet only a narrow way betther than this, I don't know. What was he but an oul' painter an' paperhanger, starvin' to save, an' usin' his cunnin' to buy up a few oul' houses, give them a lick o' paint, and charge the highest rent for th' inconvenience of livin' in them!

AYAMONN. I wish he'd keep himself and his throubles far away from me now. I've higher things to think of and greater things to do than to be attached to the agony of an old fool for ever afraid a fistful of money'll be snatched away from him. Still, he isn't a miser, for he gives kids toys at Christmas, and never puts less than half a crown on the plate in church on Sundays.

MRS BREYDON. So well he may!

AYAMON. What was he sayin' when he was here before?

MRS BREYDON. Oh, th' usual question of askin' me what I thought about the Bank of Ireland; mutterin' about somebody not payin' the rent; and that his birthday's due tomorrow.

AYAMONN [*looking at the chair*]. I'll have to get a loan of a chair with arms on, and someway make them golden to do the thing proper in the Temperance Hall; and I'll paint for the back of it, on thin cardboard, a cunning design of the House of Lancaster, the red rose, so that it'll look like a kingly seat.

MRS BREYDON. Th' killin' o' th' king be th' Duke o' Gloster should go down well, an' th' whole thing should look sumptuous.

AYAMONN. So it will. It's only that they're afraid of Shakespeare out of all that's been said of him. They think he's beyond them, while all the time he's part of the kingdom of heaven in the nature of everyman. Before I'm done, I'll have him drinking in th' pubs with them!

MRS BREYDON. I don't know that he'll go well with a Minstrel Show.

AYAMONN. He'll have to go well. If only King Henry doesn't rant too much, saw the air with his hands, and tear his passion to tatthers.* The old fool saw someone do it that way, and thinks it must be right. [*With a sigh*] I daren't attempt to recite my part now, for Oul' Brennan on the Moor's waitin' and listenin' somewhere down below; so I'll just get it off by heart. How old does he say he'll be tomorrow?

MRS BREYDON. Only seventy-six, he says, an' feelin' as if he was lookin' forward to his twenty-first birthday.

AYAMONN. Well, he won't have long to wait.

MRS BREYDON [*slyly*]. He was muttherin', too, about some air or other on the oul' piano he has at home.

AYAMONN [*springing up from where he has been sitting*]. It's one o' mine he's put an air to! [*He rushes from the room and returns in a few moments.*] He's not there; gone home, I suppose. [*Irritably*] I wish you'd told me that at first.

MRS BREYDON. I'd thry to rest a little, Ayamonn, before you go to work. You're overdoing it. Less than two hours' sleep today, and a long night's work before you. Sketchin', readin', makin' songs, an' learnin' Shakespeare: if you had a piano, you'd be thryin' to learn music. Why don't you stick at one thing, an' leave the others alone?

AYAMONN. They are all lovely, and my life needs them all.

MRS BREYDON. I managed to get on well enough without them. [*She goes over to the window and tenderly touches the fuchsia.*] There's this sorryful sthrike, too, about to come down on top of us.

AYAMONN [*sitting in the red-covered chair and reading Shakespeare – quietly and confidently*]. There'll be no strike. The bosses won't fight. They'll grant the extra shilling a week demanded.

MRS BREYDON [*now fingering the musk*]. I thought this Minstrel Show was being run to gather funds together?

AYAMONN [*impatiently*]. So it is, so it is; but only in case the strike may have to take place. I haven't much to do with it, anyway. I'm with the men, spoke at a meeting in favour of the demand, and that's all.

MRS BREYDON. You'll undhermine your health with all you're doin', tearin' away what's left of your time be runnin' afther – [*She checks herself, and becomes silent.*]

AYAMONN [*lowering his book to his lap – angrily*]. Go on – finish what you started to say: runnin' afther who?

MRS BREYDON. Nobody, nobody.

AYAMONN. Runnin' afther Sheila Moorneen – that's what was in your mind to say, wasn't it?

MRS BREYDON. If it was aself;* is there a new law out that a body's not to think of her own thoughts?

AYAMONN [*sharply*]. What have you got against the girl?

MRS BREYDON. Nothing. As a girl, I'd say she's a fine coloured silken shawl among a crowd of cotton ones. A girl I'd say could step away from the shadowy hedges where others slink along, tiltin' her head as she takes the centre of the toad for the entherprisin' light o' day to show her off to everyone. But still – [*She stops speaking again.*]

AYAMONN. Ay, but still what? You've a maddenin' way of never finishing some of your sentences.

MRS BREYDON [*braving it out*]. She's a Roman Catholic; steeped in it, too, the way she'd never forgive a one for venturin' to test the Pope's pronouncement.

AYAMONN. And who wants to test the Pope's pronouncement? Life and all her vital changes'll go on testing everything, even to the Pope's pronouncement. D'ye think I've laboured as I have, and am labourin' now, to furnish myself with some of the greatness of the mighty minds of the past, just to sink down into passive acceptance of the Pope's pronouncement? Let the girl believe what she may, reverence what she can: it's her own use of her own mind. That she is fair to look upon, charming to talk with, and a dear companion, is well and away enough for me, were she even a believer in Mumbo Jumbo, and had a totem pole in her front garden.

MRS BREYDON. There's worse still than that in it.

AYAMONN. Worse, is there? An' what may that be?

MRS BREYDON. She's th' child of a sergeant in the Royal Irish Constabulary, isn't she?

AYAMONN. Well, she can't help it, can she?

MRS BREYDON. I know that; but many have murmured again' a son of mine goin' with the child of a man crouchin' close to their enemy.

AYAMONN. Everything, it seems, is against her, save hereself. I like herself, and not her faith; I want herself, and not her father.

MRS BREYDON. The bigger half of Ireland would say that a man's way with a maid* must be regulated by his faith an' hers, an' the other half by the way her father makes his livin'.

AYAMONN. And let the whole world join them! Fair she is, and her little ear's open to hear all that I thry to say, so, were she the child of darkness aself, I'd catch her hand and lead her out and show her off to all men.

MRS BREYDON. She wouldn't be a lot to look at afther she'd wended her way through poverty with you for a year an' a day.

AYAMONN. She gives no honour to gold; neither does her warm heart pine for silks and satins from China and Japan, or the spicy isles of Easthern Asia. A sober black shawl on her shoulders, a simple petticoat, and naked feet would fail to find her craving finer things that envious women love.

MRS BRENDON. Ah, go on with you, Ayamonn, for a kingly fool. I'm tellin' you th' hearts of all proper girls glow with the dhream of fine things; an' I'm tellin' you, too, that the sword jinglin' on th' hip of Inspector Finglas, the red plume hangin' from his menacin' helmet, an' th' frosty silver sparklin' on his uniform, are a dazzle o' light between her tantalised eyes an' whatever she may happen to see in you.

AYAMONN. Tell me something else to add to my hope.

MRS BREYDON. Go on readin', an' don't bother to listen to your mother.

AYAMONN [*going over and gently putting his hands on her shoulders*]. I do listen, but I am drifting away from you, Mother, a dim shape now, in a gold canoe,* dipping over a far horizon.

MRS BREYDON [*with a catch in her voice*]. I did an' dared a lot for you, Ayamonn, my son, in my time, when jeerin' death hurried your father off to Heaven.

AYAMONN. It's I who know that well: when it was dark, you always carried the sun in your hand for me; when you suffered me to starve rather than thrive towards death in an Institution, you gave me life to play with as a richer child is given a coloured ball. [*He gently lifts up her face by putting a hand under her chin.*] Your face, your dear face that once was smooth is wrinkled now; the eyes, brown still, that once were bright, have now been dimmed by a sthrained stare into the future; the sturdy back that stood so straight, is bending. A well-tried leaf, bronzed with beauty, waiting for a far-off winter wind to shake it from the tree.

MRS BREYDON [*gently removing his hand from her chin*]. I have a tight hold still. My back can still bear many a heavy burden; and my eyes, dimmer now than once they were, can still see far enough. Well, I betther take this fancy robe from off me, lest it give me gorgeous notions.

*She takes off her robe, and leaves it carefully folded on the basket, then goes over and arranges the fire.* AYAMONN *looks thoughtfully out of the window, then takes off cloak, sword, and hat, leaving them carefully on the basket.*

AYAMONN [*musingly*]. He'll hardly come tonight in this rain. If he does, I'll get him to read the King's part, and do mine over again.

MRS BREYDON. Who's to come tonight?

AYAMONN. Mullcanny: he's searching Dublin for a book he wants to give me; and, if he got it, he was to bring it tonight – *The Riddle of the Universe.* *

MRS BREYDON. That's another one I wouldn't see too much of, for he has the whole neighbourhood up in arms against his reckless disregard of God, an' his mockery of everything solemn, set down as sacred.

AYAMONN. Oh, Tim is all right. The people are sensible enough to take all he says in good part; and a black flame stands out in a brightly-coloured world.

MRS BREYDON. You don't know them, if you say that; he'll meet with a mishap, some day, if he doesn't keep his mouth shut.

AYAMONN. Nonsense.

*She has quietly slipped a shawl around her, and is moving to the door so silently as to seem to want to prevent* AYAMONN *from noticing her movements, when the door opens and* EEADA, DYMPNA, FINNOOLA, *and several men, appear there. The three women come a little way into the room; the men stay around the door. All their faces are stiff and mask-like, holding tight an expression of dumb resignation; and are traversed with seams of poverty and a hard life. The face of* EEADA *is that of an old woman; that of* DYMPNA, *one coming up to middle age; and that of* FINNOOLA, *one of a young girl. Each shows the difference of age by more or less furrows, but each has the same expressionless stare out on life.*

DYMPNA *is carrying a statue of the Blessed Virgin, more than two feet high, in her arms. The figure was once a glory of purest white, sparkling blue, and luscious gilding; but the colours have faded, the gilt is gone, save for a spot or two of dull gold still lingering on the crown. She is wearing a crown that, instead of being domed, is castellated like a city's tower, resembling those of Dublin; and the pale face of the Virgin is sadly soiled by the grime of the house. The men are dressed in drab brown, the women in a chill grey, each suit or dress having a patch of faded blue, red, green, or purple somewhere about them.*

EEADA [*to* MRS BREYDON]. Could you spare a pinch or two of your Hudson's soap, Mrs Breydon, dear, to give the Blessed Virgin a bit of a wash? [*To all in general*] Though I've often said it's th' washin' that's done away with the bonnie blue of th' robe an' th' braver gold of its bordhers an' th' most o' th' royalty outa th' crown. Little Ursula below's savin' up her odd pennies to bring Her where She'll find a new blue robe, an' where they'll make the royalty of th' gilt glow again; though whenever she's a shillin' up, it's needed for food an' firin'; but we never yet found Our Lady of Eblana* averse to sellin' Her crown an' Her blue robe to provide for Her people's need. [MRS BREYDON *gives half a packet of soap powder. Gratefully*] Thank you, ma'am, an' though y'are of a different persuasion, Our Blessed Lady of Eblana's poor'll bless you an' your fine son for this little tribute to Her honour and circumspect appearance before the world.

THE REST [*murmuring*]. Ay, will She, an' that's a sure thing.

*They open a way for* EEADA *to pass out, with* DYMPNA *carrying the statue, following in a kind of simple procession.* MRS BREYDON *is moving slowly after them.*

AYAMONN [*who has noticed her under his eyes*]. You're not going out again, surely – on a night like this, too?

MRS BREYDON. Not really; only down the road to Mrs Cashmore's. She's not too well; I promised I'd dhrop in, and see to a hot dhrink or something for her before she wandhered off to sleep.

AYAMONN [*irritably*]. You think more of other homes than you do of your own! Every night for the past week you've been going out on one silly mission or another like an imitation sisther of charity.

MRS BREYDON. I couldn't sit quiet knowin' the poor woman needed me. I'd hear her voice all through the night complainin' I never came to give her a hot dhrink, settle her bed soft, an' make her safe for th' lonely hours of th' slow-movin' night.

AYAMONN. A lot they'd do for you if you happened to need help from
  them.

MRS BREYDON. Ah, we don't know. A body shouldn't think of that, for
  such a belief would dismay an' dismantle everything done outside
  of our own advantage. No harm to use an idle hour to help another
  in need.

AYAMONN. An' wear yourself out in the process?

MRS BREYDON [*with a sigh*]. I'll wear out, anyway, sometime, an' a
  tired ould body can, at least, go to its long rest without any excuse.

*As she opens the door to go out,* SHEILA *appears on the threshold. She is a
girl of about twenty-three, fairly tall, a fine figure, carrying herself with a
sturdiness never ceasing to be graceful. She has large, sympathetic brown
eyes that dim, now and again, with a cloud of timidity. Her mouth is rather
large but sweetly made; her hair is brown and long, though now it is
gathered up into a thick coil that rests on the nape of her neck. She is dressed
in a tailor-made suit of rich brown tweed, golden-brown blouse, and a
bright-blue hat. These are now covered with a fawn-coloured mackintosh,
darkened with heavy rain, and a hastily folded umbrella is dripping on to
the floor. She comes in shyly, evidently conscious of* MRS BREYDON'*s
presence; but fighting her timidity with a breezy and jovial demeanour.*
MRS BREYDON *tries, but can't keep a little stiffness out of her greeting.*

SHEILA. Oh! good evening, Mrs Breydon. What a night! I'm nearly
  blown to bits; and the rain – oh, the wind and the weather!

MRS BREYDON. You must be perished. Take off your mac, and come
  over to the fire. Get Ayamonn to make you a cup o' tea, and bring
  you back to life again.

SHEILA. No, really; I'm burning – the battle with the wind and the rain
  has made me warm and lively.

AYAMONN. Hey ho, the wind and the rain, for the rain it raineth every
  day.* Sit down and take the weight off your legs.

SHEILA. Not worth while, for I can't stop long. [*To* MRS BREYDON]
  Going out on a night life this, Mrs Breydon?

AYAMONN [*hastily*]. She has to go: got an urgent call from a poor sick
  neighbour.

SHEILA [*hesitatingly*]. What is it? Could . . . could I do it for you?

AYAMONN [*decidedly*]. No, no you couldn't. The woman knows my
  mother. It's only to see her safe and warm in bed for the night;
  Mother won't be long.

MRS BREYDON. Good night, Miss Sheila; perhaps you'll be here when I come back.

SHEILA. I don't think so. I must go almost at once.

MRS BREYDON. Well, good night, then. [*She goes out, and* AYAMONN *goes over to* SHEILA, *kisses her, and helps her off with the mac.*]

SHEILA. You shouldn't let your mother go out on a night like this – she's no longer a young woman.

AYAMONN. I don't like to interfere with her need to give help to a neighbour. She likes it, and it does her good.

SHEILA. But the rain's coming down in sheets, and she's got but a thin shawl round her shoulders.

AYAMONN [*impatiently*]. Oh, she hasn't very far to go. Let's think of greater things than the pouring rain and an old woman on her way to smooth pillows on a sick bed. Look ! [*he feels her skirt*] – the hem's wringing. Better dry it at the fire. Turn round and I'll unfasten it for you.

SHEILA [*forcing his hand away*]. It's nothing – you are thinking now of your own pleasure. You weren't so eager to see me when I was knocking at the door a while ago.

AYAMONN. You! But it was Old Brennan o' the Moor that was there.

SHEILA. Before him, I was there. He hammered at the door too.

AYAMONN [*angry with himself*]. And I thinking the rapping was that of a pestering neighbour! I might have guessed it wasn't, it was so gentle.

SHEILA. After trying to slip in unnoticed, there I was left with the whole house knowing I was at the door, and when I ran down, I heard them yelling that the stylish-dressed pusher was trying to get into Breydon's again! A nice time I'll have with my people when they hear it.

AYAMONN. I was doing my Shakespeare part, and didn't want disturbance, so there I was, standing stiff and breathless like a heron in a pond, keeping my dear one away from me! [*Going over and taking her in his arms*] Well, it's all over now, and here you are in my arms, safe and sure and lovely.

SHEILA [*struggling away from him*]. No, it's not all over; and don't press me so hard; don't ruffle me tonight, for I feel a little tired.

AYAMONN [*peevishly*]. Tired again? Well, so am I, more than a little tired; but never too tired to put a sparkle into a welcome for a loved one.

SHEILA. Oh Ayamonn, I do want you to be serious for one night.

AYAMONN. Very well, very well, Sheila. [*He moves away from her, and stands at the other side of the fire.*] Let us plan, then, of how we can spin joy into every moment of tomorrow's day.

SHEILA. That's why I hurried here to see you – I can't be with you tomorrow. [*There is a long pause.*]

AYAMONN. Why can't you be with me tomorrow?

SHEILA. The Daughters of St Frigid begin a retreat tomorrow, to give the Saint a warm devotion, and Mother insists I go.

AYAMONN. And I insist that you go with me. Is the Saint Frigid more to you than the sinner Ayamonn? Would you rather go to the meeting than come to see me? [*A pause.*] Would you, would you, Sheila?

SHEILA [*in a hesitant whisper*]. God forgive me, I'd rather come to see you.

AYAMONN. Come then; God will be sure to forgive you.

SHEILA. I daren't. My mother would be at me for ever if I failed to go. I've told you how she hates me to be near you. She chatters red-lined warnings and black-bordered appeals into my ears night and day, and when they dwindle for lack of breath, my father shakes them out of their drowsiness and sends them dancing round more lively still, dressed richly up in deadly black and gleaming scarlet.

AYAMONN. Sheila, Sheila, on the one day of the month when I'm free, you must be with me. I wouldn't go to a workers' meeting so that I might be with you.

SHEILA. There's another thing, Ayamonn – the threatened strike. Oh, why do you meddle with those sort of things!

AYAMONN. Oh, never mind that, now. Don't be like a timid little girl ensconced in a clear space of a thicket of thorns – safe from a scratch if she doesn't stir, but unable to get to the green grass or the open road unless she risks the tears the thorns can give.

SHEILA. Oh, Ayamonn, for my sake, if you love me, do try to be serious.

AYAMONN [*a little wildly*]. Oh, Sheila, our time is not yet come to be serious in the way of our elders. Soon enough to browse with wisdom when Time's grey finger puts a warning speck on the crimson rose of youth. Let no damned frosty prayer chill the sunny sighs that dread the joy of love.

SHEILA [*wildly*]. I won't listen, Ayamonn, I won't listen! We must look well ahead on the road to the future. You lead your life through too many paths instead of treading the one way of making it possible for us to live together.

AYAMONN. We live together now; live in the light of the burning bush. I tell you life is not one thing, but many things, a wide branching flame, grand and good to see and feel, dazzling to the eye of no one living it. I am not one to carry fear about with me as a priest carries the Host. Let the timid tiptoe through the way where the paler blossoms grow; my feet shall be where the redder roses grow, though they bear long thorns, sharp and piercing, thick among them!

SHEILA [*rising from the chair – vehemently*]. I'll listen no more; I'll go. You want to make me a spark in a mere illusion. I'll go.

AYAMONN. Rather a spark from the althar of God, me girl; a spark that flames on a new path for a bubbling moment of life, or burns a song into the heart of a poet.

SHEILA. I came here as a last chance to talk things quiet with you, but you won't let me; so I'll go. [*As he seizes her in his arms*] Let me go! [*Pleadingly*] Please, Ayamonn, let me go!

AYAMONN. I tell you it is a gay sight for God to see joy shine for a moment on the faces of His much-troubled children.

SHEILA [*fearfully*]. Oh, don't bring God's name into this, for it will mean trouble to the pair of us. And your love for me lasts only while I'm here. When I'm gone, you think more of your poor painting, your poor oul' Ireland, your songs, and your workers' union than you think of Sheila.

AYAMONN. You're part of them all, in them all, and through them all; joyous, graceful, and a dearer vision; a bonnie rose, delectable and red. [*He draws her to him, presses her hard, lifts her on to his lap, and kisses her.*] Sheila, darling, you couldn't set aside the joy that makes the moon a golden berry in a hidden tree. You cannot close your ear to the sweet sound of the silver bell that strikes but once and never strikes again!

*The door opens, and the head of* BRENNAN O' THE MOOR *looks into the room. It is a bald one, the dome highly polished; the face is wrinkled a lot, but the eyes are bright and peering. A long white beard gives him a far-away likeness to St Jerome. He is dressed in a shabby-genteel way, and wears a long rain-soaked mackintosh. A faded bowler hat is on his head.*

BRENNAN. Oh, dear, dear, dear me!


*He comes into the room showing that his back is well bent, though he still has a sturdy look about him. A strap around his body holds a melodeon on his back.* SHEILA *and* AYAMONN *separate; he rises to meet the old man, while she stares, embarrassed, into the fire.*


AYAMONN. Now what th' hell do you want?

BRENNAN [*taking no notice of* AYAMONN's *remark – taking off his hat in a sweepin bow*]. Ah, me sweet, snowy-breasted Dublin doves! Me woe it is to come ramblin' in through marjoram moments scentin' the serious hilarity of a genuine courtin' couple. I'm askin' now what's the dear one's name, if that isn't thresspassin' on others who are in a firmer condition of friendship? Though, be rights, it's a fair an' showy nosegay I should be throwin' through a shyly opened window into the adorable lady's lap.

SHEILA [*shyly*]. Me name is Sheila.

BRENNAN. Sheila is it? Ay, an' a Sheila are you. Ay, an' a suitable one too, for there's a gentle nature in the two soft sounds, an' a silver note in the echo, describin' grandly the pretty slendher lass me two ould eyes are now beholdin'.

AYAMONN [*going over and catching him by an arm to guide him out*]. I can't see you now, old friend, for the pair of us are heavily harnessed to a question that must be answered before either of us is a day older.

BRENNAN. Sure I know. An' isn't it only natural, too, that young people should have questions to ask and answers to give to the dewy problems that get in th' way of their dancin' feet?

AYAMONN [*impatiently*]. Come again, old friend, when time has halted us for an hour of rest.

BRENNAN. It isn't me, I'm sayin', that would be dense enough to circumvent your longin' to be deep down in the silent consequence of regardin' each other without let or hindrance. [*He goes towards* SHEILA, *eagerly, pulling* AYAMONN *after him.*] It's easy seen, sweet lady, that you're well within the compass of your young man's knowledge, an' unaware of nothin', so I may speak as man to lady, so with cunnin' confidence, tell me what you think of the Bank of Ireland?

AYAMONN. Oh, for goodness' sake, old man. Sheila's no intherest in the Bank of Ireland. She cares nothing for money, or for anything money can buy.

BRENNAN [*staring at* AYAMONN *for a moment as if he had received a shock*]. Eh? Arra, don't be talkin' nonsense, man! Who is it daren't think of what money can buy? [*He crosses to the door in a trot on his toes, opens it, looks out, and closes it softly again. Then he tiptoes back to* SHEILA, *bends down towards her, hands on knees, and whispers hoarsely*] I've just a little consideration of stocks and bonds nestin' in the Bank of Ireland, at four per cent – just enough to guard a poor man from ill, eh? Safe an' sound there, isn't it, eh? [*To* AYAMONN] Now, let the fair one speak out on her own. [*Twisting his head back to* SHEILA.] Safe there as if St Peter himself had the key of where the bonds are stationed, eh?

SHEILA. I'm sure they must be, sir.

BRENNAN [*with chuckling emphasis*]. Yehess! Aren't you the sensible young lady; sure I knew you'd say that, without fear or favour. [*Turning towards* AYAMONN.] What do you say? You're a man, now, of tellin' judgement.

AYAMONN. Oh, the State would have to totther before you'd lose a coin.

BRENNAN [*gleefully*]. Go bang, absolutely bang! Eh?

AYAMONN. Go bang!

BRENNAN. Bang! [*To* SHEILA] Hear that, now, from a man climbin' up to scolarship? Yehess! Stony walls, steely doors, locks an' keys, bolts an' bars, an' all th' bonds warm an' dhry, an' shinin' safe behind them.

SHEILA. Safe behind them.

BRENNAN [*gleefully*]. Ay, so. An' none of it sthrollin' into Peter's Pence. [*Chuckling.*] Wouldn't the Pope be mad if he knew what he was missin'! Safe an' sound. [*To* AYAMONN] You think so, too, eh?

AYAMONN. Yes, yes.

BRENNAN [*soberly*]. Ay, of course you do. [*To* SHEILA – *indicating* AYAMONN] A good breed, me sweet an' fair one, brought up proper to see things in their right light.

AYAMONN [*catching him impatiently by the arm*]. And now, old friend, we have to get you to go.

BRENNAN. Eh?

AYAMONN. To go; Sheila and I have things to talk about.

BRENNAN [*suddenly*]. An' what about the song, then?

AYAMONN. Song?

BRENNAN. Th' one for the Show. Isn't that what brought me up? At long last, afther hard sthrainin', me an' Sammy have got the tune down in tested clefs, crotchets, an' quavers, fair set down to be sung be anyone in thrue time. An' Sammy's below, in his gay suit for the Show, waitin' to be called up to let yous hear th' song sung as only Sammy can sing it.

AYAMONN. Bring him up, bring him up – why in hell didn't you tell me all this before?

BRENNAN [*stormily*]. Wasn't I thryin' all the time an' you wouldn't let a man get a word in edgeways. [*Gesturing towards* SHEILA] He'll jib at singin' in front of her. [*He whispers hoarsely towards Sheila*] He's as shy as a kid in his first pair o' pants, dear lady.

AYAMONN [*impatiently pushing him out of the room*]. Oh, go on, go on, man, and bring him up. [BRENNAN *goes out.*]

SHEILA [*earnestly*]. Wait till I'm gone, Ayamonn; I can't stop long, and I want to talk to you so much.

AYAMONN [*a little excited*]. Oh, you must hear the song, Sheila; they've been working to get the air down for a week, and it won't take a minute.

SHEILA [*angrily*]. I've waited too long already! Aren't you more interested in what I want to say than to be listening to some vain fool singing a song?

AYAMONN [*a little taken aback*]. Oh, Sheila, what's wrong with you tonight? The young carpenter who'll sing it, so far from being vain, is as shy as a field-mouse, and you'll see, when he starts to sing, he'll edge his face away from us. You do want to hear it, Sheila, don't you?

SHEILA [*appealingly*]. Let it wait over, Ayamonn; I can come to hear it some other time. I do want to say something, very serious, to you about our future meetings.

AYAMONN [*hastily*]. All right then; I'll hurry them off the minute the song's sung. Here they are, so sit down, do, just for one minute more.

*But she goes towards the door, and reaches it just as* OLD BRENNAN *returns shoving in before him a young man of twenty-three, shy, and loth to come in. He is tall, but his face is pale and mask-like in its expression of resignation to the world and all around him. Even when he shows he's shy, the mask-like features do not alter. He is dressed in a white cut-away coat, shaped like a tailed evening dress, black waistcoat over a rather soiled shirt-front, frilled, and green trousers. He carries a sheet of manuscript music in his hand.* BRENNAN *unslings his melodeon from his back, fusses the young* SINGER *forward; bumping against* SHEILA, *who has moved towards the door, he pushes her back with a shove of his backside; and puts* AYAMONN *to the other end of the room with a push on the shoulder.*

BRENNAN [*as he pushes* SHEILA.] Outa th' way, there! Stem your eagerness for a second, will yous? All in good time. Give the man a chance to get himself easy. [*As he pushes* AYAMONN] Farther back, there, farther back! Give the performer a chance to dispose himself. Isn't he a swell, wha'? The centre group's to be dhressed the same way, while th' corner men'll be in reverse colours – green coats, black trousers, an' white vest, see? Th' whole assembly'll look famous. Benjamin's lendin' all the set o' twelve suits for five bob, 'cause o' th' reason we're runnin' th' Show for. [*To* SHEILA – *in a hoarse whisper*] You stare at the fire as if he wasn't here. He's extravagant in shyness, an' sinks away into confusion at the stare of an eye – understand?

*She slowly, and a little sullenly, sits down to stare into the fire. The door is opened, and in comes* ROORY O'BALACAUN *with a small roll of Irish magazines under an arm. He is a stout middle-aged man, dressed in rough homespun coat, cap, and knee-breeches, wearing over all a trench coat.*

ROORY. Here y'are, Ayamonn, me son, avic's* th' Irish magazines I got me friend to pinch for you. [*He looks at the* SINGER.] Hello, what kind of a circus is it's goin' on here?

AYAMONN. Mr Brennan Moore here's organising the singers for the Minsthrel Show to help get funds in case we have to go on sthrike, Roory.

ROORY. I'm one o' th' men meself, but I don't stand for a foreign Minsthrel Show bein' held, an' the Sword of Light* gettin' lifted up in th' land. We want no coon or Kaffir* industry in our country.

BRENNAN [*indignantly*]. Doesn't matter what you stand for before you came here, you'll sit down now. Thry to regard yourself as a civilised member of the community, man, an' hold your peace for th' present. [*To the* SINGER] Now, Sam, me son o' gold, excavate the shyness out of your system an' sing as if you were performin' before a Royal Command!

ROORY [*with a growl*]. There's no royal commands wanted here.

BRENNAN [*with a gesture of disgusted annoyance*]. Will you for goodness'
  sake not be puttin' th' singer out? I used the term only as an
  allegory, man.

ROORY. Allegory man, or allegory woman, there's goin' to be no royal
  inthrusions where the Sword o' Light is shinin'.

AYAMONN. Aw, for Christ's sake, Roory, let's hear the song!

BRENNAN [*to the* SINGER, *who has been coughing shyly and turning
  sideways from his audience*]. Now, Sam, remember you're not in
  your working clothes, an' are a different man, entirely. Chin up and
  chest out. [*He gives a note or two on the melodeon.*] Now!

SINGER [*singing*].

> A sober black shawl hides her body entirely,
> Touch'd by th' sun and th' salt spray of the sea;
> But down in th' darkness a slim hand, so lovely,
> Carries a rich bunch of red roses for me.*

[*He turns away a little more from his audience, and coughs shyly.*]

BRENNAN [*enthusiastically*]. Sam, you're excellin' yourself! On again,
  me oul' son!

SINGER [*singing*].

> Her petticoat's simple, her feet are but bare,
> An' all that she has is but neat an' scantie;
> But stars in th' deep of her eyes are exclaiming
> I carry a rich bunch of red roses for thee!

BRENNAN [*after giving a few curling notes on the melodeon*]. A second
  Count McCormack* in th' makin'! An' whenever he sung 'Mother
  Mo Chree',* wasn't there a fewroory* in Heaven with the rush that
  was made to lean over an hear him singin' it!

*While* BRENNAN *has been speaking, the door has opened, and* MULLCANNY
*now stands there gaping into the room. He is young, lusty, and restless. He
is wearing fine tweeds that don't fit too well; and his tweed cap is set
rakishly on his head. He, too, wears a mackintosh.*

MULLCANNY. Is this a home-sweet-away-from-home hippodhrome,*
  or what?

BRENNAN [*clicking his tongue in annoyance*]. Dtchdtchdtch!

MULLCANNY. An' did I hear someone pratin' about Heaven, an' I coming in? [*To* BRENNAN – *tapping him on the shoulder*] Haven't you heard, old man, that God is dead?

BRENNAN. Well, keep your grand discovery to yourself for a minute or two more, please. [*To the* SINGER] Now, Sam, apologisin' for th' other's rudeness, the last verse, please.

SINGER [*singing*].

> No arrogant gem sits enthron'd on her forehead,
> Or swings from a white ear for all men to see;
> But jewel'd desire in a bosom, most pearly,
> Carries a rich bunch of red roses for me!

BRENNAN [*after another curl of notes on the melodeon*]. Well, fair damsel and gentlemen all, what do you think of the song and the singer?

AYAMONN. The song was good, and the singer was splendid.

MULLCANNY. What I heard of it wasn't bad.

SINGER [*shyly*]. I'm glad I pleased yous all.

ROORY [*dubiously*]. D'ye not think th' song is a trifle indecent?

MULLCANNY [*mockingly*]. Indecent! And what may your eminence's specification of indecency be? [*Angrily*] Are you catalogued, too, with the Catholic Young Men going about with noses long as a snipe's* bill, sthripping the gayest rose of its petals in search of a beetle, and sniffing a taint in the freshest breeze blowing in from the sea?

BRENNAN [*warningly*]. Lady present, lady present, boys!

ROORY. It ill becomes a thrue Gael to stand unruffled when either song or story thries to introduce colour to the sabler nature of yearnin's in untuthored minds.

BRENNAN [*more loudly*]. Lady present, boys!

SHEILA [*rising out of the chair and going towards the door*]. The lady's going now, thank yhou all for the entertainment. [*To* AYAMONN] I won't stay any longer to disturb the important dispute of your friends.

AYAMONN [*going over to her*]. Don't be foolish, Sheila, dear; but if you must go, you must. We'll see each other again tomorrow evening.

SHEILA [*firmly*]. No, not tomorrow, nor the next night either.

AYAMONN [*while* BRENNAN *plays softly on the melodeon to hide embarrassment*]. When then?

SHEILA. I can't tell. I'll write. Never maybe. [*Bitterly*] I warned you
    this night might be the last chance of a talk for some time, and you
    didn't try to make use of it!

AYAMONN [*catching her arm*]. I made as much use of it as you'd let me.
    Tomorrow night, in the old place, near the bridge, the bridge of
    vision where we first saw Aengus* and his coloured birds of passion
    passing.

SHEILA [*wildly*]. I can't; I won't, so there – oh, let me go! [*She breaks
    away from him, runs out, and a silence falls on the room for a few
    moments.*]

ROORY [*breaking the silence*]. Women is strange things! Elegant
    animals, not knowin' their own minds a minute.

BRENNAN [*consolingly*]. She'll come back, she'll come back.

AYAMONN [*trying to appear unconcerned*]. Aw, to hell with her!

SINGER [*faintly*]. Can I go now?

BRENNAN. Wait, an' I'll be with you in a second.

MULLCANNY [*to* AYAMONN]. I just dropped in to say, Ayamonn, that
    I'll be getting Haeckel's *Riddle of the Universe* tomorrow, afther
    long searching, and I'll let you have it the minute it comes into my
    hand.

*The door is suddenly flung open, and* EEADA, *followed by* DYMPNA *and*
FINNOOLA, *with others, mingled with men behind them, rushes into the
room in a very excited state. She comes forward, with her two companions a
little behind, while the rest group themselves by the door.*

EEADA [*distractedly*]. It's gone she is, an' left us lonesome; vanished she
    is like a fairy mist of an early summer mornin'; stolen She is be some
    pagan Protestan' hand, envious of the love we had for our sweet
    Lady of Eblana's poor!

CHORUS. Our Lady of Eblana's gone!

AYAMONN. Nonsense; no Protestant hand touched Her. Where was
    She?

DYMPNA. Safe in her niche in th' hall She was, afther Her washin',
    lookin' down on the comin's an' goin's of Her strugglin' children:
    an' then we missed Her, an' th' niche was empty!

CHORUS. Our Lady of Eblana's gone!

SINGLE VOICE. An' dear knows what woe'll fall on our poor house now.

BRENNAN. An' a good job, too. [*Passionately*] Inflamin' yourselves
    with idols that have eyes an' see not; ears, an' hear not; an' have

hands that handle not; like th' chosen people settin' moon-images an' sun-images, cuttin' away the thrue and homely connection between the Christian an' his God! Here, let me and me singer out of this unholy place! [*He pushes his way through the people, followed by the* SINGER, *and goes out.*]

EEADA [*nodding her head, to* AYAMONN]. All bark, but no bite! We know him of old: a decent oul' blatherer. Sure, doesn't he often buy violets and snowdrops, even, for little Ursula, below, tellin' her she mustn't put them before a graven image, knowin' full well that that was th' first thing she'd hurry home to do. An' she's breakin' her young heart below, now, because her dear Lady has left her. [*Suspiciously*] If Oul' Brennan had a hand in Her removal, woe betide him.

MULLCANNY [*mocking*]. Couldn't you all do betther than wasting your time making gods afther your own ignorant images?

AYAMONN [*silencing him with a gesture*]. That's enough, Paudhrig. [*To* EEADA] Tell little Ursula not to worry. Her Lady'll come back. If your Lady of Eblana hasn't returned by tonight. I'll surrender my sleep afther my night's work to search for Her, and bring Her back safe to Her niche in the hall. No one in this house touched Her.

EEADA. An' you'll see She'll pay you back for your kindness, Ayamonn – [*looking at* MULLCANNY] though it's little surprised I'd be if, of Her own accord, She came down indignant, an' slipped off from us, hearin' the horrid talk that's allowed to float around this house lately.

MULLCANNY [*mocking*]. Afraid of me, She was. Well, Ayamonn, I've some lessons to get ready, so I'll be off. I'll bring you the book tomorrow. [*To the crowd – mocking*] I hope the poor Lady of Eblana's poor'll find Her way home again. [*He goes out through a surly-faced crowd.*]

AYAMONN [*to* EEADA]. Don't mind Mullcanny. Good night, now; and don't worry about your dear statue. If She doesn't come back, we'll find another as bright and good to take Her place.

EEADA [*growling*]. The fella that's gone'll have a rough end, jeerin' things sacred to our feelin'.

*They all go out, and* AYAMONN *is left alone with* ROORY. AYAMONN *takes off his doublet, folds it up, and puts it back in the basket. He goes into the other room and comes back with oilskin coat and thigh-leggings. He puts the leggings on over his trousers.*

AYAMONN [*putting on the leggings*]. Th' shunting-yard'll be a nice place
   to be tonight. D'ye hear it? [*He listens to the falling rain, now heavier
   than ever.*]

ROORY. Fallin' fast. That Mullcanny'll get into throuble yet.

AYAMONN. Not he. He's really a good fellow. Gave up his job rather
   than his beliefs – more'n many would do.

ROORY. An' how does he manage now?

AYAMONN. Hammering knowledge into deluded minds wishing to be
   civil servants, bank clerks, an' constables who hope to take the last
   sacraments as sergeants in the Royal Irish Constabulary or the
   Metropolitan Police.

ROORY. By God, he's his work cut out for him with the last lot!


*The door is again opened and* EEADA *sticks her head into the room.*


EEADA. Your mother's just sent word that the woman she's mindin's
   bad, an' she'll have to stay th' night. I'm just runnin' round meself
   to make your mother a cup o' tea.

AYAMONN [*irritably*]. Dtch dtch – she'll knock herself up before she's
   done! When I lock up, I'll leave the key with you for her, Eeada.
   [*He lights a shunter's lantern and puts out the lamp.*]

EEADA. Right y'are. [*She goes.*]

ROORY. What kid was it sketched th' angel on th' wall?

AYAMONN. Oh, I did that. I'd give anything to be a painter.

ROORY. What, like Oul' Brennan o' th' Moor?

AYAMONN. No, no; like Angelico or Constable.*

ROORY [*indifferently*]. Never heard of them.

AYAMONN [*musingly*]. To throw a whole world in colour on a canvas
   though it be but a man's fine face, a woman's shape asthride of a
   cushioned couch, or a three-bordered house on a hill, done with a
   glory; even delaying God, busy forgin' a new world, to stay awhile
   an' look upon their loveliness.

ROORY. Aw, Ayamonn, Ayamonn, man, put out your hand an' see if
   you're awake! [*He fiddles with the books on the table.*] What oul' book
   are you readin' now?

AYAMONN [*dressed now in oilskin leggings and coat, with an oilskin
   sou'wester on his head, comes over to look at the book in* ROORY's *hand,
   and shines the lantern on it*]. Oh, that's Ruskin's *Crown of Wild Olive**
   – a grand book – I'll lend it to you.

ROORY. What for? What would I be doin' with it? I've no time to waste on books. Ruskin. Curious name; not Irish, is it?

AYAMONN. No, a Scotsman who wrote splendidly about a lot of things. Listen to this, spoken before a gathering of business men about to build an Exchange in their town.

ROORY. Aw, Ayamonn – an Exchange! What have we go to do with an Exchange?

AYAMONN [*impatiently*]. Listen a second, man! Ruskin, speakin' to the business men, says, 'Your ideal of life is a pleasant and undulating world, with iron and coal everywhere beneath it. On each pleasant bank of this world is to be a beautiful mansion; stables, and coach-houses; a park and hot-houses; carriage-drives and shrub-beries; and here are to live the votaries of the Goddess of Getting-on – the English gentleman –'

ROORY [*interrupting*]. There you are, you see, Ayamonn – th' *English* gentleman!

AYAMONN. Wait a second – Irish or English – a gentleman's th' same.

ROORY. 'Tisn't. I'm tellin' you it's different. What's in this Ruskin of yours but another oul' cod with a gift of the gab? Right enough for th' English, pinin' afther little things, ever rakin' cindhers for th' glint of gold. We're different – we have th' light.

AYAMONN. You mean th' Catholic Faith?

ROORY [*impatiently*]. No, no; that's there, too; I mean th' light of freedom; th' tall white candle tipped with its golden spear of flame. The light we thought we'd lost; but it burns again, shthrengthenin' into a sword of light. Like in th' song we sung together th' other night. [*He sings softly*]

> Our courage so many have thought to be agein',
> Now flames like a brilliant new star in th' sky;
> And Danger is proud to be call'd a good brother,
> For Freedom has buckled her sword on her thigh.

AYAMONN [*joining in*]:

> Then out to th' place where th' battle is bravest,
> Where th' noblest an' meanest fight fierce in th' fray,
> Republican banners shall mock at th' foeman,
> An' Fenians shall turn a dark night into day!*

*A pause as the two of them stand silent, each clasping the other's hand.*
AYAMONN *opens the door to pass out.*

ROORY [*in a tense whisper*]. Th' Fenians are in force again, Ayamonn;
   th' Sword o' Light is shinin'! *They go out, and* AYAMONN *closes the
   door as the* CURTAIN *falls.*

## ACT II

*The same as in Act I.*

*It is about ten o'clock at night. The rain has stopped, and there is a fine moon sailing through the sky. Some of its rays come in through the window at the side.*

AYAMONN, *in his shirt-sleeves, is sitting at the table. He has an ordinary tin money-box in his hand, and a small pile of coppers, mixed with a few sixpences, are on the table beside him. He is just taking the last coin from the slit in the box with the aid of a knife-blade. His mother is by the dresser piling up the few pieces of crockery used for a recent meal. The old one-wick lamp is alight, and stands on the table near to* AYAMONN. *Several books lie open there, too.*

AYAMONN. There's th' last one out, now. It's quite a job getting them out with a knife.

MRS BREYDON. Why don't you put them in a box with a simple lid on?

AYAMONN. The harder it is to get at, the less chance of me spending it on something more necessary than what I seek. [*He counts the money on the table.*] One bob – two – three – an' sixpence – an' nine – three an' ninepence; one an' threepence to get yet – a long way to go.

MRS BREYDON. Maybe, now, th' bookseller would give you it for what you have till you can give him th' rest.

AYAMONN [*in agony*]. Aw, woman, if you can't say sense, say nothing! Constable's reproductions are five shillings second-hand, an' he that's selling is the bastard that nearly got me jailed for running off with his Shakespeare. It's touch an' go if he'll let me have it for the five bob.

MRS BREYDON [*philosophically*]. Well, seein' you done without it so long, you can go without it longer.

AYAMONN [*with firm conviction*]. I'll have it the first week we get the extra shilling the men are demandin'.

MRS BREYDON. I shouldn't count your chickens before they're hatched.

AYAMONN [*joking a little bitterly*]. Perhaps Our Blessed Lady of Eblana's poor will work a miracle for me.

MRS BREYDON [*a little anxiously*]. Hush, don't say that! Jokin' or serious, Ayamonn, I wouldn't say that. We don't believe in any of their Blessed Ladies, but as it's somethin' sacred, it's best not mentioned. [*She shuffles into her shawl.*] Though it's a queer thing, her goin' off out of her niche without a one in th' house knowin' why. They're all out huntin' for her still.

*The door opens, and* BRENNAN *comes in slowly, with a cute grin on his face. He has a large package, covered with paper, under his arm.*

BRENNAN. Out huntin' still for her they are, are they? Well, let them hunt; she's here! A prisoner under me arm!

MRS BREYDON [*indignantly*]. Well, Mr Brennan Moore, it's ashamed of yourself you should be yokin' th' poor people to throubled anxiety over their treasure; and little Ursula breakin' her heart into th' bargain.

AYAMONN. It's god-damned mean of you, Brennan! What good d'ye think you'll do by this rowdy love of your own opinions – forcing tumult into the minds of ignorant, anxious people?

BRENNAN [*calmly*]. Wait till yous see, wait till yous see, before yous are sorry for sayin' more. [*He removes the paper and shows the lost image transfigured into a figure looking as if it had come straight from the shop: the white dress is spotless, the blue robe radiant, and the gold along its border and on the crown is gleaming. He holds it up for admiration. Triumphantly*] There, what d'ye think of her now? Fair as th' first grand tinge of th' dawn, she is, an' bright as th' star of the evenin'.

MRS BREYDON. Glory be to God, isn't She lovely! But hurry Her off, Brennan, for she's not a thing for Protestant eyes to favour.

AYAMONN [*a little testily*]. Put it back, Brennan, put it back, and don't touch it again.

BRENNAN. Isn't that what I'm going to do? Oh, boy alive, won't they get th' shock o' their lives when they see Her shinin' in th' oul' spot. [*He becomes serious.*] Though, mind you, me thrue mind misgives me for decoratin' what's a charm to the people of Judah in th' worship of idols; but th' two of you is witness I did it for the sake of the little one, and not in any tilt towards honour to a graven image.

MRS BREYDON [*resignedly*]. It's done now, God forgive us both, an' me for sayin' She's lovely. Touchin' a thing forbidden with a startled stir of praise!

AYAMONN. Put it back, put it back, man, and leave it quiet where you got it first.

BRENNAN *goes out, looking intently out, and listening, before he does so.*

MRS BREYDON. He meant well, poor man, but he's done a dangerous thing. I'll be back before you start for work. [*With a heavy sigh*] It won't take us long to tend her for the last time. The white sheets have come, th' tall candles wait to be lit, an' th' coffin's ordhered, an' th' room'll look sacred with the bunch of violets near her head. [*She goes out slowly – as she goes*] Dear knows what'll happen to th' three children.

AYAMONN *sits silent for a few moments, reading a book, his elbows resting on the table.*

AYAMONN [*with a deep sigh – murmuringly*]. Sheila, Sheila, my heart cries out for you! [*After a moment's pause, he reads*]

> But I am pigeon-livered, an' lack gall
> To make oppression bitther; or, ere this,
> I should have fatted all th' region kites
> With this slave's offal: Bloody, bawdy villain!*

Oh, Will,* you were a boyo; a brave boyo, though, and a beautiful one!

*The door opens and* OLD BRENNAN *comes in, showing by his half suppressed chuckles that he is enjoying himself. He wanders over the room to stand by the fire.*

BRENNAN [*chuckling*]. In her old place she is, now, in her new coronation robe; and funny it is to think it's the last place they'll look for her.

AYAMONN. I'm busy, now.

BRENNAN [*sitting down by the fire*]. Ay, so you are; so I see; busy readin'. Read away, for I won't disturb you; only have a few quiet puffs at th' oul' pipe. [*A pause.*] Ah, then, don't I wish I was young enough to bury myself in th' joy of readin' all th' great books of th' world. Ah! but when I was young, I had to work hard.

AYAMONN. I work hard, too.

BRENNAN. 'Course you do! Isn't that what I'm sayin'? An' all th' more credit, too, though it must be thryin' to have thoughtless people comin' in an' intherferin' with the golden movements of your thoughts.

AYAMONN. It's often a damned nuisance!

BRENNAN. 'Course it is. Isn't that what I'm sayin'? [*As the door opens*] An' here's another o' th' boobies entherin' now. [ROORY *comes in, and shuts the door rather noisily.*] Eh, go easy, there – can't you se Ayamonn's busy studyin'?

ROORY [*coming and bending over Ayamonn*]. Are you still lettin' oul' Ruskin tease you?

AYAMONN [*angrily*]. No, no; Shakespeare, Shakespeare, this time! [*Springing from his chair*] Damn it, can't you let a man alone a minute? What th' hell d'ye want now?

BRENNAN [*warningly*]. I told you he was busy.

ROORY [*apologetically*]. Aw, I only came with the tickets you asked me to bring you for the comin' National Anniversary of Terence Bellew MacManus.*

AYAMONN. All right, all right; let's have them.

ROORY. How many d'ye want? How many can you sell?

AYAMONN. Give me twelve sixpennies; if the sthrike doesn't come off I'll easily sell that number.

ROORY [*counting out the tickets which* AYAMONN *gathers up and puts into his pocket*]. I met that Mullcanny on the way with a book for you; but he stopped to tell a couple of railwaymen that the story of Adam an' Eve was all a cod.

BRENNAN [*indignantly*]. He has a lot o' the people here in a state o' steamin' anger, goin' about with his bitther belief that the patthern of a man's hand is nearly at one with a monkey's paw, a horse's foot, th' flipper of a seal, or th' wing of a bat!

AYAMONN. Well, each of them is as wonderful as the hand of a man.

ROORY. No, Ayamonn, not from the Christian point of view. D'ye know what they're callin' him round here? Th' New Broom, because he's always sayin' he'll sweep th' idea of God clean outa th' mind o' man.

BRENNAN [*excited*]. There'll be dire damage done to him yet! He was goin' to be flattened out be a docker th' other day for tellin' him that a man first formin' showed an undoubted sign of a tail.

AYAMONN. Ay, and when he's fully formed, if he doesn't show the tail, he shows most signs of all that goes along with it.

ROORY. But isn't that a nice dignity to put on th' sacredness of a man's conception!

BRENNAN [*whisperingly*]. An' a lot o' them are sayin', Ayamonn, that your encouragement of him should come to an end.

AYAMONN. Indeed? Well, let them. I'll stand by any honest man seekin' th' truth, though his way isn't my way. [*To* BRENNAN] You, yourself, go about deriding many things beloved by your Catholic neighbours.

BRENNAN. I contest only dangerous deceits specified be the Council o' Thrent,* that are nowhere scheduled in th' pages of the Holy Scriptures.

ROORY. Yes, Ayamonn, it's altogether different; he just goes about blatherin' in his ignorant Protestant way.

BRENNAN [*highly indignant*]. Ignorant, am I? An' where would a body find an ignorance lustier than your own, eh? If your Council o' Thrent's ordher for prayers for the dead who are past help, your dismal veneration of saints an' angels, your images of wood an' stone, carved an' coloured, have given you the image an' super-scription of a tail, th' pure milk of the gospel has made a man of me, God-fearin', but stately, with a mind garlanded to th' steady an' eternal thruth!

*While they have been arguing,* MULLCANNY *has peeped round the door, and now comes into the room, eyeing the two disputants with a lot of amusement and a little scorn. They take no notice of him.*

RORRY. Sure, man, you have the neighbourhood hectored with your animosity against Catholic custom an' Catholic thought, never hesitatin' to give th' Pope even a deleterious name.

BRENNAN [*lapsing, in his excitement, into a semi-Ulster dialect*]. We dud ut tae yeh in Durry* on' sent your bravest floatin' down dud in th' wathers of th' Boyne,* like th' hosts of Pharaoh tumblin' in the rush of th' Rud Sea! Thut was a slup in th' puss* tae your Pope!

MULLCANNY. You pair of damned fools, don't you know that the Pope wanted King Billy to win, and that the Vatican was ablaze with lights of joy afther King James's defeat over the wathers of the Boyne?

ROORY. You're a liar, he didn't!

BRENNAN. You're a liar, it wasn't! [*They turn from* MULLCANNY *to continue the row with themselves.*] Looksee, if I believed in the ministhration of saints on' angels, I'd say thut th' good Protestant St Puthrick was at the hud of what fell out at Durry, Aughrim, on' th' Boyne.

ROORY [*stunned with the thought of St Patrick as a Protestant*].

Protestant St Pathrick? Is me hearin' sound, or what? What name did you mention?

BRENNAN. I said St Puthrick – th' evangelical founder of our thrue Church.

ROORY. Is it dhreamin' I am? Is somethin' happenin' to me, or is it happenin' to you? Oh, man, it's mixin' mirth with madness you are at thinkin' St Pathrick ever looped his neck in an orange sash, or tapped out a tune on a Protestant dhrum!

BRENNAN [*contemptuously*]. I refuse to argue with a one who's no' a broad-minded mon. Abuse is no equivalent or lugic – so I say God save th' King, an' tae hull with th' Pope!

ROORY [*indignantly*]. You damned bigot – to hell with th' King, an' God save th' Pope!

MULLCANNY [*to* AYAMONN]. You see how they live in bittherness, the one with the other. Envy, strife, and malice crawl from the coloured slime of the fairy-tales that go to make what is called religion. [*Taking a book from his pocket*] Here's something can bear a thousand tests, showing neatly how the world and all it bears upon it came into slow existence over millions of years, doing away for ever with the funny wonders of the seven days' creation set out in the fairy book of the Bible.

AYAMONN [*taking the book from* MULLCANNY]. Thanks, Pether, oul' son; I'm bound to have a good time reading it.

MULLCANNY. It'll give you the true and scientific history of man as he was before Adam.

BRENNAN [*in a woeful voice*]. It's a darkened mind that thries tae lower us to what we were before th' great an' good God fashioned us. What does ony sensible person want to know what we were like before the creation of th' first man?

AYAMONN [*murmuringly*]. To know the truth, to seek the truth, is good, though it lead to th' danger of eternal death.

ROORY [*horror-stricken – crossing himself*]. Th' Lord between us an' all harm!

BRENNAN [*whispering prayerfully*]. Lord, I believe, help Thou mine unbelief.

MULLCANNY [*pointing out a picture in the book*]. See? The human form unborn. The tail – look, the os coccyx sticking a mile out; there's no getting away from it!

BRENNAN [*shaking his head woefully*]. An' this is holy Ireland!

ROORY [*lifting his eyes to the ceiling – woefully*]. Poor St Pathrick!

MULLCANNY [*mockingly*]. He's going to be a lonely man soon eh? [*To* AYAMONN] Keep it safe for me, Ayamonn. When you've read it, you'll be a different man. [*He goes to the door.*] Well, health with the whole o' you, and goodbye for the present. [*He goes out.*]

ROORY. Have nothin' to do with that book, Ayamonn, for that fellow gone out would rip up the floor of Heaven to see what was beneath it. It's clapped in jail he ought to be!

BRENNAN. An' th' book banned!

AYAMONN. Roory, Roory, is that th' sort o' freedom you'd bring to Ireland with a crowd of green branches an' th' joy of shouting? If we give no room to men of our time to question many things, all things, ay, life itself, then freedom's but a paper flower, a star of tinsel, a dead lass with gay ribbons at her breast an' a gold comb in her hair. Let us bring freedom here, not with sounding brass an' tinkling cymbal,* but with silver trumpets blowing, with a song all men can sing, with a palm branch in our hand, rather than with a whip at our belt, and a headsman's axe on our shoulders.

*There is a gentle knock at the door, and the voice of* SHEILA *is heard speaking.*

SHEILA [*outside*]. Ayamonn, are you there? Are you in?

BRENNAN [*whispering*]. The little lass; I knew she'd come back.

AYAMONN. I don't want her to see you here. Go into the other room – quick. [*He pushes them towards it.*] An' keep still.

ROORY [*to* BRENNAN]. An' don't you go mockin' our Pope, see?

BRENNAN [*to* ROORY]. Nor you go singlin' out King Billy for a jeer.

AYAMONN. In with yous, quick!

BRENNAN. I prophesied she'd come back, didn't I, Ayamonn? that she'd come back, didn't I?

AYAMONN. Yes, yes; in you go.

*He puts them in the other room and shuts the door. Then he crosses the room and opens the door to admit* SHEILA. *She comes in, and he and* SHEILA *stand silently for some moments, she trying to look at him, and finding it hard.*

SHEILA [*at last*]. Well, haven't you anything to say to me?

AYAMONN [*slowly and coldly*]. I waited for you at the bridge today; but you didn't come.

SHEILA. I couldn't come; I told you why.

AYAMONN. I was very lonely.

SHEILA [*softly*]. So was I, Ayamonn, lonely even in front of God's holy face.

AYAMONN. Sheila, we've gone a long way in a gold canoe over many waters, bright and surly, sometimes sending bitter spray asplash on our faces. But you were ever listening for the beat from the wings of the angel of fear. So you got out to walk safe on a crowded road.

SHEILA. This is a cold and cheerless welcome, Ayamonn.

AYAMONN. Change, if you want to, the burning kiss falling on the upturned, begging mouth for the chill caress of a bony, bearded saint. [*Loudly*] Go with th' yelling crowd, and keep them brave and yell along with them!

SHEILA. Won't you listen, then, to the few words I have to say?

AYAMONN [*sitting down near the fire, and looking into it, though he leaves her standing*]. Go ahead; I won't fail to hear you.

SHEILA. God knows I don't mean to hurt you, but you must know that we couldn't begin to live on what you're earning now – could we? [*He keeps silent.*] Oh, Ayamonn, why do you waste your time on doing foolish things?

AYAMONN. What foolish things?

*A hubbub is heard in the street outside; voices saying loudly 'Give him one in the bake'\* or 'Down him with a one in th' belly'; then the sound of running footsteps, and silence.*

SHEILA [*when she hears the voices – nervously*]. What's that?

AYAMONN [*without taking his gaze from the fire*]. Some drunken row or other. [*They listen silently for a few moments.*] Well, what foolish things?

SHEILA [*timid and hesitating*]. You know yourself, Ayamonn: trying to paint, going mad about Shakespeare, and consorting with a kind of people that can only do you harm.

AYAMONN [*mockingly prayerful – raising his eyes to the ceiling*]. O Lord, let me forsake the foolish, and live; and go in the way of Sheila's understanding!

SHEILA [*going over nearer to him*]. Listen, Ayamonn, my love; you know what I say is only for our own good, that we may come together all the sooner. [*Trying to speak jokingly*] Now, really, isn't it comical I'd look if I were to go about in a scanty petticoat, covered

in a sober black shawl, and my poor feet bare! [*Mocking*] Wouldn't I
look well that way!

AYAMONN [*quietly*]. With red roses in your hand, you'd look beautiful.

SHEILA [*desperately*]. Oh, for goodness' sake, Ayamonn, be sensible!
I'm getting a little tired of all this. I can't bear the strain the way
we're going on much longer. [*A short pause.*] You will either have to
make good, or – [*She pauses.*]

AYAMONN [*quietly*]. Or what?

SHEILA [*with a little catch in her voice*]. Or lose me; and you wouldn't
like that to happen.

AYAMONN. I shouldn't like that to happen; but I could bear the
sthrain.

SHEILA. I risked a big row tonight to come to tell you good news: I've
been told that the strike is bound to take place; there is bound to be
trouble; and, if you divide yourself from the foolish men, and stick
to your job, you'll soon be a foreman of some kind or other.

AYAMONN [*rising from his seat and facing her for the first time*]. Who told
you all this? The Inspector?

SHEILA. Never mind who; if he did, wasn't it decent of him?

AYAMONN. D'ye know what you're asking me to do, woman? To be a
blackleg; to blast with th' black frost of desertion the gay hopes of
my comrades. Whatever you may think them to be, they are my
comrades. Whatever they may say or do, they remain my brothers
and sisters. Go to hell, girl, I have a soul to save as well as you. [*With
a catch in his voice*] Oh, Sheila, you shouldn't have asked me to do
this thing!

SHEILA [*trying to come close, but he pushes her back*]. Oh, Ayamonn, it is
a chance; take it, do, for my sake!

*Rapid footsteps are heard outside. The door flies open and* MULLCANNY
*comes in, pale, frightened, his clothes dishevelled and a slight smear of
blood on his forehead. His bowler hat is crushed down on his head, his coat
is torn, and his waistcoat unbuttoned, showing his tie pulled out of its place.
He sinks into a chair.*

AYAMONN. What's happened? Who did that to you?

MULLCANNY. Give's a drink, someone, will you? [AYAMONN *gets him a
drink from a jug on the dresser.*] A gang of bowseys* made for me, and
I talking to a man. Barely escaped with my life. Only for some brave

oul' one, they'd have laid me out completely. She saved me from worse.

AYAMONN. How th' hell did you bring all that on you?

MULLCANNY [*plaintively*]. Just trying to show a fellow the foolishness of faith in a hereafter, when something struck me on the head, and I was surrounded by feet makin kicks at me!

*A crash of breaking glass is heard from the other room, and* BRENNAN *and* ROORY *come running out of it.*

ROORY. A stone has done for th' window! [*He sees* MULLCANNY.] Oh, that's how th' land lies, is it? Haven't I often said that if you go round leerin' at God an' His holy assistants, one day He's bound to have a rap at you!

BRENNAN. Keep away from that window, there, in case another one comes sailin' in.

*Immediately he has spoken, a stone smashes in through the window.* BRENNAN *lies down flat on the floor;* MULLCANNY *slides from the chair and crouches on the ground;* ROORY *gets down on his hands and knees, keeping his head as low as possible, so that he resembles a Mohammedan at his devotions;* SHEILA *stands stiff in a corner, near the door; and* AYAMONN, *seizing up a hurley lying against the dresser, makes for the door to go out.*

BRENNAN. I guessed this was comin'.

AYAMONN [*angrily*]. I'll show them!

SHEILA [*to* AYAMONN]. Stop where you are, you fool! [*But* AYAMONN *pays no attention to the advice and hurries out of the door.*]

ROORY [*plaintively and with dignity – to* MULLCANNY]. This is what you bring down on innocent people with your obstinate association of man with th' lower animals.

MULLCANNY [*truculently*]. Only created impudence it is that strives to set yourselves above the ape's formation, genetically present in every person's body.

BRENNAN [*indignantly*]. String out life to where it started, an' you'll find no sign, let along a proof, of the dignity, wisdom, an' civility of man ever having been associated with th' manners of a monkey.

MULLCANNY. And why do children like to climb trees, eh? Answer me that?

ROORY [*fiercely*]. They love it more where you come from than they do here.

SHEILA [*from her corner*]. It's surely to be pitied you are, young man, lettin' yourself be bullied by ignorant books into believing that things are naught but what poor men are inclined to call them, blind to the glorious and eternal facts that shine behind them.

MULLCANNY [*pityingly*]. Bullied be books – eternal facts – aw! Yous are all scared stiff at the manifestation of a truth or two. D'ye know that the contraction of catharrh, apoplexy, consumption, and cataract of the eye is common to the monkeys? Knowledge you have now that you hadn't before; and a lot of them even like beer.

ROORY. Well, that's something sensible, at last.

BRENNAN [*fiercely*]. Did they get their likin' for beer from us, or did we get our likin' of beer from them? Answer me that, you, now; answer me that!

ROORY. Answer him that. We're not Terra Del Fooaygeeans,* but sensible, sane, an' civilised souls.

MULLCANNY [*gleefully*]. Time's promoted reptiles – that's all; yous can't do away with the os coccyges!

BRENNAN. Ladies present, ladies present.

ROORY [*creeping over rapidly till his face is close to that of* MULLCANNY'S *– fiercely*]. We stand on the earth, firm, upright, heads cocked, lookin' all men in th' face, afraid o' nothin'; men o' goodwill we are, abloom with th' blessin' o' charity, showin' in th' dust we're made of, th' diamond-core of an everlastin' divinity!

SHEILA [*excitedly*]. Hung as high as Gilderoy* he ought to be, an' he deep in the evil of his rich illusions, spouting insults at war with th' mysteries an' facts of our holy faith!

BRENNAN [*to* SHEILA]. Hush, pretty lady, hush. [*To the others*] Boys, boys, take example from a poor oul' Protestant here, never lettin' himself be offended be a quiver of anger in any peaceable or terrified discussion. Now, let that last word finish it; finis – the end, see?

ROORY [*angrily – to* BRENNAN]. Finis yourself, you blurry-eyed, wither-skinned oul' greybeard, singin' songs in th' public streets for odd coppers, with all th' boys in th' Bank of Ireland workin' overtime countin' all you've got in their front room! Finis you!

BRENNAN [*indignantly*]. An office-boy, in a hurry, wouldn't stop to pick up from th' path before him the few coins I have. An' as for being withered, soople as you I am, hands that can tinkle a thremblin' tune out of an oul' melodeon, legs that can carry me ten miles an' more, an' eyes that can still see without hardship a red berry shinin' from a distant bush!

*The door opens and* AYAMONN *and his mother come in. She runs over to the blossoms at the window, tenderly examining the plants growing there – the musk, the geranium, and the fuchsia.*

MRS BREYDON [*joyfully*]. Unharmed, th' whole of them. Th' stone passed them by, touchin' none o' them – thank God for that mercy!

AYAMONN. What th' hell are you doin' on your knees? Get up, get up. [*They rise from the floor shamefacedly.*] Th' rioters all dispersed. [*To* MULLCANNY] Mother was th' oul' one who saved you from a sudden an' unprovided death. An' th' Blessed Image has come back again, all aglow in garments new. Listen!

*A murmur of song has been heard while* AYAMONN *was speaking, and now* EEADA, DYMPNA, FINNOOLA, *and the* MEN *appear at the door – now wide open – half backing into the room singing part of a hymn softly, their pale faces still wearing the frozen look of resignation; staring at the image shining bright and gorgeous as* BRENNAN *has made it for them, standing in a niche in the wall, directly opposite the door.* EEADA, DYMPNA, FINNOOLA, *and the* MEN *singing softly –*

> Oh! Queen of Eblana's poor children,
> Bear swiftly our woe away;
> An' give us a chance to live lightly
> An hour of our life's dark day!
> Lift up th' poor heads ever bending,
> An' light a lone star in th' sky,
> To show thro' th' darkness, descending,
> A cheerier way to die.

EEADA [*coming forward a little*]. She came back to Her poor again, in raiment rich. She came back; of Her own accord. She came to abide with Her people.

DYMPNA. From her window, little Ursula looked, and saw Her come in; in th' moonlight, along the street She came, stately. Blinded be the coloured light that shone around about Her, the child fell back, in a swoon she fell full on the floor beneath her.

1ST MAN. My eyes caught a glimpse of Her, too, glidin' back to where She came from. Regal an' proud She was, an' wondrous, so that me eyes failed; me knees thrembled an' bent low, an' me heart whispered a silent prayer to itself as th' vision passed me by, an' I fancied I saw a smile on Her holy face.

EEADA. Many have lied to see a strange thing this favoured night, an' blessin' will flow from it to all tempered into a lively belief; and maybe, too, to some who happen to be out of step with the many marchin' in the mode o' thruth. [*She comes a little closer to* MRS BREYDON. *The others, backs turned towards the room, stand, most of them outside the door, a few just across the threshold, in a semicircle, heads bent as if praying, facing towards the image.*] Th' hand of a black stranger it was who sent the stones flyin' through your windows; but ere tomorrow's sun is seen, they will be back again as shelther from th' elements. A blessin' generous on yous all [*pause*] – except th' evil thing that stands, all stiff-necked, underneath th' roof!

MULLCANNY [*mockingly*]. Me!

SHEILA [*fiercely*]. Ay, you, that shouldn't find a smile or an unclenched hand in a decent man's house!

MULLCANNY. I'll go; there's too many here to deal with – I'll leave you with your miracle.

AYAMONN. You can stay if you wish, for whatever surety of shelther's here, it's open to th' spirit seeking to add another colour to whatever thruth we know already. Thought that has run from a blow will find a roof under its courage here, an' a fire to sit by, as long as I live an' th' oul' rooms last!

SHEILA [*with quiet bitterness*]. Well, shelter him, then, that by right should be lost in the night, a black night, an' bitterly lonely, without a dim ray from a half-hidden star to give him a far-away companionship; ay, an' a desolate rest under a thorny and dripping thicket of lean and twisted whins,* too tired to thry to live longer against th' hate of the black wind and th' grey rain. Let him lie there, let him live there, forsaken, forgotten by all who live under a kindly roof and close to a cosy fire!

MULLCANNY [*with a pretended alarm*]. Good God, I'm done, now! I'm off before worse befall me. Good night, Ayamonn.

AYAMONN. Good night, my friend. [MULLCANNY *goes out.*]

BRENNAN. We're keepin' decent people out of their beds – so long, all.

ROORY. I'll be with you some o' th' way, an' we can finish that argument we had. Good night all. [*He and* BRENNAN *go out together, closing the door after them.* SHEILA *stands where she was, sullen and silent.*]

MRS BREYDON. Shame on you, Sheila, for such a smoky flame to come from such a golden lamp! [SHEILA *stays silent.*] Tired out I am, an' frightened be th' scene o' death I saw today. Dodge about how we may, we come to th' same end.

AYAMONN [*gently leading her towards the other room*]. Go an' lie down lady; you're worn out. Time's a perjured jade, an' ever he moans a man must die.* Who through every inch of life weaves a patthern of vigour an' elation can never taste death, but goes to sleep among th' stars, his withered arms outstretched to greet th' echo of his own shout. It will be for them left behind to sigh for an hour, an' then to sing their own odd songs, an' do their own odd dances, to give a lonely God a little company, till they, too, pass by on their bare way out. When a true man dies, he is buried in th' birth of a thousand worlds.

MRS BREYDON *goes into the other room, and* AYAMONN *closes the door softly behind her. He comes back and stands pensive near the fire.*

AYAMONN [*after a pause*]. Don't you think you should go too?

SHEILA [*a little brokenly*]. Let me have a few more words with you, Ayamonn, before we hurry to our separation.

AYAMONN [*quietly*]. There is nothing more to be said.

SHEILA. There's a lot to be said, but hasty time won't stretch an hour a little out to let the words be spoken. Goodbye.

AYAMONN [*without turning his head*]. Goodbye.

SHEILA *is going slowly to the door when it partly opens, and half the head of* EEADA *peeps around it, amid an indistinct murmur as of praying outside.*

EEADA [*in half a whisper*]. Th' Protestan' Rector to see Mr Breydon. [*The half of her head disappears, but her voice is heard saying a little more loudly*] This way, sir; shure you know th' way well, anyhow.

*The door opening a little more, the* RECTOR *comes in. He is a handsome man of forty. His rather pale face wears a grave scholarly look, but there is kindness in his grey eyes, and humorous lines round his mouth, though these are almost hidden by a short, brown, pointed beard, here and there about to turn grey. His black clothes are covered by a warm black topcoat, the blackness brightened a little by a vivid green scarf he is wearing round his neck, the fringed ends falling over his shoulders. He carries a black, broad-brimmed, soft clerical hat and a walking-stick in his left hand. He hastens towards* AYAMONN, *smiling genially, hand outstretched in greeting.*

RECTOR. My dear Ayamonn. [*They shake hands.*]

AYAMONN [*indicating* SHEILA]. A friend of mine, sir – Sheila Moorneen. [*Moving a chair.*] Sit down, sir.

*The* RECTOR *bows to* SHEILA; *she returns it quietly, and the* RECTOR *sits down.*

RECTOR. I've hurried from home in a cab, Ayamonn, to see you before the night was spent. [*His face forming grave lines*] I've a message for you – and a warning.

*The door again is partly opened, and again the half head of* EEADA *appears, mid the murmurs outside, unheard the moment the door closes.*

EEADA. Two railwaymen to see you, Ayamonn; full house tonight you're havin', eh?

*The half head goes, the door opens wider, and the* TWO RAILWAYMEN *come into the room. They are dressed drably as the other men are, but their peaked railway uniform caps (which they keep on their heads) have vivid scarlet bands around them. Their faces, too, are like the others, and stonily stare in front of them. They stand stock still when they see the* RECTOR.

1ST RAILWAYMAN [*after a pause*]. 'Scuse us. Didn' know th' Protestan' Minister was here. We'll wait outside till he goes, Ayamonn.

AYAMONN. Th' Rector's a dear friend of mine, Bill; say what you want, without fear – he's a friend.

1ST RAILWAYMAN [*a little dubiously*]. Glad to hear it. You know th' sthrike starts tomorrow?

AYAMONN. I know it now.

2ND RAILWAYMAN. Wouldn' give's th' extra shillin'. Offered us thruppence instead – th' lowsers! [*Hastily – to* RECTOR] 'Scuse me, sir.

1ST RAILWAYMAN [*taking a document from his breast pocket*]. An' th' meetin's proclaimed.

RECTOR [*to* AYAMONN]. That's part of what I came to tell you.

1ST RAILWAYMAN [*handing document to* AYAMONN]. They handed that to our Committee this evening, a warrant of warning.

RECTOR [*earnestly – to* AYAMONN]. I was advised to warn you, Ayamonn, that the Authorities are prepared to use all the force they have to prevent the meeting.

AYAMONN. Who advised you, sir – th' Inspector?

RECTOR. My churchwarden, Ayamonn. Come, even he has good in him.

AYAMONN. I daresay he has, sir; I've no grudge against him.

RECTOR [*convinced*]. I know that, Ayamonn.

AYAMONN [*indicating document – to* 1ST RAILWAYMAN]. What are th' Committee going to do with this?

1ST RAILWAYMAN. What would you do with it, Ayamonn?

AYAMONN [*setting it alight at the fire and waiting till it falls to ashes*]. That!

2ND RAILWAYMAN [*gleefully*]. Exactly what we said you'd do!

SHEILA [*haughtily*]. It's not what any sensible body would think he'd do.

1ST RAILWAYMAN [*ignoring her*]. Further still, Ayamonn, me son, we want you to be one of the speakers on the platform at the meeting.

SHEILA [*bursting forward and confronting the* RAILWAYMEN]. He'll do nothing of the kind – hear me? Nothing of the kind. Cinder-tongued moaners, who's to make any bones about what you suffer, or how you die? Ayamonn's his reading and his painting to do, and his mother to mind, more than lipping your complaints in front of gun muzzles, ready to sing a short and sudden death-song!

1ST RAILWAYMAN [*a little awed*]. To see Ayamonn we came, an' not you, Miss.

2ND RAILWAYMAN [*roughly*]. Let th' man speak for himself.

AYAMONN [*catching* SHEILA's *arm and drawing her back*]. It's my answer they're seeking. [*To* RAILWAYMEN] Tell the Committee, Bill, I'll be there; and that they honour me when they set me in front of my brothers. The Minstrel Show must be forgotten.

SHEILA [*vehemently – to the* RECTOR]. You talk to him; you're his friend. You can influence him. Get him to stay away, man!

RECTOR. It's right for me to warn you, Ayamonn, and you, men, that the Authorities are determined to prevent the meeting; and that you run a grave risk in defying them.

2ND RAILWAYMAN [*growling*]. We'll chance it. We've barked long
enough, sir; it's time to bite a bit now.

SHEILA [*to* RECTOR]. Warning's no good; that's not enough – forbid
him to go. Show him God's against it!

RECTOR [*standing up*]. Who am I to say that God's against it? You are
too young by a thousand years to know the mind of God. If they be
his brothers, he does well among them.

SHEILA [*wildly*]. I'll get his mother to bar his way. She'll do more than
murmur grand excuses.

*She runs to the door of the other room, opens it, and goes in. After a few
moments, she comes out slowly, goes to the chair left idle by the* RECTOR, *sits
down on it, leans her arms on the table, and lets her head rest on them.*

AYAMONN. Well?

SHEILA [*brokenly*]. She's stretched out, worn and wan, fast asleep, and
I hadn't the heart to awaken here.

RECTOR [*holding out a hand to* AYAMONN]. Come to see me before you
go, Ayamonn. Be sure, wherever you may be, whatever you may
do, a blessing deep from my breast is all around you. Goodbye. [*To
the* RAILWAYMEN] Goodbye, my friends.

RAILWAYMEN. Goodbye, sir.

*The* RECTOR *glances at* SHEILA, *decides to say nothing, and goes towards
the door;* AYAMONN *opens it for him, and he goes out through the semicircle
of men and women, still softly singing before the statue of the Queen of
Eblana's poor.* SHEILA'S *quiet crying heard as a minor note through the
singing.*

Oh, Queen of Eblana's poor children,
Bear swiftly our woe away,
An' give us a chance to live lightly
An hour of our life's dark day!

CURTAIN

## ACT III

*A part of Dublin City flowering into a street and a bridge across the river
Liffey. The parapets are seen to the right and left so that the bridge fills most
of the scene before the onlooker. The distant end of the bridge leads to a
street flowing on to a point in the far distance; and to the right and left of this
street are tall gaunt houses, mottled with dubious activities, with crowds of
all sorts of men and women burrowing in them in a pathetic search for a
home. These houses stand along another street running parallel with the
river. In the distance, where the street, leading from the bridge, ends in a
point of space, to the right, soars the tapering silver spire of a church; and to
the left, Nelson's Pillar, a deep red, pierces the sky, with Nelson, a deep
black, on its top, looking over everything that goes on around him. A
gloomy grey sky is over all, so that the colours of the scene are made of the
dark houses, the brown parapets of the bridge, the grey sky, the silver spire,
the red pillar, and Nelson's black figure.*

*On one of the bridge parapets a number of the men seen in the previous
scenes are gathered together, their expressionless faces hidden by being bent
down towards their breasts. Some sit on the parapets, some lounge against
the gaunt houses at the corner of the street leading from the bridge, and, in
one corner, a man stands wearily against the parapet, head bent, an unlit
pipe dropping from his mouth, apparently forgotten. The sun shines on
pillar and church spire, but there is no sign of sun where these people are.*

*On the pavement, opposite to where the men sit, nearer to this end of the
bridge, sit* EEADA, DYMPNA, *and* FINNOOLA, *dressed so in black that they
appear to be enveloped in the blackness of a dark night. In front of* EEADA *is
a drab-coloured basket in which cakes and apples are spending an idle and
uneasy time.* DYMPNA *has a shallower basket holding decadent blossoms,
and a drooping bunch of violets hangs from a listless hand.*

EEADA [*drowsily*]. This spongy leaden sky's Dublin; those tomby
houses is Dublin too – Dublin's scurvy body; an' we're Dublin's
silver soul. [*She spits vigorously into the street.*] An' that's what Eeada
thinks of th' city's soul an' body!

DYMPNA. You're more than right, Eeada, but I wouldn't be too harsh.
[*Calling out in a sing-song way*] Violets, here, on'y tuppence a
bunch; tuppence a bunch, th' fresh violets!

EEADA [*calling out in a sing-song voice*]. Apples an' cakes, on'y tuppence
a head here for th' cakes; ripe apples a penny apiece!

DYMPNA. Th' sun is always at a distance, an' th' chill grey is always here.

FINNOOLA. Half-mournin' skies for ever over us, frownin' out any chance of merriment that came staggerin' to us for a little support.

EEADA. That's Dublin, Finnoola, an' th' sky over it. Sorrow's a slush under our feet, up to our ankles, an' th' deep drip of it constant overhead.

DYMPNA. A graveyard where th' dead are all above th' ground.

EEADA. Without a blessed blink of rest to give them hope. An' she cockin' herself up that she stands among other cities as a queen o' counsel, laden with knowledge, afire with th' song of great men, enough to overawe all livin' beyond th' salty sea, undher another sun be day, an' undher a different moon be night. [*They drowse, with heads bent lower.*]

1ST MAN [*leaning wearily against the parapet*]. Golden Gander'll do it, if I'm e'er a thrue prophet. [*Raising his voice a little*] He'll flash past th' winnin' post like an arra from th' bow, in the five hundhred guinea West's Awake Steeplechase* Championship.

2ND MAN [*drowsily contradicting*]. In me neck he will! He'd have a chance if it was a ramble. Copper Goose'll leave him standin', if I'm e'er a thrue prophet.

EEADA [*waking up slightly*]. Prophets? Do me ears deceive me, or am I afther hearin' somebody say prophets?

DYMPNA. You heard a murmur of it, Eeada, an' it's a bad word to hear, remindin' us of our low estate at th' present juncture. Th' prophets we once had are well hidden behind God be now, an' no wondher, for we put small pass on them, an' God in His generous anger's showin' us what it is to be saddled with Johnnies-come-marchin'-home, all song an' shirt an' no surety*

FINNOOLA [*shaking her head sadly*]. A gold-speckled candle, white as snow, was Dublin once; yellowish now, leanin' sideways, an' gatherin' down to a last shaky glimmer in th' wind o' life.

EEADA. Well, we've got Guinness's Brewery still, givin' us a needy glimpse of a betther life an hour or so on a Saturday night, though I hold me hand at praisin' th' puttin' of Brian Boru's golden harp on every black porther bottle, destined to give outsiders a false impression of our pride in th' tendher an' dauntless memories of th' past.

*The* RECTOR *and the* INSPECTOR* *appear at the farther end of the bridge,* *and come over it towards where the men and women are. The* RECTOR *is dressed in immaculate black, wears a glossy tall hat, and carries a walking-stick. He has shed his topcoat, but wears his green scarf round his neck. The* INSPECTOR *is clad in a blue uniform, slashed with silver epaulettes on the shoulders, and silver braid on collar and cuffs. He wears a big blue helmet, back and front peaks silver-bordered, and from a long silver spike on the top flows a graceful plume of crimson hair. On the front is a great silver crown throned on a circle of red velvet. A sword, in a silver scabbard, hangs by his side. He is wearing highly-polished top-boots. They both pause on the bridge, the* RECTOR *looking pensively down over the parapet at the flowing river.*

INSPECTOR. It was a great wedding, sir. A beautiful bride and an elegant bridegroom; a distinguished congregation, and the Primate in his fine sermon did justice to the grand occasion, sir. Fittingly ended, too, by the organ with 'The Voice that Breathed o'er Eden'.

RECTOR [*apparently not very interested*]. Oh yes, yes; quite.

INSPECTOR. Historic disthrict, this, round here: headquarters of a Volunteer Corp in Grattan's* time – not, of course, that I agree with Grattan. A great-great-grandfather of mine was one of the officers.

RECTOR. Oh yes; was he?

INSPECTOR. Yes. Strange uniform he wore: richly black, with sky-blue facings, a yellow breast-piece, ribbed with red braid, and, capping all, a huge silver helmet having a yellow plume soaring over it from the right-hand side.

RECTOR [*smiling*]. Your own's not too bad, Mr Churchwarden.

INSPECTOR. Smart; but a bit too sombre, I think, sir.

EEADA [*whining towards them*]. On'y a penny each, th' rosy apples, lovely for th' chiselurs* – Jasus! what am I sayin'? Lovely for th' little masters an' little misthresses, stately, in their chandeliered an' carpeted dwellin'-houses; or a cake – on'y tuppence a piece – daintily spiced, an' tastin' splendid.

DYMPNA [*whining towards them*]. Tuppence, here, th' bunch o' violets, fit for to go with th' white an' spotless cashmere gown of our radiant Lady o' Fair Dealin'.

EEADA [*deprecatingly*]. What are you sayin', woman? That's a Protestan' ministher, indeed, gentleman, Dympna!

DYMPNA. Me mind slipped for a poor minute; but it's pity he'll have on us, an' regulate our lives with what'll bring a sudden cup o' tea within fair reach of our hands.

EEADA. Apples, here, penny each, rosy apples, picked hardly an hour ago from a laden three; cakes tuppence on'y, baked over scented turf as th' dawn stepped over th' blue-gowned backs o' th' Dublin Mountains.

DYMPNA. Tuppence a bunch, th' violets, shy an' dhrunk with th' dew o' th' mornin'; fain to lie in the white bosom of a high-born lady, or fit into th' lapel of a genuine gentleman's Sunday courtin' coat.

*The* RECTOR *takes a few coins from his pocket and throws them to the women, who pick them up and sink into silence again.*

INSPECTOR. Swift,* too, must have walked about here with the thorny crown of madness pressing ever deeper into his brain.

RECTOR [*indicating the men and women*]. Who are these?

INSPECTOR [*indifferent*]. Those? Oh, flotsam and jetsam. A few of them dangerous at night, maybe; but harmless during the day.

RECTOR. I've read that tens of thousands of such as those followed Swift to the grave.

INSPECTOR. Indeed, sir? A queer man, the poor demented Dean; a right queer man.

*A sleepy lounger suddenly gives a cough, gives his throat a hawk, and sends a big spit on to one of the* INSPECTOR'*s polished boots then sinks back into sleep again.*

INSPECTOR [*springing back with an angry exclamation*]. What th' hell are you after doing, you rotten lizard! Looka what you've done, you mangy rat! [*He takes hold of the lounger and shakes him sharply.*]

2ND MAN [*sleepily resentful*]. Eh, there! Wha' th' hell?

INSPECTOR [*furiously*]. You spat on my boots, you tousled toad – my boots, boots, boots!

2ND MAN [*frightened and bewildered*]. Boots, sir? Is it me, sir? Not me sir. Musta been someone else, sir.

INSPECTOR [*shaking him furiously*]. You, you, you!

2ND MAN. Me, sir? Never spit in public in me life, sir. Makin' a mistake, sir. Musta been someone else.

RECTOR. Inspector Finglas! Remember you wear the King's uniform! Quiet, quiet, man!

INSPECTOR [*subsiding*]. Pardon me. I lost my temper, I'm more used to a blow from a stone than a dirty spit on my boot.

RECTOR [*shuddering a little*]. Let us go from here. Things here frighten me, for they seem to look with wonder on our ease and comfort.

INSPECTOR. Frighten you? Nonsense – and with me!

RECTOR. Things here are of a substance I dare not think about, much less see and handle. Here, I can hardly bear to look upon the same thing twice.

INSPECTOR. There you are, and as I've said so often, Breydon's but a neat slab of a similar slime.

RECTOR. You wrong yourself to say so: Ayamonn Breydon has within him the Kingdom of Heaven. [*He pauses.*] And so, indeed, may these sad things we turn away from. [*They pass out.*]

EEADA [*thinking of the coins given*]. Two tiny sixpences – fourpence a head. Oh, well, beggars can't be choosers. But isn't it a hard life to be grindin' our poor bums to powder, for ever squattin' on the heartless pavements of th' Dublin streets!

DYMPNA. Ah, what is it all to us but a deep-written testament o' gloom: grey sky over our heads, brown an' dusty streets undher our feet, with th' black an' bitther Liffey flowin' through it all.

EEADA [*mournfully*]. We've dhrifted down to where there's nothin'. Younger I was when every quiet-clad evenin' carried a jaunty jewel in her bosom. Tormented with joy I was then as to whether I'd parade th' thronged sthreets on th' arm of a 16th Lancer, his black-breasted crimson coat a sight to see, an' a black plume droopin' from his haughty helmet; or lay claim to a red-breasted Prince o' Wales's Own, th' red plume on his hat a flame over his head.

DYMPNA. It was a 15th King's Own Hussar for me, Eeada, with his rich blue coat an' its fairyland o' yellow braid, two yellow sthripes down his trousers, an' a red bag an' plume dancin' on his busby.

EEADA. Lancers for me, Dympna.

DYMPNA. Hussars for me, Eeada.

EEADA. An' what for you, Finnoola?

FINNOOLA. What would a girl, born in a wild Cork valley, among the mountains, brought up to sing the songs of her fathers, what would she choose but the patched coat, shaky shoes, an' white hungry face of th' Irish rebel? But their shabbiness was threaded with th' colours from the garments of Finn Mac Cool of th' golden hair, Goll Mac Morna of th' big blows, Caoilte of th' flyin' feet, an' Oscar of th' invincible spear.*

EEADA [*nudging* DYMPNA]. That was some time ago, if y'ask me.

*A cheer is heard in the distance, it has a defiant and confident sound, though its echo only reaches the bridge.*

DYMPNA [*drowsily but lifting her head a little to listen*]. Wha' was that? A cheer? [*Her head droops again*] I hate the sound o' cheerin'.

*A group of* WORKINGMEN *come in. They are excited, and they speak loudly to each other.*

1ST WORKMAN [*exultingly*]. The dockers are with us to a man; and the lorry-drivers, too. They'll all be at our meetin'!

2ND WORKMAN. With their bands an' banners.

3RD WORKMAN [*timidly*]. I wonder will they call the soldiers out?

1ST WORKMAN [*loud and defiant*]. Let them; we'll stand up to them!

3RD WORKMAN [*doubtfully*]. What? Stand up against infanthry an' the bang of their bullets?

2ND WORKMAN. Ay; or against horse, fut, an' artillery – what does it matter?

3RD WORKMAN. If the soldiers are out, the police'll get tougher, knowing the power that's behind them.

2ND WORKMAN. If they do aself, what does it mather?

3RD WORKMAN [*irritably – in a half-shout*]. Nothin' seems to mather with yous two!

*The echo of a rousing cheer is heard.*

1ST WORKMAN [*exultantly*]. Hear that! Ayamonn rousin' the disthrict west from where we're standin'!

*The echo of another cheer comes from beyond the bridge.*

2ND WORKMAN [*exultantly*]. Hear that! Mick rousin' them up in the streets around the upper bridge!

1ST WORKMAN. Come on, lads! We've work to do before the real meetin' begins! [*He goes out over the bridge.*]

2ND WORKMAN. Crooning a song of death to some, ourselves, we'll be, if they thry to stop us now.

*They hurry out.* BRENNAN, *playing his melodeon has come slowly over the bridge from the far side.*

BRENNAN [*giving himself confidence*]. Evenin', ladies an' gentlemen. Good thing to be alive when th' sun's kind. [*They take no heed of what he says. He begins to sing in a voice that was once a mellow baritone, but now is a little husky with age, now and again quavering a little on the higher notes in the song. Singing*]

> I stroll'd with a fine maid far out in th' counthry,
> Th' blossoms around us all cryin' for dew;
> On a violet-clad bench, sure, I sat down beside her,
> An' tuck'd up my sleeves for to tie up her shoe.
> An' what's that to anyone whether or no
> If I came to th' fore when she gave me th' cue?
> She clos'd her eyes tight as she murmur'd full low,
> Be good enough, dear, for to tie up my shoe.

EEADA [*with muttered indignation*]. Isn't that outrageous, now on a day like this, too, an' in a sober mood!

DYMPNA. In front o' decent women as well!

1ST MAN [*waking up suddenly*]. Disturbin' me dhreams of Golden Gandher gallopin' home to win in a canther!

BRENNAN [*singing*].

> Th' hawthorn shook all her perfume upon us,
> Red poppies saluted, wherever they grew,
> Th' joyous exertion that flaunted before me,
> When I tuck'd up my sleeves for to fasten her shoe.
> An' what's it to anyone, whether or no
> I learn'd in that moment far more than I knew,
> As she lifted her petticoat, shyly an' slow,
> An' I tuck' up my sleeves for to fasten her shoe?
>
> The heathery hills were all dancin' around us,
> False things in th' world turn'd out to be thrue,
> When she put her arms round me, an' kiss'd me
>     an' murmur'd,
> You've neatly an' tenderly tied up my shoe.
> An' what's that to anyone whether or no,
> I ventur'd quite gamely to see th' thing through,
> When she lifted her petticoat, silent an' slow,
> An' I tuck'd up my sleeves for to tie up her shoe?*

*Some pennies have been thrown from the windows of the houses.* BRENNAN *picks them up, and taking off a shabby, wide-brimmed hat, bestows a sweeping bow on the houses. During the singing of the last verse of the song,* AYAMONN *and* ROORY *have strolled in, and have listened to the old man singing while they leant against the balustrade of the bridge. The scene has grown darker as the old man is singing his song, for the sun is setting.*

2ND MAN [*waking up suddenly*]. Off with you, old man, thinkin' to turn our thoughts aside from th' way we are, an' th' worn-out hope in front of us.

1ST MAN [*waking up – wrathfully*]. Get to hell outa that, with your sootherin' songs o' gaudy idleness!

EEADA. Makin' his soul, at his age, he ought to be, instead o' chantin' ditties th' way you'd fear what would come upon you in th' darkness o' th' night, an' ne'er a sword be your side either.

3RD MAN. Away with you an' your heathen songs to parts renowned for ignorance an' shame!

FINNOOLA. Away to where light women are plenty, an' free to open purple purses to throw you glitterin' coins!

BRENNAN *slings his melodeon on to his back, puts his hat back on his head, and wends his way across the bridge.*

ROORY [*as he passes*]. Isn't it a wondher, now, you wouldn't sing an Irish song, free o' blemish, instead o' one thickly speckled with th' lure of foreign enthertainment?

BRENNAN *heeds him not, but crosses the bridge and goes out. The men and women begin to sink into drowsiness again.*

AYAMONN. Let him be, man; he sang a merry song well, and should have got a fairer greeting.

ROORY [*taking no notice of* AYAMONN'S *remark – to the men and women*]. Why didn't yous stop him before he began? 'Pearl of th' White Breasts' now, or 'Battle Song o' Munster'* that would pour into yous Conn's battle-fire* of th' hundhred fights. Watchman o' Tara he was, his arm reachin' over deep rivers an' high hills, to dhrag out a host o' sthrong enemies shiverin' in shelters. Leadher of Magh Femen's Host he was, Guardian of Moinmoy, an' Vetheran of our river Liffey, flowin' through a city whose dhrinkin' goblets once were made of gold, ere wise men carried it with frankincense an' myrrh to star-lit Bethlehem.

EEADA [*full of sleep – murmuring low*]. Away you, too, with your spangled memories of battle-mad warriors buried too keep for words to find them. Penny, here, each, th' ripe apples.

DYMPNA [*sleepily – in a low murmur*]. Away, an' leave us to saunter in sleep, an' crave out a crust in the grey kingdom of quietness. Tuppence a bunch the fresh violets.

FINNOOLA [*sleepily*]. Run away, son, to where bright eyes can see no fear, an' white hands, idle, are willin' to buckle a sword on a young man's thigh.

1ST MAN [*with a sleepy growl*]. Get to hell where gay life has room to move, an' hours to waste an' white praise is sung to coloured shadows. Time is precious here.

2ND AND 3RD MEN [*together – murmuringly*]. Time is precious here.

AYAMONN. Rouse yourselves; we hold a city in our hands!

EEADA [*in a very low, but bitter voice*]. It's a bitther city.

DYMPNA [*murmuring the same way*]. It's a black an' bitther city.

FINNOOLA [*speaking the same way*]. It's a bleak, black, an' bitther city.

1ST MAN. Like a batthered, tatthered whore, bullied by too long a life.

2ND MAN. An' her three gates* are castles of poverty, penance, an' pain.

AYAMONN. She's what our hands have made her. We pray too much and work too little. Meanness, spite, and common patterns are woven thick through all her glory; but her glory's there for open eyes to see.

EEADA [*bitterly – in a low voice*]. Take your fill of her glory, then; for it won't last long with your headin' against them who hold the kingdom an' who wield th' power.

DYMPNA [*reprovingly*]. He means well, Eeada, an' he knows things hid from us; an' we know his poor oul' mother's poor feet has worn out a pathway to most of our tumbling doorways, seekin' out ways o' comfort for us she sadly needs herself.

EEADA [*in a slightly livelier manner*]. Don't I know that well! A shabby sisther of ceaseless help she is, blind to herself for seein' so far into th' needs of others. May th' Lord be restless when He loses sight of her!

FINNOOLA. For all her tired look an' wrinkled face, a pure white candle she is, blessed this minute by St Colmkille of th' gentle manner, or be Aidan steeped in th' lore o' Heaven, or be Lausereen of th' silver voice an' snowy vestments – th' blue cloak o' Brigid* be a banner over her head for ever!

THE OTHER TWO WOMEN [*together*]. Amen.

ROORY [*impatiently*]. We waste our time here – come on!

AYAMONN. Be still, man; it was dark when th' spirit of God first moved on th' face of th' waters.

ROORY. There's nothin' movin' here but misery. Gun peal an' slogan cry are th' only things to startle them. We're useless here. I'm off, if you're not.

AYAMONN. Wait a moment, Roory. No one knows what a word may bring forth. Th' leaves an' blossoms have fallen, but th' three isn't dead.

ROORY [*hotly*]. An' d'ye think talkin' to these tatthered second-hand ghosts'll bring back Heaven's grace an' Heaven's beauty to Kathleen ni Houlihan?

AYAMONN. Roory, Roory, your Kathleen ni Houlihan has th' bent back of an oul' woman as well as th' walk of a queen.* We love th' ideal Kathleen ni Houlihan, not because she is false, but because she is beautiful; we hate th' real Kathleen ni Houlihan, not because she is true, but because she is ugly.

ROORY [*disgusted*]. Aw, for God's sake, man [*He hurries off angrily.*]

EEADA [*calling scornfully after him*]. God speed you, scut!

AYAMONN [*placing a hand softly on* EEADA's *head*]. Forget him, an' remember ourselves, and think of what we can do to pull down th' banner from dusty bygones, an' fix it up in th' needs an' desires of today.

*The scene has now become so dark that things are but dimly seen, save the silver spire and crimson pillar in the distance, and* AYAMONN's *head set in a streak of sunlight, looking like the severed head of Dunn-Bo speaking out of the darkness.* *

FINNOOLA. Songs of Osheen and Sword of Oscar* could do nothing to tire this city of its shame.

AYAMONN. Friend, we would that you should live a greater life; we will that all of us shall live a greater life. Our sthrike is yours. A step ahead for us today; another one for you tomorrow. We who have known, and know, the emptiness of life shall know its fullness. All men and women quick with life are fain to venture forward. [*To* EEADA] The apple grows for you to eat. [*To* DYMPNA] The violet

grows for you to wear. [*To* FINNOOLA] Young maiden, another world
is in your womb.

EEADA [*still a little gloomily*]. Th' soldiers will be chasin' us with gun-
fire; th' polis hoppin' batons off our heads; our sons an' husbands
hurried off to prison, to sigh away th' time in gloomier places than
those they live in now.

AYAMONN. Don't flinch in th' first flare of a fight. [*He looks away from
them and gazes meditatively down the river.*] Take heart of grace from
your city's hidden splendour. [*He points with an outstreached hand.*]
Oh, look! Look there! Th' sky has thrown a gleaming green mantle
over her bare shoulders, bordhered with crimson, an' with a hood
of gentle magenta over her handsome head – look!

*The scene has brightened, and bright and lovely colours are being brought to
them by the caress of the setting sun. The houses on the far side of the river
now bow to the visible world, decked in mauve and burnished bronze; and
the men that have been lounging against them now stand stalwart, looking
like fine bronze statues, slashed with scarlet.*

AYAMONN. Look! Th' vans an' lorries rattling down th' quays, turned
to bronze an' purple by th' sun, look like chariots forging forward to
th' battle-front.

EEADA, *rising into the light, now shows a fresh and virile face, and she is
garbed in a dark-green robe, with a silvery mantle over her shoulders.*

EEADA [*gazing intently before her*]. Shy an' lovely, as well as battle-
minded!

DYMPNA *rises now to look where* AYAMONN *is pointing. She is dressed like*
EEADA, *and her face is aglow. The men have slid from the parapets of the
bridge, turning, too, to look where* AYAMONN *is pointing. Their faces are
aglow, like the women's, and they look like bronze statues, slashed with a
vivid green.* FINNOOLA *rises, last, and stands a little behind the others, to
look at the city showing her melody of colours.* FINNOOLA *is dressed in a
skirt of a brighter green than the other two women, a white bodice slashed
with black, and a flowing silvery scarf is round her waist.*

FINNOOLA. She's glowin' like a song sung be Osheen himself, with th'
golden melody of his own harp helpin'!

1ST MAN [*puzzled*]. Something funny musta happened, for, 'clare to God, I never noticed her shinin' that way before.

2ND MAN. Looka the loungers opposite have changed to sturdy men of bronze, and th' houses themselves are gay in purple an' silver!

3RD MAN. Our tired heads have always haunted far too low a level.

AYAMONN. There's th' great dome o' th' Four Courts lookin' like a golden rose in a great bronze bowl! An' th' river flowin' below it, a purple flood, marbled with ripples o' scarlet; watch th' seagulls glidin' over it – like restless white pearls astir on a royal breast. Our city's in th' grip o' God!

1ST MAN [*emotionally*]. Oh, hell, it's grand!

EEADA. Blessed be our city for ever an' ever.

AYAMONN [*lifting his right hand high*]. Home of th' Ostmen, of th' Norman, an' th' Gael, we greet you! Greet you as you catch a passing hour of loveliness, an' hold it tightly to your panting breast! [*He sings*]

> Fair city, I tell thee our souls shall not slumber
> Within th' warm beds of ambition or gain;
> Our hands shall stretch out to th' fullness of labour,
> Till wondher an' beauty within thee shall reign.

THE REST [*singing together*].

> We vow to release thee from anger an' envy,
> To dhrive th' fierce wolf an' sly fox from thy gate,
> Till wise men an' matrons an' virgins shall murmur
> O city of splendour, right fair is thy fate!

AYAMONN [*singing*].

> Fair city, I tell thee that children's white laughter,
> An' all th' red joy of grave youth goin' gay,
> Shall make of thy streets a wild harp ever sounding,
> Touch'd by th' swift fingers of young ones at play!

THE REST [*singing*].

> We swear to release thee from hunger an' hardship,
> From things that are ugly an' common an' mean;
> Thy people together shall build a brave city,
> Th' fairest an' finest that ever was seen!*

FINNOOLA *has been swaying her body to the rhythm of the song, and now, just as the last part is ending she swings out on to the centre of the bridge in a dance. The tune, played on a flute by someone, somewhere, is that of a Gavotte, or an air of some dignified and joyous dance, and, for a while, it is played in fairly slow time. After some time it gets quicker, and* AYAMONN *dances out to meet her. They dance opposite each other, the people around clapping their hands to the tap of the dancers' feet. The two move around in this spontaneous dance, she in a golden pool of light, he in a violet-coloured shadow, now and again changing their movements so that she is in the violet-coloured shadow, and he in the golden pool.*

EEADA [*loudly*].The finest colours God has to give are all around us now.

FINNOOLA [*as she dances*]. The Sword of Light is shining!

1ST MAN [*exultantly*]. Sons an' daughters of princes are we all, an' one with th' race of Milesius!*

*The dance comes to an end with* AYAMONN *and* FINNOOLA *having their arms round each other.*

EEADA. Praise God for th' urge of jubilation in th' heart of th' young.

1ST MAN. An' for th' swiftness of leg an' foot in th' heart of a dance.

2ND MAN. An' for th' dhream that God's right hand still holds all things firmly.

*The scene darkens slightly.* AYAMONN *loosens his hold on* FINNOOLA *and raises his head to listen to something. In the distance can be heard the sound of many feet marching in unison.*

FINNOOLA [*a little anxiously*]. What is it you're listenin' to?

AYAMONN. I must go; goodbye, fair maid, goodbye.

FINNOOLA. Is it goin' to go you are, away from the fine things shinin' around us? Amn't I good enough for you?

AYAMONN [*earnestly*]. You're lovely stayin' still, an' brimmin' over with a wilder beauty when you're dancin'; but I must go. May you marry well, an' rear up children fair as Emer was, an' fine as Oscar's son; an' may they be young when Spanish ale foams high on every land, an' wine from th' royal Pope's a common dhrink!* Goodbye.

*He kisses her, and goes across the bridge, passing out of sight on the farther bank of the river. The figures left behind have shrunk a little; the colours have faded a good deal, and all look a little puzzled and bewildered. The loungers have fallen back to the walls of the houses, and, though they do not lie against them, they stand close to them, as if seeking their shelter. There is a fairly long pause before anyone speaks. They stand apart, as if shy of each other's company.*

EEADA [*murmuringly*]. Penny each, th' ripe apples. Who was it that spoke that time? Jasus! I musta been dhreamin'.

DYMPNA [*in a bewildered voice*]. So must I, th' way I thought I was lost in a storm of joy, an' many colours, with gay clothes adornin' me.

FINNOOLA [*puzzled and dreamy*]. Dhreamin' I musta been when I heard strange words in a city nearly smothered be stars, with God guidin' us along th' banks of a purple river, all of us clad in fresh garments, fit to make Osheen mad to sing a song of the revelry dancin' in an' out of God's own vision.

EEADA [*murmuringly, but a little peevishly*]. For God's sake give over dwellin' on oul' songs sung by Osheen, th' way you'd be kindlin' a fire o' glory round some poor bog-warbler chantin' hoarse ditties in a sheltered corner of a windy street. [*Very sleepily*] Th' dewy violets, here, on'y tuppence a bunch – Jasus, apples I mean!

*Now the tramp-tramp of marching men is heard more plainly.*

DYMPNA [*a little more awake*]. Tuppence each, the bunch of vio – What can that be, now?

1ST MAN [*gloomily, but with a note of defiance in his voice*]. Th' thramp of marchin' soldiers out to prevent our meetin' an' to stop our sthrike.

2ND MAN [*in a burst of resolution*]. We'll have both, in spite of them!

*The scene darkens deeply now. In the pause following the* 2ND MAN's *remark, nothing is heard but the sound of the tramping feet; then through this threatening sound comes the sound of voices singing quietly, voices that may be of those on and around the bridge, or of those singing some little distance away.*

VOICES [*singing quietly*].

> We swear to release thee from hunger and hardship,
> From things that are ugly and common and mean;
> Thy people together shall build a great city,
> The finest and fairest that ever was seen.

CURTAIN

## ACT IV

*Part of the grounds surrounding the Protestant church of St Burnupus. The
grounds aren't very beautiful, for they are in the midst of a poor and smoky
district; but they are trim, and, considering the surroundings, they make a
fair show. An iron railing running along the back is almost hidden by a
green and golden hedge, except where, towards the centre, a fairly wide
wooden gate gives admittance to the grounds. Beyond this gateway, on the
pathway outside, is a street lamp. Shrubs grow here and there, and in the
left corner, close to the hedge, are lilac and laburnum trees in bloom. To the
right is the porch of the church, and part of the south wall, holding a long,
rather narrow window, showing, in coloured glass, the figures of SS. Peter
and Paul. Some distance away from the porch is a rowan tree, also in
blossom, its white flowers contrasting richly with the gay yellow of the
laburnum and the royal purple of the lilac. The rest of the grounds are laid
out in grass, except for the path leading from the gateway to the entrance of
the church. It is a warm, sunny evening, the Vigil of Easter, and the*
RECTOR *is sitting on a deck-chair, before a table, on which are some books
and papers. He is evidently considering the services that are to be held in the
church on the following day.*

*The* RECTOR *is wearing a thick black cassock lined with red cloth, and at
the moment is humming a verse of a hymn softly to himself, as he marks
down notes on a slip of paper before him. A square black skull-cap covers
his head.*

RECTOR [*singing to himself, softly*].


> As Thou didst rise from Thy grim grave,
> So may we rise and stand to brave
> Th' power bestow'd on fool or knave;
> We beseech Thee!


*The* VERGER *comes out from the porch and walks towards the* RECTOR. *He
is bald as an egg, and his yellowish face is parched and woebegone-looking.
He is a man of sixty, and shows it. His ordinary clothes are covered with a
long black mantle of thin stuff, with a small cape-like addition or insertion
of crimson velvet on the shoulders.*

RECTOR [*noticing the* VERGER *beside him*]. Hymn 625: we must have that as our opening hymn, Samuel.

SAMUEL. It's got to go in, sir.

RECTOR. As you say – it's got to go in. Did you want to speak to me, Samuel?

SAMUEL. Excuse me, sir, for what I'm agoin' to say.

RECTOR [*encouragingly*]. Yes, yes, Samuel, go on.

SAMUEL [*mysteriously*]. Somethin's afther happenin', sir, that I don't like.

RECTOR [*turning a little in his chair*]. Oh! What's that, Sam?

SAMUEL. Mr Fosther was here this mornin' runnin' a hand through th' daffodils sent for Easther, an' found somethin' he didn't like.

RECTOR. Yes?

SAMUEL. It's not for me to remark on anything that manoeuvres out in front o' me, or to slip in a sly word on things done, said, or thought on, be th' pastors, masthers, or higher individuals of th' congregation; but, sometimes, sir, there comes a time when a true man should, must speak out.

RECTOR [*with a sigh*]. And the time has come to say something now – what is it, Sam?

SAMUEL [*in a part whisper*]. This mornin', sir, and th' dear spring sun shinin' through th' yellow robes of Pether an' th' purple robes o' Paul, an' me arrangin' th' books in th' pews, who comes stealin' in, but lo and behold you, Fosther an' Dowzard to have a squint round. Seen' they're Select Vesthrymen, I couldn't ask them why they were nosin' about in th' silence of th' church in an ordinary week-day mornin'.

RECTOR [*patiently*]. Yes, but a long time ago, you said something about daffodils.

SAMUEL. I'm comin' at a gallop to them, sir.

RECTOR. Good; well, let's hear about the daffodils.

SAMUEL. Aha, says I, when I seen th' two prowlers with their heads close together, whisperin', aha, says I, there's somethin' on th' carpet.

RECTOR. Is what you have to tell me something to do with Dowzard and Foster, or the daffodils?

SAMUEL. Wait till you hear; sometimes Fosther an' Dowzard'll be to th' fore, an' sometimes th' daffodils. What can these two oul' codgers be up to? says I, sidlin' up to where they were, hummin' a hymn.

RECTOR. Humming a hymn? I'm glad to hear it; for I'd be surprised to hear either of them humming a hymn.

SAMUEL. Me it was, sir, who was hummin' th' hymn; for in a church, I like me thoughts to go wth th' work I'm doin', if you know what I mean.

RECTOR [*impatiently*]. It'll be nightfall before you get to the daffodils, man.

SAMUEL. Wait till you hear, sir. There I was gettin' close to them be degrees, when, all of a sudden, didn't Fosther turn on me, shoutin' 'Are you goin' to be a party to th' plastherin' of Popish emblems over a Protestan' church?'

RECTOR. Popish emblems?

SAMUEL. Th' daffodils, sir.

RECTOR. The daffodils? But they simply signify the new life that Spring gives; and we connect them in a symbolic way, quite innocently, with our Blessed Lord's Rising. And a beautiful symbol they are: daffodils that come before the swallow dares, and take the winds of March with beauty.* Shakespeare, Sam.

SAMUEL [*lifting his eyes skywards and pointing upwards*]. Altogether too high up for poor me, sir. [*He bends down close to the* RECTOR's *ear.*] When he seen the cross o' daffodils made be Breydon, he near went daft. [*A pause, as if* SAMUEL *expected the* RECTOR *to speak, but he stays silent.*] God knows what'll be th' upshot if it's fixed to the Communion Table, sir. [*Another slight pause.*] Is it really to go there, sir? Wouldn't it look a little more innocent on th' pulpit, sir?

RECTOR [*in a final voice*]. I will place it myself in front of the Communion Table, and, if Mr Foster or Mr Dowzard ask anything more about it, say that it has been placed there by me. And, remember, when you say Mr Foster and Mr Dowzard, it's to be Mr Breydon too. [*He hands some leaflets to Samuel.*] Distribute these through the pews, Sam, please. The arranging of the flowers is finished, is it?

SAMUEL. Yessir; all but the cross.

RECTOR. I will see to that myself. Thanks, Sam.

SAMUEL *goes off into the church, and the* RECTOR, *leaning back in his chair with a book in his hand, chants softly.*

RECTOR [*chanting*].

> May wonders cease when we grow tame,
> Or worship greatness in a name;
> May love for man be all our fame,
> We beseech Thee!

*As he pauses to meditate for a moment,* MRS BREYDON *is seen coming along, outside the hedge. She enters by the gate, and comes over to the* RECTOR. SHEILA *has come with her, but lags a little behind when they enter the grounds. The* RECTOR *rises quickly from his chair to greet* MRS BREYDON.

RECTOR [*warmly*]. My dear Mrs Breydon! Hasn't it been a lovely day? The weather promises well for Easter.

MRS BREYDON. It would be good if other things promised as well as the weather, sir.

RECTOR. We must be patient, and more hopeful, my friend. From the clash of life new life is born.

MRS BREYDON. An' often new life dies in th' clash too. Ah, when he comes, sir, speak th' word that will keep my boy safe at home, or here.

RECTOR [*laying a gentle hand on her arm*]. I wish I could, dear friend; I wish I could.

MRS BREYDON. His mind, like his poor father's, hates what he sees as a sham; an' shams are powerful things, mustherin' at their broad backs guns that shoot, big jails that hide their foes, and high gallows to choke th' young cryin' out against them when th' stones are silent.

RECTOR. Let those safely sheltered under the lawn of the bishop, the miniver of the noble, the scarlet and ermine of the judge, say unto him, this thing you must not do; I won't, for sometimes out of the mouths of even babes and sucklings cometh wisdom*

SHEILA. If what's against him be so powerful, he is helpless; so let this power go on its way of darkened grandeur, and let Ayamonn sit safe by his own fireside.

*To the left, on the path outside the hedge, the* INSPECTOR, *in full uniform, appears, evidently coming to see the* RECTOR; *on the right followed by the men and women of the previous scenes, appears* AYAMONN. *He and the* INSPECTOR *meet at the gate. The* INSPECTOR *and he halt. The* INSPECTOR *indicates he will wait for* AYAMONN *to pass, and* AYAMONN *comes into the grounds towards the* RECTOR. *The* INSPECTOR *follows, but, in the grounds, stands a little apart, nearer the hedge. The men and women spread along the path outside, and stay still watching those in the grounds from over the hedge. They hold themselves erect, now; their faces are still pale, but are set with seams of resolution. Each is wearing in the bosom a golden-rayed sun.* BRENNAN *comes and, crossing the grass, sidles over to sit down on the step of the porch.*

RECTOR [*shaking* AYAMONN's *hand*]. Ah, I'm so glad you've come; I hope you'll stay.

AYAMONN [*hastily*]. I come but to go. You got the cross of daffodils?

RECTOR. Your mother brought it to us; it will hang in front of our church's greatest promise. Come and place it there with your own loyal hands, Ayamonn.

INSPECTOR. Loyal hands engaged in rough rending of the law and the rumpling-up of decency and order; and all for what? For what would but buy blacking for a pair of boots, or a sheet of glass to mend a broken window!

BRENNAN [*from his seat on the porch's step*]. He's right, Ayamonn, me son, he's right: money's the root of all evil.

AYAMONN [*to the* INSPECTOR]. A shilling's little to you, and less to many; to us it is our Shechinah,* showing us God's light is near; showing us the way in which our feet must go; a sun-ray on our face; the first step taken in the march of a thousand miles.

INSPECTOR [*threateningly*]. I register a lonely warning here that the people of power today will teach a lesson many will remember for ever; though some fools may not live long enough to learn it.

MRS BREYDON. Stay here, my son, where safety is a green tree with a kindly growth.

MEN AND WOMEN [*in chorus – above*]. He comes with us!

SHEILA. Stay here where time goes by in sandals soft, where days fall gently as petals from a flower, where dark hair, growing grey, is never noticed.

MEN AND WOMEN [*above*]. He comes with us!

AYAMONN [*turning towards them*]. I go with you!

INSPECTOR [*vehemently*]. Before you go to carry out all your heated mind is set to do, I warn you for the last time that today swift horses will be galloping, and swords will be out of their scabbards!

RECTOR [*reprovingly – to* INSPECTOR]. I hope you, at least, will find no reason to set your horses moving.

INSPECTOR [*stiffly*]. I'll do my duty, sir; and it would be a good thing if someone we all know did his in that state of life unto which it has pleased God to call him.

RECTOR [*losing his temper*]. Oh, damn it, man, when you repeat the Church's counsel, repeat it right! Not *unto which it has pleased God to call him*, but *unto which it shall please God to call him*.

INSPECTOR [*losing his temper too*]. Damn it, man, do you believe that what the fellow's doing now is the state of life unto which it has pleased God to call him?

RECTOR [*hotly*]. I have neither the authority nor the knowledge to deny it, though I have more of both than you, sir!

*The* INSPECTOR *is about to answer angrily, but* SHEILA *catches his arm.*

SHEILA. Oh, cancel from your mind the harder things you want to say, an' do your best to save us from another sorrow!

INSPECTOR [*shaking off* SHEILA's *hand roughly, and going to the gateway, where he turns to speak again*]. Remember, all! When swords are drawn and horses charge, the kindly Law, so fat with hesitation, swoons away, and sees not, hears not, cares not what may happen.

MRS BREYDON [*angrily – up to the* INSPECTOR]. Look at th' round world, man, an' all its wondhers, God made, flaming in it, an' what are you among them, standing here, or on a charging horse, but just a braided an' a tasselled dot!

*The* INSPECTOR *hurries off, to pause, and stands outside the hedge, to the right, the men and women shrinking back a little in awe to give him a passage.*

MRS BREYDON [*to* AYAMONN]. Go on your way, my son, an' win. We'll welcome another inch of the world's welfare.

RECTOR [*shaking his hand*]. Go, and may the Lord direct you! [*He smiles.*] The Inspector's bark is louder than his bite is deep.

AYAMONN. For the present – goodbye!

AYAMONN *hurries away through the gate, pausing, outside the hedge to the left, turning to give a last look at the* INSPECTOR.

INSPECTOR. Bear back, my boy, when you see the horsemen charging!

*He goes out by the right, and* AYAMONN *goes out left, followed by the men and the women. There is a slight pause.*

RECTOR [*briskly – to banish a gloomy feeling*]. Now, Mrs Breydon, you run along to the vestry, and make us a good cup of tea – I'm dying for one. [*To* SHEILA] You'll join us, Miss Moorneen, won't you?

SHEILA [*immediately anxious*]. Oh no, thanks. I . . . I shouldn't even be here. I'm a Catholic, you know.

RECTOR. I know, and I'd be the last to ask you to do anything you shouldn't; but rest assured there's no canonical law against taking tea made by a Protestant. Off you go, and help Mrs Breydon. I'll join you in a moment.

SHEILA *and* MRS BREYDON *go off by the south wall of the church.*

BRENNAN [*as the Rector is gathering his books and papers from the table*]. Hey, sir; hey there, sir! It won't shatther th' community at large this disturbance, will it, eh?

RECTOR. I hope not.

BRENNAN [*with a forced laugh*]. No, no, of course not. Bank of Ireland'll still stand, eh? Ay. Ravenous to break in, some of them are, eh? Ay, ay. Iron doors, iron doors are hard to open, eh?

RECTOR [*going off to get his tea*]. I suppose so.

BRENNAN. Ay, are they. He supposes so; only supposes – there's a responsible man for you!

*The* VERGER *comes into the porch and bends over* BRENNAN.

SAMUEL [*in a hoarse whisper*]. Come in an' have a decko* at our grand cross.

BRENNAN. Cross? What cross?

SAMUEL. One o' daffodils for Easther, to be put in front of th' Communion Table.

BRENNAN. Popery, be God!

*Booing is heard a little distance away, followed by the rattling fall of a shower of stones.*

BRENNAN. What's that; what's happenin'?

SAMUEL [*going to back, and looking down the street*]. A crowd flingin'
   stones; flingin' them at two men runnin' for their life.
BRENNAN [*nervously*]. Let's get into the church, quick. Throuble's
   beginnin' already.

*They both go into the church, and* SAMUEL *closes the door. A crowd can be
heard booing. Men and women, among them* EEADA, FINNOOLA, DYMPNA,
*the* RAILWAYMEN, *and the Lurchers\* who were on the bridge, pass across
outside the hedge. The leader carries a red flag, and all march with
determination. They are all singing the following song.*

LEADERS [*singing*].

> If we can't fire a gun, we can fire a hard stone,
> Till th' life of a scab shrivels into a moan;

CROWD [*chorusing*].

> Let it sink in what I say,
> Let me say it again –
> Though the Lord made an odd scab, sure,
>    He also made men!

LEADERS [*singing*].

> Th' one honour he'll get is a dusty black plume,
> On th' head of th' nag taking him to the tomb;

CROWD [*chorusing*].

> Let it sink in what I say,
> Let me say it again:
> Th' scab's curs'd be th' workers, book, candle an' bell!

*They cross over and disappear. After a pause,* DOWZARD *and* FOSTER *come
running in; they hurry through the gateway, and dash over to the church's
porch.*
   DOWZARD *is a big, beefy, red-faced man, rolls of flesh pouring out over
the collar of his coat. His head is massive and bald, with jet-black tufts
behind his ear, and a tiny fringe of it combed across high over his forehead.*

FOSTER *is small and scraggy, with aggression for ever lurking in his cranky face, ready to leap into full view at the slightest opportunity. His cheeks and lips are shaven, but spikes of yellowish whiskers point defiantly out from under his chin. His voice is squeaky and, when it is strengthened in anger, it rises into a thin piping scream. Both are dressed in the uniforms of railway foremen, blue cloth, with silver buttons, and silver braid on* DOWZARD'S *peaked hat and coat-sleeves, and gold braid on those of* FOSTER. *Both have their coats tightly buttoned up on them. They take off their peaked caps and wipe sweat from their foreheads.* DOWZARD *pushes the door.*

DOWZARD. We're safe here in th' grounds; Church grounds sacred. Unguarded, verminous villains – Papists, th' lot o' them!

FOSTER [*venomously*]. On'* one o' their leaders a Select Vestryman. On' thot domned Rector stondin' by him. Steeped in Popery: sign o' th' cross; turnin' eastward sayin' th' Creed; sung Communion – be Gud, it's a public scondal!

DOWZARD. Some o' them stones scorched me ear passin' by. We shouldn't have worn our uniforms. Gave us away. I knew we were in for it when they called us scabs.

FOSTER. Scobs themselves! Smoky, vonomous bastards! I tull you I'd wear me uniform in th' Vutican. [*He unbuttons his coat and shows that he is wearing a vivid orange sash, bordered with blue.*] Thor's me sash for all tae see. You should ha' stud* with me, mon; stud like th' heroes o' Dully's Brae!*

DOWZARD [*shouting and knocking at door*]. Ey, there, in there, come out, open th' blasted door an' help a half-dead man!

*The church door is opened, and the* RECTOR, *followed by the* VERGER *and* BRENNAN, *comes out into the grounds.*

RECTOR. What's wrong; what has happened?

DOWZARD. Th' Pope's bullies with hard stones have smitten us sore. Honest men, virtuous an' upright, loyal to th' law an' constitution, have this day been smitten sore with Popish stones – oh, me poor head!

FOSTER. St Bartholomew's Day's* dawnin' again, I'm tullin' yous, an' dismumbered Protestants'll lie on all th' sthreets!

RECTOR. You can't be badly hurt when you complain so grandly.

FOSTER. Stand up for th' ruffians be makin' luttle of our hurts, so do, ay, do. [*Noticing* BRENNAN *who has edged towards the gate and is about to go away.*] Eh, you, aren't you goin' to stay an' put tustimony to the fullness o' th' Protestan' feth?

BRENNAN [*with slight mockery*]. Ay, I would, an' welcome, if I hodn't to go, forbye, at this hour on uvery day, I mak' ut a rule tae be sturdy in th' readin' of a chapther o' God's word so's I won't hold on tae worldly things too strongly. [*He goes out.*]

FOSTER [*fiercely*]. A jully-fush Protestant! [*To the* RECTOR] Look see, I tull you th' fires o' Smithfield 'ull be blazin' round Protestant bodies again, an' coloured lights 'ull be shown in th' Vatican windows soon!

DOWZARD. An' we'll be th' first to go up in th' flames.

RECTOR [*laughing contemptuously*]. Nonsense, oh, nonsense.

FOSTER [*almost screaming*]. It's not nonsense, mon! Every sable-robed Jesuit's goin' about chucklin', his honds twitchin' to pounce out on men like me here, an' Eddie Dowzard there, tae manacle us, head, hond, and fut, for th' wheel, th' thumb-screw, an' th' rack, an' then finish us up at th' stake in a hoppy Romish auto-dey-fey!* The Loyola boyos are out to fight another buttle with th' men o' King Bully!

RECTOR [*amused*]. Well, let the Loyola boyos and King Bully fight it out between them. I'm too busy to join either side. Goodbye.

FOSTER [*catching his arm as he is going – viciously*]. You're no' goin' tae be lut slide off like thot, now, with your guilty conscience, mon. There's things to be done, and things tae be ondone in yon church, there; ay, ay.

RECTOR [*quietly*]. Indeed?

FOSTER [*angrily – to Dowzard*]. Uh, speak a word, mon, on' don't leave ut all tae me.

DOWZARD. First, sir, we want you to get rid o' Breydon from the Vesthry an' from th' church.

RECTOR. Oh, indeed?

FOSTER [*almost screaming*]. It's no' oh, indeed; answer th' question – plain yes or no!

RECTOR [*coldly*]. Gentlemen, Mr Breydon stays in the Vestry till the parishioners elect someone else; as for the church, God has seen fit to make him a member of Christ, and it is not for me, or even for you, gentlemen, to say that God did wrong.

DOWZARD [*sneeringly*]. An' when did that wondherful thing hoppen?

RECTOR. At his baptism, as you yourself should know.

FOSTER [*with an agonised squeal*]. Popery, Popery, nothin' but Popery! Th' whole place's infusted with it!

*The* VERGER *appears at the porch door with the cross of daffodils in his hand. It has a Celtic shape, the shafts made of the flowers, and the circle of vivid green moss. The* VERGER *shows it to* DOWZARD, *behind the* RECTOR's *back, and* DOWZARD *sidling over, takes it from him, the* VERGER *returning into the church again.*

RECTOR. And now be good enough, Mr Foster, to let my arm go.

*In the distance, a bugle-call sounding the charge is heard.* FOSTER *lets go of the* RECTOR's *arm; and they all listen*

FOSTER [*gleefully*]. Aha, there's the bugle soundin' th' charge, an' soon the King's horses an' th' King's men'll be poundin' th' riothers undher their feet! Law an ordher in th' State an' law an' ordher in th' Church we must have. An' we're fightin' here as they're fightin' there – for th' Crown an' ceevil an' releegious liberty!

*The sound of galloping horses is heard, followed by several volleys of rifle-fire. They all listen intently for a few moments.*

FOSTER [*gleefully*]. Hear that now? Your Breydon fullow'll soon be doshin' in here for th' church to hide him.
RECTOR. The cross of Christ be between him and all harm!
DOWZARD [*dancing out in front of the* RECTOR, *holding out the cross – with exultant glee*]. The cross – a Popish symbol! There y'urre, see? A Popish symbol flourished in th' faces o' Protestant people! [*With a yell*] Ichabod!*
FOSTER [*venomously*]. I'll no stick it, no; I'll no' stick it. Look-see, th' rage kindlin' godly Luther is kindlin' me! Here, go, gimme a holt of thot. [*He snatches the cross of flowers from* DOWZARD, *flings it on the ground, and dances on it.*] Th' Bible on' th' crown! The twa on' a half, th' orange on' blue; on' th' Dagon* of Popery undher our Protestant feet!
DOWZARD [*wildly*]. Th' dhrum, th' dhrum, th' Protestant dhrum!

*While* FOSTER *and* DOWZARD *have been dancing about and shouting their last few words, the men and women have run frightened along the path, behind the hedge. Those running from the right, turn, and run back to the left; those running from the left, turn, and run back to the left again, passing each other as they run. They suddenly see the men and women*

*running about behind the hedge, and at once plunge into the porch, almost*
*knocking the* RECTOR *down.*

FOSTER [*as they fly – to the* RECTOR]. Out uh th' way, mon, out uh th'
   way!

*After a pause* EEADA *comes running through the gate, into the garden, over*
*to the* RECTOR.

EEADA [*beseechingly*]. Oh sir, please let me into the church, till all th'
   sthrife is over – no place's safe with the soldiers firin' an' th' police
   runnin' mad in a flourish o' batons!
RECTOR [*reassuringly*]. Be calm, be quiet, they won't touch a woman.
   They remain men, however furious they may be for the moment.
EEADA. Arra, God help your innocence! You should ha' seen them
   sthrikin' at men, women, an' childher. An' me own friend,
   Dympna, in hospital gettin' her face laced with stitches, th' way
   you'd lace a shoe! An' all along of followin' that mad fool, Breydon!
RECTOR. Go in, then. [*To the* VERGER, *who has come to the entrance*] See
   her safe.

EEADA *and the* VERGER *go into the church.* FINNOOLA *comes slowly along*
*the path outside the hedge, holding on to the railings as she moves, step by*
*step. When she comes to the gateway, she sinks down on the ground and*
*turns a white and distorted face towards those in the grounds.*

FINNOOLA [*painfully*]. For th' love o' God, one of you tell me if th'
   Reverend something Clinton's here, or have I to crawl a long way
   further?
RECTOR [*hurrying over to her*]. He's here; I'm he, my good woman.
   What is it you want of me?
FINNOOLA. I've a message for you from Ayamonn Breydon.
RECTOR [*eagerly*]. Yes, yes; where is he?
FINNOOLA. He's gone.
RECTOR. Gone? Gone where?
FINNOOLA. Gone to God, I hope. [*A rather long pause.*]
RECTOR [*in a low voice*]. May he rest in peace! And the message?
FINNOOLA. Yes. He whispered it in me ear as his life fled through a
   bullet-hole in his chest – th' soldiers, th' soldiers. He said this day's
   but a day's work done, an' it'll be begun again tomorrow. You're to

keep an eye on th' oul' woman. He wants to lie in th' church tonight, sir. Me hip's hurt; th' fut* of a plungin' horse caught me, an' I flat on th' ground. He sent a quick an' long farewell to you. Oh, for Christ's sake get's a dhrink o' wather! [*The* VERGER *runs for a drink.*] We stood our groun' well, though. [*The* VERGER *comes back with the water, and she drinks.*] Now I can have a thrickle of rest at last. [*She stretches herself out on the ground.*]

RECTOR. Where did you leave him? Where is he lying now? [*She lies there, and makes no answer. He picks up the broken cross of flowers and is silent for a few moments. With head bent low – sorrowfully*] Oh, Ayamonn, Ayamonn, my dear, dear friend. Oh, Lord, open Thou mine eyes that I may see Thee, even as in a glass, darkly,* in all this michief and all this woe!

*The curtain comes down to indicate the passing of some hours. When it rises again, it is evening. The lamp over the porch door is lighted, and so is the church, the light shining through the yellow robe of St Peter and the purple robe of St Paul from the window in the church's wall. The church organ is playing, very softly, a dead march. The lamp on the path, outside the hedge, isn't yet lighted. The dark figures of men and women can be faintly seen lining themselves along the hedge.* MRS BREYDON *is standing in the grounds, near to the gateway.* FOSTER *and* DOWZARD *stand on the steps of the porch. A little in front, with his back turned towards them, stands the* RECTOR, *now with white surplice over his cassock, his stole around his neck, and the crimson-lined hood of a Doctor of Divinity on his shoulders.* SHEILA, *holding a bunch of crimson roses in her hand, stands under the rowan tree. Partly behind the tree, the* INSPECTOR *is standing alone. A* LAMPLIGHTER *comes along the path, carrying his pole with the little flower of light on the brass top. He lights the lamp on the path, then comes over to peer across the hedge.*

LAMPLIGHTER. What's up? What's on? What's happenin' here? What's they all doin' now?

1ST MAN. Bringin' th' body o' Breydon to th' church.

LAMPLIGHTER. Aw, is that it? Guessed somethin' was goin' on.

1ST MAN. He died for us.

LAMPLIGHTER. Looka that, now! An' they're all accouthered in their best to welcome him home, wha'? Aw, well, th' world's got to keep movin', so I must be off; so long! [*He goes.*]

DOWZARD [*speaking to the* RECTOR's *back*]. For th' last time, sir, I tell

you half of the Vestry's against him comin' here; they don't want
our church mixed up with this venomous disturbance.

RECTOR [*without moving, and keeping his eyes looking towards the
gateway*]. All things in life, the evil and the good, the orderly and
disorderly, are mixed with the life of the Church Militant here on
earth. We honour our brother, not for what may have been an error
in him, but for the truth for ever before his face. We dare not
grudge him God's forgiveness and rest eternal because he held no
banner above a man-made custom.

FOSTER [*savagely*]. Aw, look-see, I'm no' a mon to sut down on' listen
to a tumblin' blether o' words – wull ye, or wull ye not, give intil us?

*In the distance a bagpipe is heard playing 'Flowers of the Forest'.* MRS
BREYDON's *body stiffens, and* SHEILA's *head bends lower on her breast.*

RECTOR. It is a small thing that you weary me, but you weary my God
also. Stand aside, and go your way of smoky ignorance, leaving me
to welcome him whose turbulence has sunken into a deep sleep, and
who cometh now as the waters of Shiloah that go softly,* and sing
sadly of peace.

*As he is speaking, the lament ceases, and a moment after, a stretcher bier,
bearing the covered-up body of* AYAMONN, *appears at the gateway. It is
carried down towards the church, and the* RECTOR *goes to meet it.*

RECTOR [*intoning*]. Lord, Thou hast been our refuge from one
generation to another. For a thousand years in Thy sight are but as
yesterday.* [*He chants*]

> All our brother's mordant strife
> Fought for more abundant life;
> For this, and more – oh, hold him dear.
> Jesu, Son of Mary, hear!

> Gather to Thy loving breast
> Ev'ry laughing thoughtful jest,
> Gemm'd with many a thoughtful tear.
> Jesu, Son of Mary, hear!

When Charon* rows him nigh to shore,
To see a land ne'er seen before,
Him to rest eternal steer.
Jesu, Son of Mary, hear!

*The bier is carried into the church, and, as it passes,* SHEILA *lays the bunch of crimson roses on the body's breast.*

SHEILA. Ayamonn, Ayamonn, my own poor Ayamonn!

*The* RECTOR *precedes the bier, and* MRS BREYDON *walks beside it, into the church, the rest staying where they are. There is a slight pause.*

DOWZARD. We'd betther be goin'. Th' man's a malignant Romaniser. Keep your eye on th' rabble goin' out.

FOSTER [*contemptuously*]. There's little fight left in thom, th' now. I'll no' forgive thot Inspector fur refusin' to back our demond.

*They swagger out through the gateway and disappear along the path outside the hedge, as those who carried the bier come out of the church.*

2ND MAN. That's the last, th' very last of him – a core o' darkness stretched out in a dim church.

3RD MAN. It was a noble an' a mighty death.

INSPECTOR [*from where he is near the tree*]. It wasn't a very noble thing to die for a single shilling.

SHEILA. Maybe he saw the shilling in th' shape of a new world.

*The* 2ND *and* 3RD MEN *go out by the gateway and mingle with the rest gathered there. The* INSPECTOR *comes closer to* SHEILA.

INSPECTOR. Oughtn't you to go from this gloom, Sheila? Believe me, I did my best. I thought the charge would send them flying, but they wouldn't budge; wouldn't budge, till the soldiers fired, and he was hit. Believe me, I did my best. I tried to force my horse between them and him.

SHEILA [*calmly*]. I believe you, Inspector Finglas.

INSPECTOR [*gently catching her by the arm*]. Tom to you, dear. Come, Sheila, come, and let us put these things away from us as we saunter slowly home.

SHEILA [*with a quiver in her voice*]. Oh, not now; oh, not tonight! Go you own way, and let me go mine, alone tonight.

INSPECTOR [*taking her hand in his*]. Sheila, Sheila, be sparing in your thought for death, and let life smile before you. Be sparing in thought of death on one who spent his life too rashly and lost it all too soon. Ill-gotten wealth of life, ill-gone for ever!

SHEILA [*withdrawing her hand from his gently*]. Oh, Tom, I hope you're right; you are right, you must be right.

*They have walked to the gateway, and now stand there together, the men and women along the hedge eyeing them, though pretending to take no notice.*

INSPECTOR. You'll see it clearer, dear, when busy Time in space has set another scene of summer's glory, and new-born spring's loud voice of hope hushes to silence th' intolerant dead.

SHEILA [*musingly*]. He said that roses red were never meant for me; before I left him last, that's what he said. Dear loneliness tonight must help me think it out, for that's just what he said. [*Suddenly – with violence*] Oh, you dusky-minded killer of more worthy men! [*She runs violently away from him, and goes out, leaving him with the men and women, who stand idly by as if noticing nothing.*]

INSPECTOR [*after a pause*]. What are ye doing here? Get home! Home with you, you lean rats, to your holes and haunts! D'ye think th' like o' you alone are decked with th' dark honour of trouble? [*Men and women scatter, slowly and sullenly, till only* BRENNAN, *with his melodeon on his back, is left, leaning by the gate. To* BRENNAN] Heard what I said? Are you deaf, or what?

BRENNAN [*calmly*]. I'm a Protestant, an' a worshipper in this church.

INSPECTOR. One of the elect! So was Breydon. Well, keep clear of unruly crowds – men don't wait to ask the way you worship when they raise their arms to strike.

*He goes slowly away down the path. A few moments pass, then the* RECTOR *and* MRS BREYDON *come out of the church. He arranges a shawl round her shoulders.*

RECTOR. There; that's better! My wife insists you stay the night with us, so there's no getting out of it.

MRS BREYDON. She's kind. [*She pauses to look at the rowan tree.*]

There's th' three he loved, bare, or dhrenched with blossom. Like himself, for fine things grew thick in his nature: an' lather come the berries, th' red berries, like the blood that flowed today out of his white body. [*Suddenly – turning to face the church.*] Is it puttin' out th' lights he is?

RECTOR. Yes, before he goes home for the night.

MRS BREYDON. Isn't it a sad thing for him to be lyin' lonesome in th' cheerless darkness of th' livelong night!

RECTOR [*going to the porch and calling out*]. Sam, leave the lights on tonight. [*The church, which had dimmed, lights up again.*] He's not so lonesome as you think, dear friend, but alive and laughing in the midst of God's gay welcome. Come.

*They slowly go through the gate and pass out. The* VERGER *comes from the church and swings the outer door to, to lock up for the night.* BRENNAN *comes down into the grounds.*

SAMUEL [*grumbling*]. Light on all night – more of his Romanisin' manoeuvres.

BRENNAN. Eh, eh, there; houl' on a second!

SAMUEL. What th' hell do you want?

BRENNAN. Just to sing a little song he liked as a sign of respect an' affection; an' as a finisher-off to a last farewell.

SAMUEL [*locking the door*]. An what d'ye take me for? You an' your song an' your last farewell!

BRENNAN [*giving him a coin*]. For a bare few minutes, an' leave th' door open so's th' sound'll have a fair chance to go in to him. [*The* VERGER *opens the door.*] That's it. You're a kind man, really. [BRENNAN *stands facing into the porch, the* VERGER *leaning against the side of it.* BRENNAN *unslings his melodeon, plays a few preliminary notes on it, and then sings softly*]

> A sober black shawl hides her body entirely,
> Touch'd be th' sun an' th' salt spray of th' sea;
> But down in th' darkness a slim hand, so lovely,
> Carries a rich bunch of red roses for me!

[*The rest of the song is cut off by the ending of the play.*]

CURTAIN

## SONGS IN *RED ROSES FOR ME*

### RED ROSES FOR ME

A so-ber black shawl hides her bod-y en-ti--re-ly, Touch'd by th'
sun and th' salt spray of th' sea; But down in th' dark-ness a
slim hand, so love-ly, Car-ries a rich bunch of red ro-ses for me.—

### TH' BOULD FENIAN MEN

Our cour-age so ma-ny have thought to be age-in', Now
flames like a bril-liant new star in th' sky; An' Dan-ger is proud to be
call'd a new bro-ther, Since Freedom has buckled her sword on her thigh. Then
out to th' place where th' bat-tle is brav-est, Where th'
noblest an' meanest fight fierce in th' fray, Re-pub-lic-an ban-ners shall
mock at th' foe-men, An' Fen-ians shall turn a dark night in-to day!

### OH, QUEEN OF EBLANA'S POOR CHILDREN

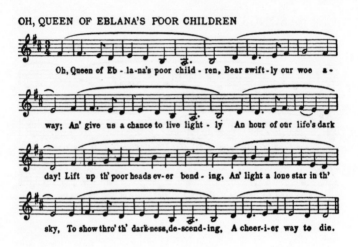

Oh, Queen of Eb - la-na's poor child - ren, Bear swift-ly our woe a-
way; An' give us a chance to live light - ly An hour of our life's dark
day! Lift up th' poor heads ev-er bend - ing, An' light a lone star in th'
sky, To show thro' th' dark-ness,de-scend-ing, A cheer-i-er way to die.

### I TUCK'D UP MY SLEEVES

I stroll'd with a fine maid far out in th' coun-try, Th'
blos-soms a - round us all cry - in' for dew;— On a
dai-sy deckt bench,sure,I sat down be-side her, An' tuck'd up my sleeves for to
tie up her shoe. An' what's that to a - ny one wheth-er or no, If I
came to th' fore when she gave me th' cue? She clos'd her eyes tight as she
mur-mured full low, Be good e-nough,dear,for to tie up my shoe.

**FAIR CITY**

Fair ci - ty, I tell thee our souls shall not slum-ber With- in th' warm beds of am - bi - tion or gain; Our hands shall stretch out to th' full-ness of la-bour, Till won-dher an' beau-ty with - in thee shall reign!

**WE BESEECH THEE**

As Thou didst rise from Thy— grim grave, So may we rise to stand and brave Th' pow'r be - stow'd on fool — or knave.— We be - seech Thee!

**THE SCAB**

If we can't fire a gun, we can fire a hard stone, Till th' life of th' scab shriv-els in-to a moan. Let it sink in what I say, Let me say it a - gain— Tho' th' Lord God made an odd scab He al - so made men!

**BROTHERS**

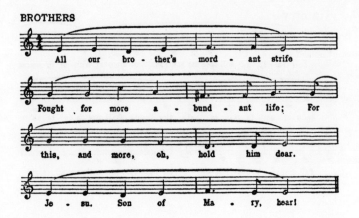

All our bro - ther's mord - ant strife

Fought for more a - bund - ant life; For

this, and more, oh, hold him dear.

Je - su. Son of Ma - ry, hear!

# Cock-a-Doodle Dandy

*To James Stephens\**
*the jesting poet with a*
*radiant star in's coxcomb*

335

## CHARACTERS

THE COCK

MICHAEL MARTHRAUN, a small farmer, now the owner of a lucrative bog

SAILOR MAHAN, once a sailor, now the owner of a fleet of lorries carrying turf from bog to town

LORNA, second young wife of Marthraun

LORELEEN, Marthraun's daughter by his first young wife

MARION, helper in Lorna's house

SHANAAR, a 'very wise old crawthumper', really a dangerous old cod

1ST ROUGH FELLOW ⎫
2ND ROUGH FELLOW ⎭ peasants working on the bog

FATHER DOMINEER, the parish priest of Nyadnanave

THE SERGEANT, of the Civic Guard

JACK, Mahan's foreman lorry driver

JULIA, Lorna's sister, a paralytic on a visit to Lourdes

HER FATHER

ONE-EYED LARRY, a peasant lad and potential sacristan

A MAYOR

A MACE-BEARER

THE MESSENGER, in love with Marion

THE BELLMAN, a kind of town crier

A PORTER, of a general store in the near-by town

## PLACE AND TIME

*Scene I* The front garden outside Michael Marthraun's house, in Nyadnanave.* Morning

*Scene II* The same. Midday

*Scene III* The same. Dusk

## SCENE I

*Part of the garden outside the house of Michael Marthraun. It is rough and uncared-for, with tough grass everywhere, sprinkled with buttercups and daisies. It is surrounded by a stone wall, three to four feet high, which is pierced by a wooden gate to the right of any visitor entering the garden. To the left, a little way from the gate, a clump of sunflowers, in full bloom, stand stiff and stately, their blossoms big as shields, the petals raying out widely and sharply, like rays from an angry sun. Glancing farther to the left, a visitor would see the gable-end of the house, with a porch jutting from it, and a window above the porch. The porch is supported by twisted pillars of wood, looking like snakes, which are connected with lattice-work shaped like noughts and crosses. These are painted a dazzling white. The framework of the window above is a little on the skew, and the sashwork holding the glass is twisted into irregular lines. A little way from the porch, towards the wall, is a dignified-looking bronze urn holding a stand-offish, cynical-looking evergreen. Farther up, near the wall, the Irish Tricolour flutters from a flag-pole. The house itself is black in colour, the sash and frame of the window in it is a brilliant red.*

*It is a brilliantly fine day in summer, and as there is nothing in the garden to provide a shade, the place is a deep pool of heat, which, seemingly, has lasted for some time, for the grass has turned to a deep yellow hue, save where the house and porch throw a rich black shadow. Stretching away in the distance, beyond the wall, is a bog of a rich purple colour, dabbed here and there with black patches. The sky above it is a silvery grey, glittering like an oriental canopy.*

*Some little distance away, an accordion is heard playing a dance tune, and, a few moments after,* THE COCK *comes dancing in around the gable of the house, circles the dignified urn, and disappears round the farther end of the gable-end as the music ceases.*

*He is of a deep black plumage, fitted to his agile and slender body like a glove on a lady's hand; yellow feet and ankles, bright-green flaps like wings, and a stiff cloak falling like a tail behind him. A big crimson crest flowers over his head, and crimson flaps hang from his jaws. His face has the look of a cynical jester.*

MICHAEL MARTHRAUN, *followed by* SAILOR MAHAN, *comes into the garden by the porch. Each carries a kitchen chair, which they set down some way from the house.* MICHAEL *is a man who is well over sixty years of age, clean-shaven, lean, and grim-looking. His lips twitch nervously whenever he forgets to keep his mouth tightly closed. He is dressed in a blackish tweed suit, and his legs are encased in black leggings. A heavy gold chain stretches across his waistcoat, and he wears a wide-leafed collar, under which a prime black bow is tied.*

SAILOR MAHAN *is a little over fifty, stouter than his companion, and of a more serene countenance. He has a short, pointed beard, just beginning to show signs of greyness. His face is of a ruddier hue, and shows that the wind and the stress of many storms have made it rugged, but in no way unpleasant. There is, maybe, a touch of the sea-breeze in his way of talking and his way of walking. He is wearing light-grey flannel trousers, a double-breasted royal blue coat, and has a white scarf round his neck, over a light-blue shirt. They come to the two chairs, and stand there facing each other.*

MICHAEL. Come out here, come on out here, where a body can talk free. There's whispers an' whispers in that house, upsettin' a man's mind.

MAHAN [*puzzled*]. Whispers? What kinda whispers?

MICHAEL. Sthrange kinds; whispers good for neither soul nor body.

MAHAN. But there's no one in the house but your wife, Lorna, Marion the maid, and your own girl Loreleen*

MICHAEL. Ay, so you think; but I know different.

MAHAN [*breezily*]. Nonsense, Mick; you're haulin' on a rope that isn't there!

MICHAEL [*raising his voice*]. You don't live in th' house, do you? [*Mahan is silent.*] You don't live in th' house, do you?

MAHAN [*raising his voice too*]. I know I don't live in it, an' if it's like what you say, I don't want to live in it!

MICHAEL. Well, then, keep quiet when a man speaks of what he knows.

MAHAN. I know as much about a whisper as you do.

MICHAEL. You know about th' whispers of wind an' wave, harmless an' innocent things; but I'm talkin' about whispers ebbin' an' flowin' about th' house, with an edge of evil on them, since that painted one, that godless an' laughin' little bitch left London to come here for a long an' leering holiday.

MAHAN. Loreleen? Why, man, she's your own daughter by your first young wife!

MICHAEL. So it was said at th' time, an' so it's believed still; but I had me doubts then, and I've more doubts now. I dhread meetin' her, dhread it, dhread it. [*With a frightened laugh*] Michael Marthraun's daughter! [*Gripping* MAHAN's *arm*] Is she anyone's daughter, man?

MAHAN [*impatiently*]. She must be somebody's daughter, man!

MICHAEL [*impatiently*]. Why must she be, man? Remember what th' Missioner* said last night: Sthrange things are foisted by the powers of evil into th' life o' man. Since that one come back from England, where evil things abound, there's sinisther signs appearin' everywhere, evil evocations floatin' through every room.

MAHAN [*puzzled*]. What kinda evocation an' significality is there?

MICHAEL [*looking suspiciously at the porch, then at the window above it, and drawing Mahan farther away from the house*]. Looka, Sailor Mahan [*he speaks furtively*], there's always a stern commotion among th' holy objects of th' house, when that one, Loreleen, goes sailin' by; an invisible wind blows th' pictures out, an' turns their frenzied faces to th' wall; once I seen the statue of St. Crankarius* standin' on his head to circumvent th' lurin' quality of her presence; an' another time, I seen th' image of our own St. Pathrick* makin' a skelp at her with his crozier; fallin' flat on his face, stunned, when he missed!

MAHAN [*doubtful, but a little impressed*]. Good God, them's serious things, Michael Marthraun! [*A pause.*] Are you sure, now, Mick, you're not deludin' yourself?

MICHAEL. Have sense, man! An' me own wife, Lorna Marthraun, is mixin' herself with th' disordher, fondlin' herself with all sorts o' dismayin' decorations. Th' other day, I caught her gapin' into a lookin'-glass, an' when I looked meself, I seen gay-coloured horns branchin' from her head!

MAHAN. No! Oh, Mick, you're fancyin' things. Lorna's a fine, upstandin' woman, an' should be respected.

MICHAEL. Are you gone on her, too? I tell you, I seen the way th' eyes of young men stare at her face, an' follow th' movements of her lurin' legs – there's evil in that woman!

MAHAN. But there's nothin' evil in a pretty face, or in a pair of lurin' legs.

MICHAEL. Oh, man, your religion should tell you th' biggest fight th' holy saints ever had was with temptations from good-lookin' women.

MAHAN [*getting nervous, and eager to change the subject*]. Looka, let's sit down, an' thry to settle about what you're willin' to pay for th' cartage of th' turf.

MICHAEL [*ignoring* MAHAN's *attempt to change the tide of talk*]. Up there

in that room [*he points to the window above the porch*] she often
dances be herself, but dancin' in her mind with hefty lads, plum'd
with youth, an' spurred with looser thoughts of love. [*As he speaks,
the sounds of a gentle waltz are heard, played by harp, lute, or violin, or
by all three, the sounds coming, apparently, from the room whose
window is above the porch. Bitterly*] There, d'ye hear that, man!
Mockin' me. She'll hurt her soul, if she isn't careful.

MAHAN. She's young enough yet to nourish th' need o' dancin'. An'
anyway, why did you insist on marryin' her, an' she so young; an'
she so gay? She was all again' it herself.

MICHAEL. She consented to it, at last, didn't she?

MAHAN. Ay, when you, her father, an' th' priest had badgered th' girl's
mind into disordered attention over th' catch she was gettin'.

MICHAEL. Oh, well you know, Sailor Mahan, that she had her blue eye
on th' fat little farm undher me feet; th' taut roof over me head; an'
th' kind cushion I had in th' bank, against a hard day.

MAHAN. I seen you meself throtting afther her from starboard to port,
from poop to quarther-deck, hoistin' before her th' fancy of ribbon
an' lace, silver-buckled shoes, an' a silk dhress for Sunday.

MICHAEL. An' what had she but a patched petticoat, a worn look, an'
broken brogues to wear to Mass on Sundays? An' didn't I give her
oul' fella fifty solid pounds so that her ailin' sisther could thravel
to Lourdes* to get undher th' aegis of th' Blessed Virgin? An'
what did I get for them but a scraggy oul' bog of two hundhred
acres?

MAHAN. An' you're makin' a good thing out of it since turf came into
its own. It's made you a Councillor, a Justice of th' Peace, an' th'
fair-haired boy* of th' clergy.

MICHAEL. As you mentioned turf, we'd bedther settle this question of
you demandin', for carting it, an exthra amount I couldn't possibly
pay.

MAHAN [*stiffness coming into his voice*]. You'll have to, Michael
Marthraun, for it can't be done now for a cent less.

MICHAEL. We'll have a drink while we're discussin'. I have a bottle of
th' best, ten years maturin', inside. Sit down there till I get it. [*He
goes into the porch and, after a few moments, comes quickly out again,
his mouth twitching, his voice toned to fear and hate.*]. That one,
Loreleen's comin' down th' stairs, an' I don't want to come too near
her. We'll wait till she goes. Let's talk of our affairs, quietly, while
she passes by. Th' thing to do, as Shanaar would tell you, when you

hear a sound or see a shape of anything evil, is to take no notice of it.
[*Whispering impatiently*] Sit down, man!

MAHAN [*sitting down – dubiously*]. Are you sure, Mick, you have a
close-hauled comprehension of th' way you're thinkin'?

MICHAEL. Ay, am I sure; as sure as I am that a cock crows!

*A cock suddenly crows lustily as* LORELEEN *appears in the doorway of the
porch. She is a very attractive young woman with an air of her own. A
jaunty air it is, indicating that it is the sign of a handsome, gay, and
intelligent woman. She is dressed in a darkish green dress, with dark-red
flashes on bodice and side of skirt. A saucy hat of a brighter green than the
dress sports a scarlet ornament, its shape suggestive of a cock's crimson crest.
Her legs – very charming ones – are clad in brown silk stockings; brown that
flashes a golden sheen.*

MICHAEL, *who has sat down, jumps startled to his feet at the sudden
sound of the cock's crow and, stretching over the table, grips* MAHAN *by the
shoulder.*

MICHAEL. What's that, what's that?

MAHAN [*startled by* MICHAEL's *frightened movement*]. What's what,
man?

MICHAEL [*trying to recover himself*]. Nothin', I heard nothin'. What was
it you were sayin'? [*In a whisper*] Get goin' on th' turf, man.

MAHAN [*mystified, but doing his best*]. You'll have to grant th' two
shillin's additional on each load, Mick. I'd work me lorries at a loss
if I took less. [*Placing an affectionate hand on* MICHAEL's *shoulder*]
An' you know well, you're such an oul' an' valued friend, I'd do it
for affection's sake, if I only could.

MICHAEL [*forgetting about* LORELEEN]. Don't I know that well, Sailor
Mahan; an' I'd do th' same, an' more, be you; but if I surrendhered
two shillin's, I might as well give you th' bog as well. I have to live,
Sailor Mahan.

MAHAN. Damn it, man, haven't I to live too? How th' hell am I goin' to
give th' men a shillin' more without th' exthra two shillin's from
you? Pray to th' saints to let them fall like rain from heaven, eh?

MICHAEL [*putting his face closer to* MAHAN's, *hotly*]. Looka here, Sailor
Mahan, you're not goin' to magicfy me into th' dhream of believin'
you're not addin', every hurryin' week, a fine bundle o' notes to th'
jubilant store you've there already, forcin' overtime on th' poor
men o' th' bank, flickin' th' notes into imperial ordher.

MAHAN [*as fiercely – standing up to say it, his face close to the face of* MICHAEL]. An' you yourself, Michael Marthraun, aren't worn away with th' punishment of poverty! Puttin' on a poor mouth, an' if you set out to count graciously all you have in hidlins, you'd be workin' many a long, glad, day, without supper or sleep, be daylight an' candle-light, till your mind centhred on th' sum dominated be th' last note fluttherin' from your fingers!

LORELEEN [*who has strolled slowly over to the gate, listening to the talk the while, turning at the gate to watch as well as listen*]. Lay not up for yourselves treasures upon earth, where moth and rust doth corrupt, and where thieves break through and steal!*

MICHAEL [*in a frightened whisper*]. Don't turn your head; take no notice. Don't pretend to hear her lyin' hallucinations!

*A young, rough-looking fellow, well-set and strong, comes running along the pathway to the gate. He is wearing dark-brown corduroy trousers, belted at waist, grey shirt, and scarf of bright green, with yellow dots. He pushes* LORELEEN *aside.*

1ST ROUGH FELLOW [*pushing* LORELEEN *out of his way*]. Outa me way, woman! [*He sees how charming she is as he swings her aside.*] Be-God, but you're th' good-lookin' lass! What are you doin' in this hole?

LORELEEN. Seeking happiness, an' failing to find it.

1ST ROUGH FELLOW. It isn't here you should be, lost among th' rough stones, th' twisty grass, an' th' moody misery of th' brown bog; but it's lyin' laughin' you should be where th' palms are tall, an' wherever a foot is planted, a scarlet flower is crushed; where there's levity living its life, an' not loneliness dyin' as it is here.

LORELEEN [*dropping him a deep curtsy*]. Thank you, sir knight, for th' silken compliments to your handmaiden. [*She turns to go out, and the* ROUGH FELLOW *hurries in through the gate, down to the two men.*]

1ST ROUGH FELLOW [*going through the gate down to where the two men are, and turning to speak up to* LORELEEN, *still standing at the gate*]. If you wait till I'm done with these fellas [*he indicates* MICHAEL *and* MAHAN] I could go to th' bend o' th' road with you, for it's meself would surrendher a long spell of heaven's ease to go a long day's journey with a lass like you!

*Another* ROUGH FELLOW *hurries in along the pathway outside to the gate, pulling* LORELEEN *aside when he finds her in his way. He wears*

*light-brown corduroy trousers, check shirt, and has a scarf of light yellow,*
*with green stripes, round his neck.*

2ND ROUGH FELLOW [*pulling Loreleen out of his way*]. Eh, there, woman
– outa me way! [*He sees, as she swings around, how charming she is.*]
Arra, what winsome wind blew such a flower into this dread,
dhried-up desert? Deirdre come to life again,* not to sorrow, but to
dance! If Eve was as you are, no wondher Adam fell, for a lass like
you could shutther th' world away with a kiss! [*He goes through the*
*gate, and down to the other men, pausing to look up at* LORELEEN *again.*
*To Loreleen*]. Wait, lass, till I'm done with these fellas, an' I'll go
with you till youth's a shadow a long way left behind!

LORELEEN [*down to the* TWO ROUGH FELLOWS]. I'm not for you, friends,
for I'm not good for decent men. The two old cronies will tell you a
kiss from me must be taken undher a canopy of dangerous
darkness. [*She kisses a hand to them.*] Goodbye [*She goes out.*]

MICHAEL ⎱ [*together*]. ⎰ What d'ye th' two of yous want here?
MAHAN  ⎰            ⎱ Why aren't yous at work?

1ST ROUGH FELLOW [*laying a hand sternly on the shoulder of* MAHAN].
Looka, you; you give us th' exthra shillin', or we leave your lorries
standin', helpless an' naked on th' roads!

2ND ROUGH FELLOW [*laying a hand sternly on* MICHAEL's *shoulder*].
Looka, you; looka that! [*He throws a cheque contemptuously on to the*
*table.*] D'ye think a good week's wages is in a cheque for tuppence?

MICHAEL. You didn't work a week, because of th' rain, an' canteen
contribution an' insurance brought your wage for the week to
tuppence.

2ND ROUGH FELLOW. Tell me how I'm goin' to live a week on
tuppence?

1ST ROUGH FELLOW. Seein' th' both of them's Knights o' Columbanus,* they should be able to say.

MICHAEL. That's a social question to be solved by th' *Rerum*
*Novarum.**

2ND ROUGH FELLOW. Fifty years old; not worth much when it was
born, an' not worth a damn now. You give a guaranteed week, or th'
men come off your bog! [*He goes off towards the gate.*]

1ST ROUGH FELLOW [*going to the gate – to* MAHAN]. Take our demand
serious, or your lorries stand still on th' highways!

2ND ROUGH FELLOW [*impatiently*]. Looka, there she is! [*He points a*

*finger in front.*] Let's hurry, an' we'll ketch up on th' fine, fair lady.
[*They hurry along the path, but suddenly stop to stare ahead.*]

1ST ROUGH FELLOW [*with awe in his voice*]. What's happenin' to her? A
cloud closin' in on her, flashes like lightning whirlin' round her
head, an' her whole figure ripplin'!

2ND ROUGH FELLOW [*frightened*]. Jasus, she's changin' into th' look of a
fancy-bred fowl! It's turnin' to face us; it's openin' its bake as big as
a bayonet! [*The crow of a cock is heard in the distance.*]

1ST ROUGH FELLOW [*frightened*]. Here, man, th' other way for us! It's
an omen, a warnin', a reminder of what th' Missioner said last night
that young men should think of good-lookin' things in skirts only in
th' presence of, an' undher th' guidance of, old and pious people.
[*The two of them hurry away in the opposite direction.*]

MICHAEL [*to* MAHAN]. Did you hear that? I'm askin' you, Sailor
Mahan, did you hear what them two graspin' rascals said?

MAHAN. I heard, but I can see no significality in it, unless th' two of
them had dhrink taken.

MICHAEL [*warningly*]. Looka, Sailor Mahan, if you aren't careful, your
wilful disbelief in things'll lead you asthray! Loreleen isn't me
daughter; she isn't even a woman: she's either undher a spell, or
she's a possessed person.

MAHAN [*with contempt*]. Aw, for God's sake, Mick, have sense, an' get
that bottle o' whiskey out to put a spell on us.

MICHAEL [*almost shouting*]. Have you forgotten already th' case of th'
Widow Malone who could turn, twinklin', into a dog or a hare,
when she wanted to hide herself? An' how, one day, th' dogs
followed what they thought was a hare that made for th' widow's
cottage, an' dived through an open window, one o' th' dogs
snappin' a leg off before it could get through. An' when th' door was
burst open, there was th' oul' witch-widow screamin' on her oul'
bed, one leg gone, with blood spoutin' from th' stump, so that all th'
people heard her last screechin' as she went sliddherin' down to
hell!

MAHAN. I heard tell of it months after, when I come back from
Valparaiso.

MICHAEL. Well, if you heard of it, you know it must have happened.
An' here you are, thinkin' only of whisky, and showin' how ready
you are to ruin me be askin' more than I'm able to give. You, a good
Christian, a Knight of St Columbanus, a student in th' Circle
studyin' th' *Rerum Novarum*, you should show a sign of charity an'

justice, recognisin' th' needs of th' people rather than your own. [*Suddenly*] Here, I'll add thruppence, an' make th' offer ninepence. Hold out th' hand, an' clinch th' bargain.

MAHAN. I'll be scuppered* if I will! You'll not use me like th' oul' father of th' good woman within, who sold you th' bog when he thought it was derelict, though you're makin' thousands out of it now.

MICHAEL. You forget I gave th' oul' cod enough to bring his other daughter to Lourdes for a cure!

MAHAN. You know th' way th' men are actin' now – goin' slow, an' doin' two journeys where they used to do three.

MICHAEL. An' aren't my men threatenin' to come off th' bog altogether? It's this materialism's doin' it – edgin' into revolt against Christian conduct. If they'd only judge o' things in th' proper Christian way, as we do, there'd be no disputes. Now let's be good sons of Columbanus – you thinkin' of my difficulties, an' me thinkin' of yours.

MAHAN. Make your offer one an' sixpence, an' I'll hoist th' pennant of agreement?

MICHAEL. I couldn't. Looka, Sailor Mahan, it would ruin me.

MAHAN [*viciously*]. You'd rather throw th' money after a tall hat so that you could controvert yourself into a dapper disturbance th' time the president comes to view th' workin' of th' turf. Talk about Loreleen castin' a spell! Th' whole disthrict'll be paralysed in a spell when your top hat comes out to meet the president's top hat, th' two poor things tryin' to keep people from noticin' what's undher them! Two shillin's, now, or nothin'. [*He sits down in disgust.*]

*Behind the wall,* SHANAAR* *is seen coming along the road; he opens the gate, and comes slowly down to where the two men are. He is a very, very old man, wrinkled like a walnut, bent at the shoulders, with longish white hair, and a white beard – a bit dirty – reaching to his belly. He is dressed peasant-wise, thin, threadbare frieze coat, patched blackish corduroy trousers, thick boots, good and strong, a vivid blue muffler round his neck, and a sackcloth waistcoat, on which hangs a brass cross, suspended round his neck by twine. A round, wide-brimmed, black hat is on his head.*

SHANAAR [*lifting his hat as he comes in by the gate*]. God save all here! God save all that may be in th' house, barrin' th' cat an' th' dog!

MICHAEL [*with great respect*]. An' you, too, Shanaar, old, old man, full of wisdom an' th' knowledge of deeper things.

SHANAAR. Old is it? Ever so old, thousands of years, thousands of years if all were told.*

MICHAEL. Me an' Sailor Mahan here were talkin' some time ago, about th' sthrange dodges of unseen powers, an' of what the Missioner said about them last night, but th' easiness of his mind hasn't been hindhered.

SHANAAR [*bending lower, and shoving his bearded face between the two men*]. If it doesn't hindher th' easiness of his mind now, it will one day! Maybe this very day in this very place.

MICHAEL [*to* MAHAN]. What d'ye say to that, now?

MAHAN [*trying to be firm, but a little uneasy*]. Nothin', nothin'.

SHANAAR [*shoving his face closer to* MAHAN'*s*]. Ah, me friend, for years an' years I've thravelled over hollow lands an' hilly lands,* an' I know. Big powers of evil, with their little powers, an' them with their littler ones, an' them with their littlest ones, are everywhere. You might meet a bee that wasn't a bee; a bird that wasn't a bird; or a beautiful woman who wasn't a woman at all.

MICHAEL [*excitedly*]. I'm tellin' him that, I'm tellin' him that all along!

MAHAN [*a little doubtfully – to* SHANAAR]. An' how's a poor body to know them?

SHANAAR [*looking round cautiously, then speaking in a tense whisper*]. A sure sign, if only you can get an all-round glimpse of them. [*He looks round him again.*] Daemones posteriora non habent – they have no behinds!

MICHAEL [*frightened a lot*]. My God, what an awe-inspiring, expiring experience!

MAHAN [*frightened too, but trying to appear brave*]. That may be, but I wouldn't put innocent birds or bees in that category.

SHANAAR [*full of pitying scorn for ignorance*]. You wouldn't! Innocent birds! Listen all: There was a cuckoo once that led a holy brother to damnation. Th' cuckoo's call enticed th' brother to a silent glade where th' poor man saw a lovely woman, near naked, bathin' her legs in a pool, an' in an instant th' holy man was taken with desire. Lost! She told him he was handsome, but he must have money if he wanted to get her. Th' brother entered a noble's house, an' demanded a hundhred crowns for his convent; but the noble was a wise old bird, an' said he'd have to see the prior first. Thereupon, th' brother up with an axe, hidden undher his gown, an' cleft th' noble from skull to chin; robbed th' noble, dhressed himself in rare velvets, an' searched out all th' rosy rottenness of sin with th' damsel till th' money was gone. Then they caught him. Then they hanged him, an', mind you [*the three heads come closer together*], while this poor brother sobbed on the scaffold, everyone heard th' mocking laughter of a girl and th' calling of a cuckoo!

*As* SHANAAR *is speaking the three last things, the mocking laughter of a girl is heard, the call of a cuckoo, and a young man's sobbing, one after the other, at first, then they blend together for a few moments, and cease.* SHANAAR *stands as stiff as his bent back will allow, and the other two rise slowly from their chairs, stiff, too, and frightened.*

SHANAAR [*in a tense whisper*]. Say nothing; take no notice. Sit down. Thry to continue as if yous hadn't heard!
MAHAN [*after a pause*]. Ay, a cuckoo, maybe; but that's a foreign bird: no set harbour or home. No genuine decent Irish bird would do a thing like that on a man.
MICHAEL. Looka here, Sailor Mahan, when th' powers of evil get goin', I wouldn't put anything past an ordinary hen!
SHANAAR. An' you'd be right, Mr Marthraun, though, as a rule, hens is always undher th' eye an' comprehension of a Christian. Innocent-looking things are often th' most dangerous. Looka th' lad whose mother had set her heart on him bein' a priest, an' one day, at home, he suddenly saw a corncrake flyin' into a house be an open window. Climbin' in afther it, he spied a glittherin' brooch on a table, an' couldn't resist th' temptation o' thievin' it. That lad spent th' next ten years in a reformatory; his mother died of a broken heart, and his father took to dhrink.

*During the recital of* SHANAAR'*s story, the 'crek crek, crek crek' of a corncrake is heard.*

MICHAEL [*in a tense whisper – to* MAHAN]. D'ye hear that, Sailor Mahan?
SHANAAR [*warningly*]. Hush! Take no vocal notice. When yous hear anything or see anything suspicious, give it no notice, unless you know how to deal with it.
MICHAEL [*solemnly*]. A warnin' we'll remember. But supposin' a hen goes wrong, what are we to do?
SHANAAR [*thoughtfully*]. It isn't aysey to say, an' you have to go

cautious. The one thing to do, if yous have the knowledge, is to parley with th' hens in a Latin dissertation. If among th' fowl there's an illusion of a hen from Gehenna,* it won't endure th' Latin. She can't face th' Latin. Th' Latin downs her. She tangles herself in a helluva disordher. She busts asundher, an' disappears in a quick column of black an' blue smoke, a thrue ear ketchin' a screech of agony from its centre!

MICHAEL [*tremendously impressed*]. Looka that now. See what it is to know! [*A commotion is heard within the house: a loud cackling, mingled with a short, sharpened crow of a cock; the breaking of delf; the half-angry, half-frightened cries of women. A cup, followed by a saucer, flies out through the open window, over the porch, past the heads of the three men, who duck violently, and then crouch, amazed, and a little frightened.*] What th' hell's happenin' now?

MARION *rushes to the door of the porch, frightened and alarmed. She is a young girl of twenty or so, and very good-looking. Her skirts come just to her knees, for they are nice legs, and she likes to show them – and why shouldn't she? And when she does so, she can add the spice of a saucy look to her bright blue eyes. Instead of the usual maid's cap, she wears a scarf-bandeau round her head, ornamented with silver strips, joined in the centre above her forehead, with an enamelled stone, each strip extending along the bandeau as far as either ear. She wears a dark-green uniform, flashed with a brighter green on the sleeves and neck, and the buttons of the bodice are of the same colour. Her stockings and shoes are black. A small, neat, white apron, piped with green, protects her uniform.*

MARION [*excitedly – to the men*]. It's flyin' about th' house, an' behavin' outrageous! I guessed that that Loreleen's cluck, cluck, cluckin' would upset th' bird's respectable way of livin'!

MICHAEL [*frightened*]. What's wrong with you, girl; what's up?

MARION. Will one of yous come in, an' ketch* it, for God's sake, before it ruins th' house?

MAHAN [*shouting*]. Ketch what, ketch what, woman?

MARION. A wild goose! It's sent th' althar light flyin'; it's clawed the holy pictures; an' now it's peckin' at th' tall hat!

MICHAEL. A wild goose? Are you sure it was a wild one?

MARION [*in great distress*]. I dunno, I dunno – maybe it's a wild duck. It's some flyin' thing tearin' th' house asundher.

MICHAEL [*trembling – to* SHANAAR]. D'ye think it might be what you know?

SHANAAR [*his knees shaking a little*]. It might be, Mr Marthraun! it might be, God help us!

MAHAN [*nervous himself*]. Keep your heads, keep your heads! It's nothin'.

MICHAEL [*beside himself with anxiety and dread – shaking* MARION *roughly by the shoulders*]. Conthrol yourself, girl, an' speak sensibly. Is it a goose or a duck or a hen, or what is it?

MARION [*wildly*]. It's a goose – no, it's a hen, it must be a hen! We thried to dhrive it out with flyin' cups and flyin' saucers, but it didn't notice them. Oh, someone should go in, or it'll peck th' place to pieces!

SHANAAR [*prayerfully*]. So long as it's not transmuted, so long as it's not been transmuted!

MICHAEL [*shaking* MARION *again*]. Where's Lorna, where's Lorna?

MARION [*responding to the shaking listlessly*]. Last I seen of her, she was barricadin' herself undher th' banisters!

MICHAEL [*pleadingly – to* MAHAN]. You've been free with whales an' dolphins an' octopususas, Sailor Mahan – you run in, like a good man, an' enthrone yourself on top of th' thing!

MAHAN [*indignant*]. Is it me? I'm not goin' to squandher meself conthrollin' live land-fowl!

MICHAEL [*to* SHANAAR – *half-commandingly*]. In case it's what we're afraid of, you pop in, Shanaar, an' liquidate whatever it is with your Latin.

SHANAAR [*backing towards the wall*]. No good in th' house: it's effective only in th' open air.

MICHAEL [*in a fury – to* MARION – *pushing her violently towards the gate*]. You go, you gapin', frightened fool, an' bring Father Domineer quick!

*All this time, intermittent cackling has been heard, cackling with a note of satisfaction, or even victory in it, interspersed with the whirring sound of wings.*

*As* MARION *rushes out through the gate, she runs into the arms of the* MESSENGER, *who carries a telegram in his hand. He clasps* MARION *tight in his arms, and kisses her. He wears a silvery-grey coat, buttoned over his breast, and trousers. On the right side of the coat is a flash of a pair of*

*scarlet wings. A bright-green beret is set jauntily on his head and he is
wearing green-coloured sandals.*

MICHAEL *and* MAHAN *have moved farther from the house, and* SHANAAR
*has edged to the gateway, where he stares at the house, ready to run if
anything happens. His hands are piously folded in front of him, and his lips
move as if he prayed.*

MESSENGER [*to* MARION]. Ah, lovely one of grace an' gladness, whose
    kiss is like a honied flame, where are you rushin' to in such a hurry?
MICHAEL [*angrily – up to the* MESSENGER]. Let her go, you – she's
    runnin' for th' priest!
MESSENGER. Th' priest – why?

*The cackling breaks into intensity, the whirring of wings becomes louder,
and a plate flies out through the window, followed by a squeal from* LORNA.

MESSENGER [*astonished, but not startled*]. What's goin' on in th' house?
MICHAEL. There's a wild goose, or somethin', asthray in th' house, an'
    it's sent th' althar bowl flyin'!
MARION. An' it's peckin' th' holy pictures hangin' on th' walls.
MAHAN. Some think it's a wild duck.
SHANAAR. It may be a hen, only a hen.
MESSENGER [*releasing* MARION, *and handing the telegram to* MICHAEL].
    Here's a telegram for you. [MICHAEL *takes it mechanically, and stuffs
    it in a pocket.*] Is it losin' your senses yous are to be afraid of a hen?
    [*He goes towards the porch.*] I'll soon settle it!
SHANAAR [*who is now outside, behind the wall*]. If you value your mortal
    life, lad, don't go in, for th' hen in there isn't a hen at all!
MESSENGER. If th' hen, that isn't a hen, in there, isn't a hen, then it
    must be a cock. I'll settle it! [*He rushes into the house.*]
MICHAEL [*in agony*]. If it's a cock, we're done!
SHANAAR [*fervently*]. *Oh, rowelum randee, horrida aidus, sed spero spiro
    specialii spam!**

*The head of the* COCK, *with its huge, handsome crimson comb, is suddenly
thrust through the window above the porch, and lets out a violent and
triumphant crow.* SHANAAR *disappears behind the wall, and* MAHAN *and*
MICHAEL *fall flat in the garden, as if in a dead faint.*

MICHAEL [*as he is falling*]. Holy saints preserve us – it's th' Cock!

SHANAAR [*from behind the wall*]. Oh, dana eirebus, heniba et galli scatterum in multus parvum avic asthorum!

The COCK's *head is as suddenly withdrawn, and a louder commotion is heard to be going on in the house; the* MESSENGER *shouting, a woman's squeal. Then silence for a few moments as puffs of blue-black smoke jet out through the window. When the smoke has gone, the* MESSENGER *comes from the house into the garden. His cap is awry on his head, his face is a little flushed, and his mouth is smiling. He carries in his right hand what might have been a broomstick, but is now a silver staff, topped with rosette of green and red ribbons. He is followed out by the* COCK *whom he is leading by a green ribbon, the other end circling the* COCK's *neck. The* COCK *follows the* MESSENGER *meekly, stopping when he stops, and moving when the* MESSENGER *moves.*

SHANAAR [*peeping over the wall*]. Boys an' girls, take no notice of it, or you're done! Talk only of th' first thing entherin' your minds.

MESSENGER [*looking with astonishment at the two men sitting up now on the ground, as far as possible from the house, and moving away when the* COCK *comes nearer*]. What's th' matther with yous? Why are yous dodgin' about on your bums? Get up, get up, an' be sensible.

MICHAEL *and* MAHAN *scramble to their feet, hurry out through the gate, and stand, warily, beside* SHANAAR. LORNA's *head appears at the window above the porch, and it is at once evident that she is much younger than her husband, very good-looking still, but the bright and graceful contours of her face are somewhat troubled by a vague aspect of worry and inward timidity. Her face shows signs of excitement, and she speaks rather loudly down to the* MESSENGER.

LORNA [*to the* MESSENGER]. Robin Adair,* take that bird away at once. Hand him over to th' Civic Guard, or someone fit to take charge of him.

MESSENGER [*up to* LORNA]. Looka, lovely lady, there's no danger, an' there never was. He was lonely, an' was only goin' about in quest o' company. Instead of shyin' cups an' saucers at him, if only you'd given him your lily-white hand, he'd have led you through a wistful an' wondherful dance. But you frightened th' poor thing!

LORNA. Frightened him, is it? It was me was frightened when I seen him tossin' down delf, clawin' holy pictures, and peckin' to pieces

th' brand new tall hat that Mr Marthraun bought to wear, goin'
with the Mayor to greet His Brightness, th' President of Eire,
comin' to inaugerate th' new canteen for th' turf workers.

MICHAEL [*enraged*]. Is it me new hat he's desthroyed?

SHANAAR [*pulling* MICHAEL's *arm in warning*]. Damnit, man, take no
notice!

MICHAEL [*turning indignantly on* SHANAAR]. How'd you like your
sumptuous, silken hat to be mangled into a monstrosity!

SHANAAR [*with concentrated venom*]. Hush, man, hush!

MARION [*who has been looking at the* COCK *with admiration*]. Sure, he's
harmless when you know him.

MESSENGER [*stroking its back*]. 'Course he is! Just a gay bird, that's all.
A bit unruly at times, but conthrollable be th' right persons. [*To the*
COCK] Go on, comrade, lift up th' head an' clap th' wings, black
cock, an' crow!*

*The* COCK *lifts up his head, claps his wings, and lets out a mighty crow,
which is immediately followed by a rumbling roll of thunder.*

MICHAEL [*almost in a state of collapse*]. Aw, we're done for!

SHANAAR [*violently*]. No notice, no notice!

LORNA [*from the window*]. God bless us, what's that? [*Down to the*
MESSENGER] Robin, will you take that damned animal away, before
things happen that God won't know about!

MESSENGER [*reassuringly – up to* LORNA]. Lovely lady, you can let your
little hands lie with idle quietness in your lap, for there's no harm in
him beyond gaiety an' fine feelin'. [*To the* COCK] You know th'
goose-step done be the Irish Militia in th' city of Cork more'n a
hundhred years ago? Well, we'll go home doin' it, to show there's
nothing undher th' sun Ireland didn't know, before th' world
sensed it. Ready? One, two – quick march!

*The* MESSENGER *and the* COCK *march off doing the goose-step.* MARION
*follows them, imitating the step, as far as the end of the garden; then she
stands looking after them, waving them farewell.* MICHAEL *and* MAHAN
*come slowly and stealthily into the garden as the* COCK *goes out. They go to
the chairs, on which they sit, exhausted, wiping their foreheads with their
handkerchiefs.* SHANAAR *comes towards them more slowly, keeping an eye
in the direction taken by the* COCK *and the* MESSENGER. *When the place is
clear, he anchors himself behind the table.*

LORNA [*down to* MARION]. Marion, dear, come on in, an' help me to
straighten things up a little. [*She goes away from the window.*]

MARION [*going slowly towards the house, after having given a last farewell
– gleefully*]. Wasn't it a saucy bird! An' th' stately way he done th'
goose-step! [*She playfully shakes* MICHAEL'*s shoulder*] Did you see it,
sir? [MICHAEL *takes no notice.*] God forgive me, but it gave us all an
hilarious time – didn't it, sir?

MICHAEL [*coldly*]. Your misthress called you.

MARION. I heard her, sir. What a clatther it all made! An' yous all
quakin', an' even Sailor Mahan there, shakin' in his shoes, sure it
was somethin' sinisther!

MAHAN [*angrily*]. You go in to your misthress, girl!

MARION [*giggling*]. Th' bould sailor lad! An' he gettin' rocked in th'
cradle of th' deep! Me faltherin' tongue can't impart th' fun I felt at
seein' yous all thinkin' th' anchor was bein' weighed for th' next
world!

MICHAEL [*loudly*]. Go to your misthress when you're told.

MARION [*giggling more than ever*]. An' oul' dodderin' Shanaar, there,
concoctin' his Latin, an' puttin' th' wall between himself an' th'
blast! Well, while yous sit all alone there in th' gloamin', yous won't
be in heart for singin'. [*She chants*] 'Only to see his face again, only
to hear him crow!' [*She runs merrily in.*]

SHANAAR [*warily – in a warning whisper*]. Watch that one!

MICHAEL. Th' ignorant, mockin', saucy face of her afther us bein' in
danger of thransportation to where we couldn't know ourselves
with agony an' consternation!

SHANAAR [*fervently*]. Sweet airs of heaven be round us all! Watch that
one, Mr Marthraun. Women is more flexible towards th' ungodly
than us men, an' well th' old saints knew it. I'd recommend you to
compel her, for a start, to lift her bodice higher up, an' pull her skirt
lower down; for th' circumnambulatory nature of a woman's form
often has a detonatin' effect on a man's idle thoughts.

MICHAEL [*pensively*]. How thrue, how thrue that is!

SHANAAR. What we have to do now, is to keep thought from dwellin'
on th' things seen an' heard this day; for dwellin' on it may bring th'
evil back again. So don't let any thought of it, *ab initio extensio*,*
remain in your minds, though, as a precaution, when I'm passin' th'
barracks, I'll acquaint the Civic Guard. Now I must be off, for I've a
long way to thravel. [*He goes as far as the gate, and returns.*] Mr
Marthraun, don't forget to have th' room, where th' commotion

was manifested, *turbulenta concursio cockolorum*, purified an' surified be an understandin' clergyman. Goodbye. [*Again he goes as far as the gate, and returns.*] Be on your guard against any unfamiliar motion or peculiar conspicuosity or quasimodical addendum, perceivable in any familiar thing or creature common to your general recognisances. A cat barkin' at a dog, or a dog miaouin' be a fire would atthract your attention, give you a shock, but don't, for th' love of God, notice it! It's this scourge of materialism sweepin' th' world, that's incantatin' these evils to our senses and our doorsteps.

MAHAN [*pensively*]. That's th' way th' compass is pointin', Shanaar – everyone only thinkin', thinkin' of himself.

SHANAAR. An' women's wily exhilarations are abettin' it, so that a man's measure of virtue is now made with money, used to buy ornaments, bestowed on girls to give a gaudy outside to the ugliness of hell.

MICHAEL [*fervently*]. Oh, how thrue, how thrue that is!

SHANAAR. An' th' coruscatin' conduct in th' dance-halls is completin' th' ruin.

MAHAN [*solemnly*]. Wise words from a wiser man! Afther a night in one of them, there isn't an ounce of energy left in a worker!

SHANAAR [*whispering*]. A last warnin' – Don't forget that six thousand six hundhred an' sixty-six evil spirits can find ready lodgin's undher th' skin of a single man!

MICHAEL [*horrified*]. What an appallin' thought!

SHANAAR. So be on your guard. Well, goodbye.

MICHAEL [*offering him a note*]. Here's a pound to help you on your way.

SHANAAR [*setting the note aside*]. No, thanks. If I took it, I couldn't fuse th' inner with th' outher vision; I'd lose th' power of spiritual scansion. If you've a shillin' for a meal in th' town till I get to the counthry, where I'm always welcome, I'll take it, an' thank you. [MICHAEL *gives him a shilling.*] Thank you kindly. [*He goes out through the gate, and along the pathway outside. Just as he is about to disappear, he faces towards the two men, and stretches out a hand in a gesture of blessing. Fervently*] *Ab tormentum sed absolvo, non revolvo, cockalorum credulum hibernica!*

MICHAEL [*with emotion*]. You too, Shanaar, oul' son; you too! [SHANAAR *goes off.*]

MAHAN [*after a pause – viciously*]. That Latin-lustrous oul' cod* of a prayer-blower is a positive danger goin' about th' counthry!

MICHAEL [*startled and offended*]. Eh? I wouldn't go callin' him a cod, Sailor Mahan. A little asthray in a way, now an' again, but no cod. You should be th' last to call th' man a cod, for if it wasn't for his holy Latin aspirations, you mightn't be here now.

MAHAN [*with exasperation*]. Aw, th' oul' fool, pipin' a gale into every breeze that blows! I don't believe there was ever anything engenderogically evil in that cock as a cock, or denounceable either! Lardin' a man's mind with his killakee Latin! An' looka th' way he slights th' women. I seen him lookin' at Lorna an' Marion as if they'd horns on their heads!

MICHAEL [*doubtfully*]. Maybe he's too down on th' women, though you have to allow women is temptin'.

MAHAN. They wouldn't tempt man if they didn't damn well know he wanted to be tempted!

MICHAEL. Yes, yes; but we must suffer th' temptation accordin' to the cognisances of th' canon law. But let's have a dhrink, for I'm near dead with th' drouth, an' we can sensify our discussion about th' increased price you're demandin' for carryin' th' turf; though, honest to God, Sailor Mahan, I can't add a ha'penny more to what I'm givin'.

MAHAN. A dhrink would be welcome, an' we can talk over th' matter, though, honest to God, Michael Marthraun, blast th' penny less I'll take than what I'm askin'.

MICHAEL [*going to the porch, and shouting into the house*]. Marion, bring th' bottle of ten years' maturin', an' two glasses! [*He returns.*] It's th' principle I'm thinkin' of.

MAHAN. That's what's throublin' me, too. [*Marion comes in with the bottle of whiskey and the two glasses. She places them on the table, getting between the two men to do so. Reading the label*] Flanagan's First! *Nyav na Nyale* – th' heaven of th' clouds! An' brought be a lass who's a Flanagan's first too!

MARION [*in jovial mood*]. G'long with you – you an' your blarney!*

MICHAEL [*enthusiastically*]. Had you lived long ago, Emer would have been jealous of you!* [*He playfully pinches her bottom.*]

MARION [*squealing*]. Ouch! [*She breaks away, and makes for the porch.*] A pair o' naughty men! [*She goes into the house.*]

MICHAEL [*calling after her*]. I forgot th' soda, Marion; bring th' siphon, lass.

MAHAN [*complacently*]. I could hold that one in me arms for a long time, Mick.

MICHAEL. Th' man would want to be dead who couldn't.

MAHAN [*enthusiastically*]. I'd welcome her, even if I seen her through th' vision of oul' Shanaar – with horns growin' out of her head!

*MARION returns with the siphon which she places on the table. The two men, looking in front of them, have silly, sly grins on their faces.*

*The ornament, which* MARION *wears round her head, has separated into two parts, each of which has risen over her head, forming two branching horns, apparently sprouting from her forehead. The two men, shyly gazing in front, or at the table, do not see the change.* MARION'*s face has changed too, and now seems to wear a mocking, cynical look, fitting the aspect of her face to the horns.*

MARION [*joking*]. Two wild men – it's afraid I am to come near yous.

MICHAEL *puts his right arm round her waist, and* MAHAN *his left one.*

MAHAN [*slyly*]. What about a kiss on your rosy mouth, darlin', to give a honied tang to th' whisky?

MICHAEL. An' one for me, too?

MARION [*with pretended demureness*]. A thrue gentleman'll rise up an' never expect a thrue lady to bend down for a kiss. [*With vigour*] Up an' take it, before yous grow cold!

*They rise from their chairs, foolish grins on their faces, settle themselves for a kiss, and then perceive the change that has taken place. They flop back on to the chairs, fright and dismay sweeping over their faces.*

MAHAN AND MICHAEL [*together*]. Good God!

*They slump in the chairs, overcome, their hands folded in front of their chests, palm to palm, as if in prayer.* MARION *looks at them in some astonishment.*

MARION. What ails yous? Was th' excitement too much for yous, or what?

MICHAEL [*plaintively*]. Saints in heaven help us now!

MARION. What's come over yous? Th' way yous slumped so sudden down, you'd think I'd horns on me, or somethin'!

MICHAEL [*hoarsely*]. G'way, g'way! Shanaar, Shanaar, where are you now!

MARION [*going over to* MAHAN, *and putting an arm round his neck*]. What about you, gay one?

MAHAN [*gurgling with fright*]. You're sthranglin' me! G'way, g'way, girl!

MARION. Looka, a kiss would do yous good. Yous think too much of th' world!

MAHAN [*chokingly*]. St Christopher, mainstay of mariners, be with me now!

LORNA *thrusts her head out from the window over the porch.*

LORNA [*down to* MARION]. Let them two oul' life-frighteners fend for themselves, an' come in. From th' back window, I can see th' crowd gathered to give Julia a send-off to Lourdes, so come in to tidy if you want to join them with me.

MARION [*half to herself – as she runs into the house*]. God forgive me – I near forgot! Here we are followin' laughter, instead of seekin' succour from prayer! [*She runs in, and* LORNA *takes her head back into the room again.*]

MICHAEL [*frightened and very angry*]. Now, maybe, you'll quit your jeerin' at oul' Shanaar! Now, maybe, you'll let your mind concentrate on higher things! Now, maybe, you won't be runnin' loose afther girls!

MAHAN [*indignantly*]. Damnit, man, you were as eager for a cuddle as I was!

MICHAEL [*lifting his eyes skywards*]. Oh, d'ye hear that! I was only toleratin' your queer declivity, like a fool. An' afther all th' warnin's given be wise oul' Shanaar! Looka, Sailor Mahan, you'll have to be more on your guard!

MAHAN [*trying to defend himself*]. How could any man suspect such a thing? We'll have to think this thing out.

MICHAEL [*with exasperation*]. Think it out! Oh, man, Sailor Mahan, have you nothin' more sensible to say than that we'll have to think it out?

MAHAN. Let's have a dhrink, for God's sake, to steady us down!

MICHAEL [*hurriedly putting bottle and glasses under the table*]. What're you thinkin' of, Sailor Mahan? We can't dispense ourselves

through a scene of jollification an' poor Julia passin' on her way to
Lourdes!

*Along the path, on a stretcher, carried by the* TWO ROUGH FELLOWS, *comes*
JULIA, *followed by* HER FATHER. *The stretcher is borne to the gate, and
there laid down, so that the head of it is flush with the gateposts, and the rest
of it within the garden. The framework of the gate makes a frame for* JULIA,
*who is half sitting up, her head supported by a high pillow. Her face is a sad
yellowish mask, pierced by wide eyes, surrounded by dark circles.* HER
FATHER *is a sturdy fellow of fifty, a scraggly greyish beard struggling from
his chin. He is roughly dressed as a poorer peasant might be, and his clothes
are patched in places. He wears a brown muffler, and a faded black trilby
hat is on his head. All the time, he looks straight in front with a passive and
stony stare.*

*Before the stretcher walks the* MAYOR, *rather stout, clean-shaven,
wearing a red robe over rough clothing; he has a very wide three-cornered
hat, laced with gold, on his head. Behind him walks the* MACE-BEARER, *a
big silver and black mace on his shoulder. He is tall, and wears a bright
blue robe, trimmed with silver, on his head is a huge cocked hat, laced, too,
with silver. These two do not enter the garden, but walk on, and stand
waiting near the house, beside the flagpole, but without the wall.*

LORNA, *followed by* MARION, *comes out of the house. Instead of the
bright headgear worn before, they have black kerchiefs, worn peasant-wise
on their heads – that is, they have been folded triangularly, draped over
their heads, with the ends tied beneath their chins.*

LORNA *runs over to the stretcher, kneels down beside it, and kisses* JULIA.

LORNA [*affectionately*]. My sister, my little Julia, oh, how sorry I am
that you have to go on this long, sad journey!

JULIA [*her voice is low, but there is a hectic note of hope in it*]. A long
journey, Lorna darlin', but not a sad one; oh, no, not a sad one.
Hope, Lorna, will have me be the hand all the long way. I go to
kneel at the feet of the ever Blessed Virgin.

LORNA. Oh, she will comfort you, me darlin'.

JULIA. Yes, she will comfort me, Lorna [*after a pause*]; an' cure me too.
Lorna, say she will cure me too.

LORNA [*stifling a sob*]. An' cure you, too.

JULIA [*to* MICHAEL]. Give me your good wishes, Mr Marthraun.

MICHAEL [*with genuine emotion*]. Julia, me best wishes go with you, an'
me best prayers'll follow all th' long way!

JULIA [*to* MAHAN]. An' you, Sailor Mahan – have you no good wish for
the poor voyager?

MAHAN [*fervently*]. Young lass, may you go through healin' wathers,
an' come back a clipper, with ne'er a spar, a sail, or a rope asthray!

FATHER DOMINEER *comes quickly in on the path outside. He is a tall, rather
heavily built man of forty. He has a breezy manner now, heading the
forlorn hope. He is trying to smile now, but crack his mouth as he will, the
tight, surly lines of his face refuse to furnish one. He is dressed in the usual
clerical, outdoor garb, and his hard head is covered with a soft, rather
widely brimmed black hat.*

FATHER DOMINEER [*as happily as he can*]. Now, now, no halts on th'
road, little daughter! The train won't wait, an' we must have a few
minutes to spare to make you comfortable. Bring her along,
Brancardiers!* Forward, in th' name o' God and of Mary, ever
Virgin, ever blessed, always bending to help poor, banished
children of Eve!

*The* TWO ROUGH MEN *take up the stretcher and carry it along the pathway
outside, the* MAYOR, *followed by his* MACE-BEARER, *leading it on.* FATHER
DOMINEER *follows immediately behind; then come* LORNA *and* MARION,
*followed by* MICHAEL *and* MAHAN.

*As the stretcher moves along the pathway outside, a band in the distance
is heard playing 'Star of the Sea', to which is added the voice of a crowd
singing the words:*

> Hail, Queen of Heaven, the ocean Star!
> Guide of the wand'rer here below!
> Thrown on life's surge, we claim Thy care –
> Save us from peril and from woe.
>
> *Mother of Christ, Star of the Sea,*
> *Pray for the wanderer, pray for me.*

FATHER DOMINEER [*enthusiastically*]. Julia will bring us back a miracle,
a glorious miracle! To Lourdes!

CURTAIN

## SCENE II

*The scene is the same as before, though the sunshine isn't quite so bright and determined. The Irish Tricolour flies breezily from its flagpole; the table and chairs stand where they were, and the bottle and glasses are still under it.*

    *No one is in the garden, all, apparently, having gone to see Julia away on her long, long journey. Away in the distance the band is playing 'Star of the Sea', and the tune can be softly heard from the garden.*

    *After a few moments,* LORNA *and* MARION *come along the path outside, enter by the gate, and cross over into the house.*

MARION [*anxiously*]. What d'ye think of th' chance of a cure?

LORNA. I'm afraid th' chance is a poor one; but we won't talk about it.

MARION [*piously*]. Well, it was a grand send-off, an' God is good.

LORNA [*coldly*]. An' th' devil's not a bad fella either.

*They both go into the house, and, a few moments later,* MICHAEL *and* MAHAN *stroll along the path, come into the garden, and go to where the table and chairs are.*

MAHAN. Well, th' anchor's weighed.

MICHAEL. It was an edifyin' spectacle, Sailor Mahan, thrustin' us outa this world for th' time bein'. Julia's asked for a sign, Sailor Mahan, an', believe me, she'll get it.

MAHAN. She will, she will, though I wouldn't like to bet on it.

MICHAEL. She'll get what she's afther – a complete cure. Me own generous gift of fifty pounds for th' oul' bog'll be rewarded; an' th' spate o' prayin' goin' on, from th' Mayor to the Bellman, is bound to get th' higher saints goin', persuadin' them to furnish a suitable answer to all we're askin'.

MAHAN [*impatiently*]. Arra, man alive, d'ye think th' skipper aloft an' his glitterin' crew is goin' to bother their heads about a call from a tiny town an' disthrict thryin' hard to thrive on turf?

MICHAEL [*indignantly*]. Looka, if you were only versed in th' endurin' promulgacity of th' gospels, you'd know th' man above's concerned as much about Nyadnanave as he is about a place where a swarm of cardinals saunther secure, decoratin' th' air with all their purple an' gold!

MAHAN [*as indignantly*]. Are you goin' to tell me that th' skipper aloft an' his hierarchilogical crew are concerned about th' Mayor, the Messenger, Marion, me, an' you as much as they are about them who've been promoted to th' quarter-deck o' th' world's fame? Are you goin' to pit our palthry penances an' haltin' hummin' o' hymns against th' piercin' pipin' of th' rosary be Bing Bang Crosby an' other great film stars, who side-stepped from published greatness for a holy minute or two to send a blessed blast over th' wireless, callin' all Catholics to perpetuatin' prayer!

MICHAEL [*sitting down on a chair*]. Sailor Mahan, I ask you to thry to get your thoughts ship-shaped in your mind.

*While they have been talking, the* MESSENGER *has come running along the path outside, and is now leaning on the gate, listening to the two men, unnoticed by them.*

MAHAN [*plumping down on the other chair – indignantly*]. D'ye remember who you're talkin' to, man? Ship-shape in me mind! Isn't a man bound to have his mind fitted together in a ship-shape way, who, forced out of his thrue course be a nautical cathastrope, to wit, videliket,* an act o' God, ploughed a way through th' Sargasso Sea, reachin' open wathers, long afther hope had troubled him no longer?

MICHAEL [*wearily*]. Aw, Sailor Mahan, what's them things got to do with th' things tantamount to heaven?

MESSENGER [*over to them*]. Mick's right – them things can't be tantamount to anything bar themselves.

MAHAN [*turning fiercely on the* MESSENGER]. What do you want? What're you doin' here? Your coalition of ignorant knowledge can't comprehend th' things we talk about!

MESSENGER [*with some excitement*]. Listen, boys – I've a question to ask yous.

MICHAEL [*with a gesture signifying this isn't the time to ask it*]. Ask it some time more convenient. An' don't refer to us as 'boys' – we're gentlemen to you!

MAHAN [*to* MICHAEL]. Looka, Mick, if you only listened to Bing Crosby, th' mighty film star, croonin' his Irish lullaby, [*he chants*] 'Tooral ooral ooral, tooral ooral ay',* you'd have th' visuality to see th' amazin' response he'd have from millions of admirers, if he crooned a hymn!

MESSENGER. I was never sthruck be Bing Crosby's croonin'.

MICHAEL [*wrathfully – to* MESSENGER]. You were never sthruck! An' who th' hell are you to be consulted? Please don't stand there interferin' with the earnest colloquy of betther men. [*To* MAHAN] Looka, Sailor Mahan, any priest'll tell you that in th' eyes of heaven all men are equal an' must be held in respect an' reverence.

MAHAN [*mockingly*]. Ay, they'll say that to me an' you, but will they say it to Bing Crosby, or any other famous film star?

MESSENGER. Will they hell! Honour be th' clergy's regulated by how much a man can give!

MICHAEL [*furiously – to the* MESSENGER]. Get to hell outa here! With that kinda talk, we won't be able soon to sit steady on our chairs. Oh! [*The chair he is sitting on collapses, and he comes down to the ground on his arse.*]

MAHAN [*astonished*]. Holy saints, what's happened?

MICHAEL [*in a fierce whisper – to* MAHAN]. Take no notice of it, fool. Go on talkin'!

MAHAN [*a little confused*]. I'll say you're right, Mick; th' way things are goin' we won't be able much longer to sit serene on our chairs. Oh! [*The chair collapses under* MAHAN, *and he, too, comes down to the ground.*]

MICHAEL [*in a fierce whisper*]. Don't notice it; go on's if nothin' happened!

MESSENGER [*amused*]. Well, yous have settled down now, anyhow! Will I get yous chairs sturdy enough to uphold th' wisdom of your talkin'?

MICHAEL [*angrily – to* MESSENGER]. There's nothin' wrong with th' chairs we have! You get outa here! Nothin's wrong with th' chairs at all. Get outa here – I don't trust you either!

MESSENGER. I've somethin' important to ask yous.

MICHAEL. Well, ask it at some more convenient time. [*To* MAHAN] It's a blessin' that so many lively-livin' oul' holy spots are still in th' land to help us an' keep us wary.

MESSENGER [*scornfully*]. An' where are th' lively holy spots still to be found? Sure, man, they're all gone west long ago, an' the whole face o' th' land is pock-marked with their ruins!

MICHAEL [*shouting at the* MESSENGER]. Where are th' lost an' ruined holy places? We've always cared for, an' honoured, our holy spots! Mention one of them, either lost or ruined!

MESSENGER [*shouting back*]. There are thousands of them, man; places

founded be Finian, Finbarr,* an' th' rest; places that are now only
an oul' ruined wall, blighted be nettle an' dock, their only glory th'
crimson berries of th' bright arbutus! Where's th' Seven Churches
of Glendalough?* Where's Durrow of Offaly, founded be Columkille himself?* Known now only be the name of the Book of
Durrow!*

MICHAEL [*ferociously*]. Book o' Durrow! It's books that have us half th'
woeful way we are, fillin' broody minds with loose scholasticality,
infringin' th' holy beliefs an' thried impositions that our fathers'
fathers' fathers gave our fathers' fathers, who gave our fathers what
our fathers gave to us!

MESSENGER. Faith, your fathers' faith is fear, an' now fear is your only
fun.

MAHAN [*impatiently*]. Let him go, Mick, an' let's have that dhrink you
mentioned a year ago.

MARION's *head appears at the window, looking down at the* MESSENGER.
*The decorations on her head have now declined to their first place.*

MARION [*down to the* MESSENGER]. Hallo, Robin Adair! [*He looks up.*]
Where are th' two oul' woeful wondhers? [*He points to where they
are.*] Oh, they've brought the unsteady chairs out, and now they've
broken them up! [*To* MICHAEL – *angrily*] You knew well th' chairs in
the hall were there only to present an appearance.

MESSENGER [*up to her*]. Oh, Marion, Marion, sweet Marion, come
down till I give you a kiss havin' in it all the life an' longin' of th'
greater lovers of th' past!

MARION [*leaving the window*]. Now, now, naughty boy!

MICHAEL [*sourly*]. You'd do well to remember, lad, the month in jail
you got for kissin' Marion, an' the forty-shillin' fine on Marion, for
kissing you in a public place at th' cross-roads.

MARION *comes from the house, goes toward the* MESSENGER, *who seizes her
in his arms and kisses her.*

MESSENGER. I'd do a year an' a day in a cold cell of pressed-in
loneliness, an' come out singin' a song, for a kiss from a lass like
Marion!

MARION. Don't think too much of me, Robin Adair, for I've some of
th' devil in me, an' th' two fostherers of fear, there, think I wear
horns on holy days.

MICHAEL [*impressively*]. See – she's warnin' you, herself, young man!

MARION [*to the* MESSENGER]. An' what has you here arguin' with them two oul' fools?

MESSENGER. I came to ask a question of them, but they were buried in their prayers. Did you see him? Did he come this way?

MICHAEL [*suddenly alarmed*]. Come where?

MAHAN [*alarmed*]. See who?

MESSENGER. Th' Cock.

MAHAN AND MICHAEL [*together*]. Th' Cock! [*They carefully creep away from the broken chairs, and stand up when they are some distance from them*]

MESSENGER. Ay. I thought he'd make for here first.

MICHAEL [*echoing the* MESSENGER]. Make for here first!

*In the distance, the loud, exultant crow of the* COCK *is heard.*

MESSENGER [*excitedly*]. There he is! Away in the direction east of th' bog! I'll go get him, an' fetch him home.

MARION [*kissing the* MESSENGER]. Bring him here first, Robin, an' I'll have a wreath of roses ready to hang round his neck.

MESSENGER [*rushing away*]. I will, I will, fair one! [*He goes off. She takes the broken chairs into the house.*]

MARION [*carrying in the chairs*]. Next time, you boyos, take out two steady ones.

MICHAEL [*horrified*]. Did you hear what she said, Sailor Mahan? Hang a wreath of roses round his neck! Well, I'll have th' gun ready! Ay, now! [*He goes over to the porch, but* MAHAN *lays a restraining hand on his arm.*]

MAHAN. What good would th' gun be? Have you forgot what Shanaar told us? Your bullet would go clean through him, an' leave him untouched. Now that we're in peace here, let's have th' dhrink we were to have, an' which we both need.

MICHAEL [*halting*]. You're right, Sailor Mahan. If he comes here, what we have to do is to take no notice. Look through him, past him, over him, but never at him. [*He prepares the bottle of whiskey and the glasses.*] There's sinisther enchantments all around us. God between us an' all harm! We'll have to be for ever on our guard.

MAHAN [*impatiently*]. Yis, yis; fill out th' dhrink for God's sake!

MICHAEL. May it give us courage. [*He tilts the bottle over the glass, but none of it spills out.*] Good God, th' bottle's bewitched too!

MAHAN. Bottle bewitched? How could a bottle be bewitched? Steady your nerves, man. Thry givin' it a shake.

MICHAEL [*who has left the bottle back on the table – retreating away from it*]. Thry givin' it a shake yourself, since you're so darin.

MAHAN *goes over to the table with a forced swagger, and reaches out a cautious hand for the bottle. As he touches it, its colour changes to a glowing red.*

MAHAN [*fervent and frightened*]. St Christopher, pathron of all mariners, defend us – th' bottle's changed its colour!

MICHAEL. There's evil things cantherin' an' crawlin' about this place! You saw th' seal on th' bottle showin' it was untouched since it left th' store. Flanagan's finest, Jamieson's best, ten years maturin' – an' look at it now.

MAHAN. How are we goin' to prevent ourselves from bein' the victims of sorcery an' ruin? You'd think good whisky would be exempt from injury even be th' lowest of th' low.

MICHAEL. It's th' women who're always intherceptin' our good intentions. Evil things is threatenin' us everywhere. Th' one safe method of turnin' our back to a power like this is to go forward an' meet it half-way. [*He comes close to Mahan, and whispers hoarsely*] Selah!*

MAHAN [*mystified and frightened at what he thinks may be something sinister*]. Selah?

MICHAEL [*emphatically*]. Selah!

MAHAN [*agonisingly*]. Good God!

MICHAEL. Now, maybe, you'll believe what th' Missioner said last night.

MAHAN [*a little dubiously*]. He might have been exaggeratin' a bit, Mick.

MICHAEL. Look at th' bottle, man! Demons can hide in th' froth of th' beer a man's dhrinkin'. An' all th' time, my turf-workers an' your lorry-drivers are screwin' all they can out of us so that they'll have more to spend on pictures an' in th' dance halls, leavin' us to face th' foe alone.

MAHAN [*abjectly*]. What's a poor, good-livin', virtuous man to do then?

MICHAEL. He must always be thinkin' of th' four last things – hell, heaven, death, an' th' judgement.

MAHAN [*pitifully*]. But that would sthrain a man's nerves, an' make life
hardly worth livin'.

MICHAEL. It's plain, Sailor Mahan, you're still hankerin' afther th'
things o' th' world, an' the soft, stimulatin' touch of th' flesh.
You're puttin' th' two of us in peril, Sailor Mahan.

MAHAN [*protesting*]. You're exaggeratin' now.

MICHAEL. I am not. I seen your eyes followin' that Loreleen when
she's about, hurtin' th' tendher muscles of your eye squintin' down
at her legs. You'll have to curb your conthradictions, for you're
puttin' us both in dire peril, Sailor Mahan. Looka what I've lost
already! Me fine silk hat torn to shreds, so that Lorna's had to
telephone th' firm for another, that I may suitably show meself
when I meet his Brightness, the President; an' looka th' whisky
there – forced into a misundherstandin' of itself be some minor
demon devisin' a spell on it! Guess how much good money I
surrendhered to get that bottle, Sailor Mahan?

MAHAN. I've no idea of what whisky is a gallon now.

MICHAEL [*impatiently*]. What whisky is a gallon now? Is there some
kinda spell on you, too, Sailor Mahan? You can't think of whisky
in gallons now; you have to think of it in terms of sips; an' sips
spaced out from each other like th' holy days of obligation.

MAHAN. An' how are we goin' to get rid of it? We're in some danger
while it's standin' there.

MICHAEL. How th' hell do I know how we'll get rid of it? We'll have to
get Shanaar to deal with it, an', mind you, don't go too near it.


*The* PORTER *appears on the sidewalk outside the wall. He is a middle-aged
man with an obstinate face, the chin hidden by a grizzled beard. He is
wearing a pair of old brown trousers, an older grey coat, and an old blue
shirt. On his head is a big cap, with a long, wide peak jutting out in front of
it. The crown of the cap is a high one, and around the crown is a wide band
of dazzling scarlet. He is carrying a parcel wrapped in brown paper, either
side of which is a little torn. He looks north, south, west, and then, turning
east, he sees the two men in the garden.*


PORTER [*to the two men*]. Isn't it handy now that I've clapped eyes on
two human bein's in this god-forsaken hole! I've been thrudgin'
about for hours thryin' to find th' one that'll claim what's in this
parcel I'm bearin', an', maybe, th' two of yous, or maybe, one of

yous, can tell me where I'll find him. I'm on th' thrack of an oul'
fella callin' himself a Councillor an' a Jay Pee.

MICHAEL. What's his name?

PORTER. That's more than I can say, for th' chit of th' girl in th' shop,
who took th' ordher, forgot to write down th' name, an' then forgot
th' name itself when she started to write it down. All I know is that
in this disthrict I'm seekin' a Mr Councillor So-an'-so; one havin'
Councillor at his head an' Jay Pee at his tail.

MICHAEL [*with importance*]. I'm a Councillor and a Jay Pee.

PORTER [*with some scorn*]. D'ye tell me that now? [*He bends over the
wall to come closer to* MICHAEL]. Listen, me good man, me journey's
been too long an' too dangerous for me to glorify any cod-
actin'!* It would be a quare place if you were a councillor. You'll
have to grow a few more grey hairs before you can take a rise
outa me!

MICHAEL [*indignantly*]. Tell us what you've got there, fella, an', if it's
not for us, be off about your business!

PORTER [*angrily*]. Fella yourself! An' mend your manners, please! It's
hardly th' like of you would be standin' in need of a silky, shinin'
tall hat.

MICHAEL. If it's a tall hat, it's for me! I'm Mr Councillor Marthraun,
Jay Pee – ordhered to be sent express by th' firm of Buckley's.

PORTER [*with a quick conciliatory change*]. That's th' firm. I guessed
you was th' man at once, at once. That man's a leadher in th'
locality, I said, as soon as I clapped me eye on you. A fine, clever,
upstandin' individual, I says to meself.

MICHAEL [*shortly*]. Hand over th' hat, and you can go.

PORTER. Hould on a minute, sir; wait till I tell you: I'm sorry, but th'
hat's been slightly damaged in thransit. [*He begins to take the hat
from the paper.*]

MICHAEL. Damaged? How th' hell did you damage it?

PORTER. Me, is it? No, not me, sir. [*He stretches over the wall towards
them.*] When I was bringin' it here, someone shot a bullet through
it, east be west!

MICHAEL. Nonsense, man, who'd be shootin' bullets round here?

PORTER. Who indeed? That's th' mystery. Bullet it was. People told
me the Civic Guards were out thryin' to shoot down an evil spirit
flyin' th' air in th' shape of a bird.

MICHAEL [*alarmed*]. Th' Cock!

PORTER [*placing the tall-hat on the wall carefully*]. An' seein' how things are, an' th' fright I got, it's welcome a dhrink would be from th' handsome bottle I see paradin' on th' table.

MICHAEL [*in a loud whisper*]. To touch it is to go in danger of your life – th' bottle's bewitched!

PORTER. Th' bottle bewitched? What sort of a place have me poor, wandherin' feet sthrayed into at all? Before I ventured to come here at all, I should have stayed at home. I'm already as uneasy as th' place itself! [*A shot is heard, and the tall hat is knocked from the wall on to the road.*] Saints in glory, there's another one!

MAHAN [*excitedly*]. It's your hat, man, th' red band on your hat!

PORTER [*to* MICHAEL – *speaking rapidly, picking the tall hat from the road and offering it to* MICHAEL]. Here, take your hat, sir, an' keep it safe, an' I'll be goin'.

MICHAEL [*frightened and angry*]. Take it back; it's damaged; take it back, fella!

PORTER [*loudly and with anger*]. Fella yourself! Is it takin' th' risk I'd be of a bullet rushin' through me instead of th' oul' hat? [*He flings it towards the two men.*] Here, take your oul' hat an' th' risk along with it! Do what you want with it; do what you like with it; do what you can with it – I'm off! [*He runs off in the direction he came from, while the two men gaze doubtfully at the hat lying in the garden.*]

MICHAEL [*tremulously*]. The cowards that are in this counthry – leavin' a poor man alone in his dilemma! I'd be afraid to wear it now.

MAHAN. Aw, give yourself a shake, Mick. You're not afraid of a poor tall hat. An' throw away ten good pounds. [*He goes toward where the hat is, but* MICHAEL *holds him by the arm.*]

MICHAEL [*with warning and appeal*]. No, don't touch it till we see further.

*The* SERGEANT *appears on the pathway outside. He has a rifle in his hands; he leans against the wall looking towards the two. He is obviously anxious, and in a state of fear.*

SERGEANT. Yous didn't see it? It didn't come here, did it?

MICHAEL [*breathless with the tension of fear*]. No, no; not yet. [*With doleful appeal*] Oh, don't be prowlin' round here – you'll only be attractin' it to th' place!

SERGEANT [*ignoring appeal*]. Three times I shot at it; three times th' bullets went right through it; and twice th' thing flew away crowing.

MICHAEL [*excitedly*]. Did you get it th' third time, did you get it then?

SERGEANT. Wait till I tell yous: sthrange things an' unruly are happenin' in this holy land of ours this day! Will I ever forget what happened th' third time I hot it!* Never, never. Isn't it a wondher an' a mercy of God that I'm left alive afther th' reverberatin' fright I got!

MICHAEL [*eagerly*]. Well, what happened when you hot it then?

MAHAN [*eagerly*]. When you hot it for th' third time?

SERGEANT. Yous could never guess?

MICHAEL [*impatiently*]. Oh, we know we'd never guess; no one can go guessin' about demonological disturbances.

MAHAN. Tell us, will you, without any more of your sthructural suggestions!

SERGEANT. As sure as I'm standin' here; as sure as sure as this gun is in me left hand [*he is holding it in his right one*]; as sure as we're all poor, identified sinners; when I hot him for th' third time, I seen him changin' into a –

MICHAEL AND MAHAN [*together*]. What?

SERGEANT [*whisperingly*]. What d'ye think?

MAHAN [*explosively*]. Oh, we're not thinkin'; we can't think; we're beyond thinkin'! We're waitin' for you to tell us!

SERGEANT. Th' soul well-nigh left me body when I seen th' unholy novelty happenin': th' thing that couldn't be, yet th' thing that was. If I never prayed before, I prayed then – for hope; for holy considheration in th' quandary; for power to be usual an' spry again when th' thing was gone.

MICHAEL. What thing, what thing, man?

MAHAN [*despairingly*]. Thry to tell us, Sergeant, what you said you said you seen.

SERGEANT. I'm comin' to it; since what I seen was seen by no man never before, it's not easy for a man to describe with evidential accuracy th' consequential thoughts fluttherin' through me amazed mind at what was, an' what couldn't be, demonstrated there, or there, or anywhere else, where mortals congregate in ones or twos or crowds astoundin'.

MICHAEL [*imploringly*]. Looka, Sergeant, we're languishin' for th' information that may keep us from spendin' th' rest of our lives in constant consternation.

SERGEANT. As I was tellin' you, there was th' crimson crest of th' Cock, enhancin' th' head lifted up to give a crow, an' when I riz th' gun to

me shouldher, an' let bang, th' whole place went dead dark; a flash
of red lightning near blinded me; an' when it got light again, a
second afther, there was the demonised Cock changin' himself into
a silken glossified tall hat!

MICHAEL [*horrified*]. A silken tall hat!

MAHAN. A glossified tall hat!

MICHAEL [*to* MAHAN – *viciously*]. Now you'll quit undher-estimatin'
what th' holy Missioner said last night about th' desperate an'
deranging thrickeries of evil things loose an' loungin' among us!
Now can you see the significality of things?

MAHAN [*going away as far as he can from the tall hat lying in the garden*].
Steer clear of it; get as far away from it as we can! Keep well abaft of
it!

SERGEANT [*puzzled*]. Keep clear from what?

MAHAN [*pointing to the hat*]. Th' hat, man, th' hat!

SERGEANT [*seeing the hat beside him, and jumping away from it*]. I was
near touchin' th' brim of it! Jasus! yous should have warned me!

MICHAEL [*close to the* SERGEANT – *in a whisper*]. Does it look anything
like th' thing you shot?

SERGEANT [*laying a shaking hand on* MICHAEL's *arm*]. It's th' dead spit
of what I seen him changin' into durin' th' flash of lightning! I just
riz th' gun to me shouldher – like this [*he raises the gun to his shoulder*]
to let bang.

*The garden is suddenly enveloped in darkness for a few moments. A fierce
flash of lightning shoots through the darkness; the hat has disappeared, and
where it stood now stands the* COCK. *While the lightning flashes, the* COCK
*crows lustily. Then the light as suddenly comes back to the garden, and
shows that the* COCK *and the hat have gone.* MICHAEL *and* MAHAN *are seen
to be lying on the ground, and the* SERGEANT *is on his knees, as if in prayer.*

SERGEANT. Holy St Custodius, pathron of th' police, protect me!

MICHAEL [*in a whisper*]. Are you there, Sailor Mahan?

MAHAN [*in a whisper*]. Are you there, Michael Marthraun?

MICHAEL. I'm done for.

MAHAN. We're both done for.

SERGEANT. We're all done for.

MAHAN. Th' smell of th' sulphur an' brimstone's burnin' me.

MICHAEL. Now you'll give up mockin' Shanaar, if it's not too late. You seen how Marion's head was ornamented, an' it'll not be long till Lorna has them too.

SERGEANT [*now sitting down, so that he is to the left of* MICHAEL, *while* MAHAN *sits to the right of him, so frightened that he must blame someone*]. We'll have to curtail th' gallivantin' of th' women afther th' men. Th' house is their province, as th' clergy's tired tellin' them. They'll have to realise that th' home's their only proper place.

MICHAEL. An' demolish th' minds that babble about books.

SERGEANT [*raising his voice*]. Th' biggest curse of all! Books no decent mortal should touch, should never even see th' cover of one!

MICHAEL [*warningly*]. Hush! Don't speak so loud, or th' lesser boyo'll hear you!

SERGEANT [*startled*]. Lesser boyo? What lesser boyo?

MAHAN [*whispering and pointing*]. Th' boyo in th' bottle there.

SERGEANT [*noticing it for the first time*]. Why, what's in it?

MICHAEL. Th' best of whisky was in it till some evil spirit put a spell on it, desthroyin' its legitimate use.

SERGEANT [*unbelievingly*]. I don't believe it. Nothin' could translate good dhrink into anything but what it was made to be. We could do with a dhrink now. [*He advances cautiously towards the table.*]

MICHAEL [*excitedly*]. Don't meddle with it, man; don't stimulate him!

*The* SERGEANT *tiptoes over to the table, stretches his hand out, and touches the bottle. He immediately lets out a yelp, and jumps back.*

SERGEANT. Oh! Be-God, it's red hot!

MAHAN [*angrily*]. You were told not to touch it! You're addin' to our dangers.

MICHAEL [*shouting*]. Good God, man, couldn't you do what you're told! Now you've added anger to its impositional qualities!

SERGEANT [*nursing his hand*]. Aren't we in a nice quandary when an evil thing can insconce itself in a bottle!

MICHAEL. Th' whole place's seethin' with them. You, Sergeant, watch th' road north; you, Sailor Mahan, watch it south; an' I'll keep an eye on th' house. [MAHAN *goes to one end of the wall, the* SERGEANT *to the other, and both stretch over it to look different ways along the road. During the next discussion, whenever they leave where they are, they move cautiously, crouching a little, as if they were afraid to be seen; keeping as low as possible for security*]. One of us'll have to take th' risk, an' go for Father Domineer at once. [*He waits for a few moments, but no one answers.*] Did yous hear me, or are yous lettin' on to be deaf? I said one of us'll have to go for Father Domineer. [*There is no reply.*] Are you listenin' to me be any chance, Sailor Mahan?

MAHAN. I heard you, I heard you.

MICHAEL. An' why don't you go, then?

MAHAN [*coming down towards* MICHAEL – *crouching low*]. Nice thing if I met th' Cock barrin' me way? Why don't you go yourself?

MICHAEL. What about th' possibility of me meetin' him? I'm more conspicuous in this disthrict than you, an' th' thing would take immediate recognisance of me.

SERGEANT [*coming down towards them – crouching too*]. Me an' Sailor Mahan'll go together.

MICHAEL [*indignantly*]. An' leave me to grapple with *mysteriosa Daemones* alone? [*He turns his face skywards*] Oh, in this disthrict there's not a sign of one willin' to do unto another what another would do to him!

MAHAN [*fiercely*]. That's a lie: there isn't a one who isn't eager to do to others what others would do to him!

*The* BELLMAN, *dressed as a fireman, comes in, and walks along on the path outside. He has a huge brass fireman's helmet on his head, and is wearing a red shirt and blue trousers. He has a bell in his hand which he rings loudly before he shouts his orders. The three men cease their discussion, and give him their full attention.*

BELLMAN [*shouting*]. Into your houses all! Bar th' doors, shut th' windows! Th' Cock's comin'! In the shape of a woman! Gallus, Le Coq, an' Kyleloch, th' Cock's comin' in th' shape of a woman! Into your houses, shut to th' windows, bar th' doors!

*He goes out in the opposite direction, shouting his orders and ringing his bell, leaving the three men agitated and more frightened than ever.*

SERGEANT [*frantically*]. Into the house with us all – quick!

MICHAEL [*hindering him – ferociously*]. Not in there, you fool! Th' house is full o' them. You seen what happened to the whisky? If he or she comes, th' thing to do is to take no notice; if he or she talks, not to answer; and take no notice of whatever questionable shape it takes. Sit down, quiet, th' three of us.

*The three men sit down on the ground –* MICHAEL *to the right, the* SERGEANT
*to the left, and* MAHAN *in the centre.*

MICHAEL [*trembling*]. Now, let th' two of yous pull yourselves
together. An' you, Mahan, sing that favourite of yours, quietly, as if
we were passing th' time pleasantly. [*As* MAHAN *hesitates*] Go on,
man, for God's sake!

MAHAN [*agitated*]. I can't see how I'll do it justice undher these
conditions. I'll thry. [*He sings, but his voice quavers occasionally.*]

> Long time ago when men was men
> An' ships not ships that sail'd just to an' fro-o-o,
> We hoisted sail an' sail'd, an' then sail'd on an' on to
>     Jericho-o-o;
> With silks an' spice came back again because we'd
>     nowhere else to go!

MICHAEL AND SERGEANT [*together*].

> Go, go!

MAHAN [*singing*].

> Th' captain says, says he, we'll make
> Th' pirates where th' palm trees wave an' grow-o-o,
> Haul down their sable flag, an' pray, before we hang
>     them all, heave yo-ho-ho;
> Then fling their bodies in th' sea to feed th' fishes down
>     below!

MICHAEL AND SERGEANT [*together*].

> Low, low!

*A golden shaft of light streams in from the left of the road, and, a moment
afterwards,* LORELEEN *appears in the midst of it. She stands in the gateway
staring at the three men squatted on the ground.*

LORELEEN [*puzzled*]. What th' hell's wrong here?

MICHAEL [*in a whisper – motioning* MAHAN *to continue*]. Go on, man.

MAHAN [*singing – with more quavers in his voice*].

An' when we've swabb'd th' blood away,
We'll take their hundhred-ton gunn'd ship in tow-o-o;
Their precious jewels'll go to deck th' breasts of women,
    white as snow-o-o;
So hoist all sail an' make for home through waves that lash
    an' winds that blow!

MICHAEL AND SERGEANT [*together*].

Blow, blow!

LORELEEN *comes into the garden, and approaches the men. The golden light follows her, and partly shines on the three singers.*

LORELEEN [*brightly*]. Singin' is it the three of you are? Practisin' for the fancy-dress ball tonight, eh? Ye do well to bring a spray of light, now and again, into a dark place. The Sergeant's eyes, too, whenever Lorna or me passes by, are lit with a light that never was on sea or land. An' th' bould Sailor Mahan is smiling too; only Dad is dour [*She glances at the bottle on the table.*] The song is heard, th' wine is seen, only th' women wanting. [*She runs over to the porchway and shouts into the house*] Lorna, Marion, come on down, come out here, an' join th' enthertainment!

LORNA *and* MARION *come trotting out of the house into the garden. They are both clad in what would be called fancy dress.* LORNA *is supposed to be a gypsy, and is wearing a short black skirt, low-cut green bodice, with a gay sash round her waist, sparkling with sequins. Her fair arms are bare. Her head is bound with a silver and black ornament, similar in shape to that already worn by* MARION. *Her legs are encased in black stockings, and dark-red shoes cover her feet.* MARION *is dressed as a Nippy,\* a gay one. She has on a short, bright-green skirt, below which a black petticoat peeps; a low-cut bodice of a darker green, and sports a tiny black apron to protect her costume. She wears light-brown silk stockings and brown shoes. Outside the white bandeau round her head she wears the ornament worn before. The two women stare at the three men.*

LORNA [*vexatiously*]. Dhrunk is it? To get in that state just when we were practisin' a few steps for tonight's fancy-dress dance! [*She notices the bottle.*] Looka th' dhrink left out in th' sun an' air to dhry! [*She whips up the bottle, and places it inside on the floor of the porch.*] An' even th' Sailor Mahan is moody too! [*She goes over to the* SERGEANT, *standing behind him, and lays a hand on his head. She is now in the golden light which shines down on the* SERGEANT *too.*]

> I saw a ship a-sailing, a-sailing on th' sea;
> An' among its spicy cargo was a bonny lad for me!

*The* SERGEANT *rises slowly, as if enchanted, with a foolish look of devotion on his face, till he stands upright beside* LORNA, *glancing at her face, now and again, very shy and uncertain. While this has been happening,* LORELEEN *has gone to* SAILOR MAHAN, *and now stands behind him with a hand on his head.*

LORELEEN [*down to* SAILOR MAHAN].

> I saw a man come running, come running o'er th' lea,
>    sir,
> And, lo, he carried silken gowns
> That couldn't hide a knee
> That he had bought in saucy towns;
> An' jewels he'd bought beyond th' bounds
> Of Asia's furthest sea.
> And all were lovely, all were fine,
> An' all were meant for me!

SAILOR MAHAN *rises, as if enchanted, till he stands upright beside* LORELEEN, *slyly looking at her now and again.*

MARION. Aw, let's be sensible. [*She sees the gun.*] What's th' gun doin'? Who owns th' gun?

SERGEANT. It's mine. I'm on pathrol lookin' to shoot down th' demon bird loose among innocent people.

MARION. Demon bird loose among innocent people! Yous must be mad.

SERGEANT [*indignantly*]. We're not mad! It's only that we were startled when th' darkness came, th' lightning flashed, an' we saw Mr Marthraun's tall hat turnin' itself into th' demon bird!

LORNA [*mystified*]. Th' darkness came, th' lightning flashed? A tall hat changin' into a demon bird!

MICHAEL [*springing to his feet*]. Ay, an' this isn't th' time for gay disturbance! So go in, an' sthrip off them gaudy things, an' bend your mind to silent prayer an' long fastin'! Fall prostrate before God, admittin' your dire disthress, an' you may be admitted to a new dispensation!

LORNA [*to* MICHAEL]. Nonsense! Your new tall hat was delivered an hour ago, an' is upstairs now, waitin' for you to put it on. [*To* MARION] Take that gun in, dear, outa th' way, an' bring down th' tall hat to show him he's dhreamin'.

MARION *takes up the gun, and goes into the house with it, as* MICHAEL, *in a great rage, shoves* MAHAN *aside to face* LORNA *fiercely*.

MICHAEL [*loudly*]. Who are you, you jade,* to set yourself up against th' inner sight an' outer sight of genuine Christian men? [*He shouts*] We seen this thing, I tell you! If you knew what you ought to know, you'd acknowledge th' thrained tenacity of evil things. Betther had I left you soakin' in poverty, with your rags coverin' your thin legs, an' your cheeks hollow from mean feedin'. Through our bulgin' eyes, didn't we see th' horrification of me tall hat turnin' into th' demonised cock? Me tall hat, you bitch, me own tall hat is roamin' round th' counthry, temptin' souls to desthroy themselves with dancin' an' desultory pleasures!

MAHAN [*gripping* MICHAEL'*s arm*]. Aw, draw it mild, Mick!

MICHAEL [*flinging off* MAHAN'*s hold*]. Go in, an' take them things, showy with sin, off you, an' dhress decent! [*He points to* LORELEEN] It's you who's brought this blast from th' undherworld, England, with you! It's easy seen what you learned while you worked there – a place where no God is; where pride and lust an' money are the brightest liveries of life! [*He advances as if to strike her, but* MAHAN *bars his way*]. You painted slug! [MARION *comes from the house, carrying a fresh, dignified tall hat, noble in its silken glossiness. She offers it to* MICHAEL *who jumps away from it.*] No, no, take it away; don't let it touch me.

MARION *puts the hat on the table, and the three men stare at it, as if expecting something to happen.*

LORNA [*darting into the porch, and returning with the bottle. It has gone
back to its former colour*]. Let's have a dhrink to give us courage to
fight our dangers. Fetch another glass, Marion.

MARION *goes in, and returns with a glass.* LORNA *uncorks the bottle, and
takes up a glass to fill it.*

MICHAEL [*warningly*]. Don't meddle with that dhrink, or harm may
come to us all!

LORNA [*recklessly*]. If I can't wrap myself in th' arms of a man, I'll wrap
myself in a cordial. [*She fills the glass, then she fills another one, and
gives it to Loreleen; then she fills a third, and gives it to Marion.*] Here,
Loreleen. [*Loreleen takes the glass.*] Here, Marion. [MARION *takes the
glass from her.*]

MAHAN [*doubtfully, and with some fear*]. I wouldn't, Lorna, I wouldn't
dhrink it – there's some kind of a spell on it.

LORNA. Is there, now? I hope to God it's a strong one! [*Raising her
glass*] Th' Cock-a-doodle Dandy!

MARION AND LORELEEN [*raising their glasses – together*]. Th' Cock-a-
doodle Dandy!

*The three women empty their glasses together.* LORNA *fills her glass again,
and goes over to the* SERGEANT.

LORNA [*offering the glass to the* SERGEANT]. Dhrink, hearty man, an'
praise th' good things life can give. [*As he hesitates*] Dhrink from th'
glass touched by th' lips of a very fair lady!

SERGEANT [*impulsively*]. Death an' bedammit, ma'am, it's a fair lady
you are. [*He takes the glass from her*] I'm not th' one to be short in
salutin' loveliness! [*He drinks, and a look of delightful animation
gradually comes on to his face.*]

LORELEEN [*who has filled her glass again – going over to* SAILOR MAHAN,
*and offering him the drink*]. Here, Sailor Mahan, man of th' wider
waters, an' th' seven seas, dhrink! [*As he hesitates*] Dhrink from th'
glass touched by th' lips of a very fair lady!

MAHAN [*taking the glass – impulsively*]. Here's a one who always yelled
ahoy to a lovely face an' charmin' figure whenever they went sailin'
by – salud! [*He drinks, and the look of animation gradually comes onto
his face too.*]

MARION [*who has filled her glass the second time – going over to* MICHAEL *and offering him the drink*]. Dark man, let th' light come to you be dhrinkin' from a glass touched be th' red lips of a fair young maiden!

MICHAEL [*who has been watching the others enviously – taking the glass from her*]. Gimme it! I won't be one odd. Yous can't best me! [*He drinks it down greedily. A reckless look steals over his face.*]

*During the last few moments,* LORNA *has been humming a tune, which has been taken up by an accordion, very softly. Then the* MESSENGER *appears on the pathway outside, and it can be seen that he is the player. He sits sideways on the wall, still playing softly a kind of a dance tune.*

MICHAEL [*to* MARION]. In our heart of hearts, maid Marion,* we care nothin' about th' world of men. Do we now, Sailor Mahan?

MAHAN [*cautiously – though a reckless gleam is appearing in his eyes too*]. We all have to think about th' world o' men at times.

MICHAEL. Not with our hearts, Sailor Mahan; oh, not with our hearts. You're thinkin' now of th' exthra money you want off me, Sailor Mahan. Take it, man, an' welcome! [*Enthusiastically*] An' more! You can have double what you're askin', without a whimper, without a grudge!

MAHAN [*enthusiastically*]. No, damnit, Michael, not a penny from you! We're as good as bein' brothers! Looka th' lilies of th' field, an' ask yourself what th' hell's money!

MICHAEL [*excitedly*]. Dhross, be God! Dhross, an' nothin' else! [*To* MARION] Gimme that hat there!

*She gives it to him. He puts it on, puts an arm round her waist, and they begin to move with the beat of the music. As* MICHAEL *puts his arm around her waist, the ornament on her head rises into a graceful, curving horn, but he does not notice it.*

*At the same time, the* SERGEANT, *having put an arm round* LORNA, *moves in the dance, too. As he does so, the ornament on her head, too, becomes a curving horn, but he does not notice it. Then* MAHAN *goes over stealthily to* LORELEEN, *who is watching the others, and stabs her shyly in the ribs with a finger. She turns, smiles, takes hold of his arm, and puts it round her waist. Then the two of them join the others in moving round to the beat of the music, the cock-like crest in* LORELEEN'S *hat rising higher as she begins to move in the dance.*

*After a few moments, the dance quickens, the excitement grows, and the*

*men stamp out the measure of the music fiercely, while the three women
begin to whirl round them with ardour and abandon. While the excitement
is at its height, a loud, long peal of thunder is heard, and in the midst of it,
with a sliding, rushing pace,* FATHER DOMINEER *appears in the gateway, a
green glow enveloping him as he glares down at the swinging dancers, and
as a loud, lusty crow from the* COCK *rings out through the garden.*

*The dancers, excepting* LORELEEN, *suddenly stand stock still, then fall
on one knee, facing the priest, their heads bent in shame and some dismay.*
LORELEEN *dances on for some few moments longer, the music becoming
softer, then she slowly ends her dance to face forward towards the priest, the*
MESSENGER *continuing to play the tune very softly, very faintly now.*


FATHER DOMINEER [*down to those in the garden – with vicious intensity*].
Stop that devil's dance! How often have yous been warned that th'
avowed enemies of Christianity are on th' march everywhere! An' I
find yous dancin'! How often have yous been told that pagan poison
is floodin' th' world, an' that Ireland is dhrinkin' in generous doses
through films, plays, an' books! An' yet I come here to find yous
dancin'! Dancin', an' with th' Kyleloch, Le Coq, Gallus, th' Cock
rampant in th' disthrict, desthroyin' desire for prayer, desire for
work, an' weakenin' th' authority of th' pastors an' masters of your
souls! Th' empire of Satan's pushin' out its foundations everywhere, an' I find yous dancin', *ubique ululanti cockalorum ochone,
ululo!*\*

MESSENGER [*through his soft playing of the accordion*]. Th' devil was as
often in th' street, an' as intimate in th' home when there was nor
film nor play nor book.

FATHER DOMINEER. There was singin' then, an' there's singin' now;
there was dancin' then, an' there's dancin' now, leadin' innocent
souls to perjure their perfection. [*To* LORELEEN] Kneel down, as th'
others do, you proud an' dartin' cheat, an' beg a pardon!

LORELEEN [*obstinately*]. I seek no pardon for th' dance that's done.

FATHER DOMINEER [*turning away from her*]. Seek for it then when
pardon hides away.

MICHAEL. Oh, what have I done! I've bethrayed meself into a sudden
misdoin'!

MAHAN. *Mea culpa*, me, too, Father!

FATHER DOMINEER. Oh, Michael Marthraun, an' you, Sailor Mahan,
Knights of Columbanus, I come to help yous, an' I catch yous in th'

act of prancin' about with shameless women, dhressed to stun th'
virtue out of all beholdhers!

MICHAEL. It was them, right enough, Father, helped be th' wine, that
done poor me an' poor Sailor Mahan in! I should have remembered
that a Columbanian knight told me a brother Columbanian knight
told him another brother has said that St Jerome told a brother once
that woman was th' gate of hell! An' it's thrue – they stab a man with
a knife wreathed with roses!

FATHER DOMINEER. Get up, get up, an' stand away from me; an' let ye
never be loungers again in th' fight for good against evil. [*They all
rise up humbly, the women to one side, the men to the other, and go back
some way, as the priest comes into the garden.* LORELEEN *strolls defiantly
over to the table, and sits sideways upon it. To* MAHAN] An' now, Sailor
Mahan, a special word for you. On my way here, I passed that man
of yours who's livin' in sin with a lost an' wretched woman. He
dodged down a lane to give me th' slip. I warned you, if he didn't
leave her, to dismiss him – did you do so? [MAHAN *is silent.*] I have
asked you, Mahan, if you've dismissed him?

MAHAN [*obstinately*]. I see no reason why I should dismiss me best
lorry-driver.

FATHER DOMINEER [*coldly*]. You don't see a reason? An' who are you to
have any need of a reason in a question of this kind? [*Loudly*] I have
a reason, an' that's enough for you!

MAHAN [*defensively*]. He's a fine worker, Father, an' th' nation needs
such as him.

FATHER DOMINEER [*loudly*]. We're above all nations. Nationality is
mystical, maundering nonsense! It's a heresy! I'm the custodian of
higher interests. [*Shouting*] Do as you're told – get rid of him!

MICHAEL [*wheedling*]. It's all right, Father – he'll do what your
reverence tells him. Sailor Mahan's a thrue Columbanian.

MAHAN [*angrily – to* MICHAEL]. He won't do what his reverence tells
him!

*Down the path outside comes the* LORRY-DRIVER, *a man of thirty years of
age. He doesn't look a giant, but there is an air of independence and
sturdiness about him. He is wearing a leather jacket, a pair of soldier's
khaki trousers, and an oily-looking peaked cap. His face is tanned by the
weather, and his upper lip is hidden by a well-trimmed moustache. He
hesitates for a moment when he sees* FATHER DOMINEER; *but, stiffening a
little, he continues his walk to the gateway, into the garden. He stands a*

*little way from* MAHAN, *looking at him, evidently having something to say to him.*

FATHER DOMINEER [*sneeringly*]. Ah, the gentleman himself has arrived. [*To the man*] We were just talking of you, my man. I have told Mr Mahan to dismiss you. You know why. You're a scandal to th' whole place; you're a shame to us all. Either leave this woman you're living with, or go to where that sort of thing's permitted. [*Loudly*] You heard me?

LORRY-DRIVER [*surlily*]. I heard you.

FATHER DOMINEER [*impatiently*]. Well?

LORRY-DRIVER. I come to speak with Mr Mahan, Father.

MAHAN [*quickly*]. Me, Jack! Oh, yes; what's the throuble now?

LORRY-DRIVER. Plenty, sir. The turf-workers have left th' bog, an' we've no turf to load. Th' delegate says he sent a telegram to Mr Marthraun, sayin' th' men would leave th' bog, if no answer came within an hour.

MESSENGER. He did, an' I delivered it.

MICHAEL. Damnit, but I forgot about it! The tension here put it out of me mind!

FATHER DOMINEER [*catching the* LORRY-DRIVER *by an arm*]. Never mind turf or tension now. Are you going to go from here?

LORRY-DRIVER [*obstinately*]. I'll go, if Mr Mahan tells me to go.

FATHER DOMINEER [*in a fury*]. Isn't it a wondher God doesn't strike you dead! I tell you to give the wretched woman up, or go, an' that's enough for either Sailor Mahan or you. [*He shakes the* LORRY-DRIVER's *arm.*] Will you give that wretched woman up; will you send that woman of yours away?

LORRY-DRIVER [*resentfully*]. Eh, don't be pullin' th' arm outa me!

FATHER DOMINEER [*his fury growing*]. Did you send that woman away; are you going to do it?

LORRY-DRIVER [*shaking his arm free, and stepping back*]. Aw, let go! I didn't an' I won't!

FATHER DOMINEER [*in an ungovernable burst of fury*]. You wretch, would you dare to outface your priest? Get out of me sight!

*He lunges forward, and strikes the* LORRY-DRIVER *swiftly and savagely on the side of the head. The man falls heavily; lies still for a moment; tries feebly to rise; falls down again, and lies quite still.*

MAHAN [*frightened*]. He's hurted, Father; you hot him far too hard.

FATHER DOMINEER [*frightened too – with a forced laugh*]. Nonsense! I just touched him. [*He touches the fallen man with his foot.*] Get up, get up – you're not that much hurt.

MAHAN [*bending over the* LORRY-DRIVER, *and placing a hand on his breast*]. I'm afraid he's either dyin' or dead, Father!

FATHER DOMINEER *runs over agitatedly to the fallen man, kneels down beside him, and murmurs in his ear. Then he raises his head to face the others.*

FATHER DOMINEER [*to the others*]. Yous all saw what happened. I just touched him, an' he fell. I'd no intention of hurting him – only to administer a rebuke.

SERGEANT [*consolingly*]. Sure, we know that, Father – it was a pure accident.

FATHER DOMINEER. I murmured an act of contrition into th' poor man's ear.

MESSENGER [*playing very softly*]. It would have been far fitther, Father, if you'd murmured one into your own.

CURTAIN

## SCENE III

*It is towards dusk in the garden now. The sun is setting, and the sky shows it. The rich blue of the sky has given place to a rich yellow, slashed with green and purple. The flagpole stands black against the green and yellow of the sky, and the flag, now, has the same sombre hue.*

*The big sunflowers against the wall have turned into a solemn black, too; the house has a dark look, save where a falling shaft from the sun turns the window above the porch into a golden eye of light. Far away, in the depths of the sky, the evening star can be faintly seen.*

*In the distance, for some time, the sounds of drumming, occasionally pierced by the shrill notes of a fife, can be heard.*

MAHAN *is sitting at the table, busy totting up figures on papers spread out before him, his face knotted into creases of anxiety and doubt.*

LORNA *and* MARION *are leaning against the wall, away from the gateway, and near the house. Their gay garments are covered with dark hooded cloaks to temper the coolness of the evening air.*

LORNA. They all seem to be out on th' hunt – police an' soldiers, with th' bands to give them courage. Th' fools!

MARION. D'ye think they'll get him? Th' place'll lose its brightness if th' Cock's killed.

LORNA. How can they desthroy a thing they say themselves is not of this world? [*She goes over to* MAHAN, *and stares at him for a moment.*] It's cooler. The sun's settin'.

MAHAN [*hardly noticing*]. Is it? I didn't notice. I'm busy. Everything thrust through everything else, since that damned Cock got loose. Th' drouth now dhryin' everything to dust; the turf-workers refusin' to work, th' women thinkin' only of dancin' an' dhress. But we'll lay him low, an' bury him deep enough to forget he ever came here!

LORNA. Th' men on th' bog work hard; they should get all you've got to give them.

MAHAN [*resentfully*]. An' why th' hell shouldn't they work hard? Who'd keep th' fires of th' nation burning, if they didn't?

LORNA. They work for you, too; an' for Michael. He's got a pile in th' bank, an' rumour says you've got one too.

MAHAN [*whining*]. Michael may: I never had, an' I'm losin' th' little I had since I lost me best lorry-dhriver – blast th' hand that hot him!

[*The* COCK *suddenly glides in, weaving a way between* MAHAN *at the table, and* LORNA, *circling the garden, and finally disappearing round the gable-end of the house; the dance tune softly keeps time with his movements. Jumping to his feet*] What was that? I thought I saw him prancin' by me!

LORNA [*startled too*]. What was what?

MAHAN. Th' Cock in his black plumage, yellow legs, an' crimson crest!

MARION [*who has gone tense*]. You put th' heart across me! I thought you meant th' poor dead man. [*She turns to look along the road again.*]

LORNA [*to* MAHAN]. There's little use worryin' over figures till you settle with th' men.

MAHAN [*irritably*]. That's Mick's business, that's Mick's business!

MARION [*running over to whisper excitedly to* LORNA]. Here they are – Father Domineer an' Mr Marthraun comin' along th' road!

MAHAN [*irascibly*]. Aw, what does that Father Domineer want comin' here when we've so much to think about! Delayin' things! I want to get away from here before it gets dark.

LORNA. Didn't you know they're goin' to purge th' poor house of its evil influences?

MAHAN [*irritably*]. Oh, can't they do first things first?


*Along the pathway outside come* FATHER DOMINEER *and* MICHAEL, *followed by a lad. The lad is* ONE-EYED LARRY. *His face is one alternately showing stupidity or cunning, according to whomsoever may be speaking to him. Where his left eye was is a black cavity, giving him a somewhat sinister look. He is lanky and rather awkward-looking. He is wearing a black cassock or soutane, piped with red braid, and is bare-headed. He is carrying a small bell, a book, and an unlighted candle. He shuffles along after the two men, and follows them into the garden.*


FATHER DOMINEER. We'll banish them, never fear, Michael, before I have to leave th' parish because of that unhappy accident. I've faced worse. Be staunch. Th' bell is powerful, so is th' book, an' th' blessed candle, too. [*He glances at the women.*] Let yous women keep to th' farther end of th' garden. [*He glances at* MAHAN.] We won't be long, Sailor Mahan. [*Suddenly, as he,* MICHAEL, *and* ONE-EYED LARRY *reach the porch*] Where's that other one?

MICHAEL. Is it Loreleen, me daughter, Father?

FATHER DOMINEER. She's no daughter of yours, Michael. [*Bending down to whisper warningly*] Get rid of her, get rid of her – she's dangerous!

MICHAEL. How get rid of her, Father?

FATHER DOMINEER. Pack her off to America!

MICHAEL [*respectfully – as they are about to go into the house*]. I'll go first, Father.

FATHER DOMINEER [*setting him gently aside*]. No, no; mine th' gap of danger.*

*The three of them go in, the priest first, then* MICHAEL, *and, lastly,* ONE-EYED LARRY. MARION *and* LORNA *move over to the farther side of the garden.*

LORNA. It's all damn nonsense, though Michael has me nerves in such a way that I'm near ready to believe in anything.

MAHAN. Waste of time, too. It'll take a betther man than Father Domineer to dhrive evil things outa Eire.

MARION. Messenger says he's only addin' to their number, an' soon a noddin' daffodil, when it dies, 'll know its own way to hell. [*The roll of a drum is heard and a great booing.* MARION *runs to the wall to look over it, and up the road. Excitedly*] A girl runnin' this way, hell for leather. My God, it's Loreleen!

*After a few moments,* LORELEEN *runs along the pathway outside, and dashes in through the gateway to* LORNA, *who catches her in her arms. Clumps of grass and sods of turf, and a few stones follow* LORELEEN *in her rush along the road.*

LORELEEN [*out of breath*]. God damn th' dastards of this vile disthrict! They pelted me with whatever they could lay hands on – th' women because they couldn't stand beside me; th' men because there was ne'er a hope of usin' me as they'd like to! Is it any wondher that th' girls are fleein' in their tens of thousands from this bewildhered land? Blast them! I'll still be gay an' good-lookin'. Let them draw me as I am not, an' sketch in a devil where a maiden stands!

LORNA [*soothingly*]. Be calm, child! We can't go in, for Father Domineer's inside puttin' things in ordher. [*Releasing* LORELEEN] I'll run along th' road to them disturbers, an' give them a bit o' me mind! [*She catches hold of* MARION'S *arm*] Come on, MARION! [*She and* MARION *rush out along the road, and pass out of sight.*]

LORELEEN [*staring at the house*]. He's inside, is he? That's not where th' evil is, th' gaum,* if he wants to know.

MAHAN [*seriously*]. Come here, Loreleen; nearer, for I've something to say to you. [*As she does not stir, he grips her arm, and draws her farther from the house.*] We might be heard.

LORELEEN [*suspiciously*]. What do you want, Sailor Mahan? You're not of one mind with them who chased me?

MAHAN [*a little embarrassed*]. Aw, God, no! Me sails of love are reefed at last, an' I lie quiet, restin' in a lonely harbour now. I'm too old to be flusthered with that kinda folly. I just want to warn you to get outa this disthrict.

LORELEEN [*bitterly*]. Why must I go? Is it because I'm good-lookin' an' gay?

*But the bold* MAHAN *isn't indifferent to the charms of* LORELEEN. *So he goes on to show* LORELEEN *the youthfulness of his old age; that his muscles are still strong, his fibres flexible. He becomes restless, and walks about, occasionally glancing at the house, nervous at what may be happening inside. When he comes to a chair, he nonchalantly swings a leg over the back of it, turning on the foot of the same leg to swing the other one back again. These actions, like the conversation, though not done in a hurry, are done quickly, as if he wanted to say all he had to say before any interruption.*

MAHAN [*swinging a leg over a chair*]. Partly because you're good-lookin' an' partly because of th' reckless way you talk. Remember what happened to poor Jack. I'd clear out if I were you. [*He vaults on to the table, swings round it on his backside, and vaults from it on the opposite side, a little stiffly.*]

LORELEEN. How'm I to clear out? I've no money left. Th' forty pounds I had, Dad put into his bank for me, an' now won't give me a penny of it, because he says if I got it, I'd go to England; an' if I went to England, I'd lose me soul, th' shaky, venomous lout! An' I keep quiet because of Lorna. [*Hurriedly, as Mahan is stiffly climbing a few feet up the flagpole*] Oh, don't be doin' th' monkey on a stick! Maybe you could help me? Could you, would you!

MAHAN [*sliddering from the pole, swinging a leg over a chair, and coming closer to her*]. Now that's what I'd hoped you'd say. This is th' first time I've caught you alone. I'll give you what you need, an' you can weigh anchor, an' be off outa this damned place. Listen, darlin':

you steal out tonight to th' Red Barn, west of th' Holy Cross, an' I'll dhrive there with what'll get you as far as you want to go. [*He suddenly puts an arm round her in a kind of clutch.*] Jasus, you have lovely eyes!

LORELEEN [*trying to pull his arm away*]. Oh, Sailor Mahan, don't do that! Let me go – someone may see us!

MAHAN [*recklessly*]. You deserve to be ruffled a bit! Well, will you come to th' Red Barn, while th' rest are goin' to th' dance, an' save yourself? Yes or no!

LORELEEN. Maybe, maybe; yes, yes, I'll go. Let go your clutch!

*The house shakes; a sound of things moving and crockery breaking comes from it; several flashes of lightning spear out through the window over the porch; and the flagpole wags drunkenly from side to side.*

   MARION *and* LORNA *appear on the pathway outside the wall, and hurry along into the garden just as* ONE-EYED LARRY *comes running out of the house, his face beset with fear. His one eye takes in the picture of* LORELEEN *breaking away from* MAHAN. LORELEEN *turns aside from* ONE-EYED LARRY, *while* MAHAN, *embarrassed, turns to face him.*

ONE-EYED LARRY [*excitedly*]. It's startin' in earnest! There's a death-sthruggle goin' on in there! Poor Father Domineer's got a bad black eye, an' Micky Marthraun's coat is torn to tatthers!

LORNA [*hurrying into the garden*]. What's happened, what's happenin'?

MAHAN [*with dignity – to* ONE-EYED LARRY]. Misther Marthraun in your mouth, me lad.

LORELEEN [*mischievously*]. Let th' lad tell his funny story.

ONE-EYED LARRY [*turning on* LORELEEN]. It's funny to you because you're in league with th' evil ones! [*To the others*] One o' Father Domineer's feet is all burned be a touch from one o' them, an' one o' Mickey's is frozen stiff be a touch from another. [*To* MAHAN] Maybe you'd ha' liked me to have lost me other eye while you were warmin' yourself in that one's arms! [*He points to* LORELEEN.]

MAHAN [*furiously*]. You one-eyed gett,* if you had two, I'd cyclonise you with a box!

LORELEEN [*unmoved – a little mockingly*]. An' how did th' poor lamb lose his eye?

MAHAN [*indifferently*]. Oh, when he was a kid, he was hammerin' a bottle, an' a flyin' piece cut it out of his head.

ONE-EYED LARRY [*venomously*]. You're a liar, that wasn't th' way! It was th' Demon Cock who done it to me. Only certain eyes can see him, an' I had one that could. He caught me once when I was spyin' on him, put a claw over me left eye, askin' if I could see him then; an' on me sayin' no, put th' claw over th' other one, an' when I said I could see him clear now, says he, that eye sees too well, an' on that, he pushed an' pushed till it was crushed into me head.

LORELEEN [*mockingly*]. What a sad thing to happen!

*The house shakes worse than before, and seems to lurch over to one side. The flagpole wags from side to side merrily; there is a rumble of thunder, and blue lightning flashes from the window. All, except* LORELEEN, *cower together at the far end of the garden. She stands over by the wall, partly framed by the sable sunflowers.*

MARION [*full of fright*]. Sacred Heart! Th' house'll fall asundher!

LORELEEN [*gleefully*]. Let it! It's th' finest thing that could happen to it!

ONE-EYED LARRY [*trembling violently*]. It's now or never for them an' for us. They're terrible powerful spirits. Knocked th' bell outa me hand, blew out th' candle, an' tore th' book to threads! Thousands of them there are, led be th' bigger ones – Kissalass, Velvethighs, Reedabuck, Dancesolong, an' Sameagain. Keep close. Don't run. They might want help. [*Screeches like those of barn owls are heard from the house, with the 'too-whit too-whoo' of other kinds, the cackling of hens, and the loud cawing of crows. Frantically pushing his way to the back of the others*] Oooh! Let me get back, get back!

*The house shakes again; the flagpole totters and falls flat; blue and red lightning flashes from the window, and a great peal of thunder drums through the garden. Then all becomes suddenly silent. They all hang on to each other, shivering with fear, except* LORELEEN, *who lights a cigarette, puts a foot on a chair, leans on its back, looks at the house, and smokes away serenely.*

LORNA [*tremulously*]. Why has th' house gone so silent suddenly?

ONE-EYED LARRY [*from the rear*]. They've either killed th' demons, or th' demons has killed them.

MARION. God save us, they must be dead!

LORELEEN [*with quiet mockery*]. Welcome be th' will o' God.

LORNA [*suddenly – with great agitation*]. Get back, get back! Run! There's something comin' out!

*She,* MARION, *and* ONE-EYED LARRY *race for the gateway, rush onto the sidewalk, and bend down, so that only their heads can be seen peeping over the wall.* MAHAN *shrinks back to the far end of the garden, and* LORELEEN *remains where she is.*

*From the house, sideways, through the now lurching porch, come* FATHER DOMINEER *and* MICHAEL. *Both are limping,* FATHER DOMINEER *on his left foot,* MICHAEL *on his right one.* DOMINEER *has a big black eye, his coat is awry on his back, and his hair is widely tossed.* MICHAEL'S *coat hangs in tatters on him.* FATHER DOMINEER'S *face is begrimed with the smudges of smoke, and both look tired, but elated.*

ONE-EYED LARRY *at once runs out, and takes his place reverently behind them, standing with his hands folded piously in front of his breast, his eyes bent towards the ground.* MAHAN *straightens up, and* LORNA *and* MARION *return to the garden.* LORELEEN *remains as she was.*

FATHER DOMINEER [*as he enters with* MICHAEL]. Be assured, good people, all's well, now. The house is safe for all. The evil things have been banished from the dwelling. Most of the myrmidons of Anticlericus, Secularius, an' Odeonius* have been destroyed. The Civic Guard and the soldiers of Feehanna Fawl* will see to the few who escaped. We can think quietly again of our Irish Sweep. Now I must get to my car to go home, and have a wash an' brush up. [*To* MARION *and* LORNA] Off you go into the house, good women. Th' place, th' proper place, th' only place for th' woman. Straighten it out, and take pride in doing it. [*He shoves* MARION *towards the porch*] Go on, woman, when you're told! [*To* MICHAEL] You'll have to exert your authority more as head of the house.

MICHAEL [*asserting it at once – to* LORNA]. You heard what Father Domineer said. Go on; in you go, an' show yourself a decent, God-fearin' woman.

FATHER DOMINEER [*trying to be gracious – to* LORNA]. Th' queen of th' household as th' husband is th' king.

MARION *has gone into the house with a sour-looking face, and* LORNA *now follows her example, looking anything but charmed.*

FATHER DOMINEER [*turning to* LORELEEN]. And you – aren't you going in to help?

LORELEEN [*quietly*]. No, thanks; I prefer to stay on in the garden.

FATHER DOMINEER [*thunderously*]. Then learn to stand on the earth in a more modest and suitable way, woman! [*Pointing to ornaments on crest of hat and breast of bodice*] An' do you mind that th' ornaments ye have on of brooch an' bangle were invented be th' fallen angels, now condemned to everlastin' death for worshippin' beauty that faded before it could be clearly seen? [*Angrily*] Oh, woman, *de cultus feminarum malifico eradicum!**

MICHAEL. That one's mind is always mustherin' dangerous thoughts plundered outa evil books!

FATHER DOMINEER [*startled*]. Books? What kinda books? Where are they?

MICHAEL. She has some o' them in th' house this minute.

FATHER DOMINEER [*roaring*]. Bring them out, bring them out! How often have I to warn you against books! Hell's bells tolling people away from th' thruth! Bring them out, *in annem fiat ecclesiam nonsensio,** before th' demoneens we've banished flood back into th' house again!

MICHAEL *and* ONE-EYED LARRY *jostle together into the porch and into the house to do* FATHER DOMINEER'S *bidding*.

LORELEEN [*taking her leg down from the chair, and striding over to* FATHER DOMINEER]. You fool, d'ye know what you're thryin' to do? You're thryin' to keep God from talkin'!

FATHER DOMINEER. You're speakin' blasphemy, woman!

MAHAN. What do people want with books? I don't remember readin' a book in me life.

MICHAEL *comes back carrying a book, followed by* ONE-EYED LARRY *carrying another.* FATHER DOMINEER *takes the book from* MICHAEL, *and glances at the title-page.*

FATHER DOMINEER [*explosively*]. A book about Voltaire! [*To* LORELEEN]. This book has been banned, woman.

LORELEEN [*innocently*]. Has it now? If so, I must read it over again.

FATHER DOMINEER [*to* ONE-EYED LARRY]. What's th' name of that one?

ONE-EYED LARRY [*squinting at the title*]. *Ullisississies,** or something.

FATHER DOMINEER. Worse than th' other one. [*He hands his to* ONE-EYED LARRY] Bring th' two o' them down to th' Presbytery, an' we'll desthroy them. [LORELEEN *snatches the two books from* ONE-EYED LARRY. ONE-EYED LARRY *tries to prevent her, but a sharp*

*push from her sends him toppling over.* LORELEEN, *with great speed,
darts out of the gateway, runs along the pathway, and disappears.
Standing as if stuck to the ground*] Afther her, afther her!

MICHAEL [*astonished*]. Me legs won't move!

MAHAN AND ONE-EYED LARRY [*together*]. Nor mine, neither.


*As* LORELEEN *disappears, the* COCK *suddenly springs over the wall, and
pirouettes in and out between them as they stand stuck to the ground.*

*Cute ears may hear the quick tune, played softly, of an accordion, as the*
COCK *weaves his way about. The* SERGEANT *appears running outside, stops
when he sees the* COCK, *leans over the wall, and presents a gun at* MICHAEL.


MICHAEL [*frantically – to* SERGEANT]. Not me, man, not me!


*Terribly excited, the* SERGEANT *swings the gun till it is pointing at* MAHAN.


MAHAN [*frantically*]. Eh, not me, man!


*After the* COCK *has pirouetted round for some moments, while they all
remain transfixed, the scene suddenly goes dark, though the music continues
to sound through it. Then two squib-like shots are heard, followed by a
clash of thunder, and, when the garden enjoys the light of early dusk again,
which comes immediately after the clap of thunder, the music as suddenly
ceases.*

*The returning light shows that* FATHER DOMINEER *is not there; that*
MICHAEL *and* MAHAN *are stretched out on the ground; and that* ONE-EYED
LARRY *is half over the wall, his belly on it, his legs trailing into the garden,
his head and shoulders protruding into the road.*


MICHAEL [*moaning*]. Shot through the soft flesh an' th' hard bone!

MAHAN [*groaning*]. Shot through th' hard bone an' th' soft flesh!

ONE-EYED LARRY [*shouting*]. Mrs Marthraun, Marion, we're all killed
   be th' Cock an' th' Sergeant!


LORNA *and* MARION *come running out of the house over to the two prostrate
men.*


LORNA. What's happened? Where's th' Sergeant?

ONE-EYED LARRY [*sliddering over the wall, frantic with fear*]. I seen him
   runnin' off when he'd shot us all! I'm goin' home, I'm goin' home!

Father Domineer's been carried off be th' Demon Cock – I'm off!
[*He runs swiftly down the road, and disappears.*]

LORNA [*bending over* MICHAEL]. Where were you hit? D'ye think
there's a chance of you dyin'?

MICHAEL [*despairingly*]. I'm riddled!

LORNA [*feeling his body over*]. I can't see a speck of damage on you
anywhere, you fool.

MARION [*who has been examining* MAHAN]. No, nor on this fella either.

MICHAEL. I tell you th' bullet careered through me breast an' came out
be me back!

MAHAN. An' then tore through me back an' came out be me breast!

LORNA. What darkness was One-eyed Larry talkin' about? An' Father
Domineer carried off be the Cock! Me nerves are all gettin'
shatthered. It's all very thryin'. [*She pokes* MICHAEL *roughly with her
foot.*] Here, get up, th' both of yous. There isn't a thing wrong with
either of you.

MAHAN [*sitting up cautiously, and feeling in his breast pocket*]. What th'
hell's this? [*He pulls out a bullet bigger than a cigar.*] Looka, Michael
Marthraun, th' size of th' bullet that went tearin' through you an'
then through me! [*Very devoutly*] Good angels musta gone along
with it, healin' all at th' same time that it tore our vitals.

MICHAEL [*as devoutly*]. Some higher an' special power musta been
watchin' over us, Sailor Mahan. Sharin' a miracle, now, Sailor
Mahan, we're more than brothers.

MAHAN [*fervently*]. We are that, now; we are indeed. I'll keep this
bullet till th' day I die as a momento of a mementous occasion!

LORNA [*impatiently*]. Get up, get up. An' don't disturb us again while
we're practisin' for the fancy-dhress dance tonight in th' hope of
winning a spot prize.

MICHAEL [*furiously to her*]. You'll win no spot prize, an' there'll be no
dance till that Demon Cock's laid low! [*To* MAHAN – *piously*] Thrue
men we are, workin' in a thruly brotherly way for th' good of th'
entire community – aren't we, Sailor Mahan? That's what saved us!

MAHAN [*as piously*]. We are that, Michael; we are indeed; especially
now that we've settled th' question finally so long disputed between
us.

MICHAEL [*suspiciously, a note of sharpness in his voice*]. How settled it?

MAHAN. Be you arrangin' to give me, not only what I was askin', but
twice as much.

MICHAEL [*sarcastically*]. Oh, did I now? That was damned good of me!

[*Angrily*] No, nor what you were askin' either. D'ye want me to ruin meself to glorify you? An' didn't I hear a certain man promisin', nearly on his oath, he'd give his lorries for next to nothin' to serve th' community?

MAHAN [*shouting*]. When I was undher a spell, fosthered on me here! I'm goin', I'm goin'. I'll argue no more! [*He goes out by the gate and along the road, pausing as he is about to disappear.*] For th' last time, Michael Marthraun, are you goin' to do th' decent for th' sake of th' nation, an' give me what I'm askin'?

MICHAEL [*with decision – quietly*]. No, Sailor Mahan, I'm not. [*He shouts*] I'd see you in hell first!

MAHAN [*as he goes*]. A sweet goodbye to you, an' take a dhrug to keep from stayin' awake o' nights thinkin' of the nation's needs!

LORNA [*persuasively*]. Be reasonable, Michael. You're makin' enough now to be well able to give him all he asks.

MICHAEL [*savagely seizing her arm*]. Listen, you: even though you keep th' accounts for me, it's a law of nature an' a law of God that a wife must be silent about her husband's secrets! D'ye hear me, you costumed slut?

LORNA [*freeing herself with an effort*]. Don't tear th' arm out of me! If you want to embalm yourself in money, you won't get me to do it!

*The sound of the wind rising is heard now – a long, sudden gust-like sound, causing Michael to do a sudden rush towards the gate, pressing himself back all the time, and gripping the wall when he gets to it. The two women do not notice the wind.*

MICHAEL. Jasus! that was a sudden blast!

LORNA [*wondering*]. Blast? I felt no blast.

MARION [*shaking her head*]. He's undher a spell again.

ONE-EYED LARRY *comes running along the road outside, excited and shouting. He is holding on tensely to the waistband of his trousers.*

ONE-EYED LARRY [*without the wall*]. A miracle, a miracle! Father Domineer, outa th' darkness, was snatched from th' claws of the Demon Cock, an' carried home safe on th' back of a white duck!

LORNA [*amazed*]. On th' back of a white duck? When will wondhers cease! They're all goin' mad!

MICHAEL [*clapping his hands*]. Grand news! Was it a wild duck, now, or merely a domestic one?

ONE-EYED LARRY. Wild or tame, what does it matther? It carried him cheerily through th' sky, an' deposited him dacently down on his own doorstep!

MICHAEL [*with deep thought*]. It might well have been one of me own sensible ducks that done it.

ONE-EYED LARRY [*coming to the gate*]. Wait till I tell yous. Th' Demon Cock's furious at his escape, an' he's causin' consthernation. He's raised a fierce wind be th' beat of his wings, an' it's tossin' cattle on to their backs; whippin' th' guns from th' hands of Civic Guard an' soldier, so that th' guns go sailin' through th' sky like cranes; an' th' wind's tearin' at the clothes of th' people. It's only be hard holdin' that I can keep me own trousers on!

MICHAEL [*eagerly*]. Th' wind near whipped me on to th' road a minute ago.

*The* BELLMAN *enters on the pathway outside, and meets* ONE-EYED LARRY *at the gateway, so that the two of them stand there, the one on the left, the other to the right of it.*

*The collar and one arm are all that are left of the* BELLMAN'*s coat, and his shirt has been blown outside of his trousers. He is still wearing the brass hat. His right hand is gripping his waistband, and his left carries the bell that he is ringing.*

BELLMAN [*shouting*]. Get out, get in! Th' Demon Cock's scourin' th' skies again, mettlesome, menacin' molestifyin' monsther! Fly to your houses, fall upon your knees, shut th' doors, close th' windows! In a tearin' rage, he's rippin' th' clouds outa th' sky, because Father Domineer was snatched away from him, an' carried home, fit an' well, on th' back of a speckled duck!

ONE-EYED LARRY [*startled into anger*]. You're a liar, it wasn't a speckled duck! What are you sayin', fella? It was a pure white duck that carried th' Father home!

BELLMAN [*angrily – to* ONE-EYED LARRY]. Liar yourself, an' you're wrong! It was a speckled duck that done it; speckled in black, brown, an' green spots. I seen it with me own two eyes doin' th' thrick.

ONE-EYED LARRY [*vehemently*]. I seen it with me one eye in concentration, an' it was a duck white as th' dhriven snow that brought him to his domiceel.

LORNA. I'd say white's a sensible colour, an' more apter for th' job.

MICHAEL. I'd say a speckled duck would look more handsome landin' on a doorstep than a white fowl.

MARION [*thoughtfully*]. I wondher, now, could it have been Mr McGilligan's tame barnacle goose?

MICHAEL [*explosively*]. No, it couldn't have been Mr McGilligan's tame barnacle goose! Don't be thryin' to scatther confusion over a miracle happenin' before our very eyes!

*The* SERGEANT *comes rushing in along the pathway outside the wall, and runs into the garden through the gateway, roughly shoving the* BELLMAN *and* ONE-EYED LARRY *out of his way. His cap is gone, a piece of rope is tied round his chest to keep his coat on; and, when he reaches the gate, all can see that he wears no trousers, leaving him in a long shirt over short pants. He is excited, and his face is almost convulsed with fear and shame.*

SERGEANT [*shoving* ONE-EYED LARRY *and* BELLMAN *aside*]. Outa me way, you fools! [*Rushing into the garden – to* MICHAEL] Give me one of your oul' trousers, Mick, for th' love o' God! Whipped off me be a blast of th' wind me own were. When I seen them goin', me entire nature was galvanised into alarmin' anxiety as to what might happen next.

MICHAEL. A terrible experience! What's to come of us, at all!

SERGEANT [*tearfully*]. Why isn't Father Domineer here to help? He doesn't care a damn now, since he was carried home, safe an' sound on th' back of a barnacle goose!

ONE-EYED LARRY [*dumbfounded and angry*]. A barnacle goose? What are you sayin', man? It was a dazzlin' white duck that brought him home.

BELLMAN [*to* ONE-EYED LARRY]. I'm tellin' you it was a specially speckled duck that done it.

SERGEANT [*emphatically*]. It was a goose, I'm sayin'. Th' Inspector seen it through a field-glass, an' identified it as a goose, a goose!

LORNA [*amused – laying a hand on* MARION'*s shoulder*]. Look at him, Marion. All dollied up for th' fancy-dhress dance!

MARION [*hilariously*]. It's lookin' like th' blue bonnets are over th' bordher!*

MICHAEL [*angrily – to the* SERGEANT]. Get into th' house, man, an' don't be standin' there in that style of half-naked finality! You'll find some oul' trousers upstairs. [*Turning on* LORNA *and* MARION *as the* SERGEANT *trots timidly into the house*] You two hussies, have yous no semblance of sense of things past an' things to come? Here's a sweet miracle only afther happenin', an' there yous are, gigglin' an' gloatin' at an aspect in a man that should send th' two of yous screamin' away! Yous are as bad as that one possessed, th' people call me daughter.

*The sound of the wind now rises, swifter, shriller, and stronger, carrying in it an occasional moan, as in a gale, and with this stronger wind comes the* MESSENGER, *sauntering along outside the wall, sitting down on it when he reaches the end farthest from the house. Nothing in the garden is moved by the wind's whistling violence, except* MICHAEL, *the* BELLMAN, *and* ONE-EYED LARRY (*who have been suddenly hustled into the garden by the wind*). *These three now grip their waist-bands, and begin to make sudden movements to and fro, as if dragged by an invisible force; each of them trying to hold back as the wind pushes them forward. The* MESSENGER *is coaxing a soft tune from his accordion; while* MARION *and* LORNA *are unaffected by the wind, and stand staring at the men, amused by their antics.*

MICHAEL [*a little frantic*]. Listen to th' risin' evil of th' wind! Oh, th' beat of it, oh, th' beat of it! We know where it comes from – red wind on our backs, black wind on our breasts, thryin' to blow us to hell!

BELLMAN [*gliding about, pushed by the wind; holding on to his trousers with one hand, while he rings his bell with the other one*]. Fly into th' houses, close th' windows, shut th' doors!

ONE-EYED LARRY [*gliding in opposite direction*]. We can't, we can't – we go where th' wind blows us!

MESSENGER. What ails yous? I feel only th' brisk breeze carrying the smell of pinewoods, or th' softer one carryin' th' scent of th' ripenin' apples.

MICHAEL [*to the women, while he holds fast to his waist-band*]. Get in, an' sthrip off them coloured deceits, smellin' of th' sly violet an' th' richer rose, sequestherin' a lure in every petal! Off with them, I say, an' put on a cautious grey, or th' stated humbleness of a coal-black gown! [*The* SERGEANT *comes from the house wearing* MICHAEL's *best black Sunday trousers. He comes from the porch shyly, but the moment he steps into the garden, his face flashes into a grim look, and he grabs hold of the waist-band, and glides about as the others do.* MICHAEL, *seeing the trousers – with a squeal of indignation*] Me best Sunday black ones! Couldn't your damned plundherin' paws pounce on something a little lowlier to wear?

BELLMAN. Get into th' houses, shut to th' doors, close th' windows!

FATHER DOMINEER *suddenly appears on the pathway outside, and stands at the gateway looking into the garden. A gust of wind, fierce and shrill, that preceded him, declines in a sad wail, and ceases altogether, leaving a sombre silence behind it.* FATHER DOMINEER's *hair is tossed about; he has a wild look in his eyes, and he carries a walking-stick to help him surmount the limp from the hurt he got when warring with the evil spirits.*

FATHER DOMINEER [*stormily*]. Stop where yous are! No hidin' from the enemy! Back to hell with all bad books, bad plays, bad pictures, and bad thoughts! Cock o' th' north, or cock o' th' south, we'll down derry doh down him yet.* Shoulder to shoulder, an' step together against th' onward rush of paganism! Boldly tread, firm each foot, erect each head!

ONE-EYED LARRY, MICHAEL, BELLMAN AND SERGEANT [*together – very feebly*]. Hurraah!

FATHER DOMINEER. Fixed in front be every glance, forward at th' word advance!

ONE-EYED LARRY, MICHAEL, BELLMAN AND SERGEANT [*together – very feebly*]. Advance!

FATHER DOMINEER. We know where we're goin', an' we know who's goin' with us.

MICHAEL. The minsthrel boy with th' dear harp of his country, an' Brian O'Lynn.

BELLMAN. Danny Boy an' th' man who sthruck O'Hara.

ONE-EYED LARRY. Not forgettin' Mick McGilligan's daughter, Maryann!*

*Sounds of fifing and drumming are heard, mingled with the sound of booing, a little distance away.*

FATHER DOMINEER [*jubilantly*]. Listen to th' band! We're closin' in; we're winnin'! [*He puts a hand up to shade his eyes, and peers forward.*] They've collared one of them! Aha, a woman again! [*A*

*pause.*] A fine, familiar one too. [*He shouts*] Lead th' slut here,
Shanaar, right here in front of me!

*He goes through the gateway, and waits in the garden for things to come.*

SHANAAR *appears on the pathway, followed by the* TWO ROUGH
FELLOWS *dragging* LORELEEN *along. She is in a sad way. Her hair is
tumbled about; her clothes are disarranged; her bodice unbuttoned, and her
skirt reefed half-way up, showing a slim leg, with the nylon stocking torn.
One of the* ROUGH FELLOWS *is carrying her hat with its cock-like crest in his
hand. A blood-stained streak stretches from a corner of an eye half-way
down a cheek. Her face is very pale, and intense fright is vividly mirrored in
it. She is dragged by the arms along the ground by the men, led by*
SHANAAR, *to where the priest is standing. When she is nicely placed before
him, she hangs her head, ashamed of her dishevelled state, and of the way
she has been pulled before him. Other men and women follow them in, but
are checked from crowding the pathway by an order from the priest. The*
MESSENGER *rises from his seat on the wall, and comes near to where the men
are holding* LORELEEN. *He has placed the carrying straps of his accordion
over his shoulders, and now bears the instrument on his back.* MICHAEL, *the*
BELLMAN, *and* ONE-EYED LARRY *stand some way behind the priest.*
MARION *and* LORNA *have started to come to* LORELEEN's *assistance, but
have been imperiously waved back by* FATHER DOMINEER, *and have
retreated back towards the house, where they stand to stare at what
happens.* SHANAAR *stands at the gateway, gloating over the woeful
condition of* LORELEEN.

FATHER DOMINEER [*to those following the men dragging in* LORELEEN].
Go back; keep back there! Give th' honied harlot plenty of space to
show herself off in.
SHANAAR [*down to* FATHER DOMINEER]. Tell her off, Father; speak to
her in th' name of holy Ireland!
FATHER DOMINEER [*to* SERGEANT]. You go, Sergeant, an' keep them
from coming too close; [*to* SHANAAR] an' you, Shanaar, stand at the
opposite end to keep any others from pressing in on us. [*To the men
holding* LORELEEN] Bring her a little closer. [*The men drag her closer.*]
FATHER DOMINEER. Now, jerk her to her feet. [*The men jerk her
upright.*] Well, me painted paramour, you're not looking quite so
gay now; your impudent confidence has left you to yourself. Your
jest with heaven is over, me lass! [*To the men*] How did you ketch
her?

1ST ROUGH FELLOW [_with pride_]. We've been on her tail, Father, for some time. We ketched her in a grand car with a married man; with a married man, Father, an' he thryin' to put an arm round her.

2ND ROUGH FELLOW [_butting in to share the pride of capture_]. So we hauled her outa th' car, and hustled her here to you.

LORNA [_running over to the man nearest to her, and catching his arm_]. Let th' poor lass go, you cowardly lout! I know you: your whole nature's a tuft of villainies! Lust inflames your flimsy eyes whenever a skirt passes you by. If God had given you a tusk, you'd rend asundher every woman of th' disthrict!

FATHER DOMINEER [_angrily – to_ LORNA]. Get back to your place, woman! [_Shouting, as she hesitates_] Get back when I tell you!

LORNA _moves slowly away from_ LORELEEN's _side and goes into the house._

MARION [_as she follows_ LORNA _into the house_]. Dastard Knights of Columbanus, do noble work, an' do it well!

LORELEEN [_to_ FATHER DOMINEER – _appealingly_]. Make them let me go, Father, an' let me get into th' house! It was Sailor Mahan promised me enough to take me away from here that made me go to him. I shouldn't have gone, but I wanted to get away; [_brokenly_] get away, away! Five pounds he gave me, an' they took them off me, with th' last two pounds of me own I had left.

FATHER DOMINEER [_savagely_]. Sailor Mahan's a decent, honest soul, woman! A man fresh for th' faith, full of good works for clergy an' his neighbours. [_He bends down to hiss in her ears_] An' this is th' man, you sinful slut, this is th' man you would pet an' probe into a scarlet sin!

LORELEEN. I only wanted to get away. I wanted to get away from Sailor Mahan as much as I wanted to get away from all here.

FATHER DOMINEER [_to the_ TWO ROUGH FELLOWS]. Where's Sailor Mahan?

1ST ROUGH FELLOW. Th' people pelted him back to his home an' proper wife, Father, an' he's there now, in bed, an' sorry for what he thried to do.

LORELEEN [_plaintively_]. Make them give me back th' last few pounds I had.

FATHER DOMINEER [_to the_ ROUGH FELLOWS]. You shouldn't have handled Sailor Mahan so roughly. Where's the money?

2ND ROUGH FELLOW. We tore it up, Father, thinkin' it wasn't fit to be handled be anyone of decent discernment.

LORELEEN [*emphatically*]. They didn't; they kept it. [*Stifling a scream*] Oh, they're twisting me arms!

FATHER DOMINEER [*cynically*]. Don't be timid of a little twinge of pain, woman, for, afther th' life you've lived, you'll welther in it later. [*To the* TWO ROUGH FELLOWS] Yous should have kept th' money to be given to th' poor.

MESSENGER [*coming over to the* ROUGH FELLOW *on* LORELEEN's *right – calmly*]. Let that fair arm go, me man, for, if you don't, there's a live arm here'll twist your neck instead. [*With a shout*] Let it go! [*After a nod from the priest, the* 1ST ROUGH FELLOW *lets* LORELEEN's *arm go. The* MESSENGER *goes quietly round to the* 2ND ROUGH FELLOW.] Let that fair arm go, me man, or another arm may twist your own neck! Let it go! [*The* 2ND ROUGH FELLOW *sullenly does so.*] Now stand a little away, an' give th' girl room to breathe. [*The* TWO ROUGH FELLOWS *move a little away from* LORELEEN.] Thank you. [*To the priest*] Now, Father, so full of pity an' loving-kindness, jet out your bitther blessin', an' let th' girl go. An' thry to mingle undherstandin' with your pride, so as to ease th' tangle God has suffered to be flung around us all.

FATHER DOMINEER [*fiercely – to the* MESSENGER]. Keep farther away, you, for th' crowd is angry and their arms are sthrong! We know you – enemy to th' glow of tradition's thruth, enemy to righteous reprobation, whose rowdy livery is but dyed in rust from th' gates of hell! [*To* LORELEEN] An' you, you'd hook your unholy reputation to a decent man's life. A man, like Sailor Mahan, diligent in his duty, th' echo of whose last prayer can ever be heard when another worshipper enters th' church. You'd sentence him to stand beside you, you shuttle-cock of sin!

LORELEEN [*roused to indignation*]. Oh, end it, will you! You fail in honesty when you won't make them give me back what they robbed from me. When you condemn a fair face, you sneer at God's good handiwork. You are layin' your curse, sir, not upon a sin, but on a joy. Take care a divil doesn't climb up your own cassock into your own belfry!

FATHER DOMINEER [*furiously*]. You'll dhribble th' blackness of sin no longer over our virtuous bordhers! [*He hisses the words out*] *Stipendium peccati mors est!*\* Get away from here quicker than you came, or it's in your coffin you'll be – in your coffin, your coffin!

SHANAAR [*from the gateway*]. A merciful sentence, an aysey* one, for a one like her!

LORELEEN [*half defiantly*]. How am I to go where I'd like to go, when they took all I had off me? How am I to go for miles with me clothes near rent from me back, an' frail shoes on me feet?

FATHER DOMINEER [*putting his face closer to hers*]. Thrudge it; thrudge on your two feet; an' when these burn an' blister, go on your knees; an' when your knees are broken an' bruised, go on your belly; crawl in th' dust, as did th' snake in th' Garden of Eden, for dust is th' right cushion for th' like of you! [*He raises himself erect, and commands in a loud voice*] Go now!

LORELEEN *turns away, goes slowly through the gateway, and along the road outside. As* LORELEEN *reaches the gate,* LORNA *runs out of the house. She is wearing a dark-red cloak, and carries a green one over her arm. She has a fairly large rucksack strapped on her back.*

LORNA [*calling as she runs out of the house*]. Loreleen! [LORELEEN *halts but does not turn her head.*] Loreleen, I go with you! [LORNA *shoves* FATHER DOMINEER *aside at the gateway, nearly knocks* SHANAAR *over, and hurries to* LORELEEN. *Draping the green cloak over* LORELEEN's *shoulders*] I go with you, love. I've got a sthrong pair of shoes in the sack you can put on when we're free from th' Priest an' his rabble. Lift up your heart, lass: we go not towards an evil, but leave an evil behind us! [*They go out slowly together.*]

FATHER DOMINEER [*taking the* SERGEANT *by the arm*]. Let her go quietly to her own. We'll follow some of the way to prevent anyone from harming her. [*Down to* MICHAEL] Be of good cheer, Michael; th' demon is conquered – you can live peaceful an' happy in your own home now.

*He goes out with the* SERGEANT, *followed by all who may be there, except* MICHAEL, *the* MESSENGER, *and* SHANAAR.

*The* MESSENGER *goes back to the wall, sits on it sideways, takes the accordion from his back, and begins to play, very softly, the air of 'Oh, Woman Gracious'.* SHANAAR *leans on the wall from the outside, looking down at* MICHAEL, *who is now seated gloomily on a chair beside the table, an elbow resting on it, his head resting on the hand.*

SHANAAR [*down to* MICHAEL]. His reverence never spoke a thruer

word, Mick, than that of you'd have happiness an' peace now. You
were a long time without them, but you have them now.

MICHAEL [*doubtfully*]. Maybe I have, Shanaar, an', God knows, I need
them. [*He pauses for a moment, thinking*] I wondher will Lorna come
back?

SHANAAR [*emphatically*]. Oh, devil a come back! You need have no fear
o' that, man. An' fortunate you are, for a woman's always a menace
to a man's soul. Woman is th' passionate path to hell!

MESSENGER [*playing softly on his accordion and singing*].

> Oh, woman gracious, in golden garments,
> Through life's dark places, all glintin' go;
> Bring man, in search of th' thruth tremendous,
> Th' joy that ev'ry young lad should know.

> Then come out, darlin', in reckless raiment,
> We'll dance along through Ireland gay,
> An' clip from life life's rich enjoyments,
> An' never want for a word to say.

[MARION *has come into the porch, and now stands at the door, watching
the* MESSENGER. *She is covered to her knees by a bright-blue cloak.*]

> Cling close to youth with your arms enthrancin',
> For youth is restless, an' loth to stay;
> So take your share of th' kisses goin',
> Ere sly youth, tirin', can slink away!

[MARION *crosses the garden towards the gate, and is about to go through it
when the* MESSENGER *catches her by the arm.*] Would you leave me
here, alone, without a lass to love me?

MARION [*gently removing the hold of his hand on her arm*]. Your voice is
dear to me; your arm around me near seals me to you; an' I'd love to
have –

MESSENGER [*quickly*]. Your lips on mine!

MARION. But not here, Robin Adair, oh, not here; for a whisper of love
in this place bites away some of th' soul! [*She goes out by the gateway,
and along the road taken by* LORNA *and* LORELEEN. *The* MESSENGER
*stays where he is, wistful and still. Just before she goes*] Come, if you
want to, Robin Adair; stay, if you will.

SHANAAR [*to the* MESSENGER]. Stay, Messenger. Take a warnin' from a
wise oul' man, a very wise oul' one, too. [*He turns his head to look
peeringly to the left along the road*] What's this I see comin'? If it isn't
Julia, back from Lourdes, an' she on her stretcher still! I'd best be
off, for I've no inclination to thry a chatter with a one who's come
back as bad as she was when she went. [*He bends down nearly double,
so as not to be seen, and slyly and quietly steals away.*]

*After a pause,* JULIA *comes in on her stretcher, carried by the* TWO ROUGH
FELLOWS *as before,* HER FATHER, *silent and stony-faced, walking beside
her. The stretcher is laid down in the garden just inside the gate.* JULIA *is
covered with a rug, black as a winter's sky, and its sombre hue is enlivened
only by the chalk-white face of the dying girl. The* MESSENGER *has gone
from the gateway, and now stands in a half-to-attention, military way, a
little distance from the stretcher, looking down at* JULIA. JULIA'S FATHER
*stands, as before, behind her head.* MICHAEL *sits, unnoticing, elbow on
table, his head resting on his hand.*

JULIA [*in a toneless voice – to no one in particular*]. Lorna, I want Lorna.
MESSENGER [*gently*]. She's gone, Julia.
JULIA. Gone? Gone where?
MESSENGER. To a place where life resembles life more than it does
here.
JULIA. She's a long way to go, then. It's th' same everywhere. In
Lourdes as here, with all its crowds an' all its candles. I want
Loreleen.
MESSENGER. She's gone with Lorna, an' Marion's followed them both.
JULIA. Then there's no voice left to offer even th' taunting comfort of
asking if I feel better.
MESSENGER. There's Michael Marthraun there.
JULIA [*after a long look at Michael*]. He, poor man, is dyin' too. No-one
left, an' th' stir there was when I was goin' – th' Mayor there, with
all his accouthered helpers; th' band playin'; Father Domineer
spoutin' his blessin'; an' oul' Shanaar busy sayin' somersaultin'
prayers; because they all thought I would bring a sweet miracle
back. [*She pauses.*] There was no miracle, Robin; she didn't cure
me, she didn't cure me, Robin. I've come back, without even a
gloamin' thought of hope. [*She pauses again; with a wan smile*] I can
see your whole soul wishin' you could cure me. Touch me with your
questionable blessin' before I go.

MESSENGER [*very softly*]. Be brave.

JULIA. Nothin' else, Robin Adair?

MESSENGER. Evermore be brave.

JULIA [*after a pause*]. Dad, take me home.

*The* ROUGH FELLOWS *take up the stretcher and carry it out, the stony-faced* FATHER *following in the rear without a word.*

MICHAEL [*raising his head from his hand to look at the* MESSENGER]. Maybe Lorna might come back. Maybe I mightn't have been so down on her fancy dhressin'.

MESSENGER [*tonelessly*]. Maybe she will; maybe you mightn't.

MICHAEL [*tonelessly too*]. It'll be very lonely for me now. All have left me. [*He takes a set of rosary beads from his pocket, and fingers them.*] I've no one left to me but th' Son o' God. [*He notices the* MESSENGER *settling the accordion comfortably on his back, and watches him going to the gate.*] Are you goin' too?

MESSENGER [*shortly*]. Ay.

MICHAEL. Where?

MESSENGER. To a place where life resembles life more than it does here.

MICHAEL [*after a pause*]. What, Messenger, would you advise me to do?

MESSENGER [*turning at the gate to reply*]. Die. There is little else left useful for the likes of you to do.

*He swings his accordion comfortably before him, and plays a few preliminary notes. Then he starts to sing softly as he goes away along the pathway outside; while* MICHAEL *leans forward on to the table, and buries his head in his arms.*

MESSENGER [*singing and accompanying himself on the accordion – as he is going off*]

> She's just like a young star out taking the air –
> Let others be good or be clever –
>
> With Marion gay, a gay flower in her hair,
> Life becomes but a pleasant endeavour.

When building a city or making the hay,
I'll follow her close as night follows day,

Or lads follow lasses out nutting in May,
For ever and ever and ever!

CURTAIN

## SONGS IN *COCK-A-DOODLE DANDY*

### STAR OF THE SEA

Hail, Queen of Heav'n, the o - cean Star! Guide of the wand-'rer here be - low! Thrown on life's surge, we claim thy care, Save us from per - il and from woe. Mo - ther of Christ, Star of the Sea, Pray for the wan - der - er, pray for me.

### WHEN MEN WAS MEN

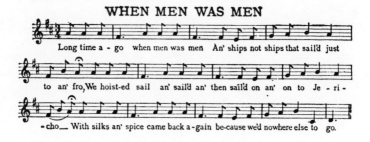

Long time a - go when men was men An' ships not ships that sail'd just to an' fro, We hoist-ed sail an' sail'd an' then sail'd on an' on to Je - ri - cho With silks an' spice came back a - gain be-cause we'd nowhere else to go.

### LORELEEN'S SHANTY

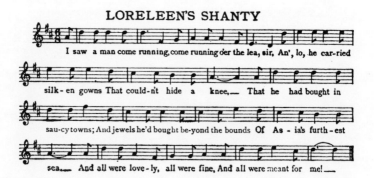

I saw a man come running, come running o'er the lea, sir, An', lo, he car-ried silk - en gowns That could-n't hide a knee, That he had bought in sau-cy towns; And jewels he'd bought be-yond the bounds Of As - ia's furth - est sea, And all were love - ly, all were fine, And all were meant for me!

## MUSIC FOR COCK'S DANCE

## OH, WOMAN GRACIOUS

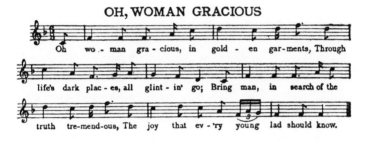

Oh wo - man gra - cious, in gold - en gar - ments, Through life's dark plac - es, all glint - in' go; Bring man, in search of the truth tre-mend-ous, The joy that ev - 'ry young lad should know.

## MARION

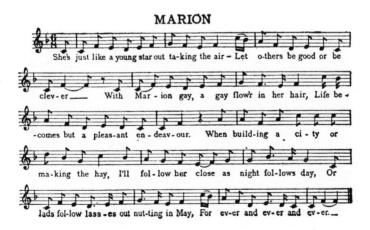

She's just like a young star out ta-king the air — Let o-thers be good or be clev-er.___ With Mar - ion gay, a gay flow'r in her hair, Life be - comes but a pleas-ant en - deav-our. When build-ing a ci - ty or ma-king the hay, I'll fol - low her close as night fol-lows day, Or lads fol-low lass - es out nut-ting in May, For ev-er and ev-er and ev-er.___

# The Bishop's Bonfire

## A Sad Play within the Tune of a Polka

Cad dhéanfamaoid feasta gan adhmad,
Atá deire na g-coillte ar lár.*


*To Susan gone and Susan here**

## CHARACTERS

DICK CARRANAUN (known as the PRODICAL), a mason
RICHARD RANKIN, another mason
COUNCILLOR (later COUNT) REILIGAN
THE VERY REV. TIMOTHY CANON BURREN
MANUS MOANROE
DANIEL CLOONCOOHY
KEELIN, Councillor Reiligan's daughter
CODGER SLEEHAUN
FATHER BOHEROE, a curate
FOORAWN, Councillor Reiligan's other daughter
LIEUTENANT MICHAEL REILIGAN, Councillor Reiligan's son
A RAILWAY PORTER


## PLACE AND TIME

*Act I*. Councillor Reiligan's house – outside window of drawing-room.
   Time: about 6 p.m. on an autumn evening.
*Act II*. The drawing-room of Councillor Reiligan's house. Time: later
   the same evening.
*Act III*. The same. Time: still later.

## ACT I

*The garden of* COUNCILLOR REILIGAN's *house. It is not a grand garden, but it is undergoing improvements. A red brick wall is being built at the back. At present it goes two-thirds of the way across the garden, part of it passing behind the house opposite, which is to the right. The finished part has a wrought-iron gate in its centre. To the left the remainder of it is being built, and is only half-way up to where the coping will be when it is finished. A platform runs along this part on which the masons stand while laying a string course to lift it higher. A few plants, a desperate aspect on them, have been planted along by where the wall has been built. Near the garden's centre is a portly, metal garden urn, moulded into twists and twines, set on a pedestal of new yellow brick. It stands pompously on its pedestal, though looking a little embarrassed that its one use is only to stand and not to serve. Behind the urn is a pile of bricks waiting to be moulded into the part of the wall the masons are building. To the left of the bricks is a rough bench on which a sack of cement stands. A little apart from the urn is a wheelbarrow with a long-handled shovel thrust into it, the blade resting in the barrow, the handle stretched out over the wider end of the barrow. The part of the house seen juts out from the right, crosses the garden diagonally, and mostly consists of a large semi-bow window opening on to the garden. Branches of an ash-tree spread out between the end of the house and the wall passing behind it, and under it can be seen, or partly seen, a garden chair with a gaily coloured canvas back and seat. Behind the wall, and through the iron gate, the fields and meadows belonging to* REILIGAN *stretch out to the view, and, beyond them, the skyline of the town's buildings, the highest of them, the church spire, thrusts itself up, looking like a stony stork rising from a fleecy nest of cloud. It is a warm, sunny day in the beginning of autumn, when nature gives a last rally and sings a song of colour before winter brings death to flower and field.*

DICK CARRANAUN – *known as* PRODICAL – *and* RICHARD RANKIN *are standing on the scaffold, each with a trowel in a right hand which they, alternatively, rattle and scrape over the surface of the wall's top.* RANKIN *is a man of about forty, long and lanky, a little bent at the knees, much more apparent when he is walking. His cheeks are reddish-brown, his head bald (he is now wearing a bowler hat, once black, but now turning green, and with its brim frayed by years and use) except for a mousy tuft over either ear and a faint ridge of the same hair at the base of the skull. He wears dark tweed trousers, stained with cement, brown waistcoat, and dark-blue shirt, fading now into a lighter blue colour. His eyebrows are so pale that they are*

*visible only when one is close to him, consequently, when his hat is off, his*
*face and head look somewhat like a bony skull in which the brown eyes still*
*burn, for he is what is known as a 'voteen', one somewhat obsessed with a*
*sense of ever-present sin, and his nostrils frequently sniff the fogs of hell. He*
*neither drinks nor smokes, and his one interest in women is to keep as far*
*away from them as possible. He chooses rather to pray than to whistle when*
*at work. He has the high, falsetto voice of a man unmade.*

PRODICAL *is long and lanky too, but whereas* RANKIN's *face is woeful*
*and sour, the* PRODICAL's *is sour and pugnacious. He, too, becomes*
*pregnant with a sense of sin after coming out of a drinking-bout, and, at*
*times, when he is in the centre of it. He is always deciding to give up drink*
*altogether, but – in spite of numerous pledges – never quite succeeds. A*
*thick, iron-grey moustache straddles his upper lip. He wears a blue*
*dungaree over his trousers, a patterned cotton shirt, and dirty red braces*
*keep his under trousers in a safe position. His iron-grey hair, bushy and*
*uncombed, is protected by a bowler hat of fading brown, and, as the day is*
*hot, he at times takes this off to wipe his forehead and the beading sweat*
*from the rim of the hat. Both masons wear common heavy boots, stained*
*with mortar.*

RANKIN [*dolefully*]. Daniel's gone long enough to have loaded a dozen
    waggons of hay since. He's stoppin' away a long time.
PRODICAL [*indifferently*]. He can stop away for ever, if he likes, far as I
    care. [RANKIN *is silent.*] An' you want the job to end so's to get away
    from me, eh? [RANKIN *is silent.*] Clamin' to be on your own. You
    can't abide to be near a decent, God-fearin' mortal whose one failin'
    is an occasional drink. [RANKIN *is silent.*] Not a word outa him! I try
    desperate to keep from it, but the strain's too much at times.
    [*Loudly*] You wouldn't want me to suddenly shoot asunder, would
    you? [*Wiping his forehead on the inner rim of his hat*] We couldn't idle
    on a better day. [*A pause.*] I haven't let a drop pass me lip these three
    days. I try desperate. [*Loudly*] You wouldn't like to see me burstin'
    asunder, would you? Have you no pity?
RANKIN. I am what I am.

COUNCILLOR REILIGAN *appears at the window, opens it, and allows* THE
VERY REVEREND TIMOTHY CANON BURREN,* *Parish Priest of Bally-*
*oonagh, to step out into the garden. The* COUNCILLOR *follows him. There*
*is a great scraping of trowels over the wall by the masons. The* CANON *is a*

*short man, below middle height, plump, and a little awkwardly built. His legs are short so that he seems to trot when he walks. The upper part of his head is perfectly round, but the jaws are rather coarsely square-set. His face is ruddy and deep lines flow from either wing of his nose to the curves of his lower lips; his upper lip is deep and protruding. His clothes seem to be ill-fitting; coat a little too big, the trousers coming down only a little below his boot-uppers. The two things about him that are spick and span are his collar and the canonical flash of purple under his chin. He wears a soft black hat, and carries an untidy-looking umbrella.*

COUNCILLOR REILIGAN *is a short man, less than medium height, stocky and sturdy, now developing an imposing paunch. His face is ruddy, weather-beaten, and wrinkled, looking older than his fifty-five years. He has small, piercing, pig-like eyes, and his chin and neck are hidden by a red beard, now turning grey. Reddish hair on his head has receded from the front so that the front half of his head is bald. He is dressed in morning clothes, frock coat, striped trousers, all a little too baggy for him, except that part of his clothing enclosing his waist. He is the biggest money-man in the district, a loyal pillar of the clergy, and has a great power and influence in the affairs of the state – the local member of the Dail\* could never climb into a seat without the backing of* COUNCILLOR REILIGAN. *He carries in his hand a silk tall-hat which he puts on when he enters the garden.*

CANON [*with finality*]. Manus Moanroe is not a person to have about the place, Councillor. I've said so before. You should remember he had an eye on your Foorawn\* before he became a seminarist and before she entered the convent. You know the scamp he has become since he flung his vocation away, and since he served in the English air force.

REILIGAN [*apologetically*]. I know, I know: an unfortunate poor man. Maybe, Canon, there's not much harm in him. He's been a godsend to me. With his checkin' things comin' in and things goin' out, and his wary way of keepin' me accounts, he musta saved me more'n half a thousand pounds.

CANON. You think too much of mere money-making, Councillor. I must remind you that there are more important things than even half a thousand pounds.

REILIGAN [*meekly*]. I know, Canon; sure, I know that; though Father Boheroe\* thinks something of Manus.

CANON [*with cold anger*]. *I* am Parish Priest of Ballyoonagh, Reiligan!

REILIGAN [*meekly*]. Sure, I know, Canon. I know [*To escape, he turns on the masons.*] What are the two of yous doin', standin' there motionless like gorged gulls airin' themselves on a quay-wall? Yous know the church tower has to be built well as the wall.

RANKIN [*in his high, falsetto voice*]. We're waitin' for Daniel to bring us the bricks.

PRODICAL [*in his deep baritone*]. Waitin' for Daniel to bring us the mortar.

REILIGAN [*mimicking them in turn*] Waitin' for Daniel to bring us the bricks; waitin' for him to bring us the mortar. [*Furiously*] Hop off the platform an' get them yourselves!

RANKIN. Masons is supposed to have the things brought to them.

PRODICAL. That's a labourer's job.

CANON [*to* RANKIN]. We're all labourers, Rankin. When you are working for the Councillor, Rankin, however menial the job may be, you are serving God. We want you masons for the church tower; so get a move on.

RANKIN [*jumping down and running to the bricks*]. Yis, Canon.

REILIGAN [*looking at his gold watch*]. We better be goin', Canon, if we're to be in time to meet Monsignor Mulligan. [*As they go towards the gate*] The wall'll look fine when it's finished. When it is, I'm goin' to have it covered with climbin' roses.

CANON [*petulantly*] Roses? Pshaw! What put such a useless idea into you head? Ballyoonagh hasn't the time to go wading through roses. Roses cost money, Councillor. The church needs money more than your wall needs roses!

REILIGAN. I know, I know, Canon; I only thought a rose here an' there might do no harm.

CANON. They mightn't and they might. They might provoke envy. Put nodding roses in this garden, and it wouldn't be long till others wanted nodding roses in theirs. I don't want the needs of our church to lie hidden in the petals of a rose.

REILIGAN. I know, Canon, I know. I like roses, tho' I don't know why: a foolish wish, Canon, right enough; but somehow, I always longed for a rose to lie in me Sunday coat.

*They go out by the gate, and pass by behind the wall, only their heads and shoulders showing.*

CANON [*as they pass on behind the wall*]. The coat's better without one. The wall itself, even, wasn't really needed. You'll have to guard yourself, Michael, against pride and vanity. Your wall will do fine without your roses. Roses indeed!

*They pass out on path behind the wall, the* CANON *leading the way, commenting on the roses; the* COUNCILLOR *meekly following.*

RANKIN [*indignantly*]. Roses indeed! We all know what happened before in a beautiful garden among the roses. Can't he plant ivy? It grows quicker, looks as well, costs nothin', an' sinful love can't quicken in it. Roses indeed! Our Blessed Lady's rose enough for Ballyoonagh.

PRODICAL [*contemptuously*]. Roses! Maybe it's roses he wants! Isn't he stuck-up enough without a rose gildin' a coat! I always liked a rose, says he. Goin' about himself like a blasted bonnie bunch of roses o! The Canon soon put an end to his dream. [*He takes up a brick from those that* RANKIN *has carried to the platform, and goes to lay it.*]

RANKIN [*whipping it from the* PRODICAL, *and laying it on his end of the wall*]. Eh, there, that's mine. Get your own bricks.

PRODICAL [*indignantly – as* RANKIN *is bedding it*]. You're a nice Christian cut-throat, denyin' a buttie* a few bricks! [*Admonitorily*] Remember what your Canon said that when you served oul' Reiligan, you served God; so as I'm servin' Reiligan, by servin' me, you're servin' God, too. [*He snatches the brick back angrily and starts to set it in his own part of the wall.*] Good Catholic an' all as you call yourself, you're not goin' to be let bounce yourself into an authority you've no legal or Christian right to! I'll not be bounced.

RANKIN [*indignantly*]. It's you's a bouncer, but I'm not goin' to stand you bouncin' away the bricks I carried over for meself! I'll not be bounced either!

PRODICAL *has tapped the brick home with the tip of the handle of his trowel, and now goes to take another brick from those beside* RANKIN; *but* RANKIN *pushes him away so that he has to jump down from the scaffolding.* RANKIN *then takes the brick* PRODICAL *has set, and starts to bed it in his own part of the wall.*

PRODICAL [*angrily getting back on to the scaffold and sending* RANKIN *off it with an angry push*]. Mind who you're pushin'! You're exhibitin' a nice kind of Catholic conduct.

RANKIN [*getting back on to the scaffold*]. I am what I am, but you'll not lord it over me. It's my brick – I carried it.

PRODICAL. It's not your brick an' it's not my brick; it's nobody's brick; if it's anybody's brick, it's God's brick.

RANKIN [*gripping* PRODICAL *by an arm and reaching for the brick which* PRODICAL *holds behind his back*]. It's mine rightfully. It's in my charge for the moment. Gimme it.

PRODICAL [*trying to pull his arm free*]. It'll do you good to be denied. The brick hasn't been designated to you. Let go!

RANKIN. You let go! It hasn't been designated to you either. Let go!

PRODICAL. I won't let go!

RANKIN. You'll have to let go!

*RANKIN pulls PRODICAL to the left, PRODICAL pulls RANKIN back to the right, their struggle bringing them to the edge of the scaffold, till one of the struggles forces them to jump off the scaffolding together.*

*MANUS has come in, and is seen behind the wall. He enters the garden by the gate, goes over to the barrow, sits down on a handle, and watches the couple disputing. He has a notebook and pencil in his hand. MANUS MOANROE is thirty or so, tall and well built. He looks slovenly now, with a beard of a week's growth, and a face lined more than his years warrant, warped by a sad and sullen look. He is wearing old air-force trousers, frayed at the bottoms, coarse boots beginning to go at the toes; his cotton shirt is soiled, and one torn sleeve but comes to the elbow. At the moment he is wearing neither waistcoat nor coat, though an old grey felt hat covers his head, its flabby brim pulled down over his eyes.*

*PRODICAL and RANKIN stand bunched together as if they were about to begin a bout of wrestling, one angry face glaring at the other equally angry one.*

PRODICAL [*gripping* RANKIN *by the shoulders and shaking him*]. I'll wrastle you if you want to wrastle! I'll bring back your Catholic conscience, you holy hoodlum, muckin' me about like you were on a prairie outa sight of God an' scholarship!

RANKIN [*now shaking the* PRODICAL *who has grown tired of shaking* RANKIN, *and is now panting*]. Call me what you like, but say nothin' against me religion! [*In a squeal*] 'Gainst me religion, see!

*Though gripping themselves in the manner of wrestling, the two boyos content themselves with shoving each other to and fro in a semi-rhythmic movement to the accompaniment of their arguments,* MANUS, *from his seat on the barrow, conducting the movements with mock gestures.*

PRODICAL [*vehemently*]. True religion isn't puffed up, you bastard; it's long-sufferin' an' kind, an' never vaunts itself like you do;* true religion doesn't envy a man a brick, you rarefied bummer!

MANUS [*angry and exasperated – flinging his notebook at them*]. Give over your fightin' for bricks of clay, the way Reiligan fights for the gold ones, you god-frightened fools! [*He gets up, and pushes them asunder.*] You spoilers of men's hopes and men's fancies; you curses on Ballyoonagh where the rust of hell is on everything that's done there.

PRODICAL [*indignantly – retreating to the scaffolding*]. What're you? Who are you to talk? You didn't do much for yourself. A dirty leaf torn out of a book. A labourer, no more, now. Now you're here, you bring us the mortar and the bricks we need.

MANUS [*picking up his notebook, and returning to the barrow – wearily*]. Oh, go to hell!

PRODICAL. You'd better do it. When we're done here, we're wanted to work on the church tower, and the Canon's in a hurry. He said so.

RANKIN [*sharp and strong falsetto*]. The Canon said so.

MANUS. And God stops talking to listen when the Canon speaks. Aw, go to hell, and carry the Canon along with you; [*fiercely*] on your backs takin' turns with the carrying, bring yourselves to hell, and bear the Canon with you!

DANIEL CLOONCOOHY *is seen coming behind the wall. He opens the gate, and enters the garden. He is young, twenty-five or so, and good-looking in a rugged way. His face is open and innocent, though sometimes shadowed with a furtive look; neither sure of himself nor sure of his future. He wears flannel trousers, tweed waistcoat, and carries an old grey coat over an arm. When he is in the garden, he drapes the coat over the wall, and goes to the barrow, sits down on it, opposite side to* MANUS, *takes out a cigarette, lights it, and begins to smoke.*

PRODICAL [*to* DANIEL]. Come on, Daniel, more bricks; hurry up! Attaboy! You couldn't have been that long tumblin' hay. We have a wall to build, lad; a duty to do.

RANKIN. More mortar, Daniel; come on, hurry up! We have our consciences to mind.

DANIEL [*to* MANUS, *ignoring the call – intensely and delightedly*]. The Codger has discovered a keg, Manus – a beauty! The wood was swellin' with the soaked-in juice left behind. He's drenched it gently with more'n half a gallon of boilin' water, an' left it to mature in the sun. I've tasted it, an' it's like the fire of love meltin' into dew.

MANUS. I know. I found the keg. He's bringing it here.

PRODICAL [*impatiently*]. Come on, Dan; more bricks here. We have to hurry. We have to get goin' on the church tower.

RANKIN. Canon said so.

PRODICAL. Some bricks, Dan. When we're done here, we've got to tackle the church tower.

RANKIN. More mortar, Daniel. Here today; church tower tomorrow. The Canon said so.

MANUS [*to* DANIEL]. Go on, Dan. [*He rises from sitting on the barrow.*] We have to keep building our temples higher and higher till the shouting of heavenly pride encases and hides the growling-grumble of men. The church tower, Dan; the church tower! [*He pushes* DAN *to the bricks.*] Go on! God is waiting. He mustn't be made to stand in a queue. [DANIEL *takes the barrow and trundles it under the ash-tree round to the back of the house. Manus looks at the pile of bricks, and glances at the bag of cement. Jotting down a few figures*] Another thousand bricks should do the job, and with the cement at the back, this bag here'll be enough.

DANIEL *returns to the farther end of the scaffolding with mortar in the barrow. He shovels some of it onto the mortar-board that lies between the masons; then shoves the barrow away to where it had been before.*

PRODICAL [*calling to where* DANIEL *has gone*]. Bricks now, Dan.

RANKIN [*calling as* PRODICAL *did*]. More bricks, Dan.

DANIEL *comes back, goes over to the bricks, and is about to collect them for the masons, when* KEELIN *appears at the window, and beckons him.* KEELIN *is a handsome lass of twenty-five. Her hair is a ripe auburn, more red than brown, and it surrounds her head in great fuzzy clusters, standing out from it so that it looks like a burning bush. Her figure is slim, though her breasts be buxom. She is dressed in a dark-green skirt, reaching just to her knees, a white blouse, amber nylon stockings, black shoes, and a lighter green apron, trimmed with dark red, protects her skirt and the front of her blouse from damage during housework.*

KEELIN [*beckoning to* DANIEL – *lovingly and softly*]. Come on in, Dan. They want your help to shift a wardrobe in a bedroom.

DANIEL *runs over and hurries into the house by the window.* KEELIN *blows a kiss to* MANUS, *a gracious kiss.*

RANKIN [*working last brick on scaffold into wall*]. Last brick goin' in, Dan. More bricks, more bricks.

KEELIN [*in a loud, sharp, and authoritative voice*]. Richard Rankin!

RANKIN [*wheeling round to face her at the sound of authority*]. Yis, Miss Keelin?

KEELIN [*roguishly lifting her skirt to above her knees*]. How do you like my nylons, darling?

RANKIN [*with an hysterical moan of shame-filled anguish*]. Ooh no; [*he wheels convulsively to turn his back to her.*] I didn't look, I didn't see!

KEELIN. Yes, you did.

RANKIN. No, I didn't.

MANUS [*to* KEELIN]. The nylons aren't as handsome as the legs, Keelin.

RANKIN [*revolving round to look at her again*]. I was taken unawares, I was. [*He revolves agitatedly to face away from her.*] So I was, I was. [*He revolves to look at her again – almost shouting.*] I won't look, I won't, I won't! [*He revolves again till he is facing away.*] Shoo her away, men. [*In a faint voice*] Oh, do, please! [*Exhausted, he half leans, half lies over the wall.*] I'm dizzy, I'm dazzled!

PRODICAL. God, man, take it easy! [*Shaking him*] You're not goin' to die.

MANUS [*with animation – to* KEELIN]. That was a sudden sight to make a young heart thrill thinking of things to come, and an old heart tremble thinking of things gone by!

KEELIN *bows to* MANUS, *blows him another kiss, points at* RANKIN, *and goes in again, leaving the window ajar.*

PRODICAL [*glancing round garden, and seeing no* DANIEL]. God damn it – where's that bastard, Dan, gone to now!

MANUS [*bitterly*]. Gone into the house and into hell, where his one aching desire will be to get Keelin into his arms, and her one desire to find herself there; but nothing will come to them save, maybe, an accidental touching of hands.

PRODICAL [*mocking*]. Them two'll never kiss in front of the Councillor's face or behind his back either. [*Down to* MANUS] Keelin's reckoned a lady, an' the moon will never shine on them two with their heads too close together.

MANUS [*fiercely*]. Shut up, you two wizened wisps of dust! You shadows of coming events to Daniel and to me! [*He sits dejectedly on the barrow's handles, musingly.*] Keelin, Foorawn, Daniel, me, you are on the swift way to become but dusty questions that life has never answered. No frond of a child's laugh shall ever spring from us.

PRODICAL [*down to him – scornfully*]. Have sense, man! Isn't it the laugh of the town an' district, him loungin' after Keelin, an' you loungin' after Foorawn?

MANUS [*fiercely*]. Shut up, I say, you neon light of ignorance and ruin! Oh, Foorawn, Foorawn, time shall toss wrinkles on to your sweet face, shall wither your breasts, shall bring your knees to a bending; but no bonny breeze of life shall ever blow your skirt aside.

PRODICAL [*down to* MANUS]. If it's all the same to you, Manus, we want no double-meanin' talk here.

MANUS. Oh, listen to them, look at them. Two of the people of God's hand, two sheep of his pasture! Away, you slimy touch of hell!

PRODICAL [*in a semi-shout*]. We believe in God, an' you don't!

RANKIN *has got down from scaffold and has gone over to the window.*

RANKIN [*at the window, calling plaintively into the room*]. Daniel, Daniel!

MANUS. I don't know which of you's the bigger bum* – him who thinks he's given to heaven, or you who know you're given to drink.

PRODICAL [*getting off the scaffold and going to* RANKIN *by the window – loudly and defiantly as he goes*]. I believe in God, an' you don't. [*Prodding* RANKIN's *arm*] Eh, Dick? We believe in God, an' he doesn't, don't we?

RANKIN [*plaintively*]. I don't want to be entered into the talk. He is what he is; you are what you are; I am what I am. I don't want to be led into a tangle of talk.

PRODICAL [*indignantly*]. Are you afraid to stand up for your religion, or wha'? We believe in God, an' he doesn't, don't we?

RANKIN [*with a plaintive yelp*]. Yis! [*Plaintively calling into the room*] Daniel, Daniel!

PRODICAL [*impatiently*]. Damn it, man, a mouse wouldn't hear that

call. Put some force into it, an' make it reverabate* through the
house. [*Shouting*] Daniel!

RANKIN [*just as plaintively as before*]. Daniel!

PRODICAL [*shouting*]. Daniel! Damn you, are you comin'? [*To* RANKIN]
Call out together – loud! Now!

PRODICAL [*loudly*]  
RANKIN [*plaintively*] } [*together*]. Daniel!

MANUS, *who has been risen from the barrow, and has gone to the left to
watch westwards, now meets the* CODGER* *coming in gloriously with a keg
on his left shoulder.*

*He is heard singing before he is seen, and continues when he appears.*

CODGER [*singing*].

Ah, them were the days when th' sickles were keen,
Th' barley bright yellow, the grass a rich green;
When our feet beat th' road on th' way to cut corn,
An' the dew turn'd the world to a diamond-clad morn.*

*The* CODGER *is eighty-four years old; but carries his age about with him in a
jaunty and defiant way. He is tall, thin, and wiry, his face deeply seamed
with many wrinkles from weathers and old age, and is strongly tanned, and
as tough as leather. His head is covered with a crisp, thick mop of white
hair, his upper-lip hidden by a white moustache, and his chin by a
shovel-shaped white beard; his dark eyes are alert and sparkling. He wears
old black trousers, caught up and held in place by a leather belt ornamented
and heavy with many brass badges of British regiments, a gaily chequered
cotton shirt, without a waistcoat, and his white hair is half covered by an
old, soiled, grey trilby hat. His old brown coat is slung over his right arm,
and his right hand holds the shaft of a hay-fork which he is trailing behind
him.*

*As he is crossing,* DANIEL *comes hurrying out of the house by the window,
shoving aside* RANKIN *and the* PRODICAL, *his eyes fixed on the keg the*
CODGER *is carrying.*

DANIEL [*shoving* RANKIN *and* PRODICAL *aside*]. Mind yourselves; get
outa the way.

PRODICAL [*seeing the keg*]. Ah, me sowl man,* Codger!

DANIEL [*running in front of* CODGER]. Come on, me sowl man – we'll dump it behind the laurels.

*He goes off past the ash-tree.* RANKIN *and the* PRODICAL *go back to the scaffold, get up on it,* RANKIN *scraping wall with his trowel, the* PRODICAL *fascinated by the keg.* MANUS *goes along with the* CODGER, *who halts beisde the ash-tree, and looks at it.*

CODGER [*gazing at the tree*]. The ash is beginnin' to shed its leaves already. Odd, how the old leaves drop so early an' the young ones come so late.

MANUS [*quoting*].

> Delaying as the tender ash delays
> To clothe herself when all the woods are green.*

CODGER [*fervently*]. Yet I love it; love it better than the beech herself.

MANUS. The ash, Codger, gave the wood for the shafts for the spears of the ancient Greeks, and for the pikes we used ourselves to free Ireland through the sad year of Ninety-eight.

DANIEL [*appearing round the tree – impatiently*]. What the hell's keepin' yous? Come on, Codger, with the keg.

*The* CODGER *goes on round the tree, followed by* MANUS. PRODICAL *is looking longingly after them. He gets down from the scaffold, is about to follow, but climbs back again, and keeps looking towards where they have gone.* RANKIN *is busy scraping the top of the wall, with one eye watching the* PRODICAL.

RANKIN [*persuasively*]. Be careful, man. Look the other way, Prodical. Have a little spiritual spunk, an' act as if the gin-keg wasn't there.

PRODICAL [*firmly*]. It is there, isn't it? I didn't call the keg into being, did I? I haven't the power to conjure the keg into bodiless existence, have I? I can't work miracles, can I? Your likes or dislikes isn't goin' to control the progress of the world. The keg's here now, an' can't be avoided, can it? We'll have to suffer it, like it, or dislike it.

RANKIN. There's the church tower to think of, too.

PRODICAL. That's a perspective contingency; a *primae facie*.* That other subject's a factuality of here and now.

RANKIN. You said a short time ago that it was goin' to be never again
with you.

PRODICAL [*protestingly*]. I'm not to blame for you overhearin' silent
things. What I murmured was sotto vossie.* I'm not a factotum to
me own whisperin's into me own ear.

RANKIN. It wasn't said sotto vossie. It was outspoken, an' next door to
a vow.

PRODICAL [*indignantly*]. It was no vow It had no habiliments of any
vow on it. It was a *sub rosa** understandin' or misunderstandin' with
meself.

RANKIN [*plaintively to* PRODICAL]. Your good angel's trying to pull you
back, Prodical; but if you once get to the keg, you're cornered!
It's an occasion of sin, an' may do immortal harm to your poor
soul!

PRODICAL [*coming over to* RANKIN *and thrusting his face upwards towards*
RANKIN – *indignantly*]. Looka, me good angel, I won't have you
hoverin' over me soul like a saygull over a fish too deep for a dive
down! I'm not goin' to let foreign bodies write down messages on
me soul the way a body writes down things on a Christmas card.
[*Preparing to jump from the scaffold*] Me soul's me own particular
compendium. Me soul's me own spiritual property, complete an'
entire, verbatim in all its concernment. [*He jumps down to the
ground, and goes to the tree.*]

RANKIN [*calling after him*]. If you'd only listen, you'd hear your good
angel callin' you back from the keg!

PRODICAL [*halting and turning round – annoyed at being checked*].
What's it to an angel if I go calmly after a keg? What's it to an angel
if I trot after a keg? [*He returns swiftly to the edge of the scaffold, and
glares angrily at* RANKIN.] What is it to the angel if I go at a gallop
after a keg?

RANKIN [*his back turned to* PRODICAL]. Aha, you're waverin'. You're
half afraid. I hear the shakin' in your voice.

PRODICAL [*beside himself with rage*]. You buttoned-up delusion, there's
ne'er a quiver in me voice! It's dense with concentration, but it's
under calm control.

RANKIN. Listen to your good angel's warnin'!

PRODICAL [*loudly*]. How the hell d'ye know what me own angel's
thinkin'? How d'ye know me own good angel isn't smilin'? How
d'ye know me own angel doesn't know what I do or don't do is me
fate? [*He goes again towards the tree.*]

RANKIN [*firmly – turning to shout after the* PRODICAL ]. My angel's tellin'
me to urge you to listen to your own angel's warning!

PRODICAL [*shouting back from where he stands at the tree*]. I'm not goin'
to have your angel interferin' with my angel! A keg here, or a keg
there, is no proper positive subject for an angel to bother about.

RANKIN [*positively*]. Like it or no, your good angel's at your elbow
drawin' you back from the curse in the keg!

PRODICAL [*in a wild shout*]. Listen you an' listen all! I don't want, an'
I'm not goin' to have, an angel always be me side to tap me on the
shoulder every time I stir! Tap tap tap!

*He makes off around the ash-tree, after the keg.* RANKIN *stands silent on the
scaffolding for a few moments; then he takes off his hat, and indulges in a
prayer; after the prayer, he gets down to the ground, goes over to the bricks,
carries some of them over to the scaffold, comes back to them, pauses, takes
off his hat again, and begins to pray.* KEELIN *comes to the window, looks
out and around the garden.*

KEELIN [*to* RANKIN]. Where's Dan? [*He takes no notice, but continues to
pray. She watches* RANKIN *for a moment, and then goes softly over to
him.*] Sweet man, d'ye never get tired prayin'? [*He is startled, slides
his hat back on to his head, but keeps his back turned to her.*] You know,
Mr Rankin, too much of a good thing may be bad for a man, while a
little of a bad thing may be good for him.

RANKIN [*resentful*]. God knows what is good for me.

KEELIN [*coaxingly*]. Don't be so sure: what you think God is thinkin'
may be only your own thinkin' formed in your own mind to satisfy
and please yourself. The other day, Foorawn said what you said to
Father Boheroe, but he laughed, laughed at her. The priest
laughed. D'ye know what he said?

RANKIN [*going at a jog trot to the ash-tree, halting there, cupping his hands
over his mouth, and calling*]. Daniel!

KEELIN [*following and standing behind him*]. Father Boheroe said that a
man learns what's good for him by experience; an', often, a woman
as well as God knew what was good for a man. So there!

RANKIN [*doing a jog trot back to the bricks, and lifting some to the
scaffold*]. I haven't time to talk; I have to get on with me work.

KEELIN [*following him*]. How d'ye know God lets you know what He
believes is good for you, anyhow?

RANKIN [*confused and embarrassed*]. You should know yourself – be mortification, prayer, and what the priest says.

KEELIN [*mocking*]. What about Father Boheroe then? He told me once that what a priest says to a layman isn't always evidence. He said too that a lot of what crawthumpers* like you tell us God said to them is nothin' but a conceited an' ignorant mind blatherin' to itself. Think of that!

RANKIN [*suddenly, stiff-standing, suspicious – vehemently*]. I don't want to think of it! [*Slyly*] You seem to do a lot of talkin' with Father Boheroe.

KEELIN [*cautiously*]. I do some talkin' as you do yourself. What about it?

RANKIN [*slyly with a touch of malice*]. Doesn't sound proper for a priest to talk too much to a good-lookin' girl. I seen a young swalla* this mornin'. Flyin' swift he was like he was carousin' close to heaven.

KEELIN [*hilariously*]. Now you do a carousin' close to earth, fancy boy. Never mind the flying swalla – there's a far prettier birdie standin' beside you now. It's nice to know Father Boheroe thinks me good-lookin', an' nicer, darling, when you look at me, you think so too.

RANKIN [*head bent lower still*]. I didn't look at you, I don't look at you. The swalla musta been a young one; alone there, up so high, dancin' like in a wide, wide space of blue light.

KEELIN [*teasingly*]. Look at me, now, an' never mind the swalla. You must have looked at me to know I'm good-lookin'.

RANKIN. I never looked; not the way I looked at the swalla. The knowin' about it came out in the talk I heard from others. I never looked; only at the swalla up high away from man in a wide world of his own.

KEELIN. You're just tryin' to be shy, dear. Now's your time to have a long ravishin' look at me. [*She slips round to face him.*] Look at me the way you looked at the dancin' swalla.

RANKIN [*swiftly turning his back to her – confused*]. Your Da wants to put roses along the wall. Roses along the wall, the wall. Can't he put ivy there instead? Looks as well; costs nothin'.

KEELIN. Yes, yes, ivy would be grand, an' then, like the ivy, I'd cling to thee!*

RANKIN [*agitated and confused*]. Yis, yis; no, no, no! The wall. Oh, go away, Miss. [*With as loud a shout as he is capable of*] Daniel!

KEELIN [*reproachfully*]. Now, don't be so rude as to turn your back on a good-looking lady. Here, do something to keep you from the sin of idleness. [*She slips round to face him, pulls up her skirt as far as her knee, and shows a trim leg in a nylon stocking.*] Stoop down and tie my shoe-lace tighter, and mind you, no naughty tricks! Look, and let yourself live for a minute!

RANKIN *gives a shuddering, frightened start when he sees the nyloned leg, jerks his head up from the sight, looks* KEELIN *in the eyes for a second, then viciously spits in her smiling face. Surprised and startled, she jumps back, searching frantically in a pocket for a handkerchief.* RANKIN *hurries away to the scaffold, jumps up on it, picks up his trowel, plunges it into the mortar remaining on the mortar-board, and appears to be very busy.*

KEELIN [*violently wiping her face with her handkerchief*]. You dirty, evil-minded lugworm! You huckster* of hollow an' spiteful holiness! You get! [*She hurries to the window, turning when she gets there, to throw a few more angry words at him.*] Looka the fella who wants to be great with God! Christ, you'll make a commotion when you get, you get, to where you're goin'! Crawlin' to heaven the way the snake crawled outa Eden! Damn you, you God's remorse for men!

RANKIN [*almost wailing*]. Daniel! [*To* KEELIN] I'll tell the Canon all you said, me lassie.

KEELIN [*furiously*]. Tell the Bishop, you canting cod; tell the Pope, you blob of dung! [*She goes into the house by the window, closing it angrily after her.*]

*After a pause through which* RANKIN *works at the wall,* FATHER BOHEROE *saunters in by the path behind the wall. When he comes in by the gate, we see that he is in his early thirties, and of middle height. His clerical clothes are old and beginning to fade, with creases in coat, vest, and trousers; only the white collar is without one. His face is a rugged one, surmounted by a thoughtful, wrinkled brow; but his eyes are bright, searching at times, but often somewhat sad and thoughtful; though they are not incapable of a roguish twinkle or two when he sees or hears some foolish thing said or done by some foolish mortal. His boots are strong ones, dusty and somewhat muddy with much walking. He wears no hat, but his dark and bushy hair protects his head well from rain or sun. A man of the world as well as a man of God. He strolls over to where Rankin is working.*

FATHER BOHEROE. Good day, mason.

RANKIN [*whipping off his hat*]. Good day, Father.

FATHER BOHEROE. Put your hat on. It's warm today. Where are your butties?

RANKIN [*righteously*]. I'm sorry to say, Father, that they're all gathered round a keg, among the laurels, drinking.

FATHER BOHEROE [*brightly*]. Ah, trying to get a glimpse of heaven through the wrong window. We often do that, too, through false piety, or through foolish sin. So that was why I heard Keelin shouting as I came along – urging them to come back to their work?

RANKIN. I wasn't listenin'; I thought I heard a voice. I was busy thinkin' only of the work I was doin'.

FATHER BOHEROE. The work; ah yes, the work. Never-ending work, yet few fruits come from it. [*Musing*] Just a little life. No colour, no thought; lean cattle, thin milk; worn-out meadows giving dusty hay; not a single building calling a halt for a look at it; not even the tawdry church.

RANKIN [*shocked*]. The church, Father? Oh, Father, the church. I'd be afraid to say anything against a sacred place.

FATHER BOHEROE [*impatiently*]. All places are sacred, man; the church we pray in, the homes sheltering us, the shops where we get the things we need to go on living, the halls we dance in; yea, the very place we walk on is holy ground. Work, too, is holy, but only when it's reasonable. Work, Rankin, can bless, but it can blast, too, as it is blasting little Keelin, who should be living with a gay young lad in a house of her own.

RANKIN. Keelin, is it? Anyone here'll tell you, Father, there's ne'er a man in Ballyoonagh fit to marry into the family.

FATHER BOHEROE. They say that, do they? An' what does God say, I wonder?

RANKIN [*frightened*]. I dunno. [*He moves to part of platform nearest to ash tree – calling*] Daniel! [*To* FATHER BOHEROE] Ballyoonagh's holy, Father, an' we have to put down anything that doesn't fit into what we know God doesn't like.

FATHER BOHEROE [*suddenly catching hold of* RANKIN *as if he were frightened*]. Whisht! Did you hear that sound of rending?

RANKIN [*greatly startled*]. What sound? Oh, what sound of rending, Father?

FATHER BOHEROE. The sounds of clawing hands, of pious fools tearing God's good manners into little pieces!

RANKIN [*gasping*]. Sacred Heart, you frightened me! I dunno, I dunno; I was only thinkin' of Keelin an', an', an' of Dan an' of meself.

FATHER BOHEROE. Ay, of Keelin, of Dan, and of yourself. Keelin's a fine girl but works too hard for too little. Too much work misfits a soul for heaven and for here, Rankin. Keelin's a grand girl, an' should have a wide an' merrier corner in life. Too much formal prayer, Rankin, sometimes makes a soul conceited; and merriment may be a way of worship!

RANKIN [*viciously*]. It's mostly merriment with her right enough. It's often said, Father, she does very queer things at times.

FATHER BOHEROE. Is it, now? Oh, well, it was said of our Blessed Lord that He did very queer things at times. Maybe He did; maybe she does too. If I only knew her moments of merriment, I'd join her. [*Suddenly – to* RANKIN] Are you in love with Keelin by any chance?

RANKIN [*fiercely*]. What, me? That one! No, I amn't, I amn't, I amn't! A one that waits only for the beck of a finger to laurel herself with light livin'! [*With clenched teeth*] I hate the evil Eves who send men sidling into sin!

*Before* FATHER BOHEROE *can get out of his surprise at Rankin's vehement protests, the* CODGER *appears, returning to the garden by the ash-tree. He is trying to walk upright like a guardsman. His eyes have something of a wild light in them, excited rather than drunk, but, all the same, half-lit with diluted gin. He goes towards the heap of bricks, the hay-fork over his shoulder like a gun.*

CODGER [*jovial but dignified*]. Good morrow, good Father; good morrow again. Rare day. Day for the beatin' of a big drum! Brrum brrumm! I'm the sole Sleehawn left standin' here in Ballyoonagh. Wife dead (rest her soul), two daughters an' three sons away, away in America, leavin' me the one lone, mohican* Sleehawn left standin' in Ballyoonagh, Fly away, Peter, fly away, Paul; fly away, Susan, fly away all – a fly-away country,* this of ours. Father; this country of ours. Man has to set his face to face things, eh, Father? God's more than a mere melodeon-player. Yis, man has more to do than just sing for his supper. Be rights, I should be helpin' with the hay. Hay, is it? God! No heart in the soil, no heart in the grass that tops it. Hay from grass that never had a life. I suppose I shouldn't say these things, Father, to you, anyhow.

FATHER BOHEROE. Why not, Michael, when they're true? God is unhappy when we don't do what we can with what He gives us.

CODGER [*emphatically*]. 'Course He is! A man's more than a mayfly; though the dance of the mayflies itself has a midget glory of its own. [*He sits down on the bricks.*] That's what we have now – a midget glory: [*pauses – musingly and liltingly*] slower and slower and slower the wheel swings, lower and lower and lower the reel rings.*

*DANIEL now comes in marching as the* CODGER *marched in before him. He goes to the bricks, takes up two, goes to scaffold, and dumps them down on it. He returns to the bricks for more, never bending as he marches.*

CODGER [*taking out an old pipe, and lighting it*]. Take it easy, Daniel, take it easy.

*The* PRODICAL *now comes in marching as the two before had done. He goes to mount the scaffold, but though able to balance on two legs, he fails to do it haughtily on one, so he loses his balance, and suddenly grips hold of* RANKIN, *who holds on to the wall, and so the* PRODICAL *manages to pull himself up, pull himself together, and, at last, stand as erect on the platform as he had stood on the ground.*

PRODICAL [*as he loses balance*]. Woa! False step. Uups a daisy!* I feel fine, gentlemen. Men at work, Father. No finer sight in nature. No, none. [*Shoving* RANKIN *from him*] Move over, an' let a man get goin'. [*He does mime movements of a dance.*] You promenade down the centre an' split the way in two, go through the open window, an' swing your Sindy Sue!*

DANIEL [*to* FATHER BOHEROE]. You know, Father, that the Bishop is comin' to Ballyoonagh; comin' to his own home town; Bill Mullarkey that was;* the one who older people know as a kid runnin' wild through the streets of Ballyoonagh.

FATHER BOHEROE [*unimpressed*]. Is he? Oh, yes; I remember the Canon told me about it. A great time coming.

CODGER. Faith, Bill Mullarkey'll be handier with a hay-fork than he'll ever be with a crozier.

PRODICAL [*to* CODGER]. No blasphemin', you. [*To* FATHER BOHEROE] Manus told us, Father. I feel fine. He's comin' all right; comin' in his purple cassock, golden mitre, an' satin shoon. Nothin' grander – purple an' gold, with the sheen of satin on them all.

RANKIN. A great time coming.

CODGER. What are the things that God gives to one man to the things God gives to all? What's the gold on a bishop's mitre to the gold on the gorse? The sheen of his satin shoon to the feel of a petal on the wildest rose? What's a bishop's purple to the purple in the silky plume of the speary thistle?

PRODICAL. Still an' all, the Bishop'll bring a few golden days to Ballyoonagh.

CODGER. Ay, golden days of penance an' prayer [*indicating* RANKIN] for God's gaum* there; but not for me. Me golden days is over. [*He chants gaily and a little gloomily*]

Ah, them were th' golden days with an arm round a waist,
When everything shone so shy an' gay;
When a man had heart to toss the girls as well as time to toss th' hay –
Oh, them were th' days when life had something fine to say!

PRODICAL [*warningly*]. Now, now, Codger! [*To* FATHER BOHEROE] Ay, an' Reiligan has a gang sweatin' mill-streams buildin' a great bonfire to light a welcome to the comin' Bishop, an' piles of bad books an' evil pictures on top of it are to go away in flames.

RANKIN [*stuttering with rage*]. Pitch them in, all in – bad pictures, bad books – pitch them into the burnin' bonfire!

CODGER. Reiligan ought to pitch his hay into it, too, for there's none of God's growin' in it. [*He rises up from sitting on the bricks.*] Be God, I'll go an' tell him!

KEELIN [*appearing at the window*]. Me Da's on the phone, Father. He asked if you were here. I seen you from a window upstairs. He says he has news for you. Will you come in, Father?

CODGER [*to* FATHER BOHEROE]. In with you, Father, an' tell him to do the decent thing be makin' a bonfire of Ballyoonagh, Bishop, books an' all!

FATHER BOHEROE *crosses over and goes in by the window with* KEELIN *to the house.*

PRODICAL [*gaily*]. Now then, let's get goin'! Come on, Dan, loads of brick an' mortar till we cope the wall, an' cry *finis*.

DANIEL [*indicating bag of cement on the bench – to the* CODGER]. Come on, an' give's a hand to carry this to the barrow.

CODGER [*contemptuously*]. Give you a hand! Didja hear him? [*Angrily*] Why, man, when I was your age, I'd carry that between me finger an' me thumb! Put it on your back, man, an' show you're no cissy.*

DANIEL [*resentfully*]. You put it on your back, if you're so eager.

CODGER. Ay, an' carry it where it's to go, without losin' a breath.

DANIEL [*sneering*]. You crazy old fool, you can't even handle your rosary beads without puffin'!

CODGER [*shoving* DANIEL *from the sack*]. Get outa th' way! I'll show you! [*He turns his back to the sack, and grips it by the lugs.*] I'll show yous all!

PRODICAL [*over to the* CODGER]. You let that alone, an' go back to your harmless hay!

CODGER [*giving the sack a vicious tug on to his back – as he starts on his journey*]. I'll show yous all!

DANIEL [*frightened – warningly*]. Steady! [CODGER *starts off at a trot facing towards the window; the weight is too much for him, and his trot grows into a gallop; he has to run to save himself from falling on his face. The others watching him are stupefied,* DANIEL *standing stiffly upright,* PRODICAL *bending forwards from the scaffold, his mouth wide open;* RANKIN, *seeing what is going to happen, turns his back, crosses himself, takes off hat and bends his head in prayer. Calling after the* CODGER *in a frightened effort to stay the rush*] Eh!

*As the* CODGER *comes near to the window,* REILIGAN *enters on the path behind the wall, sees what is happening, and stares across the wall in bewildered amazement. The* CODGER *turns half-sides on reaching the window, hits it with a bang, and the window bursts open, so that the* CODGER, *sack and all, goes on headlong into the room.*

REILIGAN [*agonisingly*]. Oh, what's this, what's this? What's the rascal done? [*To the others*] You muted jays, who ordered him to carry a sack of cement through me grand drawin'-room; over me carpet, me new carpet, laid special for the Bishop? [*The* PRODICAL *is busy with the wall, back turned to the world and* REILIGAN; RANKIN, *though working, is still praying;* DANIEL *is busy stretching up from the ground to fumble with the bricks on the scaffolding, his back, too, turned towards* REILIGAN. *All remain silent. Furious*] Answer! One of yous! Who told the Codger to make a passage-way through me drawing-room to carry stuff to the east side of the house? [*Silence. He pulls the*

PRODICAL *off the scaffold.* ] Oh, come off the scaffold, an' answer me, man!

PRODICAL [*resentfully*]. He had to go somewhere! He was in before I started to wonder where he was goin'!

DANIEL [*solemnly*]. He musta taken the wrong turnin'.

REILIGAN [*still in agony*]. Ooh! An' I wanted Keelin to help in pluckin' fifty ducks for tomorrow's market! Now, she'll be all night cleanin' me new carpet laid down to make the world soft under the Bishop's feet! [*He jumps up onto the platform, and pushes* RANKIN *so violently in the back that he is bent in two over the top of the wall.* ] You, you prayin' gaum, you answer!

RANKIN. I dunno; I wasn't watchin'.

REILIGAN [*shoving him aside – disgustedly*]. You prayer-gasper, if you prayed less, you'd see more! [*He jumps from the scaffold, his glance catching sight of the bricks. He pulls* DANIEL *over to them.* ] Didn't I say them bricks were to be put behind the house? Can't you see they're spoilin' the look of the lovely urn? [*He looks into the urn.* ] Oh, which of you monkey-souled jays are shovin' cigarette butts an' old papers into me garden urn, makin' a dust-bin of it? [*He pushes* DANIEL'*s head down towards the urn.* ] Looka there. Who threw them in? D'ye hear me askin'? Is your tongue palsied, or what?

DANIEL [*sullen*]. Eh, steady, there.

REILIGAN [*furious*]. Clean it out, out, an' take the bricks away!

KEELIN *appears at the window, her dress and her face dusty with dry cement. She has a sweeping-brush in her hand, and is half tearful.*

KEELIN. What the hell did yous let the Codger do? The carpet's half-way ruined, yella with cement; dust over everything when the sack burst. The brush is no good – instead of brushin' it out, it brushes it in. [*She shakes the brush, and a cloud of cement dust floats into the garden.* ]

REILIGAN. Clean if off, girl, clean it off! Get the carpet clean, an' then go to give a hand to the pluckin' of the fifty ducks for tomorrow's market.

KEELIN [*indignantly*]. I'll do no such thing. I've been long at you to get one of them machines pluckin' a bird in a few seconds that would take us an hour to do.

REILIGAN [*furious*]. That's what yous all want – machines! So's yous all can sit soft on your backsides watchin' the machines workin'.

[*Angrily and impatiently*] Get the carpet done first, girl; get the carpet clean!

KEELIN. I don't know how I'm goin' to do it. It'll take me all night. It's in a terrible state. An' we're as bad. It's all in our eyes an' up our noses.

REILIGAN [*near out of his mind*]. A terrible state! [*To the others*] Didjas hear that, you bunch of destituted owls! Near a ton of raw cement spilled over, lashed down, on me new carpet, an' not a soul of yous lifted a finger to save it! Yous didn't hear, did yous? [*In a great shout*] She'll be up all the night cleanin' it! A new carpet that I had laid down so's the Bishop could walk over the room with dignity an' warmth. A carpet alight with colour an' alert with good taste.

KEELIN [*dolefully*]. It'll never be the same carpet again.

REILIGAN [*in agony*]. Never be the same carpet again! Didjas hear that? Not a sigh of a sound from any of yous! An' I left the Codger quietly tossin' over the hay [*He jumps on to the scaffold, catches* RANKIN *by the shoulders, and shakes him.*] What was the Codger doin' here, what was the Codger doin' here?

RANKIN. I dunno; he didn't say.

REILIGAN. He didn't say, an' you didn't ask him. [*He grips the* PRODICAL *and shakes him.*] What was the Codger doin' here, you?

PRODICAL [*angrily*]. How the hell do I know?

KEELIN [*impatiently*]. Aw, Da, for goodness' sake, send someone in to carry the Codger out, an' take away the burst bag before the cement eats into the carpet.

REILIGAN [*furiously*]. Eatin' into it while yous stand there dodderin' into doin' nothin' to help. [*With a yell*] Go on, go on in, an' try to save what's left of me new carpet! [*He pushes* PRODICAL *towards the window.*] Go on, you. [*He pushes* DANIEL *towards the barrow.*] Get the barrow, man, to wheel the sack away. [DANIEL *wheels the barrow to the window. The* PRODICAL *goes into the room.* RANKIN *stays on the scaffold, his back turned towards the turmoil.* KEELIN *lingers at the window.* REILIGAN *in a rage jumps on to the scaffold, catches hold of* RANKIN, *and pulls him on to the ground. Pushing* RANKIN *towards the window*] Oh, you menacer, turn your face to where the trouble is, an' not be lardin' your skimpy soul with maudlin mumbles, settin' the saints above wonderin' why they aren't deaf. Come outa your booze of prayin' for a minute to help our Christian humanity on its way!

REILIGAN *shoves him into the house after the* PRODICAL. DANIEL *wheels the barrow to the window.* PRODICAL *and* RANKIN *come out carrying the burst bag of cement which they place on the barrow, and* DANIEL *wheels it away behind the house, past the ash-tree, coming back to the garden with the barrow when he has left it there.*

*As the work goes on,* FOORAWN *comes past the ash-tree, and comes out into the garden. As she comes out to the garden,* MANUS *is following her but stops beside the ash-tree, and leans against it, watching her.* PRODICAL *and* RANKIN *have gone back into the house to get the* CODGER. FOORAWN *is tall and handsome, twenty-seven years of age. She has large blue eyes, brown hair that shows reddish gleams within it; it is thick and long, and is pulled back from a white, narrow forehead, to be arranged in a thick bun resting on the nape of her white neck. She tries to give her fair face a look of resolute and austere serenity. She is dressed in a black, tailor-made suit, which is meant to be solemn and sober, but which plainly hints at the slim, trim figure beneath it. A thin gold chain encircles her neck, its two ends meeting to hold up a red enamel cross hanging on her breast. A blue mantle covers part of her glossy brown hair, and a belt of the same colour encircles her waist. The men, whenever they pass her, lift their hats respectfully in tribute to her reputation for piety, and in reverence for the vow of perpetual chastity with which she has burdened herself. She tries to keep her eyes turned modestly towards the ground, but doesn't always succeed, for her years are few and her heart is young and yearning. She looks the other way, but steals a glance or two at* MANUS, *then drops her look to the ground at her feet again.*

FOORAWN [*to* REILIGAN]. I'm goin', Da, to say a few short prayers to bless the Bishop's welcome. [*She notices his agitation.*] What's goin' on here? What's happened?

REILIGAN [*to* FOORAWN – *irritably*]. All right, all right, go, but get outa the way! It's desolation's goin' on here, that's what; so go on, you, for prayers are no use here now.

MANUS [*loudly, and with some mockery in his voice, from his place near the tree*]. An' say a few, too, for the Bishop's bonfire!

*She flashes a timid and longing look at* MANUS, *but quickly lets her glance fall towards the ground again.*

FOORAWN [*to* REILIGAN]. I won't be long, Da. [*She goes out by the gate.*]

KEELIN [*as* FOORAWN *goes towards the gate, and is walking off behind the wall – maliciously*]. If I know anything, there's silk knickers an' nylon stockin's under the skirt that feels so sober an' looks so black. Why doesn't your old threadbare mouth order her to help a little about the house?

REILIGAN [*angrily*]. You know why. She belongs to God, an' is separated from menial work – her for prayer an' you for work. [*More angrily*] Go in, I tell you, an' finish the carpet, an' then get on with the pluckin' of the ducks! [*He pushes her in.*]

*Now the* PRODICAL *and* RANKIN *come out to the garden, helping the* CODGER *out of the room. His face and clothes show how well the sack of cement had scattered its dust. They let him sink down to sit by the window, and recline himself against its sash. He reclines quiet, his eyes closed.*

PRODICAL [*advising*]. Leave him quiet, now, till he gets back his *status quo*.

REILIGAN [*angrily – down to Codger*]. Why are you here? Why didn't you stay turnin' the hay? You knew what the turnip-fly has done – more than half the crop riddled an' useless. How'r we goin' to winter-feed the cattle without the good help of the hay? [*Shouting*] Why'd you come here to demonstrate destruction? Why didn't you stay with the hay?

CODGER [*without the opening of an eye*]. God, he calls the hay hay!

REILIGAN. Ay, an' prime hay too! Hay full of ripe juice got from the sun, purveyin' fat nourishment to me cattle, an' afterwards, fat nourishment to man through the milk the cattle give!

CODGER [*wearily*]. Hay? Dust that the weary cattle can't chew. There isn't a sign in any meadow even of clover or of vetch. Meadows that haven't felt the rousin' rift of a plough for fifty years.

REILIGAN. It's my land, isn't it?

*The* CANON *comes along behind the wall, and stops at the gate to listen.*

CODGER [*eyes shut*]. Meadows a medley of mayweed an' of dock, with rushes creepin' in from the brook's bank. Grass that's tired of life before it's quarter grown. He calls his cattle cattle! The best of them cross-eyed with the strain of spillin' out a few hundred gallons a year; spillin' out what all know is an illusion of what it ought to be; with every passer-by turnin' his head aside so's not to see the tormented look on their gobs an' they complainin' silently to God against the dawn's lift-up of another day.

REILIGAN. Even so, even if your lie was truth, it's me own loss, for I own them all.

CODGER. You own them all. You own the land, own the tavern, own the shirt-factory, own the dance-hall, own the store, an' God help us, you own the people too. You're a menace to the world, Reiligan.

*The* CANON *has come over from the gate, and now stands looking down on the shut-eyed* CODGER.

CANON [*prodding* CODGER *in the ribs with umbrella*]. What's that I hear you sayin', Codger Sleehawn, what's this I hear you sayin'? Why aren't you attendin' to the hay? To your master's hay?

CODGER [*with mock reverence*]. Oh! the Canon's voice. The Church an' State's gettin' together. I was bearin' a bag of cement, Canon, an' some bum shoved me in the wrong direction.

PRODICAL [*who with* RANKIN *has drifted back to working at the wall*]. He's a bit delirious. After a little rest, Canon, he'll be back to his *status quo*.

CANON [*prodding the* CODGER *again*]. Remember when you speak to Councillor in the future, you will be speaking to a Count, for His Holiness has honoured us all by making the Councillor a Count of the Papal Court.

CODGER [*eyes still closed*]. A Count is it? [*Lifting his hat – with mock piety*] Ballyoonagh lifts herself up a step nearer to heaven!

CANON [*roughly*]. An' no more talk, Sleehawn, about the Count's land or the Count's cattle; or his good hay either.

CODGER [*a touch of mockery in his tone of voice*]. Good land, Canon, an' finest hay I've seen in a generation; nothin' like it, caught in the urge of the sun an' yieldin' to the tender kiss of the dews the nights give. [*He sniffs.*] I can get the smell of the hay from here: fuller an' sweeter than any scent from a far-off land where there's camphor an' rare gums tricklin' from the trees, givin' a forest all the grandeur of a grove of roses bushed about with thyme.

FATHER BOHEROE *comes to the window with a glass of liquor in his hand. He offers it to the* CODGER.

FATHER BOHEROE [*offering glass to* CODGER]. Keelin sent this out to you.

CODGER [*shrinking*]. What is it – water?

FATHER BOHEROE. No, no: the best of brandy.

REILIGAN [*dismayed*]. Brandy? Is it the Bishop's brandy – Good God! That damned girl! To give the like of that brandy to the like of him! [*He rushes into the house.*]

CODGER [*taking the glass eagerly*]. A grand girl, God bless her! The scent of camphor and thyme is in her goodness, an' her look in the morning, or when the evenin' comes, is as the simple grandeur of Sharon's rose; ay, an' her comin' an' goin' carries grace along, and is lure enough to make a man turn his head to look, an' his mind to a grabbin' thought to get her.

CANON [*quietly – to* FATHER BOHEROE]. He didn't need brandy. I wish, when you get a chance, Father [*indicating the* CODGER], you'd put a curb on this mischievous old mouth.

FATHER BOHEROE. It may be a disturbing old mouth, Canon; but I wouldn't say it was a mischievous one.

CANON [*impatiently, but quietly*]. Your Parish Priest says it is mischievous, and it is – mischievous and unruly.

FATHER BOHEROE. We have authority, Canon, for believing that old men may sometimes see visions; and what the Codger sees has been seen by others.

CANON [*about to enter house*]. Visions? The Codger's visions are compounded of ignorant and impudent guff. Visions, me neck! [*A pause.*] And look, Father Boheroe, a priest would do well to beware of seeking promotion in his mind from spiritual ambition; and hesitate before he hangs a tassel of honour upon any emotional fancy. Please come in, Father Boheroe. Looks as if I had more than one mischievous and unruly man in my parish. [*They both go in.*]

CODGER [*scornfully*]. A Count! His Holiness honours Ballyoonagh be makin' Reiligan a Count. A Count, be God! [*He holds his glass of liquor out from him, and calls*] Dan! [DANIEL *turns towards him, as* RANKIN *suddenly gets off the scaffold, and goes out by the gate, his hat off, his head bent in prayer. Fervently*] Happiness to Miss Keelin Reiligan and [*he pauses*] to another! [*He drinks.*] Prime stuff. Bishop's brandy, right enough. [*He utters a half-cry*] Jasus, me back aches! [*A pause.*] Count Mick – can you imagine it!

PRODICAL [*in a listening attitude*]. Whisht! The Angelus!* You can hear it faintly when the breeze blows this way. [*Indeed, the sound of the bell is faintly heard at irregular intervals till the twelve strokes are struck.*]

DANIEL [*indignantly*]. An' the louser, Rankin, heard it, and left, without sayin' a word.

MANUS [*who has been standing by the tree, drinking from a mug*]. Blow for lunch, lads. And there's more in the keg, if any of you'd like a cooler; with a bottle of the Bishop's brandy in it to give the drink a body: for they shall not muzzle the oxen that are treadin' out the corn.*

*He comes over the heap of bricks, and sits down on them.*

*The rest eagerly make for the way to the keg, marching not quite so stiffly as before; but still with signs of exaltation, the* CODGER *bringing up the rear. He pauses at the tree, and turns towards* MANUS.

CODGER [*to* MANUS]. Aren't you comin' too?

MANUS [*quietly*]. I'll join you in a few minutes, old friend.

CODGER [*softly and feelingly*]. Waitin' for a chance to see her. A union would be a blossomy blessin' to yous both. May God smile on you, Manus, and the lassie too. Waitin' is hard an' watchin' is hard and wonderin' is harder still. [*A pause.*] A Count, be God! [*He goes.*]

FOORAWN *comes in by the path behind the wall, comes through the gateway, sees* MANUS, *goes a little aside to avoid him, but he moves, too, and the two of them stand face to face; he looking steadily at her, she, after a long glance, turning her gaze to the ground, pulling her mantle more closely round her face.*

MANUS. Foorawn!

FOORAWN [*in a slightly frightened voice*]. Oh, Manus, don't stop me; let me go quietly in for both our sakes. I never thought I'd meet you.

MANUS [*firmly*]. You knew I'd be near. You saw me as you were going. You hoped to meet me. You wanted to meet me. You meant to meet me!

FOORAWN. No, no, I didn't. When you stopped me yesterday, I beseeched you not to trouble me again.

MANUS. You wanted to see me yesterday; you wanted to see me today. You would like to see me till your eyes were old, and could see no more.

FOORAWN [*poignantly*]. God forgive me! Don't torment me, Manus. Let me go quietly into my refuge. I am now under the pure white moon of heaven. Gone for ever from you, Manus. Look at me all in black an' blue. I am no longer a lure to your seeking eyes.

MANUS. Oh, you cannot hide the lure of your figure under a tenebrae cloak,* or masquerade your handsome face under a hiding hood. Oh, Foorawn, my love and my longing for you go under them all.

FOORAWN. Go away from me! I prayed to help you on your way to the priesthood; and while I was praying, you were creeping from your intention during the slow, cold hours of an early morning, leaving your name marked down as dead in the sacred register of the College; an' then, an' then you ran off to become one of the English air-force.

MANUS. Where I flew towards death at every chance I got so that I might die from all that had happened; but God laughed, and presented me with a medal; and when in another chance, I pushed closer to death, He laughed again, and added a silver bar to ripen the ribbon.

FOORAWN. Look at you now; oh, look at you now!

MANUS. Yes, look at me now. [*He takes her arm gently, and draws her towards him.*] A man with the same soul, the same mind, the same defiance of shabby life [*he gathers her into his arms*], and the same outlasting and consuming love for Foorawn, my [*he kisses her*] own, and for ever.

FOORAWN [*pulling herself out of his arms*]. No, no! I must go. I belong to God now, and Him only can I serve.

MANUS [*bitterly*]. That's pride and fear speaking. You think God couldn't do without you; at a loss when He can't find you. Go on, then, heaping up pound after pound for foreign missions that bring a sly storm of harm to the ebonised African in the sun's centre, and the icy-homed Eskimo in the shroudy snows of the north.

FOORAWN [*halting at the window – surprised*]. What pounds are you talking about?

MANUS. The notes heaped up for the good greed of the Church in the bureau-drawer under the votive light. The key's under your bodice on your breast within where the cross is lying on your breast without. [*Bitterly*] Cross and key to keep you cold, lying where my hand ought to be to keep you warm.

FOORAWN [*coldly*]. Your words are wild and your words are bitter. Your words are like the words in the books that will burn to ashes in the Bishop's bonfire. Manus, you are a bad man.

MANUS [*bitterly*]. And in the ashes that the fire will leave will be the ashes of our love; of mine for you, of yours for me; and Daniel's love for Keelin and hers for him.

FOORAWN [*going in by the window*]. A very bad man!

MANUS *makes to go after her angrily, but finds* FATHER BOHEROE *standing in his way. They face each other for a moment, then* MANUS *turns and goes slowly back to the heap of bricks to sit down on them, resting his head in his hands.*

FATHER BOHEROE [*from near the window – softly*]. Be a man, Manus. She is too deep now in the vainglory of her chastity to come to you.

MANUS [*impatiently*]. Oh, you! You who stifle and tangle people within a laocoön of rosary beads!*

FATHER BOHEROE. I wish, not to tangle them with rosary beads, Manus, but to join them with life. . . . Come, let yourself fall in love with life, and be another man.

MANUS [*sarcastically*]. At peace with all things.

FATHER BOHEROE. At war with most things.

MANUS. You are a kind, good man, Father. [*He pauses.*] Would you do me a great favour?

FATHER BOHEROE [*eagerly*]. Of course I would. You've but to tell me what it is, Manus.

MANUS [*tonelessly*]. Just leave me alone.

FATHER BOHEROE *goes slowly to the gate, opens it, and passes out to the path behind the wall. He halts there, leaning thoughtfully over the wall's top.*

*The others,* PRODICAL, DANIEL, *and* CODGER, *come back to the garden by the ash-tree, the* CODGER *leading, the butt of the hay-fork's handle in his hand, the prongs trailing along the ground behind him. His eyes are glazed and dreamy, but he walks more erect than ever, though his steps, now and again, are unsteady. He goes to the heap of bricks and sits down on them, on the opposite side from* MANUS, *so that his head or hat is only seen, with the hay-fork, prongs upward, rising up beside him like a trident.* DANIEL *goes over to the gate, walking more stiffly than before, and stands there looking pensively out over the fields. The* PRODICAL *goes over to the scaffold, and sits down upon it, head erect and eyes alight with an inarticulate defiance of the world.*

PRODICAL [*to the world and to* FATHER BOHEROE]. Prodical Carranaun demands a wider world, Father Boheroe; a world where a man can roar his real opinions out; where night becomes a generous part of a day, where rough seas tumble in on a lonely shore. Prodical Carranaun is far above the meanin' of Reiligan's roses and Reiligan's wall!

DANIEL [*gazing out over the fields – half to himself*]. I'm in a mood for work no longer. Let work go hang. I'll go stretch meself in a meadow, an' go listen, listen to the lark singin'. The lark, wha'? Yes, the lark singin' in the clear air, clear air of the day, wha'?*

CODGER [*musingly*]. You do well, Dan. The lark's a bonnie bird; Our Lady's hen singin' near all the year round. But for all her singin', the lark has her troubles like the rest of us, a lot of sorra; all kinds, like the rest of us. Even in love when she waits an' waits an' waits for the mate that sometimes never comes back to the nest. An' we're all like the birds that way: sorra after the loved one's gone outa sight or gone from ken. Father Boheroe there could tell you that. [*After a pause, he lilts quietly and softly*]

> My Bonnie's gone over the ocean,
>     My Bonnie's gone over the sea;
> My Bonnie's gone over the ocean,
>     Oh bring back my Bonnie to me.

DANIEL *and the* PRODICAL *join the* CODGER *in the chorus –* DANIEL *at the chorus's second line, the* PRODICAL *at the third, so that from the third line they are singing together;* FATHER BOHEROE *listening as he leans by the gate;* MANUS *sitting lonely on the bricks; his hands under the chin of his bent head.*

> Bring back, bring back,
> [DANIEL *joining in*] Oh, bring back my Bonnie
>     to me, to me;
> [PRODICAL *joining in*] Bring back, bring back,
> Oh, bring back my Bonnie to me.*

CURTAIN

## ACT II

*The drawing-room of* COUNCILLOR REILIGAN's *house is a large one, and everything in it is new, except the things that are newer, and the newest that are now being added to adorn the Bishop's stay. At the back is the big bow window, black plushy curtains at either side, with a white pelmet over them, looking out to the garden, and we can see from it a wide and elegant branch of the ash-tree, beginning to look black in the deepening dusk; the heap of bricks is there too, and the urn in front of them. Behind them all is the wall and the gateway, the path behind it, and the fields stretching away to the town. The window through which people come and go is open to the garden, for the evening is fine and balmy though the autumn is wending a way to its ending. Some few birds are still faintly twittering, and at some distance the cawing cries of the rooks are heard, not loud, but clear, flying home for rest and sleep. All is calm and peaceful without, though there is bustle and some anxious hurryings within.*

*To the right of the window is an upright piano, covered with an old sheet, and another sheet covers a big sideboard to the left of the window. On a ledge, or bracket, beside the piano, is a telephone. A table to seat six or seven stands somewhat to the middle of the room; it is a mahogany one, and has been polished so that the surface shines like a brightened mirror. There are six or so chairs set round the room, their seats cushioned with dark-green cloth, mahogany-backed and mahogany-legged.*

*The fireplace, a large and wide one, is to the right, and is curbed by a shining brass fender with heavy, brightened brass poker, tongs, and coal-shovel. There are paper and sticks and coal set there so that a great blazing fire may be kindled any minute in the grate to warm up a room that is used only to receive important visitors. The mantelpiece has a two-set piece of prancing bronze horses, one at either end, and in the centre a gilded clock that does go. Over them, on the wall, is a big picture of a Pope which REILIGAN says is a striking likeness of Pio Nino. Between the piano and the window is a narrow bureau, also of mahogany, with narrow drawers, and a desk-like top. It is half a prie-dieu, for a ledge for kneeling juts out at the bottom, softened for kneeling by a black-covered cushion. Over this, on the wall, is a bracket holding a votive light; above, on a smaller bracket, is the small statue of Saint Casabianca, who has a black face, wears a scarlet robe, and carries a golden crown in one hand. Over the floor is a thick beige carpet, partly covered with old sheets, particularly giving a protective covering to the carpet from the door to the right of the fireplace, leading to the rest of the house, and the door on left, leading to the kitchen basement, the hall, and the front entrance.*

*At one end of the table are writing-paper, pen, and ink.*

*When we see the scene, we find* RANKIN *looking down at the hearthstone, once a plain slab of slate, now a gorgeous hearthstone of green, yellow, and white tiles that he has laid there. He has a trowel in one hand, a chamois-cloth in the other. The* CODGER *is carrying out a mortar-board by the window.* RANKIN *bends down, and gives the tiles another polish with the cloth.*

RANKIN [*to the* CODGER]. You can tell them they can light the fire now any time they like. It's all firmly set.

CODGER. It needs one. With all its newness, the room's musty, and with all its image and its holy picture, it smells of mercy as much as the County Court.

*The* CODGER *goes out by the window with the mortar-board;* RANKIN *goes to the window and peeps out after him, then slides to the bureau, and, taking away the kneeling-cushion that lies before it, kneels down on the ledge to pray.*

RANKIN [*scornfully as he removes the cushion*]. Cushion! [*Softly and with suppressed intensity*] Holy St Casabianca of Allahoona, pray for us, that Ballyoonagh may be blessed by the Bishop's comin' soona –

*The door to the right flies open, and in rushes* LIEUTENANT MICHAEL REILIGAN. *He is in full marching order, steel helmet, English pattern, dark-green uniform, Sam Browne belt, sword slung on one side, revolver in holster on the other.*

LIEUTENANT [*breathlessly*]. Where's me Da; did you see me oul' fella?

RANKIN [*who has jumped up to his feet – sheepishly*]. I dunno; no, I dunno. [*The* LIEUTENANT *flies out by the door on left.* RANKIN *tiptoes to it, peeps out after the officer, closes it carefully, returns to the prie-dieu, kneels down again, and begins to pray. Praying*] Holy St Casabianca of Allahoona, pray for us that the Bishop's bonfire may light such a flame in Ballyoonagh soona –

*The door on the left flies open, and* KEELIN *rushes into the room.* RANKIN *springs to his feet, and stands sheepishly near to the prie-dieu.*

KEELIN [*breathlessly*]. Didja see me Da? Where's the Count Reiligan?

RANKIN. I dunno, Miss Keelin; no, I dunno.

KEELIN [*petulantly*]. Looks like this Bishop's visit is goin' to be a curse instead of a blessin'!

*She rushes out by the door on the right, leaving it open after her.* RANKIN *tiptoes over to it, peeps out, returns to the prie-dieu, kneels down, and begins to pray again.*

RANKIN [*praying*]. Holy St Casabianca of Allahoona, pray for us that the Bishop's bonfire may light such a blaze in all the hearts in Ballyoonagh that men may no longer think of women, or women think of men, soona –

COUNT REILIGAN, *still in his morning suit and top hat, appears at the window, stares at* RANKIN *for a moment, and then flares into indignation.*

REILIGAN [*angrily*]. What the hell are you doing at that pray doo?* [*As* RANKIN *jumps up, frightened and embarrassed*] That pray doo is the private perquisite of Miss Foorawn, and not meant for one of your stattus. [*He comes closer to* RANKIN.] That's Miss Foorawn's special saint; [*indicating statue*] an' no one in the house prays to him but her. See? Understand? [*As* RANKIN *remains silent, with bent head*] Oh, for God's sake, man, say something, so's I'll know you savee!*

RANKIN [*feebly*]. Yis.

REILIGAN. Yis what?

RANKIN [*with rising falsetto*]. I understand!

REILIGAN [*roughly*]. Well, then, try to act accordin'! Even Miss Foorawn herself has decided not to use it while the Bishop's living here for two or three nights as his headquarters. Get that? [*He waves a hand round the room*] This whole room's the Bishop's perquisite while he's here, and we're relegatin' the room and all that's in it to the Bishop's stattus, furnishin' him with a sittin'-room an' private oratorium for his security and comfort while his stay honours our much-loved town of Ballyoonagh. Understand? [*Impatiently – as* RANKIN *stays silent*] Oh, for God's sake, say something to show you savee!

RANKIN [*very lowly*]. Yis.

REILIGAN [*shouting*]. Yis what, man! Yis which!

RANKIN [*shouting in falsetto*]. Yis that! I understand!

REILIGAN [*shouting*]. Well, act accordin' then. [*Looking at the hearth*]
Ah, now that's lookin' fine now! You're done here, so come along
an' help with the paintin' of the hall. You're done here, so come on.
[*Pushing him*] Oh, on, on; no dilly-dallying

*As they are about to go out by the door on the left,* DANIEL *appears at the
opposite door. He is carrying a square pedestal of polished black wood with
a raised circular rim within its top, evidently there to make a statue's stand
secure.*

DANIEL. Here, Count, is the box for the Saint somebody or other to
stand on.
REILIGAN. Put it on the table. [*As* DANIEL *dumps it near the edge –
angrily*] Gently, you careless tit, an' don't scratch me table. In the
centre, you fool; in the centre of the table!
RANKIN [*imitating in falsetto*]. In the centre of the table, fool!
REILIGAN [*impatiently pushing* RANKIN *out by the door, and following
him*]. Oh, you! Interferin' gob, you! What's it to you whether it's in
the centre or at the side? Oh, come you an' help with the painting of
the hall! I've told you before; I'm tellin' you again, we've no use
now for a dilly-dallier!

*As* DANIEL *measures the pedestal into the perfect centre of the table,*
LIEUTENANT REILIGAN *comes in by the door on right, and for a moment
watches* DANIEL's *manoeuvres.*

LIEUTENANT [*cordially*]. Hello, Dan, me son.
DANIEL [*turning round – more cordially*]. Oh, hello, Mick.

*The* LIEUTENANT *crosses the room and hangs the holstered revolver by its
sling from a hook in the wall to the left of the votive light.*

LIEUTENANT. This thing's rubbin' me hip. It'll be safe here, Dan.
Should be beside a saint.
DANIEL. Dunno, Mick, if it's always safe to leave a gun within reach of
a saint these days.
LIEUTENANT [*laughingly*]. Now, Dan, no mockery! Seen me oul' feller
anywhere?
DANIEL [*as cautiously*]. Just gone out be that door.
LIEUTENANT. What sort of a gob had he on him? Gay, or what?

DANIEL. Uneasy. He's feelin' the flow of the money away from him. All he's spendin' on the Bishop's the core in the talk of the town. All he's doin' and all he's bringin' to diversify the house is the centre, too, of the town's sight an' hearin', like a rocket of coloured stars let loose in a deep dark sky.

LIEUTENANT [*as confidently as he can*]. He'll spend a little more when I get to him, for I must find a tenner* somewhere.

DANIEL. A tenner? Why only a tenner? Why not tap him for more than a tenner? A tenner won't go far.

LIEUTENANT. Ay, Dan, for with me an officer in charge of the Guard of Honour to meet the Bishop, an' the glory hangin' round the house now, I have to keep up my stattus in the Officers' Mess.

DANIEL [*emphatically*]. Of course you have! You need to keep a Guard of Honour round your stattus.

LIEUTENANT [*as emphatically*]. An' I'm goin' to! A waterfall of money flowin' for a Bishop, an' him denyin' his son a tiny tenner; his own son, mind you, Dan.

DANIEL. His own son: yis, I know, I know. It's little short of a visible mystery, Mick.

*The* CODGER *comes in by the door on right carrying a pot of green paint in one hand and a big paint-brush in the other. He appears almost at the same moment as the* PRODICAL *is seen at the window, carrying a huge duck, fully plucked, and ready for roasting, on a wide dish. The* CODGER *halts at one end of the table,* PRODICAL *at the other.*

PRODICAL. The finest duck of the fifty for the Bishop.

LIEUTENANT [*somewhat enviously*]. Looks like they're goin' to regale the laddo with a whole regalia of things. Must be costin' the oul' fella a packet. An' his own son shakin' a shillin' in a pocket.

CODGER. Bill Mullarkey under a bishop's robe's a different one to the one I knew with a patch on the seat of his trousers. Makes a helluva difference when the hand that held a hay-fork now grips a crozier! An' withal his golden mitre and his purple petticoat, he's Bill Mullarkey still.

LIEUTENANT [*to* DANIEL *who is polishing the pedestal with a cloth*]. What's that there you're polishin'?

DANIEL. A stand for a big statue, coloured fair an' gilded nobly, of some saint that no mortal in Ireland never heard of.

CODGER. The one thing increasin' in Ireland – the population of stone an' wooden saints.

LIEUTENANT. What's his name? Maybe I'd know the fella.

DANIEL. I was told it, but it's gone outa me mind now. A curious name – something concerned with a bugle or something.

LIEUTENANT. A bugle? How could it be a bugle?

DANIEL [*thinking*]. Some kinda musical thing it was anyway.

CODGER [*prompting*]. Fiddle, drum, cornet?

LIEUTENANT. Saxophone, oboe?

PRODICAL [*placing his duck on the table as the* CODGER *has already placed his pot of paint and his brush*]. Dulcimer, maybe?

DANIEL [*thinking hard*]. Wait now – let me think; yes, the fella was a soldier who played a buck, a buckineeno* in the old Roman Army.

CODGER. An' what kinda spiritual stir is a sinner's goin' to get out of a buckineeno. Somethin' sinister in it to me. We'll be all well served with a bishop an' a buckineeno.

DANIEL [*in an air of great secrecy*]. Hush! Listen! No word to go from here. The buckineeno boyo is the private patron of the Bishop, and his statue always fronts him while he's thinkin'. If he's thinkin' right, the buckineeno blows a steady note; if his thinkin's goin' wrong, the buckineeno quavers. The Canon told the Count, Count told Foorawn, Foorawn told Keelin, an' Keelin told me.

PRODICAL [*snorting contemptuously*]. Pah!

DANIEL. What are you pahhin' outa you for, Prodical! Looka the way this house has prospered be the prayers made to St Casabianca be Miss Foorawn. [*He gestures towards the statue on the bracket over the bureau.*]

PRODICAL [*taking up the dish and the duck, and about to go out*]. Pah!

CODGER. Buckineeno or no buckineeno, clear or quaverin', I can't see Bill Mullarkey thinkin' at all.

DANIEL [*resentfully*]. There's more in it than Pah! The way the country's in, we need all the help we can get from the saints.

LIEUTENANT. That's all right – up to a point, Dan; but what we want now is soldiers an' not saints. How best are we goin' to act if tens of thousands of Russian paratroopers came droppin' down from the Irish skies on to Tara's Hill or the Mountains of Mourne. You haven't to think twice to see the pickle we'd be in then.

CODGER. It would be better an' fitter for us to guard against the swarms of green flies an' swarms of black flies that drop from our Irish skies, an' slaughter the crops.

DANIEL [*indignantly – to* CODGER]. Aw, don't be an eejut.* Go on, Mick.

LIEUTENANT. You see, Dan, we're too small to fight the Russians on our own – we'd have to have help.

DANIEL. We're twice too small – we'd have to have help: you're right there.

LIEUTENANT. No use, either, of looking to allies too far off, like Italy or France – they'd take years to come.

PRODICAL [*who has become interested, and has placed the duck and the dish back on the table again*]. So they would, so they would.

LIEUTENANT. You see, men, Ireland's so important, geographically, that, in a war, the Russians would need to take her over within an hour, within an hour. Does that ring a bell?

DANIEL [*convinced*]. Yis; a whole peal of them. But then, wha'?

LIEUTENANT. Well, man, we'd have to get help at once.

PRODICAL. Then what about England?

LIEUTENANT. England! Why, man alive, she'd be fightin' for her life, an' couldn't let us have even a policeman from point-duty! I'm an Army Officer; I know these things.

DANIEL [*wisely – to Prodical*]. You see, Prodical? He's an Army Officer – he knows. [*To* LIEUTENANT]. Well, then, wha', Mick?

LIEUTENANT. America's our only man, Dan, for what we need is swarms an' swarms of jeeps.

CODGER [*incredulous*]. Jeeps?

LIEUTENANT. Yes, jeeps; each with a driver, a spare driver, a commander, an' a wireless operator. Every able-bodied man in Ireland in a jeep here an' a jeep there, with a sten gun, a hammer an' pliers, headphone, an' a jeepsie walkie-talkie – that's the one solution, Dan.

CODGER [*testily*]. An' what would the ordinary cars an' pedestrians do, an' the roads buzzin' with jeeps? There wouldn't be a man, woman, child, or chicken left alive in the country!

DANIEL [*rapping the table*]. Order, order, Codger; order!

LIEUTENANT [*hotly – to the* CODGER]. An' even if they were all done in aself, wouldn't death on our own roads be better than exportation be the Bolsheviks to an unknown destination?

CODGER. What exportation are you walkie-talkiein' about?

DANIEL. Don't talk like an eejut, Codger.

LIEUTENANT [*hotly*]. Looka, a nation like Russia that did so much to her own people wouldn't cast a thought about eliminatin' a few thousand Irishmen an' Irishwomen, or wait to think twice about exportin' the rest of us.

CODGER [*fiercely*]. An' where would the Bolsheviks find the ships an' trains to export four millions of us? Siberia's a long way off, if you ask me!

LIEUTENANT [*to the* CODGER]. Looka, man, the Bolsheviks wouldn't be dreamin' of Siberia, an' the Isle of Man only a few feet away from our green border.

DANIEL [*to* CODGER]. Aha, that's bet you! You see, now, Codger, don't you?

CODGER [*vehemently*]. No, I don't see now! If Russia be anything like what the clergy make it out to be, any Russians flutterin' down from the Irish skies on to our emerald sod will be poor divils seekin' an asylum.

PRODICAL. An asylum? It's a lunatic asylum you must be meanin'?

CODGER [*rattily*]. No, no, man; an ordinary asylum, an ordinary asylum!

PRODICAL. There's no ordinary asylum. When anyone says we've taken a certain party to the asylum, we mean a lunatic asylum, don't we?

CODGER. Yes, yes; but –

PRODICAL. There's no but about it. An asylum's an asylum – there's no but about it.

CODGER [*raising his voice*]. I'm tellin' you, there's different asylums; for instance, a deaf an' dumb asylum!

PRODICAL [*raising his voice higher than the* CODGER]. The paratroopers droppin' from our skies won't be deaf an' dumb, will they?

DANIEL [*louder than the other two*]. Order, order – let Mick speak!

LIEUTENANT [*resignedly*]. Aw, let the eejuts talk, Dan.

PRODICAL [*angrily – to the* LIEUTENANT]. Eejut yourself! Wantin' to flood the country with jeeps! Will you tell us who's goin' to provide the hundreds of thousands of jeeps to go gallopin' round, an' lay out every man-jack an' every woman-lizzie of us, dead as mackerel on the roads of Eireann, bar the boyos who have the good fortune to be sittin' in them?

CODGER [*fiercely – to* LIEUTENANT]. An' if we put into every one of them a driver, a spare driver, a commander, and a wireless operator with his walkie-talkie, addin' all them laid out flat an' dead on the roads, will you tell us who's goin' to look after the common things that have to be done to keep the country goin'?

PRODICAL [*to* LIEUTENANT]. Aha, you're silent now. That's bet you!

LIEUTENANT [*in a rage as he goes swift from the room, banging the door after him*]. Aw, go to hell, you pair of eejuts!

CODGER. You see, he turns to abuse when he's bet. Couldn't face up to unconfutable arguments.

PRODICAL. Him an' his jeeps! Another thing – while America might be droppin' the jeeps, what's to prevent the Bolshies at the same time from droppin' their paratroops an' fillin' the jeeps as they touch down, to let them go scamperin' all over the roads?

CODGER [*emphatically*]. Nothin'. An', maybe, takin' over the Turf Board, the Tourist Association, the Hospitals Sweep, the Catholic Young Men's Society, the Protestant pulpits, an' the President's residence; endin', maybe, with the plantin' of a Red Flag in the hand of St Patrick's Statue standin' helpless on a windy hill in the centre of the lonely Plains of Meath!

DANIEL. Don't be actin' the eejut, Codger!

CODGER [*angrily*]. Who's actin' the eejut?

DANIEL [*as angrily*]. You are, the way you're talkin'!

CODGER [*close up to him*]. Eejut yourself!

DANIEL [*placing a hand to* CODGER's *chest, and shoving him backwards*]. Aw, go away!

CODGER [*rushing back, putting a hand to* DANIEL's *chest, and shoving him backwards*]. You go away!

DANIEL [*swiftly returning, and giving the* CODGER *a fiercer shove backwards*]. You go away!

PRODICAL [*remonstrating*]. Gentlemen, easy! Can't yous see yous are turnin' your own opinions into *ipso factos*?*

*The door to the right suddenly opens, and* REILIGAN, *with* FOORAWN *behind him, comes into the room. When he sees the three men, a look of surprised anger floods over his face.*

REILIGAN [*angrily*]. What's this, aw, what's all this? The bricks, too, left lyin' still in me garden! Good God, is this the way you're helpin' the work to welcome the Bishop? Looka the paint on the mahogany table, and the Bishop's duck beside it suckin' in the fumes, with the hall little more than half painted, an' all hands wanted to give the finishin' touches to the Bishop's bonfire. You know we haven't a single minute to spare, not a single minute, mind yous. From this out, there's to be no talkin'; and if anyone does talk, everybody is to listen to nobody. Anyone – no one – mind yous! [*The three men stand mute.*] Damn it, are yous listenin' to me?

CODGER. Damn it, you; weren't you after sayin' no one was to listen to no one.

REILIGAN [*wildly*]. Not to me; I'm not no one! Not to me. Yous are all to listen to me. Nobody's to listen to anyone, but everybody's to listen to me!

CODGER [*mockingly serious*]. Listen to him, lads; yous are all to listen to him.

REILIGAN [*with a roar – to* PRODICAL]. Take the duck down to the cook! [*A roar – to* DANIEL] Take the paint to Rankin in the hall!

*A* RAILWAY PORTER *appears at the window; a middle-aged man with whiskers under his chin, a wide mouth, and spectacles helping a pair of weak eyes. He is dressed in yellow or black corduroy trousers, the same material in a cotton-sleeved waistcoat, and he wears a peaked cap, circled by a red band, on his head. He looks worn out, and there is a settled look of fright on his face. He leans against the window's side, half-way into the room, half-way out of it. His eyes twitch open, twitch shut again, many times, rapidly, and he is out of breath for a time.* PRODICAL, *on his way out with the duck, and* DANIEL *with the paint, pause, and stay to listen, one putting the paint back on the table, and the other putting back the duck.*

REILIGAN [*impatiently*]. What is it? What is it you want? What d' yeh want?

PORTER [*panting*]. Give a man a breeze, man!

REILIGAN [*after a pause, while they look at him for a few moments*]. Well, me man, what do you want? Have you a message or wha'?

PORTER [*half to himself*]. All right in a praying procession, but weighin' heavy on the poor shoulder of your own responsibility. Poor sinner, poor sinner that I am! Him irksome to me, me irksome to him. He knew I was a toss-up for heaven or hell; head or a harp.* So he kept blowin'; oh, me poor ears – a piercin' blast! [*a fierce blast from a horn or a cornet is heard by the* PORTER.] Just like that!

REILIGAN [*mystified*]. Just like what?

PORTER [*ignoring him*]. Ran all the way to the polis station to get shut of him. Had his hooks dug into me from start to finish. [*Pressing his hands over his ears*] Oh, me ears! Buzzin' brazen still. Every time I thought of a drink, or a comic line from a song, he plunged the bell over me ear, an' blew his best.

REILIGAN. Blew his best? Who did?

FOORAWN. Who blew his best?

PORTER [*wistfully*]. He did.

REILIGAN. Who did?

PORTER. He did. Loud an' long, or sudden, sharp, an' sinister.

CODGER [*impatiently*]. Who blew long an' loud? Shake yourself, Hughie Higgins, shake yourself, man!

REILIGAN. Who blew sharp, sudden, an' sinister?

PORTER. He did: the one with the big, big body an' the little, little head; knocked me outa me downy dream; the boyo with the bookaneeno.*

REILIGAN. Boyo with the bookaneeno?

FOORAWN. The bookaneeno?

PRODICAL. Bookaneeno?

PORTER. Them they call saints is right enough on a pedestal, half-hidden in a church frustrated with its own dimness; but out in the light, they're dazzlin', an' there's danger in the dimension of their shinin'. Dimpled dangers the lot of them. [*With conviction*] No, no; I'd rather look for heaven in a cracked lookin'-glass at home. I'm breathin' quiet now at last. We're both safe now: me here, him in the polis station waitin' for someone to carry him home here. [*In an awed whisper*] Whistist, the lot of yous carefully; a question: is this bookaneeno boyo goin' to be a fixture in Ballyoonagh? I'd like to be warned.

REILIGAN [*still mystified*]. Looka, me man, what are you complainin' of, an' what's the matter with you?

PORTER [*to* REILIGAN]. An' with you' too? What's the matter with you an' me is a world's question. We're all flyin' about on consequential an' bewildered wings. Even when singin' a song, a man's a sighin' sinner. A little whisky now would buoy me up, and make me fancy meself safe in the world's welter.

FOORAWN [*severely*]. There's no whisky in this house for you, an' better for you if there was none outside of it either.

PORTER [*quietly resentful*]. Whatever whisky I take is got in your own Da's tavern, Miss. No whisky in the house; no nothin'; no light in a window, no welcome at a door. [*To* FOORAWN] I don't want to listen to you; don't want to go too near to you, for you're one of the higher ones hearin' woe in the first cry comin' from a cradle. They're queer, these holy men an' holy women. Never have a minute's peace if you let them get you thinkin'. Give one of them

ones a chance to get a grip on you, an' he'll have you worryin' God
for help to do what you should be damn well able to do yourself
without botherin' God at all.

FOORAWN [*thrusting herself forward*]. You're speakin' blasphemy!

PRODICAL [*echoing her*]. Yis – blasphemy.

CODGER. If you ask me, the poor man's beginnin' to say sense at last!

DANIEL [*firmly*]. Hush, Codger! We've got to be careful. A holy house
has unholy enemies.

REILIGAN [*finding an excuse*]. It's drink. He's not himself. He's coloured his mind with drink, and it's separatin' into pictures like ones
in a stained-glass winda. It's drink.

PORTER. An' what else have we; we who see nothin', we who hear
nothin'; an' work hard: what else have we but drink to give us a
coloured dream or two?

FOORAWN. You have prayer, bad man.

PORTER [*suddenly coming to alert life, and standing full front before the
crowd, waving his hands excitedly, moving a step forward, a step back,
a step forward again*]. Listen, you blatherers!\* A question for yous,
a question! Does a prayer lift you up or get you down? Are these
prayin' people right an' proper in a world like this at all? How'd you
like one of them to start on you, an' you sittin', glass in hand,
listenin' to some gazebo\* singin' a shut-eyed song? Or one of them
with a hand on your shoulder, freezin' a body, an' you trying to
shout victory to your county football team? Would you feel at ayse
to shout? I'm a wild man when I think of these things. I'm askin'
yous something, Is prayer good for you? I don't mean the odd nod
of the head most of us give to God, but the prayer that's the real
McCoy\* – does it lift a man up, or does it cast a man down? [*They
stand, as they have stood for some time, in a semicircle around him,
gaping, stiff and still, only moving back a step or two when he has come
closer, waving his hands.*] There's no answer; [*in a wail*] there's no
answer! We don't feel comfortable with them here, we won't feel
comfortable with them there. What are we doin' but weavin' a way
through life, content with an odd prayer to propel us towards where
none of us wants to go! How'r we to know if we're comin' up
upstream, or goin' down downstream? [*He catches sight of the big
duck on the dish on the table.*] Jasus! Who owns the massive duck?

REILIGAN [*breaking from the spell – angrily, to* PRODICAL]. Didn't I tell
you long ago to take the Bishop's duck to the cook, an' not leave it
exposed to the gaze of the whole world? Take it down! [*To* DANIEL]

An' you take that pot of paint to where the hall's bein' done, an' then put your uniform an' slippers on so's you'll be used to them when the time comes to act. [*To the* PORTER] An' you, get out and bring here whatever you left at the polis station.

PRODICAL *goes out with the duck;* DANIEL *goes out with the paint; the* CODGER *makes to follow, but* FOORAWN *catches his coat, and holds him back.*

PORTER. I sent the man called Rankin, paintin' the hall, holier an' hardier than any here, barrin' the lady, to fetch what wouldn't come with me. [*He stiffens and becomes alert.*] I feel it comin'! [*He runs a hand over head, chest, and legs.*] Tremors here, tremors there: I feel him comin'! [*He listens.*] Nearer. The Saint of the Bookineeno! [*At a little distance, a steady blast comes from a horn or cornet.*] Hear that?

REILIGAN *takes his hat off, and, after hesitating,* CODGER *does the same.*

REILIGAN [*alert and uneasy*]. Hear what?
FOORAWN AND PORTER [*together*]. The blast from his buckineeno!
REILIGAN [*uneasily*]. I'll go. I've a lot to do elsewhere. You, Foorawn, can safely settle the saint down. I'll go. [*He makes for the door.*]
CODGER [*making to follow*]. Me, too.
FOORAWN [*pulling him back*]. You stay here with me, Codger.
PORTER [*uneasily*]. I'm goin', too. I'm goin' now. He doesn't like me. I unsettle him, an' him me. [*To* FOORAWN] There are other things I have to bring from the railway station. I'm off now be the back way, if you don't mind, Miss?
FOORAWN [*pointing to door left*]. That way.
PORTER [*going out*]. There's hardly one of these saints that doesn't want to be a conquering hero. Forced to serve this holy jack or that holy jill. Crosses have odd shapes sometimes. We're all staggerin' about among mysteries!
CODGER [*uneasily*]. Time is drivin' me on to ninety, Miss, an' it might be a shock if me thoughts provoked blasts from the bookineeno.
FOORAWN [*soothingly*]. Have no fear, as long as I'm here. You're not a bad man, Codger, rather a dear, indeed. Ah! [FOORAWN's *exclamation is caused by the appearance of* RANKIN *at the window with the statue, covered with a white cloth, in his arms. He carries it into the room.*] Here, on its pedestal, Mr Rankin; softly; take the cloth off –

up! We welcome thee, St Tremolo, to our home! Make us worthy of
you; pray for us all, an' help dear Codger to be a good man.

*They lift the cover cautiously from the statue when they have placed it on
its pedestal. The statue is a big one, about three feet high, and its form takes
the shape of a modern sculpture and somewhat fantastic. The body is
barrel-like, the legs are short and fat, the head tiny, and all is dressed in
the uniform of a Roman legionary. The one ecclesiastical sign the figure has
is his red-hair tonsure. The horn or buccina is of silver or polished brass,
and is coiled round the body, the bell flowing over the right shoulder. They
look at it for a moment or two,* RANKIN *and* FOORAWN *close up, the* CODGER
*at a distance.*

FOORAWN. It was sin that weighed the railway porter down, and not
the statue, for it's quite light, an' all holla underneath.
CODGER [*surprise in his voice and some doubt*]. Holla? A holla* statue; a
holla saint. All Hollas Eve* – me mind's wanderin'.
FOORAWN [*to* RANKIN]. And how does the town look, Mr Rankin?
RANKIN [*enthusiastically*]. Never seen it lovelier! The whole town's a
flapping of flags, an' coloured streamers everywhere, with a great
arch of paper flowers at the cross-roads whose centre is a golden
mitre and crossed keys of silver; an' a tall, white candle stands up in
every window.
FOORAWN. Hear that, Codger? We've got them all – mitre an' keys for
our Bishop of Bishops, roses for our Lady, an' candles for God!
Clap hands, clap hands, till our Bishop comes home! [*She slaps*
RANKIN *on the back vigorously*] Clap hands, you! [*He does so timidly.*]
Clap hands, Codger! [*She slaps him on the back vigorously.*] Clap
hands, all! [*The* CODGER *claps briskly.*] Hundreds of little fires from
the candles an' one great blaze from the bonfire! Clap hands!
CODGER [*losing control of himself*]. Yis, yis, Miss! [*He blows a wild kiss
towards the window.*] We'll flip a kiss to the candles [*he whirls round
in a dance*], an' dance a ring round the bonfire!
FOORAWN [*restraining him*]. Codger, Codger, please! What would me
Da say if he came in, an' saw you jig-actin' in th' Bishop's room! An'
no kissin' to candles, an' no dancin' round th' bonfire either; no,
nor no annoyin' of th' air or the Bishop's ears with any of your
titterin' songs. [*To* RANKIN] You go, now, an' help with the buildin'
of th' bonfire. [*To the* CODGER *as* RANKIN *goes*] Help me take the

sheets from the carpet an' off th' furniture so's to be ready when Keelin comes to polish it all up.

CODGER. Lovely carpet, Miss; no sulkiness in it under a footfall. An archangel could trot across it in his bare feet without feelin' a sting.

FOORAWN. Not a bit too good for the good Bishop, though you near ruined it with cement when you fell be th' window.

CODGER [*bitterly*]. Some lousy bum shoved me in the wrong direction, Miss.

FOORAWN [*helping him and showing him how to fold the sheets neatly*]. Stretch it out. Now fold in two. No more coarse talk, Codger. Now come to meet me so's to fold again – that's it! Yes, Ballyoonagh will have a new lease of spiritual life; and you must help, Codger. No more drinking.

CODGER [*tonelessly*]. I must give up the drinkin'.

FOORAWN [*firmly*]. Smoking, too.

CODGER. Smoking, too.

FOORAWN. An' senseless singin' as well, Codger. Fold in two. Now come to me – that's it.

CODGER [*dubiously*]. I don't know how I'm goin' to give up the singin'; I've been singin' all me life. After all, Miss, the birds sing, the angels sing, an' I don't see why the poor oul' Codger shouldn't sing too.

FOORAWN [*firmly*]. You're neither bird nor angel, Codger, but only a poor old man on his way to th' tomb. God forbid we'd lose you, but, then, we're all steppin' our way to th' tomb.*

CODGER. We are, we are; goose-steppin' it, right enough, Miss.

FOORAWN [*gaily*]. Goose-steppin' it there, Codger, yis, an' lively, too – quick march, man! [*She links her arm in his, and they go goose-stepping round the room.*]

CODGER [*hilariously*]. Step be step! Steady ordher; left right, left right; march on, march on!

FOORAWN [*gaily*]. To th' tomb!

CODGER [*gaily lilting the 'Marseillaise'*]. Lal de lal lal lal da dee, lal da lal lal da dee; march on, march on!

*A wailing blast comes from the bookineeno.* FOORAWN *hears it, stops her steps in a flash, pulls her arm from the* CODGER's, *and starts away from him in a frightened manner. The* CODGER *stops, too, astonished, a leg cocked up in the air, staying there for a few moments, before he slowly lets it down again.*

FOORAWN [*angry and frightened*]. Stop this nonsense; stop it, fool! Didn't you hear?

CODGER [*puzzled*]. Hear it? Hear what, Miss?

FOORAWN [*peevishly*]. No, you didn't hear; you weren't listenin'. Oh, Codger, you shouldn't, you shouldn't coax poor souls to places where they don't want to go; to sayin' things that shouldn't be done; to doin' things that shouldn't be said. We must fall serious, so that every step will be a new arrival an' a different departure.*

CODGER. A lot in that, oh, a lot, Miss: here we come, an' there we go.

FOORAWN [*solemnly*]. But listen, Codger: If we want to go from where we think we are, we must go to where we can't get;* we must set out early before the dew declines, before the sun rises, before life's fun starts; always remembering that joy, within the light or under the darkness, is joy under the frock of death.

CODGER [*trying to be fervent*]. Yis. How right you are! You're right there, right enough! Couldn't be righter.

FOORAWN [*helping to take cover off piano, or to fold a sheet*]. Now, the last one. Take them all to the lumber-room. The last. Sad word, Codger. Maybe this visit will be someone's last chance. The song sung is the song unheard, the song unsung. The song unsung is the song heard, the song sung.*

CODGER [*enthusiastic*]. You're right there, Miss! [*In a half-reverie*]. How true an' terrifyin' is all you're after sayin', Miss: enough to make this bugle here hum till it's hot – for years; yis, for years to come! [*Looking at statue. He touches it, and immediately two short, sharp blasts from the bookineeno are heard. He jumps back, startled.*] Jasus! He doesn't like me either! Hear them two venomous blasts! He doesn't want me here. I'd better go.

FOORAWN [*startled, too, and irritated*]. Why did you touch it? Better go, quick as you can. [*She places bundle of linen in his arms*] There – off you go! [*She opens the door for the* CODGER *carrying the bundle of linen, and near hidden by it. He goes out.* FOORAWN *crosses to the other door, opens it, looks out to call* KEELIN. *Calling*] All ready, Keelin, to come and polish away!

*She crosses then to the other door, and follows the* CODGER *as* KEELIN *enters by the door opposite, followed by* DANIEL, *both of them carrying chamois dusters in their hands.*

*As* DANIEL *is polishing the table at one end and* KEELIN *at the other, the*

RAILWAY PORTER *appears at the window carrying an inlaid and gaudily decorated stand desk. He calls to them.*

PORTER [*calling out*]. Eh, there! [*He turns his back to them on the threshold of the window.*] Take this thing off me spine. Hall full of pots an' ladders, so had to come here. [*As they take it off his back*] That desk's called a Buhl:* a piece you won't see every day in the best of places, an' never in Ballyoonagh; not till now. It's for the Bishop's bedroom. [*Indicating statue of Tremolo – in a whisper*] I see you have the Bookineeno boyo safely bedded.

KEELIN. Yis. Isn't the Buhl lovely!

PORTER. Decked out with rare mother-o'-pearl patterns, here an' there, bits of enamelled metals, fancifully turned, this one blue, that one green – be God, he should be able to write a lovely pastoral with a thing like that under his pen!

KEELIN [*to Daniel*]. Help me carry it out of the way, Dan, into the hall.

*They carry it across the room to the door on the left, pass out into the hall, leave the desk there, and return to the room.*

PORTER [*as they are carrying desk out*]. Wait till yous see the chair I have in the van for yous. I'll get it now. Don't be talkin'! [*He goes off to get the chair.*]

KEELIN [*as they come back to the room*]. A chair, too, for the Bishop. Sure, he'll be goin' from one glory to another in this house. I hope his bonfire an' his blessin' will do us some good.

DANIEL [*gleefully*]. It's done good be throwin' us together more, anyhow. I've been able to come into the house; able to see you alone, like now; an' able to put me arm around your waist like this. [*He puts an arm around her.*]

KEELIN [*snobbily, though no way displeased that his arm's around her*]. Don't forget, Daniel, I'm a lady, that me Da's a Count, an' gave me a high convent education, an' that we live in a grand house, while the Clooncoohys sheltered under a slate roof for the first time, me Da says, when Rural Authorities built them a council house outa the ratepayers' money.

DANIEL [*undaunted, knowing that Keelin loves him*]. What's it matter whether a man's born under turrets or under a thatch? It's the man with the gay heart that rides the waters an' the winds; who shakes life be the hand when life looks fair, an' shakes her be the shoulder when she shows a frown.

KEELIN [*pushing his arms from her waist*]. He's comin' back.

*The* PORTER *comes to the window carrying the chair, a gorgeous, slim armchair, all crimson rep, with gilded framework and legs. The crimson back is ornamented with fleurs de lis surmounted by a silver crown.*

PORTER. Here 'tis, half throne, half chair, curvin' nicely in the seat to suit the Bishop's backside. Bill Mullarkey, won't you please come home.* Looks like this place'll be his heart's first home

KEELIN. Bring it in, please.

*The* PORTER *carries it in over the window's threshold, but as soon as he has stepped into the room, three short, sharp blasts come from the cornet, or horn. He drops the chair, and hurries out by the window again.*

PORTER [*agitatedly*]. Didja hear that? Has it in for me, that laddo.

KEELIN [*surprised*]. Hear what? What ails you?

PORTER [*wiping sweat from his forehead*]. Are yous deaf? Didn't yous hear the blasts from the boyo's buckineeno? The minute I set a foot into the room. [*He takes a docket from his pocket and offers it to* KEELIN] Here, sign for desk an' chair, an' let me be off while I'm safe. [KEELIN *takes the docket, goes to the end of the table where pen and ink are, signs it, and gives it back to the* PORTER. *With a sigh of relief*] Thanks. [*He catches* DAN *by an arm, and draws him closer.*] Listen, me poor boy. [*He catches* KEELIN *by an arm, and draws her closer.*] Listen, me poor girl. Listen both, cautiously: Yous have a larboard watch ahoy laddo in this distracted house. Keep a kee veev* over your thinkin'. When you talk of this an' not of that, let your voices be as low as a murmurin' wind among the willows. Listen both: never let a single thing yous say about a certain party rise above the surface of a whisper. Hush! Goodbye, poor girl; poor boy, goodbye!

*He steals away on tiptoe, and* KEELIN *stands thoughtfully for a moment.* DANIEL *comes over to her, and puts an arm round her.*

KEELIN. Oh, Dan, I don't know, I don't know; our love has many enemies.

DANIEL [*puzzled*]. Enemies? What are you talking about? There's only your Da.

KEELIN [*indicating the statue*]. There's this; there's the Canon; there's all of your own class who are envious of you; and there's my own dark pride warning me against marrying beneath me.

DANIEL [*huffily*]. Oh, well, if you think that, let's say goodbye.

KEELIN [*sharply*]. Don't be a fool, Dan! You know it was dinned into me since I was a toddler. You mustn't play with those children, dear; they aren't fit for you. Then by the nuns, telling me I was a lady, and mustn't do anything unladylike. I can't get rid of the feelin' at the first go.

DANIEL [*ardently*]. Let your love falsify your own feelin', Keelin, an' leave me to deal with the Count, your Da, the Canon, an' the town!

KEELIN [*doubtfully*]. Oh, don't try to be too brave, too sudden, Dan. It won't be easy, it won't be easy.

DANIEL [*confident*]. Just you wait. We're not goin' to let ourselves die in the gloom of Ballyoonagh.

KEELIN. Oh, Dan, there's gloom in the outside world as well as in little Ballyoonagh.

DANIEL. Sure, I know. I've travelled England an' a bit of Scotland, and found gloom dulling the life of Scot an' Briton. But, here and there, torches flamed in the gloom lighting a way out of it, while here we have to praise an' worship the gloom that stifles us. In the world outside, we would find hours like them we knew as children, when climbing a tree we made the branches merry steps away from childhood's hardship, when we thought the rustling of leaves the lesser lilt of life, and when the stars above were nothing less than our own thoughts gleaming.

KEELIN. If the world outside's so good, why did you come back to Ballyoonagh?

DANIEL [*fervently holding her in his arms*]. I came back because you were here.

KEELIN. No, Danny, no!

DANIEL. Yes, Keelin, yes. Down in foundation, up among the girders, the figure and face of Keelin were always beside me.

FATHER BOHEROE *appears at the window, a tired look in his soft eyes, a half-sad, half-amused smile crinkling his sensitive mouth. He stands just outside watching the couple.*

KEELIN [*half struggling to free herself, but finally nestling down within* DAN's *arms*]. No, Danny, no!

DANIEL [*bending his head down to her upturned face*]. Yes, Keelin, yes!

KEELIN. You mustn't, Danny; you really mustn't.

DANIEL. Mustn't what?

KEELIN. Mustn't say such things; and you mustn't kiss me.

DANIEL [*kissing her several times*]. I know I mustn't! Oh, Keelin, if we could only stay like this for ever!

KEELIN. Life couldn't let us stay together like this for ever, Dan, dear. It wouldn't be good for us; but if we be constant an' brave, we might be together like this for a long, long time.

FATHER BOHEROE. For a long, long time. [*With mock seriousness*] Aha, I've caught the pair of you.

*The couple break away from each other, and stand embarrassed, then go back to the table polishing,* KEELIN *at one end, and* DANIEL *at the other.*

DANIEL [*confused and penitent*]. Excuse me, Father, I forgot meself. I shouldn't have done it. I wasn't thinkin'.

KEELIN. You didn't forget yourself, Dan. You done what I wanted you to do. You were thinkin' an' there was no harm in the delight of the kisses you gave me!

FATHER BOHEROE. Keelin is right. No need to be penitent, Danny; a man in a woman's arms may indeed be close to God.

DANIEL [*shocked*]. Oh, Father, such a thing to say! I forget at times that Miss Keelin here's so far above me in her bringin' up, an' that her father's a Count now, a big man an' the right-hand man of Canon Burren. Who am I to think of his daughter?

KEELIN [*pathetically*]. There's all that against us, Father. Oh, what can we do? We can't go on; we can't go on.

FATHER BOHEROE [*in a loud and imperative voice – suddenly*] Listen!

DANIEL *and* KEELIN *stand intent, listening, for a few moments.*

KEELIN [*in an awestruck whisper*]. What is it, Father; what is it?

FATHER BOHEROE. I heard God laughing, Keelin.

KEELIN [*shocked*]. God laughing? Oh, Father, how could God laugh?

FATHER BOHEROE. He's laughing now, Keelin. What else can He do, except destroy the lot of us?

DANIEL [*solemnly*]. Laughing at what, Father?

FATHER BOHEROE. Laughing at the punch and judy show of Bally-oonagh, at you, Keelin, for thinking your Da governs your soul and body; at you, Danny, for giving Count Reiligan a higher place than God might give him. Laughing at me, too. Oh, who are you to dream today of a greater tomorrow! Who am I to dream of it either!

KEELIN. It's nice to dream, an' it does us good; but when we come out of our dream, we daren't think of what it told us.

FATHER BOHEROE. Well, my children, if you daren't think of what your dream has told you, remember the bonfire, the things for the Bishop's comfort; see you do your duty well. [*To* DANIEL] Give up Keelin. [*To* KEELIN] Give up Dan. Goodbye to you both. [*He goes towards the window.*]

KEELIN [*convulsively clutching* DANIEL'*s arm*]. No, no; I won't give Danny up! I'm not frightened, Father, not a bit frightened.

DANIEL [*putting his arm round her*]. Nor am I frightened! I refuse to be frightened! If the future gives us a gay gown, we'll wear it, an' be glad; if the future weaves us one of mourning, we'll wear it, too, an' go on bravely wherever life may lead us

KEELIN [*softly – looking up at* DANIEL]. Wherever life may lead us, we go together.

DANIEL [*looking down at her*]. Together!

FATHER BOHEROE [*delightedly – half dancing towards the piano*]. That's the stuff, children! You are both now in the fierce flow of what the poets have glorified in a thousand songs. Through time and through eternity, you will never feel quite the same glad glow again. [*He plays the soft notes of a waltz very softly on the piano.*] Get to yourselves the courage to last it out. You've escaped from the dominion of the big house with the lion and unicorn on its front;* don't let yourselves sink beneath the meaner dominion of the big shop with the cross and shamrock on its gable.* Whatever comes, refuse to be frightened, and take whatever the glow may bring, be it the mourning habit or the golden gown!

KEELIN AND DANIEL [*together*]. The mourning habit or the golden gown!

FATHER BOHEROE [*playing in a more lively way*]. Grand! Boot and saddle and away! Blue bonnets, blue bonnets over the border!*

KEELIN AND DANIEL [*together*]. Blue bonnets over the border!

KEELIN *and* DANIEL *have come into the rhythm of the music, and now, close together, with their arms around each other, they move quietly and dreamily about the room in front of the table. When they are well under the music's spell, the door on the right flies open, and in comes the* COUNT *excited, and with a look of fury on his face; he is followed by the* CANON, *now Monsignor, whose face carries on it a look of angry exasperation.*

DANIEL *pulls wildly away from* KEELIN'S *hold, which he succeeds in doing, though she holds him tightly to her for a few moments.*

DANIEL *retreats backwards before the angry glare from the* COUNT.

FATHER BOHEROE *continues to play the piano, but very softly now.*

REILIGAN [*furiously*]. What's this? [*He rushes over to* DANIEL, *grips him by the shoulders, and shakes him.*] Who told you to do a belly-to-belly dance with me lady daughter? God in heaven, the like of you, you dung-scented menial, to wind your arms around a lady!

DANIEL [*frightened*]. I didn't mean it, I didn't really. I musta been mad, sir.

REILIGAN [*as furiously as ever*]. Get outa me house, outa me employment, outa me sight!

FATHER BOHEROE [*rather loudly*]. Blue bonnets are over the border!

KEELIN [*running over and catching* DANIEL'S *arm*]. We love each other! I won't let you, won't let anyone, take Dan away from me!

DANIEL [*roughly forcing her hand from his arm*]. For God's sake, girl, have sense, an' don't make things worse!

REILIGAN [*gripping* KEELIN *roughly, swinging her around, and giving her a pushing fling that sends her, almost spinning, to the other end of the room where she subsides into the half throne, half chair*]. Disgrace to your father, disgrace to your sister, you jade, shameless an' shockin'! I'll deal with you later.

FATHER BOHEROE [*going over to where* KEELIN *sits, almost silently sobbing on the chair, and laying a gentle hand on her shoulder*]. You are a liar, Reiligan, regarding your daughter. She is a disgrace to no truth, to no virtue.

REILIGAN [*wrathfully*]. You encouraged them, did you, Father Boheroe?

FATHER BOHEROE [*quietly but firmly*]. I gave them my blessing, and left another hovering over all they intended to do.

REILIGAN. It's not for me to say you scatter your blessin's curiously, Father Boheroe. I'll leave all that to the Right Rev. Monsignor Burren.

CANON [*after a pause – to* DANIEL]. Go now, Clooncoohy, and help with the Bishop's bonfire; and, tomorrow, come at nine o'clock to the Presbytery – I must have a talk with you.

DANIEL [*submissively*]. Yis, Canon.

REILIGAN [*explosively*]. Monsignor, you lug!* Our Canon's a Monsignor, now.

DANIEL [*apologetically*]. I'm very sorry, Canon, I didn't know.

CANON [*unceremoniously pushing him out by the door – impatiently*]. Oh, go on, man! [*To* REILIGAN] Clooncoohy won't offend again. Come, Count, we must have a talk. [*As* REILIGAN *steps aside to allow the* CANON *to go out first*] No; you first, my dear man. [*The* COUNT *goes out while the* CANON *pauses by the door.*]

REILIGAN [*as he is going out – to* FATHER BOHEROE]. May I say, Father Boheroe, that I'd rather you didn't bang about the piano I've had tuned up and polished bright for the Bishop.

CANON [*quietly to* FATHER BOHEROE]. You're clever, Father – and sincere, I hope – but your cleverness seems only to make persons more unhappy than they were. I'm afraid I cannot commend the way you try to lead my poor people towards illusions. Can't you understand that their dim eyes are able only for a little light? Damn it, man, can't you see Clooncoohy can never be other than he is? You're very popular with our people, but remember that the love they may have for you doesn't come near the fear they have for Reiligan [*he pauses*] or the reverence they must show for their Parish Priest.

FATHER BOHEROE [*as quietly as the* CANON]. There's Keelin to think of as well as Clooncoohy, Canon Burren. God help us, Monsignor, for by fear, we have almost lost our love for our neighbour; even our worship is beginning to have the look of the fool's cap and the sound of the jester's bells.

CANON [*sarcastically*]. I seem to hear the tinny tinkle of the bells in what you say. [*With meaning.*] I think, Father Boheroe, it is near time for you and me to have a friendly chat with our Bishop. [*He goes out, shutting the door behind him.*]

FATHER BOHEROE [*tenderly – to* KEELIN]. My poor child, my poor child.

KEELIN [*brokenly*]. What am I to do, Father; oh, what am I to do! Dan hadn't the courage to stand up to them. Dan has forsaken me, forsaken me! I will never marry. I will die as I am; I love him, an' he's lost to me now!

FATHER BOHEROE. My poor child!

*The room suddenly flashes into darkness, a cold wind sweeps through it, and when the light comes again, it comes only to the sad and pensive density of dusk.*

KEELIN [*startled – with a sudden shuddering shiver*]. What was that, Father? [*She clutches his arm.*] A shiver cold and powerful through my body, into my soul.

FATHER BOHEROE [*shivering too*]. Cold and powerful through my body, into my soul as well.

KEELIN [*frightened*]. What is it? What was it, Father?

FATHER BOHEROE. It was, my child, a long, sad sigh from God.


CURTAIN

## ACT III

*Still the drawing-room in* REILIGAN's *house; all spruced and spiced now for the Bishop's stay there. An electric light, covered with a light-green shade, hangs from the ceiling over the table. Near the fireplace is a standard lamp whose shade is white, and a small stand lamp on the sideboard is decked out with a yellow shade. There are table-mats on the table ready for any hot plates that may be put there. The brandy in a decanter stands on the sideboard with a bottle of soda-water and another bottle of brandy beside it. It is night-time, and the window stands half open, for the air is very warm, and even a few birds are still twittering in the ash tree.*

*The* PRODICAL *is sitting, very dignified indeed, in a chair by the head of the table. He is dressed in the uniform of a waiter, apron and all. He wears a piece of chamois folded on his head, so as (he thinks) it may look like a mitre.*

*DANIEL is dressed like a waiter, too, though the suit is too baggy for him as* PRODICAL's *is too tight, and the trousers a little too short.*

*DANIEL is fussing at the sideboard, evidently pretending to be waiting on the Bishop. He suddenly stands rigid, stiff to attention.*

DANIEL [*shouting fiercely*]. Silence! me Lord Bishop, Bill Mullarkey, is about to spake!

PRODICAL [*pompously*]. Dan, me son, take me epicpiscopal advice, an' keep your young innocent puss\* outa the whisky-tumbler, out of a bad book, an' keep far from the girls, for a young bitch's enfiladin' blessin' is the devil's choicest curse!

DANIEL. Sound Christian doctrine, Right Reverend. Would you like any more soup, your reverence, holy man, benevolent Bishop?

PRODICAL. Bring me another glass of brandy, fella.

DANIEL. I will that. [*He pours one for* PRODICAL.] An' one for meself. [*He pours another and fetches it to the* PRODICAL.] There y'are. [*He goes back to sideboard, lifts the glass, and turns towards the* PRODICAL.] To the Bishop, the Bishop's bonfire – to hell with the two of them!

KEELIN *comes into the room carrying a piece of music and a chamois duster in her hand. She passes by* DANIEL *without a look or a word, and goes to the piano, which she opens, and places the music on the rest. The sheet of music shows the title of 'Kiss Me, Kate'.\* There is a silent pause.*

PRODICAL [*remonstratively*]. You're gettin' too furious, Dan. We're riskin' what we needn't risk. We're steppin' into where curious things may be whirrin' about. [*Taking the comic mitre from his head*] I don't feel easy trying to make a cod of the Bishop's visit, and the image of St Tremolo with his eyes out on sticks watchin' us. You'd never know what might happen.

*The* CODGER *has appeared at the window carrying a lantern in his hand. He lingers there, watching and listening to those in the room.*

DANIEL. Let anything happen; let everything happen! I'm a hard case when I'm roused. I'm reckless. [*Bragging to restore his lost reputation with* KEELIN] No fear in me of him stickin' his neck out. The whole house is bloomin' with statues. Doesn't matter to me. I won't be long here. When the fun's over, I'm off. [KEELIN *becomes interested, and listens intently.*] I'm not goin' to stay as a pot-walloper in Ballyoonagh. Dan Clooncoohy was made for something better. I've enough saved to keep me a fortnight, so when the Bishop's bonfire's blazed its way to black soot and grey ash, I head for England's shore.

KEELIN [*who has stolen nearer and nearer to him as he speaks – with an intense appeal*]. I've some saved, too, sewn up in the mattress of me bed; thirty pounds an' more! Oh, Danny, take me with you! The money's all yours; I'm all yours – oh, Danny, do!

DANIEL [*ignoring her – to* PRODICAL]. Let's be goin', Prod – there's more to be done yet.

*PRODICAL has been going towards the door, and now passes out;* DANIEL *has been delayed for a moment by* KEELIN'S *hold on an arm.*

KEELIN [*with anguish in her appeal, as he shakes her hold off, and follows the* PRODICAL]. Oh, Danny, do!

*But he goes out without a yea or nay, and quietly shuts the door after him, leaving her standing disconsolate, her breast heaving with silent sobs. After a pause, the* CODGER *comes into the room, leaves his lantern thoughtlessly down on the fresh, grand carpet, and goes over to where she is standing.*

CODGER [*gently*]. Me poor little girl, me poor little child! There's small use of me sayin' you're better without him. [*He stays silent for a*

*moment, then says vehemently*] Jasus! If I was only half me age, I'd
gather you up in me arms, carry you outa th' house, out of th' town,
out th' country to th' nearest port, where you could live with a few
bits of furniture, a bright fire, an' geraniums in the window!

KEELIN [*brokenly*]. Oh, Codger, I'm to be pitied, for Danny's nigh
broken me heart! I was ready to defy them all.

CODGER [*viciously*]. An' they tell me there's a statue of Ireland's hero,
Cuchullain, somewhere up in Dublin.* [*Pathetically*] Oh, Keelin,
Keelin me darling, I'm Irish an' ashamed of it.

KEELIN [*suddenly putting her arms round the* CODGER, *and kissing him on
the cheek*]. Oh, Codger, dear Codger, I wish to God that you were
me Da!

*The clang of an opening and shutting gate is heard in the garden.*

CODGER [*stroking* KEELIN'*s hair*]. Me poor child; we'll talk again when
things are quieter; talk a lot. There's someone comin' now.

*They separate;* KEELIN *going to the piano which she starts polishing; the*
CODGER *to the lantern on the carpet, as the* CANON – *now Monsignor* –
*appears at the window, and comes into the room.*

CANON [*seeing the lantern*]. Ah, a dirty lantern on the good carpet! Slap
it down – anywhere will do! Clumsy, thoughtless fellow! Why isn't
it alight in the garden to give a glimpse of gate and pathway?

CODGER [*brusquely*]. No oil; goin' to get some now, Canon.

CANON [*testily*]. Monsignor, my man; 'tis Monsignor now.

CODGER [*shortly*]. I know; but you'll always be the Canon to me. [*Exit*
CODGER]*

CANON. Something even less than a Canon to him. [*To* KEELIN] Surly,
disrespectful old man, the Codger. Don't listen too leniently,
Keelin, to that old rascal's gab.* Well, still busy, my child.

KEELIN. Yes, Monsignor – as you can see.

CANON [*graciously*]. I was just talking to the Bishop's brother, Farmer
Mullarkey: a good man, young and active lad.

KEELIN. Hardly a lad; why, he's well over fifty, Father.

CANON [*testily*]. That's not considered old these days. He was asking
about you, Keelin. [*A pause.*] A strong farmer, and anxious to settle
down: to marry. He likes you, my daughter, and a girl could go
further and fare worse for a husband.

KEELIN [*facing the* CANON]. He doesn't care a damn about me! He's in debt to me Da, and him an' me Da want to join their property.

CANON [*with decision*]. And a very sensible thing to do, child. You should think about it. Two hundred acres of good land, thirty head of fine cattle, pigs, and poultry; fine crops of wheat, and barley, a commodious barn, nearly new, and green pastures for many more animals. Joined to you in the holy Sacrament of Matrimony, my daughter, the son-in-law of the Count and the brother of the Bishop would be next in power to the Count himself; and, when the Count goes, as we all must go one day, you and he would lead the day-to-day life of Ballyoonagh.

REILIGAN *appears opposite to the door near which* KEELIN *is standing, facing the* CANON, *who is standing at the window side of the table, with a hand resting on the head of St Tremolo. Reiligan is in the full uniform of a Papal Count – short jacket, long trousers, braided cuffs and collar, elegant sword, feathered cocked hat, and all.* KEELIN *ignores him, keeping her look fixed towards the* CANON.

KEELIN [*passionately*]. I don't want his acres of good land, I don't want his fine cattle, his crops of wheat an' barley, his pigs or his poultry, his long an' lofty barn, or his grassy-green fields either! [*She goes to the door, opens it, ready to go out, turning back to stare straight again at the* CANON.] I don't want old grey-headed Paul Mullarkey, with or without the Sacrament of Matrimony. [*In a passionate shout*] I want me Danny! [*She goes wildly out, banging the door hard after her.*]

REILIGAN [*furiously*]. There's a convent-educated girl for you – the rebellious little bitch! Wants her Danny, does she? Be God, whatever happens, she won't get her Danny!

CANON [*soothingly*]. No, no, Count, she won't get her Danny. And, now, Michael, be patient. She is very young, and she believes she has suffered a great loss. Time will tell her differently. What she thinks is love will soon be but a thought in the darkness, fainting into nothingness in the daylight of commoner feeling. It is a common thing for the young to think that their way is wiser and brighter than God's way.

REILIGAN. Last thing they think of now is God's way. Mullarkey himself doesn't help much. For a man of fifty-eight, he should be ashamed of himself, tellin' me once he'd as lief have his pipe beside him as any woman. If it wasn't for the hold I've over him he wouldn't look over a hedge at Keelin.

CANON. He'll soon be glad to come into the house, Michael, so don't worry. Let Keelin be for the time being. Her Danny won't bother you again – I've made sure of that; he saw the error of his way.

REILIGAN. A real lady livin' with a lout! I can't get the meanin' of them even thinkin' they could ever come together.

CANON. Well, don't try to get the meaning. Even the Book God is writing will have very little meaning for us till it's finished.

CODGER [*heard calling from the garden*]. Think of what you're doin', think of what you're doin', man!

*The* PRODICAL *comes to the window, followed by the* CODGER, *who stands a little way from the window in the garden.* PRODICAL *comes into the room. He is excited and a look of tense determination sours his face. He is a little breathless.*

REILIGAN [*irritably – to* PRODICAL]. Well, what d'ye want, what d'ye want now?

PRODICAL [*pushing him carelessly aside*]. Not you, not you – Monsignor. [*To the* CANON] Heard you were here, an' hurried here to catch you. Afraid I'd miss you. I must get rid of it. I'm lost if I don't; must shove it outa sight, outa me mind. I'm lost if I don't.

CODGER [*loudly – from near the window – to* PRODICAL]. You're lost, too, if you do. Better, be far, man, to be lost with it than to be lost without it!

CANON [*impatiently – to* PRODICAL]. Well, what is it, what is it you want? Get rid of what?

PRODICAL [*to the* CANON]. Wait a minute, you! [*To the* CODGER] Go away; I won't listen to you. You're a menace to me.

CODGER [*loudly – to the* PRODICAL]. An hour after it's done, you'll be comin' to ask me why did I let you do it.

CANON [*indignantly – to* CODGER]. Go away, and let Carranaun speak. [*To* PRODICAL] Now, my son, what is it?

CODGER [*ignoring the* CANON – *to* PRODICAL]. You sorrow before you do anything, an' you sorrow when it's done. You're puttin' years on yourself with your perpetual sorrowin'!

PRODICAL [*out to the* CODGER]. I'm not sorrowin' now. I'm full of elation at me own resolution not to be beaten be a bottle. For the time bein', Codger, you're just Satan tryin' to wheedle me into sin.

CODGER. You're wheedlin' yourself, Prodical; you're wheedlin' yourself into a right disaster.

CANON [*testily – to* PRODICAL]. What's wrong? What are you trying to wheedle yourself from, man?

PRODICAL [*ignoring* CANON *– to the* CODGER]. You're bad company. You're always imposin' yourself in the way of me vow.

REILIGAN [*angrily – to* PRODICAL]. Monsignor Burren's askin' you a question, man.

PRODICAL [*loudly and angrily*]. Let him wait a minute! [*To the* CODGER] A minute after makin' a resolution, I always find you in front of me, or hear you hailin' me from behind. You're my menacin' ubique.* You may well take it easy, for you don't sorrow as I sorrow. You bury your sorrows in a song, while my sorrowin's like the moanin' of the harbour bar on a misty an' a mournful night.

CODGER [*vehemently – to the* PRODICAL]. Can't you give it to me, an' I'll dispose of it for you? Don't sully a comrade's love with the test of a sour behaviour. You'll never see it again till it's dead.

CANON [*shaking* PRODICAL's *left arm*]. Dispose of what, my son?

REILIGAN [*shaking his right arm*]. Till what's dead?

CODGER [*to* REILIGAN *and* CANON]. Oh, shut it, will yous, for a minute? [*To the* PRODICAL] Mind you, you'll live to be sorry for your wild notion. Let me take care of it.

PRODICAL [*decisively*]. I will not. I'm not goin' to furnish you with the means of committin' a sin I'm tryin' to escape meself.

CANON [*impatiently shaking the* PRODICAL's *arm*]. What is all this about, man? I and the Count have things to discuss, and can't wait here all night – what is it!

PRODICAL [*after rummaging in his tail pocket and taking out a pint bottle of whisky, which he displays to all in the room*]. This is what it's all about. I've taken a vow never for ever to drink again; an', to make sure, an' rid meself of temptation, I want you, kind Monsignor, to present this bottle of danger to the sacred St Tremolo standin' there in the table's middle, appealin' to men to be sensible and be sober.

CODGER [*appealingly – to* PRODICAL]. Throw it to me, Prodical. Be sensible even at the eleventh hour – throw it to me!

CANON [*graciously*]. St Tremolo's always on the watch to warn, and, when his warning's heard, is always ready to help. Besides, we mustn't have any nonsense during the Bishop's visit. Give me the bottle.

PRODICAL [*earnestly – but hesitating to give the bottle*]. We're all part of the Bishop's bonfire, flaming up with feelin's of welcomin' good will. I wouldn't like the Bishop to notice me noddin'.

CODGER [*sarcastically*]. It might do the Right Reverend a lot of good to see a part of the real life in the town he comes to bless!

CANON [*angrily – to the* CODGER]. Be off, you mischievous poacher on men's desire to do good deeds! You wicked man! I warn you the time is near at hand when the cold clay of death will fill that vicious mouth of yours. [*To* REILIGAN] Oh, Count, break your silence into a reprimand.

REILIGAN [*shouting at the* CODGER]. Take yourself off! What are you doing here, anyway?

CODGER. Been cleanin' out your *de profundis* urn,* an' am waitin' to be told whereabouts in the garden I'm to put the lighted lantern.

REILIGAN [*angrily*]. On the bricks, mouth; on the top of the bricks! Do it, an' be off!

CANON [*amiably – to the* PRODICAL]. Give me the bottle, my son. [PRODICAL *hands him the bottle, and the* CANON *lifts the statue, and puts the bottle into the hollow under the legs and cloak of the figure. Putting the bottle away.*] In you go! You are out of season, now you are out of sight and out of mind.

PRODICAL [*firmly*]. Out of sight an' mind, wha'? Yis.

CANON [*patting* PRODICAL *between the shoulders*]. Your temptation's imprisoned in a holy place, now; and you are free.

PRODICAL [*with dubious assurance*]. Free, Canon, wha'? Yis, free!

CODGER [*shouting from without the window*]. No!

CANON [*patting* PRODICAL's *shoulder*]. And safe, my son.

PRODICAL [*somewhat dubiously*]. Safe, too.

CODGER [*shouting from outside*]. No!

PRODICAL [*shouting out to the* CODGER]. Yis!

CODGER [*who hasn't stirred from the window – dismally*]. They've got you now where they want you, Prodical. What'll you do when the band plays, the people cheer, the bonfire blazes, an' the Bishop comes waltzin' into the town, an' you with a dry tongue in a dusty mouth, parched, an' powerless to feel anything but a desire for a *domine vobiscum* death.* [*He leaves the window, lantern in hand, and goes over to the pile of bricks to fix it there.*]

REILIGAN [*suddenly listening intently*]. Whist! Is that them? No, not yet. [*To the* CANON] The cattle, Father. [*Looks at his wrist-watch.*] Jerry the cowman should have had them home more than an hour ago. I'm anxious. Left them to gawk at the flags in the town, maybe. Rushin' to see the flags, rushin' to hear the band practisin', rushin' to see the bonfire, regardless of the cattle! [*Shouting to the* CODGER] Eh, you, slip down along the road, an' see can you see any sign of Jerry with the cows! [*He listens again. The sound of the lowing of cattle is heard, faintly at first, then louder as they come nearer to the house, then fading away as they pass on their way to the byres. He runs to the window and shouts to the* CODGER.] It's all right, Codger – they're here! [*He peers out into the garden.*] Oh, he's gone now! He'll go clamping down the road now; *he'll* have to look at the Bishop's bonfire; he'll stop to listen to the band practising; he'll be everywhere but where he's wanted! [*to the* PRODICAL] After him, you, an' bring him back before he gets to tavern or town.

PRODICAL [*with dismay*]. Me, is it? What the hell d'ye think I am? A fine sight I'd look gallopin' down the road in these garments! I feel bad enough sequestered in a sequestered house, without runnin' out to show meself under the public stare of the stars. Send someone commonly accoutred to do your biddin'.

REILIGAN [*shouting*]. Where're the others, where're the others to send!

PRODICAL [*shouting just as loud*]. How the hell do I know?

CANON. Boys, boys! [*Laying a friendly hand on* PRODICAL'S *arm*] We must all leave off shouting, for it would distress the Bishop if he heard us shouting at each other. Besides, you look very attractive in the suit that's to be worn while helping to serve the Bishop's meals. [*Soothing* REILIGAN *with a pat on the arm*] Take it easier, Count; try to take it easier. It's trying, very, but we must be calm: no shouting, please.

REILIGAN [*furiously*]. I'll hunt some of them out! [*He makes for the door on the right, and, as he reaches it, a tremendous kicking is heard on the door to the left. Turning back in anguish*] Oh, who's kicking all the good paint off the newly painted door? [*He rushes to it, pulls it open, and* RANKIN *staggers in, carrying a tall palm in a tub, painted with circular bars of yellow and white. Furiously – to* RANKIN] You jellybrained eejut, what d'ye mean kickin' a newly painted door to pieces? [*He notices that* RANKIN *is wearing boots.*] Oh, looka the boots he's wearin'! [*He runs to the door and examines it.*] Looka, the paint's scattered, an' even the wood is bruised. Look at it, look at it!

RANKIN [*who has placed the palm on the near end of the table, and has come over a little way to glance at the door*]. It isn't much. I had to get it open someway. A little lick of paint an' it'll look as well as ever.

REILIGAN [*fiercely*]. What're you wearin' your boots for? Where's the slippers I gave you? Where's your slippers, where's your slippers?

RANKIN [*gloomily*]. They're in the back pocket of me tailed-coat, if you want to know. They were cuttin' the feet off me.

REILIGAN. Let them, then. You're not to cross this room again without your slippers on you. [*He now notices that the palm is standing on the table.*] Ooh! Looka where he put the palm! [*He grips hold of* RANKIN *and forces him to the palm and the tub.*] Borin' right down into the polished wood of me table! Take it off, take it off, take it off!

RANKIN [*protestingly – dragging the tub into his arms*]. I had to lay it somewhere!

REILIGAN. Don't drag, don't drag it, man! The table! [*When* RANKIN *has the tub in his arms.*] Oh, looka, looka the table! Junks out of it!

RANKIN [*plaintively*]. Open the door here, open the door.

CANON [*shouting*]. Get out of our sight!

RANKIN [*less plaintively*]. Open this door, then, or this palm'll be plungin' about on the carpet!

REILIGAN [*hastening to the door, opening it, and pushing* RANKIN *out*]. Go on, get out, you Jezebel's get! and put the slippers on. [*To the* PRODICAL] You go, Prodical, get a chamois duster, and try to get these scratches out of the table. And get Rankin to put his lick of paint on the bruised door, an' make sure he puts the palm in the porch outside the front door. [PRODICAL *goes out.*]

CANON. Careless fools. They have me heart-scalded, Count. No regard for anything: see a window-pane cracked – push it in! See a banister loose – pull it out!

REILIGAN. They'll make everything unfit for the Bishop by the time they're done doin' violence to them. [*He comes to the table and bends over the list on it.*] Almost everything at hand now. Manus has forgotten nothing. Let me see. Four hot-water bottles haven't come yet, an' the rug to go by the Bishop's bed. Yes, an' the wine. That isn't ticked off either. [*A kicking by a heavy boot, harder than that done by* RANKIN, *is heard again on the door to the left.*] Good God! Again! The door'll be down! [*He rushes over to it, and* DANIEL *staggers into the room, carrying a palm in a tub similar to the one already borne in by* RANKIN. *Madly*] Looka the door again! In another spot too! The whole panel's pattered and battered.

DANIEL [*staggering, gives a complete turn, glances at the door, and wheels again to go on his journey*]. Oh, that? A little lick of paint'll put that right. [*He wheels round in a circle to turn and answer Reiligan, the palm held at a right angle, a left angle, as he struggles to keep it upright.*]

CANON [*shouting*]. Careful, you fool!

REILIGAN [*moaningly*]. Another lick of paint! They'll never be satisfied. They're distillin' destruction all over the place! [*Daniel, when
he comes near to the door on the right, plonks the palm on the end of the
table nearest to it, and goes to the door to open it for himself, as* REILIGAN
*turns, and sees him do it. Frantically*] Aw, the table! Tear that too!

DANIEL [*as he goes staggering out*]. It's nothin'. You can put a plate over
it or somethin'.

REILIGAN [*sinking into a chair*]. A plate over it or somethin'! Aw,
what's the use of the Bishop comin'? What's the use of tryin' to
bring a little culture into the town? It only adds to a body's sorra!

CODGER [*heard singing outside in the garden*]:

> The rose that is fresh in the vase today
> Will be flung away, fadin', tomorrow;
> An' ev'ry song sung be a singer gay
> Has in it the seed of a sorra.

[*Appearing at the window, looking into the room, and speaking to*
REILIGAN] Will I light the lantern now?

REILIGAN [*testily*]. Light it, light it, an' be damned to you!

CODGER [*going back into the garden*]. Righto. [*He sings again*]

> Go away, get away, sorra, go!
> No foot hastens forward to meet thee;
> Come in the midnight or come at cock-crow,
> No hand will be stretch'd out to greet thee!*

CODGER *lights the lantern. The red panel of glass is towards the window,
so that it looks like a red eye watching those in the room. The other panels,
white glass, shine out and show dimly the gateway, the wall, maybe the
urn, and, maybe, parts of the elegant, branching ash-tree, looking dark
now from the window view.*

CANON [*bitterly*]. Listen to him! You'd think butter wouldn't melt in
his mouth. I often wonder, Reiligan, why you keep that vicious-
mouthed old man in your employment.

REILIGAN. Well, Monsignor, he's the best man in all the country
round to trim a rick or thatch one. A clever hand with the scythe, as
well as knowing the soil in every field for miles round, what you can

sow in this field, and can't in that one. A right good man, too, with the cattle when the cowman's away, and a sheep-shearer still that no one near can match. Clever, too, with hammer, saw, an' chisel at all but first-class work. And he's well over eighty, Father. No; no one but God can shift the wily old Codger from Ballyoonagh.

CANON. Things belonging to Caesar, Count. Remember there are still things of God. A favourite of Father Boheroe, too. A fine choice, I must say. Another pet of his is Manus Moanroe, another fine choice.

REILIGAN. A gifted fella, too, Father, as clever on the business end of a farm as the Codger is at the hand-work. Pity he isn't a good Catholic. Yes, a gifted man. The Codger, too. Bad Catholics, bad Catholics, but gifted.

CANON [*bitterly*]. The devil's very lavish with his gifts to those who serve him, Michael. [*Briskly*] But we must think of little now but the Bishop's visit. That's what concerns us now, Michael. When that's over, we can talk of the Codger and of Moanroe.

REILIGAN [*as briskly – getting on to his feet*]. The Bishop's visit – you're right, Monsignor; we can't leave anything to chance. Now where the hell's that Prodical? He went out for a chamois an hour ago, and he isn't back. Listening, I suppose, to Dan telling him how he near battered down oul' Reiligan's door, with the Prodical drinking it all in, to spread it, later on, over the whole town. [*He leans on the table and buries his head in his hands.*] The malicious bastards! An' all I've done for them! Like a father to some of them. What would the town be like, if it wasn't for Reiligan?

CANON [*laying a hand on his shoulder – soothingly*]. The Prefect of our Confraternity mustn't lose courage. When our anxiety and excitement have passed, Michael [*with grimness*], we'll do our best to put the fear of God in them! They understand only the harsh word and the lash from the whip. The low-minded always envy the successful and the good.

REILIGAN [*raising himself from the table*]. Looka, Monsignor, a lot of them would twist themselves into a big laugh if this house fell in on itself while the Bishop was comin' up the pathway. Oh, a venomous bunch, the most of them. [*As the* PRODICAL *comes in with the chamois*] Ah, here you are at last. Get to work, man, get to work.

PRODICAL [*easily*]. All in good time. The four hot-water bottles have come, and the rug, too. An' Foorawn wants someone in the kitchen to pluck plover an' peel potatoes. [*Looking at the table*] It'll take more'n chamois to take these furrows outa the table.

REILIGAN [*irritably*]. Oh, try, man, try, before you start cryin'.

PRODICAL [*indignantly*]. Cryin'? Who's cryin'? Nothin' easier than to cover the rents with a plate or somethin'.

CANON [*who has gone to the window, looked out into the garden, and come back again*]. The Codger's not in the garden now. I thought he might be the one who could help in the kitchen.

FOORAWN [*appearing at the door*]. Da, send someone down to the kitchen to peel potatoes an' pluck plover. Dan won't go; says he's no cook's mate.

REILIGAN [*to the* CANON]. You see, Father, how they're gettin' outa hand? Any of them who've ever been in England almost expect you to call them Mister now. [*To* FOORAWN] Well, search out the Codger.

FOORAWN. Oh, I've already asked him: he won't do it either.

REILIGAN [*sarcastically*]. An' what did that old gentleman say?

FOORAWN [*uneasily*]. I wouldn't care to say what he said.

REILIGAN [*impatiently*]. Go on – out with it, out with it!

CANON [*encouragingly*]. Go on, daughter; don't be afraid. We can partly guess what the reprobate might say.

FOORAWN. He said that if the holy Monsignor plucked the plover, he'd peel the spuds.

REILIGAN. An' had me own daughter, devoted to perpetual chastity, nothin' to say to the oul' blasphemer?

FOORAWN. Of course she had: she told him no one would think of expecting holy hands that held holy things should be set to pluck a plover.

REILIGAN. An' what did he say to that homer, eh – the infidelian dastard?

FOORAWN [*uneasily*]. No, no. He said somethin' shockin'; something that frightened me.

CANON. You mustn't be frightened at what such an old rascal would say. We should get to know the full scope of the irreverent ruffian's mind. What did he say, Foorawn?

FOORAWN. He said, Father, that since the holy hands of Christ washed the feet of His Disciples, the half-holy hands of the Canon shouldn't be afraid to peel a spud.

CANON [*firmly*]. You hear, Count?

REILIGAN. Terrible that such a one should be let go on fermentin' mockin' thoughts of sacred things in the holy quietness of Ballyoonagh!

*They are all shocked – except the* PRODICAL, *who is puzzled – and remain silent. Then the chanting voice of the* CODGER *is heard in the garden again.*

CODGER [*singing in the garden*]

> Ah, where is the laughter rich of children mad at play?
> Gone, too, is the lover and his lass
> From all the hawthorn's fragrance in the month of
>     June or month of May.
> Where, where is the time when life had something
>     fine to say?*

CANON. Hear him! [*jeeringly*] The lover and his lass. What a filthy mind the sly old fool has!

*Now the* CODGER *is seen before the window, just as* FATHER BOHEROE *comes into the garden by the gate. He comes over to the* CODGER *who is carrying a branchy, big geranium, topped with many lovely clusters of scarlet flowers. He holds it up for all in the room to see, while* FATHER BOHEROE *stands beside him.*

CODGER [*holding the geranium forth*]. Here's the geranium for your urn. A handsome plant. Lovelier than the Count in all his glory, and lovelier than the Monsignor would be, either, were he dollied up in the scarlet robe of a cardinal. God's work, gentlemen an' lady.

FATHER BOHEROE. Helped by man, my friend; it's a cultivated plant. God and man together.

CODGER. Helped be man, right enough. Man has to finish what God begins. Lovely blossoms: red as the wrath of God; red as the holy blood of Christ sprinklin' mercy over all, unknown to some I know in Ballyoonagh.

CANON [*coldly, but fiercely*]. Go to your own, for you blaspheme even in your saner sayings. You make a contraband of God's mercy, you vicious void in God's kingdom!

REILIGAN [*coming nearer to the window, and facing the* CODGER]. Set it in the urn, without more ado, and then go.

CODGER [*taken by surprise*]. Go? Go where?

REILIGAN. Outa the garden; outa any property of mine. I've no more need of you. Your evil thoughts or your croakin' voice isn't goin' to be heard any more again in any place owned be Reiligan. So off you go!

FOORAWN [*agitatedly*]. Oh, no, no! The Codger's a good old man: we all love the Codger.

FATHER BOHEROE [*putting a hand on the shoulder of the* CODGER *furthest from him, so that it looks as if he had an arm around him*]. Monsignor, Monsignor, we are stripping Joseph of his coat of many colours again. Oh, I fear, I fear we do wrong to diminish the usefulness, or admonish the honesty, of a brave man.

CODGER [*to* FATHER BOHEROE]. Never mind, Father. [*To* REILIGAN] Your loss, Count, well as mine. The old age pension'll keep me in bread, tea an' onions, an' what more does an old man want? In me time, I've fasted far more than the Bishop who's comin', or the Monsignor who's here. I'll set the flower in the urn, for there's no ill will between me an' the geranium; then, I'll go.

CANON. Go then, and no more talk.

PRODICAL. No, no; the Codger's never goin' to be a stranger in the town of Ballyoonagh. It's a tiring shame!

FOORAWN. It's a shame!

CODGER *goes into the garden, and may be seen putting the plant into the urn.*

REILIGAN [*violently*]. Your concern isn't with the Codger. You mind your own work!

FOORAWN [*impatiently*]. Who's goin' to do the plover and the potatoes then?

REILIGAN [*as impatiently*]. What about Keelin? Get Keelin, get Keelin!

FOORAWN. Oh, she's in a mood; won't do anything; won't bless herself even.

KEELIN *appears at the door left as* DANIEL *appears at the door right.*

KEELIN [*vehemently*]. The Bishop can peel his own spuds!

DANIEL [*vehemently*]. The Bishop can pluck his own plover!

REILIGAN [*furiously*]. Be off, the two of you! We don't need yous. We've one here darin' an' dyin' to do both. [*To* PRODICAL] You go, oul' son, to the kitchen, an' do the spuds an' the plover.

PRODICAL [*in shocked and pained surprise*]. Me?

REILIGAN [*impatiently*]. You, yes, you; you, you. Off to the kitchen with you!

CANON [*warningly*]. Count, Count, speak more mildly like a good man to another good man.

REILIGAN [*ignoring the* CANON]. Go on an' don't stay to argue – I'm orderin' you!

PRODICAL [*a gleam coming into his eyes*]. Y'are, are you?

CANON [*smoothly*]. Not ordering, no, not ordering; just appealing to your generosity, Prodical.

FATHER BOHEROE [*amused*]. Let the Bishop do with bread and do without the plover.

CANON [*to* FATHER BOHEROE]. Please, Father Boheroe, if you've nothing constructive to say, say nothing.

DANIEL [*from the door right*]. Let the Bishop peel his own spuds!

KEELIN [*from the door left – in a shout*]. Let the Bishop pluck his own plover.

CANON [*angrily*]. Children, children, don't be acting the goat! St Tremolo's ashamed of you; St Casabianca's ashamed of you; I'm ashamed of you. [*To the* PRODICAL] Mr Carranaun, be sensible.

PRODICAL [*indignantly – to the* CANON]. Would you like to dispel your stattus in order to pluck plovers an' peel spuds!

CANON [*appealingly*]. It's for the Bishop, my son, for the Bishop. Peeling spuds for a Bishop, or plucking plovers for a Bishop, only adds to our stattuses, my dear man.

PRODICAL [*violently*]. I won't be wheedled! [*He unties the strings of his apron.*] I won't do it! [*He flings the apron at* FOORAWN.] Let the lady put this on for a change. After an age of prayer, a spot of honest work'll do her soul good!

CANON [*almost putting an arm round the* PRODICAL]. My dear Protestant friend, this is a rare occasion; only this once; you will, won't you?

PRODICAL [*yielding*]. Maybe this once, then.

CANON [*all smiles*]. My dear friend, thanks. [*To* DANIEL] And you, too, Dan, come along and join us.

DANIEL [*coming in hesitantly*]. Well, maybe, this once.

CANON. Grand. We must be a united family for this coming event. [*To* KEELIN] You, too, daughter, come on in and join us.

KEELIN [*as she goes, slamming the door behind her*]. I hope yous'll all be settled spiced in hell, soon, the whole of yous hungry, with flocks of plucked plovers yous can't catch flyin' round yous!

CANON [*undismayed*]. Never mind her, children. We mustn't get angry. A united family. Irish, too; and the Irish aren't at their best

when they're angry; only when they're smiling; smilin' through.
[*The* CANON *has picked up* PRODICAL's *apron, and has begun to tie it
back round* PRODICAL's *waist, as he lilts his little flattering ditty, in a
half-nasal, semi-husky voice.*]

> When Irish eyes are smilin',
> Sure it's like a morn in spring;
> In the lilt of Irish laughter,
> You can hear the angels sing.

[REILIGAN, DANIEL, *and the* PRODICAL *join in, rather sheepishly, while*
FATHER BOHEROE *and* FOORAWN *look on, and listen, amused and a little
scornful.*]

> When Irish hearts are happy,
> All the world seems bright and gay,
> When Irish eyes are smilin',
> Sure, they steal your heart away!*

*During this singing the* CODGER *has appeared at the window and has
gapingly listened to the chanting, a good measure of scorn in his looking. He
carries in one hand a saw and a hammer, and over one shoulder a scythe
and a hay-fork. The blade of the scythe is heavily sheathed in sacking so as
to protect anyone from injury.*

CODGER [*mockingly*]. A happy, holy family! [*Flings the hammer into the
room*] There's your hammer. [*He flings the saw in*] There's your saw.
[*He flings the hay-fork in*] There's your hay-fork. Take them up and
treat them kindly while your eyes are smiling. The scythe's me
own. Give me regards to your bishop. [*He turns away and goes slowly
off down the path, and out by the gate, singing*]

> Ah, bless'd be the day when I follow'd the plough,
> An' the birds follow'd me with a peck and a bow,
> Though I'm bending low now, an' I feel, ah so old,
> Me heart is still young an' me spirit's still bold.*

CANON [*as the gate clangs shut*]. That's the last of the old ruffian, thank
God. Him and his songs!
FATHER BOHEROE. I wish I could put into my prayers the spirit he puts

into his songs. I'm afraid, Monsignor, God listens more eagerly to the songs of the Codger than He does to our best prayers.

REILIGAN. I'm sorry at losin' the Codger, but he must be nearin' his end anyhow. [*To* PRODICAL *and* DANIEL – *indicating saw, hammer, and hay-fork*] Take them things outa the way with yous, please. [PRODICAL *and* DANIEL *pick them up, and go off carrying them out.*]

CANON [*testily*]. Oh, let's get on with what we've to do. [*He looks at the list at the end of table.*] Gilded looking-glass, right; rug and hot-water bottles, right. Oh, the wine isn't ticked off – has it come?

FOORAWN [*at door – calling into hall*]. Is the wine come yet?

PRODICAL [*heard asking up the hall*]. Is the wine come yet?

VOICE [*farther on*]. No, wine isn't come yet.

PRODICAL [*calling back*]. No, wine isn't come yet.

FOORAWN [*from the door to* CANON]. No, wine isn't come yet.

MANUS *enters, morose and sullen, by the door where* FOORAWN *is standing. She backs a little way, and half extends her hands to him, then takes them slowly back. He passes by without apparent notice, and goes to the end of the table where the papers are. He carries a thin ledger which he lays down on the table beside the papers. He is dressed as he was before, but now wears an old air-force, buttonless top-coat over his old shirt. He wears the old hat still pulled down over his eyes. The* CANON *eyes him coldly, but* REILIGAN *greets him with forced geniality.*

REILIGAN [*cordially*]. Well, Manus, me lad, everything all right?

MANUS. All serene. Everything has come, including the wine. You can all turn your minds to cheering. [*He goes to the sideboard, fills out a generous glass of brandy, adding a splash of soda-water.*]

CANON [*deprecatingly*]. That's the Bishop's brandy, Moanroe. I chose it myself for him.

MANUS [*coolly*]. Did you? [*He lifts the glass*] To Manus Moanroe! [*He drinks.*] Ah, fine! You've a good taste in brandy, Monsignor. [*He returns to the table, and glances through a few pages of the ledger.*] Everything, Count, is set down in best accountant's style. This entertainment's going to cost you a pretty penny. Never mind – all for the glory of God's Bishop and the honour of Ballynoonagh. Have a look at it, Count, and see if it's all right.

REILIGAN. No time now, Manus, oul' son; we'll look over it when things have settled down. Tomorrow, maybe.

MANUS. I won't be here tomorrow. [*Goes to sideboard, fills out a glass of brandy again, and drinks it.*] To me own Godspeed! I'm leaving Ballyoonagh tonight – now.

FOORAWN [*with a self-stifled catch in her voice*]. Oh, Manus!

REILIGAN [*trying to disbelieve it*]. Nonsense! You couldn't leave me – me right-hand man. Look at the state you're in, an' you've no money. [*He puts a hand affectionately on the shoulder of* MANUS] Your goin' would leave the stars over Ballyoonagh lonely.

MANUS [*to* REILIGAN]. I've enough money waiting for me; don't worry. Bar the Codger, you are the only man who ever told me there were stars over Ballyoonagh. I've never seen them meself. There's never been but one star in Ballyoonagh for me. I go now. [*He points to the ledger.*] There's the ledger made up to the last penny of today's accounting. [*He goes to the sideboard, and fills himself out another drink.*] A drink at the door! The Bishop won't grudge it to me. I like to do a thing thoroughly, if I do it at all.

CANON [*bitterly*]. Pity you weren't thorough enough to follow the way to the glory and honour of the priesthood, the time you were at College, after the then Bishop had paid your fees. The time you slunk off, away from the College, and away from Ballyoonagh.

*There is a tense pause as* MANUS *stands stiff, the glass half-way to his mouth. His eyes flash, but he shakes the anger off partly by a reckless shrug of his shoulders.*

FATHER BOHEROE [*to* MANUS *and to all*]. Those words are black against charity and truth, Manus. They are false to charity, and you must not weave them into a cold and dreary cape to drag your shoulders down.

MANUS [*with a bitter laugh – drinking*]. To Manus Moanroe, the dead priest! [*Coldly – to the* CANON] I had more exciting times, in many places far away from Ballyoonagh. [*He tosses the glass into the fireplace.*] When I think of the Bishop who's coming, and look at the Monsignor who's here, I'm glad I escaped from the honour and glory of the priesthood! [*He goes towards the window.*]

FOORAWN [*anguished*]. Oh, Manus, Manus, don't be so bitter!

MANUS [*without looking at her*]. Goodbye!

REILIGAN [*as he goes*]. I'm sorry, very sorry, Manus.

*He goes out by the window, crosses the garden, opens the gate, and the clang of its shutting can be heard as he closes it, and goes out of sight.*

CANON [*with decision*]. A very good riddance!

*The telephone on the ledge beside the bureau rings, and* REILIGAN *takes the call.*

REILIGAN [*into the mouth-piece*]. Yes? Oh, yes, Councillor. Lovely, is it? It should be. Round towers, shamrocks, an' wolf dogs all done to the life, huh? Grand. Me and the Monsignor will be down in five minutes. Right. [*He replaces the receiver – to* CANON] The Councillors are waitin' in the Parish Hall for us to top the Illuminated Address with our names. Secretary Mulvey says it's lovely. In a beautiful golden frame. The Bishop will be a proud man.

CANON [*briskly*]. We'll go now, Count.

REILIGAN. Me car's outside. [*They go out by the door on the right.*]

FOORAWN. Aren't you goin' to put your name on the address, Father Boheroe?

FATHER BOHEROE. I haven't been asked. You saw yourself, my dear: the Count and the Monsignor pretended to notice that I wasn't here. My name has been banished from among the wolf dogs, the shamrocks, and the round towers. [*He sits in a chair by the table, close to the image of St Tremolo.*] Oh, Foorawn, I am something tired of it all.

FOORAWN. Tired of what, Father?

FATHER BOHEROE. Of all the gilded foolishness claimed to come so gleefully from God.

*He puts his arms on the table and wearily lays his head down between them.* FOORAWN *pours some brandy into a glass, adds soda-water, and brings the drink to* FATHER BOHEROE.

FOORAWN [*touching his shoulder timidly, but affectionately*]. Drink this wee drop, Father, an' stiffen away your weariness.

*He raises his head, looks at the glass for a few moments, hesitates, then takes the glass from her, and drinks the brandy.*

FATHER BOHEROE. Thanks, Foorawn, agradh;* I needed it. God help us, it's poor some of the things are that give us courage to stand up, and go on.

FOORAWN. It's so, Father, that you take too little, an' Manus takes too much.

FATHER BOHEROE. Ah, yes; poor Manus! Meeting with him'll torment you no more. He's gone, and Ballyoonagh will be an empty place to you, now.

FOORAWN [*firmly, but with twitching lip*]. I'm glad he's gone. I hope I never set eyes on him ever again!

FATHER BOHEROE [*after a pause*]. Not so long ago, Foorawn, he was your lover, and you were his lass.

FOORAWN [*fiercely*]. That's long ago, an' dead, an' dim, an' gone for ever!

FATHER BOHEROE. It was but yesterday to him; and, if you would only say truth, it was but yesterday to you.

FOORAWN [*passionately*]. I have forgotten it; I must forget it!

FATHER BOHEROE. You have not forgotten it; you can never forget it.

FOORAWN [*appealingly*]. Oh, Father Boheroe, help me to persuade myself that I've forgotten it all. Help me; pity me; do not hinder me.

FATHER BOHEROE. I am not able to help you, but I do not hinder you; would not hinder you.

FOORAWN. But you say things to remind me of what is all over, an' say nothing to help me to forget it all.

FATHER BOHEROE. I cannot help you to forget what you can never forget yourself. You love Manus now as you loved him once. He is still an image bright in your eyes, deep in your heart. If you could change the image to the man, and hold him in your arms for a year and a day, the colours might dim, the light from it be less; it would become a common man full of anxiety and fret, of sorrow today, of laughter tomorrow; a life offending you, hurting you, even, at times; but the common man would help you to laugh, too, help you to love when a child crept into your arms; a love you may miss unto tears in the years that are to come.

FOORAWN [*resentful, but moved*]. You talk curious, Father; talk as if I had thrown me vow away, and had hidden meself in Manus Moanroe's arms!

FATHER BOHEROE. You haven't thrown your vow away; you would be afraid to do it; but you are in his arms, all the same.

FOORAWN [*vehemently*]. I am not! The Monsignor, when he was Canon, has praised me often an' often; an' the very Bishop comin' here has praised me once.

FATHER BOHEROE. I can hear the two wordly and ambitious men speaking. God help us! You've only to read his pastorals to see that Bill Mullarkey with a bishop's robe on his back, a bishop's ring on his finger, and a bishop's mitre on his head, is Bill Mullarkey still. [*A pause.*] Ask him to release you from your foolish vows, Foorawn. Be brave.

FOORAWN [*shocked*]. Oh, Father Boheroe! Don't say such things. You know the Bishop would never consent to release me from my vow. I daren't ask him.

FATHER BOHEROE. Then ask God, my daughter.

FOORAWN. Ask God? How could I ever possibly know that God wouldn't be angry with me for breaking my vow?

FATHER BOHEROE. How did you know that God was pleased when you took it?

FOORAWN. The Canon told me, the Bishop told me.

FATHER BOHEROE. Oh, yes, the Bishop and the Canon. I forgot them. They hear everything that God says.

FOORAWN [*with uneasy indignation*]. What kind of a priest are you, sayin' such things! Muddlin' a young girl's mind against turnin' her face to God, an' turnin' her back on the world, the flesh, an' the devil.

FATHER BOHEROE. Ah, Foorawn, it is easy to turn one's back on things, but it is better and braver to face them. I shall never turn my back on a beautiful world, nor on the beautiful flesh of humanity, asparkle with vigour, intelligence, and health; and as for the devil, what we often declare to be the devil is but truth who has at last mustered the courage to speak it.

FOORAWN. You aren't much help to God. You seem to feel for none. I've noticed you with the Prodical, ignoring his needs. Once, he seemed to be knocking at the door of our church, and you never tried to open it to him.

FATHER BOHEROE [*rising to his feet – a little impatiently*]. Oh, don't worry about the Prodical – he's safer than you or I.

FOORAWN [*shocked*]. Safer than us!

FATHER BOHEROE [*moving towards the window*]. He has helped to build hospitals where the sick shelter, homes where we live, churches even where we worship; he serves God as a mason better than I do in my priesthood, or you in your chastity.

FOORAWN [*with some sarcasm*]. A great fella indeed! Are you goin' to watch the Bishop's bonfire?

FATHER BOHEROE. I had forgotten the bonfire. No, Foorawn, my road goes in an opposite direction, where, though there be no cedars, at least, I shall walk under the stars. Come with me, and, maybe, we shall find something to say that will encourage us to go more firmly through the woe of life.

FOORAWN [*in shocked amazement*]. An' supposin' someone saw us walkin' together on a lonely road in the dead of the night-time?

FATHER BOHEROE [*with mock seriousness*]. That would be terrible, Foorawn! We are dead people, and must learn to lie circumspectly in our shrouds.

FOORAWN [*reproachfully*]. You try to mock me, but should mock yourself. You have tried, and failed, Father. You have failed poor Keelin.

FATHER BOHEROE. I did my best.

FOORAWN [*bitterly*]. You have given no help to me, Father.

FATHER BOHEROE. I did my best.

FOORAWN. Or to Manus either.

FATHER BOHEROE. Or to him, though God knows I'd dearly like to help you both. [*With some scorn*] Here in the room, Foorawn, you have two saints, and neither the one here [*he indicates St Tremolo*], nor that one there [*he indicates St Casabianca*], opened a gob,* or blew the bookineeno, to say a word, or give a sign of help. When we have problems, Foorawn, ourselves are the saints to solve them. Our weakness – and our strength.

FOORAWN [*opening the door on right to go out*]. You frighten me sometimes, Father. I'm going. Good night, Father Boheroe.

FATHER BOHEROE [*appealingly*] Foorawn, Foorawn, don't be too hard on a poor priest unable to work a miracle!

FOORAWN [*coldly as she goes out, and shuts the door behind her*]. Goodbye, Father.

FATHER BOHEROE *goes out into the garden as the* PRODICAL *comes in by the door on left.*

PRODICAL [*out to* FATHER BOHEROE]. Off to watch the Bishop's bonfire, Father?

FATHER BOHEROE [*calling back – angrily*]. Oh, to hell with the Bishop's bonfire!

PRODICAL [*surprised and shocked*]. Oh? What ails him, now, I wonder? A lot of the glamour's goin' into gloom. [*He peers out into the garden, then puts some fingers into his mouth, and gives a long, shrill whistle. After a few moments, the* CODGER *appears before him.*]

CODGER. I'm here, me son; waitin'. [*He turns to gaze into the distance.*] Looka all the twinklin' lights from the lanterns carried be them comin' up the valleys and down the hills to meet the Bishop an' watch his bonfire blazin'! Twinklin' lights. Man-made stars risin' a little from the earth, but never soarin' too high.

PRODICAL [*fussily*]. Let's not bother now about twinklin' lights or blazin' bonfires. You know the ordeal in front of us. What we have to do is to snatch the bottle I hid under the bookineeno boyo; for without it, we'll be destitute.

CODGER. It was a maniacal thing to do! Are they all gone to see the bonfire?

PRODICAL. Yes, though I'm not sure about Foorawn. I seen her puttin' on her cloak, takin' it off, an' puttin' it on again. [*He comes in, creeps close to the* CODGER, *and whispers*] Listen – we'll do it in darkness to confuse him. Hum one of your tunes as if we were only casually reconnoiterin'.

CODGER [*turning out the light*]. A good idea. I'll lift, you snatch. [*He hums a bar or two of 'My Bonnie' – suddenly*] Now! [*He lifts the statue with a swift movement, and the* PRODICAL *snatches the bottle away from under it. At the same moment the Bookineeno gives out a long, wailing, trumpet-like bar of sound.* CODGER *dumps the statue back on to the table swiftly. Making for the window*] Saint Michael, head of the fightin' angels, keep him off me! [*The* PRODICAL *and the* CODGER, *with the bottle of whisky, rush out, and disappear around by the ash-tree.*]

*A pause. When the running sound of the footsteps has gone from a hearing, and the wail of the Bookineeno has died down,* MANUS *is seen outside in the garden. A cloth cap is now on his head, the peak pulled well down over his eyes. He takes the lantern from the top of the bricks, and, carrying it with him, enters the room by the window. He stands to listen for a few moments, pulling his cap down further over his eyes, then goes to the bureau, over which the votive light burns, and the Saint stands. He takes a steel chisel from a pocket, and prises a drawer open, and takes a bundle of notes from it. He looks at the bundle to read an inscription on a slip attached to it.*

MANUS [*reading – mockingly*]. For God and Church. For Manus and his doxies now. She forgot to write that down. Wants me to be barren as herself. [*He catches sight of the gun as he puts the notes into a pocket. He takes the gun from its holster, and slips it into another one.* ] St Casabianca, you're a bad boy: over the money and beside the gun. The lack of a gun and the loss of the money will make you a little more like a saint. [*He wheels to face the door on right as* FOORAWN *enters, switching on the light as she comes into the room. The two stare at each other speechless for a few moments. Recovering himself*] Oh, what a surprise!

FOORAWN [*coldly*]. What are you doing there?

MANUS [*pouring out a glass of brandy and offering it to her*]. Have a drink, dear; it'll make you warmer in your voice.

FOORAWN. I don't drink.

MANUS. More for meself. [*He drinks.*]. Forgot. You don't drink, smoke, dance, go to a cinema, read bad books, or ever swear. You are a real puritanical bitch, but [*he pauses for a moment*] you are a very beautiful one.

FOORAWN [*as coldly as before*]. What are you doin' there, Moanroe?

MANUS. Damn it, can't you see, Foorawn, daughter of Reiligan? I'm stealing a little from a lot stolen from many.

FOORAWN. It wasn't stolen; it is money saved from the reward given for honest work done.

MANUS [*hilariously*]. For work done! For setting up an appearance of sanctity, you mean, before a front of fraud!

FOORAWN [*angry now*]. Fraud! What fraud, you gaspin' throw-away from the Church eternal! What fraud, you rusty drunkard! What fraud?

MANUS [*quietly and firmly*]. The fraud of clericals forbidding drink in the dance-halls, though here, in Ballyoonagh, drinkers from Reiligan's tavern go to the dance-hall to dance, and dancers from Reiligan's dance-hall go to Reiligan's tavern to drink; the fraud of Reiligan's town stores where there's nothing in spirit or manner to show that life's more than meat, and the body than raiment; the fraud of his mean meadows where his bunchy cattle low their woe to God for want of grass; the fraud of his shirt-factory where girls work but to earn enough to leave the land, and where there's more melody in the heart of a machine than in the heart of its minder.

FOORAWN [*more calmly than before*]. Having said your say, lustiest fraud of them all, leave the money back where you got it, an' go.

MANUS [*mildly*]. You ask too much, my love.

FOORAWN [*appealingly*]. Manus, what you do is sacrilege.

MANUS. I'm a bad one, sweetheart, but you are wrong, my sombre musk rose – the notes haven't been consecrated.

FOORAWN. It's you are wrong; the drawer was blessed top, bottom, and on either side by the Canon himself.

MANUS. Ah, how readily the Canon would bless any place where money lay! For him the cosy parlour and the glass of grog; for him no part in the rainfall at morning and the dewfall at night. But blessing is different from consecration. If the Canon complains, tell him Manus took the notes from their sacred hiding-place as David took the shewbread from the holy altar.* [*He moves towards the window. She rushes over and grabs hold of him.*]

FOORAWN [*struggling with him*]. Give them back, and go your wicked way!

MANUS [*flinging her from him*]. Oh, let me go, you mournful, empty shell of womanhood!

FOORAWN [*running to the telephone, and whipping up the receiver*]. I'll get the police! I'll watch you hauled to jail; I'll have you finished in this whole district, in this whole land!

MANUS. So that's your love and that's your charity, Foorawn's love and Foorawn's charity, you sounding cymbal, you junk of tinkling brass!* [*Wildly, a deep menace in his voice, taking the gun from his pocket*] Get away from that! D'ye hear? Drop that phone, you bitch!

FOORAWN [*wildly and passionately*]. I'll settle you for ever, you spoiled priest! [*He fires at her. She drops the telephone, seems stunned for a second. Then she goes to the table-end where the ledger and the papers are and, pressing a hand to her side, sinks down on the chair that stands there. As she staggers to the chair*] You ruffian! Oh, Manus, darling, I think I'm dying. [*She takes up a pen, and writes some words on a paper lying on the table.*] Give me the gun – quick – before I go! The gun! [*He offers it to her in a dazed way, she takes it in a hand, Manus staring at her, sinking forward over the table.*]

MANUS [*very low*]. Go on, shoot me, before the strength of hate leaks away from your weakening white arm.

FOORAWN [*softly – half to herself, half to* MANUS]. Oh, Manus, I loved you once. I love you now. I love –

*She dies. He switches off the light, giving the room darkness, showing more plainly the red glare in the sky from the Bishop's bonfire. He crosses over and replaces the receiver on the telephone; comes back to where she sits on the chair, her head and shoulders resting on the table, her arm and the hand, holding the gun, stretched out, half encircling the statue of St*

*Tremolo. He takes up the paper on which she had written, takes it up slowly, and looks over it.*

MANUS [*reading slowly and softly – in stifled anguish*]. 'I can bear this life no longer. Goodbye all. Foorawn.' [*He slowly places the paper back on the table.*] Oh, my poor Foorawn! My sombre musk rose; my withered musk rose now!

*The sound of distant cheering is heard as* MANUS *lifts the lantern and goes towards the window. Before he reaches it, the sound of the* CODGER's *voice is heard speaking to the* PRODICAL *in the garden.* MANUS *goes softly to the side of the window, pressing himself against the curtain, and holding the lantern so that its light cannot be seen by anyone outside.*

CODGER. There goes the Bishop's bonfire blazing high! An' the cheerin' – the Bishop has come to Ballyoonagh!

PRODICAL [*irritably*]. Never mind the Bishop or the Bishop's bonfire! I'm your friend, not the Bishop. With our bottle of wine an' bottle of whisky, and a tasty snack in my little shanty, we'll keep the night aglow by a tait-a-tait* talk about the woes an' wonders of the world. Go on with your singin', Codger, an' shorten the road before us. A Count now, begod!

CODGER. He wouldn't like it if he knew we were takin' a short cut through his lovely garden. Window open, an' all dark. [*Exclaiming*] Begod, the lantern's gone from the top of the bricks!

PRODICAL [*impatiently*]. Never mind about the lantern, the Bishop, or the Bishop's bonfire or the Bookineeno boyo now – them's trivial things! I'm your friend now, amn't I? am I, or amn't I? We have to think of what we have to do with the woes an' wonders of the world. Come on, an' go on with the song you were singin', for I'm in a mournful mood.

CODGER. We're all in a mournful mood, merrily mournful all. [*Singing*]

> Last night as I lay on me pilla,
>   Last night as I lay on me bed
> Last night as I lay on me pilla,
>   I dreamt me dear Bonnie was dead.

CODGER AND PRODICAL [*singing together*].

>     Bring back, bring back,
>        bring back my Bonnie to me,
>     Bring back, bring back,
>        O bring back my Bonnie to me.

*When the song has died away, Manus takes up the lantern, goes out into the garden, and replaces it on top of the bricks; then he comes back to the window, closes it, and goes slouching away out of sight; while the Bishop's bonfire flames higher and more brightly, and the cheers are heard a little more clearly.*

### CURTAIN

## SONGS IN *THE BISHOP'S BONFIRE*

### THE ROSE THAT IS FRESH

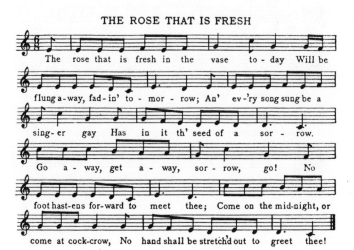

The rose that is fresh in the vase to - day Will be flung a - way, fad - in' to - mor - row; An' ev - 'ry song sung be a sing - er gay Has in it th' seed of a sor - row. Go a - way, get a - way, sor - row, go! No foot hast - ens for - ward to meet thee; Come on the mid - night, or come at cock-crow, No hand shall be stretch'd out to greet thee!

### MY BONNY'S GONE OVER THE OCEAN

My Bon - ny's gone o - ver the o - cean, my Bon - ny's gone o - ver the sea, My Bon - ny's gone o - ver the o - cean, Oh, bring back my Bon - ny to me. Bring back, bring back, Oh, bring back my Bon - ny to me, to me, Bring back, bring back, Oh, bring back my Bon - ny to me.

## AH, BLEST BE THE DAY

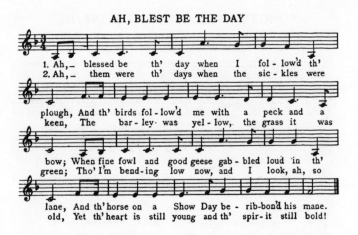

1. Ah,— blessed be th' day when I fol-low'd th' plough, And th' birds fol-low'd me with a peck and a bow; When fine fowl and good geese gab-bled loud in th' lane, And th' horse on a Show Day be-rib-bon'd his mane.

2. Ah,— them were th' days when the sic-kles were keen, The bar-ley was yel-low, the grass it was green; Tho' I'm bend-ing low now, and I look, ah, so old, Yet th' heart is still young and th' spir-it still bold!

## WHEN IRISH EYES ARE SMILING

When Ir-ish eyes are smil-in'___ Sure it's like a morn in spring;___ In the lilt of Ir-ish laugh-ter, You can hear the an-gels sing.___ When Ir-ish hearts are hap-py,___ All the world seems bright and gay,___ When Ir-ish eyes are smil-in'___ Sure, they Steal_ your heart a-way.___

## AH, THEM WERE THE GOLDEN DAYS

Ah, them were th' gold - en days with an
Oh, where is th' laugh - ter rich of

arm a-round a waist ____ When ev-'ry-thing shone so shy an'
chil-dren mad at play. ____ Gone, too, is the lov - er an' his

gay; ____ When a man had heart to toss th'
lass ____ from all the haw - thorns frag - rance

girls as well as time to toss th' hay— Ah
in the month of June or month of May. Ah,

them were th' days when life had some-thing fine to say! ____
where is the time when life had some-thing fine to say! ____

# Notes on the Plays

## THE SHADOW OF A GUNMAN

The action of the play takes place in May 1920 at the height of the Anglo-Irish war, fought between the British forces and the Irish Republican Army. Here, the former are represented by an irregular militia of Black and Tans and Auxiliaries, recruited for counter-terrorist activities in support of the regular troops and the Royal Irish Constabulary. By mid 1920 the ordinary people of Ireland, many of whom had been initially hostile to the revolutionaries (as can be seen in *The Plough and the Stars*), had become far more sympathetic to them – and openly antagonistic to the forces of the Crown, mostly as a result of the conduct of the irregular troops who often behaved far more lawlessly than the Auxiliary does in *The Shadow of a Gunman*.

ACT I

3 *A return room*: an extra room added to a tenement, eked out of space not originally intended for a room for habitation. A return is an architectural term for 'the part of a wall or continuous moulding, frieze, etc. which turns away (usually at right angles) from the previous direction'.

3 *Hilljoy Square*: Mountjoy Square, Dublin, where the playwright lived for some months in 1920–21.

3 '*the might of design . . . beauty everlasting*': quotation from a speech that begins 'I believe in Michael Angelo, Velasquez, and Rembrandt', delivered by the dying painter Louis Dubedat in the fourth act of Bernard Shaw's *The Doctor's Dilemma*.

4 *Or when sweet Summer's . . . life is only ours*: stanza from 'Sun-shadows', early poem by O'Casey, printed in *Windfalls* (London, 1934) p. 25. There are minor changes in the latter, which closes 'For each is dead, and joy and life are ours.'

4 *a bedlam*: a madhouse, corruption of 'Bethlehem', from Bethlehem Hospital, used as an insane asylum from 1547.

4 *oul' ones bawl at a body*: old people shout at one.

4 *Morpheus*: God of Dreams in Greek mythology.

4 *Somnus*: God of Sleep and brother of Death.

4 *The Angelus:* Roman Catholic devotion in honour of the Annunciation, beginning with the words 'Angelus Domini nuntiavit Mariae'. It is recited thrice daily, usually at 6 a.m., noon, and at 6 p.m. to the sound of the Angelus bell. Here, presumably, it is the noon Angelus that Shields has 'missed'.

5 *Oh, Kathleen ni Houlihan, your way's a thorny way*: quotation taken from a patriotic poem, 'The Passing of the Gael', by Ethna Carberry (1866–1902) published in her popular collection *The Four Winds of Eirinn* (Dublin, 1902) pp. 109–10. Kathleen ni Houlihan is one of the poetic names for Ireland.

5 *Ah me! alas, pain, pain ever, for ever!*: refrain spoken by Prometheus in Shelley's *Prometheus Unbound*, I, 23, 30 and 635.

5 *the Black and Tans*: irregular fighting force of 5800 armed men recruited by the British authorities for counter-terrorist activities in Ireland after 1919, so named because their uniforms were a mixture of black and khaki clothes.

6 *there's great stuff*: that is, they are well made.

6 *Cuchullain* or 'Cuchulain': Irish 'Cú Chulainn', literally 'the hound of Chulainn'. As a young boy the hero killed Chulainn's hound and, in consequence, was forced to serve as watchdog and bodyguard. He is the most important legendary Irish warrior whose heroic deeds are embodied in the great Gaelic prose saga known as the *Táin Bó Cuailnge*, or 'The Cattle Raid of Cooley' (see also note to 'Deirdre' on p. 504), contained in the Red Branch or Ulster cycle of tales. These were transmitted orally in the early Christian period in Ireland, then transcribed by monks and incorporated in late manuscripts in the eleventh and fifteenth centuries. Cuchullain was, reputedly, king of Muirthemne, in what is now County Louth.

6 *Keep your hair on*: don't get excited.

6 *Knocksedan*: in County Dublin.

6 *a cod*: a fool.

7 *Goodbye . . . ee*: echo of a famous line from one of the most popular British army songs from the First World War, written by Weston and Lee (see fuller reference to the song in a note to p. 192).

7 *knocking about now*: living at the present time.

7 *Irish Republican Brotherhood*: founded by James Stephens (see note below) on 17 March 1858, this secret underground revolutionary organisation (of which O'Casey was a member from about 1907 to late 1913 or early 1914) was known for its militancy; its leaders master-minded the 1916 Easter Rising.

7 *rifle levy*: a contribution towards the cost of arms.

7 *James Stephens*: nationalist politician (1824–1901), founder in 1858 of the Irish Revolutionary Brotherhood (which later became the Irish Republican Brotherhood) and instigator of nineteenth-century Fenian movement. Stephens is not to be confused with his younger namesake, the poet and storyteller (see note to p. 335).

7 *Pro-Cathedral*: the main Roman Catholic Church in Dublin.

7  *Dark Rosaleen*: poetic name for Ireland (used when patriotic references in literature were forbidden by the authorities) and title of one of James Clarence Mangan's best known poems, a translation of one of Ireland's most famous political songs 'Róisín Dubh'.

7  *Balor of the Evil Eye*: one of the great prehistoric mythical figures in early Gaelic saga literature, also known as Balor Bailcbhéimneach and Balor Na mBéimeann (of the Blows). Leader of the Fomorians, mythical early inhabitants of Ireland, he was defeated in an epic battle by Lugh Lámhfhada and his people, the Tuatha Dé Danann, who proceeded to take over the country.

7  *A half tall hat*: in general shape, like those worn at weddings and on fashionable occasions, but much lower in the crown.

8  *gostherin'*: that is, gostering, from *gauster*, *goster*, dialect survival of ME *galstre*; to behave in a noisy, boisterous, or swaggering fashion; to brag or boast; boastful and idle speech.

8  *green, white, an' yellow*: colours of the Irish national flag (though the yellow is actually orange in the Irish flag).

8  *billickin'*: bilking, not paying money owed.

8  *Be me sowl*: upon my soul.

9  *troglodytes*: prehistoric cave-dwellers (note later description of Mrs Grigson as a tenement 'cave-dweller').

9  *blow*: complain.

9  *got the wind up*: that is, is scared.

10  *rookery*: crowded tenement house.

10  *Banba*: poetic name for Ancient Ireland, as is 'Inisfail' (isle of destiny), referred to in the song subsequently sung by Shields (p. 10). Banba, one of the female druids of the Tuatha Dé Danann, asked the Milesians upon their conquest of Ireland to name the island after her (as did Fotla and Eriu or Erin).

10  *Oh, proud were the chieftains . . . the salt of our soil*: first three lines from the immensely popular 'Lament for the Milesians' by Thomas Davis, published in *The Spirit of the Nation* (Dublin, 1843, with countless editions subsequently). In Davis's poem it reads '*proud* Innis-Fail'. The Gaelic line means 'That is pity, without heir in the company' i.e. what a pity that there is no heir remaining of their company (from a note to the poem by Davis himself).

10  *Fury*: one of the goddesses of Greek mythology sent by Tartarus to punish crime.

10  *tam o' shanter*: round woollen or cloth cap, full in the crown but fitting closely round the brows.

11  *lashins*: more than enough.

11  *a Hooley*: an entertainment with dancing.

11  *two-pair back*: rooms at the back of a tenement, on the second storey.

11  *melodeon*: a kind of accordion, small organ with suction-operated reeds.

11  *weeshy*: very small, tiny.

11  *dawny*: sickly, delicate.

11  *the men o' '98*: the United Irishmen, who rebelled in 1798.

12  *One day, when Morn's half-open'd eyes ... The Golden Celan-*
    *dine*: stanza quoted from an early poem by O'Casey, 'A Walk with
    Eros', published in *Windfalls* (London, 1934) p. 7, where the last line
    refers to 'The queenly celandine.'

13  *Annie Laurie*: the poem 'Annie Laurie' was not written by Burns but
    by William Douglas of Finland at the end of the seventeenth century.
    James Grant in his Preface to *The Scottish Cavalier* says that the
    original woman who inspired Douglas was one of the four daughters
    of Sir Robert Laurie, the first baronet of Maxwelton, to whom
    'Douglas inscribed those well-known verses and that title air which
    now bear her name and are so wonderfully plaintive and chaste for the
    time.' She did not marry her ardent lover – who is supposed to have
    been killed in Flanders though this has not been confirmed
    historically – but, instead, was wedded to Alexander Fergusson of
    Craigdarroch in 1709. She is also the mother of the triumphant hero
    in Burns's poem 'The Whistle'.

13  *Robert Emmet*: Irish patriot (1778–1803) who tried to induce
    Napoleon and Talleyrand to support Irish independence. He led a
    rising in which he attempted to seize Dublin Castle and capture the
    Viceroy, in consequence of which he was tried by court-martial and
    hanged. See also note to 'She is far from the land' on p. 508.

14  *'grasp this sorry scheme of things entire, and mould life nearer to the heart's*
    *desire'*: quotation from *The Rubáiyat of Omar Khayyám* by Edward
    Fitzgerald (1809–83).

14  *dungarees*: overalls, usually made of denim.

14  *minded*: cared about.

15  *There's no flies on Tommy*: he is sharp and doesn't miss anything.

15  *burgeons*: Minnie really means 'burdens'.

15  *a nod's as good as a wink to a blind horse*: that is, there is no need to say
    anything; we understand.

15  *High upon the gallows tree ... when for Ayryinn dear we*
    *fall!*: extremely popular patriotic poem in the nineteenth century
    (then virtually the Irish 'national anthem' among nationalists); text
    by T. D. Sullivan, published in the *Nation* for 7 December 1867;
    often reprinted in broadsides – sometimes under the title 'The
    Manchester Patriot Martyrs'. 'Ayryinn' is Owen's pronunciation of
    'Erin' – that is, Ireland.

15  *he also serves who only stands and waits*: adaptation of the last line of
    Milton's celebrated sonnet 'On His Blindness'.

16  *as Sarsfield said at the battle o' Vinegar Hill*: a force of United Irishmen
    were defeated at this spot (near Wexford) in 1798. The remark
    exposes the speaker's ignorance. Sarsfield died more than a century
    earlier (in 1693); he had fought in the Jacobite wars in Ireland, had
    gone to France and was killed at the Battle of Landen.

16  *disremembered*: forgot.

16  *wan of*: one of.

17  *nor*: than.

17  *cock*: look.

17 *we know our own know*: that is, we know what we know (that Davoren is an IRA gunman).
17 *fairity*: honesty, truthfulness.
18 *the top sayin'*: the form of address.
18 *some swank*: showing off.
19 *Republican Courts*: courts set up by the IRA from about 1919 onwards.
19 *foreign Courts*: that is, the British (and then still the only 'official' law courts in the land).
19 *childer*: children.
20 *a Primmy Fashy Case*: that is, *prima facie*, at first sight based on an initial impression.
20 *Sinn Fein Amhain*: we ourselves alone.
20 *the sowl-case*: that is, the soul case, slang for the body.
21 *'clare*: declare.
21 *mallavogin'*: a good telling off, a verbal mauling; from Irish 'malavogue' (also written 'malivogue'); according to Joseph Wright's *The English Dialect Dictionary* (London, 1903) this means to punish in some dire but undefined way; to beat, chastise.
21 *a make*: in one of his footnotes to a song in the first volume of *The Mercier Book of Old Irish Street Ballads* (Cork, 1967) James N. Healy says that 'a make' is the slang term for one-third of a penny; generally, however, the phrase (origin unknown) seems to have signified a halfpenny.
22 *particularated*: particularised.
22 *mandamus*: a judicial writ issued from the Queen's Bench division as a command to an inferior court.
22 *interpretate*: interpret.


ACT II

24 *The cold chaste moon . . . yet still the same*: Shelley, 'Epipsychidion', lines 281–4.
24 *When night advances . . . beautiful and happiest things are dead*: stanza quoted from an early poem by O'Casey, 'Sunshadows', published in *Windfalls* (London, 1934) p. 25.
25 *digs*: rented lodgings.
25 *curfew*: the British imposed a curfew in Dublin from July 1920 until a treaty was signed in December 1921; all city-dwellers without special permission were forbidden to be outdoors after 8 p.m.
26 *Whisht!*: quiet! listen! used all over Ireland in such phrases as 'hold your whisht', that is, be silent. It is the Irish word *tost*, with the first *t* aspirated as it ought to be, which gives it the sound of *h*. The same word is found everywhere in Scotland and is used by Robert Burns in his poem 'The Vision'.
27 *'I do not mourn . . . he fell in his Jacket Green'*: sardonic reference to a nationalist ballad, 'The Jackets Green', by the Limerick poet Michael Scanlan. The full text may be found in James N. Healy's *The Mercier*

*Book of Old Irish Street Ballads*, II (Cork, 1969), where the song is entitled 'The Jacket Green'.

27 *British Tommy with a Mons Star*: the reference is to a battle-hardened veteran of the Great War; the award was specially struck to honour those who served in France before 23 November 1914; Mons was one of the earliest of the great bloody battles in that war and something of a defeat for the Allies.

28 *The village cock . . . salutation to the morn*: Shields's attribution is correct, though it is 'twice' and not 'thrice' that the cock crows in Shakespeare's play.

28 *Paternosters*: The Paternoster ('Our Father') is the Lord's Prayer.

28 *De Profundis*: cry from the depths of sorrow (from the opening words of Psalm 130).

28 *'The Soldiers' Song'*: ballad by Peadar Kearney or O'Cearnaigh (1883–1942), which became the Irish national anthem after independence. The song was written in 1907.

28 *plug*: shoot.

28 *blowin' about*: boasting about.

30 *there I'll leave you!*: I'll let you guess.

31 *sign or light*: that is, not a glimpse.

31 *a sup taken*: here, clearly, a too modest phrase for a considerable consumption of alcohol.

31 *he's too far gone in the horns*: that is, he is too old to change his ways now.

31 *them Societies*: life insurance companies.

32 *mindin' you*: that is, taking any notice of you.

32 *fit to take a fall out av*: capable of bringing him down a peg or two.

33 *goughers*: cheats, swindlers.

33 *Tone, Emmet an' Parnell*: Theobald Wolfe Tone: nationalist (1763–98), founded the Society of United Irishmen. He attempted to organise a force from France to invade Ireland. Captured by the British after a naval engagement off Lough Swilly, he committed suicide. For Emmet, see note to reference on p. 500. Charles Stewart Parnell (1846–91): Irish nationalist leader, who united Irishmen in Ireland and America to fight for Home Rule. He was imprisoned as an agitator, but was released on condition that he denounced violence. His imprisonment brought him increased popularity among his supporters and he was popularly regarded as 'the uncrowned King of Ireland'. He converted Gladstone to Home Rule, and with the help of the Liberal Party overthrew the Conservative Government in 1886. Though the end of his life found him fighting bitterly a losing battle, Parnell succeeded in bringing the conception of Home Rule within the bounds of practical possibility.

34 *King William . . . battle av the Boyne*: William of Orange (1650–1702) defeated James II at the battle of the river Boyne in 1690.

34 *An' dud ya go . . . what flower can vie with Erin's Or. . .*: well-known Ulster song, entitled 'The Orange Lily – O', that is almost a sectarian hymn among Orangemen. Text is given in Colm O Lochlainn, *Irish*

*Street Ballads* (Dublin, 1939; repr. 1952). His note indicates that the words were taken from a printed ballad sheet; no author is given. He says, 'Learnt in Belfast, 1912, where it was a very popular tune with pipe bands because of the excellent scope it offered to drummers.'

35 *a traneen*: a scrap, a straw, something worthless.
35 *blower*: one who talks far too much.
35 *the Staff*: officers of the IRA.
36 *Mills bombs*: Oval hand grenades, named after their inventor.
38 *if they do aself*: if they do, anyway.
38 *Tommies*: regular British soldiers, as opposed to the irregular Black and Tans (see note to reference on p. 8) and Auxiliary forces.
38 *awd*: hard (this speech and others by the Auxiliary are, presumably, in a Cockney idiom).
38 *koind blowke*: kind bloke (man).
39 *a lingo of its ahn*: a language of its own.
39 *prawse*: price.
39 *little bit too ikey*: a little too cunning, too clever.
39 *no curer*: that is, nothing to relieve his hangover.
39 *flitter*: scatter.
40 *blaguards*: blackguards.
40 *Moody an' Sankey*: well-known nineteenth-century American evangelists, who made trips to Britain in 1873 and 1883.
41 *the Auxsie*: the Auxiliary policeman.
42 *They're after gettin'*: that is, they have discovered.
44 *She did it off her own bat*: on her own initiative.
44 *the silver cord is loosened and the golden bowl . . . broken*: cf. Ecclesiastes 12:6.
44 *poltroon*: French, *poltron*, Italian, *poltrone* – spiritless coward; a mean-spirited, worthless wretch; a craven.

# JUNO AND THE PAYCOCK

The action of the play occurs at the height of the civil war between the newly independent Irish Free State and the Republican Irregulars (the Diehards, who refused to accept the 1921 treaty between the British and the Free State government). In classical mythology Juno was the only 'married' wife of Jupiter, the philandering king of the gods. The peacock was her bird; the 'eyes' on its tail represent the hundred eyes of her messenger, Argus, who spied on her husband's infidelities.

ACT I
47 *beyant*: beyond.
47 *Finglas*: suburb on outskirts of Dublin.

48 *paycock*: peacock.

48 *a Diehard*: militant opponent of the 1921 Treaty between the British and Irish Free State governments by which the Anglo-Irish war was brought to an end.

48 *boul'*: bold (here used, ironically, for 'fine').

49 *Novena*: religious devotion lasting for nine days.

49 *to walk out*: to go on strike.

49 *borry*: borrow.

49 *on tick*: goods obtained on credit.

50 *Easter Week*: armed insurrection in Dublin at Easter, 1916; this turning-point in recent Irish history is dramatised in the third and fourth acts of O'Casey's *The Plough and the Stars*.

50 *the fight in O'Connell Street*: during the Black and Tan war of 1920 (the situation realised in *The Shadow of a Gunman*).

50 *Free State*: the Irish Free State, set up by the Treaty of 1921, comprised twenty-six southern countries of Ireland, with a parliament in Dublin and (until 1938) the status of a Dominion of the British Empire.

50 *snug*: private room or alcove in a public house (tavern).

51 *Sweet spirit, hear me prayer . . . pray. . .er!*: part of an aria from *Lurline*, an opera by W. V. Wallace (1812–65).

51 *affeydavey*: affidavit, written statement, confirmed on oath.

51 *Deirdre of the Sorras*: the legendary doomed (hence 'Sorrows') lover from one of the best-known stories in the ancient *Táin Bó Cuailnge* or 'Cattle Raid of Cooley' saga: 'The Sons of Usna', one of the 'Three Sorrowful Stories of Erin'. Deirdre was the daughter of Feidhlimidh, harper to Conchobhar, High King of Ulster. It was prophesied that her beauty would prove fatal to heroes. Conchobhar, intending her for his wife, kept her in solitude. By accident she was seen by Naoise, eldest of the three sons of Usna; they fell in love, and with the help of his brothers, Ardan and Ainnle, Naoise carried off Deirdre to Scotland. The brothers, having been enticed back to Ireland, were treacherously put to death by Conchobhar, Deirdre killed herself and the king's treachery brought disaster to his kingdom. See also note to 'Deirdre' in Act I of *Cock-a-Doodle Dandy*, on p. 530 in the present collection.

51 *grousin'*: grumbling.

52 *the cup that cheers but doesn't*: misquotation (as so often in this play, where it is a deliberate strategy) from *The Task*, Book IV ('The Winter Evening') by William Cowper (1731–1800): 'the cups / That cheer but not inebriate'.

52 *butty*: pal, workmate; also spelt 'buttie' by O'Casey (see p. 535).

53 *the blow o' dinner*: whistle blown to stop work at dinner-time.

53 *lashins o' time*: plenty of time; abundance, great quantities; 'lashings and leavings' – plenty and to spare.

53 *for want of a nail . . . the man was lost*: somewhat garbled account of 'proverb' attributed to Herbert's *Jacula Prudentum*, in which a battle is lost through the loss of a horseshoe nail.

54 *gallivantin'*: gadding about.

55 *knock out*: find out.

55 *pereeogative*: Boyle's mispronunciation of 'prerogative'.

55 *cushy*: easy, see also note to reference on p. 521.

56 *wake*: funeral celebration.

57 *clicked with*: suddenly fallen in love with.

57 *Micky Dazzler*: common Dublin expression for what Americans would call a 'flashy dresser' (as here); usually applied to men, though Richard Wall, in an article in *Place, Personality and the Irish Writer* (Gerrards Cross, 1977), claims that it can also apply to women and has a specifically sexual implication.

57 *hillabaloo*: hullabaloo; unseemly commotion.

58 *chiselurs*: Dublin slang for 'children'.

58 *bringin' their father's grey hairs . . . sorra to the grave*: Genesis 42:38, 44:29 and 31. Tom Taylor uses this biblical quotation for similarly comic purposes – this time in the mouth of a garrulous London working-class woman – in his play *The Ticket-of-Leave Man* (London, 1863).

58 *chassis*: chaos (Boyle's own idiosyncratic pronunciation).

58 *When the robins nest agen . . . agen!*: from an American ballad by F. Howard.

59 *tatheraraa*: sound of a knock on the door.

59 *in the kisser*: in the face.

59 *bog o' Allen*: a group of morasses, about 238,500 acres in area, stretching from within seventeen miles of Dublin to very close to the Shannon.

59 *return room*: see note to reference on p. 497.

59 *The Doll's House, Ghosts an' The Wild Duck*: problem-plays of Henrik Ibsen (1828–1906), the Norwegian dramatist; each one, though the titles could be said to suggest stories for children, shows characters (like Mary herself) trapped within families or marriage, from which they can only free themselves by finding their true identities.

59 *Elizabeth, or Th' Exile o' Sibayria*: a popular moral tale about filial piety by Madam Sophie Cottin (Marie Risteau, 1770–1807); the actual title is *Elizabeth, or the Exiles of Siberia*.

60 *Virol*: brand name for a nutritious food preparation intended for babies and convalescent adults.

60 *a Wicklow man*: County Wicklow is a rural area contiguous to Dublin; there is a traditional rivalry between the two; it is here used as a disdainful reference.

61 *livin' in the Chapel*: throughout Ireland it is customary to call a Protestant place of worship a 'church', and that belonging to Roman Catholics a 'chapel'. P. W. Joyce has a most interesting commentary on this practice: see *English as We Speak It in Ireland* (Dublin, 1910) pp. 143–9. He concludes, 'The term "chapel" has so ingrained itself in my mind that to this hour the word instinctively springs to my lips when I am about to mention a Catholic place of worship; and I always

feel some sort of hesitation or reluctance in substituting the word "church".' A nineteenth-century broadside, entitled 'A Discussion between Church and Chapel', demonstrates the antagonism between the two: see Georges-Denis Zimmermann, *Songs of Irish Rebellion* (Dublin, 1967) pp. 198–9.

61 *the people in '47*: reference to the Irish famine of 1845–7, caused by blight to the country's staple diet, the potato crop.

61 *Parnell*: see note to reference on p. 502.

61 *hell wasn't hot enough nor eternity long enough to punish the Fenians*: quotation from a well-known denunciation of the revolutionary Irish organisation in a sermon by Archbishop Moriarty of Kerry in 1867. The Fenians (named after the Fiana or Fianna, the legendary warrior band led by Finn MacCumhaill that is supposed to have guarded Ireland in the third century) were an association of Irishmen in Ireland and America formed in the middle of the nineteenth century to secure Home Rule. *Fian* is Irish for a warrior or champion.

61 *mulin'*: working hard (like mules).

61 *craw-thumpin'*: beating the breast, sarcastic reference to a person who makes a public demonstration of piety. See also note to 'crawthumpers' (p. 536).

61 *Confraternity*: religious group devoted to the worship of the Sacred Heart.

61 *marlin-spike*: iron spike used by sailors in splicing ropes.

62 *How can a man . . . the temples of his god?*: lines from 'Horatius' in *Lays of Ancient Rome* by Thomas Macaulay (1800–59).

62 *if you gently touch . . . soft as silk remains*: lines from 'Verses Written on a Window' by Aaron Hill.

63 *collogin' together*: hobnobbing confidentially, a heads-together conversation; from 'colloge', an Irish form of the Latin or English word 'colloquy,' to talk and gossip in a familiar, friendly way.

63 *thrun*: thrown.

64 *Boy Scout*: *not* the innocuous Baden-Powell Boy Scouts but one of the Fianna, the junior branch of the IRA.

65 *Sorra many*: not many; sorra – that is, sorrow – used as a negative, is a euphemism for 'devil'.

66 *the St Vincent de Paul Society*: religious society which distributes charity among the poor. St Vincent de Paul (c. 1581–1660) was a French Roman Catholic saint who founded the Lazarists.

66 *NT*: National Teacher (Irish diploma, not a university degree).

66 *a wet . . . a jar . . . a boul*: all terms for a drink or a glass of something alcoholic (a bowl).

66 *Guh sayeree jeea ayera*: a rough phonetic rendering of a Gaelic phrase, *Go Saoraidh Dia Éire* – 'God Save Ireland.'

67 *had a slate off*: colloquialism for 'not right in the head', mad.

67 *aw rewaeawr*: au revoir.

67 *O, me darlin' Juno . . . you're all the world to me*: Boyle's personal adaptation of lines from 'Jennie, the Flower of Kildare' (music by

James E. Stewart, words by Frank Dumont). Text is in *Good Old Songs We Used to Sing* compiled by J. C. H. Ditson (London, 1895).

ACT II

68   *moke*:  donkey.

68   *attackey*:  attaché.

68   *riz on the blankets an' table*:  Maisie Madigan has raised money for Boyle by pawning blankets and, presumably, a tablecloth.

68   *bob*:  coin worth one shilling.

69   *the two Musketeers*:  his error, presumably, for the Three Musketeers (in Alexander Dumas's novel of that name) – Athos, Porthos and Aramis, who had the motto 'One for all and all for one.'

69   *I met with Napper Tandy, an' he shuk me be the han'*:  quotation from the early nineteenth-century patriotic ballad 'The Wearing of the Green' ('I met with Napper Tandy, and he took me by the hand, / Saying, how is old Ireland? and how does she stand? / She's the most distressful country that ever yet was seen; / They are hanging men and women for wearing of the green.') James Napper Tandy (1740–1803) helped Wolfe Tone to found the Society of United Irishmen in 1791. He was tried for treason after attempting a revolutionary landing in the Isle of Aran in 1798, but was reprieved and allowed to go to France, where he died. *shuk* is 'shook', of course.

69   *the heart o' the rowl*:  a decent chap.

69   *that bummer*:  a worthless idle fellow; in Ireland, particularly in the north, *to bum* meant to cart turf to market, hence *bummer* was a person whose living was so earned; in time this came to mean anyone who did odd jobs for a living and, in a pejorative sense, one who cadged a living anyhow – and often by doing no work at all; it is characteristic of O'Casey's humour in this play that two real bummers should be criticising as one another person who, clearly, is not one at all. The word 'bum' as a general term for a layabout, shiftless kind of fellow probably entered the United States as a derivative from 'bummer'; see note to 'bum' (p. 535).

69   *Soggart Aroon*:  Irish *sagart a rún*:  dear or darling priest.

69   *gawkin'*:  gaping, and looking foolish because he gapes.

69   *Where ignorance's bliss 'tis folly to be wise*:  quotation from Gray's 'Ode on a Distant Prospect of Eton College'.

69   *The Story o' Irelan'*:  history book by A. M. Sullivan. (J. L. Sullivan was the famous American pugilist! Boyle and Joxer frequently make such mistakes while criticising the ignorance of other people.)

70   *a Boney's Oraculum*:  a cheap booklet published in bygone days containing a wide variety of oracular statements, which circulated in millions among the poorer classes. It told fortunes of those who shuffled and dealt playing-cards, interpreted dreams, and prophesied the future of individuals. It was named after Napoleon because of his alleged faith in the stars, particularly his own.

71 *allanna*: here used as a general term of endearment, it comes from *alanna*, my child, vocative case of Irish 'a leanbh', my child.

71 *Consols*: Government Securities of Great Britain consolidated into a single stock in 1751.

72 *when we got the makin' of our own laws*: that is, under the Anglo-Irish Treaty of 1921.

72 *A Theosophist*: Theosophy, a system of religious belief derived primarily from Eastern mysticism, was founded by Madame Blavatsky in 1875.

72 *the Vedas*: four sacred books of the Brahmans containing prayers and hymns, from *veda* meaning knowledge.

72 *the Prawna*: Prana, the life principle of Theosophy; it is a Sanskrit word meaning *breath*.

73 *Yogi*: a believer in Yoga, an ascetic Eastern philosophy, who aspires to spiritual knowledge by divorcing himself from all physical and material contacts.

73 *Charlie Chaplin and Tommy Mix*: stars of the silent screen in comedy and the western; Chaplin subsequently made the transition to the talking movies, of course.

75 *a bit o' skirt*: vulgar term for a girl; Mrs Madigan is presumably so familiar with such terms that she no longer can see them as vulgar.

75 *puff*: (of breath, presumably), life.

75 *skelpin'*: a spanking, a beating.

76 *signs on it*: according to P. W. Joyce, in *English as We Speak It in Ireland* (London, 1910), this phrase is used to express the result or effect or proof of any proceeding. It is a translation from Irish, in which *rian* means 'track', 'trace', 'sign', and 'signs on it' (or 'sign's on it') is *ta a rian air* ('its sign is on it').

76 *Nil desperandum*: nothing is to be despaired of (Latin).

76 *ball o' malt*: glass of whisky.

76 *'Home to our Mountains'*: aria from Verdi's opera *Il Trovatore* (1853).

77 *Gawn*: go on (word of encouragement), cf. the Cockney 'garn', as used by Eliza Doolittle in Shaw's *Pygmalion*.

77 *doty little nook*: cosy (dinky) little place.

77 *If I were a blackbird . . . Willie's white breast*: traditional Dublin street ballad. A large number of Irish political broadsides celebrate national heroes under the guise of birds; the blackbird at times stood for a Jacobite or a rapparee (see entry under *loudubh* in Father Dinneen's Irish dictionary). In the Samuel French acting edition of *Juno and the Paycock* (supervised by O'Casey) this song is changed to Thomas Moore's 'The Young May Moon'.

78 *'An' You'll Remember Me'*: aria from the opera *The Bohemian Girl* (1843), words by Alfred Bunn (1796–1860) and music by M. W. Balfe (1808–70). Melodies by Moore and Balfe were probably the most popular concert-pieces in Dublin in the nineteenth and early twentieth century; they are pervasive in the writings of James Joyce, for instance.

78 *She is far from the lan' . . . lovers around her are sighin'*: 'She is Far from

the Land', one of Thomas Moore's *Irish Melodies* (1808). The heroine here is Sara Curran, daughter of John Philpot Curran, the lawyer who defended Wolfe Tone, Lord Edward Fitzgerald and other United Irishmen; she was the sweetheart of Robert Emmet (see also note to Emmet reference on p. 500).

78  *I have heard the mavis singin'* . . . *born*:  from 'Mary of Argyle', who is, supposedly, Burns's 'Highland Mary'. The style is, consciously, that of Burns but words and music are by two Englishmen, Charles Jeffries (1807–65) and Sydney Nelson (1800–62); a mavis is a thrush.

79  *Whisht*:  silence, see note to reference on p. 501.

79  *the Republicans*:  that is, the Diehard Republicans, waging war on the Free State forces; hostile to the Dominion status conferred by the Treaty of 1921, they wanted an independent thirty-two county Irish Republic.

80  *Free State soldier son*:  the Irish Free State army fought against the Diehard Republicans.

80  *take away our hearts o' stone* . . . *an' give us hearts o' flesh*:  Ezekiel 11:19 and 36:26.

81  *collandher*:  'made a colander of', i.e. riddled with holes by bullets.

81  *wake*:  a watch held over the dead body, usually in the home, prior to church services and burial, often accompanied by festive drinking.

81  *Let me like a soldier fall* . . . *to th' ball!*:  quotation from a nineteenth-century opera popular in Dublin and London, where it was first staged in 1845 – *Maritana* by W. V. Wallace (1812–65), so entitled after its Spanish gypsy heroine. The aria in question is 'Yes, let me like a soldier fall'; the same snatch of melody is also quoted in *The Silver Tassie* (see p. 230 in the present collection of plays).

81  *CID*:  Criminal Investigation Department (counter-espionage squad within police force), originally a British creation. There is still a unit with this title in the British police-force, though it is no longer concerned with espionage.

81  *a copper*:  penny coin.

82  *folly*:  follow.

82  *'If You're Irish, Come into the Parlour'*:  cheap ballad of fake Irish sentiment heartily detested by O'Casey; note its juxtaposition to the funeral. The satirical use of 'When Irish Eyes are Smiling' in *The Bishop's Bonfire* is comparable to O'Casey's practice here.

82  *Civic Guard*:  Free State policemen.

83  *the Pillar*:  Nelson's column in O'Connell Street, Dublin, prominent landmark demolished by a bomb in 1966.

83  *gave the bend*:  provided (treacherous) information.


ACT III

85  *wan*:  literally 'one', that is, person.

85  *Sorra mend you!*:  you've got what you deserve.

85  *blood out of a turnip*:  remark of common usage: attributed to Frederick Marryat in *Japhet in Search of a Father*.

86 *Sloane's Liniment*: old, established commercial remedy for easing muscular aches and pains.

86 *The Messenger . . . News of the World*: the former is a pious Catholic newspaper, the latter a British scandal sheet, much preoccupied with 'juicy' law-cases, mostly of a sexual or violent nature.

86 *chapel*: Roman Catholic church; see note to reference on p. 505.

87 *red rex*: one penny, perhaps from red (copper) and the king's head on one side.

87 *a make*: see note to reference on p. 501.

87 *him that goes a borrowin' goes a sorrowin'*: in common usage but attributed to Thomas Tusser in 'September Abstract'.

87 *juice*: tuppence (two pennies), probably from 'deuce'.

87 *an honest man's the noblest work o' God*: quotation from Alexander Pope's *An Essay on Man*, IV, 248; also quoted in Burns's 'The Cotter's Saturday Night', line 166.

87 *climb up my back*: take advantage of me.

88 *redshank*: a (speedy) game-bird, like a snipe; phrase used in the sense of doing something in great haste.

89 *man's inhumanity to man makes countless thousands mourn*: from Robert Burns's 'Man Was Made to Mourn', lines 55–6.

89 *a barny*: brief (and usually violent) talk on an unpleasant subject.

89 *Come in the evenin' . . . come without warnin'*: quotation from 'The Welcome', poem by Thomas Davis in *The Spirit of the Nation* (Dublin, 1843, and countless reprints).

89 *formularies*: Mrs Madigan really means 'formalities'.

89 *me uncle's*: the pawnbroker.

90 *a sup taken*: a little (or more) drunk.

90 *twisther*: twister, a crook, a liar.

90 *The anchor's weighed . . . me*: romantic song from the opera *The Americans* (1811) by John Braham (1777–1856).

91 *a gradle*: a great deal, probably from rushing the phrase in hurried speech.

92 *St Anthony an' the Little Flower*: St Anthony of Padua (1195–1231), one of the most popular of all saints in Ireland as elsewhere, he has the reputation of finding lost belongings. St Theresa of Lisieux (1873–97) advocated the Little Way of Goodness in small things in daily life and is known as the Little Flower of Jesus.

92 *a Child of Mary*: member of a Roman Catholic confraternity for the young, called the Children of Mary.

92 *swank*: dandy.

93 *The thick*: fool, idiot (from 'thick-skulled', presumably).

93 *whack*: share.

93 *banjax*: mess-up, from verb meaning to ruin, to defeat, to destroy. 'Banjaxed' means broken, smashed, out of order: Anglo-Irish intensive since c. 1920; blend of '*banged* about' and '*smashed*'? See Eric Partridge, *A Dictionary of Slang and Unconventional English*, II: Supplement (London, 1961). The word appears to be a favourite of Samuel Beckett's.

97 *An' we felt the power . . . a violin out of tune*: lines quoted from an early
poem by O'Casey, 'A Walk with Eros', published in part in *Windfalls*
(London, 1934), p. 16. The first six lines are printed in *Windfalls*; the
second stanza of six lines appears in a typescript of the poem among
the playwright's papers (now in the Berg Collection of the New York
Public Library); the first two lines of the third stanza were printed in
*Windfalls*, but the last four lines appear only in the version in this
play.

98 *Irregulars*: from the Diehard faction of the IRA.

98 *beads*: rosary beads (the implication is that Johnny will need to pray
before he is executed).

99 *polismen*: policemen.

100 *take away . . . hearts o' flesh*: see note to reference on p. 509.

100 *The last o' the Mohicans*: Uncas, the Indian chief, in the novel of that
title by James Fenimore Cooper (1789–1851).

100 *Put all your troubles . . . smile, smile, smile!*: misquotation from a
popular British marching (and recruiting) song from the Great
War.

101 *Ireland sober is Ireland free*: a sardonic reference to a well-known (in
Ireland) saying of the nineteenth-century Temperance advocate
Father Matthew.

101 *Chains an' slaveree*: quotation from Robert Burns's 'Scots, Wha Hae'.
According to the accompanying stage direction Joxer stretches
himself on the bed at this point; meanwhile, the heroic poem he
quotes continues 'welcome to your gory bed' (probably a private joke
by O'Casey).

101 *a flying column*: Irish republican guerrilla force, a special commando
force.

101 *Breathes there a man . . . me native lan'!*: quotation from the opening
lines of canto vi of Walter Scott's poem 'The Lay of the Last
Minstrel':

> Breathes there the man, with soul so dead,
> Who never to himself hath said,
> This is my own, my native land!

101 *'Willie Reilly an' His Own Colleen Bawn'*: an old sentimental
nationalist story and ballad of a rich young lady's love for a 'rebel',
and how she saved him from condemnation and transportation.
William Carleton's novel *Willy Reilly and His Dear Colleen Bawn*
(1855) was based loosely on this poem as well as on knowledge of
Gerald Griffin's *The Collegians* (1829), the novel of an Irish girl
drowned by her husband so that he might marry a wealthy woman.
The same work inspired Boucicault's *Colleen Bawn* (1861) and
Benedict's opera *The Lily of Killarney*. 'Colleen Bawn' means, in
Irish, blonde or fair-haired girl.

# THE PLOUGH AND THE STARS

The action of the play spans the years 1915 to 1916 and culminates in the Easter Week Uprising in Dublin in 1916. The title is taken from the name of the flag of the Irish Citizen Army (see note on page 513); O'Casey was secretary to the Army and, early in 1914, drew up its constitution.

**ACT I**

105 *'The Sleeping Venus'*: painting by Giorgione Barbarelli (1478–1510).

105 *Robert Emmet*: see note to reference on p. 500.

105 *'The Gleaners'* . . . *'The Angelus'*: cheap popular prints of paintings by Jean François Millet (1814–75), who specialised in pictures of peasants at work.

105 *claw-hammer*: hammer having a head with one end curved and cleft for drawing nails.

105 *'oil'*: alcohol (probably whisky).

106 *seedy*: shabby.

106 *jerry hat*: a bowler hat (from its shape).

106 *Arnott's*: well-known dressmaker's and tailor's shop in Dublin.

107 *judy*: Dublin slang for girl; see also note on p. 521.

107 *glad-neck*: with low-cut neckline.

107 *just been after*: just that minute been.

107 *a babby-house*: doll's house, baby house i.e. spick-and-span, not a thing out of place; a hint perhaps that Nora is pregnant?

108 *foostherin'*: fussing, engaged in a futile manner, footling.

108 *'Great Demonstration . . . at eight o'clock'*: Wording of the handbill here closely follows that of a notice in the *Irish Worker* for a meeting actually held on 25 October 1914: see O'Casey's *Story of the Irish Citizen Army* (Dublin, 1919) p. 54; repr. in *Feathers from the Green Crow: Sean O'Casey, 1905–1925* (Columbia, Missouri, 1962) p. 228. The 'Irish Republic' was not in existence at this time, of course.

108 *up th' pole*: 'on the wagon' – not drinking alcohol.

108 *a Mormon*: strange, exotic fellow (very few, if any, in Ireland in 1915!); a member of a religious sect in the United States calling itself 'The Church of Jesus Christ of Latter-Day Saints', founded in 1830 by Joseph Smith, who claimed to have had a revelation in favour of polygamy.

108 *best*: get the upper hand of.

108 *Red Hand o' Liberty Hall*: insignia of Irish Transport and General Workers' Union, whose headquarters were at Liberty Hall (they still are, though the building bearing this name is a new edifice, built in the 1960s). Clitheroe is enrolled in the Irish Citizen Army, the armed militia within the trade union originally formed in 1913 to protect members on strike or in demonstrations from police brutality.

O'Casey, an early supporter of the Army, particularly during the
1913–14 Dublin Lockout, resigned from its executive council in the
summer of 1914.

108 *Sam Browne belt*:   so named after British army officer who invented it;
a leather waist-belt and cross-strap over one or even both shoulders.

109 *figaries*:   elaborate ornamentation, often used in relation to notions,
fancies, vagaries; Mrs Gogan means filigree decoration.

109 *get his goat*:   that is, annoy him.

110 *threspassin'*:   sinful.

110 *fermentin'*:   boiling over.

110 *the covey*:   Dublinese for a smart alec, a know-all person.

111 *th' Plough an' th' Stars*:   flag of the Irish Citizen Army – the plough on
the banner symbolised labour, the stars represented the aspirations of
the Labour Movement.

111 *in seculo seculorum*:   should be *in saecula saeculorum*, for ever.

111 *songs o' Tara*:   the early Irish kings, priests, and bards used to
assemble in consultation in the regal palace at Tara, in County
Meath, where wandering poets recited songs and sagas at festive
gatherings.

111 *manifestin' forth*:   proof of.

112 *twart*:   thwart.

112 *th' man o' Java*:   a Dutch scientist discovered in Java the fossilised
remains of what he called *Pithecanthropus Erectus* (Erect Ape-man),
which he believed to be a creature half-way between man and the
higher apes.

113 *aself*:   itself.

114 *animosities*:   i.e. belittling remarks.

114 *Dear harp o' me country . . . freedom an' song*:   one of the *Irish Melodies*
of Thomas Moore (1779–1852).

115 *a free pass*:   i.e. an invitation.

115 *flit*:   move.

115 *bowsey*:   drunken.

115 *'ill*:   will.

115 *meet . . . with an encore*:   i.e. get as good as you give.

115 *Jenersky's Thesis on th' Origin, Development an' Consolidation of th'
Evolutionary Idea of th' Proletariat*:   a parody of the names of
Communist authors and treatises.

116 *You're a whole man*:   that is, a fine fellow and a good tradesman.

116 *throllop*:   trollop, baggage, whore.

117 *bargin'*:   being abusive.

117 *guzzle*:   throttle.

117 *he'd see me righted*:   he'd stand up for me.

117 *sorra fear*:   little fear.

117 *the Foresters*:   the Irish National Foresters, a sort of patriotic friendly
society, the southern equivalent of an Orange lodge; O'Casey wrote
of it in the 1932 stage edition that it is 'merely a benevolent Society,
and those who wear the costume worn by Peter are a subject of
amusement to intelligent Irishmen'.

118 *assed*: asked.

119 *Oh, where's the slave . . . before us*: from 'O! Where's the Slave So Lowly', one of Thomas Moore's *Irish Melodies*.

119 *varmint*: i.e. vermin.

119 *Now, yout hat's on, your house is thatched*: a country expression usually addressed to children.

120 *snotty*: to be indignant in an unpleasant manner.

122 *General Jim Connolly*: James Connolly (1868–1916), socialist and trade-union organiser; commander-in-chief of the Irish Citizen Army and, in Easter Week, of all the insurgent forces in Dublin; executed following the 1916 Rising.

123 *Commandant Clitheroe . . . Com.-Gen. Connolly*: if the commanding general's orders of the day here appear far-fetched – at least for the months preceding the Easter Rising – it should be noted that the playwright is writing of events he knew as a former member of the Irish Citizen Army's executive council. His book *The Story of the Irish Citizen Army* (Dublin and London, 1919) recounts other incidents similar to this one, which may also be found there (pp. 55–6): 'One day everyone entering Liberty Hall was startled to read on the notice-board that that night the Irish Citizen Army was to make an attack upon Dublin Castle [the headquarters of British rule there], and many a conjecture was formed as to the seriousness of the purpose indicated on the notice-board. At midnight out marched the Citizen Army under their leaders. . . . But it was only a test, and these practices continued making the members used to sudden calls, and generally preparing them for the heavy struggle that was soon to break the gentle and heavy sleepiness of Dublin City.'

124 *'The Soldiers' Song'*: see note to reference on p. 502. This stage direction is not found in the first edition of the play; it was first added to the 1932 acting edition published by Samuel French.

125 *'It's a Long Way to Tipperary'*: popular British Army marching (and recruiting) song during the Great War.

125 *th' arrow that flieth . . . that wasteth be day*: see Psalm 91:5–6. V. 4 has significance, too, in its relevance to Bessie Burgess's prayer at the end of Act III (p. 517).

126 *titther*: small scrap.


ACT II

127 *a half of whisky*: a small or single tot.

127 *glad-neck*: see note on p. 512.

127 *Curse o' God on th' haporth*: God damn the little I've earned.

127 *dials*: faces.

127 *spoutin'*: orating.

128 *It is a glorious thing . . . and slavery is one of them*: this speech and others by the Voice in this act embodies phrases taken from well-known orations by Padraic Pearse, leader of the 1916 Rising; in particular, from 'The Coming Revolution', 'Peace and the Gael' and

his funeral oration at the graveside of O'Donovan Rossa in Bodenstown (see note on p. 515). The speeches may be found in Pearse's
*Political Writings and Speeches* (Dublin, 1916, and numerous editions) pp. 98–9, 136–7, and 216–17. The speech here is extracted
from 'The Coming Revolution', pp. 98–9. See also note on Pearse in
reference on p. 516.

128  *'The Soldiers Song'*:  see note on p. 514.

128  *Wolfe Tone*:  see note to reference on p. 502. The grave is in
Bodenstown cemetery, County Kildare.

129  *we rejoice in this terrible war . . . there is no redemption*: 'this terrible
war' is the First World War (1914–18); the quotation is from Padraic
Pearse's speech 'Peace and the Gael', delivered in December 1915
and published in his *Political Writings and Speeches*, p. 216. The Irish
Volunteers, founded in 1913, was the major armed nationalist body
before 1916; its members (compared to the predominantly blue-
collar Irish Citizen Army) were mainly white-collar workers.

130  *glass o' malt*:  double shot of whisky, a full measure.

130  *Jiggs*:  cartoon character widely syndicated in British newspapers.

131  *shinannickin' afther*:  running after.

131  *mot*:  Dublin slang for a girl, usually in a disreputable sense.

131  *a tittle*:  a tickle.

131  *adorers*:  knees.

132  *pilgrimage to Bodenstown*:  location of cemetery (in Bodenstown,
County Kildare) in which Wolfe Tone's body is buried and where
annual national parades (with speeches) were and still are held.

132  *scabbin' it on*:  blacklegging along with – workers' strike expression.

132  *aroree boree alis*:  Aurora Borealis, the Northern Lights.

132  *asy*:  easy.

133  *poor little Catholic Belgium*:  phrase taken from recruiting posters
designed to appeal to Catholic Irishmen.

133  *bevy*:  group, bunch.

133  *flappers*:  frivolous young women dedicated to the social whirl.

133  *a woman that is loud an' stubborn . . . not in her own house*:  Proverbs
7:11 (the full biblical context makes explicit the strength of Bessie's
attack on Mrs Gogan, for the woman there, with whom she is
compared, has 'the attire of an harlot' and is 'subtil of heart').

134  *The last sixteen months . . . welcome the Angel of God!*:  phrases taken
from Pearse's speech 'Peace and the Gael', printed in his *Political
Writings and Speeches*, pp. 216–17.

134  *St Vincent de Paul man*:  see note to reference on p. 506; visitors were
sent to check the home circumstances of families in receipt of
charitable help from the society.

135  *precept upon precept . . . there a little*:  Isaiah 28:10,13.

135  *weddin' lines*:  marriage certificate.

135  *dawny*:  weakly, sickly, delicate; small, tiny (also written 'dony',
south of Ireland dialect).

137  *a right gom*:  stupid, a proper idiot (sometimes spelt 'gaum' by
O'Casey); according to P. W. Joyce the word comes from a

shortening of the words 'gommul', 'gommeril' and 'gommula' (from the Irish *gamal*, *gamaille*, *gamairle* and *gammarail*), a simple-minded fellow, a half fool.

137 *thrim*: trim, neat.

138 *th' Shan Van Vok!*: Irish, *An Sean Bhean Bhoct* (the Shan Van Vocht), literally 'the poor old woman', i.e. Ireland – a revolutionary song, composed in 1798, which has been called 'The Irish Marseillaise'.

138 *th' Boorzwawzee*: the bourgeoisie, the middle class.

138 *holla*: hollow.

138 *skelp*: blow; possibly from the Irish *sceilp*, a slap.

138 *bobby's*: police in Ireland – as in Britain generally – were known as 'bobbies' or 'peelers' from Sir Robert Peel (1788–1850), Chief Secretary for Ireland, who in 1814 introduced a coercion bill under which he created the Peace Preservation Force.

138 *chancers*: tricksters, liars.

138 *Karl Marx*: German socialist philosopher (1818–83); expelled from Prussia, he settled in London, where he wrote *Das Kapital*, an exposition of his theories of political economy, in which he attacked the capitalistic system and advocated class warfare to abolish it.

139 *prate*: idle chatter.

139 *I have you well taped*: I have you sized up.

139 *bate th' puss*: beat the face.

139 *pass-remarkable*: pass insulting remarks.

140 *lowser*: low, mean parasite, probably from 'louse'.

140 *snots*: mucus from the nose.

140 *bowsey*: truculent, disreputable fellow.

140 *a fair hunt*: give me fair play, a reasonable chance.

140 *malignified*: maligned, insulted and abused.

140 *clatter*: blow.

141 *Our foes are strong . . . never be at peace!*: passages from Pearse's funeral oration at the graveside of O'Donovan Rossa, printed in his *Political Writings and Speeches*, pp. 136–7. The 'Fenian dead' are the Irish revolutionaries fallen in battle, or martyred in other ways.

142 *the Assembly*: the British Army calls it the 'Fall-in'.

ACT III

143 *the area*: small sunken court giving access to the basement of a tenement dwelling.

143 *put much pass*: attach much importance.

144 *folly*: follow.

144 *Nelson's Pillar . . . Parnell Statue*: prominent landmarks in Dublin's main thoroughfare, O'Connell Street.

144 *assin'*: asking.

145 *General Pearse*: Padraic Henry Pearse (1879–1916), educationalist and man of letters, was leader of the 1916 Rising; extracts from his political speeches comprise much of the material for the platform orator in Act II (see notes to pp. 128, 129, 134 and 141). He was active

in the Gaelic League, the Irish Volunteers and the Irish Republican Brotherhood; edited *An Claidheamh Soluis*, the official organ of the Gaelic League; was the headmaster of St Enda's (Dublin); and wrote poems, stories and plays. He was executed for his part in the Easter Week rebellion.

145  *shanghaied*:   to be press-ganged; to 'shanghai' is to render a man insensible before shipping him as a sailor, a practice once common in the Chinese city of that name.

145  *th' boyo hasn't a sword on his thigh now*:   reference to Peter Flynn, as he was seen in Acts I and II; the comparison is with the Minstrel Boy, the brave young hero of the poem in Moore's *Irish Melodies*.

145  *where the wicked are at rest*:   parody and reversal of the hymn line.

146  *tossed*:   dishevelled.

146  *He is to be butchered*:   Nora here echoes the words of the platform orator in Act II.

146  *stabbin' in the back*:   Bessie, a loyalist, believes the rebels are letting down the British forces (which include her own son, fighting in France) at war with Germany.

146  *jilt*:   trifle with.

146  *judgements are prepared*:   again, the scriptural echo.

146  *a power o'*:   many.

148  *only for Fluther*:   had it not been for Fluther.

148  *tossers*:   strips of wood for tossing coins in the air, used for playing 'two up'.

148  *Heads, a juice. Harps, a tanner*:   pitch-and-toss expressions. Juice (that is, deuce), twopence; tanner, sixpence. Irish coins had a harp on one side, the head of the British monarch on the other.

150  *Wrathmines*:   genteel pronunciation of Rathmines, a middle-class Dublin suburb.

150  *howl*:   whole.

151  *game*:   lame.

151  *Dunboyne*:   village about ten miles from Dublin.

151  *jamb*:   projecting masonry.

152  *live with from backside to breakfast time*:   coarse way of saying that she knows her neighbours well and intimately.

152  *kinch*:   twist.

152  *Sorra mind I'd mind*:   I would not mind at all.

152  *met with a dhrop*:   were injured or killed.

152  *mot's*:   see note to reference on p. 515.

153  *cuban heels*:   then fashionable square heels (financially out of the reach of the tenement dwellers).

154  *kind and merciful . . . is alive again!*:   cf. Mary's song of thanksgiving in Luke 1:48, and the parable of the prodigal son, Luke 15:24.

155  *Th' Minsthrel Boys . . . out of their hands*:   further mocking references to Moore's famous song.

158  *thrim*:   trim, put a stop to.

159  *Oh, God . . . th' shadow of Thy Wings!*:   Psalms 17:8; 57:1; 63:7; and 91:4.

ACT IV

160   *you'll only bring a nose on the house*:   you'll have someone suspecting you of being a sniper.

160   *pimpin'*:   spying, peeping out (no sexual overtones).

160   *Brian Boru*:   'Brian of the Tribute' (926–1014). Having subdued Munster and Leinster and defeated the Danes established around Dublin, he gradually extended his domain till he became *árdrí*, or high king, of Ireland. At the age of eighty-eight, after a victory over the Danes at Clontarf, he was slain in his tent.

161   *Spuds*:   spades.

161   *snuffed it*:   died.

161   *hand runnin'*:   consecutively.

162   *spread that out*:   make it last longer.

162   *whipped away*:   captured or killed.

162   *civvies*:   an ordinary (civilian) suit.

163   *th' Imperial Hotel*:   the Irish Citizen Army made its last stand here, an ironic circumstance in that it belonged to the implacable enemy of trade unionism in Ireland, William Martin Murphy.

163   *our General*:   Commandant Connolly.

165   *sorrow may endure for th' night, but joy cometh in th' morning*:   Psalm 30:5.

165   *Lead, kindly light . . . an' lost awhile*:   hymn written by John Henry Cardinal Newman (1801–90), well known to Protestants.

166   *trench-tool*:   short-handled, small-bladed implement for digging foxholes.

167   *cheese it*:   stop it.

168   *I'd make 'em all join hup*:   reference to conscription then being introduced in England; though threatened, it was never introduced into Ireland.

168   *Shinners*:   Sinn Fein Republican Sympathisers (Irish, *sinn fein*, ourselves alone).

169   *a hot shop*:   i.e. very dangerous.

169   *hearse-man*:   coffin bearer.

169   *redjesthered*:   registered.

169   *th' Man above*:   a reference to Jesus or God, commonly used in Ireland and the British Isles.

169   *sliddherin'*:   slippery.

169   *picaroons*:   ruffians.

170   *scrawls o' chaps*:   poor wretches of men.

175   *cup of scald*:   cup of tea.

175   *scoff*:   eat (or drink) greedily.

175   *They were summoned . . . Till the boys come 'owme!*:   'Keep the Home Fires Burning', a song by Ivor Novello, popular among British troops during the Great War (1914–18).

## THE SILVER TASSIE

The action of the play takes place during the Great War, clearly opening some time after that conflict had commenced: c. 1916–18. The Dublin Fusiliers had departed for service in France at the end of Act I of *The Plough and the Stars*. *The Silver Tassie* realises the drama associated with a group of them.

ACT I

179 *Notes*:  these, absent from the first edition, were written especially for the 1949 stage version.

181 *Man walketh . . . who shall gather them*:  Psalm 39:6. In the first edition (1928) two further verses from Psalm 39 and two verses from Psalms 9 and 60 were also incorporated into this speech by Susie.

182 *the wicked go down into hell, an' all the people who forget God*:  Psalm 9:17.

182 *An account of every idle word shall be given at the last day*:  Matthew 22:36.

184 *You'd run before a great wind . . . calling you to repentance and faith*:  1 Kings 19:11–12.

184 *call on the mountains to cover you*:  Luke 23:30 and Revelation 6:16.

185 *turn from his wickedness and live*:  Ezekiel 28:32.

187 *A cockatrice . . . hatched out of a cock's egg*:  garbled account of Isaiah 59:5.

187 *'Adestay Fidellis'*:  'Adeste Fideles' ('O Come All Ye Faithful') – hymn of anonymous authorship with origins in France or Germany that has become a popular Christmas carol in recent years; the best known English translation is by Canon Frederick Oakeley; the musical score exists in manuscript at Clongowes College, Ireland. The hymn must have been well liked by O'Casey: he introduced it into two other plays – *The Star Turns Red* (London, 1940) and *The Drums of Father Ned* (London, 1960).

189 *Lion and Unicorn standing on their Jew ay mon draw*:  description of the British coat of arms, a lion and a unicorn on each side of a crown above emblems for each of the four nations within the United Kingdom; the Royal motto is 'Dieu et mon droit' – 'God and my right'.

190 *harder for a camel . . . kingdom of heaven*:  Matthew 19:24; Luke 18:25.

192 *your cheery amee*:  British army French, presumably for 'your loving friend' (*cheri* and *ami*).

192 *napoo*:  nothing doing, finished, gone, dead; British soldier's slang (of World War I vintage) for something that is of no use or does not exist; it is the attempted representation of the French phrase *il n'y en a plus*, 'there is no more of it'. Most notably, it is given ironic utterance in the Song 'Good-bye-ee' by Weston and Lee (c. 1917), an army song that

was used to conclude the final scene of the anti-war play *O What a Lovely War*: 'Bonsoir old thing, cheerio, chin-chin,/ Napho, toodle-oo, goodbye-ee.'

192  *Ring-papers*: wedding-licence that would entitle the owner to a government allowance or, in the event of death or disability, a pension.

194  *DCM*: Distinguished Conduct Medal, an award struck in the First World War for the common ranks.

194  *Harry [joyous and excited]*: at this point in an early typescript version of the play O'Casey made the note *'Quicker tempo to end* [of act]'.

196  *bow themselves down in the House of Rimmon*: 2 Kings 5:18.

197  *spread*: feast, banquet.

199  *Gae bring to me . . . my bonnie lassie*: song by Robert Burns entitled 'Go Fetch to Me a Pint o' Wine.'

### ACT II

201  *And the hand of the Lord . . . a valley of dry bones*: inversion of incident in Ezekiel 37:1–10.

201  *'Kyr . . . ie . . . Christie . . . eleison'*: Lord have mercy upon us . . . Christ have mercy upon us.

201  *'Gloria in excelsis . . . bonae voluntatis'*: Glory be to God on high, and on earth peace to men of good will.

201  *'Accendat in Nobis Dominus ignem sui amoris, et flammam aeternae caritas'*: 'May the Lord enkindle in us the fire of His love, and the flame of everlasting charity' – prayer from the Incensation of the Offerings of bread and wine in the service of mass.

202  *red-cap*: military policeman.

203  *Crécy*: site in northern France of one of the famous victories (in 1346) of the Black Prince during the Hundred Years' War between France and England.

203  *Conchie*: conscientious objector, one who refused active service during the war on religious or ethical grounds, though many served in various medical or nursing roles.

203  *seperytion moneys*: army allowance for wives of men on active service.

204  *'shun!*: attention!

204  *Estaminay's*: cockney pronunciation for 'estaminet', a small French café selling alcohol.

205  *infra dignitatem*: literally, 'under the dignity or glory', beneath one's dignity.

206  *RC Station*: Red Cross Station.

206  *mug*: stupid person or, as here, a victim.

207  *scrap*: fight, battle.

207  *Ay one in the kingdom of the bawmy*: foremost among the mentally insane.

207  *grousing*: complaining.

207 *cushy*: having things easy, probably with implication of reclining on soft cushions.

207 *duckboard*: wooden pathway put down to combat the mud of the trenches.

207 *judy*: girl, usually one with loose morals; in Anglo-Chinese circles a native courtesan.

208 *Tottenham Hotspur*: professional football team based in north London suburb.

211 *red-tabb'd squit*: abusive reference to an army officer; 'red-tabb'd' refers to the flashes on an officer's epaulettes; a 'squit' is a small insignificant person.

212 *Per omnia saecula saeculonum*: literally 'from century to century', that is, 'for all times' or 'for ever and ever'; the phrase is presumably the speaker's garbled recollection of the ending of a prayer in the old Latin Mass ('*Saeculorum*' should really be '*Saeculum*').

213 *Comprenneemoy, Tray bong*: pidgin French (*comprenez-moi, très bon*).

213 *Bond Street*: fashionable London shopping-area.

216 *Grant them all the peace of death*: after celebration of the Mass the priest intones the refrain 'Grant them eternal rest, O Lord'; the Staff-Wallah's 'prayer' here is an ironic echo of this benediction.

217 *Only flashes are seen; no noise is heard*: additional stage direction first appended to stage version in 1949, presumably based on experience of Raymond Massey's 1929 stage production in London.


ACT III

218 *'Mater Misericordiae, ora pro nobis'*: Mother of Mercy, pray for us.

218 *how are the mighty fallen and the weapons of war perished!*: 2 Samuel 1:19 and 25.

219 *VAD*: Voluntary Aid Detachment.

222 *fag*: cigarette.

224 *DSO*: Distinguished Service Order, award restricted to commissioned officers.

226 *tips*: advice, counsel.

228 *VC*: Victoria Cross – the most prestigious of British military awards for valorous conduct.

230 *You know th' oul' song – Let Me Like a Soldier Fall!*: quotation from an aria in W. V. Wallace's opera *Maritana* (see fuller note on p. 509); this speech and the preceding one were added to the text of the stage version first published in 1949.

232 *Forasmuch as ye do it unto the least of these my brethren, ye do it unto me*: Matthew 25:45.

232 *for wonderful He is in His doing toward the children of men*: cf. Psalm 66:4; this biblical quotation (and others in the 1928 version that have been deleted in the present text) gives clear evidence that O'Casey used the Anglican *Book of Common Prayer* as well as the 1611 Authorised Version of the Bible. In the former, Psalm 66:4 reads, 'O come hither, and behold the works of God; how *wonderful* He is in His

doing toward the children of men.' The AV, on the other hand, says, 'He is *terrible* in his doing toward the children of men.'

232  *Salve Regina, mater misericordiae . . . benedictum fructum ventris tui* – : this is one of the post-communion prayers after Low Mass – 'Hail, Holy Queen, Mother of Mercy; hail, our life, our sweetness and our hope! To Thee do we cry, poor banished children of Eve; to Thee do we send up our sighs, mourning and weeping in this vale of tears. Turn then, most gracious advocate, thine eyes of mercy towards us; and show unto us the blessed fruit of Thy womb, Jesus.'

232  *Nobis post hoc . . . o dulcis Virgo Maria!* :  After this our exile, Oh clement, oh loving, oh sweet Virgin Mary!

ACT IV

234  *for even creeping things can praise the Lord!* :   cf. Psalm 148:10.

234  *the day cometh when no man can play* :   bitter reverse of the biblical: 'The night cometh, when no man can work' (John 9:4).

235  *a cod* :   a deception, sham, humbug.

241  *the blood that was shed for you and for many for the commission of sin!* :   words used in the Anglican Communion service and in the Roman Catholic mass – where, however, it is *remission* and not *commission* of sin, as follows: 'this is my blood of the New Testament, which is shed for you and for many, for remission of sins'. The service is here quoting from the words of Christ in Matthew's gospel, see 26:28.

241  *lift up thine eyes unto the hills* :   Psalm 121:1.

241  *He whirls round in the chair to the beat of the tune* :   this effective piece of stage business was added to the stage version, presumably on the basis of experience of the original 1929 London production.

242  *The Lord hath given . . . Blessed be the Name of the Lord* :   Job 1:21; also quoted in the Anglican burial service in *The Book of Common Prayer* (1559), well known to O'Casey.

246  *pimp* :   spy (see also note on p. 518).

248  *Jessie, Teddy Foran and Harry Heegan . . . must go on living* :   this speech is not found in the first edition; it was first added to the stage version of 1949.

248  *Swing into the dance . . . We a full life on the flow!* :   the text of Maxwell's lyric is considerably changed from the first version (1928), where the music is a tango instead of, as here, a waltz.

# RED ROSES FOR ME

This is the most obviously autobiographical of O'Casey's plays, embodying relationships and events that occurred in his early manhood from about 1911 to 1917; Ayamonn Breyden is a somewhat idealised self-portrait whose relationships with his mother, his girl-friend and the local Protestant minister are further delineated in *Drums under the Windows* and *Inishfallen, Fare Thee Well*. The railway strike took place in 1911, while O'Casey was still employed by the Great Northern Railway of Ireland, but experiences from the 1913 Dublin Lockout are also realised in the action of the play.

ACT I

258   *St Burnupus*:   in reality, St Barnabas' Church, North Wall, Dublin: Church of Ireland place of worship for O'Casey in his teens and early manhood; here, he taught Sunday school as well as being a regular communicant for many years; it was demolished in 1966.

260   *Ay, an' for much more slaughter . . . say I sent thee hither!*:   dialogue embodying Gloucester's murder of the King in Shakespeare's *King Henry the Sixth, Part Three*, v., vi., 59–67.

261   *Brennan on the Moor*:   Irish outlaw hero whose role is somewhat similar to that of the English Robin Hood, found in the popular traditional Irish ballad bearing his name – see, for example, 'Brennan on the Moor' in *More Irish Street Ballads*, ed. Colm O Lochlainn (Dublin, 1965) pp. 144–5.

262   *saw the air . . . tear his passion to tatthers*:   phrases from Hamlet's speech to the players, *Hamlet*, III.ii.10.

263   *aself*:   itself.

264   *a man's way with a maid*:   Proverbs 30:19.

264   *a dim shape now in a gold canoe*:   this image and the lyric of 'Red Roses for Me' were the inspiration for the creation of this play, for which O'Casey's original title was *At Sea in a Gold Canoe*.

265   *The Riddle of the Universe*:   once popular pro-Evolution book by Ernst Haeckel (1834–1919); originally entitled *Die Welträthsel*, its full title in English is *The Riddle of the Universe at the Close of the Nineteenth Century* (London, 1900).

266   *Eblana*:   ancient poetic name for Dublin.

267   *Hey ho, the wind and the rain, for the rain it raineth every day*:   quotation from the clown Feste's song at the conclusion to Shakespeare's *Twelfth Night*, v.i.387–9.

274   *avic's*:   literally, in Irish, 'my son's'; from the vocative of *mac*, i.e. *a mhic*, my son; the meaning is uncertain in this context.

274   *the Sword of Light*:   in Gaelic, 'an Claidheamh Soluis', symbol for regeneration and, as such, used as the title for the Gaelic League journal, edited by Padraic Pearse (see note on p. 516). There, it was a symbol for the revival of the Irish language. It was also associated by O'Casey with 'the sword of the Lord and of Gideon; it was on the sword's hilt that the knights took their vows before they set sail to deliver the Holy Land from the infidel' and with 'the Sword of the Spirit' – see his essay 'Purple Dust in Their Eyes' in *Under a Colored Cap* (London, 1963) p. 271.

274   *coon or Kaffir*:   pejorative references to black people in, respectively, North America and South Africa.

275   *A sober black shawl . . . red roses for me!*:   original lyric by O'Casey to a traditional air; its writing preceded the play bearing its name.

275   *Count McCormack*:   John McCormack (1884–1945), extraordinarily popular Irish tenor; the title of count in the Papal peerage (awarded to him by the Vatican in 1928) is here used mockingly by O'Casey.

275   *Mother Mo Chree*:   popular and sentimental nineteenth-century Irish ballad whose title means 'mother dear', from Irish *mo croidhe*, literally 'my heart'.

275   *fewroory*:   furore.

275   *hippodhrome*:   ironic reference to the music-hall tradition, in which such songs were often performed in nineteenth-century England.

276   *snipe's*:   a snipe is a long-beaked bird.

277   *Aengus*:   Oengus or Angus Og, Gaelic god of love and youth, a symbolic figure much loved by O'Casey, he is given a splendid poster in the Tóstal procession in a later play, *The Drums of Father Ned* (London, 1960). Various Gaelic myths associate Aengus with birds and human beings transformed into birds: his wife, Caer, had originally been bewitched into a bird and Aengus took the form of one when wooing her.

279   *Angelico or Constable*:   Fra Angelico (c. 1400–55), one of the leading Italian painters in the first half of fifteenth century, adopted in his frescoes and altarpieces principles of Renaissance art established by Brunelleschi and Masaccio and codified by Alberti. John Constable (1776–1837), with J. M. W. Turner, dominated British landscape-painting in the early nineteenth century; his work at its best reconciles directness of personal observation with rules of composition learned from seventeenth-century masters. Both artists were much admired by the young O'Casey, who had originally wanted to be a painter himself – another personal touch in a highly autobiographical play.

279   *Ruskin's Crown of Wild Olive*:   John Ruskin, Victorian man of letters (1819–1900) and art-critic, whose social criticism strongly influenced the playwright's thinking in early manhood. *The Crown of Wild Olive* was first published in 1866.

280   *Our courage . . . Fenians shall turn a dark night into day!*:   quotation from 'The Bold Fenian Men', nineteenth-century patriotic ballad.


ACT II

284   *But I am pigeon-livered . . . bloody, bawdy villain!*:   Hamlet, II.ii.588–91.

284   *Will*:   William Shakespeare (1564–1616).

285   *Terence Bellew MacManus*:   nationalist and revolutionary (1823–60). MacManus worked as a successful shipping-agent in England until 1843, when he joined the Young Ireland Movement upon his return to Ireland. He was with William Smith O'Brien and John Blake

Dillon at the skirmish with police at Ballingarry, County Tipperary, in July 1848 that brought the rising of that year to an inglorious end. Initially sentenced to death for treason, his sentence was commuted to transportation for life to Van Diemen's Land (now Tasmania). With Thomas Meagher, he escaped from there in 1852 and settled in San Francisco, where he lived in poverty until his death eight years later. His body was brought to Ireland and, following a huge funeral organised by the Fenian Movement, was buried in Glasnevin cemetery, Dublin, on 10 November 1861, despite vehement opposition from Cardinal Cullen.

286  *Council o' Thrent*:   the Council of Trent, the long-term deliberations of a council of Roman Catholic bishops (1545–63); the nineteenth council (meeting) of the bishops of the Roman Church, it overhauled and tightened its doctrines and discipline following the onslaughts of the Reformation. Though there were attempts at reconciliation with the Protestant world, the Council in effect promoted the division between the two. Many extremist positions were rejected but reactionary measures such as the drawing-up of an index of forbidden books were commended, though left for Pope Pius IV to complete.

286  *Durry*:   Ulster pronunciation of 'Derry' – that is, Londonderry in Northern Ireland – famous for a siege in which the Protestant garrison successfully held out against a Catholic army in 1689.

286  *Boyne*:   reference to the site of the famous battle, where on 12 July 1690 the Protestant William II defeated the forces of the Catholic James II.

286  *slup in th' puss*:   slap in the face.

288  *sounding brass an' tinkling cymbal*:   see note on p. 539.

289  *one in the bake*:   a blow to the nose (beak).

290  *bowseys*:   rough, disreputable louts.

292  *Terra Del Fooaygeeans*:   inhabitants of Tierra del Fuego (land of fire), at the southernmost tip of the South American continent, here used to denote outlandish and uncivilised people.

292  *Hung as high as Gilderoy*:   reference to the hero in a popular Scottish ballad bearing that name. The protagonist was Patrick MacGregor, a noted Highland robber and cattle-rustler, executed with five of his gang near Edinburgh in 1638. He was usually called Gillie Roy – that is, the Red Roy – from the colour of his hair; hence the designation 'Gilderoy', under which he has become almost as famous as Rob Roy or Robin Hood.

294  *whins*:   gorse-bushes.

295  *Time's a perjured jade . . . must die*:   in a discussion of this neo-Elizabethan passage with the present editor some years ago O'Casey noted that there is a mistake in gender here – 'jade' is invariably female and the reference should be 'an' ever *she* moans a man must die'.

ACT III

300   *West's Awake Steeplechase*: ironic reference in the context of a
       horse-race – 'the West's awake' is a popular refrain from a
       nineteenth-century patriotic ballad by Thomas Davis foretelling the
       political and spiritual reawakening of Ireland.

300   *The* RECTOR *and the* INSPECTOR: subsequent references to the Primate
       and to Dean Swift suggest that Clinton and Finglas are walking
       towards the river Liffey after attending a wedding in St Patrick's
       (Church of Ireland) Cathedral in the impoverished Liberties district
       of Dublin.

301   *Grattan's*: Henry Grattan (1746–1820), orator, politician and lawyer.
       One of the most eloquent orators of his time, he was the moving spirit
       of the Irish Parliament from 1782 until, under pressure from the
       British government, it dissolved itself by the Act of Union in 1800.
       Though he would be thought essentially conservative in comparison
       with politicians such as Wolfe Tone or John Mitchel, Grattan is
       viewed unfavourably by Inspector Finglas presumably because the
       politician vigorously opposed the union with Britain.

301   *chiselurs*: Dublin slum word for children.

302   *Swift*: Jonathan Swift (1667–1745), prose satirist and poet, was Dean
       of St Patrick's Cathedral, Dublin, 1713–45. Defender of liberty and,
       consequently, a powerful critic of English exploitation of Ireland, he
       was much loved by many of the common folk, who (as the Rector says
       in this scene) gave him a popular hero's funeral in Dublin.

303   *Finn MacCool . . . Goll Mac Morna . . . Caoilte . . . and Oscar of the
       invincible spear*: redoubtable heroes of the legendary Fianna (from
       *fian*, Irish for champion or warrior), a military force which sup-
       posedly guarded Ireland in the third century; the mythical Finn
       MacCumhaill or Finn MacCool was its leader. The role of these
       warriors in the saga literature is akin to that of the Knights of the
       Round Table in the Arthurian tradition.

305   *I stroll'd with a fine maid . . . her shoe?*: lyric by O'Casey to a
       traditional air.

306   *'Pearl of th' White Breasts' . . . 'Battle Song o' Munster'*: patriotic songs
       celebrating past Hibernian achievements.

306   *Conn's battle-fire*: another mythical hero prominent among the war-
       riors of the Fianna.

307   *her three gates*: Dublin's coat of arms bears upon it the representation
       of three castles.

308   *St Colmkille . . . Aidan . . . Lausereena . . . Brigid*: Columcille or
       Columba (c. 521–97) was of the blood royal and might well have
       become High King of Ireland had he not chosen to be a priest. His
       truly adventurous and vital personality has given rise to many
       legends. A splendid sailor, he was a poet (in Latin and Irish) as well as
       a man of action. With twelve companions he founded the famous
       monastic settlement at Iona in Scotland in AD 563, from which
       southern Scotland and northern England were evangelised, and a
       monastery at Durrow in County Offaly. St Aidan (Aedhan), or

Maedoc of Ferns, is known to have died in AD 626. According to legend, he came from Connaught to study at St David's monastery in Wales; returning to Ireland, he built a monastery at Ferns, in County Wexford, and became a bishop. The identity of St Lausereena is more difficult to ascertain. There are two Irish saints named Laserian and one of these may be meant here. The better known is Laserian or Molaisse and (probably) Lamliss, bishop and founder of the abbey of Leighlin; he built a cathedral there about 622 and died in 638. The other Laserian (or Laisren) was third abbot of Iona, AD 600–5; a cousin of Columcille, he was also Abbot of Durrow, and for these reasons it may be he to whom Finnoola is referring here. St Brigid or Bride, who flourished in the second half of the fifth century, was probably born at Faughart, near Dundalk in County Louth. She had the same love of nature and power over the animal kingdom traditionally displayed by Celtic saints. Daughter of a Leinster chieftain, she ranks as the most remarkable Irishwoman of the fifth century. Brought up a Christian, she became a nun and was a pioneer of Irish feminine monasticism in that she was the innovator of community life for women. It is now the fashion to decry the numerous Brigidine legends for their naive credulity and contradictions but they remain valuable for their delineation of a strongly defined character that is familiarly Irish; consistently, they depict Brigid as generous and gay, vehement and energetic, and always compassionate towards the poor. She is popularly supposed to be buried in Downpatrick in the same grave as Patrick and Columcille. Her cult, strong in Brittany as well as Ireland, appears to have appropriated features from a pagan namesake who was a goddess of fire.

308 *the' bent back of an oul woman as well as th' walk of a queen*: reference to W. B. Yeats's early patriotic play, *Cathleen ni Houlihan*, whose aged heroine assumes 'the walk of a queen' when the young men are prepared to lay down their lives for Ireland (see note on p. 498 on Kathleen ni Houlihan).

308 *Ayamonn's head set in a streak of sunlight, looking like the severed head of Dunn-Bo speaking out of the darkness*: O'Casey's protagonist is poet as well as warrior, like the Fenians of old with whom he is persistently linked in the play. Donn-bó or Dunn-Bo, a warrior-poet, is described in Eleanor Hull's *Pagan Ireland* (Dublin, 1923) as a handsome youth who was famous as singer and story-teller. On the eve of a battle the warriors asked him to sing for them but he refused, saying he would do so within twenty-four hours. Later, he fought and died alongside the King of Erin, who was also killed in the engagement. That evening a warrior found Donn-bó's severed head singing because it had been commanded to so do by 'the King of the Plains of Heaven' to make music for the King of Erin. The head promised to sing for the hosts of Leinster 'when my minstrelsy here is done'; the warrior subsequently carried the head to the feasting-place of the men of Leinster, where it was set on a pillar. 'Then Don-bó', the story goes,

'turned his face to the wall, that the darkness might be around him', and sang so sad a song that 'all the host sat weeping at the sound of it'. The story obviously meant much to O'Casey, who makes use of several parallels in Ayamonn's latterday martyrdom. He also celebrated Donn-bó's story in the Tóstal preparations in his later drama *The Drums of Father Ned* (London, 1960), though acknowledging there (through the words of one of his Irish patriots, who obviously has never heard of Dunn-Bo) that many present-day Irishmen no longer have the awareness of their ancient gods and heroes that the young O'Casey's contemporaries possessed (see *The Drums of Father Ned*, pp. 77–8).

308 *Songs of Osheen and Sword of Oscar*: Osheen (or Oisin), son of Finn MacCumhall, leader of the Fianna; Oscar was Oisin's son.

311 *Fair city . . . finest that ever was seen*: lyric by O'Casey to a traditional air. In the earliest typescript draft the song was to be sung to the melody, not of 'a Gavotte, or an air of some dignified and joyous dance' as here (and in all published versions), but to 'that of the jig, "The Humours of Bandon" '.

311 *th' race of Milesius*: mythical tribe embodying the splendours and achievements of the early Gaels, celebrated in Thomas Davis's poem, 'Lament for the Milesians', and Charles Robert Maturin's novel *The Milesian Chief* of 1811. Reputedly the ancestors of the present Irish race, the Milesians were a third wave of colonising invaders who conquered the Tuatha Dé Danann, as the latter had defeated the Fomorians. Supposedly, they were descended from a Scythian nobleman, Mile, expelled from Egypt, who came to Ireland by means of Spain.

312 *Spanish ale foams high . . . wine from th' royal Pope's a common drink*: images celebrating Ireland's early Christian civilisation derived from the well-known patriotic poem 'Dark Rosaleen' by James Clarence Mangan (1803–49), based on an eighteenth-century Irish poem (see note on p. 499).

ACT IV

316 *daffodils that come . . . and take the winds of March with beauty*: quotation from Shakespeare's *The Winter's Tale*, IV.iv.118–20.

317 *out of the mouths of even babes and sucklings cometh wisdom*: Psalm 8:2 and Matthew 21:16.

318 *our Shechinah*: a glorious vision, the divine presence; in Jewish literature *shekinah* meant the direct presence of God among men, in the Tabernacle or temple, immediately overshadowing and protecting His people. Ezekiel, in Ezekiel 40–8, has a vision in such terms of the restored temple at Jerusalem. Later Jewish writers referred to God's luminous presence as 'the glory of the shekinah', literally 'divine abode'.

320 *a decko*: a peep, a quick look.

321 *the Lurchers*: these are the men (elsewhere in the text referred to as

'loungers') who were sitting on the parapets and lounging at the street corners near the bridge across the River Lifey in the third act.

322 *On'*: And.

322 *stud*: stood.

322 *th' heroes o' Dully's Brae!*: Ulster pronunciation of Dolly's Brae, near Banbridge in County Down, where on 12 July 1849 a skirmish between Catholic Ribbonmen and Orangemen followed the former confronting an Orange Order rally; thirty Catholics were killed and the incident became (as here) part of Orange folklore.

322 *St Bartholomew's Day's*: the reference is to the slaughter of Huguenots in France ordered by Charles IX at the instigation of his mother, Catherine de Médicis; beginning on 24 August 1572, the incident (in which casualties are variously estimated at between 2000 and 100,000 deaths) has become known as the Massacre of St Bartholomew.

323 *auto-dey-fey!*: *auto da fé*, public indictment of persons tried by Spanish Inquisition and usually burned at the stake.

324 *Ichabod*: literally, in Hebrew, 'Where is the glory?' – that is, really, that there is no glory; name of a child (in I Samuel 4:21–2) so called after the defeat of Israel and the capture of the Ark of the covenant by the Philistines. Dowzard seems to be using the term very loosely here, possibly as a general term of reproach for what he (wrongly) sees as the clergyman's 'defeatism', his 'surrender' to idolatry.

324 *Dagon*: typically an hysterically garbled account from a biblical incident (Judges 16:23); Dagon was the god of the Philistines; here it is invoked as a god of superstitious idolatry.

326 *fut*: foot.

326 *even as in a glass, darkly*: I Corinthians 13:12.

327 *the waters of Shiloah that go softly*: the prophet Isaiah contrasts the gently flowing waters of Shiloah with the mighty torrent of the river Euphrates, the former symbolising divine aid and the latter the naked power of Assyrian arms (here, such tranquillity is contrasted to the brutality of the strike-breaking forces).

327 *a thousand years in Thy sight are but as yesterday*: Psalm 90:4.

328 *Charon*: ferryman in classical mythology who conveys souls of the dead across the Styx.

## COCK-A-DOODLE DANDY

This play, while it re-creates events that actually occurred in Ireland during the 1940s – the killing of a man by a priest was the subject of legal action while in another court case, a young man was imprisoned and fined for kissing a woman in a public place – also looks back to the Ireland of O'Casey's youth in a spirit of extravagant burlesque. Beneath the hilarious fantasy, however, lies heartbreak and tragedy.

335 *James Stephens*:   Irish poet and man of letters (1880 or 1882–1950), not
to be confused with the nineteenth-century nationalist politician (see
note on p. 498). O'Casey dedicated the play to Stephens when he
heard from their mutual publisher–friend Harold Macmillan, that
the poet was depressed and unable to write; within a year of the play's
publication Stephens was dead.

336 *Nyadnanave*:   Irish, *nead na naomh*, literally 'Nest of Saints', but the
name also incorporates in typical O'Casey fashion the ironic pun
'Nest of Knaves'.


SCENE I

338 *your own girl Loreleen*:   the name suggests a siren, calling up echoes of
the Lorelei, a maiden who threw herself into the Rhine in despair
over a faithless lover and became a siren luring fishermen to
destruction. Clemens Brentano created the legend in its essentials in
his novel *Godwi* (1800–2), though it is best known outside Germany
through a number of nineteenth-century songs and poems, especially
Heinrich Heine's poem 'Ich weiss nicht was soll es bedeuten'.

339 *the Missioner*:   a 'mission' is being held in the neighbourhood – that is,
visiting clerical speakers make a brief 'moral blitz' on the region
seeking to reawaken faith and censure moral backsliding by means of
hell-fire sermons.

339 *St Crankarius . . . St Pathrick*:   here, as in *The Bishop's Bonfire*,
O'Casey's saintly hierarchy includes a number of hilarious eccentric
creations as well as figures venerated in his native land. St Patrick,
patron saint of Ireland (fl. fifth century AD), went there from Britain
as a slave when he was sixteen years of age; he is now venerated in
both ecclesiastical and popular tradition as the national apostle who
converted most, if not the whole, of Ireland to Christianity. *The
Confession of St Patrick* is a document of unquestioned authenticity
but Thomas F. O'Rahilly argues in *The Two Patricks* that only two
events in the saint's life can be dated and even those only approxi-
mately: his coming to Ireland about 461 and his death round about
492.

340 *Lourdes*:   place in south-west France which, from the second half of
the nineteenth century, became the object of pilgrimages undertaken
by sick people in search of a holy cure; it is the site of a neo-Byzantine
church and basilica built in the 1870s and 1880s to commemorate
several alleged appearances of the Virgin Mary to a peasant girl,
Bernadette Soubirous, between February and July in 1858. In his
autobiographical *Sunset and Evening Star* (1954), O'Casey is strongly
critical of what he saw to be the gaudy present-day promotion of
Lourdes as a place for jet-set pilgrimage, believing that the hopes and
fears of many sick people were being exploited for commercial gain.

340 *th' fair-haired boy*:   the favourite; the person in favour, whether man or
boy.

342 *Lay not up . . . where thieves break through and steal*:   Matthew 6:19.

343 *Deirdre come to life again*: Deirdre, the prophetically doomed lover in 'The Sons of Usna', one of the best known of the 'Three Sorrowful Stories of Erin'. See fuller note to 'Deirdre of the Sorrows' (p. 504).

343 *Knights o' Columbanus*: a society of Roman Catholic laymen dedicated to good works in honour of the Irish monk and saint Columbanus (AD 543–615).

343 *th' Rerum Novarum*: an encyclical letter published by Pope Leo XIII in 1891 on the condition of the working classes in which he rejected the idea of state ownership of the means of production.

345 *scuppered*: (British slang) to be overwhelmed, surprised or even massacred, from ME *skoper*. There is, probably something of a private joke by O'Casey here. 'Sailor' Mahan, like 'Captain' Boyle in *Juno and the Paycock*, often spices his speech with nautical expressions. He may well think (wrongly) that to be scuppered is a sailor's expression meaning to be sunk or drowned, from the 'scuppers', a drain at the edge of a deck exposed to the weather to allow accumulated water to drain out of a boat into the sea or into the bilges.

345 *Shanaar*: in Irish *shan ahr* means 'old man', but it is highly probable that O'Casey also wants to invoke, satirically, the biblical 'Shinar' or 'Sennaar', the Babylonian region of the Tigris–Euphrates basin near the Persian Gulf that is traditionally associated with the land of many confused tongues and, most notably, the tower of Babel. Shanaar's superstitious incantations are calculated to confuse and awe his listeners.

346 *Ever so old, thousands of years, thousands of years if all were told*: the quotation is a refrain from W. B. Yeats's early poem 'A Faery Song', published in the poet's collection entitled *The Rose* (London, 1893).

346 *I've thravelled over hollow lands an' hilly lands*: echo of a phrase from W. B. Yeats's poem 'The Song of Wandering Aengus', also published in Yeats's early volume of poetry entitled *The Rose*.

348 *Gehenna*: hell, with a pun on 'hen'.

348 *ketch*: catch.

350 *Oh, rowelum randee . . . specialii spam*: tower-of-Babel gibberish compounded of (mostly) Latin words, like Shanaar's subsequent invocations; the incongruous reference to 'spam', a scarce tinned meat product prized by poorer people in Britain during the Second World War, is a reminder that *Cock-a-Doodle Dandy* was written soon after that war had come to an end.

351 *Robin Adair*: idealised figure of romance, here compounded by his being in love with 'Maid Marion', who clearly has her origin in the Robin Hood saga. The lovely Irish folksong 'Eibhlin a Ruin', 'Eileen a Roon' (see note on p. 536), is known in Scotland as 'Robin Adair'. The latter was a real person – and an Irishman at that – whose romantic story is told entertainingly by S. J. Adir Fitz-Gerald in *Stories of Famous Songs* (London and Philadelphia, 1901) I, pp. 38–45. The words of the best-known song celebrating Adair were written about 1850 by Lady Caroline Keppel; the first stanza reads as follows:

What's this dull town to me?
    Robin's not near;
He, whom I wish to see,
    Wish so to hear.
Where's all the joy and mirth,
    Made life a heaven on earth?
O! they're all fled with thee,
    Robin Adair.

352 *lift up the' head and clap th' wings, black cock, an' crow*: quotation loosely based on lines from W. B. Yeats's play *The Dreaming of the Bones*:

Red bird of March, begin to crow!
Up with the neck and clap the wing,
Red cock; and crow!

The lines are also to be found in Yeats's untitled poem 'Why should the heart take fight', but O'Casey is less likely to have met them in their only publication, *The Variorum Edition of the Poems of W. B. Yeats*, ed. Peter Allt and R. K. Alspach (London and New York, 1968) pp. 781–2.

353 *als initio extension*: literally, Latin for 'at the very beginning'.

354 *cod*: deceiver, cheat.

355 *blarney*: smooth talk, flattering speech.

355 *Emer would have been jealous*: Emer, the beautiful wife of Cuchulain (see note on p. 498), was jealous of his infidelities with many women, and particularly of his association with Fand, wife of the sea-god Mariannan.

359 *Brancardiers*: origin uncertain but probably from French *brancard*, a litter, and originally a horse litter; here, clearly, pedestrian carriers bearing a home-made litter.

SCENE II

361 *videliket*: *videlicet*, *Latin* for 'namely', 'that is to say'.

361 *'Tooral ooral ooral, tooral ooral ay'*: the refrain of a lullaby sung by Bing Crosby in a pietistic film (much disliked by O'Casey) entitled *The Bells of St Mary's*.

363 *places founded by Finian, Finnbar*: St Finian (d. 579) established a monastery at Mooville, County Down; St Finbar (d. 633) founded a monastery round which grew the city of Cork.

363 *th' Seven Churches of Glendalough*: Glendalough, 'the valley of two lakes', in County Wicklow, contains the remains of two churches dedicated to St Kevin, Reefert Church, St Mary's Church, St Kieran's Church, Trinity Church, and the Cathedral of SS. Peter and Paul.

363 *Durrow of Offaly, founded be Columkille himself*: Columcille, or

Columba (521?–97), founded an important monastery at Durrow in County Offaly in AD 553; see also note to reference on p. 526.

363   *the Book of Durrow*:  finely illustrated gospel from the mid seventh century, now in the library of Trinity College, Dublin. The work shows the first incontrovertible blending of Irish and Germanic (or Saxon) influences – the style often known as Hiberno-Saxon. The book is traditionally associated with Durrow, County Offaly, and was probably produced in a sciptorium at the Columban monastery there. However, the strong Saxon influence evident in, for instance, the style of the animal interlace has led some contemporary scholars to believe that the book was made in Northumbria; there are striking similarities with the animal-interlace decorations on some of the jewellery discovered at the seventh-century Saxon burial site of Sutton Hoo in England.

365   *Selah!*:  Hebrew word often recurring in the Psalms, supposed to be a liturgical or musical direction, probably a direction to raise the voice or, perhaps, indicating a pause.

367   *cod-actin'*:  deceptive play-acting.

369   *I hot it!*:  I hit it; past tense of to hit, now seldom used in English speech.

374   *a Nippy*:  a waitress in a cheap restaurant or teahouse; originally, in the early 1930s, a registered trademark for a waitress in Lyons's restaurants and teahouses, whose dress was invariably skimpy in the fashion of the 1930s.

376   *jade*:  a woman, in opprobrious use, from a horse of inferior breed or a vicious one (Icelandic *jalda*, a mare); see also note on p. 525.

378   *maid Marion*:  Marthraun's reference associates Marion, his servant, with the Robin Hood folk tradition; it is therefore appropriate that her lover in the play should be 'Robin Adair'. Maid Marion is, traditionally, consort to the outlaw in Robin Hood. Her association with this folk hero of poems and ballads is post-medieval, however: by the sixteenth century the Robin Hood stories were frequently mimed as part of the May games and Marion was most often associated with Robin, as is appropriate in a celebration which may have originated in a fertility cult – which O'Casey almost certainly wishes to invoke in his play. Marion appears in none of the medieval ballads.

379   *ubique ululanti cockalorum ochone, ululo!*:  a mixture of dog Latin and Irish approximating to 'everywhere crying out "Cockalorum", alas alas!'; *ochone* is an Irish form of 'alas' and so is *ullilu*, an interjection of sorrow equivalent to 'alack and well-a-day'.

SCENE III

385   *th' gap of danger*:  Irish, *bearna baoghal*, traditional Gaelic phrase, much used in epic sagas, and more than a trifle incongruous in the present context.

386  *th' gaum*: stupid, idiotic (also spelt 'gom' by O'Casey; see note on p. 515).

387  *gett or 'git'*: common term of abuse nowadays, in North America as in Britain; originally meant (in Irish dialect, north and south) a bastard child.

389  *Odeonius*: comic reference to the Odeon, a commonly used name for cinemas, especially in the 1930s and 1940s.

389  *Feehanna Fawl*: that is, Fianna Fáil, 'soldiers of destiny', Irish political party founded in 1927 by Eamon de Valera and, from 1932, the governing-party in power for most of the time.

390  *de cultus feminarum malifico eradicum*: dog Latin approximating to 'concerning women's dress I will root out evildoers'.

390  *in annem fiat ecclesiam nonsensio*: if this gibberish has any meaning it is 'for a year let the church be nonsense'.

390  *Ullisississies*: James Joyce's novel *Ulysses* (1922).

395  *It's lookin' like th' blue bonnets are over th' bordher!*: Allan Ramsay, when he came across 'Blue Bonnets over the Border', inserted it in his *Tea-Table Miscellany* and labelled it 'ancient', little knowing that the poem was writen by Sir Walter Scott, who founded it on 'General Leslie's March to Longmarston Moor'. The Scots troops commonly wore blue cloth caps so that Scottish and blue-cap became synonymous terms for many years.

397  *Cock o' th' north, or cock o' th' south, we'll down derry doh down him yet*: here and in several subsequent speeches there are snatches from popular songs.

397  *We know where we're going . . . not forgetting Mick McGilligan's daughter, Maryann!*: these lines are compounded of the mythology of popular songs, including Thomas Moore's Minstrel Boy and the Danny Boy of the sentimental lyric set to the *Londonderry Air*. Brian O'Lynn figures in some popular ballads as an Irish Casanova; in others as a labourer who always finds excuses for not working. In another ballad, Mick McGilligan's daughter has a face like a Connemara moon, feet like two battleships, and hair on her chest like a man's. 'We know where we're goin'' here is a comic adaptation of a tender line from an Ulster love-song, 'I know where I'm going but the dear knows whom I'll marry.'

400  *Stipendium peccati mors est!*: 'the wages of sin is death' (Romans 6:23).

401  *aysey*: easy.


## THE BISHOP'S BONFIRE

Social and cultural sterility, the strict censorship of minds and conduct as well as of books, the increased power of the Roman Catholic Church and large-scale emigration were prominent concerns in Ireland in the 1940s and 1950s. The spiritual and moral atmosphere in which such conditions were bred is the subject of this play, which continues the critical analysis of contemporary Ireland that was begun in *Purple Dust* and maintained in *Cock-a-Doodle Dandy*.

409 *Cad dhéanfamaoid . . . na g-coillte ar lár*: an explanation of the quotation on the title-page was provided by O'Casey in a letter dated 24 March 1955 to Thomas Mark of Macmillan (his publisher),

> The Irish motto is the first two lines of a famous and rather lovely Irish lament; one for the loss of chieftains fled away from Ireland to France and Spain; the beginning of the flight of the 'wild Geese'. The best English I can think of is:
>
> > What shall we do for timber
> > Now that the last tree in the forest is down?
>
> This poem, 'Kilcash' (the Irish title is 'Cill Chais'), may be found in a fine translation by Frank O'Connor in his collection of Irish poetry, *Kings, Lords, and Commons* (London, 1959). Its relevance to O'Casey's theme in this play is pointed by the Codger's reference to contemporary Ireland being 'a fly-away country' (p. 428).

409 *To Susan gone and Susan here*: the dedication is to O'Casey's mother, who died in 1918, and to his daughter, born in 1939.

ACT I

412 *Burren*: the parish priest is named after a stony and barren part of the Clare–Galway country in the west of Ireland; the Burren is now a nature reserve, with many rare wild flowers and vegetation not found elsewhere in Ireland or the British Isles.

413 *the Dail*: that is, Dáil Éireann, the Irish parliament.

413 *your Foorawn*: Foorawn, in Irish, means cold, frigid.

413 *Boheroe*: Irish for 'Red Road'.

415 *buttie*: friend, comrade, work-mate; also *butty*, see note on p. 504.

417 *True religion isn't puffed up . . . never vaunts itself like you do*: Pauline phrases taken from I Corinthians 13:4.

420 *bum*: down-and-out, derelict, a shiftless person. See also note on 'bummer' (p. 507).

421 *reverabate*: reverberate.

421 *the codger*: old fellow, chap; here, an obviously affectionate portrait. of one who could be included among W. B. Yeats's 'golden codgers'; an odd or eccentric yet lovable old person; in British dialect, the word connotes a mean or miserly person (perhaps a corruption of 'cadger'?) but, clearly, this is quite the opposite of O'Casey's meaning or that of Yeats in his late poem 'News for the Delphic Oracle', where 'the

golden codgers' include Oisin, Pythagoras and Plotinus in an ironic vision of an after-life according to neo-Platonic doctrine.

421  *Ah, them were the days . . . a diamond-clad morn*:  lyric by O'Casey to a traditional musical air.

421  *me sowl man*:  my soul man, soul mate.

422  *Delaying . . . when all the woods are green*:  quotation from Tennyson, *The Princess*, IV.88–89.

422  *primae facie*: *prima facie* (see note on p. 501).

423  *sotto vossie*: *sotto voce*, Italian for a low tone intended not to be overheard.

423  *Sub rosa*:  under express or implied pledge of secrecy.

425  *crawthumpers*:  hostile allusion to pietistic breast-beaters, people who are ostentatiously devotional; see also note on p. 506.

425  *swalla*:  swallow.

425  *Like the ivy, I'd cling to thee*:  parodic reference to sentimental and popular Victorian love song.

426  *huckster*:  a cheaply mercenary person, here used as a general term of abuse.

428  *one, lone mohican*:  reference to James Fenimore Cooper's novel *The Last of the Mohicans*.

428  *a fly-away country*:  reference to the problem of emigration from Ireland at that time (1940s and 1950s) which was increasingly seen as a social dilemma.

429  *slower and slower . . . lower the reel rings*:  snatch from traditional Irish song known as 'The Spinning Wheel', whose melody and words are meant to accompany the rhythm of a spinning-wheel (as in the quoted words here, where the tired spinning-woman's words and actions become slower and slower); the full English text of the song is quoted in O'Casey's later play *The Drums of Father Ned*, Act I (London, 1960) pp. 22–3.

429  *Uups a daisy*:  common British slang expression, self-admonition accompanying a stumble in one's footing, meaning 'steady there'; origin uncertain, though it may be an adaptation of an expression in a once popular music-hall song, 'Hands, knees and boomps-a-daisy', where the singers accompany the words by clapping their hands together, slapping knees and, on 'boomps-a-daisy', bumping posteriors together.

429  *You promenade down . . . an' swing your Sindy Sue*:  most probably, directions for a kind of square dance, but which one is uncertain.

429  *Bill Mullarkey, that was*:  the Bishop's secular surname embodies symbolic overtones; 'mullarkey' or 'malarkey' (origin unknown), insincere or foolish or pretentious talk or writing designed to impress and usually to distract attention from ulterior motives or actual conditions.

430  *God's gaum*:  a gaum (sometimes spelt 'gom' by O'Casey) is one who is stupid, an idiotic person – here, an unthinking voteen or religious devotee.

431 *show you're no cissy*: 'cissy' is British slang for an effeminate man, invariably used in a pejorative manner.

437 *The Angelus*: here, it is the 6 p.m. Angelus (see fuller note on p. 498).

438 *they shall not muzzle the oxen that are treadin' out the corn*: Deuteronomy 25:4; also I Corinthians 9:9; and 1 Timothy 5:18.

439 *a tenebrae cloak*: a dark and gloomy cloak, presumably, from the name given to the Roman Catholic office of Matins and Lauds for Thursday, Friday and Saturday of Holy Week.

440 *a laocoön of rosary beads*: a confusing (and dangerous) tangle of rosary beads; named after the priest of Apollo at Troy who warned his compatriots against the Wooden Horse and who, with his two sons, was strangled by serpents (hence this image of entrapment) sent by Athena.

441 *the lark singin' in the clear air . . . of the day, wha?*: allusion to a song by Thomas Moore (much loved by O'Casey) from Moore's *Irish Melodies*.

441 *My Bonnie's gone over the ocean . . . Oh, bring back my Bonnie to me*: traditional British folk-song, probably from the north of England.


ACT II

444 *pray doo*: prie-dieu (pidgin French).

444 *savee!*: savez (pidgin French).

446 *a tenner*: ten pounds (Irish currency).

447 *a buckineeno*: *buccina* (Latin), a crooked trumpet. Also spelt in this play 'bookineeno', 'bookaneeno'.

448 *eejut*: idiot.

450 *ipso factos*: another comic use of Latin, *ipso facto* means, literally, 'by that very act or fact'.

451 *head or a harp*: the two sides to an Irish coin.

453 *blatherers*: spouters of nonsense; people who utter vulgar, foolish and boastful speech; from 'blather' or 'bladdher', idle and foolish talk. In the north of Ireland and in Scotland the word is 'blether' – as in Robert Burns's poem, 'The Vision'.

453 *gazebo*: English dialect for a show, gaping-stock; any object which attracts attention. P. W. Joyce, in *English as We Speak It in Ireland* (London, 1910), says that it can also mean a tall building, a tall object or even a tall awkward fellow – all objects that attract attention to themselves, of course.

453 *the real McCoy*: the genuine article, the real thing, a slang expression which seems – according to *A Dictionary of Americanisms on Historical Principles*, ed. Mifford M. Mathews (Chicago, 1951) – to be of American origin. It is possible, however, that it may be a transatlantic confusion of McCoy for MacKay. There are two branches of clan MacKay: those in Inverness-shire and those in Argyll. The northern MacKays are actually MacDhais, or Davidsons; thus the MacKays of Argyllshire are the real thing. Aodh, son of Morgan – the Morgan

clan chief – is the original MacKay. In Gaelic, MacAo(i)dh is equated with MacKay. Thus, Aodh is the original MacKay, with each subsequent son or ally becoming a member of his clan.

455 *holla*: hollow.

455 *All Hollas Eve*: All Hallow's Eve.

456 *our way to th' tomb*: ironic reference to Ronald Duncan's pietistic masque *This Way to the Tomb* (London, 1946); here, as in the subsequent allusions to T. S. Eliot's *Four Quartets*, O'Casey is mocking then-fashionable literary propaganda on behalf of High Church Anglican religion.

457 *every step will be a new arrival an' a different departure*: here, and elsewhere in this scene, the parodic reference is to T. S. Eliot's poem *Four Quartets* (London, 1937–44), which O'Casey much admired as a work of art but disliked for what he saw as its support for a resigned acceptance of things as they are, in the guise of 'God's will'.

457 *If we want to go . . . to where we can't get*: further parodic reference to T. S. Eliot's poem.

457 *The song sung is the song unheard . . . the song sung*: parody of similar phrases in *Four Quartets*.

458 *a Buhl*: furniture with elaborate inlaid work of woods, metals, tortoiseshell, ivory and so on, named after A. C. Boulle or Boule (1642–1732), French cabinet maker.

459 *Bill Mullarkey, won't you please come home*: comic adaptation of a line in a popular American song – 'Oh Bill Bailey, won't you please come home'.

459 *Keep a kee veev*: Keep on the *qui vive* (French challenge: 'who's there?'), maintain a sharp lookout, watch out for.

462 *the big house with the lion and unicorn on its front*: Britain – that is, British government, from the British coat of arms.

462 *the big shop with the cross and shamrock on its gable*: Ireland – that is, modern Ireland dominated, in O'Casey's view, by middle-class shopkeeping values and puritanical Roman Catholic control.

462 *Blue bonnets . . . over the Border!*: reference on p. 534.

464 *you lug!*: derogatory term used for an ignorant person, possibly from the slang term for an ear or could it be from lugworm?

ACT III

466 *puss*: Irish *pus*, the mouth and lips; always used in dialect in an offensive or contemptuous sense.

466 *'Kiss Me, Kate'*: title of song from American musical bearing the same name; with music by Cole Porter, the work is based loosely on Shakespeare's *The Taming of the Shrew*.

468 *there's a statue of Ireland's hero, Cuchullain, somewhere up in Dublin*: the Codger knows very well where in Dublin stands the statue of Cuchullain (see note on p. 498 for details of Ireland's legendary warrior) – it is in the main post-office in O'Connell Street, where Pearse proclaimed an Irish Republic in Easter Week 1916. Cuchul-

lain had long been a potent symbol for Pearse; in the words of W. B.
Yeats:

> When Pearse summoned Cuchulain to his side,
> What stalked through the Post Office?

The statue is itself memorably celebrated in verse in Yeats's late play
*The Death of Cuchulain*:

> Are those things that men adore and loathe
> Their sole reality?
> What stood in the Post Office
> With Pearse and Connolly? . . .
> Who thought Cuchulain till it seemed
> He stood where they had stood? . . .
> A statue's there to mark the place,
> By Oliver Sheppard done.

468  [*Exit* CODGER]:   stage direction added by editor.

468  *gab*:   idle talk.

471  *You're my menacin' ubique*:   *ubique* (Latin), everywhere, wheresoever;
here with the sense of assailed or threatened from all sides. The
previous sentence explains it: 'I always find you in front of me, or
hear you hailin' me from behind.'

472  *your de profundis urn*:   an exaggeratedly gloomy urn seems implied by
this phrase.

472  *a domine vobiscum death*:   almost certainly this is a death reconciled
with the Church and with God. The phrase *Dominus vobiscum* (the
Lord be with you) occurs frequently in the old Catholic liturgy.

475  *The rose that is fresh . . . stretch'd out to greet thee!*:   lyric by O'Casey to a
traditional air.

478  *Ah, where is the laughter . . . something fine to say?*:   lyric by O'Casey to
a traditional air.

481  *When Irish eyes are smilin' . . . they steal your heart away!*:   the kind of
vacuous sentimental song that O'Casey detested.

481  *Ah, bless'd be the day . . . me spirit's still bold*:   lyric by O'Casey to a
traditional air.

484  *agradh*:   Irish term of endearment – 'my love'; vocative of *grádh*, love.

487  *gob*:   mouth.

490  *as David took the shewbread from the holy altar*:   cf. 1 Samuel 21:1–6.

490  *sounding cymbal . . . tinkling brass*:   hysterical inversion of Pauline
images from the 1611 Authorised Version of 1 Corinthians, 13:1,
where it is said that without love and charity one becomes like
'sounding brass or a tinkling cymbal'.

491  *tait-a-tait*:   *tête-à-tête*, private conversation or interview, usually between two people.

# Select Bibliography

PLAYS

*Two Plays: 'Juno and the Paycock', 'The Shadow of a Gunman'* (London and New York, 1925).
*The Plough and the Stars* (London and New York, 1926).
*Juno and the Paycock* (London, 1928).
*The Silver Tassie* (London and New York, 1928).
*The Shadow of a Gunman*, acting edition (London and New York, 1932).
*Juno and the Paycock*, acting edition (London and New York, 1932)
*The Plough and the Stars*, acting edition (London and New York, 1932).
*Within the Gates* (London, 1933; New York, 1934).
*Five Irish Plays: 'Juno and the Paycock', 'The Shadow of a Gunman', 'The Plough and the Stars', 'The End of the Beginning', 'A Pound on Demand'* (London, 1935).
*The Star Turns Red* (London, 1940).
*Purple Dust* (London, 1940).
*Red Roses for Me* (London, 1942; New York, 1943).
*Oak Leaves and Lavender* (London, 1946; New York, 1947).
*'Juno and the Paycock' and 'The Plough and the Stars'* (London, 1948).
*Cock-a-Doodle Dandy* (London, 1949).
*Collected Plays*, volumes I and II (London, 1949).
*Collected Plays*, volumes III and IV (London, 1951).
*The Bishop's Bonfire* (London and New York, 1955).
*Red Roses for Me*, acting edition (New York, 1956).
*Purple Dust*, acting edition (New York, 1957).
*Three Plays: 'Juno and the Paycock', 'The Shadow of a Gunman', 'The Plough and the Stars'* (London, 1957).
*The Drums of Father Ned* (London and New York, 1960).
*'Behind the Green Curtains', 'Figuro in the Night', 'The Moon Shines on Kylenamoe'* (London and New York, 1961).
*Three More Plays: 'The Silver Tassie', 'Purple Dust', 'Red Roses for Me'* (London and New York, 1965).
*The Harvest Festival* (New York and Gerrards Cross, 1980).
*The Complete Plays of Sean O'Casey*, 5 vols (London, 1984).

AUTOBIOGRAPHIES

*I Knock at the Door* (London and New York, 1939).

*Pictures in the Hallway* (London and New York, 1942).
*Drums under the Windows* (London, 1945; New York, 1946).
*Inishfallen, Fare Thee Well* (London and New York, 1949).
*Rose and Crown* (London and New York, 1952).
*Sunset and Evening Star* (London and New York, 1954).
*Mirror in my House: The Autobiographies of Sean O'Casey*, 2 vols (New York, 1956).
*Autobiographies*, 2 vols (London, 1963).
*Autobiographies*, 2 vols with an index (London, 1981).

### OCCASIONAL WRITINGS

*The Story of the Irish Citizen Army* (Dublin and London, 1919).
*Windfalls: Stories, Poems and Plays* (London and New York, 1934).
*The Green Crow* (New York, 1956; London, 1957).
*Feathers from the Green Crow: Sean O'Casey, 1905–1925*, ed. Robert Hogan (Missouri, 1962; London, 1963).
*Under a Colored Cap* (London and New York, 1963).
*Blasts and Benedictions*, ed. Ronald Ayling (London and New York, 1967).

### LETTERS

*The Letters of Sean O'Casey*, ed. David Krause, 3 vols, vol. I: *1910–1941* (New York and London, 1975); vol. II: *1942–1954* (New York and London, 1980); vol. III: *1955–1964* (in press).

### BOOKS AND ARTICLES ON O'CASEY

(a) *General*

Armstrong, William A., *Sean O'Casey* (London, 1967).
Ayling, Ronald (ed.), *Sean O'Casey: Modern Judgements* (London, 1969).
——, 'Popular Tradition and Individual Talent in Sean O'Casey's Dublin Trilogy', *Journal of Modern Literature*, II (1972) 491–504.
——, 'Sean O'Casey and the Abbey Theatre, Dublin', *Sean O'Casey: Centenary Essays*, ed. David Krause and Robert G. Lowery (Gerrards Cross, 1980) pp. 13–40.
——, ' "Two Words for Women": a Reassessment of O'Casey's Heroines', *Woman in Irish Legend, Life and Literature*, ed. S. F. Gallagher (Gerrards Cross and Totowa, N.J., 1983) pp. 91–114.
——, and Michael J. Durkan, *Sean O'Casey: A Bibliography* (London, 1978; Seattle, 1979).
Fallon, Gabriel, *Sean O'Casey: The Man I Knew* (London, 1965).
Goldstone, Herbert, *In Search of Community: The Achievement of Sean O'Casey* (Cork and Dublin, 1972).

Lady Gregory, Augusta, *Lady Gregory's Journals, 1916–1930*, selection edited by Lennox Robinson (London, 1946); complete text edited by Daniel J. Murphy is to be issued in two volumes of which vol. I only has appeared. *Lady Gregory's Journals*, vol. I: *1916–1925*, ed. D. J. Murphy (Gerrards Cross, 1978).

Hogan, Robert, *The Experiments of Sean O'Casey* (New York, 1960).

*Joseph Holloway's Abbey Theatre: A Selection from his Unpublished Journal*, ed. Robert Hogan and Michael J. O'Neill (Carbondale and London, 1967).

*Irish University Review* (special issue: 'Sean O'Casey, Roots and Branches') X, no. 1 (Spring 1980).

Kilroy, Thomas (ed.), *Sean O'Casey: A Collection of Critical Essays* (Englewood Cliffs, N.J., 1975).

Kosok, Heinz, *Sean O'Casey: Das dramatische Werk* (Berlin, 1972).

Krause, David, 'The Principle of Comic Disintegration', *James Joyce Quarterly*, VIII (1970) 3–12.

——, *Sean O'Casey: The Man and his Work* (London and New York, 1975; enlarged edition of book first published in 1960).

——, *The Profane Book of Irish Comedy* (Ithaca, N.Y., and London, 1982).

Mikhail, E. H., *Sean O'Casey: A Bibliography of Criticism* (London, 1972).

Mitchell, Jack, *The Essential O'Casey: A Study of the Twelve Major Plays of Sean O'Casey* (New York and Berlin, 1980).

O'Casey, Eileen, *Sean* (London, 1971; New York, 1972).

Sanger, Wolfgang R., 'To Hell with So-Called Realism: the Later Plays of Sean O'Casey', *Etudes Irlandaises*, VI (1981) 43–59.

Snowden, J. A., 'Sean O'Casey and Naturalism', *Essays and Studies*, XXIV (1971) 56–68.

Starkie, Walter, 'Sean O'Casey', *The Irish Theatre*, ed. L. Robinson (London, 1939) pp. 147–76.

Williams, Raymond, *Drama from Ibsen to Brecht* (London, 1968).

Zimmermann, Georges-Denis, *Songs of Irish Rebellion: Political Street Ballads and Rebel Songs, 1780–1900* (Dublin, 1967).

(b) *The Shadow of a Gunman*

Armstrong, William A., 'History, Autobiography, and *The Shadow of a Gunman*', *Modern Drama*, II (1960) 417–24.

Casey, Paul Foley, 'The Knocking Motif in Sean O'Casey's *The Shadow of a Gunman*', *Literatur in Wissenschaft und Unterricht*, XIII (1980) 170–5.

O'Maoláin, Michael, 'That Raid and What Went with it', *Essays on Sean O'Casey's Autobiographies*, ed. Robert G. Lowery (London and New York, 1981) pp. 103–22.

Rollins, Ronald G., 'O'Casey and Synge: the Irish Hero as Playboy and Gunman', *Arizona Quarterly*, XXII (1966) 217–22.

Schrank, Bernice, 'Poets, Poltroons and Platitudes: a Study of Sean O'Casey's *The Shadow of a Gunman*', *Mosaic*, XI (1977) 53–60.

——, ' "You needn't say no more": Language and the Problems of Communication in Sean O'Casey's *The Shadow of a Gunman*', *Irish University Review*, VIII (1978) 23–37.

Worth, Katharine, 'O'Casey, Synge and Yeats', *Irish University Review*, X (1980) 103–17.

(c) *Juno and the Paycock*

Armstrong, William A., 'The Integrity of *Juno and the Paycock*', *Modern Drama*, XVII (1974) 1–9.

Ayling, Ronald, 'Patterns of Language and Ritual in Sean O'Casey's Drama', *Anglo-Irish Studies*, II (1976) 25–44.

——, '*Juno and the Paycock*: a Textual Study', *Modernist Studies*, II (1976) 15–26.

Durbach, Errol, 'Peacocks and Mothers: Theme and Dramatic Metaphor in O'Casey's *Juno and the Paycock*', *Modern Drama*, XV (1972) 15–25.

Fricker, Robert, 'Sean O'Casey: *Juno and the Paycock*', *Das moderne englische Drama: Interpretationen*, ed. Horst Oppel (Berlin, 1966) pp. 181–200; rev. edn (Berlin, 1976) pp. 188–207.

Kaufman, Michael W., 'O'Casey's Structural Design in *Juno and the Paycock*', *Quarterly Journal of Speech*, LVIII (1972) 191–8.

Kosok, Heinz, 'Sean O'Casey, *Juno and the Paycock*', *Dramen des 20 Jahrhunderts für den Englisch unterricht in der Sekundarstufe II*, ed. Hans Weber (Frankfurt, 1982).

Schrank, Bernice, 'Dialectical Configurations in *Juno and the Paycock*', *Twentieth-Century Literature*, XXI (1975) 438–56.

(d) *The Plough and the Stars*

Armstrong, William A., 'The Sources and Themes of *The Plough and the Stars*', *Modern Drama*, IV (1961) 234–42.

Ayling, Ronald, 'Character Control and "Alienation" in *The Plough and the Stars*', *James Joyce Quarterly*, VIII (1970) 29–47.

——, 'Ideas and Ideology in *The Plough and the Stars*', *Sean O'Casey Review*, II (1976) 115–36.

——, 'History and Artistry in *The Plough and the Stars*', *Ariel*, VIII (1977) 73–85.

De Baun, C. Vincent, 'Sean O'Casey and the Road to Expressionism', *Modern Drama*, IV (1961) 254–9.

Kaufman, Michael W., 'The Position of *The Plough and the Stars* in O'Casey's Dublin Trilogy', *James Joyce Quarterly*, VIII (Fall 1970) 48–63.

Krause, David, 'Some Truths and Jokes about the Easter Rising', *Sean O'Casey Review*, III (1976) 3–23.

Lindsay, Jack, '*The Plough and the Stars* Reconsidered', *Sean O'Casey Review*, II (Spring 1976) 187–95.

Lowery, Robert G., 'Prelude to Year One: Sean O'Casey before 1916', *Sean O'Casey Review*, II (Spring 1976) 92–102.

McHugh, Roger (ed.), *Dublin 1916* (London, 1966).

O'Casey, Sean, '*The Plough and the Stars* in Retrospect', *Blasts and Benedictions*, ed. Ronald Ayling (London and New York, 1967) 95–8.

Schrank, Bernice, 'The Low and the Lofty: a Comparison of Sean O'Casey's

*The Plough and the Stars* and Denis Johnston's *The Scythe and the Sunset'*, *Modern Language Studies*, XI (1980–1) 12–16.

——, ' "Little Ignorant Yahoo": the Theme of Human Limitations in O'Casey's *The Plough and the Stars'*, *Etudes Irlandaises*, VI (1981) 32–42.

——, ' "The Nakedness o' th' Times": Dressing-up in *The Plough and the Stars'*, *Canadian Journal of Irish Studies*, VII (1981) 5–20.

Thompson, William Irwin, *The Imagination of an Insurrection; Dublin Easter 1916: A Study of an Ideological Movement* (New York, 1967).

(e) *The Silver Tassie*

Ayling, Ronald, *Continuity and Innovation in Sean O'Casey's Drama: A Critical Monograph* (Salzburg, 1976).

Brandt, G. W., 'Realism and Parables: from Brecht to Arden', *Contemporary Theatre*, ed. J. R. Brown and Bernard Harris (London, 1962) pp. 33–55.

Doyle, Jacqueline, 'Liturgical Imagery in Sean O'Casey's *The Silver Tassie'*, *Modern Drama*, XXI (March 1978) 29–38.

Kleiman, Carol, *Sean O'Casey's Bridge of Vision: Four Essays on Structure and Perspective* (Toronto, Buffalo, N.Y., London, 1982).

Kosok, Heinz, 'The Revision of *The Silver Tassie'*, *Sean O'Casey Review*, V (1978) 15–18.

Kreps, Barbara, 'The Meaning of Structure and Images in Sean O'Casey's *The Silver Tassie'*, *Studi dell' Istituto Linguistico*, II (1979) 195–210.

Massey, Raymond, *A Hundred Different Lives* (London, 1980).

O'Casey, Sean, 'W. B. Yeats and *The Silver Tassie'*, *Blasts and Benedictions*, ed. Ronald Ayling (London and New York, 1967) pp. 99–102.

——, '*The Silver Tassie'*, *Blasts and Benedictions*, ed. Ronald Ayling (London and New York, 1967) 103–7.

Pasachoff, Naomi S., 'Unity of Theme, Image and Diction in *The Silver Tassie'*, *Modern Drama*, XXIII (March 1980) 58–64.

Peterson, Richard F., 'Polishing Up *The Silver Tassie* Controversy: Some Lady Gregory and W. B. Yeats Letters to Lennox Robinson', *Sean O'Casey Review*, IV (Spring 1978) 121–9.

Smith, Winifred, 'The Dying God in the Modern Theatre', *Review of Religion*, V (March 1941) 264–75.

Templeton, Joan, 'Sean O'Casey and Expressionism', *Modern Drama*, XIV (May 1971) 47–62.

Williams, Simon, 'The Unity of *The Silver Tassie'*, *Sean O'Casey Review*, IV (Spring 1978) 99–112.

(f) *Red Roses for Me*

Aickmann, Robert Fordyce, 'Mr Sean O'Casey and the Striker', *Nineteenth Century*, CXXXIX (April 1946) 172–5.

Armstrong, William A., 'Sean O'Casey, W. B. Yeats and the Dance of Life', *Sean O'Casey*, ed. Ronald Ayling (London, 1969) pp. 131–42.

Kleiman, Carol, *Sean O'Casey's Bridge of Vision: Four Essays on Structure and Perspective* (Toronto, Buffalo, N.Y., London, 1982).

MacAnna, Tomas, 'An Interview about the Later O'Casey Plays at the Abbey Theatre', *Irish University Review*, x (Spring 1980) 130–45.

Malone, Maureen, '*Red Roses for Me*: Fact and Symbol', *Modern Drama*, IX (September 1966) 147–52.

Rollins, Ronald, 'Finn Again: O'Casey Resurrects Celtic Heroes in *Red Roses for Me*', *Irish University Review*, x (Spring 1980) 52–58.

Stock, A. G., 'The Heroic Image: *Red Roses for Me*', *Sean O'Casey*, ed. Ronald Ayling (London, 1969) pp. 126–30.

(g) *Cock-a-Doodle Dandy*

Armstrong, William A., 'The Irish Point of View: the Plays of Sean O'Casey, Brendan Behan and Thomas Murphy', *Experimental Drama*, ed. W. A. Armstrong (London, 1963).

MacAnna, Tomas, 'An Interview about the Later O'Casey Plays at the Abbey Theatre', *Irish University Review*, x (Spring 1980) 130–45.

O'Casey, Sean, 'Cockadoodle Doo', *Blasts and Benedictions*, ed. Ronald Ayling (London and New York, 1967) pp. 142–5.

Pasachoff, Naomi, 'O'Casey's Not Quite Festive Comedies', *Eire-Ireland*, XII (1977) 41–61.

Rollins, Ronald, 'Clerical Blackness in the Green Garden: Heroine as Scapegoat in *Cock-a-Doodle Dandy*', *James Joyce Quarterly*, VIII (Fall 1970) 64–72.

Worth, Katharine, *The Irish Drama of Europe from Yeats to Beckett* (London and Atlantic Highlands, N.J., 1978).

Zeiss, Cecelia, 'Sean O'Casey's Final Tragicomedies: a Comment on the Dramatic Modes Employed in *Cock-a-Doodle Dandy* and *The Bishop's Bonfire*', *Studies in Anglo-Irish Literature*, ed. Heinz Kosok (Bonn, 1982) pp. 278–86.

(h) *The Biship's Bonfire*

Armstrong, William A., 'The Irish Point of View: the Plays of Sean O'Casey, Brendan Behan and Thomas Murphy', *Experimental Drama*, ed. W. A. Armstrong (London, 1963).

O'Casey, Sean, 'Bonfire Under a Black Sun', *The Green Crow* (London, 1957) pp. 122–45.

——, 'O'Casey's Drama-Bonfire', *Blasts and Benedictions*, ed. Ronald Ayling (London and New York, 1967) pp. 138–41.

Zeiss, Cecelia, 'Sean O'Casey's Final Tragicomedies: a Comment on the Dramatic Modes Employed in *Cock-a-Doodle Dandy* and *The Bishop's Bonfire*', *Studies in Anglo-Irish Literature*, ed. Heinz Kosok (Bonn, 1982) pp. 278–86.